PENNSYLVANIA NATURALLY

Acknowledgements

We gratefully appreciate the following for their assistance in making this publication possible:

U.S. Department of Agriculture
National Resource Conservation Service
Morris Arboretum / University of Pennsylvania
U.S. Forest Service
U.S. Environmental Protection Agency
U.S. National Park Service
Pennsylvania Department of Natural Resources
The Nature Conservancy
Harvard University
The Pennsylvania State University
The University of Wisconsin
University of Kentucky
The Center for Plant Conservation
Missouri Botanical Garden

Plant images courtesy of the U.S. Department of Agriculture and the University of Kentucky

PENNSYLVANIA NATURALLY

ISBN 978-0986276606

© Copyright 2016, The Pennystone Project

All rights reserved. No part of this publication may be reproduced or transmitted in any form or by any means, electronic or mechanical, without permission from The Pennystone Project. Contact us at http://www.pennystone.com.

Pennsylvania Naturally

Geoffrey Mehl
The Pennystone Project

Pennsylvania Naturally

Contents

1. Introduction
Natural Light Levels • About Soils • Sustainability • Preservation • Restoration • Conservation • Feeding Your Forest

9. Down and Dirty
More than Dirt • How to Identify Your Soil • Soil Textures • Sands, Silts, Clays • Drainage • Permeability • Moisture • Reactivity • Flooding and Ponding • Soil Foundations • Calcareous Soils • Wetlands • Parent Materials

21. What Do They Call...
Uplands, Lowlands • Slope Elements • Mountain and Hill Features • Slopes in Three Dimensions • Streams and Drainage Systems • Riparian Features • Fans and Deltas • Terraces and Steps • Stream Features and Processes • Stream Types • Wetlands • Lakes and Ponds • Depressions and Basins • Glacial Features • Drift and Till • Outwash Features • Dunes • Elemental Geomorphology

43. Neighborhoods
Foundations of Ecoregions • Major Areas • Piedmont and Coastal Plain • Appalachian Ridge and Valley • Unglaciated Allegheny Plateau • Northwestern Glaciated Allegheny Plateau, Erie Lake Plain • Unglaciated High Allegheny Plateau • Northeastern Glaciated Plateau • Blue Ridge Mountains

68. Eco-communities
Major Systems and Plant Lists • Dry Oak Forests • Barrens, Talus Slopes, Boulderfields • Dry Oak-Hickory Forests • Chinkapin-Red Cedar-Redbud Woodlands • Sugar Maple-Basswood Forests • Pine-Hemlock-Oak Forests • Mesic Red Oak Forests • Northern Hardwood Forest • Hemlock-Oak Forests • Mesic Hemlock-Hardwood Forests • Rich Hardwood Forests • Piedmont Mesophytic Forest • Serpentine Barrens • Erie-Ontario Lake Plain • Wetlands – Meadows, Fens, Seeps, Swamps, Depressions, Shrublands, Palustrine Wetlands • Bogs • Riparian Zones and Floodplains • Models for Raingardens • Lakes, Ponds, Marshes

141. Pennsylvania Soils
Soil series descriptions, including topographic positions, characteristics, composition, current use and major trees, taxonomy; not included: urban land, for which no details are available.

231. Pennsylvania Native Plants
Alphabetical list of 2,000 species by latin name, common name, type of plant, perennial/annual, natural habitat and preferences, cultivation suggestions.

Introduction

For more than four decades, we've heard with increasing urgency the call for greater environmental responsibility, including the horticultural practices in our own back yards. The case for resource conservation and sustainability has been well made by many, so there's no need to recite it once more.

Regrettably, advocates tend to be mired in simplistic solutions: rip up the lawn, banish the hybrids, toss in a rain garden, throw down a sack of wildflower seed, get out of the way and let Nature heal itself with sturdy, no-care wildflowers that take care of themselves. Add anecdotal personal examples from scattered locations around the country and off we go to rescue the planet. Here's a plan for a butterfly garden, a rain garden, a border, a mini-meadow. It's easy, it's simple, it's quick and it's fun.

Kind of a shame that it won't work.

So our discussion is not about the *why* — we get it — but rather the *how*. Our assumption is that natural landscaping and native plant gardening enthusiasts are receptive to information from an array of science disciplines that form a mosaic of expertise. Our goal is to provide the tools that give the average gardener confidence and control in landscape management that leads to success and satisfaction, no matter what the scale of the project.

Our discussion concerns Pennsylvania, which is, in fact, a *landscape* — a defined tract with a surface area — of about 29.5 million acres. It has more than 83,000 miles of streams and rivers (second highest in the the United States). It straddles five major eco-regions, has more than 360 different kinds of soils found in thousands of combinations, is home to nearly 2,000 species of native plants and a dozen major types of forest systems. It has been farmed, mined, logged, industrialized and urbanized for more than four centuries and the resulting changes to the land surface are *landscaping*.

Similarly, the lot under our feet is also a *landscape*, defined by the deed, and how we shape it — erecting a house, installing a patio, making a walkway, organizing a garden, is also *landscaping*. The border garden with a flat of marigolds, the foundation planting in front of the house, the patch of beefsteak tomatoes and zucchinis, the lawn where the kids play are all *landscapes*.

For our purposes, a *natural landscape* is an area used for plants or materials that would be considered natural to the habitat. We think first of living plants, but should also include such materials as a log from a fallen tree, boulders that have been frost-heaved to the surface or rolled downhill from higher elevations, the leaf litter deposited by trees on site. If we import stone and it's the kind of stone normally found on such sites, a bit of a stretch, but okay; if it's concrete block and pavers to build a retaining wall, sorry, doesn't count.

Landscaping paths diverge when natural materials are organized in an artificial way versus a *wildscape*, where those same materials are presented in a reasonably faithful representation of the habitat. A garden is, by definition, a managed landscape for a specific purpose — generally *aesthetic* or artistic, but also *productive* (a vegetable garden) or *botanical* (a collection of species for scientific or educational

> **The advantage of a natural landscape, however, is that less resources will be devoted to its survival and more on grooming and management.**

How natural light levels are defined

Almost all growing guides to native species include a general guide to required light levels. While these are imprecise, they offer landscapers useful guidelines and may require site-specific interpretation. As a general rule, lean toward high light levels if uncertain. Many *ephemerals* straddle light requirements in deciduous forest, taking advantage of sun to part sun in early spring to bloom and set seed, then becoming part shade plants as leaf cover fills out. Some go dormant in early summer, while others — especially if moisture is sufficient — may remain in leaf well into the growing season but go dormant when it becomes too dry.

Sun - unobstructed sunshine for a least eight hours daily. *Full sun* suggests constant sunshine from sunrise to sunset.

Part sun - unobstructed sunshine for several hours daily, especially at midday or afternoon, when the sun's rays are strongest. Glade-loving species and some westward-facing woods edge plants congregate in these situations. Whether those hours of sunshine are in the morning or afternoon can make a difference.

Part shade - unobstructed sunshine for several hours a day, but most often in the mornings, when the sun's rays are gentle. These are species likely to be found on the east side of thickets and edges. An important secondary definition implies *dappled shade*, that is, somewhat rapidly moving pools of sunshine that penetrate the canopy. If it persists for an hour or more, it starts to become part sun.

Shade - light that is shrouded often by high or thin deciduous canopies, sometimes with very rapidly moving pools of sunlight. A variant is *full shade*, which implies much lower light levels, such as those found in conifer stands.

---

purpose). And thus, if we organize and manage natural materials for a pleasing design as a foundation planting across the front of the building, it's still a *natural landscape*. If we crave the sensation of a state or natural park and construct a garden to suggest it, we have a *wildscape* that is also a natural landscape.

Indeed, we can subdivide all aesthetic garden designs into two categories: two and three dimensional. The former is intended to be looked at from a convenient distance — read that curb appeal or border gardens — while the latter is intended to be immersive. We surround our sitting area with a landscape as a decoration or shelter, but we can also turn it into one or more botanical rooms through which we wander and enjoy. Specifically how they are designed and presented is entirely up to the owner, as with any traditional design, so natural landscapes can be anywhere between classic suburban to unabashed wilderness, from formal European and English cottage to subtle Asian asymmetrical.

The bottom line potential of natural landscaping, no matter which direction the designer takes, is resource conservation that stewards water and protects soils, but also shelters an enormous range of other living creatures from microscopic to mammalian. The butterfly and bumble bee don't care how the garden is designed, just as long as the necessary species is there. With shrewd plant selection, artificial fertilizers and irrigation are no longer required and with attentive landscape management, groundwater supplies are enhanced — a good thing if our water comes from an on-site well.

But how to efficiently and effectively design a natural landscape?

The baseline design comes directly from our own personal sense of what a great garden looks like — an impression from somewhere in our past, an image in a book or periodical, a concept that supports our lifestyle. We might not be able to list from that image each specific species, but we know what it looks like and just need some kitchen table time sifting through possibilities. Wildscapers have a larger challenge; their impression is probably from a memorable scenic view they've seen. It's virtually impossible to replicate that impression in a back yard. *However...*

In few places in the world are gardens so energetically developed than in Japan. From tiny court-

Why landform and soil terms are important

A great deal of attention in the next section of our discussion relates to terms — soils, landforms and features. Further along, we'll tour the major ecoregions of the state and become acquainted with subsections and their unique characteristics.

At first glance, this might appear dreary and mundane, perhaps even irrelevant. After all, a hill is a hill and dirt's dirt — and most of the dirt in the state is lousy anyway. Some of it seems terribly arcane and may very well be included "just in case," a sort of FYI that's handy for showing off at the neighborhood barbeque.

In fact, the complicated features of the state individually and collectively create distinct habitats that support entire systems of plant life. These in turn serve as models for the natural landscape, which can be vastly different not only around the state, but sometimes within just a mile or two.

Our goal, of course, is the dream of every gardener: The List. Tree, shrubs, herbaceous plants ideal for our specific backyard, plus those just on either side of ideal that might work with a little effort. Secondarily, we recognize that gardeners like to stretch the boundaries and model different habitats.

If it sounds far-fetched, consider life on a dry upland slope that also just happens to include the house and garage roofs, the driveway and maybe the patio as impervious surfaces producing bursts of stormwater runoff. One of the trendy design features in environmentally-conscious scheme is a rain garden — a shallow closed depression that serves as a temporary retention basin to allow stormwater to drain gracefully into the soil rather than into the street. But rain gardens can be far more sophisticated and useful features if we consider them in the context of rills, floodplains, headslopes and ephemeral streams, potentially servicing seasonal wetlands or perhaps supporting a generally *xeric*, or extremely dry, habitat. Some homeowners have installed backyard ponds, complete with pumped babbling brooks and these, too, can be developed as habitats out of the normal sequence of drainage systems. And there are enthusiasts who enjoy the challenge of rock gardens; they might very well be on a suburban lot in the lower slope of the Piedmont, but will find delight in modeling summit barrens and talus fields.

Because we don't know everyone's specific interest or inclination, it's all here to digest and consider — along with a wide array of starter lists for general habitats and the specific habitat interests of all the plants. These can be fairly specific, for example: *found on upper side slopes and nose slopes in gravelly to sandy loams.* Or perhaps *backswamps, wet meadows and bottomlands that are high in marl.* Or perhaps *riparian terraces and benches above major rivers and along larger streams.*

Knowing the lingo used in the sciences related to environment is an asset to success in the garden, a tool just as useful as a trusty shovel or a favorite rake.

yard gardens in many homes to deeply spiritual presentations for meditation and ceremony to sprawling stroll gardens that take landscaping to very high art, designers tease magnificence from natural materials. When one famous designer held court for Americans eager for a set of off-the-shelf plans, he pointed out how impossible that might be. All gardens, he said, are designed specifically for a site and with a specific message in mind. The object is for a visitor to discover the subtle philosophy, and it often relates to the culture of his native Japan. But, while we might adopt some of the design practices and artistic sophistication, we as Americans might do well to present our own cultural values — *or suggestions of ecoregions of value to us*. Not replicate. Not miniaturize. *Suggest*.

If this sounds far-fetched, consider the goal of a good National Park Service trail: to take the visitor on a journey of discovery from point of interest to point of interest. We might not be able to put that sprawling vista in our suburban back yard, but we can *suggest* it with the artistic organization of natural materials, to capture the feel and sense of it.

Those hoping for an "oh-so-easy" or "no-care" garden by turning to natural landscaping are likely to be disappointed. A garden is a garden and it requires all the usual care and maintenance one might normally expect. The advantage of a natural landscape, however, is that less resources will be devoted to its survival and more on grooming and management. That, in turn, enhances the pleasure we seek in such an enterprise.

Natural landscapes are not packaged in convenient kits or flats at garden centers, three for ten bucks on special. The hunt for stock can be maddening or exciting, depending on how we want to look at it; sacks of seed might work in some locations, but our goal is to plan site-specific and localized habitats can be very unique and challenging. The depth of expertise comes only from research and a willingness to learn, as with any style of gardening; with knowledge, however, comes both empowerment and enlightenment and consequently personal growth. The result in the field will only be as attractive as we are willing to make it with straightforward work — the sweat and toil that makes recreational activity worthwhile, and allows us, at day's end, to stand back and admire achievement.

Digging in

At the root of endless variations of habitats, from very common to very distinct, are the many different kinds of soil throughout the state. For more than a century, soil scientists have mapped and defined soils by exacting criteria and continue to refine them. Major groupings of soil types have been divided into 360 unique *soil series*, or families. Like all families, they have names, lineage, characteristics, style and locations where they're likely to be found. And there are variations on the theme, in the context of slopes and combinations with nearby neighbors.

What makes it the most significant baseline for landscaping is that the soil research includes the type of habitat as well as some of the characteristic trees found on it. When we compare these to the habitats that plant communities prefer *plus* the ecological organization of forests, we begin to see whole palettes of plants to use for a garden that will be successful in that specific habitat. In other words, we have vital clues for sustainable landscape design.

Even if our design includes non-native plants, an understanding of natural habitat will yield informed and confident planning as well as awareness of how far we're straying from truly sustainable.

Most of Pennsylvania's soils are silt loams, tending toward acidic, and generally formed from shale, sandstone, and limestone, although siltstone, dolomite, and some metamorphic-igneous material appears as well. Soils can vary dramatically in narrow bands, especially in the Appalachians, and become complex pot-potpourri in areas impacted by glaciation. Organic matter within the top 12 inches is rarely above two percent — but decaying vegetation on the surface can result in completely different forest systems. Soils range from excessively to very poorly drained. The consequences of all this variety are endless variations of habitat from very common to very unique.

This brings us to our next critical juncture: finding common ground in the thicket of expressions related to natural landscaping, which comes with an astonishing array of terms that can carry different shadings, depending on the context, the source and often the agenda.

It's helpful to pause for just a moment to consider expressions we'll encounter often in the course of the discussion — not just definitions, but interpretations that can be helpful in our design efforts.

Heading the list are *sustainability, conservation, preservation and restoration.*

Sustainability

In it's simplest terms, *sustainabililty* is conserving an ecological balance by avoiding depletion of, or permanent damage to, natural resources.

Among the more fashionable adjectives attached to landscape design is *sustainable*. At first glance, we might infer that our careful and perhaps even costly design will stay just the way it is without a great deal of effort on our part.

"Easy-care" is attractive to a lot of gardeners. Everyone wants things easy, and home improvement projects ought to be "once-and-done." And so we often lump comforts into sustainability: the garden doesn't require much weeding, won't be bothered by many pests — especially insects but in Pennsylvania especially deer — hardly ever needs watering, always looks nice.

From an environmental viewpoint, we tend to lump gardens into an "either-or" category — i.e. the garden is sustainable or it isn't. These days, to be fashionably "green" it behooves us to fix that which isn't correct and win that gold star of approval.

From the standpoint of encouraging people to think sustainability, the arbitrary nature of this definition is doomed. Gardeners enjoy their hostas, glads, lilies, tulips, azaleas, forsythias, peonies and roses, sustainable or not. And it's not likely that a gardener in an epiphany is going to tear up years of work and dispatch it to compost because it's not perfectly sustainable.

Complicating matters is the ability to measure

> **Because there is, ultimately, no such thing as a truly sustainable garden ... we might find it more helpful to consider sustainable as both a goal and a sliding scale.**

or define natural resources, of which water is perhaps the most commonly cited. Assume a half-acre garden that requires an inch of precipitation per week; during a droughty period, we might irrigate it with 6,500 gallons of water — open the tap and let it run full bore for 18 hours. From our own well, it'll work as long as the water table regenerates that much within the period of use or shortly thereafter. If the well is downslope, we simply draw from the aquifer above and those at higher elevations are simply out of luck. The higher the well on the slope, the more we rely on water that has already fallen as precipitation. By contrast, if we're on a municipal or regional water system, we're pulling water from the community supply and that works only as long as the source can replenish it *and without harming other users of the same supply.*

Because there is, ultimately, no such thing as a truly sustainable garden — there are way too many matters that demand landscape management to avoid a jumbled disaster — we might find it more helpful to consider sustainable as both a goal and a sliding scale.

To accomplish environmental responsibility, we strive for the most prudent use of resources possible. Individual circumstances and unique situations demand compromise for a larger purpose; we sometimes have to adjust our perfection passion for pragmatic reasons: a new plant must be watered in; a gift from a good friend or family member must have a home, even though it's not terribly high on the sustainability list. And gardeners always over reach, ever hopeful that the full-sun plant might do okay in that patch that gets pretty decent light (but in reality is more part shade).

Our individual design may include species that are less than ideal for the specific site, some delicate species that demand a little extra support, or existing materials that are respectable but not perfect. So our garden, as a whole, gets an eight on a scale of ten, fairly decent and certainly better than a four. If we are shrewd with organic layer management, we can stretch the limits of the garden in terms of species range — an artificial adjustment that might bump the score up to an eight-point-five. We might develop beds to sustainable perfection, but accept a turfgrass path as means to enjoy it, dropping our score to six-point-eight, the pH we need to maintain for our grass to look nice.

In nature, landscapes are never truly sustainable. The enemy is *succession* — the long-term consequence of competitors for space gradually altering the ecological community and evolving toward a *climax* system in which the toughest, biggest, sturdiest take over the entire patch of ground. In even the most forbidding patch of open ground, plants gain a foothold and, as they grow, cause their own eventual demise by making the habitat suitable for rivals. And at the opposite end of the spectrum, the most well entrenched climax forest is not immune to change; disease, age, fire, storms, even animals all cause extensive damage that results in openings — and the cycle begins again.

Succession is measured in large blocks of time, generally well beyond the design range of most gardens, but is always present in the natural world. By virtue of holding succession to a given point in time — weeding, thinning, making adjustments — we enforce sustainability in artificial ways.

As a result, it's probably not useful to dwell on sustainability as an absolute standard. Yet we know that the more sustainable a landscape is, the better the garden in both an environmental and routine maintenance context.

Preservation

One effective approach to protecting natural resources is not to exploit them at all, but rather step aside and allow nature to do what nature knows best — a hands-off policy. Some suggest a jumpstart by eliminating lawns, unsustainable gardens, certainly invasives and seeding with wildflower mixes designed for sunny to shady circumstances.

The persuasive argument here is that we share the planet with many creatures, many food chains, many habitats and — just like the climate generally — it's not a good idea to damage entire systems that which we do not fully understand.

Collectively we preserve some natural landscapes, especially those with significant beauty or unique character, to varying degrees. A wilderness area is undeveloped and left for study; a state or national park is managed only to the extent that visitor safety and convenience demands. A shrewd local government gathers the land along an active floodplain for quasi-recreational, sometimes educational, use and at the same time prevents costly damage resulting from periodic floods.

Preservation demands a hands-off approach, encouraging natural succession and in its purest context is sometimes called *deep ecology*.

The problem for landscaping enthusiasts is obvious. A garden by definition is an artistic expression with some form of unified design. A preservation site is just the opposite. One might even say there is no garden at all, just a weedy disarray. That might work well in a region of wild habitat, but tends to stir controversy in suburban neighborhoods simply because it diminishes the property values of neighbors with well-groomed landscapes.

Restoration

Landscapes that have been severely damaged, perhaps even destroyed, by human activity or vast infestations of invasives attract restoration enthusiasts eager to return a site to its original natural beauty. This is especially popular with both wetlands — or areas that should be wetlands — and *riparian* areas along rivers and streams. Perhaps as much as fifty percent of the attention given to ecological communities is devoted to wetlands and stream edges and understandably so. Both of these play crucial roles in the health of freshwater systems.

The tug of "putting it back the way it was" is an admirable one, no matter what the habitat. We

Feeding your forest

Forests are like any other feature in nature. They do just fine if we simply stay out of the way. It's a remarkable process of balance and conservation. During the growing season, leaves change in chemical composition from complicated mechanisms to flower, set seed, grow. As the seasons turn, the leaves are converted into an organic chemical mix designed to accomplish much more.

When it's time to pack it up for the winter, a single layer of cells at the base of each leaf stem causes the leaf to be disconnected and tumble to the ground. It may join discarded branches, limbs, even entire trees on the forest floor. The trash is hardly that. Now the leaf has the exact chemical composition to fertilize that tree. It creates a thick blanket of mulch designed to keep competitors for resources at bay. It's highly acidic and, when it gets wet, makes rainfall a potent chemical designed to dissolve nutrients both above the topsoil and release minerals in the ground to be harvested by the root system.

Because leaves are a perfect mulch, they hold enormous volumes of water, even during extended drought. This serves to cool the forest and limit temperature extremes during the growing season, act as a reservoir to even the availability of moisture to roots, and smooth out temperature fluctuation in the topsoil itself.

Under the messy collection of recognizable litter, we find a rotting and often quite wet mass that still displays familiar shapes. Below that there's a brownish layer often less than an inch thick in which all the nutrients for the tree are stacked up for delivery.

Because trees are prudent managers of water — full grown they can use a hundred gallons a day just to operate — the entire organization of the forest is devoted to conservation. Hold onto *all* the water for immediate use above, secondary use in the topsoil and leftovers, trapped in subsoil, can only head one direction: down to the water table (and the business end of our well or municipal water supply).

The entire process of extracting nutrients from the soil is aided and abetted by vast armies of fungi, insects, bacteria, even small mammals who function in anonymity as elements of an enormous living system.

Trees live and trees die, and when their turn comes they crash to the floor and become part of the next generation, an endless cycle.

Some may have already guessed: take away the leaves in the fall to keep our lawn looking nice and we take away all the natural food and operating system of the forest itself. Further, to keep the lawn looking nice, we often must apply lime to raise the pH to lawn-happy 6.8, when in fact the forest really likes it at a much lower point. And we feed our lawn with high-nitrogen fertilizers ideal for grass but not for trees. Much research continually affirms that the best possible fertilizer for a given kind of tree are the leaves themselves. The tree is genetically programmed to actually alter the chemical composition of its leaves over the course of a growing season, finishing up with just the right balance to make food for a couple of seasons down the road.

broke it; we should fix it. It's not so important that, over time, natural succession will turn an old hayfield into fine oak forest. Our goal is to put it in right now.

A good example of enthusiasm for restoration centers around the American chestnut (*Castanea dentata*). For most of history, as much as 25 percent of old-growth forest in the eastern United States was chestnut — *huge* trees — until importation of Chinese chestnut and genetic tinkering unleashed a fungus for which the native trees had no defense. Within 50 years, the species was virtually

> **Picking a date is one thing. Knowing for certain what was growing there is something else.**

wiped out, and since that time, oaks have come to dominate the same forest landscapes. But in an exhaustive breeding effort, advocates hope to bring a blight-resistant chestnut back, so those original forests can be restored.

Chestnut illustrates one of the difficulties with restoration — we might want to put it back, but can't without chestnut or any number of other species that have gone extinct, are extirpated, or are just commercially unavailable. And the question looms: restore it to what point in time? Pre-European settlement? A hundred years ago? Fifty? Picking a date is one thing. Knowing for certain what was growing there is something else.

A lot of research explores ecological communities — but these are sample plots, generally a hundred feet square, and from them much larger inferences are drawn. Taken collectively, they only include a small fraction of all the species native to the region. Others use field sightings and historical records to determine whether a species is native to the state or not and create distribution maps — but these, too, are samplings and based on data of more recent time.

Professionals involved in restoration are also concerned with *ecotypes,* the specific genetic variants that are ideal for a given site. Specifications for restoration often require that the materials brought in must be correct and may indicate that stock has to come from a range of perhaps fifty miles or less.

Finally, "putting it back" is one thing — especially when dealing with invasives — but keeping it intact requires a long-term commitment to maintenance with all the practical matters most gardeners can fully appreciate.

However, the sum of the research gives us a reasonable foundation to build upon, a fairly solid and reasonable list that provides variety for design and sustainability for the environment. All we need to do, once again, is avoid the temptation of absolutes.

Conservation

In a conservation landscape, success is found through the wise and prudent management of resources. The strict rules of restoration do not apply. The strict hands-off practice of preservation are not a hindrance. Conservation and sustainability share a common goal.

Those concerned with the broader environmental community, such as pollinators and the full food chain for wildlife, can grasp that it's perhaps not as ideal as a totally wild landscape but comes close. A bumblebee doesn't really care how the garden is organized; it only needs the plants to be there. The downside can come with the urge to design only with plants we find attractive. Within plant communities, a succession of flowering occurs from early spring to late autumn, providing an ongoing supply for pollinators. It's almost as if each plant species takes its turn to benefit the several generations of insects such as bees. Skipping species that are lower in aesthetics creates holes in the continuum and suggests that landscapers concerned with pollinators may wish to be more tolerant of less attractive plants in their design.

Overall, a broader plant palette and the opportunity to organize design clearly make conservation landscaping the most plausible. It does not make a landscape maintenance free because weeding remains a constant, and the right plant in the right habitat will reproduce energetically. Some are more placid but others are aggressive spreaders that require constant supervision to avoid taking over the entire garden. The residential gardener sees these chores as the puttering that makes a garden a recreational endeavor, but the commercial property owner regards it as overhead and the municipal authority see it as a budget issue.

However, a wisely planned, properly stocked, simply developed natural landscape is always less time consuming and less expensive than working with non-sustainable exotics and to at least some extent support rather than diminish the larger environment.

DOWN AND DIRTY

When we think of a good garden soil, our imagination typically goes straight toward a rich, black humus just loaded with the possibilities of huge vegetable crops and stunning flowers. When we think of the soil in our back yard, we more often than not sigh with disappointment. It's hard. It's full of rocks. It's either excessively drained or poorly drained. It's acidic. It's not very fertile.

And it's perfect.

Our orientation toward soil, thanks to enthusiasts of organic farming and an energetic horticulture industry, leans toward *mollisols,* one of the more important of the dozen major types of soil found worldwide. The name itself, which comes from the Latin *mollis,* or soft, suggests first-rate dirt. And indeed it is; more than 20 percent of the land area of the United States — and just 7 percent worldwide — is fortunate to have mollisols, which rank as the best agricultural soils of all.

In Pennsylvania, however, these "ideal" soils are relatively scarce. Just one tenth of a percent of the entire state features mollisols, virtually all of them on active floodplains.

The key to the stereotypical rich organic soil are development over a very long time by prairie grasses. These endure relatively harsh conditions by putting roots extremely deep into the ground; as plants conclude a life cycle, the roots decompose into a very thick layer high in organic matter.

Pennsylvania soils are more typical of what's found in forests. These are *mineral soils* — quite literally rock that's been ground up by a variety of forces to create three components: sand, silt and clay. The exact blend, or *texture,* determines whether it's a sandy loam, a silty loam, a silty clay, etc. Compounding soil texture is parentage. Some soils have higher concentrations of limestone and dolomite, while others are derived from sandstones and shales. The former tend to be higher in pH while the latter tend to be more acidic.

The different varieties of soil statewide each have very significant implications for landscaping. Of course, the "ideal" soil is the one we'd like to have to grow the plants we prefer. But in natural habitats, there are no "good" or "bad" soils — just different and resulting in different kinds of plant communities. Understand the soil and half the battle for a successful landscape is won.

Not quite so simple

We often think of soil as just "dirt" — the stuff where a plant puts its roots as kind of an anchor that, in turn, suck up nutrients to feed the plant and help it grow. Better dirt, better plants — and so gardeners are open to modifying the soil (usually by working in organic matter), amending the soil (usually with fertilizers) or watering the soil (the premise being that if it's dry, the plant is unhappy and droops, whereas if it's wet, it thrives).

But it's a bit more complicated that that.

What we often disparage as poor soil or just plain dirt is actually an exotic brew of weathered rock that has widely variable chemical composition. Precisely how changes occur dramatically impact what kinds of plants will grow and thrive on the surface.

Precipitation seeps through a relatively thin layer of decomping plant litter typically structured in such a way as to create an even flow of familiar materials — nitrogen, potash and phosphorus head the list — into the mineral soil where the roots are. The blend on the surface has its own exotic concoction of organic chemicals depending on what it is. Pine needle litter is quite different than, for example, leaves of oak or hickory trees.

As water passes through, it becomes acidic,

Identifying your soil

For many decades, the USDA has been mapping and cataloging soils throughout the United States, primarily to assist farmers and forest managers, civil engineers, and the military not only with the topography but the nature of soils in a variety of use contexts. What used to be the US Soil Survey is now part of the National Resource Conservation Service (NRCS).

Today, this trove of information is available to anyone with just a few clicks of a mouse. In a matter of a couple of minutes, any landscaper can get a very clear picture of what they're dealing with in areas as small as fractions of a building lot.

Here's the path (as of this publication date): http://websoilsurvey.sc.egov.usda.gov/App/HomePage.htm

The site requires some patience when navigating into the "area of interest" (AOI), which can be displayed as an ordinary street map or an aerial image of the property. The prize is a soil survey map showing the boundaries of soil groups and codes identifying the soil. Example: OxB for "Oquaga-Lackawanna channery loam on a 3 to 8 percent slope."

Some basic information will be immediately available in the name and description, but researching the series yields much more. In our example, the survey site identifies both Oquaga and Lackawanna — a consequence of soils being patches too small to map efficiently but so close together that attributes of both can be used. Most are a single series, making the task easier. In Montgomery County, for instance, "BnA" is Birdsboro silt loam on a 0 to 3 percent slope; Birdsboro is the series to investigate (they're all in an appendix)

In urban areas, where soils have been so disturbed for so long, some sites will have variants on "Urban" soil. Best bet: look for the nearest identified series and work with that.

As a reference, a county-by-county list of all soil codes is kept at our companion website, www.pennystone.com/soils, as well as step-by-step in working with soil survey maps.

---

which is essential to help dissolve the fine rock around the roots and release a host of trace minerals that can be quite different depending on the chemical structure of the soil and how long the water lingers within the air spaces around grains of rock.

Yet this is only the beginning; soil itself is teeming with life in many forms. We immediately think of chipmunks, voles, mice and other small mammals, and then possibly a variety of other creatures — beetles, worms and the like. Yet a single gram of soil can host *millions* of bacteria, fungi and other microscopic creatures, hard at work on tiny habitats, making life possible further up the food chain. It's such a complicated process that the relationship between all this life is still a matter of conjecture and is a long way from understood.

Over thousands of years, plants have evolved to work with the blend and thus are borne habitats suitable for plant communities. In other words, if we alter it in the *slightest way*, we risk messing things up for an *entire system*.

This is soil conservation in its most basic sense — as well as the core explanation as to why adapting to habitat and working with the natural collection of species works better than trying to control the habitat and change it to suit a whim.

From the top down

We can think of soil as a sort of layer cake with a stack of components important to everything growing on the surface. These layers are called *ho-*

Topsoil

Soil textures — the ratio of sands, silts and clays — impact drainage, with sands the most permeable and clays the least. In specific soil descriptions, soils are always identified as to the type of loam. Silt loams are the most common in Pennsylvania.

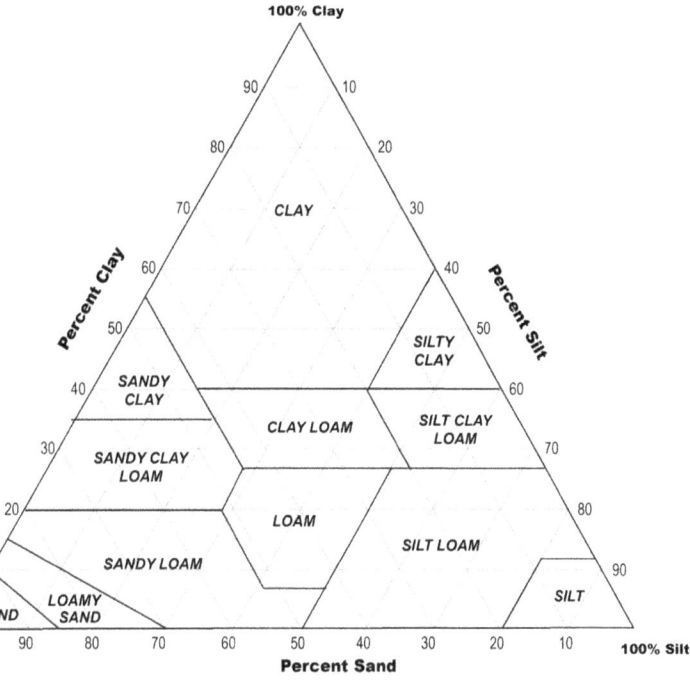

Soil texture summary

In order of increasingly fine particles: sand, loamy sand, sandy loam (all three which may be further subdivided as coarse, fine or very fine), loam, silt loam, silt, sandy clay loam, clay loam, silty clay loam, sandy clay, silty clay, and clay.

rizons, and each plays part in hospitality to plant life.

A typical *pedon* — or patch of soil has, from the top down, a series of horizons that serve particular functions:

- O Horizon — Organic matter in various stages of decomposition, sometimes subdivided into Oi, Oe and Oa to represent layers that are well recognized (freshly fallen leaves), partially decomposed (generally wet and rotting but still somewhat recognizable) and humus (so fully decomposed that they are no longer recognizable).
- A Horizon — What we know as *topsoil*. The upper part of the soil and the best material for plant growth. In most areas of Pennsylvania, it has between 1 and 7 percent organic matter, most typically about 2 percent by dry weight.
- E Horizon — The *eluviation* layer, in which soil material from topsoil, especially minerals, transfers or leaches into lower levels by downward movement of water.
- B Horizon — What we know as *subsoil* and often stony.
- C Horizon — The *regolith* layer composed primarily coarsely broken rock from parent material just below it.
- R Horizon — What we know as bedrock, solid and impermeable.

A good basic loam

A *loam* is a soil composed mostly of sand and silt with a smaller amount of clay — somewhere in the range of 40, 40 and 20 percent by dry weight, respectively. These are the vast middle range of soils in the USDA textural classification triangle and likely where our garden soil is likely to be found.

Sand is defined as rock or mineral fragments ranging from 0.05 millimeters to 2.0 millimeters in diameter (anything larger is considered gravels). We find sandy soils to be easily worked, well drained and quick to warm up in the spring. Because they keep the soil from compaction, water easily passes to improve drainage and counter clay and organic matter, which impedes flow and retains water, respectively.

Silt ranges from 0.05 down to 0.002 millimeter. Silt particles and are the most efficient source of minerals for plants. It is easily and most commonly transported in water (as well as ocean currents) and is fine enough to be moved great distances by wind as dust.

Clay is less than 0.002mm in diameter. How much and what kind of clay effects fertility and physical condition of the soil, including the ability to react chemically and retain water. Clays are responsible for shrink-swell potential and therefore drainage, as well as plasticity, ease of soil dispersion and permeability (also known as *saturated hydraulic conductivity*).

Because the proportions of loam can vary, we can further define loam soils into meaningful categories: sandy loam, silty loam, clay loam, sandy clay loam, silty clay loam and loam. As a group, these soils share features important to our landscape plans because they contain more humus, moisture and nutrients than sandy soils, are better drained and accept more water and air than silty soils and are easier to work than clay soils.

Moderately coarse textured soil includes coarse sandy loam, sandy loam, and fine sandy loam.

Moderately fine textured soil includes clay loam, sandy clay loam, and silty clay loam.

A loam soil with just a bit of organic matter — about two to three percent — makes a splendid soil for food production.

The more extreme corners of the soil texture triangle have distinct characteristics that affect plant life found there.

Sands — specifically sand and loamy sand — are at least 85 percent sand and less than 10 percent clay. In general habitat parlance, these are *coarse textured soils*. *Sandstone* is a sedimentary rock containing dominantly sand-size particles. Sands, comprised mostly of quartz, comes in grades that are especially useful in designs involving rock gardens, barrens and rain gardens:

Very coarse — 1.0 to 2.0mm
Coarse — 0.5 to 1.0 m
Medium — 0.25 to 0.5mm
Fine — 0.10 to 0.25mm
Very fine — 0.05 to 0.10mm

Silts — soil that are 80 percent or more silt and less than 12 percent clay. *Siltstone is* sedimentary rock made up of dominantly silt-sized particles.

Clays – Soils that are 40 percent or more clay, less than 45 percent sand, and less than 40 percent silt. *Fine textured soils* include sandy clay, silty clay, and clay. Shale is a sedimentary rock formed by the hardening of a clay deposit; *slate* is shale that has undergone metamorphic change, sometimes involving volcanic ash.

Soil moisture

Soils are categorized in a range of moisture regimes that have enormous impact on the types of plants suitable for a given site. General factors involved include soil texture (which impacts drainage), moisture holding capacity (often related to organic matter), position in relationship to the water table (typically, the higher, the drier), and position in relationship to sunlight (north and east-facing slopes tend to be cooler and more moist while south and west facing slopes tend to be warmer and drier).

Drainage

Another important feature of soil is *drainage* — the natural frequency and duration of periods of partial to complete saturation. As a general rule, the higher the position on a slope, the faster a soil is drained because soils tend to more coarse and because the water table is so much lower.

There are helpful definitions for various kinds of drainage used in both soil science and ecology, which directly impacts the types of plant communities that will do well on a given site. When we identify our soil, the drainage class is included. The seven classes of natural soil drainage defined by the

Soil Terminology 101

Soils have *taxonomy*, just like plants, beginning with 12 great orders and then classification depending on a uniform set of geological standards. Naming conventions create terms that at first appear intimidating — such as "Aquic Fragiudepts" — just like the exotic Latin constructions that put different species of plants into their proper botanical bin.

The very specific identification of a soil — sort of like the common name of a plant — is happily in plain English and often referencing a geographic location. So we have Lackawanna, Allegheny, Berks, Funkstown and others. Just as plants have "species," soils have "series."

Just as biologists strive to perfect animal and plant taxonomy, geologists do the same with soils. Over time, they've developed an elaborate set of definitions for scientific precision, far more than most landscapers would ever need to consider.

But the broad picture does help, simply because the terms show up in cross references with ecological research, and in discussion, we bump into the terms related to soils all the time — their structure, drainage, composition, moisture, movement.

NRCS are:

- ***Excessively drained:*** Water is gone very rapidly; these are usually very coarse textured, rocky or shallow soils, sometimes on steep slopes, and never exhibit mottling related to wetness.
- ***Somewhat excessively drained:*** Water is gone rapidly; these are usually sandy and rapidly pervious soils, sometimes shallow and sometimes so steep that much of the water received is lost as runoff. They also never exhibit mottling related to wetness.
- ***Well drained:*** Water drains away readily, but not rapidly; these are generally medium textured soils, mainly free of mottling. An important requirement is that moisture is available to plants throughout most of the growing season, and wetness does not block growth of roots for significant periods during most growing seasons.
- ***Moderately well drained:*** Water drains somewhat slowly during some periods, often because of a slowly pervious layer below the surface or there is periodically high amounts of precipitation. Such soils are wet for brief periods during the growing season, but occasionally be wet enough to impact most mesophytic crops.
- ***Somewhat poorly drained:*** Water drains slow enough that the soil is wet for extended periods during the growing season, often due to a slowly pervious layer, a high water table, nearby seepage, continuous rainfall or some combination of all. The soil is wet enough to inhibit growth of mesophytic crops unless artificial drainage is provided.
- ***Poorly drained:*** Water drains so slowly that the soil is saturated periodically during the growing season or remains wet for extended periods often due to a slowly pervious layer, a high water table, nearby seepage, continuous rainfall or some combination of all. Although the soil is not continuously saturated in layers below plow depth, ponding is severe that growing agricultural crops almost certainly requires artificial drainage.
- ***Very poorly drained:*** Water drains so slowly that free water is found at or on the surface during most of the growing season. These are usually level to depressed areas and are frequently ponded. Without artificial drainage, most mesophytic crops cannot be grown. Very poorly drained soils are commonly level or depressed and are frequently

ponded.

Permeability

The ease of how water moves downward through the soil is *permeability,* and, again, there is no good or bad — just reality and the consequences of how it impacts the plant community. It's measured as the number of inches per hour that water moves down through saturated soil. Terms describing permeability and often cited in soil descriptions are:

Very slow — less than 0.06 inches per hour
Slow — 0.06 to 0.2 inches per hour
Moderately slow — 0.2 to 0.6 inches per hour
Moderate — 0.6 to 2.0 inches per hour
Moderately rapid — 2.0 to 6.0 inches per hour
Rapid — 6.0 to 20.0 inches per hour
Very rapid — more than 20 inches per hour

Available moisture

Another helpful factor in evaluating soils to match plant requirements is *available moisture,* also known as available water capacity. This relates to the ability of a soil to hold water and keep it available for use by most plants. Expressed as inches of water per inch of soil, it's usually considered in a 60-inch soil profile or to a limiting layer — the latter being an underground feature that keeps water from saturating any further and, in effect, makes it a shallow soil.

The technical definition is the amount of soil water at field moisture capacity and the amount at wilting point, but for gardeners it gives a more specific definition of "dry-mesic-moist," and also helps identify wetlands, either seasonal or year-round.

There are five classes of capacity:
Very low — 0 to 3 inches
Low — 3 to 6 inches
Moderate — 6 to 9 inches
High — 9 to 12 inches
Very high — more than 12 inches

Soil reaction

The relative acidity, neutrality or alkalinity of a soil is measured in pH values. A pH value of 7.0 is precisely neutral, and soils in the range of 6.5 to 7.3 are often referred to as *circumneutral.* This is a logarithmic, not linear, scale, which means that a pH value of 5.0 is ten times more acidic than 6.0.

In the context of natural habitats and plant preferences, there are ranges often cited for each species, sometimes the upper and lower limits and sometimes a preference.

A given soil series can vary somewhat statewide, but a specific soil map unit, such as the precise one for our back yard, is much more narrowly defined.

There are some spots with extremely acidic soils, but none in Pennsylvania that are alkaline.

Terms related to pH:
Extremely acid — below 4.5
Very strongly acid — 4.5 to 5.0
Strongly acid — 5.1 to 5.5
Medium acid — 5.6 to 6.0
Slightly acid — 6.1 to 6.5
Circumneutral (or simply neutral) – 6.5 to 7.3
Mildly alkaline — 7.4 to 7.8
Alkaline — 7.9 to 8.4
Strongly alkaline: 8.5 to 9.0
Very strongly alkaline: 9.1 and higher

The organic soil component

Soil organic matter is plant and animal residue at various stages of decomposition.

The standard for measuring organic content is a percentage by weight of soil material less than 2 millimeters in diameter. Many forest soils are surprisingly lean in organic matter, with just one to two percent being relatively common.

In a normal forest ecosystem, a series of layers of decomposing organic materials - generally leaf litter, twigs and branches, last season's herbaceous plant matter and the remains of a variety of animal life create layers. At the top is fresh material, and at the bottom is a thin veneer of completely decomposed matter that provides nutrition to plant roots below as chemicals leached into the soil by water.

In agricultural practice, organic soil content is maintained, perhaps enhanced, by returning crop residue to the soil; decorative landscapes are routinely amended with the addition of imported humus and surfacing with rapidly decomposing mulches.

It is reported that soil with more than six percent organic matter will likely have virtually no stormwater runoff, but high organic content is not always a good thing. An overload of nutrients can cause excessive growth and ultimate weakness in some herbaceous species and can be toxic to others. Soils very high in organic content also subside upon drying and cause destabilized root systems, and because of high porosity will need larger volumes of water on a sustained basis to recover.

Humus improves porosity of fine textured soils and binds together particles in coarse-textured soils. These properties enhance internal drainage and aeration and increase field capacity of the soil.

A correct balance creates an efficient soil, primarily because of water-retention capacity, the promotion of soil organism activity, and as a nutrient source. Nature regulates this process with thick layers of forest litter in varying stages of decomposition. Fresh material on top acts as an insulation to stabilize soil temperature and reduce transpiration rates. It also captures and holds passing water supplies for sustained support of the active system below.

Older material is modified by microbial and fungal activity, which breaks materials down into workable humus. Water passing though often forms mild acids to transport mineral content toward roots and also breaks down the mineral content in the soil - all providing a complex chain of organic compounds to sustain the plant.

Trees in particular are exceptional models of recycling, drawing a specific blend of compounds from the soil, using them temporarily in the active phase of growth, both for structure and to assist in phytochemical processes that produce flowers, seed and new growth. When leaves are discarded in the fall, the mineral content of the leaf has changed and returns the materials to the soil surface for use in future years.

Soils and too much water

Engineering and agriculture professionals have understandable interest when too much water is predicted in any given soil.

As a result, soil series descriptions assembled by the National Resource Conservation Service of the U.S. Department of Agriculture pay careful attention to how well drained a soil might be, how easily water flows through it well below the surface, and issues of ponding and flooding.

These last two possibilities interest ecologists and conservationists because these are zones where wetland species often concentrate. Native plant landscapers designing water features ranging from artificial ponds to rain gardens will also find such zones to be helpful models.

Flooding is a temporary inundation of an area caused by overflowing streams, from stormwater running off adjacent slopes, or by ocean tides. Water that stands for a short period after rainfall or snow melt is not typically considered flooding. Sites that grow in flood-prone areas are useful for landscape rills and rain gardens because they can withstand inundation for varying periods of time.

Ponding is standing water in a closed depression and includes swamps and marshes. Water exits by deep percolation, transpiration, evaporation or some combination of all three. Swales, bioretention basin and rain gardens are built specifically for the potential of ponding.

Frequency of occurrences in the context of soil science relates to the number of events anticipated in an average year.

Flooding values include:

None - not probable; the chance of flooding is nearly 0 percent in any year. Flooding occurs less than once in 500 years.

Very rare - very unlikely but possible under extremely unusual weather conditions, less than 1 percent chance in any year.

Rare - unlikely but possible under unusual weather conditions, with a 1 to 5 percent chance in any year.

Occasional - occurs infrequently under normal weather conditions, with a 5 to 50 percent chance in any year.

Frequent - likely to occur often under normal weather conditions, with a more than 50 percent chance in any year but less than a 50 percent chance in all months in any year.

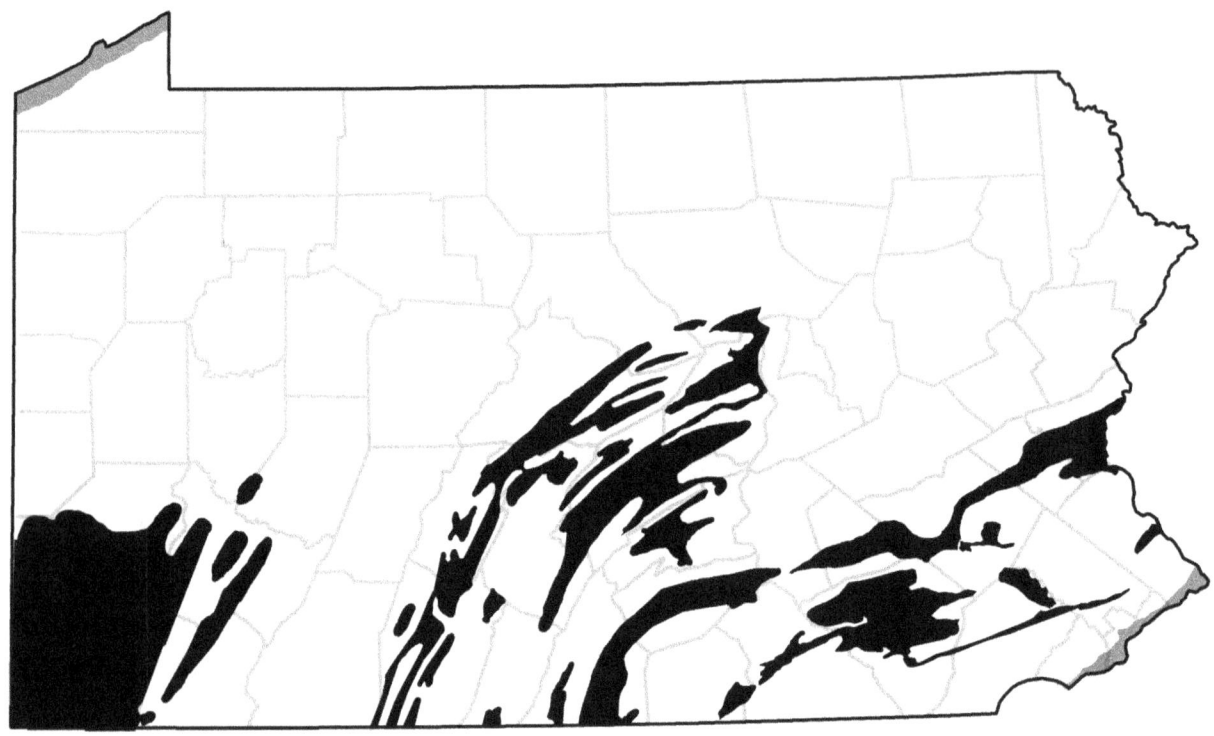

Soil foundations of Pennsylvania. Above, areas whose soils are limestone; thin gray corner bands are unconsolidated sediments. Below, soils from sandstone bedrock.

Soil foundations of Pennsylvania. Above, areas whose soils are of sandstone origin. Below, soils from igneous and metamorphic rock, including serpentine.

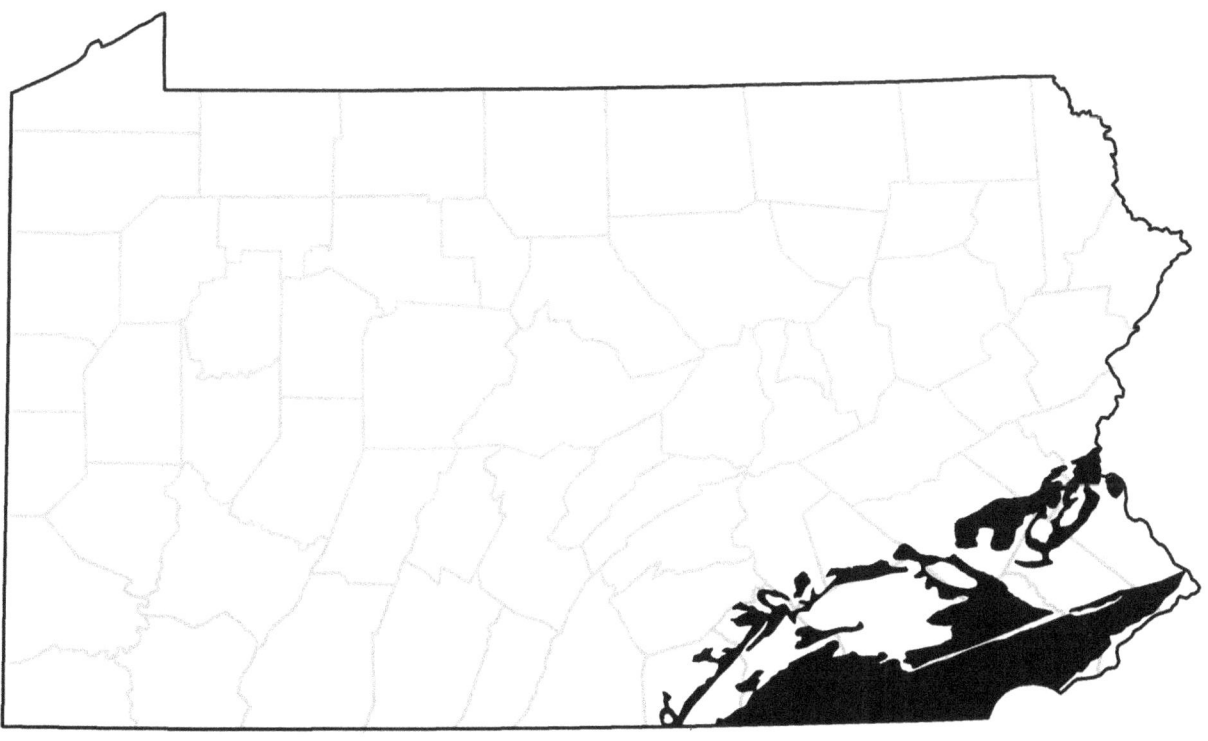

Very Frequent - likely to occur very often under normal weather conditions, with a chance of more than 50 percent in all months of any year.

Ponding values include:

None - not probable; the chance of ponding is nearly 0 percent in any year.

Rare - unlikely but possible under unusual weather conditions, with a nearly 0 percent to 5 percent chance in any year.

Occasional - occurs, on average, once or less in 2 years, with a 5 to 50 percent chance in any year.

Frequent - occurs, on average, more than once in 2 years, with a more than 50 percent chance in any year.

An overview of wetlands

About half of the researched ecological communities in the region are classified as wetlands, a distinction with serious ramifications for permitted land use and responsibilities - so much so that precisely what defines a wetland is as much a legal issue as an environmental one.

It's not surprising that so much attention is given to wetlands — these are critical features in the freshwater supply chain and we ignore their importance at our peril.

We often think of wetlands in the context of open swamps and marshes, lake and pond edges, bogs and the active channel of rivers and streams. But geologic anomalies create a number of other habitats that lead to distinct ecological communities. These include woodland swamps, seeps, fens, and even some wet meadows.

The common thread is that significant amounts of water are very close by, either laying on, just at or right under the surface and very often mucky soils are hosts to plant species that like it much more than damp.

Swamps can be any area of low, saturated ground - usually because of poor drainage or high water tables - and sometimes covered with water, with or without the accumulation of peat. They are similar to *marshes*, which can be periodically wet to continually flooded with shallow water and are

---

What's a wetland?

The full, formal definition of a wetland:

A wetland is an ecosystem that depends on constant or recurrent, shallow inundation or saturation at or near the surface of the substrate. The minimum essential characteristics of a wetland are recurrent, sustained inundation or saturation at or near the surface and the presence of physical, chemical, and biological features reflective of the recurrent, sustained inundation or saturation. Common diagnostic features of wetlands are hydric soils and hydrophytic vegetation. These features will be present except where specific physicochemical, biotic, or anthropogenic factors have removed them or prevented their development. - (National Research Council, 1995 p. 55)

---

often dominated by sedges, cattails, rushes and hydrophytic plants. Stagnant water left in poor drainage areas behind natural floodplain levees and the adjacent slopes are called *backswamps*.

Bogs are waterlogged, spongy ground that attracts sedges, heaths and especially mosses such as sphagnum. These are usually highly acidic, low-nutrient sites with strong potential to develop into peat. *Fens*, on the other hand, are waterlogged but often circumneutral to slightly alkaline, and often considered closely related to very wet meadows. Reeds and rushes are more common.

When moisture is substantial under the surface but somewhat more dry than fens, *meadows* are the common result. To remain as open ground and not become forested, substantial water flow often demolishes trees and shrubs trying to get started. Meadows are often found on the floodplains of high volume rivers, where seasonal flooding and ice scour cleanses the surface. When clogged by unexpected occurrences or the activity of creatures like beavers even small stream blockages cause meadows to develop because the ground becomes too saturated for trees to grow.

> ## Calcareous soils
>
> Pennsylvania includes vast quantities of calcareous soils — most commonly limestone, but also dolomite — as evidence of long periods of history in which much of the state was a shallow sea.
>
> Most limestone, technically forms of calcium carbonate, comes from the skeletal remains of marine organisms. A similar type of rock, dolomite, is believed to come from the influence of magnesium-rich groundwater on lime mud and limestone and is technically calcium magnesium carbonate.
>
> These soils tend to have higher pH levels than siltstone, shale and especially sandstone, but because they dissolve in water tend to erode quickly and are primarily responsible for *karsts* — vast networks of underground drainage systems in which sinkholes and caves are common.

Where aquifers leak in small areas, we find springs or the lesser-flow *seeps,* where reflow or lateral subsurface flow keeps the surface saturated during dry periods. An substantial seep may be less than an acre in size, but a unique ecological community nonetheless.

Wetland indicators

Soil surveys concentrate on drainage — and now permeability — in the taxonomic context and in *available moisture* to a depth of 60 inches in county-by-county samples. Additional factors include seasonal fluctuations in water tables, especially during winter, and frequency of flooding and/or ponding. These additional factors are critical in soils where underground obstructions sometimes causes water to perch — making what should be a dry, well-drained soil a potential *palustrine* wetland. The results can become quite precise in narrowly defined areas, but a larger view suggests that most soils can be defined as dry to mesic, mesic to moist and wetland, with a special category for those along streams and rivers (*riparian*).

Research conducted by the U.S. Fish and Wildlife Service evaluates many plants on the probability that the will occur in wetlands or not. These *indicators* provide the landscaper with additional clues for site consideration because they tend to describe how wet or dry a site might be. Cultivation for many — but regrettably not all — plants include wetland indicator designation; again, these create suggestions and criteria for plant choices in a garden.

Definitions include:

Obligate wetand (OBL) — almost always occurs in wetlands; a 99 percent chance under natural conditions.

Facultative wetland (FACW) — usually occurs in wetlands but sometimes in non-wetlands; a 67 to 99 percent likelihood.

Facultative (FAC) — equally likely to appear in wetlands or non-wetlands; a 34 to 67 percent likelihood in wetands.

Facultative upland (FACU) — usually found in non-wetlands, a 67 to 99 percent probability, but occasionally found in wetlands, a 1 to 33 percent probability.

Obligate upland (UPL) — almost always occurs in non-wetlands under natural conditions, a probability of more than 99 percent.

These descriptions are sometimes accompanied by a positive (+) or negative (-) sign which indicates the frequency leans toward the wetter (+) or drier (-) ends of the category.

Moisture categories

Soil moisture expressions can be roughly matched with wetland indicators to assist our evaluation of a soil against the wetland indicators for many plant species. These are:

Xeric — Extremely dry, often because of excessive drainage; moisture availability very low; dries very rapidly after precipitation;

wetland indicator UPL.

Dry — Dry, typically because of rapid drainage; moisture availability low; dries soon after precipitation; wetland indicator FACU to UPL.

Mesic — Somewhat moist, with adequate moisture retention throughout the year; available moisture is moderate; dries at a moderate pace; wetland indicator FAC.

Moist — Remains moist to slightly wet for most of the season, with slow to somewhat poor drainage; available moisture moderate to high; dries slowly; wetland indicator FACW.

Hydric — Wet for substantial periods or often inundated by water; drainage is poor to very poor and the water table can be at or near the soil surface for most of the year; never really dries; indicator OBL. A soil need only be saturated for a portion of the year to be rated as hydric.

Types of parent materials

All mineral soils are formed by the effects of weathering of rock; given the time and energy source, even the hardest boulder will eventually be just a pile of sand, silt or clay. In soil descriptions, which of several different parenting processes can make a difference in the character of the soil and the habitats that result, as well as offering design suggestions for models of these types of habitats.

Residuum is partly to fully weathered or unconsolidated mineral material accumulated from the disintegration of bedrock in place; residual soil material found where it was created.

Colluvium is unsorted and unconsolidated soil and rock transported or deposited at the base of slopes or on side slopes as a result of either mass movement, or local and runoff. These can be dramatic — such as an abrupt landslide — or more subtle, such as long-term flattening or cutting back of a hill. A landscape representing the base of the slope would likely include a variety of rock and soil to suggest colluvium.

Alluvium is unconsolidated soil and rock deposited by flowing water, including sand, silt, clay, gravel, boulders or any mixture of these. *Slope alluvium* is a special term referring to sediments gradually moved downslope by non-channel alluvial process - that is, slope wash - and characterized by particle sorting. Rivers and streams continually cut and transport enormous amounts of material in three ways: *dissolved load*, in which such rock as limestone is actually carried in solution; *suspended load*, in which the force of moving water carries the material in the current; and *bed load*, in which the force of moving water pushes heavy material along the stream bed. With more velocity and volume, material moves downstream. When the pace slows, materials are deposited along the stream. Landscape representations of streams would routinely feature a variety of river stone organized in such a way as to indicate how the material flowed in.

Lacustrine sediments are deposited at the bottoms of lakes, especially in the context of ancient glacial lakes that vanished when lakes retreated but left broad open plains of glacial outwash. These tend to be high concentrations of sands and silts in a very smooth to slightly rolling pattern.

WHAT DO THEY CALL...

With our own soil information in hand, we begin to wonder about the sometimes colorful, even amusing, references that describe it.

For example, Kensington silt loams are found on "sideslopes, noseslopes, headslopes and interfluves of till plains." On the other hand, we find Lackawanna loams on "nearly level to steep glaciated hillslopes and ridges of the Allegheny Plateau."

These expressions, from the NRCS Glossary of Landform and Geologic Terms, describe with great precision the nature and location of specific soils — and just happen to be also used to describe habitat sites for most plants. From the site descriptions, we can also infer a great deal — especially about relative soil moisture. For example, available moisture on the higher elevations of nose slopes and summits will tend to be sparse, while soils on lower elevation footslopes will be much more mesic to moist. Summits and interfluves tend to be exposed to harsher weather, while coves and toeslopes tend to be sheltered and, as a result, cooler.

Plants are more generalists than soils and can usually survive in a variety of locations. But preferences — where they really do well — can be another matter and get quite specific.

As we develop our personal plant list, knowing the details about our site clearly gives us an advantage when considering plants.

Uplands, Lowlands

The most basic line of demarcation between types of landscape sites are *lowlands* and *uplands*, broad and informal terms that essentially define areas that water flows into (lowlands) rather than comes from (uplands).

Lowlands are low-lying, comparatively level land, often in the vicinity of water. This is most classically the tidal marshes found close to sea level, but it can also mean higher elevation floodplains, swamps and depressions. It's fairly common for floodplains to operate within a series of terraces on either side of the stream or river channel that often define what we know as annual, periodic or once-in-a-century flooding. These areas generally make poor choices for building sites and gardens — although floodplains are historically occupied as villages surrounded the easiest navigation routes and are attractive for agricultural purposes. Lowlands are generally excellent opportunities for publicly owned conservation and recreation sites, so it's a good idea to encourage government officials to invest in them. There are more than 83,000 miles of rivers and streams in Pennsylvania, the most outside of Alaska, and to conservationists, protecting stream quality is a very big deal.

Of interest to all landscapers, however, are many lowland features — especially floodplains — because when we create rain gardens, we are, in fact, modeling these to help manage local stormwater runoff. Through the shrewd management of stormwater, we not only make our landscapes sustainable, but we support the efforts of those concerned about stream quality.

Uplands, by contrast, are higher ground, i.e., all those parts of hills, ridges and mountains, low and high, steep and gentle, smooth and bumpy. The very lowest parts of slopes, adjacent to lowlands, are often lumped in with the lowland because of potential flooding, but technically remain elements of the upland. It is here that almost everyone lives and works and gardens. Plants suitable for just about every type of site are often described as being found on uplands, such as "rich, mesic upland sites."

Almost always, "upland" implies some sort of slope. Although level ground is level in some locations, it more likely is a gentle to very steep slope. Soil map units sometimes divide large blocks of the same soil series into gradients, with 0 to 3 percent grades being the flattest. Grades under 15 percent are popular for building sites, but many slopes can routinely range much steeper, up to and including sheer cliffs.

Geographers consider slopes in two dimensional and three dimensional terms, the former being looking at a profile of a cross section and the latter being a downward-looking view that reveals contour lines of elevations.

Slopes in profile

If we cut vertically through a hillside, we see it profile, or two dimensions and in Pennsylvania, these hills generally follow a fairly standard shape: rounded on top, a convex curve near the summit, a somewhat straight line down the center and a concave curve at the bottom.

In full scale, the location of a site will affect habitat, so it's worth understanding. As we shape the surface for design purposes, our suggestions of much larger surfaces by modeling these contours adds authenticity to our finished look.

Among the most common description of preferred habitat is *hillslope*. the generic term for the steeper part of a hill from summit to the base, and often used to describe habitat options anywhere on the hill (including most ridges). An example might be "the species is found on dry to mesic *hillslopes*." Less frequently used is *mountain slope*, which means the same thing, but on a mountain.

In profile, all hillslopes have five key elements:

- **Summit** — the topographically highest position of a hillslope profile, with an almost level to slightly convex, relatively wide surface. The technical difference between a summit and a *crest* is that the latter is much more narrow and tends to be linear in shape; here the slope shoulders come quite close together. Both mountains and hills can have summits, while narrow ridges usually have crests.
- **Shoulder** — the profile position near the top of a hillslope that features a convex and highly erosional surface, and which forms the transition zone from the summit to the backslope. The name is reference to the shape of a human shoulder, which it often resembles. Both summits and shoulders tend to have thin, coarse and well drained soils — an important qualifier for xeric to dry landscape sites, and it is often in these areas that barrens occur.
- **Backslope** — The part of a hillslope profile that forms the steepest and usually linear middle part of a slope, found between the shoulder and the footslope below. If there are *free faces*, or cliffs, they will be found in this part of the slope. Erosional forces here include *mass movement*, or landslides, *colluvial action*, such as falling rocks, and running water, especially stormwater runoff from above. Precisely how the water crosses the area can have a dramatic impact on evolution of the slope and the types of plants that grow on it. As a general rule, backslopes tend to be more dry near the top and more mesic near the bottom, and successful vegetation can significantly reduce erosion and improve moisture levels of the local soil.
- **Footslope** — The concave surface at the bottom of a hillslope, this is an important transition zone between areas of erosion and transport above (shoulder and backslope) and areas of deposition further downhill. This is the area where *talus* — a mass of rock fragments often found at the base of cliffs

> **A slope, also called slope gradient or gradient, is defined as the inclination of the land surface from the horizontal.**
>
> **Steepness of a slope is in percent — the vertical distance divided by the horizontal distance, then multiplied by 100.**

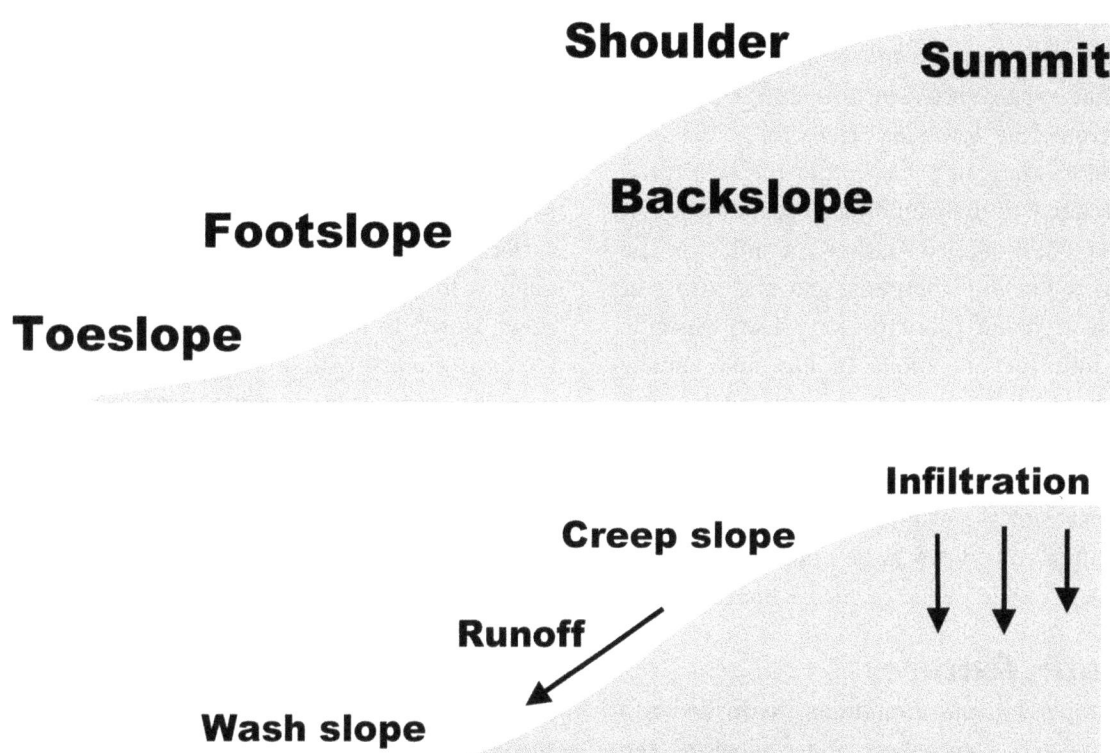

Above: physical elements of a slope often used in habitat descriptions. References to *hillslope* implies any part of the slope above the toeslope. Below: The same slope from an *erosional* point of view.

and very steep slopes — collects. Most of the soils found here are *colluvium,* having formed from the disintegration of talus or brought down as soil via erosion from above. It is generally mesic to possibly moist because of the depth of erosional materials gathered here. The name is a reference to the concave curve of the human foot at the ankle.

Toeslope — The very bottom, gently inclined area that marks the transition from hillslope to valley floor. They are only slightly concave, and most are virtually linear in grade. This is the area where colluvium from upslope erosion gathers, tends to be deepest and richest soil on the slope and because groundwater levels are high, also tends to be mesic to moist. Because this margin of colluvium can sometimes resemble a floodplain terrace, it is often included in the broader description of "lowland," but is still technically part of the hillslope.

Mountains and hills

A subtle, but sometimes significant, difference in habitat and soil references distinguishes mountains from hills, and to complicate matters even more, the terms can have local and somewhat arbitrary definitions.

For our purposes, a *mountain* is an elevated land surface that rises more than 1,000 feet above the surrounding lowlands, usually with sides greater than 25 percent gradient and may feature substantial exposure of bare rock. It has a nominal summit, can occur individually or in a group to form a chain or range, and was probably created by tectonic or volcanic activity, but differential erosion is a possible creation factor.

On the other hand, a *hill* is an elevated land surface that ranges between 100 and 1,000 feet above surrounding lowlands. Here the slopes are typically more than 15 percent, and the summit is nominal relative to the bounding slopes, most often a rounded, well-defined outline. A hill can be defined as a *low hill* (between 100 and 300 feet high) or a *high hill* (300 to 1,000 feet). Specific types of hills include *knolls* (a low and usually small, rounded hill), *mounds* (a rounded low hill usually less than 10 feet high and constructed of earth materials), and *hillocks* (low hills between 10 and 100 feet with slopes ranging from 5 to 30 percent and often considered to be *microfeatures* of a landscape).

Mountain features

From top to bottom, mountains are divided into specific zones by geographers and geologists. The *mountain top* is a relatively level and gently sloped part featuring bare rock, residuum or nearby colluvial material, and the very highest point is the *peak*. Between the top and the base we find the *mountain slope* or *mountain flank*, which is comprised of long, complex backslopes and relatively steep side slopes. These present a wide variety of colluvial surfaces and complex hydrology just below the surface, often leading to creep and landslides. The flank can be subdivided into segments: upper, middle and lower thirds. At the lowest end of the mountain slope we find the *mountainbase*, featuring concave aprons or wedges of colluvial materials, extending onto valley floors where it eventually merges with alluvium. The *mountain valley* tends to be V-shaped and in the process of erosion by streams or U-shaped, indicating it's been modified by a glacier and featuring either a till or alluvial base.

In three dimensions

If we look straight down on a hill or ridge, the feature takes on a more three-dimensional form usually shown as contour lines on topographic maps.

As mentioned above, uplands are areas where water comes *from*. The journey of water is the primary force behind Pennsylvania's current and still evolving topography. How cleverly we use this resource is the foundation of sustainable landscape design.

A simple experiment illustrates the much larger principles. If we lay a sheet of paper on a smooth surface and push the opposite edges inward, we quickly form a very neat, virtually symmetrical ridge. Now let's consider the summit and a gloomy forecast: cloudy with a very strong possibility of rain. Our paper ridge is going to get wet, and water will always obey the laws of gravity. A single drop lands at the exact summit of our ridge — so exact, in fact, that it might pause before choosing which side to roll down.

In geology, this spot is an *interfluve*, that decision making point where water could go either way. In Pennsylvania, it could easily mean a choice between the Allegheny and Susquehanna watersheds. Our drop could wind its way into the Ohio River system, then the Mississippi and eventually pass through New Orleans into the Gulf of Mexico. Or it could roll eastward, down into the Chesapeake Bay and out into the Atlantic. Along the way, it will of course advance the cause of erosion, perhaps being the tipping point drop for a massive rock slide into a valley or as seemingly insignificant as tweaking the bedload of a stream by a fraction of an inch.

But at that moment of decision, at the top of the paper ridge, the drop of water will detect the slightest variable that results in a pathway. Improved by one drop, the next one takes the new, less resistant route and the pathway is eroded a bit more. Now drops from the side can join in and cut a bit more. The result is a *headslope* and as centuries pass, the persistent drops *dissect* the ridge to form what looks like a V-shaped *cove*. More and more water from along the way gravitates into the ephemeral run at the center of it all (the head of a stream, hence the name of the slope) and away from the part of the ridge that escaped all the cutting — what's called a *nose slope*.

In our brief impact on the environment, the rill we might create at the base of a downspout forms

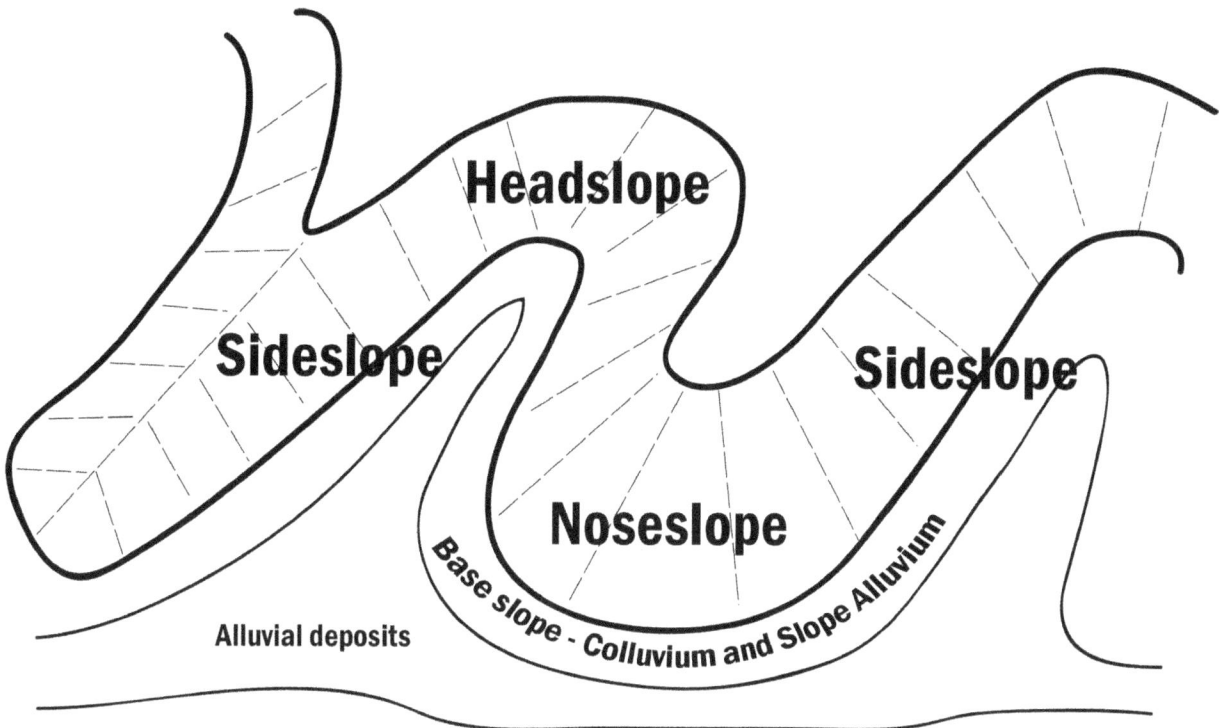

Looking down on a part of a *dissected* ridge. Runoff will go away from the *noseslope* and toward the *headslope* whenever it can, making noseslopes drier and headslopes richer and more moist. On sideslopes, runoff heads straight down as *sheetwash*.

an elemental headslope, and how we engineer the flow of water away from the building creates mini-habitat opportunities. If the drainage route is broad and gentle, it will more resemble a floodplain. If it's steep, make it v-shaped and include stone material for a lining to speed up the flow for landscape effect. The center point of what will become the water channel, by the way, is properly called a *thalweg* and defines the route the water will take.

Two entirely different habitats emerge within a very short distance of each other. The headslope, or cove, is rich with organic matter and fine soils from either side. Sheltered from extremes of weather, it becomes a cool, moderate, generally moist place ideal for a wide range of species that relish this level of comfort. By contrast, the nose slope might have been spared the deformation but is left with much more coarse soils, much less water, and must face weather extremes — especially direct sun and heat. So this becomes a dry, even xeric, habitat, best for species that prefer harsh conditions.

Sometimes there's a straight line of slope that divides headslope from noseslope, a bit of transition. These are called *sideslopes* and in some situations become the homes of very distinct habitats, depending on how steep the slope is and how much *sheetwash* comes down from above — stormwater runoff that goes straight down the hill in a straight line, as quickly as it can. Sheetwash with any degree of regularity, volume and force can literally peel the soil and, with it, vegetation, right away from the bedrock. And then it will begin carving up the rock.

But wily landscapers have already come up with a "yes, but..."

Exactly. All the fallen logs, branches, twigs and especially leaves act like a giant sponge to suck up a lot of passing water and hang onto it. Instead of racing away downhill, much of the rainfall is diverted into the soil, as we discussed earlier in the basics of feeding a forest.

Meanwhile, damage to the sideslope has been minimized. What damage was done winds up at the bottom, in the *base slope*, as *colluvium* that blends with *alluvium* deposited by the local stream in one of its recent floods. And so it finishes as welcome material for species that like a richer, deeper, more moist blend of dirt.

Not all slopes take a direct line to the bottom. Erosion can be irregular and bedrock resistance variable. The result are *benches*, upon which pockets of *depressions* can take shape, especially in areas mauled by glaciers. These may be just a bit moist and richer than the surrounding terrain, but they can also be "drainage problem" spots, especially in the spring. The culprit can be a surge of runoff that is held or blocked from moving along. But more likely it's a *fragipan*, a layer of soil so dense that even tree roots and certainly water find difficult to penetrate. If the fragipan is relatively shallow, water can *perch* on it for extended periods. The result is that the low spot becomes increasingly saturated, even to the point of ponding, until summer and slow drainage resolves the matter.

Many ecologists find these *palustrine* areas enchanting for the unique communities that take root and thrive in it. Many farmers find them distressing and often install artificial drainage to clear them, and many developers do likewise to make them suitable construction sites. It's an expensive alternative to working with it; those fortunate enough to have one may find them most intriguing as landscape opportunities and contribute to the general quality of life by recognizing that flowing water sometimes pauses to keep the larger community balanced.

Our brief journey brings us back to lowlands, most commonly a *valley floor*. This is a nearly level to perhaps gently sloping surface where we find an assortment of *terraces* constructed by floods and wear of the flowing water. The flood plain itself may feature steps and terraces, natural levees — possibly with attendant *backswamps,* and a wide range of stream channel possibilities, depending on gradient and flow throughout the seasons.

As we shall see, however, it's a dynamic and ever shifting land feature with may design possibilities for natural gardens.

Streams and drainage systems

Pennsylvania's 83,000 miles of streams comprise drainage systems that can often be traced back to their *head*, or point of origin, most often found at the upper reaches of a slope or valley. These represent the highest point of a *fluve* or *drainageway,* described as a linear or elongated depression along which water flows at some time.

In fact, if one were to establish a line from the lowest points at any given latitude on a slope, one would map out a *thalweg,* which serves as the very bottom of a channel from its starting point near the highest point of any landform to the nearest ocean. An important feature of drainageways are that they can not exhibit a defined channel - for example, swales and *headslopes* - or have a small defined channel, as in the case of *low order streams*.

The highest point, from which water flows in at least opposite directions, is called an *interfluve,* typically found on the *summit* or *crest* of a hill or ridge, a comparatively level or gently sloped area but one that feeds at least two drainageways. Low points on ridges between heads of streams flowing in opposite directions are called *saddles*.

As soon as water begins to flow in an organized pattern, erosion begins, and with it the dissection discussed above. Contour lines are usually concave curves, and while the slope can range from simple to complex, it nonetheless tends to gather colluvium and slope wash sediments - also known as *slope alluvium* - and generally be more moist than surrounding areas. Headslopes contain the drainageway and pull water away from adjacent nose slopes.

Low order streams are the smallest and unbranched of tributaries for larger streams. Streams with a designated order of "one" eventually converge with another and the segment becomes order "two." The junction of two second-order streams results in an order three stream, continuing upward until becoming the highest stream order before entering an ocean (e.g., the Delaware and Susquehanna River systems; the Allegheny, while substantial, merges into the Ohio, which in turn joins the Mississippi).

A *drainage basin* is defined as an area bordered by a distinct drainage divide and occupied by a *drainage system*, which can mean a region as large as the entire Delaware River drainage system or as small as a single low order stream.

Each steam's collective drainage system typically falls into one of several categories of *drainage patterns,* depending on the plan view of a configuration or arrangement cased by local geologic structure and materials, geomorphic materials and the geomorphic history of the region. Also sometimes called a drainage network, these typically include three within Pennsylvania:

Dendritic - a very common pattern in which tributaries join a gently curving main stream at acute angles, which resembles the branching habit of a deciduous tree. This pattern results where the primary stream receives several tributaries that are in turn fed by even smaller tributaries and suggests streams flowing across horizontal rock strata and the homogenous soils typical of landforms found on soft sedimentary rock or crystalline rocks that offer even resistance to erosion.

Trellis - a relatively common pattern that results when generally parallel main streams, such as those found in adjacent valleys to ridge lines, intersect at or nearly at right angles to their tributaries. Those tributaries are in turn served by long, secondary tributaries and short gullies that arc parallel to the main stream. This produces a plan view that suggests a trellis and often occurs where beveled edges of alternating soft and hard rock outcrop in parallel lines - particularly in interbedded sedimentary rock where folded-mountain topography is found.

Deranged - A clearly disordered drainage pattern with non-integrated streams suggesting an absence of control by underlying structure and bedrock found on relatively young landscapes with a flat to slightly rolling topographic surface and a typically high water table. This results in comparatively few and irregular streams with low numbers of short tributaries and which flow out of an into depressions featuring lakes, ponds, marshes, bogs and swamps. These often regional streams meander through the area but generally do not influence drainage, and surfaces between streams are often swampy. Deranged systems are most often found in glaciated areas on thick till plains and moraines, but can also develop on established floodplains and coastal plains.

Each of these represents a modeling opportunity for the movement of stormwater through the garden, and dendritic patterns are likely the most common. On the other hand, a path layout involving right-angle intersects with the main path invites trellis structure and all the possibilities of landscaping that go with it.

Riparian features

Coming from the Latin *ripa*, meaning river bank, the expressions *riparian zone* or *riparian area* represent the interface between streams and rivers and the adjacent land. One of the 15 major terrestrial biomes on the planet, riparian areas are a serious matter to ecologists, conservationists and civil engineering because of the role they play in habitat biodiversity, soil conservation and critical influence on fauna and aquatic ecosystems. They can be grasslands, woodlands, wetlands and even non-vegetative. Those concerned with the health of these regions often refer to them as riparian buffer zones.

Although sometimes referred to as "bottomland" (an obsolete and informal term), riparian areas include a *floodplain,* possibly a natural *levee* (also known as an *earth dike*) and potential *backswamp*, and a variety of *terraces.*

A *floodplain* is defined as a nearly level plain created from sediments (alluvium) deposited during regular flooding as well as the lateral migration of streams (including rivers). Small plains can be known as *alluvial flats,* while very broad to extensive ones can be known as *alluvial plains.*

Streams sometimes create natural *levees* along edges, but more often the feature is an artificial embankment designed to confine stream flow to the channel. Levee is the preferred expression for "floodwall." Natural levees evolve on both sides of the channel when, during floods, the stream must deposit the coarsest part of the load. Natural levees generally exhibit a gentle slope away from the river and toward the surrounding floodplain, with the highest elevation very close to the river bank.

When an overloaded stream breaks through a levee, materials are deposited on the floodplain, especially coarse-grained material, to become a *floodplain splay.*

The area between natural levees and nearby valley sides or terraces often becomes a large, marshy to swampy area across a large natural depression called a *backswamp* and layers of silt and clay deposited there are known as *backswamp deposits*. This differs from a *slackwater,* or still to quiet body of water, which is in stream rather than outside of the levee.

Two types of wetlands are often found in riparian areas, but are more affected by groundwater levels and poor drainage than periodic flooding:

Swamps are low and saturated ground either intermittently or permanently covered with water and predominantly covered with water and tend to be populated by shrubs and trees; an accumulation of peat is possible, but not necessary.

Marshes are periodically wet or continually flooded areas with the surface not deeply submerged. These tend to be populated by sedges, rushes, cattails and other *hydrophytic,* or species that grow in standing water, plants.

When designing rain gardens, these models take us away from the stereotypical shallow depression and open up an enormous set of design possibilities. How much we flood, how often, to what depth and for what period of time implies a variety of plants and opportunities for overall appearance.

Fans and deltas

An *alluvial fan*, which is typically shaped like an open fan or segment of a cone, is an outspread area of loose alluvial materials, sometimes with gentle slopes, that were deposited by a stream where water is no longer kept to a narrow, rigid channel. This can be where the stream widens dramatically after it leaves a narrow valley, or where it merges with a larger stream. The steepest part will be near the apex that points upstream and slopes run in a gentle, convex shape outward (downstream) with a gradual decrease in gradient.

Fan piedmonts are formed when mountain-front alluvial fans blend into one generally smooth slope, with or without undulating surfaces or from accretions of fan aprons.

A *fan apron* forms when relatively young alluvium and soils cover part of an older fan piedmont and sometimes alluvial fan surfaces. These are generally further downslope and thicker than fan collars. The material buries older soils that traceable to the fan apron edge; there the older soil emerges as land surface, also called *relict soil*.

A *fan collar* is made up of short, thin, relatively young alluvial layers on the very upper part of a major alluvial fan. Mantles bury older soil traceable to the edge of the collar where the older soil emerges as a *relict soil*.

A *fan skirt* is an area of smooth, small alluvial fans from gullied cuts into the fan piedmont. These merge laterally, but can also be extensions of inset fans that merge with each other and the basin floor near toeslopes.

A *delta* is a fan-shaped and nearly flat area of alluvium deposited near or at the mouth of a stream as it enters a body of more quiet water like a lake or sea. Within the nearly level *delta plain are* numerous smaller channels that allow the stream to break into even smaller sections and dissipates.

Deltas are most dramatic when streams enter an *estuary,* such as the Delaware and Chesapeake Bays. Here fresh water mixes with seawater and encounters the impact of tides. Estuarine deposits are typically fine-grained sand, silt and clay of both marine and fluvial origin, often including decomposed organic matter and laid down in brackish water. Coves, bays, inlets and lagoons found along these areas often result in very distinct and unique ecosystems.

But in our back yard, the fan we create at the end of a rill from a downspout becomes a distinctive garden feature, not to be overlooked in a natural design.

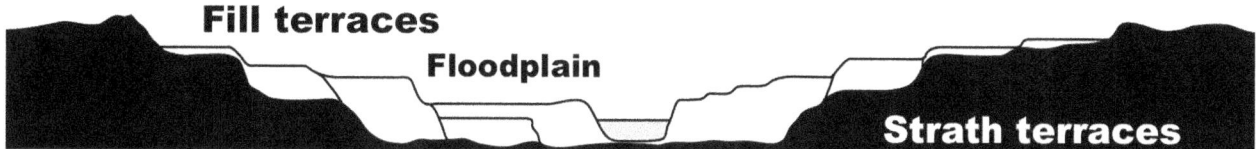

Basic elements of a riparian zone. At the center (in gray) is the *active channel,* surrounded by a series of terraces. Those cut into bedrock by the stream or river are *strath terraces,* while those created by deposition of alluvial materials are *fill terraces.* Just to the left of our channel is the *active floodplain,* the part of the valley that will be flooded first. There is often a natural levee along the channel, which may or may not survive a serious flooding event. If it does, and the floodplain drains very slowly, a *backswamp* is the result. This land feature is an excellent model for a backyard rain garden.

Terraces and steps

Different than *stream terraces* are *floodplain steps,* a flat alluvial surface that is *below* the 100-year flood level and often inundated by the current stream or impacted by fluvial scour or sediment deposition. These may be single or multiple steps and are also known as cut terraces or cut-and-fill terraces. Steps were originally called *first bottoms,* an informal term describing the lowest flood-plain steps to experience routine flooding, but the term was deemed obsolete because the frequency of flooding was inconsistently defined. The horizontal surfaces are called *treads* and the vertical surfaces are known as *risers (terrace slope* is not a recommended term).

The step-like surfaces *above* the 100 year flood stage are called *terraces* or *stream terraces.* These are often described as being *paired* or *unpaired,* a reference to a matching or non-matching terrace on the opposite bank. Adjacent to floodplain steps we find *fill terraces,* made up of alluvial materials that are rarely if ever flooded, having been laid down much earlier (and higher) in the history of the active channel. Sometimes these are beneath current floodplain deposits, in which case they are called *buried fill terraces* or *nested fill terraces.* Fill terraces are also known as *aggradational* terraces — they are being built up by alluvial deposits.

All terraces consist of a flat to slightly sloping surface called a *tread,* which is bordered on one side by a steeper, descending slope called a *riser* or *scarp.* It is possible to have a tread bounded on all sides by a descending riser, and narrow terraces are sometimes called *benches.*

Fill terraces can be 300 feet thick or more and represent the result of an existing valley being filled with alluvium, typically a consequence of an influx in bed load because of glaciation or change in the power of the stream that created the valley. Until a point of equilibrium is reached, the stream will continue to deposit material and then it will begin to transport it again. This point can be reached quickly or over very long periods of time, depending on the exact and shifting circumstances.

Strath terraces develop from the stream *downcutting* through the bedrock. As this process continues, the valley may widen and the channel may move laterally. When the downcut forms a deeper valley, many strath terraces are no longer subjected to the flooding that may have left thin veneer of alluvium, usually less than 10 feet thick with coarse gravels just above bedrock.

Cut and strath terraces are also known as *degradational* terraces — they are being slowly degraded by the force of the moving water.

As these sites are adjacent to the bases of slopes, *colluvium* - materials reaching the base of a slope under the force of gravity - may mix (or *interfinger)* with the abandoned alluvium, and a new round of erosion begins. Strath terraces are often referred to as *high terraces.*

When the stream downcuts evenly on both sides, it may create *paired terraces* found at the same elevation on opposite sides of the channel. If the stream encounters more resistant material on one side, *unpaired terraces* - single terraces with no corresponding terraces on the resistant side - are the result.

Thus, if we construct a basic depression for use as a rain garden, we may wish to consider a series of terraces that are flooded to varying degree — a brief shower affects the first bottom, then successive terraces as the torrent increases; the higher terraces will be the first to drain, impacting plant selection.

Stream features and processes

From the faintest trickle at the top of a headslope to massive forces entering estuaries, moving water is more responsible for altering landforms than any other geomorphic activity, as well as creating a number of specialized landforms that host unique plant communities.

Earth materials of all kinds are constantly being moved, if ever so slightly. A raindrop falling on a hillside creates a tiny impact crater, and with it the surface soil is shifted slightly downslope. Groundwater dissolves limestone and seeps onto the surface, displacing the adjacent surface moisture that, in turn, begins a journey to the sea. A brief rainfall erodes a tiny bit of rock and trickles down to join faint runoff. At the instant of movement, these materials become sediments.

This article discusses the basic terms and processes related to *fluvial geomorphology* - that is, how moving water creates various landforms which result in various plant habitats.

These sediments are commonly described as *alluvium*, which is properly defined as unconsolidated fragments (or *clasts*) of pre-existing rock - including gravel, sand, silt, clay in various combinations - deposited by running water. Sediments on the move include materials found in:

Suspended load — all organic and inorganic matter carried in suspension by moving water

Dissolved load — all organic and inorganic matter carried *in solution* by moving water; literally minerals that have been dissolved from water contacting surface materials.

Bed load — coarse materials like stones and gravel that move along the stream bottom by rolling or sliding.

Rivers and streams are consequently measured in terms of:

Capacity — the maximum load that can be transported related to its discharge, often calculated in cubic feet per second; the more water flowing, the greater the capacity to haul sediment.

Competence — the maximum size of particles capable of being hauled; the stronger the flow, the larger the particles that can be transported in suspension or bed load. As a general rule, competence increases as a square of velocity, so if the velocity doubles the force of the water increases four times; if it triples, the force is up nine-fold.

In addition to dissolved load, which can typically represent about 20 percent of the capacity, streams continually pick up and drop solid materials from the *channel* (which may be enlarged during a flood event). Stream channels are defined as the hollow bed where a natural body of surface water flows or may flow, typically enclosed by banks or splayed across a fan surface.

When the water flows fast, more particles are picked up than dropped; when it slows, more particles are dropped than picked up. The amount of material moved by rivers is significant. Even smaller streams have the capacity to move tons of dissolved load daily, and it is estimated that the Mississippi River *every day* moves more than *1.3 million tons of sediment* into the Gulf of Mexico.

The City of Philadelphia is built on materials that washed down the Delaware River from melting glaciers.

Within relatively constant flow (typically measured in cubic feet per second, or *cfs*), the narrowing of channel by adjacent topography results in greater depth and/or velocity. As the channel widens, water depth becomes more shallow and/or velocity decreases. The former serves to increase load and the latter causes load to exceed the ability of the stream to move it, resulting in deposition.

As streams continually *downcut* the materials at the bottom of the channel, the shape of the bed can vary considerably and plays an important role in the health of the stream:

- **Runs** are stream sections where the flow is relatively even and unimpeded. While current may be swift, the surface is smooth.
- **Riffles** form where the underlying rock is more resistant to erosion. The stream becomes relatively shallow (one to three feet) and a likely place for under-surface obstructions like large rocks to collect. As water flow is compressed and then quickly drops, velocity increases. This results in areas of noticeable turbulence, even rapids; the combination of turbulence and velocity oxygenates the water.
- **Pools** just below riffles form where rock is less resistant to erosion and the force of water coming over a riffle magnifies the force on the stream bed. Because the water deepens, velocity drops. Pool sections are, from upstream to down stream, are called tongue, throat, belly and tail

The combination of riffles and pools create a important feature of cold water streams, particularly for such fish as trout. The riffle is where many species of insects reproduce or grow to maturity - but the velocity of the moving water pushes many into the adjacent pools in a form of biological drift to feed the fish. Best feeding locations for fish are the tongue and the tail of a pool, with choices depending on warm temperatures and the corresponding need for oxygen found at the tongue versus the conservation of energy and ultimate safety from predators at the tail. If food is abundant, fish may move away from riffles and pools to feed in runs.

Coldwater streams are the primary systems within a watershed making their health extremely important to all of the connected streams, rivers and ultimately, lakes throughout the watershed. These vitally important coldwater streams act to control excess sediment and nutrients from entering the lower portions of a watershed, which means better overall water quality, biodiversity and improved recreational opportunities. They are also vital in controlling water levels, whether it is in times of drought or in the event of a flood. A healthy coldwater system will sustain the larger, lower portions through a steady base flow from the headwaters. Their importance also extends to terrestrial wildlife as the native vegetation that binds the *riparian zones* are effective wildlife corridors.

If our landscape plan involves an artificial stream, these channel features are good models to add realism to the design.

Types of streams

Commonly named rivers, creeks, brooks, runs, many hundreds of briefly to permanently flowing water systems are responsible for much of Pennsylvania's varied landscape in networks of *drainage systems*, but ultimately, they are all *streams*.

A stream is any body of water that runs, under the force of gravity, to progressively lower levels in a somewhat narrow but well-defined channel on the ground surface, in a subterranean cavern, or beneath a glacier that usually includes a mixture of water and dissolved, suspended or entrained material.

Stream types include:

- **Perennial stream** - a stream that flows continuously throughout the year with a surface that is usually lower than the water table of the adjacent region. These include *rivers*, described as a natural, freshwater surface stream of substantial volume and generally with a permanent base flow with a defined channel moving toward a larger river, a lake, or the sea.
- **Intermittent stream** - a stream that can be dry for three or more months of the year, with a channel generally lower than the local water table, which flows only when it receives base flow during wet periods or groundwater discharge from melting snow or other occasional surface or shallow subsurface sources. These include *creeks*, which are generally larger than a brook but smaller than a river.

Ponds and pools

Water features are attractive to landscapers, the more energetic of whom often install backyard ponds, sometimes with pumped water flow through a circulating stream. In the parlance of natural design, a *pond* is defined as a body of fresh water found in a small depression, typically smaller than a lake but larger than a pool. A pool is also a natural body of standing water, but more commonly found in a marsh or a depression puddle following rain.

Of great interest to ecologist are *vernal pools*, which are closed-depression seasonal ponds that support semi-aquatic to aquatic ecosystems, usually in the spring, but dry out in summer to fall. These wetlands are often the result of snow melt perched on dense fragipans with no outlet or by high seasonal groundwater levels.

***

Ephemeral stream - typically a small stream that flows only after precipitation; it gets no lengthy water supply from snow melt or other sources and has a channel that is always above the water table. These include *brooks* and *runs,* described as very small ephemeral streams, especially resulting from a spring or seep, which conducts less water and for shorter distances than a creek.

A common variant is a *braided stream*, which features multiple channels that interweave as a result flow being repeatedly divided and converged around inter-channel bars, suggesting the strands of a complex braid. Typically limited to wide, shallow streams that feature steep gradients, high bed load, non-cohesive bank material and follow a fairly straight line. The cross sections of channels tend to be more shallow, broader, less stable with steeper slopes than *meandering channels.* Braided stream is preferred over the sometimes used "braided channel."

Bars result from ridge-like accumulations of gravel, sand or other alluvium within the channel, along banks or at the stream mouth when reduced velocity results in deposition. Types include channel and meander bars. A secondary reference is to ridges, banks or other mounds of sands and gravels built up by waves and currents on coastal shorelines, especially in estuaries or just offshore from beaches; these are typically submerged at high tide.

In *bar and channel topography,* a recurring pattern of small, threadlike ridges between 18 inches and six feet high, divided by shallow troughs are unevenly spaced across low-relief floodplains, typically less than 6 percent slopes. Common on meandering floodplains, the micro-elevation variances are defined by the competency of the stream, and the bars are usually coarser sediments contrasting with fine-textured sediment in the troughs.

Other types of water courses used by ephemeral to permanent water flow include:

Ravines - small stream channels that are often V-shaped, narrow and steep sided, larger than a gully.

Gullies - steep sided small channels result when intermittent water flow, usually after heavy rains or ice-snow melt, cuts into unconsolidated materials. Deeper than 18 inches, a gully can impede wheeled vehicles and are too deep to be obliterated by ordinary tillage.

Rills - very small channels with erosion-created sides cut into unconsolidated materials as a result of concentrated but intermittent water flow, usually during and right after moderate rain or after snow-ice melt. These tend to be less than 18 inches deep and can be obliterated by ordinary tillage practices.

Ditches - open and rarely paved channels excavated to move water for drainage or irrigation to or from a landscape. These can include modified natural waterways and tend to be smaller than canals.

Wetlands

In addition to the much more common riparian landscapes, Pennsylvania has a variety of wetlands, rich in plant species and interest by ecologists simply because the role these areas play in freshwater supply and special habitats. Some properties have seasonally-wet areas, primarily in the form of *ponding* that invite very unique landscaping to support conservation efforts.

Others may find these types of habitats useful when developing models such as back yard ponds, often with pump-assisted or stormwater drainage flow.

Descriptions of plant habitats often include many of the terms discussed here.

Generally found in lowlands are a variety of unique wetlands in addition to streams and rivers, some of which may be of interest to specialty garden models.

Lacustrine, palustrine

In soil survey work, "water" is the generic map unit for any open body of water that does not support rooted plants.

A wide variety of water-related features appear in Pennsylvania, including:

Lacustrine areas: Lakes, ponds and pools
Palustrine areas : Swamps, bogs, fens, marshes, and floodplains (discussed separately)

Lacustrine features

Permanently standing bodies of fresh water in surface depressions rank from the largest to the smallest:

- **Pool** - a small natural body of standing water, including standing stagnant water in a marsh, but also a temporary puddle in a depression following a rain. A *vernal pool* is a naturally occurring seasonal pond in a closed depression that can support an aquatic or semi-aquatic ecosystem adapted to the annual cycles of standing water in spring and dry beds in summer and fall.
- **Pond** - usually smaller than a lake and larger than a pool; also an artificial, small body of water used as a water supply source.
- **Lake** - larger than a pond and too deep to allow vegetation (except subaqueous vegetation) to take root completely across the water. Lakes have distinct features that may be of interest when modeling them in small scale as backyard ponds.
- **Lake terrace** - a relatively narrow shelf, partially built and partially cut, created along a lake shore in front of a scarp line sometimes exposed if water levels decline.
- **Lake bed or lake plain** - bottom of a lake, but also flat to gently undulating surface made up of fine-grain sediments deposited in a former lake.
- **Lake shore** - a narrow strip of land in contact with or bordering a lake, especially the beach.
- **Lacustrine deposits** - sediments and chemical precipitates deposited on lake beds.

Palustrine features

A *bog* is typically spongy, waterlogged ground that consists mostly of mosses and contains acidic, decaying vegetation (sedges, sphagnum and heaths) that have the potential of developing into peat.

- **Highmoor** bogs are found in upland with a surface covered by sphagnum moss; because of the high water retention of the moss, the health of the bog is more dependent on precipitation than the local water table. These are often described as a *raised peat bog* or a *blanket bog*.
- **Lowmoor bogs** occur slightly above or just at the water table, on which it relies for the accumulation and preservation of peat, mostly from the remains of reeds, sedges, shrubs and a variety of mosses.
- **Muskegs** are typically sphagnum bogs with grassy tussocks or hummocks found in wet, poorly drained boreal regions, featuring deep accumulations of organic material. They are most frequent in areas of permafrost.
- **String bogs** are peat areas featuring narrow

ridge of peat that are roughly parallel, interspersed with minor depressions that can contain shallow pools. The ridges are commonly three to 10 feet wide, up to three feet high and can be nearly a mile long. The ridges are usually better drained and allow shrubs and trees to take root.

Common soils in bogs are often called *muck*, which consists of highly decomposed organic matter in which the original plant material is no longer recognizable (or *sapric*). Muck typically has higher mineral content and is generally darker in color than peat. *Mucky peat* is organic material at an intermediate decomposition state where plant material can be recognized (or *hemic*). Herbaceous peats include *moss peat, woody peat,* and *sedimentary peat* (floating aquatic material, animal waste, some mineral soil).

A *fen* is spongy, usually waterlogged ground that contains alkaline decaying vegetation, such as reeds, that eventually develop into peat. These are sometimes found in sinkholes of karst regions. *Marl fens* include substantial amounts of a combination of clay and calcium carbonate, typically showing as a mucky grey-white material.

A *marsh*, typically covered by sedges, cattails, rushes or other hydrophytic plants, is found in areas that are periodically to continually flooded, but with a surface that is not deeply submerged. *Low marshes* are generally bare, flat ground on the seaward side of a salt marsh and generally subjected to tidal flooding; sometimes called a *mud flat*.

A *seep* consists of generally small areas in which water flows slowly out of the land surface. Although they are too small to be considered springs, the flow is enough to keep the surface soil nearly saturated during dry periods.

A *swamp* is a region of saturated low ground that can be permanently or intermittently covered with water and generally populated by trees and shrubs, with or without a peat accumulation.

Pocosins are large wet areas found on nearly level interfluves in the Atlantic Coastal Plain. They feature distinct vegetation relative to adjacent areas and may be comprised of organic or mineral soils. The term is a Native American expression for "swamp on a hill."

A *swale* is an open, shallow depression in unconsolidated materials that does not have a defined channel but can direct surface and subsurface flow into a drainageway. The soils are usually more moist and thicker than the surrounding area.

A *rill* is a water channel with steep sides so shallow that it can be obliterated by ordinary tillage. They form in the earliest stages of erosion from intermittent water flow, typically during and after rain or ice-snow melt. In sustainable development, rills can be cut into paved materials to direct stormwater runoff in a desired direction.

Depressions and basins

Often considered the model for rain gardens, basins and depressions are widely varied landforms that generally include areas where drainage enters and, if only for a little while, lingers. A basin is sometimes also defined as a "low area of the Earth's crust, of tectonic origin, in which sediments have accumulated."

Popular rain garden designs involve the excavation of soil to form a large, shallow pan, typically to accept runoff from roofs by directing downspout flow into them. During stronger storms, the pan fills and slowly discharges into the soil rather than running off into stormwater collection systems.

A *closed depression* is without a natural outlet for surface drainage; examples include sinkholes; topographic maps would show a complete loop in contour lines. An *open depression* has at least one natural outlet for surface drainage; areas of lower ground would be obvious on a topographic map where an incomplete loop is shown.

In rain garden applications, where water is left to seep into the ground, it would be closed; where stormwater can rise to a point and then depart by a rill, it would be open.

In nature, these may or may not be lowlands - an area of low, comparatively level ground in contrast to adjacent higher areas (uplands), most commonly valley floors and alluvial flats.

Basins can include lowlands, but also ancient glacially-related alluvial (flowing water) and lacustrine (lakes and ponds) regions that are rarely, if ever, flooded. Floodplains dominate areas where through-drainage systems are well-developed and these rarely include lake plains. A basin floor generally grades mountainward toward the edges of piedmont slopes and include all the eolian, alluvial and erosional landforms below the piedmont slope; and basin-floor remnants are the lower-most and nearly level parts of basin floors dissected after stream erosion.

Slightly different implications involve depressions, which represents a somewhat sunken, low-lying part of the surface, oftentimes surrounded by higher ground. These tend to be more localized features and are often caused by glaciers digging out the surface or by surface collapses resulting when minerals below the surface are washed away and the land settles.

Because of the potential consolidation of water and drainage issues, depressions can host unique plant communities, but because they are by definition a collection point for fine-textured and hence slowly-draining soils, they create something of a challenge for rain garden designers. Splendid when wet, the conditions of dry periods may cause problems for plant populations and advocates of rain gardens remind us that it should completely drain within 72 hours if we are to avoid mosquitos. Sandy soils drain more quickly, but are not necessarily suitable for depression-loving plants (that may secondarily benefit from water tables being near the surface for substantial periods of the year and hence moist to wet).

Shallow, open depressions in unconsolidated materials lacking a defined channel are called *swales*. While no specific channel is evident, water can travel overland or subsurface into an adjacent drainageway. Soils in swales are usually moister and thicker compared to surrounding soils, a consequence of erosion and accumulation.

Swales can also be shallow and small closed depressions in ground moraine deposits unevenly deposited by glaciers. These are elements of swell and swale topography, which is a combination of well-rounded, small hillocks and closed-depression swales. Typically scattered irregularly across low-relief ground moraine with slopes commonly less than 2 to 6 percent, this topographical effect is a subdued, undulating surface, with variances in elevation less than 20 feet.

The expression "swale" is sometimes applied to the trough-like depressions between beach ridges, usually parallel to the coastline, but a more correct term is interdune.

Potholes are closed depressions ranging from 3 to 80 feet deep, mostly circular or elliptical found on till plains, recessional moraines or outwash planes. Pothole lakes occur on disintegration moraines and typically include intermittent or seasonal ponds and marshes.

The consequences of ice

Pennsylvania has endured continental glaciation several times, the most recent two called *Illinoian,* about 770,000 years ago, and *Wisconsinan,* which lasted 100,000 years and ended about 10,000 years ago.

Although the Illinoian extended a bit further into northeastern and northwestern parts of the state, it was the Wisconsinan that left the most dramatic impact: people.

We're familiar with concerns about melting glaciers — the global impact of climate involving ice sheets and the freshwater supply issues involving alpine glaciers. The latter begin when snow does not melt in the summer and is added to during the following winter. The weight of it compresses the base into ice, and ice obeys the laws of gravity, carving out U-shaped valleys and providing a considerable ongoing supply of fresh water from perpetual melt at the bottom edge.

An ice sheet is an altogether different matter. By definition, you don't have one until the ice covers at least 20,000 square miles, which is precisely what the *Laurentide Ice Sheet* did. Sea levels — not to mention the entire surface of the land underneath the ice — sank dramatically and allowed the first humans to cross into North America, reaching present-day Pennsylvania just as the ice began to leave and the region was a vast tundra, rather like Arctic features today, including permafrost and sparse forest for thousands of years.

A popular analogy to the flow of continental

glaciers is that of pancake batter being poured onto a griddle - it spreads from the center outward and sometimes forms irregular edges called *lobes*. Two distinct lobes from different directions impacted Pennsylvania.

> The *Erie Lobe* flowed southward from Lake Ontario and Lake Erie to cover the northwestern corner of the state
>
> The *Champlain Lobe* flowed southwest from Lake Champlain to cover the northeastern corner of the state

The unglaciated area in between is known as the *Salamanca Reentrant*.

Each lobe made a different mark. Because the general terrain in the Lake Erie region is far more gently rolling, glacial flow was less impeded and deposits were spread out fairly evenly. At the other end of the state, however, the intense folding and steep ridges resulting from tectonic collisions impeded the glacial path. Here the glaciers carved through ancient valleys, leaving a familiar U-shaped path and pushing billions of tons of material with it. Glacial retreat was even more messy, sometimes with those valleys completely filled with debris and changing the course of rivers.

A good analogy to glacial deposits — called *till* — can be found in the early springtime at any shopping center parking lot. Over the course of the winter, snow removal crews create mountains of material scraped from the pavement. Once looking pristine white, the mass becomes more and more grey as the snow melts and the lot debris picked up with the snow becomes more concentrated. Eventually, a few inches of dust and gravel remains to be collected and hauled away.

Glaciers are the same thing, just a bigger scale and when they melt, enormous volumes of liquid water carry the rubble sometimes huge distances from the terminal point. But a retreating glacier also drops its load in place. In northern Pennsylvania, these deposits can be not just the few inches of a parking lot, but up to hundreds of feet thick. Among the silts and sands left in the wake are boulders that can be as big as a house. When huge blocks of ice were briefly trapped under a mound of till, the end result were *kettles* that sometimes became lakes or bogs.

Down the line, *glacial outwash* tumbled out to fill valleys in conventional *fluvial* processes.

Although the northern corners were directly covered by ice sheets, the impact of glaciers statewide is profound. Enormous volumes of melting ice created lakes and streams that moved huge amounts of outwash well into the central portions of the state and developed drainage patterns that extend all the way to the Atlantic Ocean.

About drift

Drift is a broad term that applies to all mineral material - such as boulders, gravels, sand, silt and clay - transported by a glacier and then *deposited directly by or from the ice or by running water that comes from a glacier*. It's unstratified till that forms moraines, or g*laciofluvial deposits*, which are sediments deposited and sorted by streams flowing from melting ice. As sediment layers stratify, they form *outwash plains* and such varied landforms as *valley trains, deltas, kames, eskers* and *kame terraces. Erratics* are rock fragments, ranging in size from pebbles to blocks as large as a house, carried by the ice and deposited at a considerable distance from its source, usually found on completely different bedrock. Drift is the preferred expression, rather than "glacial drift."

About till

Till is an unsorted, unstratified blend of clay, silt, sand, gravel, stones and boulders deposited directly by a glacier that came from distant sites, without subsequent reworking by melt water. The expression "glacial till" is redundant, since the sediments that make up till are glacial.

Important types of till include:

> **Ablation till** - relatively permeable, loose, earthy material deposited when nearly static glacial ice melts away; it can be contained in the glacier or have accumulated on the glacier surface. This is the material most common in northeastern and northwestern corners of the state.
>
> **Subglacial till** - accumulated in or by the bottom parts of a glacier, especially dense,

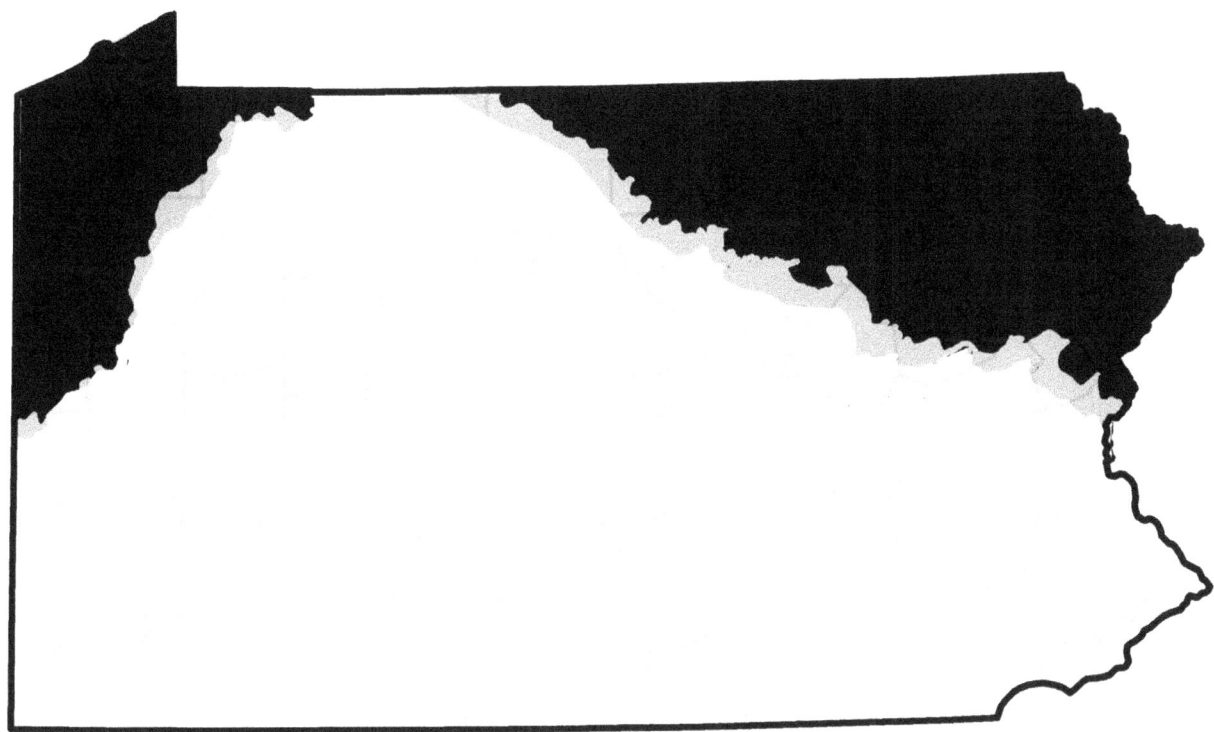

Extent of continental glaciation in Pennsylvania. The lighter gray reflects the furthest advance of the ancient Illinoisan event, while the black shows the more recent Wisconsinan, about 10,000 years ago. The ice came from two lobes of the same glacier. In the northwest, the effect was *depositional*, while in the northeast, the glacier was *erosional*. Both areas are blanketed with deep till.

clay-rich and firm till that contains many coarse rock fragments dragged beneath a moving glacier and left on bedrock or other glacial deposits. Also known as *basal till*.

Lodgment till - A subglacial till that is characterized by a compact, easily split structure of coarse fragments that feature long axes usually parallel to the direction of ice flow.

Flow till - A usually surface till that has been modified and transported by plastic mass flow. Also known as slump till.

Melt-out till - Materials deposited by slow melting of stagnant ice rich in debris that is buried well enough to inhibit deformation caused by gravity, which preserves the structures as they came from the parent ice.

Glacial processes and features

Glaciation of a region produces landforms, common and unusual, that can dramatically affect subsequent plant communities or create specialized habitats for highly localized communities. In addition to varied soils, topographies, including drainage patterns, are significant.

Distinct zones of glacial consequences help identify the nature and impact of glaciation: till deposits, left as the glacier retreated; margin features, created along the leading edge of the glacier; and outwash features, from materials flushed away from the glacier by melt water pouring from the glacier.

Geologists divide glacial features into two areas:

Intramorainal - deposits and phenomena that are found within the area defined by moraines, that is, occupied by the glacier.

Extramorainal - deposits and phenomena that occur outside of the area occupied by the glacier and its lateral and end moraines.

Till deposit features

Moraines can take many shapes - ranging from

nearly flat plains to distinct ridges - but share the common characteristic of being accumulations of unsorted, unstratified glacial drift that were deposited by direct action of glacial ice. The materials are predominantly till, but *kame moraines* are composed of stratified outwash. They are subdivided into several types:

- **Disintegration moraine** - randomly arranged and chaotic mounds and pits, with many abrupt vertical and lateral changes in unconsolidated material of varying lithology, these formed from drift at the top of the glacier. As underlying ice melted, the drift collapsed into the wide variety of shapes caused by melting and water flow from underneath. Slopes are often unstable and steep, and old stream courses and lake depressions are often mixed in with ridges. Common are collapsed lake plains, formed when sediment gathered in lakes at the top of a melting glacier eventually collapsed under melting ice, leading to distortions of the original lake sediment. Also included are collapsed outwash plains, which formed when outwash plains were created on the ice and then collapsed when the underlying ice melted. Again, this creates contortion and folding of the layers of sediments.
- **Ground moraine** - extensive, low relief areas of till with a gently rolling surface and usually bordered by the furthest ends of recessional or end moraines. It is also popularly known as a till plain, especially in soil and plant community discussions. The term ground moraine can also refer to a layer of unsorted mineral debris and rock beneath, in or dragged along beneath a glacier and deposited at points of accumulation or by release from melting stagnant ice.
- **Kame moraine** - usually an end moraine, typically of outwash material, that includes many low mounds, knobs, hummocks or short and irregular ridges (kames) that were built from stratified sand and gravel left by a subglacial stream, typically in fans or deltas at glacier margins. These moraines can also be a group of kames found along the front of a stagnant glacier that usually include remnants of an old outwash plain that was built by rapidly wasting or stagnant ice.
- **Lateral moraine** - composed of rock fragments or colluvial accumulation stripped from valley walls by glacial abrasion, then built into a moraine resembling a ridge on the side margins of the valley.
- **End moraine** - accumulations of material, typically forming a ridge, deposited at the outer margins of a glacier that is actively flowing at any given time (glaciers sometimes advance and recede depending on smaller climate periods).
- **Terminal moraine** - an end moraine that identifies the furthest advance of a glacier, which usually features a huge bow-shaped or concentric ridge, or a complex of ridges, that are underlain by till and other types of drift.
- **Recessional moraine** - a type of lateral or end moraine that was created during major pauses of the final retreat of a glacier. It may include moraine built during minor readvances, but nonetheless in the overall retreat phase of the glacier.

Other landforms

As glaciers advance, their impact on terrain being covered up is varied and considerable. As they drag through valleys of any size, the original V-shape created by stream erosion is rounded into a distinct U-shape when valley sides are simply sheared off. If they cross a valley from side to side, they can completely fill it with till hundreds of feet deep that, among other things, will completely rearrange stream systems in the region.

Glacial lakes caused by differential melting often developed on the surface of glaciers and filled with sediments, but also occur in basins where drainage is blocked by morainal dams or in bedrock after glacial erosion - such as scouring or quarrying. In northwestern parts of the state, large areas of relatively smooth ground and silty soils are the remnants of these lakes.

Drumlins are elongated, oval hills, ridges or

mounds that are low and smooth with a core of bedrock or drift, feature a blunt nose facing the direction from which the ice approached and a gentler slope tapering in the opposite direction. The longest axis always points to the general direction of glacial flow because these occur in the streamline flow and are molded on the bottom of the glacier through a combination of erosion and deposition. They are more common in New York State, but the expression occasionally turns up in habitat discussions.

Outwash features

Outwash is a term referring to layers of sediments, primarily sand and gravel, that have moved away from a glacier by melt-water streams and deposited in front of or well beyond the end moraine of the glacier. Coarser material is deposited closer to the ice, while finer materials are pushed further, hence the description "sorted." The term "glacial outwash" is considered redundant.

Outwash deposits featuring kettles or potholes on the surface, resulting from burial of ice in outwash and collapse during a subsequent thaw, are called *pitted outwash*.

Outwash areas are further defined:

Outwash delta - composed of glaciofluvial sediments, these form where an outwash river laden with sediment empties into an open lake, often a proglacial lake. Coarser material forms very gently dipping *topset beds* (less advanced and a top layer), while finer textures are found in more deeply dipping *foreset beds* (further advanced into the delta and to some extent buried by the topset layer).

Outwash fan - accumulated materials that have been deposited by melt water streams in front of end or recessional moraines; when they combine, they form an *outwash plain*.

Outwash plain - A broad lowland region composed of coarse-textured glaciofluvial material, usually low in relief and in its original gradient. Outwash plains are typically smooth, but when marked by a number of irregular depressions like potholes and kettles are called *pitted outwash plains*.

Outwash terrace - a bank of outwash with a flat top and an abrupt scarp or riser that extends along a valley downstream from an outwash plain or terminal moraine, typically an element of a narrow, long section of outwash within a valley called a *valley train*. When these terraces are pockmarked with many kettles and potholes, they are called *pitted outwash terraces*.

Dune features

Dunes create specialized habitats along the shores of major bodies of water, such as Lake Erie. These take the form of low mounds, ridges, hills or banks and are composed of subaerially deposited, windblown material, mostly sand. They can be barren and consequently capable of moving from place to place or covered with vegetation that stabilizes the surface but retains a characteristic shape.

Not surprisingly, a collection of terms define parts of dunes and maybe of interest to those landscaping within this unique habitat range.

Collectively, dunes form a *dune field*, which includes both stabilized and moving dunes, as well as *interdune* areas and swamps, ponds and lakes that result when migrating dunes block waterways.

A *dune lake* occupies both a basin formed by a blowout, or a basin created when dunes block a stream.

An *interdune* is a somewhat flat surface - either sand covered or sand-free - between dunes, and an *interdune valley* consists of flat areas between very large dunes near the local groundwater table if one is present.

Dune slack is a trough or damp depression found between dunes in a dune field or shoreline dune ridge, caused by intersecting the capillary fringe of the local water table - that is, a moist kind of interdune.

Dune traces are a series of semi-concentric to linear micro-ridges and intervening dune troughs that are found on either an interdune or dune slack exposed by dune migration.

Dunes take a variety of shapes and forms and can include:

Foredune - the typically somewhat stabilized

coastal dune or ridge that runs parallel to the shoreline at either than landward margin of the beach, the shoreward face of a beach ridge, or the landward limit of the highest tide.
- **Barchan dune** - A dune that has a crescent shape with the tips pointing downwind (leeward), creating a convex windward side, usually organized in chains extending in the dominant wind direction.
- **Parabolic dune** - A crescent-shaped dune with the tips pointing upwind (windward), which creates a concave windward side; when perfectly developed, the ground plan approximates a parabolic shape.
- **Shrub-coppice dune** - A very small and streamlined dune formed around brush or clump vegetation.
- **Longitudinal dune** - Narrow but long dunes that are typically symmetrical in cross section and are generally parallel to prevailing wind directions. Commonly steeper and wider on the windward side and tapering to a point on the lee side. These usually form behind obstacles in places where there is a strong and constant wind and a lot of sand, and can be about 10 to 15 feet high, but up to 60 miles long.
- **Seif dune** - A very large, elongated longitudinal dune or chain of dunes with a sharp crest featuring curved slip faces that result from infrequent but strong cross winds, as much as 700 feet high and ranging from 1,500 feet to more than 60 miles long.
- **Transverse dune** - An asymmetrical dune elongated perpendicular to prevailing wind, with a gentle windward and steep leeward slope; the leeward slope is commonly at or near the angle of repose of sand and such dunes often form where there is sparse vegetation.

Geomorphology 101

The keys to what makes Pennsylvania's habitats so varied and complex are rooted in the distant past. It began simply enough with a handful of substantial volcanoes scattered along a line extending from Adams to Northampton Counties at a time when the state straddled the equator and Philadelphia would have been on the southwest corner of the state.

Over millions of years, the tectonic plate rotated counterclockwise about 90 degrees and drifted northwest — but not without a few continental collisions and a lot of mountain building. At one time, the Piedmont itself was an impressive range mountains, rivaling the present-day Andes and Himalayas at the eastern end of shallow seas, mucky swamps, and shallow seas again.

As the growing North American continent rose and fell, those vast flat areas were layered with sand, limestones, and silt over and over into a sort of layered cake.

Then came the collision with North Africa in the age of the super-continents. The effect of the encounter can be illustrated with a kitchen table experiment. Have an assistant in one corner, about Erie, hold a tablecloth firm so it cannot move. Now slowly push from Philadelphia toward the assistant. Very soon a series of ridges begins to form — in fact, closest to Philadelphia, the ridges may fold over on each other to illustrate the formation of the Piedmont. Further inland, the waves of ridges are more gradual and broader, but the land itself is nonetheless lifted upward to form the Allegheny Plateau. Where the ridges remained packed tightly together but not folded over we find the Appalachians.

As the surface buckled, it often fractured to form impressive peaks and high valleys — but remember, most of the newly-exposed rock along these shattered hinge lines is sedimentary and very susceptible to erosion. So the ridges and valleys smoothed out — helped on three occasions by continental glaciers entering from the northwest and northeast.

The result were relatively thin bands of alternating sandstone, limestone and shales on a variety of slopes carved even more — dissected — by flowing water over a period of more than 200 million years. As recently as 10,000 years ago, when people migrated in from points west, the state was still very much a tundra-like habitat with a lot of permafrost.

The forest systems we enjoy today are, in geologic time, relatively new.

The persistent forces of erosion are nearly as dramatic as the consequences of tectonic collision. The total picture adds up to *geomorphology* — a science that investigates how landforms were created and the ongoing process of change.

The relevance to landscapers using native species is two-fold: Those developing conservation/restoration gardens may find insight into specialized habitats that result from landforms and their ongoing change. Those modeling, replicating or suggesting habitats may find useful clues in habitat construction that leads to successful plant communities.

As we have seen, two of the several different kinds of geomorphic processes are responsible for the actual creation of the landmass we call home:

Igneous processes resulting from volcanic eruptions and distribution of volcanic material, such as those found in southeastern Pennsylvania, but also heating and reprocessing sedimentary rock to form metamorphic rock areas such as the delicate serpentine barrens in the southeast, and

Tectonic processes involving the collisions of continental plates leading to uplifting and folding of bedrock, but also earthquakes that can raise or lower large regions in a matter of minutes, such as escarpments along the Hudson River Valley.

Also impacting the surface are:

Aeolian processes or erosion, transport and deposition by wind; some *loess* pockets in Pennsylvania are caused by fine soil moved by air, and

Biological processes including events caused by living organisms interacting with landforms, ranging from biochemical to mechanical processes such as burrowing, tree throw, beaver dams, and bedrock fracturing by roots.

But much of the activity that shapes the land comes in three forms:

Mass movement - A wide variety of means for rock and soil to move downslope as a consequence of gravity; ranges from dramatic brief events like landslides to very slow soil creep.

Fluvial erosion, transport and deposition - Erosion of rock and movement of soil materials by water from one location to another; this can include glacio-fluvial processes either directly by ice or glacial outwash.

Karst solution - Bedrock changes from solid to liquid state when combined with water — especially carbonates like limestone and dolomite; as a liquid, it is moved elsewhere and eventually precipitates back into solid state.

Mass movement

Impacting all ecoregions in Pennsylvania, mass movement - formerly called mass wasting - can range from very slow to rapid events. Water, ice and air may play an important role in causing weakness in the upland structure, but gravity will actually move the material.

Some of the factors that affect potential for mass movement include weakening of material by weather, abrupt changes in water content, changes in vegetation cover (especially blowdowns), overloading and changes in the angle of the slope. Factors that often enhance slope stability are relative dryness of soils and sturdy root systems of covering plant material.

Basic slow events:

Solifluction – when freeze-thaw cycles cause water-saturated regolith to peel away and slowly slide downhill, especially common during permafrost (in Pennsylvania, permafrost persisted for thousands of years following glaciation).

Creep - A combination of small movements over long periods of time that cause soil and rock to gradually succumb to gravity and slide downslope; on steeper slopes, the process is faster.

Some rapid events include:

Landslides (landslips) - When heavy rain loosens material that can then move down-

hill.
- **Flows** - Movement of soil and regolith that resembles fluids, such as mudflows, avalanches and debris flows, usually caused by water, air or ice.
- **Topples** - When blocks of rock are loosened, often by freeze-thaw activity, and fall away from a slope.
- **Falls** - When regolith cascades down a slope usually caused by undercutting by water along streams or on steep slopes loosened by rain, plant-root wedging, expanding ice or earthquakes. The material that falls to the base of the slope is called *talus*.

Fluvial processes

An important feature of streams and rivers is the movement of sediment as well as water through bed, suspended and dissolved load. The rate of sediment transport varies with availability of sediment and the *stream discharge* (how much water flows through a cross section per second, usually in terms of cubic feet, cubic meters or acre-feet). Periodic flooding becomes an important variable.

The pattern and nature of sediment deposition greatly impacts the ecology of the riparian area; even periodic flood and ice scour creates opportunities for entire plant communities.

Additionally, rivers are capable of eroding rock to create new sediment from their own bed load, channel materials and surrounding hillslopes. Consequently rivers are considered as setting the base level for large-scale landscape evolution in areas unaffected by glaciers, such as *dissection* of uplands to form new ridges and valleys.

As rivers and streams flow across the land, they typically increase in size and continually merge with other streams and rivers to form networked drainage systems.

Glacial processes

Glaciers cause direct and indirect landscape change. When ice sheets approached northern Pennsylvania from two directions (distinct *lobes* of a continental glacier spread out over many thousands of square miles), abrasion and plucking of underlying rock altered the shapes of valleys, impacted drainage systems and during retreat deposited vast amounts of till.

Where glaciers moved over valleys in a perpendicular way, till deposits can be very deep and sometimes completely fill the valley. When they followed the general directions of valleys, deposits tend to be thinnest on the higher elevations and thicker below - often a result of subsequent fluvial erosion. When glaciers retreated in spurts, the deposits take the form of moraines.

Indirect processes are a consequence of the enormous amount of water flowing from a melting glacier and the resulting outwash fields that can extend considerable distances from the terminal point of glaciation.

Karsts

Karsts are closed depressions, sinkholes, caves and underground drainage created when limestone, gypsum or other soluble rocks are dissolved and washed away. The solutions tend to have higher soil pH and therefore affect plant communities along the surface flow. Karst solutions can be physical (when rock minerals go directly into solution without transformation) or chemical (when weak, usually carbonic, acid reacts with the minerals and forms solutions. In Pennsylvania karsts are common in the Southern Allegheny Plateau, the Northern Ridge and Valley, the Northern Glaciated Allegheny Plateau, the Blue Ridge Mountains and the Allegheny Mountains, all of which have limestone deposits.

NEIGHBORHOODS

Pennsylvania's widely varied habitats are rooted in the ancient past, when the earth's crust jostled for position and periodically collided. Layers of different kinds of sediments, hardened into rock over millions of years, were crumpled like tinfoil to form at least two breathtaking mountain chains. When erosion, mostly by water, took over, those layers, now tilted and deformed, were gradually exposed to produce the patchwork of soils and landforms of today.

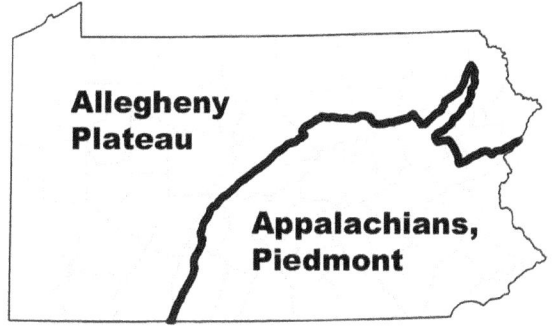

Tectonic damage was most intense in the southeast, while the north and western two thirds of the state was less severely wrinkled and more uplifted, only to have huge parcels rearranged by at least three periods of continental glaciers. The bottom line is an enormous array of soil types and land features that creates countless habitats, some specific, some variations on a larger theme.

Because sustainable landscaping by definition implies collaborating with rather than controlling a habitat, we turn first to regions in progressive steps.

The first logical subdivision is the Allegheny Front — an escarpment that follows a wiggly line from Bradford County in the southwest to Monroe County in the northeast. This is the general dividing line between the most severe collision crunching and the more rolling but uplifted terrain of the Allegheny Plateau. The Allegheny Plateau side includes a narrow band of the Erie and Ontario Lake Plain, generally in Erie County, which features some very specialized habitats.

On the southeastern side are the narrow ridges and valleys of the northern Appalachians in a curving band just east of the front. As we move eastward, we encounter the Piedmont, once a craggy line of mountains that rivaled the Rockies but have since eroded into the foothills of the Appalachians, and at the very corner, in and around Philadelphia, the Atlantic Coastal Plain. Crossing the state line from Maryland toward the center of the state, the region also includes the very northern tip of the Blue Ridge Mountains.

A secondary subdivision of the state results from continental glaciation. For our purposes, we'll consider the last two of at least four ice ages: Illinoian from 198,000 to 128,000 years ago and Wisconsinan from 110,000 to 10,000 years ago.

These dramatically rearranged surfaces in the northeast and northwest in different ways. Although both came ice sheets as much several thousand feet thick that spread in all directions from the Hudson Bay in Canada, individual lobes entered Pennsylvania from two directions. In the west, it curled in on a line from Lake Ontario to Lake Erie and then slightly southeast. In the east, it flowed in from Lake Champlain and New England in a southwesterly flow.

Because the land surface was smoother in the west, the glaciers deposited materials more evenly and deeply. The eastern area, however, featured obstacles that required the glacier to erode surfaces and push them outward, dropping them only when in retreat and unevenly so.

If we were to overlay the glaciated regions onto the areas divided by the Allegheny Front, we form four relatively distinct regions of Pennsylvania:

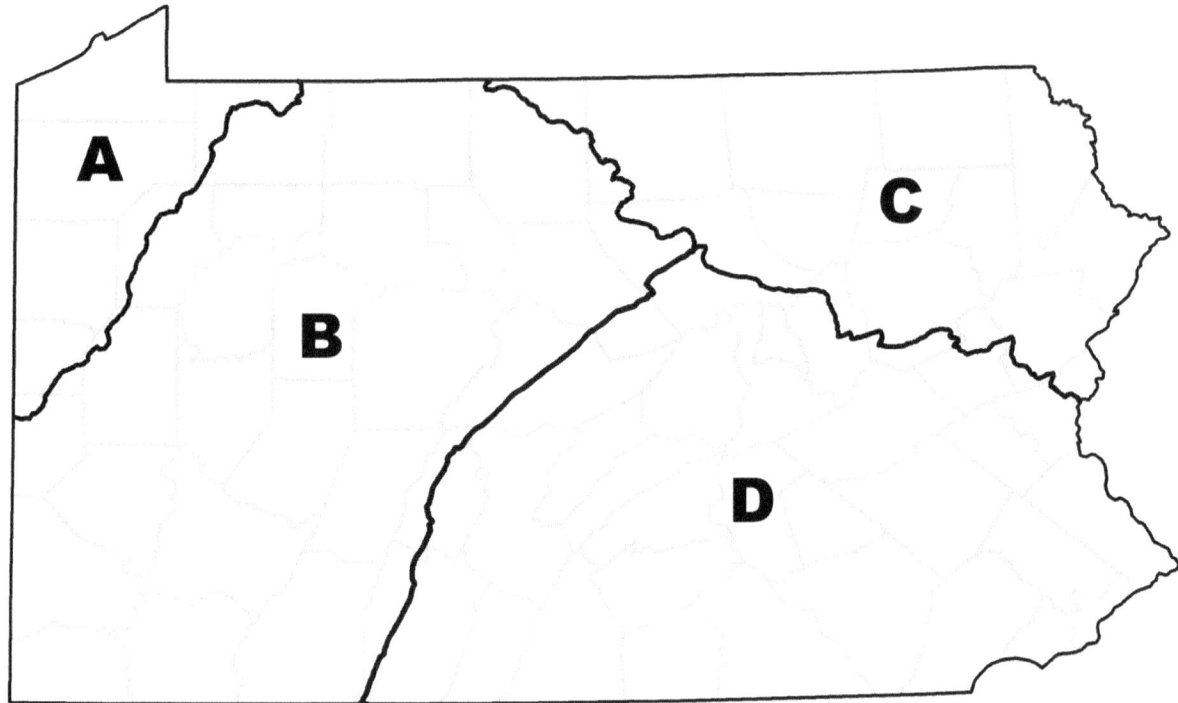

A. Northwestern Glaciated Plateau; B - Unglaciated Plateau; C - Northeastern Glaciated Plateau; D - Appalachians, Piedmont, Coastal Plain

Appalachians/Piedmont/Coastal Plain/
 Blue Ridge Mountains
Unglaciated Allegheny Plateau
Northwestern Glaciated Plateau / Erie Lake
 Plain
Northeastern Glaciated Plateau

Further subdivisions within those regions now become more manageable to consider in detail. Major soil associations fit into these zones. The combination of soil characteristics and landform position are key elements to plant habitats and species with regional orientations tend to consolidate along these lines. Ecologists who investigate ecological communities tend to sort distribution on the same general lines.

With each of the zones we discover the full range of habitats, from xeric to wetland, from barrens to floodplain, from rocky to fertile — all issues for landscapers to be considered with care. But these subdivisions regionalize soil, plant and ecological data to simplify the task.

As we investigate the four regions, we will consider general characteristics, general soil patterns, natural vegetation, climate and current land use and environmental issues for each.

Because of the richness of information for each, some sections are broken down further — most notably the Unglaciated Allegheny Plateau (Pittsburgh Plateau, Allegheny Mountains) and Appalachian-Piedmont (Ridge and Valley, Blue Ridge Mountains, and Piedmont, the latter including both the Reading Prong and Atlantic Coastal Plain area found in Pennsylvania). Discussion of the Northwestern Glaciated Plateau includes the Erie Lake Plain, while that of the Northeastern Glaciated Plateau includes the Wyoming Valley portion of the Ridge and Valley region.

These summaries are organized to provide an overview, climate information, a sense of topography, general types of vegetation, a summary of current use and environmental issues, and the sites of major soil series. For example, in the ridge and valley region, Hazleton soils are often found on convex upper thirds of backslopes, shoulders and summits, from which we can infer xeric to dry habitats and are probably acidic. Laidig soils, by contrast, are found on lower to middle slope benches and footslopes of limestone valleys, suggesting a more mesic to moist habitat that may be more circumneutral.

Piedmont and Coastal Plain

General Description

Consisting of open valleys and irregular plains among low, rounded hills, the Northern Piedmont is a maturely dissected low-relief plain in final stages of fluvial erosion, where rivers and streams are close to base level and tend to meander and braid. The plain, a hilly to rolling surface with a few higher ridges that can reach 1,200 feet, slopes gently toward the Atlantic coast.

It is the remnant of very ancient mountains that have completely eroded away. At the end of the mountain building era that created the Appalachians further west, the Piedmont became a deposition area for sediments moving south and east from the new chain, which originally rose as high as 16,000 feet.

The gentle topography is punctuated by areas of rock more resistant to erosion — intrusive igneous dikes and sills — that form somewhat sharp ridges. Steeper slopes tend to be on higher elevation ridges or side slopes adjacent to drainageways.

The area includes a broad, structural basin that forms a lowland plain on a southwest to northeast line and extends into Lower New England section. Most of the area is above the "fall line" - the boundary between coastal plain sediments and the crystalline bedrock of the interior uplands.

Further west, bedrock is more typically limestone. The ancient coastal mountain chain, called "tectonic highlands," had a major impact on what is now the Appalachians and the Allegheny plateau. At varying times, that area was a shallow seabed — hence the limestone — and sometimes a flat alluvial plain with meandering or braided drainage patterns, hence the shale and siltstone. Coastal beaches moved back and forth over millions of years, resulting in layers of sandstone.

When tectonic plates collided to create the ridge and valley region in a series of tight folds, the general effect in the Piedmont was to crush and overfold anticlines and synclines into the complex shapes they are today.

Along the northern boundary of the Piedmont and the southern edge of the Lehigh Valley — primarily from west of Reading to Easton on a line south of Allentown and Bethlehem — a thin band of metamorphic and igneous rock appears. The Northeastern Highlands extends toward New England and is composed moderately fertile, slightly acidic residuum to form dissected, rugged, crystalline hills distinct from the Central Appalachians on the northwest and the Northern Piedmont on the southeast. Summits range from 700 to 1,000 feet, about 200 to 500 feet above intervening valleys.

Within the Piedmont and Coastal Plain are several distinct areas:

Triassic Lowlands — Featuring wide, undulating ridges and nearly level broad valleys, the Triassic Lowlands plain is underlain and delineated by sedimentary rock and features local relief of only 30 to 200 feet within elevation ranges of 175 to 600 feet. It is higher than the Piedmont Limestone/Dolomite Lowlands and lower than the Piedmont Uplands and the Diabase and Conglomerate Uplands, and not as deeply dissected as the Piedmont Uplands.

Presently used mostly for farming, the soils would have suited oak-hickory forest. Because the soils are less acidic and richer in calcium and magnesium than soils from non-sedimentary rock, hickory (*Carya* spp) is more abundant here than elsewhere in the Piedmont, but red maple (*Acer rubrum*) and black gum (*Nyssa sylvatica*) is less common; they prefer the more acidic soils with lower calcium and magnesium levels found over metamorphic rocks.

Diabase and Conglomerate Uplands — Stony, wooded steep ridges and hills formed from highly resistant igneous (diabase), heat-altered sedimentary or sedimentary rock characterizes an irregular string along the Blue Ridge and Ridge and Valley front, toward a larger pool in southern Berks County. Elevations are usually from 300 to 1,150 feet but can reach as high as 1,300 feet; local relief varies from 50 to 650 feet.

Diabase soils tend to be more difficult to farm, which results in more common used for pasture or oak-hickory forest. On soils where there are diabase intrusions, acid-loving plants are absent, which results in a distinctive regional plant palette. On steeper surfaces or areas covered by rocks and boulders, woodland is common. Where diabase soils are not an issue, the land is more suited for general agriculture.

Piedmont Uplands — This area is underlain by metamorphic rock and exhibit higher elevations and high relief compared to the rest of the region. Narrow valleys, irregular plains, low ridges and rounded hills are the norm. Toward the southwest along the Susquehanna River, relief increases and gorges contain high-gradient streams. Along the fall zone in the east, exposed bedrock shows a mix of metamorphic and sedimentary rock, high stream gradients, islands and falls. The area also includes chrome soils formed from serpentinite, low in calcium but high in magnesium, chromium and nickel. The resulting barrens support specialized vegetation of dry oak-pine forests and grasslands.

Piedmont Limestone/Dolomite Lowlands — Limestone, dolomite and shale bedrock form both a high-yielding aquifer and unique and very fertile soils. Mostly limestone and carbonate have been weathered to form a nearly level to slightly undulating terrain with little dissection and relief that is less than 125 feet. While the original vegetation would have been oaks and some oak-hickory-pine stands are found near the Susquehanna River, all of this area has been converted to agriculture.

Delaware River Terraces and Uplands — Technically a part of the Atlantic Coastal Plain, this area includes a thin band along the lower Delaware River in lower Bucks, Montgomery and Philadelphia counties. Low, nearly level terraces — with elevations less than 60 feet and local relief of only about 35 feet — feature an ocean-modified climate and long growing season. The narrow region is marshy and swampy, immediately adjacent to the Delaware estuary and bay. In its natural state, we would find habitats such as intertidal and saltwater marshes as well as sluggish meandering streams, with many areas saturated or flooded during the growing season. While regulations have reduced wetland loss since the 1970s, much of the original habitats have been eradicated by erosion, dredging, filling and embankment construction.

Like the Lake Erie Plain in the far northwest, soils of this thin band are identified as "unconsolidated sediments." Alluvial and estuarine sand and silt are underlain by unconsolidated and easily-eroded Quaternary gravels, sands and silt, in contrast to the Lower Paleozoic schist and gneiss of the Northern Piedmont on the opposite side of the fall line. Surface features include beaches, barrier beaches, beach ridges, dunes, marshes and low terraces, usually on poorly drained mesic and thermic Ultisols and Histosols. Appalachian Oak Forest is found on northerly uplands and Oak-Hickory-Pine Forest populate southern areas.

Soils

Soils above bedrock tend to be residuum on ridges and hilltops, with colluvium on slopes and alluvium in valleys. Stream floodplains are predominantly well drained and tend to be deep.

The most fertile soils throughout the Piedmont are found in the northern end, where agricultural diversity has limited erosion and over-cropping. The most challenging soils are found on serpentine barrens, but well documented plant lists are available to support local landscapers.

Unconsolidated stream alluvium of gravel and sand fills major river valleys, especially the Delaware Valley. Some deep, weathered ancient till can be found in the extreme northeast.

Hills are residuum, such as:

Chester — upper slopes and upland divides

Duffield — nearly level to steep hillsides

Gladstone — rolling foothills and upland divides

Glenelg — nearly level to very steep well dissected uplands

Glenville — level to sloping upland flats, footslopes or near drainageway heads

Manor — backslopes, shoulders and summits of hills

Mt. Airy — on strongly dissected uplands of the inner Piedmont Plateau, in complexes with Manor loams

Neshaminy — nearly level to very steep upland slopes

Parker — gentle to steep slopes of ridges and hills

Penn — nearly level to steep and moderately dissected uplands

Footslopes and drainageways:

Readington — nearly level to sloping concave hillsides, upland flats, stream heads and drainageways

On the coastal plain area, soils are very deep, excessively to poorly drained and mostly loamy to sandy.

Coastal plain terraces and flats — fluvio-marine deposits including:

Sassafras — sideslopes and summits of hills in the Atlantic coastal plain

Woodstown — upland marine and old stream terraces

Coastal plain uplands — near-shore marine

Once a mountain chain

Had we arrived at major moments in geologic history, we would have discovered a coastline far different than today. This is the oldest part of what we call Pennsylvania — originally a string of volcanic islands lounging along the equator. But even as the new continent bumped and crunched its way to the present latitude, staggering landforms evolved and disappeared.

At one point, we would have found the site for Philadelphia in a mountain chain rivaling the Alps of Europe, with snow-capped peaks reaching 15,000 feet. Methodically they were ground down by erosion, filling out a vast plain with huge quantities of sediments. The present-day Appalachians came next, with the crunching of tectonic plates so severe in the southeastern part of the state that ridges were literally folded over one another and the new mountain range took shape.

Again, time takes its toll, and as the Appalachians eroded away, the materials moving downslope smoothed the surface even more and gave the region its present name. *Piedmont* comes from the French, meaning "foothills" and is named for the Piedmont region of Italy, a lowland that abuts the Alps (the Latin phrase "*pedem montium*" means "foot of the mountain."

and silty loess deposits:

    Matapeake — upland interfluves and side slopes of the Atlantic Coastal Plain in Bucks County

    Mattapex — swales, flats, depressions and marine terraces on nearly level surfaces in the Atlantic Coastal Plain

Coastal plain hills and relict stream terraces — silty deposits on broad flats:

    Beltsville — upland coastal plain on summits, shoulders and backslopes of broad interstream divides (interfluves and sideslopes)

Natural vegetation

The oak-hickory forest system covers the entire region.

Natural vegetation of the Piedmont prior to European settlement was primarily oak and hickory with American chestnut, ash, walnut, elm and yellow-poplar as associates. Maple dominated wet bottomlands.

Today, the primary forest systems are oak-hickory, with some sugar maple-mixed hardwoods and hemlock-mixed hardwoods and, in the Susquehanna River valley, oak-hickory-pine. Major regional species include chestnut oak, white oak, red oak, hickories, ash, American elm and yellow-poplar (particularly common on northeast-facing slopes). Black walnut and black cherry prefer the well-drained flood plain soils and eastern red cedar is common in areas of abandoned cropland.

Scattered serpentine barrens occur in Lancaster, Chester and Delaware Counties. Here, chrome soils formed from serpentinite, low in calcium but high in magnesium, chromium and nickel. The resulting barrens support specialized vegetation of dry oak-pine forests and grasslands. Among the species reported: Blackjack oak (*Quercus marilandica*), post oak (*Quercus stellata*), black oak (*Quercus velutina*), Virginia pine (*Pinus virginiana*), pitch pine (*Pinus rigida*), greenbriar (*Smilax rotundifolia*), and a number of prairie grasses and herbs, some of which are threatened and rare. Grazing, quarrying, and suburban development are threats to these unique habitats.

On the Atlantic Coastal Plain, vegetation is primarily pines and hardwoods, such as loblolly, Virginia and shortleaf pine, northern and southern red oak as well as black, scarlet, pin and willow oak, walnut, yellow-poplar, sweetgum and red maple.

Climate

Annual precipitation ranges from 37 to 52 inches, with most of it in spring and early summer. Ten to 14-day droughts are common in summer. Snowfall ranges from 27 to 40 inches on average and mean annual temperature ranges from 40 to 55 degrees F, with a growing season of 160 days (north) to 250 days (south).

Use and issues

About 25 percent of the region is privately held forest, while 40 percent is used for agriculture and 32 percent is urban development and growing rapidly. Many former dairy operations have become horse and "hobby" farms near suburban edges. Of primary concern is impact from conversion of farmland, especially prime land, to urban and suburban use and the consequential effect on streams and general soil quality. Ample water supplies farm, urban and industrial use, but expanding urban development is impacting water yields by reducing groundwater recharge rates.

Much of the coastal plain region is dominated by Philadelphia and its suburbs, generally on the fall line next to the Delaware River estuary, resulting in extensive pollution and habitat change, concerns that continue today. Among currently endangered species found here are arrowhead (*Sagittaria calycina*), coast violet (*Viola brittoniana*), riverbank quillwort (*Isoetes riparia*) and swamp beggar-ticks (*Bidens bidentoides*).

In the Piedmont, primary concerns relate to the conversion of non-urban land (especially prime farmland) to urban use and the associated degradation of stream and soil quality, while in the coastal plain the issues center around loss of marshes and related wetlands.

Appalachian Ridge and Valley

The Ridge and Valley section of the northern Appalachians is a folded and faulted area of parallel sandstone and shale ridges and narrow to broad limestone and shale valleys, carved from anticlines, synclines and thrust blocks.

Defining the western boundary is the Allegheny Front, a steep, high ridge; on the east lies the Great Valley lowland.

The region reaches its greatest width on a line from southeast of Harrisburg to just northwest of Lock Haven and narrows between the higher Blue Ridge Mountains and the higher and less deformed Allegheny and Cumberland plateaus.

Ridges are strongly sloping to very steep and feature narrow, rolling crests. Valleys are level to strongly sloping. The western side is predominantly hilly to very steep and much steeper and rougher than the rolling and hilly eastern side.

Elevations range from 330 to 985 feet in the alleys and 1,310 to 2,625 feet on mountains and ridges. Local relief ranges from 15 to 165 feet in the valleys, with ridges rising about 650 feet above adjacent valleys.

On a northeast to southwest line, the landforms were created by tightly folded and intensely faulted bedrock. Surfaces are affected by the underlying bedrock. Although the pattern is parallel valleys and ridges, a zig-zag pattern formed in central Pennsylvania when resistant strata were compressed into plunging folds during mountain-building periods, then eroded.

Ridge crests are conglomerate bedrock and resistant sandstones, while the valleys are underlain by less resistant limestones and shales. The orientation of topography runs on a northeast to southwest line; streams follow less resistant types of rock and cut through more resistant rock at 90 degree angles to form water gaps. Most of these are along intensive fracturing zones.

The parallel patterns encourage trellised stream networks because topography guides active downcutting streams to enter valleys in a perpendicular way. Larger rivers, like the Susquehanna, cross the structure by cutting deep gorges in the ridges. This leads to high-gradient streams in water gaps and ridge slopes, and gentle gradient, meandering and warmer streams in the valleys.

The result: valleys that vary in both agricultural potential and microtopography. Those formed from limestone and dolomite have smoother shapes and lower drainage density than those from shale, which often show a distinctive rolling topography. Soils from limestone are fertile and hence good for agriculture, while those formed from shale have lower farming potential unless they are calcareous.

In Pennsylvania, the region is subdivided into five distinct areas found in alternating bands throughout the chain:

Northern Limestone/Dolomite Valleys - base-rich soil, muted terrain, low drainage density, and limestone, dolomite, and calcareous shale bedrock. Characterized by level to undulating broad and fertile valleys with extensive farming, these valleys are built over limestone and dolomite, interbedded with carbonates from other rocks (including shale). Examples include the Great Valley and the Nittany Valley. Sinkholes, underground streams and other karst features are common, and streams offer gentle gradients with good year-round flow. Local relief varies from 50 to 500 feet. Current woodlands tend to be limited to steeper areas and are Appalachian Oak forest in the north and Oak-Hickory-Pine forest in the south.

Northern Shale Valleys - neutral to acidic

valley and low hill soils developed from shales and siltstones. More extensive rolling valleys and low hills are underlain by siltstone, shale and fine grained sandstone to form the Northern Shale Valleys, which extend to near the James River in Virginia. Local relief ranges from 50 to 500 feet. These valleys are both folded and faulted, and because underlying rock is not as permeable as nearby limestone, the surface streams tend to be larger and soil erosion more pronounced. Poorer than the soils of the Limestone/dolomite valleys because they are derived from acidic shale, there nonetheless remains substantial soil variability. Some soils are more calcareous than others, and farming predominates. Natural vegetation is Appalachian Oak forest in the north and Oak-Hickory-Pine forest in the south. Woodland tends to be found on steeper slopes, which includes scattered shale barrens on very steep south and west-facing slopes in Huntingdon, Fulton and Bedford counties that are one of the most rare types of habitat in the state.

Northern Sandstone Ridges - Ridge contour lines are straight and parallel, not irregular like those of the Northern Dissected Ridges. With elevations ranging from 1,000 to 4,300 feet and local relief from 500 to 1,500 feet, these steep, high and forested ridges are characterized by narrow crests and high-gradient and acidic streams flowing into narrow valleys. Interbedded and folded sandstone and conglomerate were folded to form the ridges, but some less resistant rocks like siltstone and shale may form sideslopes. Residuum soils can vary considerably over close distances. Soils tend to be poor and sandy, and limitations include stoniness, fertility and slope angle. Appalachian Oak Forest and Oak-Hickory-Pine Forest in the south.

Northern Dissected Ridges - morphologically distinct from the sharp ridges and narrow valleys of the Northern Sandstone Ridges. Underlain by interbedded, folded, sedimentary rock that includes siltstone,

these dissected ridges are described as "broken" and "almost hummocky" and range from 800 to more than 4,100 feet in elevation with local relief from 200 to 1,150 feet. Streams tend to be less acidic than with Sandstone Ridges. Appalachian Oak Forest dominates in the north and Oak-Hickory-Pine forest in the south. Forest covers most of the region, but some land is in pasture. Shale barrens, among the most rare in Pennsylvania are found on steep south and west-facing slopes in Huntingdon, Fulton and Bedford Counties. They feature stunted *Juniperus virginiana* (eastern red cedar), *Pinus virginiana* (Virginia pine) and *Quercus prinus* (chestnut oak); shrub thickets including *Crataegus uniflora* (hawthorn), *Prunus alleghaniensis* (Allegheny plum), *Gaylussacia baccata* (huckleberry), and herbaceous vegetation that include *Taenidia montana* (mountain parsley), *Phlox subulata* (moss pink), *Senecio antennariifolius* (barrens ragwort); *Viola pedata* (Birdfoot violet) and *Trifolium virginicum* (Kate's mountain clover).
- **Anthracite** - areas underlain by anthracite-bearing stratam, and low woodland density, in the Wyoming Valley in the extreme north. While technically considered a part of the Ridge and Valley region, the area was among those glaciated and is discussed in the section on the glaciated northeast.

Soils

Soils range from shallow to very deep, excessively to moderately well drained, and loamy to clayey. Most formed in residuum or colluvium from limestone (which can be cherty), sandstone or shale. Over most bedrock - chiefly shale, siltstone, sandstone, chert and carbonates - lies a veneer of unconsolidated materials.

Side slopes and ridges - steep and very steep, shallow to very deep, well drained, such as:
- Berks - rounded summits, shoulders, and backslopes of dissected uplands
- Calvin - hillslopes, side slopes and summits of ridges
- Dekalb - level to very steep ridges and uplands, with slopes typically convex
- Hazleton - upper third of backslopes, shoulders and summits, typically convex
- Klinesville - gently to very steeply sloping convex hillslopes on dissected ridges and valley sides
- Lehew - nearly level to steep ridges and mountain side slopes
- Weikert - gentle to very steep convex dissected uplands, sometimes in complexes

Limestone valleys - nearly level to sloping, very deep, well drained, medium textured to fine textured, such as:
- Hagerstown - floors of valleys and adjacent hillsides
- Duffield - nearly level to steep hillsides
- Edom - gently sloping to dissected steep hillslopes
- Carbo - gentle to very steep upland valleys and ridges
- Washington - nearly level to steep ancient till plains within limestone valleys, often with many shallow and closed depressions

Lower footslopes of ridges and in valleys - gently sloping to sloping, deep and very deep, well-drained and moderately well drained medium to fine textured soils such as:
- Bedington - nearly level valleys to steep, convex uplands and on sideslopes of ridges and hills
- Frankstown - gentle to steeply sloping uplands in limestone valleys
- Leck Kill - level to very steep and usually convex upland slopes
- Mertz - gently to steeply sloping middle and upper parts of chert ridges
- Murrill - benches, fans, footslopes and lower backslopes
- Buchanan - nearly level to very steep terraces and concave sections of mountain footslopes
- Laidig - lower to middle slope benches and footslopes

Floodplains along drainageways - nearly level to gently sloping, very deep, well drained to poorly drained, medium textured to fine textured soils such as:

- Chagrin - on floodplains that receive alluvium from upland areas of shale, siltstone, sandstone, limestone and low-lime glacial drift
- Lobdell - nearly level floodplains, usually in areas of Wisconsinan or Illinoian glaciation but also in some unglaciated valleys
- Tioga - higher floodplain positions with gradients less than 3 percent

Climate

Average annual temperature ranges from 39 to 57 degrees, with frost-free periods varying from 140 to 220 days, an average of 180 days. Latitudes and elevations are the variance factors.

Precipitation ranges from 30 to 45 inches, with maximum amounts in late winter through early summer and the minimum in fall and amounts depend on the precise position in the Allegheny Mountains rain shadow. Near the transition point to the Allegheny Plateau, rainfall can be as much as 60 inches.

Because 20 to 30 percent of the annual precipitation comes as snow, the area's streams are most active in spring; many dry up in summer and will not be recharged until October to November. Stream patterns are trellis-shaped and reflect the regular folding of the geomorphology; they tend to be more alkaline and productive than in the Allegheny Mountains. Wetlands are scare.

The consequence, because of the rain shadow, is that vegetation tends toward the xeric side of mesic. Included are Appalachian oak forest, oak-hickory-pine forest and some northern hardwood forests.

Formerly a bastion of American chestnut, the region is now dominated by oaks, with these general trends:

- Red and white oaks are on more productive and mesic sites
- Eastern white pine and white oak are on lower portions of slopes
- Scarlet and black oak suggest drier sites
- Oaks are mixed with pitch, table mountain or Virginia pines on the driest sites.

Natural vegetation

Predominantly hardwood forest, with major species including white, red and black oak, hickories and associated upland hardwoods. Scarlet oak, chestnut oak, and scattered pines (Virginia, pitch, shortleaf and eastern white) are common on more shallow soils and on southern aspect slopes. Yellow-popular, red oak, red maple and other moisture preferring species are concentrated in sheltered coves, footslopes and slopes with northerly aspects.

Use and issues

About 55 percent is forested, most in private ownership of small to medium-sized holdings; about 30 percent is in agriculture, and 10 percent is urbanized. Water erosion, sedimentation and maintenance of organic matter are the primary issues. Most farming operations are grazing and hay production on river floodplains and in limestone soil areas. Extensive logging between 1880 and 1920 stripped the landscape and created erosion problems. On reforested sites, timber production continues, along with recreational fishing, hunting, camping and hiking. At present, extractive industries - notably coal - prevails.

Unglaciated Allegheny Plateau

This region is subdivided into two distinct areas — the Pittsburgh Plateau in the far southwest and the Allegheny Mountains to the east and north.

Pittsburgh Plateau

A well-dissected plateau with narrow, level valley floors, rolling ridgetops and hill to steep ridge slopes are the primary characteristics of the Pittsburgh Plateau. Elevation ranges from 650 feet to 1,310 feet, with local relief in the 330-foot range toward the south but less in the north. Narrow level valleys and sloping ridgetops are separated by steep to very steep long side slopes. Old glacial drift deposits are found in some of the major river valleys in the north.

The basic structure of this area of the Allegheny Plateau is flat rather than folded, but heavily eroded to form dramatic surface features. Among the distinct landforms are hummocky or gouged topography resulting from strip mining operations.

While the region was not covered by ice, it was dramatically impacted by glaciers. Tributaries of three major pre-glacial streams were blocked by advancing ice sheets to the northwest. Substantial sediments, deposited in ancient valley lakes, spread into valleys here when ice sheets departed.

The current dendritic drainage system comes from complex rearrangement that evolved over long periods of time. It results in no natural lakes, but many streams that feed the Ohio River system. Some are underlain by shallow sand, silt or gravel alluvium but others, found in pre-glacial valleys, are often filled with very deep glacial outwash. Small ephemeral springs are common.

Low intensity fires historically occur every five to 10 years, while high intensity fires average intervals of 50 years. These impact dry ridges and south and west-facing slopes more often than moist slopes facing north and east and creek bottoms.

Climate

In addition to insect and tree diseases, climate events often include ice storms in winter, occasional tornadoes, and regular inundation of major floodplains. Droughts are common. Average annual precipitation ranges from 34 to 45 inches, but can reach 51 inches at higher elevations along the eastern edge; maximum precipitation occurs in midsummer, with minimums in early autumn and winter. Average annual temperature range is 48 to 56 degrees F, and the frost free period ranges from 165 (southwest) to 215 days, with an average of 190 days in the south and 185 in the north.

Soils

Soils in the region are moderately to very deep, loamy, and range from very poorly to excessively drained. Soils to the north tend to be derived from shale, sandstone and coal and acidic. Moving southward, the soils become more circumneutral because of the influence of limestone and sandstone. High elevation soils are commonly formed from stone weathered in place. Toward the bases of slopes, soils were formed from stone moved to the base by weather or gravity. Along streams, soils are derived from sediments carried by water.

Common soils found in the area include:

Higher elevations

Berks — rounded summits, shoulders, and backslopes

Cavode — broad, level to somewhat steep ridgetops, sideslopes and benches

Clarksburg — nearly level valley flats to concave, somewhat steep hillslopes

Culleoka — narrow crests of ridges and steep hillsides

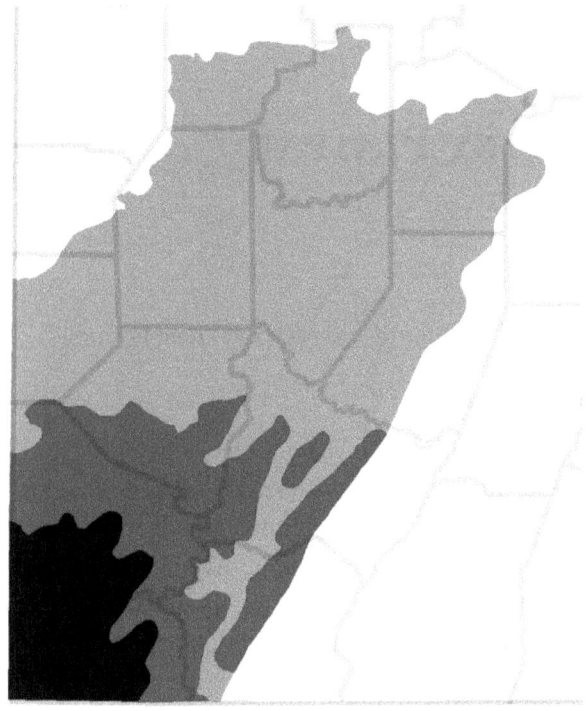

Dekalb — level to very steep ridge slopes, typically convex
Dormont — backslopes and hill summits
Gilpin - level to very steep convex slopes, usually in complexes with other soils
Guernsey — sideslopes and benches
Hazleton — upper third of backslopes, shoulders and summits, typically convex
Lowell — benches, footslopes, sideslopes and ridgetops
Rayne — hillsides and ridgetops
Upshur — ridgetops, benches and hillsides
Weikert — gentle to very steep convex dissected uplands, sometimes in complexes with related soils
Westmoreland — nose slopes, headslopes, hillsides and interfluves
Wharton — nearly level to steep upland slopes and broad summits

Footslopes and alluvial fans

Ernest — upland footslopes, hillslopes, head slopes and base slopes
Shelocta — mostly concave, gently sloping to steep benches, footslopes and mountainsides
Guernsey — sideslopes and benches

Along major streams

Chagrin — on floodplains that receive alluvium from upland areas of shale, siltstone, sandstone, limestone and low-lime glacial drift
Chavies — long, narrow to broad, nearly level to steep stream terraces where flooding is rare to never
Monongahela — stream terraces of old alluvium
Newark — nearly level floodplains and upland depressions
Philo — nearly level floodplains

Surface mining areas

Bethesda — on almost level to slightly sloping interfluves, base slopes, head slopes and benches, as well as very steep nose slopes and side slopes
Fairpoint — very steep sideslopes, benches and nearly level ridgetops
Sewell — nearly level to gently sloping benches, gently to strongly sloping hillslopes and steep outslopes (north)

Natural vegetation

Appalachian Oak Forest is the primary forest system, with some Mixed Mesophytic Forest in the extreme south and some Northern Hardwood Forest in the extreme northeast, with lesser amounts of mixed oak forest, oak-hickory-chestnut forest, oak-pine forest, hemlock forest, beech forest, and floodplain and swamp forest systems.

Dominant canopy species include white, black oak and northern red oak and shagbark, bitternut, pignut and mockernut hickory throughout. Along ridgetops in the north are oaks, black gum, flowering dogwood, sassafras, Virginia pine, pitch pine and shortleaf pine. In the south, scarlet oak, chestnut oak, hickory and scattered Virginia pine, shortleaf pine and white pine are found on dry ridges in ares with shallower soils. Yellow poplar, black walnut, red oak, red maple and other moisture-preferring species are found on north-facing slopes, sheltered coves and on footslopes.

Land use and issues

The impact of man includes stream channelization, lock construction and dams, and dumping industrial waste, sewage, mine waste and soil. With about half the land forested, most slopes have repeatedly been logged. Land sufficiently level for agricultural use has been cleared, especially in creek bottoms and along ridgetops, but sites with poor soils and erosion issues tend to be abandoned and left to natural succession. Other land is used for urbanization (including industrial development) notably along the Ohio River and major tributaries.

In the north, nearly two thirds of the region is forested, the bulk of it in farm woodlots, state and national forest and large commercial holdings. Grasslands comprise 14 percent of land use, mostly privately held. About 22 percent is under cultivation, urbanized or used for mining. Primary soil resource issues are sheet and rill erosion, land slippage and subsidence as well as riverbank erosion, gullying, surface compaction and reductions in surface organic content from farming and mining. Grazing and cultivation has led to slope erosion and upland top soil tends to be absent to thin, but the environmental impacts of bituminous coal mining and oil and gas production are more common.

In the south, about half the area is farming, primarily from beef cattle and dairy associated with hay, grassland and cultivated crops. More than one-half is forested, with timber an important commercial venture in some areas. Urban development is expanding along the Ohio River and major tributaries, with much cropland converted to urban use, most notably the Pittsburgh metropolitan area, thus siltation and industrial pollution is a concern. Large acreage blocks are owned or leased for surface coal mining. Major soil resource issues include sheet and rill erosion in pastures, land slippage, mining subsidence, stream bank erosion and reduction of organic matter on cropland. A variety of agricultural conservation practices are in use. Extraction of oil in the west and gas in the east, as well as acidic bituminous mine drainage and industrial pollution, have impacted stream habitats.

Allegheny Mountains

The eastern third of the Allegheny Plateau is a transition zone between the flatter western part and

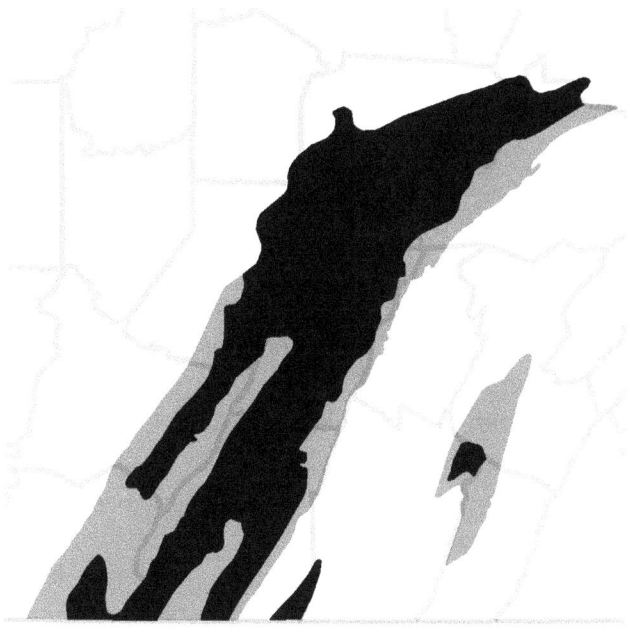

the Appalachian Ridge and Valley region to the east. As such, the terrain becomes more rugged, especially in the south. A thin band of the Ridge and Valley section that creates the Allegheny Front, is included in the region.

The front is an escarpment that essentially separates the extensive folding in the southeast to the more general uplift of the plateau to the west.

In the Forested Hills and Mountains section on the southern end, narrow valleys are interspersed with very steep-sided and highly dissected hills, mountains and ridges. The region was formed from resistant conglomerate and sandstone, often exposed at the surface, but in some areas were gently folded into a series of anticlinal ridges.

The Uplands and Valleys section to the north are characterized by a woodland-agriculture mosaic on rounded hills and low ridges. Here the region is a dissected upland plateau formed from nearly horizontal shales, siltstones, sandstones and bituminous coal.

Covering the top third of the unglaciated Allegheny Plateau, the high plateau features rounded hills, low mountains and narrow valleys from a deeply dissected plateau remnant, with extensive forests on nutrient-poor residual soils, mostly shales. Bedrock is nearly horizontal, but dissection has led to a rugged terrain with steep valley sides, entrenched streams and many waterfalls. Valleys were carved by immense volumes of glacial melt water. Most of the soils are steep, stony, acidic and low in fertility.

Soils

Regional soils are moderately to very deep, excessively well drained to somewhat poorly drained, loams formed in residuum and colluvium, sometimes including till in the north washed down from glaciated areas on both sides.

Footslopes and alluvial fans

Buchanan - nearly level to very steep terraces and concave sections of mountain footslopes, from colluvium

Ernest - upland footslopes, hillslopes, head slopes and base slopes, from colluvium

Cookport - moderately steep side slopes and broad, nearly level to gently sloping ridgetops, from residuum.

Hills and ridges

Cavode - broad, level to somewhat steep ridgetops, sideslopes and benches

Dekalb - level to very steep ridges and uplands, with slopes typically convex

Hazelton - upper third of backslopes, shoulders and summits, typically convex, formed in residuum

Gilpin - level to very steep convex dissected uplands, often hillslopes and in complexes with other soils

Hartleton - sideslopes and convex uplands

Leck Kill - level to very steep and usually convex upland slopes

Rayne - hillsides and ridgetops

Wharton - nearly level to steep slopes on uplands, residuum and/or till.

Mandy — nearly level to very steep broad ridgetops and upper slopes of mountains

Mining areas

Cedarcreek - level to gently sloping benches and hillslopes, as well as steep outslopes in strip mining areas

Climate

Average annual precipitation can vary from 33 to 68 inches, increasing toward the south and with elevation. Most precipitation is in spring and summer, with the least in the autumn; average annual temperature is 43 to 54 degrees, with frost-free periods averaging 160 days and ranging from 115 to 205 days. It decreases with both elevation and northerly direction.

Natural vegetation

Habitats in the southern region support mostly high quality hardwoods, with combinations varying with elevation:

Lower elevations - oak, black cherry, yellow-poplar, maple and other associated hardwoods; white pine, Virginia pine and black walnut occur, but are less common.

Intermediate elevations - sugar maple, black cherry, red oak.

Higher elevations - red spruce, hemlock, birch and maple

In the north, forests trend toward northern hardwoods. On moist sites, eastern hemlock and American beech-hemlock forests are common, while better drained sites tend to host American beech-sugar maple forests. Forest associates typically include: red maple, sweet birch, black cherry, white ash, yellow birch, eastern white pine and tuliptree.

Use and issues

In the south, about 75 percent in forest, of which 68 percent is privately owned. About 15 percent is used for farming and 5 percent is urbanized. Concerns include sheet and rill erosion, slippage and stream bank erosion, mining-related subsidence, gullying and stream pollution.

In the northern area, most of the land is forested and used for recreation including hunting and fishing, wildlife habitat, production of forest products and oil and gas production. Oil extraction and surface coal mining degrading stream habitats is a concern.

NORTHWESTERN GLACIATED PLATEAU, LAKE PLAIN

On four occasions, edges of continental glaciers spread into northwestern Pennsylvania, rearranged the surface and deposited vast amounts of till in a variety of ways. The region is described as a *dissected glaciated plateau* — meaning the original area of the Allegheny plateau has been carved by flowing water into its present landforms.

Very ancient glaciations are a matter of speculation, but the more recent two (Illinoian between 196,000 and 128,000 years ago and Wisconsinan between 110,000 and 12,000 years ago) have been well mapped and measured.

Consequences of glaciation are three distinct areas: a thin, flat lake plain along the shore of Lake Erie that ends with an escarpment on the southeast edge and, within the Allegheny Plateau itself, a lowland in the vicinity of Lake Pymatuning and a larger drift plain that extends toward the boundary of glaciation on the east and south. Geographers and environmentalists often consider the Lake Plain as a distinct region, part of a thin band surrounding Lake Erie and Lake Ontario, but for our landscaping purposes it's easier to consider it as part of the larger glaciated plateaus because most of the habitats are similar.

The lobe of the thick sheet of ice that spread southwestward from Lake Ontario and then curled into Pennsylvania is defined as a *depositional* glacier, in contrast to the *erosional* glaciation of northeastern Pennsylvania. The difference is that while ice coming down from the New England area had to plow through and smooth out a more irregular surface, the westerly route had less resistance because it was flatter to begin with. This allowed the ice to deposit more till, while glaciation on the eastern end had the effect of removing material and releasing it at the terminal point.

Five different kinds of till have been identified

in the northwest, along with vast streams of stratified drift.

Wisconsinan tills — Ashtabula, Hiram, Lavery and Kent — are described as thick, gray and clayey to silty soils that cover more than 75 percent of the surface. Topography is commonly gentle undulations, but in some areas there is a combination of knob-and-kettle landscapes with thin soil. The Illinoian till, Titusville, is gray to brown, thin, clayey to sandy and covering between 10 and 25 percent of the surface, with the topography more reflective of underlying bedrock.

The stratified drift is sands and gravels in eskers, kames and kame terraces, mostly in valleys. In formerly ice-dammed valleys, soils trend toward clay and silt. Along Lake Erie, lake clays and beach sands and gravels tend to dominate.

Along Lake Erie, a rolling to nearly level series of deposits from ice sheets and lakes covers horizontally-bedded sedimentary rock. Common features include ancient beach ridges, hummocky moraines, kettles and kames. Many valleys cut into the bedrock point northwest, the direction of retreating glaciers.

An important water divide in this section separates drainage into that which flows toward the Gulf of St. Lawrence and the Gulf of Mexico. Stream gradients, underlain by deep, coarse sand and gravel glacial outwash, range from steep headwater streams to low-gradient rivers feeding the Ohio River or Lake Erie. A number of small natural lakes and wetlands such as bogs and marshes are common features in the glaciated landscape.

Generally, till and drift blanket the upland bedrock. Lower slopes are covered by colluvium and valley floors are with alluvium and materials once on the bottoms of glacial lakes.

Pymatuning Lowlands

The Pymatuning Lowlands are level to undulating terrain, with a relief of less than 150 feet. It features many wetlands and flat-bottomed broad valleys mantled by glacial outwash and alluvial and lacustrine deposits. Low gradient streams in the region and Pymatuning Lake reflect the low-relief terrain.

Hiram till dominates the lowland area and fragipans are common, compounding drainage issues. The general topography, climate and soil makes the region well-suited for the dairy industry, and on well-drained outwash soils crops can include oats, wheat, potatoes and corn. Very poorly drained sites are most commonly wooded to brushy idle land and wetlands.

Low Lime Drift Plain

Ground moraines, rolling terrain, broad valleys, kettles, kames and poorly drained depressions are key features and are covered by Kent till from the late Wisconsinan age covers acidic, sedimentary rock of varying types and age. Most soils are poorly drained because of fragipans and are rocky near the surface, acidic not very fertile.

Lake deposits are common along the northern edge, where climate moderates and natural vegetation changes. Toward the east, Kent till declines and so does dairy farming. To the southwest, around the Pymatuning Lowlands, terrain becomes flatter and wetter.

The Erie Lake Plain

Flatness with shallow entrenchment of drainage is a key characteristic of the Erie Lake plain, which is a combination of level to gently rolling till plain and flat lake plain. Some broad low gravelly ridges run parallel to the shoreline and tend to be northwest sloping and hint at the shorelines of two ancient glacial lakes. Moraines, 50 to 200 feet thick, cover about half of the section are till. The remainder is from either Wisconsinan lake deposits of muck, peat, marl, silt and clay or the sands that formed prehistoric beach dunes and ridges. Streams in the region tend to be shallow with low gradients and deranged drainage patterns because of low topography and glacial influence.

Regional soils

Soils, formed from till and lacustrine material, are acidic Alfisols and some Inceptisols.

Across the region, soils are Alfisols from glacial outwash and till, as well as glacial lake sediments and stratified drift deposits (especially kames and eskers) over bedrock of alternating sandstone, siltstone and shale. Shale tends to be most dominant near Lake Erie and along the border with Ohio. Along streams, alluvial deposits can lie over glacial materials.

Soils are very deep, loamy to clayey, and range from well to poorly drained. Various land features and major soil types include:

- Canfield — moderately well drained interfluves, headslopes, nose slopes and sideslopes on till plains and moraines
- Chili — well drained outwash plains and terraces, kames and beach ridges
- Frenchtown — poorly drained broad flat areas, base slopes, depressions and along natural

drainageways on till plains

Mahoning — somewhat poorly drained till plains

Platea — somewhat poorly drained sideslopes, shoulders and summits on till plains and moraines

Ravenna — poorly drained areas at or near the lowest landscape positions of Wisconsinan age till plains

Sheffield — poorly drained large flats and depressions on till plains

Venango — somewhat poorly drained convex flats, slight rises, low summits, shoulders and sideslopes of till plains and moraines

Wooster — well drained convex slopes on till plains and moraines

Natural vegetation

Three major forest systems are found in the region: Northern Hardwood, Beech-Maple and Appalachian Oak.

Beech-Maple Forest dominates the lake plain and wetter soils in the southwestern area of the region, while the remainder tends to be Northern Hardwoods Forest.

Beech forest is dominated by American beech, sugar maple, red oak, white ash and white oak. Secondary species include American basswood, shagbark hickory, and black cherry. In poorly drained flatlands, American beech and sugar maple are common and some mesophytic oak-sugar maple and oak forest types are reported. Other types found in the region include maple-ash-oak swamps and wet beech, beech-sugar maple, oak-maple and mixed oak forests.

In the Pymatuning Lowlands and the Low Lime Drift Plain, natural vegetation would lean toward Northern Hardwood Forest on better-drained sites, while Beech-Maple Forest dominates elsewhere.

Shrub swamps and swamp forests are extensive in the lowlands and feature *Cephalanthus occidentalis* (buttonbush); *Cornus amomum* (silky dogwood); *Rhus vernix* (poison sumac), and *Rosa palustris* (swamp rose). Common to swamp forests are: *Acer rubrum* (red maple); *Pinus strobus* (white pine); *Larix laricina* (larch). Among marsh species reported here are *Carex* spp. (sedges); *Cladium jamaicense* (sawgrass); *Phragmites communis* (reed grasses); *Typha* spp (cattails).

In the Low-Lime Drift Plain, natural vegetation includes Northern Hardwood forests in better-drained sites and Beech-Maple Forest elsewhere. Along the eastern edge of the Low-Lime Drift plain, near the limit of glaciation, Appalachian Oak Forest appears. Marshes, swamps and bogs are typical in areas of poor drainage, and two endangered species are found in alkaline meadows: *Lobelia kalmii* (Kalm's lobelia) and *Trollius laxus* (spreading globe flower).

On the Erie Lake Plain features habitats for a variety of forest types, including northern hardwood, beech-maple and elm-ash, but beech-maple dominates. More localized vegetation types are pitch pine-heath barrens, oak openings, hemlock-northern hardwood forest and maple-basswood forests and, in the eastern edge, beech-maple mesic forests. The plain contains habitat considered rare and unique and home to as many as 35 species ranked as rare in Pennsylvania.

Climate

Annual precipitation averages 34 to 50 inches, most heavily in summer months; annual temperature ranges from 44 to 51 degrees F, with a growing season ranging from 145 to 215 days, averaging 180 days.

On the lake plain, precipitation averages between 27 and 45 inches, increasing from west to east, and evenly distributed throughout the year. Lake effect snow is between 40 and 80 inches each winter, and mean annual temperature ranges from 45 to 52 degrees F, and the growing season varies between 140 and 160 days.

Proximity to the lake results in more winter cloudiness, delayed coastal freezing, an increased growing season and greater snowfall. Here the 194-day growing season is three to 10 weeks longer than elsewhere in the adjacent Low Lime Drift Plain. The lake's climate impact is pronounced within five to six miles, but vanishes at 8 to 16 miles from the shoreline.

Climate disturbances on the lake plain include

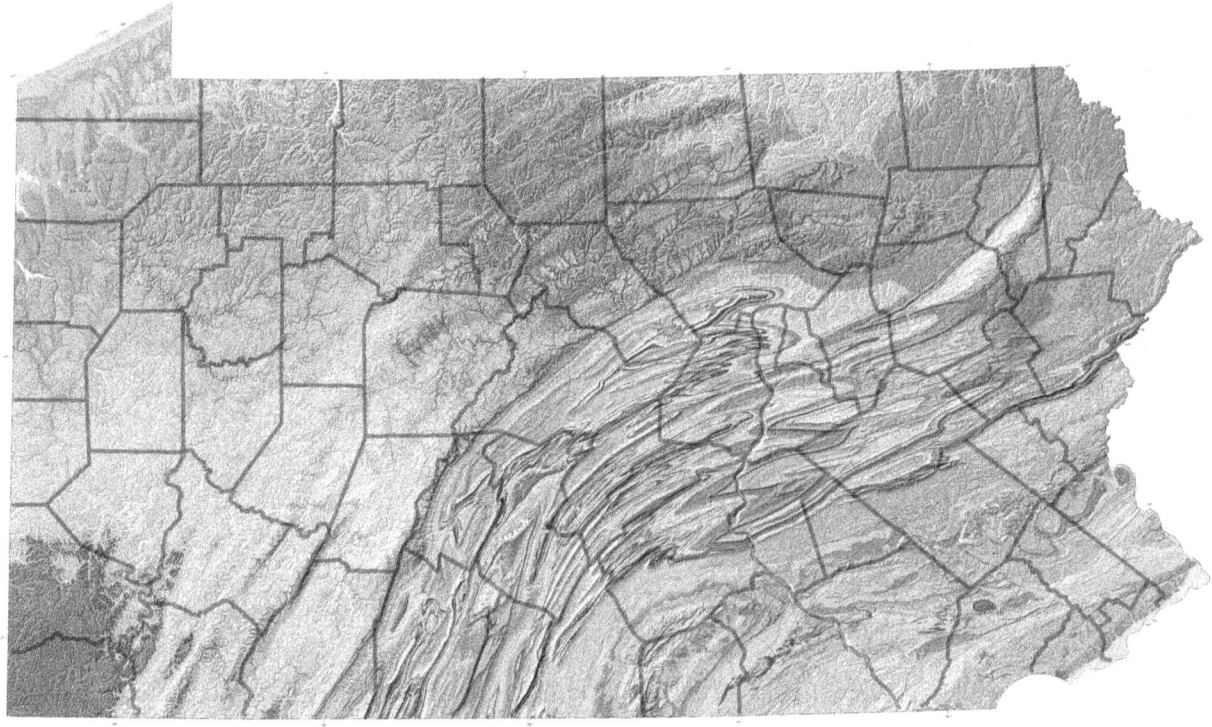

A relief map of Pennsylvania with an overlay of county boundaries

occasional tornadoes, but more frequent winter ice storms; some swamp forests, wet prairies and marshes are flooded during several months of the year, and periodic floods and droughts can impact areas near streams and rivers. Disease concerns include Dutch elm, chestnut blight and ash dieback; fires tend to be small and scattered.

Environmental Issues

About 50 percent of the land is used for agriculture (orchards, vineyards and vegetable farming, but more commonly dairy) and about 28 percent is forested, mostly small woodlots and almost all in private ownership with some large holdings devoted to watershed protection; another 21 percent is urban development. Primary concerns are sheet and rill erosion, storm water runoff sedimentation and maintenance of organic matter/productivity of soils. Erosion and stream pollution are local issues.

Impacting regional forests, especially in ravines and on dissected slopes are insects and diseases, as well as windstorms. Terraces and floodplains are also disturbed by drought and fire, but less severely than upland forests.

Unglaciated Allegheny High Plateau

A deeply dissected plateau terminating at the Allegheny Front, the Unglaciated High Allegheny Plateau features steep slopes as well as level to gently rolling plateau remnants in the far north. Elevation ranges from 980 feet in the lowest valleys to between 1,970 and 2,620 along ridge crests, with local relief in the 330 to 980-foot range. Although the western edge was covered by at least two pre-Wisconsinan glaciations, there is no evidence of smoothing by glaciers, and hilltop elevations increase in a northeastward direction to a range of 1,700 to 2,200 feet. This insures a humid but cool climate; precipitation is higher in the west.

Over time, erosional forces have dissected the plateau into prominently incised ridges and valleys that create a dendritic drainage pattern. Fast-moving streams in channels controlled by exposed bedrock flow toward:

- The Allegheny River and subsequently the Ohio and Mississippi systems
- The Susquehanna Rivers and ultimately to the Chesapeake Bay.

Other surface water is in the form of wetlands in alluvial areas, benches, heads of drainageways and depressions. Springs and seeps are numerous.

Here the folding consequences of continental plate collisions resulted in wide but relatively low folds on a northeast to southwest line and elevation ranges from 1,000 to 2,000 feet. Local relief can range from 100 to 670 feet. Upper Devonian, Lower Mississippian and Pennsylvanian bedrock is a series of sandstone, siltstone, shale, conglomerate, coal and sometimes limestone.

Overlying the bedrock is a layer of unconsolidated materials that includes alluvium in narrow valley bottoms, colluvium on steep hillsides and residuum on flat to gently sloping uplands. In wider valleys, gravel, sand, silt and clay are found in thicker deposits.

These soils are parented by local sandstone, siltstone and shale, moderately to very deep, excessively well drained to somewhat poorly drained, loams that are steep, stony, acidic and low in fertility.

Footslopes and alluvial fans --Buchanan and Ernest series formed in colluvium and the Cookport series, formed on ridge residuum.

Hills and ridges — Cavode, Dekalb, Hazelton, Gilpin, Hartleton, Leck Kill, Rayne and Wharton series formed from residuum and/or till. The Mandy series is found at high elevations.

Mining areas - Udorthents, such as Cedarcreek series, in mesic areas of surface coal mining.

Vegetation

Natural vegetation is primarily Northern Hardwood Forest, with a perimeter of Appalachian Oak. Lakes and marshes common to the glaciated plateau less frequent, but some intermixed bogs are reported. On moist sites, eastern hemlock and American beech-hemlock forests are common, while better drained sites tend to host American beech-sugar maple forests. Forest associates typically include:

- Red maple
- Sweet birch
- Black cherry
- White ash
- Yellow birch
- Eastern white pine
- Tuliptree
- Cucumber tree

Combinations varying with elevation:

Lower elevations - oak, black cherry, yellow-poplar, maple and other associated hardwoods; white pine, Virginia pine and black walnut occur,

but are less common.

Intermediate elevations - Sugar maple, black cherry, red oak.

Higher elevations - Red spruce, hemlock, birch and maple

Climate

Aaverage annual precipitation can vary from 33 to 68 inches, increasing toward the south and with elevation. Most precipitation is in spring and summer, with the least in the autumn; average annual temperature is 43 to 54 degrees, with frost-free periods averaging 160 days and ranging from 115 to 205 days. It decreases with both elevation and northerly direction.

Use and issues

About 75 percent in forest, of which 68 percent is privately owned. About 15 percent is used for farming and 5 percent is urbanized. Concerns include sheet and rill erosion, slippage and stream bank erosion, mining-related subsidence, gullying and stream pollution.

Most of the land is forested and used for recreation including hunting and fishing, wildlife habitat, production of forest products and oil and gas production. Common oil extraction and surface coal mining in the south, degrading stream habitats, is a concern.

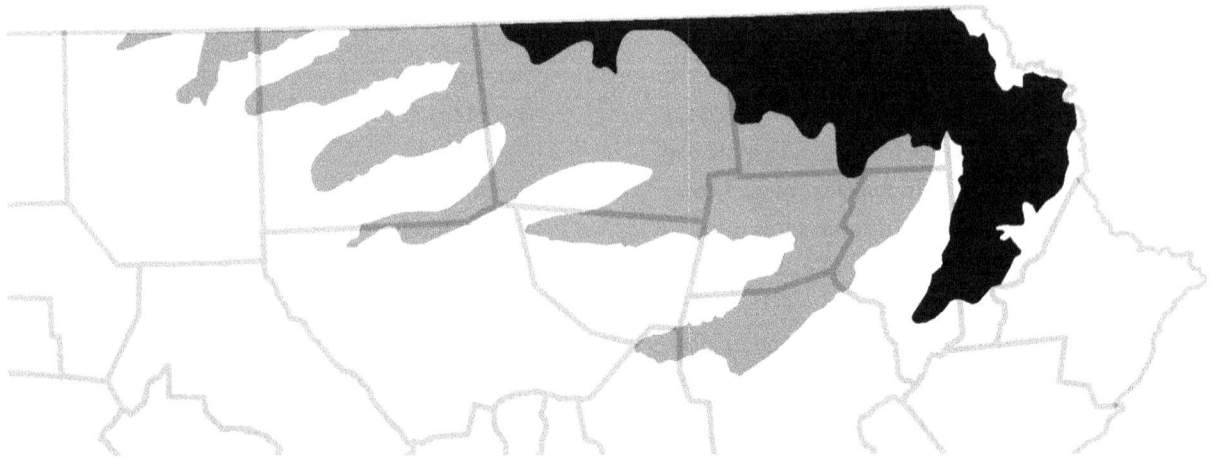

Glaciated Low Plateau

Northeastern Glaciated Plateau

The portion of the northeastern glaciated Allegheny Plateau is a nearly level to moderately sloping, dissected plateau with narrow, steep-walled valleys and smooth valley floors. Three major river systems — Susquehanna, Allegheny and Delaware — originate on the plateau in New York and are well established rivers when they enter Pennsylvania.

Substantial amounts of glacial drift and outwash — much of it sand and gravel — covers the region, especially valley floors, with some glacial lake sediment and ice-contact and stratified drift in the valleys. Virtually the entire region is blanketed by Olean Till, a moderately thick, gray to grayish-red, and sandy glacial deposit. Along the very southwestern edge, the remnants of more ancient tills are browner and contain more clay, but feature better developed topsoil.

The entire region was most recently covered by the Lake Champlain-Hudson River Lobe of a continental ice sheet more than 1,000 feet thick, and the irregular topography of the region is covered with a variety of features, including moraines, drumlins, kames, kettles, eskers and glacial scour. In contrast to northwestern Pennsylvania, glaciation here was erosional rather than depositional; the ice sheet encountered a hilly terrain caused by folded bedrock and had the effect of smoothing it out. In the northwest, glaciers encountered little resistance and toward the terminal point made much more substantial deposits of till.

The northeast region is defined by escarpments, east-facing in this area, and is gently rolling with high hills and steep valleys, a consequence of extensive dissection of the plateau by erosional forces. Upland areas are characterized by high gradient and bedrock-controlled streams, leading to numerous waterfalls and rapids. Poorly drained uplands and valleys are marked by swamps and marshes.

The complexity of the region becomes apparent

Glaciated High Plateau

when it is further subdivided into several distinct areas. In a general line from northwest to southeast are the Glaciated Allegheny High Plateau, Glaciated Low Plateau, Appalachian Northern Sandstone Ridges and Appalachian Anthracite regions in the Wyoming Valley, then the Pocono High Plateau and the Pocono Low Plateau, ending with the Shale Valleys region of the Appalachians in southeastern Monroe County. Toward the northeast is the Northeastern Uplands and, in a thin band along the Delaware River, the Low Catskills. Toward the southwest, features of the very north end of the Appalachian ridge and valley region appear, specifically Northern Shale Valleys, Northern Sandstone Ridges and Northern Dissected Ridges.

High and Low Plateaus

The Glaciated Allegheny High Plateau is mostly forested, with elevations ranging from 1,900 to 2,300 feet, whereas the Low Plateau is 1,300 to 1,800 feet and extensively used for farming. The smoothing effect of glaciation has created many closed depressions and blocked valleys that contain small lakes and shallow ponds. While the high plateau features resistant bedrock, the lower plateau is less so and features many broad valleys; both are less deformed than the sandstone ridges to the south.

On the high plateau, glacial drift is stony, acidic, often steep and low in fertility. Lower elevation soils are described as leached and stony with fragipans and, consequently, poor drainage, and bogs and marshes are common.

A very small portion of the Low Catskills, less than five miles wide, forested and highly dissected, hugs the Delaware River in the extreme northeastern corner of the state. Cliffs and steep-walled valleys with high-gradient streams are common and the Olean Till soils are, again, characterized by stoniness, shallowness, low fertility, and acidity. Combined with rugged terrain and a very short growing season, the land is best suited for forest.

Ridge and Valley pieces

A narrow extension of the Central Appalachians along the Susquehanna River at elevations under 825 feet bisects the plateau, along a line from Wilkes-Barre to northeast of Scranton in Wayne County. On either side of the Anthracite coal region is northern shale valley featuring acidic valley and low hill soils developed from shales and sandstones, while the central line is underlain by anthracite-bearing strata, mine-waste soils and low woodland density.

On the southwestern line of the region, the familiar ridge and valley topography of the Appalachians crosses glaciated zones at just about the extent of Wisconsinan glaciation and into ancient till deposits. Shale valleys straddle both sides of a long sandstone ridge, Blue Mountain in the southeastern edge of the glaciated area as well. The area to the southeast of the ridge is part of the Lehigh Valley, while to the north it is part of the Blue Mountain Section of Monroe County.

Pocono High and Low Plateaus

The Pocono High Plateau is a forested highland with local relief ranging only from 50 to 175 feet, smoothed by glacial advances and retreats to a morainal topography with many hummocks and potholes over undeformed, noncabonate strata and bounded by an escarpment of over 300 feet. Glacial and artificial lakes are common.

Further southeast, the Pocono Low Plateau is a glaciated, forested plateau smoothed by ice sheets that altered drainage and formed many shallow wetlands and kettle lakes. Because underlying soils are less resistant than the high plateau, the region hill crests are lower by 500 to 700 feet and feature a combination of till, glacial outwash, glacial lake deposits and recent alluvium over shale, siltstone and sandstone. These, too, tend toward poor drainage, acidity, stoniness and low fertility. Many streams of varying sizes have dissected the landscape into a variety of surface features. The limited areas underlain by Illinoian till support the ecologically significant Pocono till barrens.

Across the northeastern corner of the estate, dissected and glaciated uplands feature low rolling hills with moderate relief and slope. About half the area is wooded, and lakes and bogs are common.

Because the local sandstones are more resistant to erosion, the general elevations are higher. The strata is less deformed, leading to less relief and lower forest density. Wetlands — especially swamps — can be very typical of low relief areas, notably in the Morris-Wellsboro and Morris-Wellsboro-Oquaga soil associations.

Soils

Soils can range from shallow to very deep and well to very poorly drained, but loamy. Among major soils in the region:

Hills and dissected plateaus
Arnot — valley sides, with slopes ranging from gentle to nearly vertical
Lordstown — nearly level to very steep hillsides and hilltops in bedrock-controlled dissected uplands
Oquaga — level to very steep hillslopes

Hills and till plains
Bath — gentle to steep mountain and ridge hillslopes
Lackawanna — nearly level to steep glaciated hillslopes and ridges
Mardin — backslopes, shoulders and broad summits of glaciated hills
Swartswood — nearly level to very steep upland slopes
Wellsboro — nearly level to steep glaciated slopes
Wurtsboro - level to moderately steep glaciated slopes
Chippewa — nearly level depressions with concave surface shapes in till deposits
Morris — slightly concave uplands and till plains
Norwich — seeps, depressions and low-relief till plains
Volusia — entle to steep concave to planer slopes on lower valley sides and on broad divides

Natural vegetation

Hardwood forest is the most common, with the amount of oak species increasing from east to west, particularly where soils are dry and shallow. In more moist locations, conifers such as white pine appear as well as aspen, hemlock, northern white cedar and black ash.

On higher elevations and toward the north, Northern Hardwood forest systems dominate and mix with some floating peat and kettlehole bogs, swamps and marshes. In lower elevations, toward the Appalachians, Appalachian Oak forests become the norm.

An important exception are the mesic to hydric Pocono till barrens that abut xeric ridgetop barrens, over sandstone. Among the species found in the glacial till barren shrublands are scattered *Pinus rigida* (pitch pine) *Quercus ilicifolia* (scrub oak), *Kalmia angustifolia* (sheep laurel) and *Rhododendron canadense* (rhodora).

In the Anthracite region, Appalachian Oak forest were the natural forest, mixed with some Northern Hardwoods Forest. Cherry and birch are currently recolonizing some of the mined areas. On higher elevations away from the Susquehanna River, the region trends toward Northern Hardwood Forest.

Climate

Annual precipitation ranges from 30 to 45 inches, but up to 64 inches in high elevations; most falls as snow. Average annual precipitation is 40 to 50 degrees F, with frost-free periods ranging from 130 to 200 days and averaging 165 days, depending on elevation.

Use and issues

About 61 percent is in forest, mostly second and third growth and most privately held, with another 27 percent in agriculture and 8 percent in urban development. Water erosion, soil wetness and nonpoint stream sedimentation are concerns. The sandstone and shale aquifer in the region is important; water from the former is soft while from the latter it is most often hard. Common oil extraction and surface coal mining in the south, degrading stream habitats, is a concern.

BLUE RIDGE MOUNTAINS

The Blue Ridge Mountains are a relatively narrow band of mountain ridges with high local relief and steep side slopes and channel gradients, underlain by deformed, igneous rock on the east and sedimentary rock on the west.

These rugged mountains present narrow valleys – although some broad valleys exist — and sharp crests atop steep slopes. Deep and intricate stream dissection is a common theme; rivers and streams and their tributaries often flow through gorges and mountain gaps.

They are, in fact, the eroded core of the Appalachian Mountains, a very ancient fold exposed during the most recent uplift of the continent. Each highland, made up of crystalline rock, is distinct from the adjoining lowlands.

In Pennsylvania, the region is subdivided into the Northern Igneous Ridges on the easterly side of the band and the Northern Sedimentary and Metasedimentary Ridges on the western edge. The region is technically the northeast-plunging nose of the Catoctin-Blue Ridge anticline and the single ancient ridge extends from Adams and Franklin Counties in Pennsylvania well into Georgia.

On the east side, steep and well-dissected northern igneous ridges are separated by coves and high gaps, with elevations eranging from 1,000 to 1,600 feet in Pennsylvania and local relief maximizing at about 1,300 feet.

On the west side, a series of high, steep ridges with deep, narrow valleys ranges from 1,300 to 2,000 feet in elevation, with local relief as high as 1,000 feet, formed from erosion-resistant sedimentary and metasedimentary rock.

Soils

The general pattern of soil lineage is residuum on ridges and mountain tops, colluvium on lower slopes and alluvium in valleys. Soils range from deep to very deep and from fine-textured clays to sandy loams, generally mesic. Boulders and bedrock outcrops are common but not extensive on upper slopes.

Steep mountain slopes – low fertility soils, such as:

Edgemont — nearly level to very steep ridge and mountain slopes

Myersville — nearly level to very steep mountainside slopes

Highfield — slopes up to 50 percent, mountain crests and intermountain valleys

Catoctin — nearly level to steep ridges and sideslopes

Duffield — nearly level to steep hillsides

Arendtsville- on dissected upland hillslopes, ranging from gentle to steep

Footslopes and coves – mostly from colluvium:

Thurmont — footslopes, colluvial fans, benches and stream terraces

Hagerstown — floors of valleys and adjacent hillsides

Along narrow streams – tend to be frequently flooded:

Comus — floodplains

Codorus — nearly level slopes of floodplains

Natural Vegetation

These ridges remain extensively forested with the oak-hickory forests of southern Pennsylvania, but agriculture is common on South Mountain on Arendtsville soils. The region's habitats are well suited for Appalachian oak, southeastern spruce-fir and northern hardwood forests. Oaks dominate

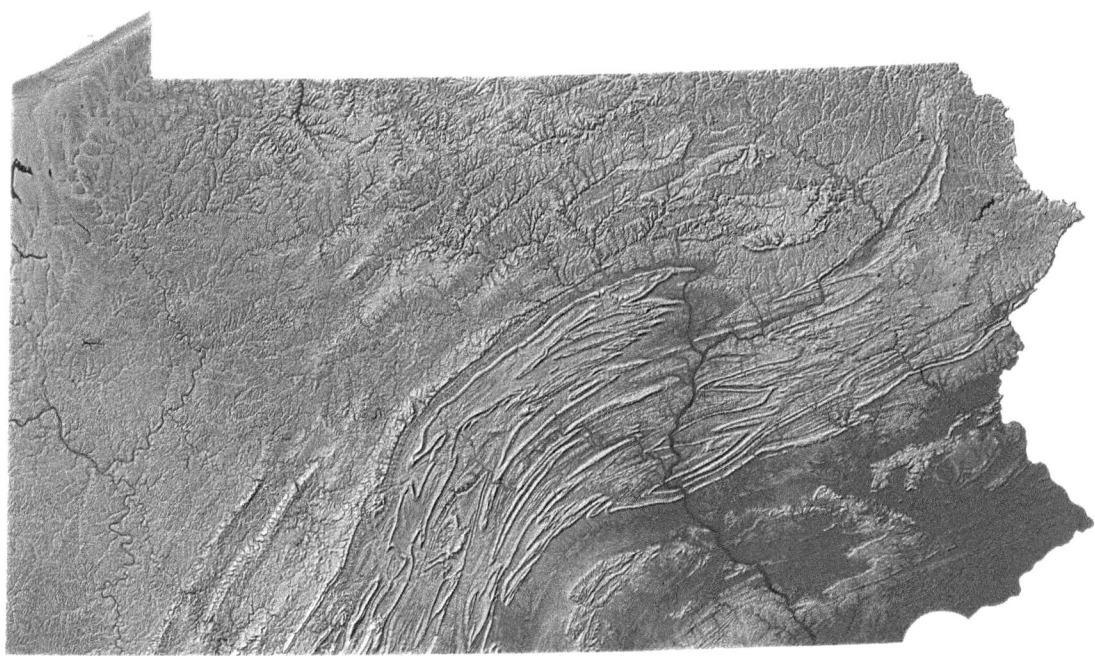

An illustration of elevations in Pennsylvania

montane cold-deciduous broadleaf forest, with black, white and chestnut oaks on dry mountain slopes. Pitch pine is a ridge top component, and mesophytic species such as northern red oak, red maple, yellow-poplar and sweet birch dominate valleys and moist slopes. Higher elevation mesic sites host northern hardwoods, such as sugar maple, basswood and buckeye; drier sites will be dominated by northern red oak.

Common understory species include dogwood, hornbeam, pawpaw, sassafras, persimmon, greenbrier, leatherwood, mountain laurel, rhododendron and witch hazel. Cover combinations often include:

    white pine-hemlock
    chestnut oak
    white-oak-red oak-hickory
    northern red oak
    basswood-white ash
    yellow-poplar-white oak-northern red oak
    loblolly pine-shortleaf pine

Climate

Precipitation averages 36 to 45 inches, but can reach more than 60 inches at highest elevations; annual temperature range is 49 to 56 degrees, with a frost-free season averaging 195 days and ranging from 165 to 225 days, depending on latitude and elevation.

Use and issues

About 60 percent is in forest, of which 10 percent is federally-owned (national parks and forests), with 27 percent in agricultural use and 9 percent urbanized. Erosion along poorly constructed and maintained access roads is a major concern, with runoff sediments and urban development leading to stream pollution.

Chief natural disturbances are fire, wind, ice and precipitation. Lightning-spawned fire is more prevalent in some areas, as well as bursts of intense wind that leads to blowdowns on mountain slopes. Winter ice storms damage tree crowns, and surges of precipitation results in localized scouring and erosion, followed by downstream flooding and the associated siltation and sedimentation. Chestnut blight devastated forests between 1920 and 1940, forever altering the composition of the region. Gypsy moth infestation has the potential to seriously impact the newly dominant oaks.

Distribution of Major Forest Systems in Pennsylvania

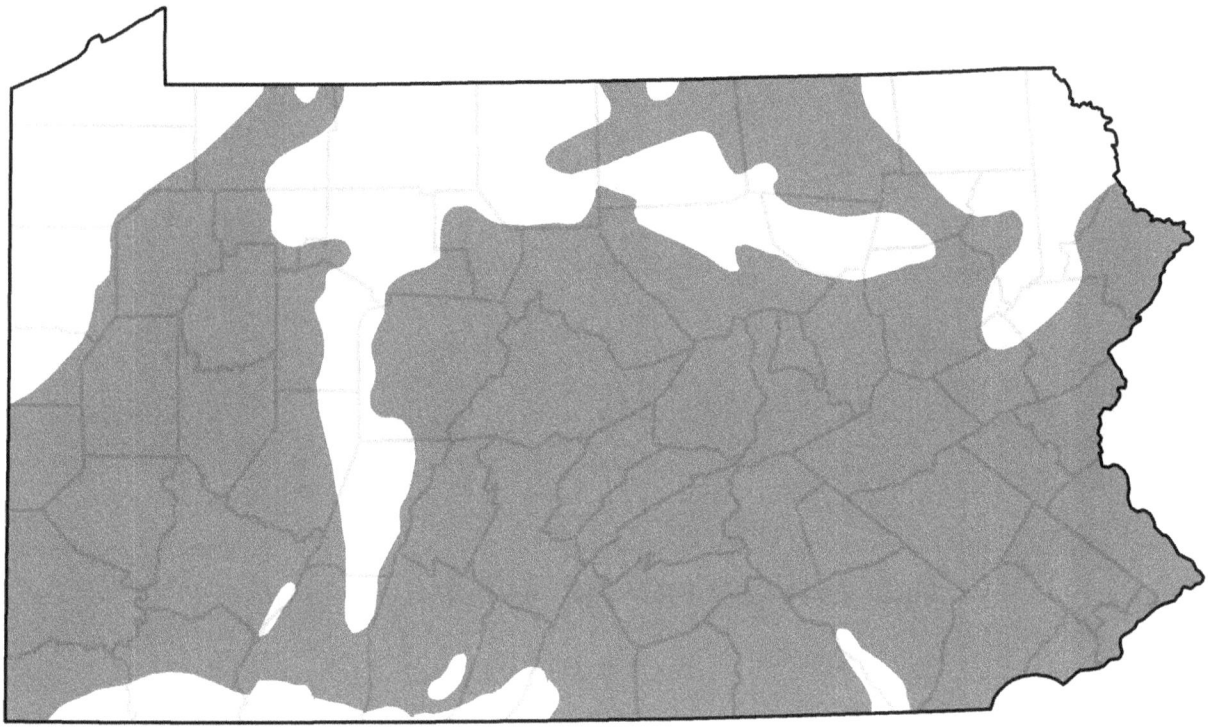

Above: Appalachian Oak forests dominate the Pennsylvania Landscape. Below, other major systems include Northern Hardwood (light gray), Beech-Maple (northwest); Mixed Mesophytic (southwest), and Oak-Hickory (along the southern boundary.

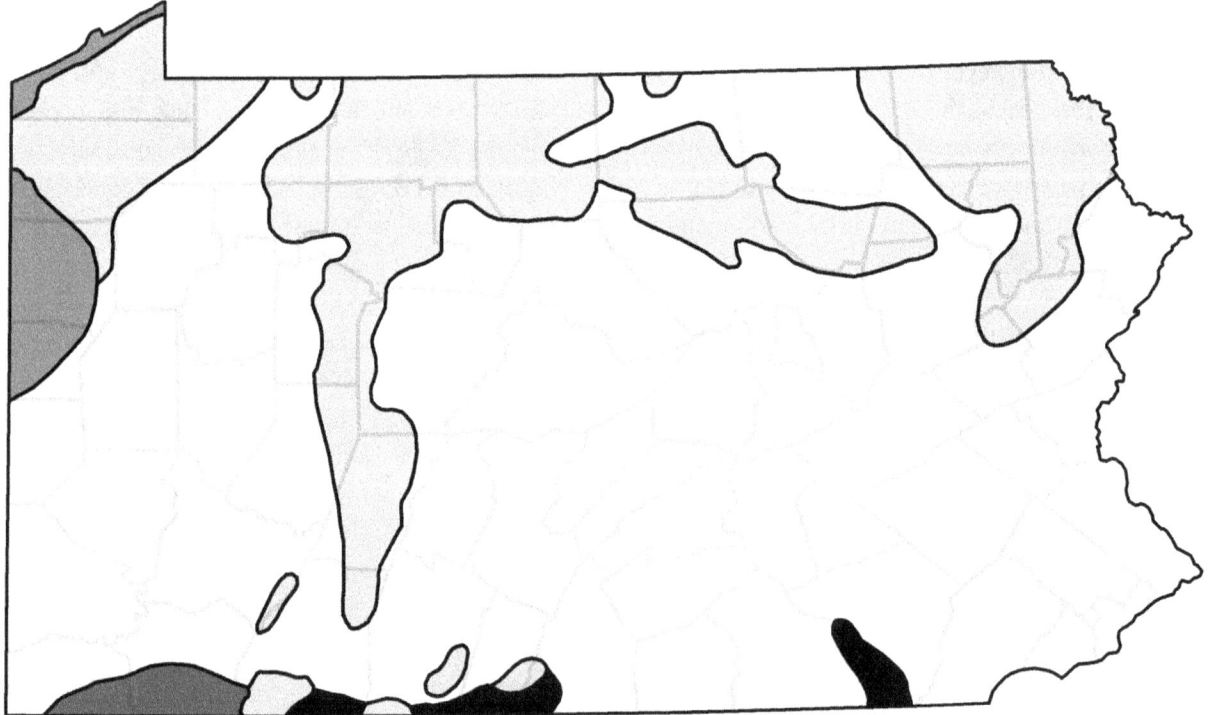

DRY OAK FORESTS

Oak forests and woodlands vary in composition and by region, but share many major characteristics. The key players are constant: chestnut oak (*Quercus prinus*), black oak (*Quercus velutina*), scarlet oak (*Quercus coccinea*), white oak (*Quercus alba*) and red oak *(Quercus rubra)*.

Dry oak forests have common habitat themes: xeric summits and high elevations of steep, often convex slopes and ridges, mostly on warm aspects, with well drained, rocky to sandy, infertile, very acidic soils that can be so thin that bedrock is exposed. Sites are over sandstone, shale and sometimes siltstone.

Some oak forests in the western two-thirds of the state occur on steep but concave slopes that are downslope from xeric sites, but upslope from richer coves. They often face north to southeast, are a bit more protected from weather extremes, have higher calcium levels in the soil but nonetheless remain acidic. Chestnut and red oaks share dominance and the understory tends to be more mesic. Yet overall, the species census is much the same as other oak forests.

In terms of liking it dry, chestnut and black oak have a distinct advantage: they can handle the most shallow soils of the group (36 and 40 inch minimums) and, with scarlet oak, savor the xeric, sun-soaked faces of south and west facing slopes. White and red oaks can hold their own if the soil is a bit deeper, but tend to congregate on the cooler side of the ridge and thrive partway down the slope.

Red oak is more common in sheltered slopes facing north while scarlet prevails on open or exposed sites, especially those timbered or subjected

Sugar Maple Variation

In glaciated areas of northwestern Pennsylvania, on rich and sandy loams that tend toward acidic, white, red and chestnut oaks can share canopy dominance with sugar maple. This suggests the soil is in the 5.5 to 6.5 pH range — the bottom end for sugar maple and the high end for chestnut oak, with soils of a medium to coarse texture.

For authenticity, the ratio of oaks to sugar maple is about three to one, with shagbark hickory *(Carya ovata)*, American beech *(Fagus grandifolia)*, tuliptree *(Liriodendron tulipifera)* and black gum *(Nyssa sylvatica)* as excellent associate choices.

These kinds of habitats are ideal sites for an impressive array of small trees and tall shrubs, such as serviceberry *(Amelanchier arborea)*, American hornbeam *(Carpinus caroliniana)*, redbud *(Cercis canadensis)*, flowering dogwood *(Cornus florida)*, American hazelnut *(Corylus americana)* and American hop hornbeam *(Ostrya virginiana)*.

For authentic touches in the herbaceous layer, be sure to include wild sarsaparilla *(Aralia nudicaulis)*, fibrousroot sedge *(Carex communis)*, Pennsylvania sedge *(Carex pensylvanica)*, rattlesnake weed *(Hieracium venosum)*, whorled yellow loosestrife *(Lysimachia quadrifolia)* and starry false lily of the valley *(Maianthemum stellatum)*.

to fire in the past 100 years.

Of the primary species, minimum pH is around 4.5 – but maximum for chestnut oak and black oak is 6.5, while white oak can go to 6.8, scarlet to 6.9, and red oak to 7.3. In terms of preferences, chestnut is at the low end of the scale, while white oak is toward the higher end, but ideal ground for oaks is always less than 6.5, and all oaks need between 36 and 48 inches of soil in which to grow.

Because of thick layers of decaying leaves, oak forests in the wild are lean at the shrub and herbaceous levels. Where soil pH is 5.5 or less, brushy stands of mountain laurel *(Kalmia latifolia)* can develop long term. This slow-growing ericaceous species — and the state flower of Pennsylvania — thrives through a vast network of fine roots in the thin soil under the humus layer. Very drought tolerant and a model for slow-growing, acid loving ericads, it can take 20 years to reach a height of five feet.

Options for trees are broad, with sassafras *(Sassafras albidum)*, white pine *(Pinus strobus)* and red maple *(Acer rubrum)* perhaps the most common. Black gum *(Nyssa sylvatica)* is a regular in eastern Pennsylvania, while sourwood *(Oxydendrum arboreum)* is more typical in the west. But designers should also consider hickories, black cherry, ash, sugar maple and sweet birch *(Betula lenta)* as good possibilities for these sites and in more sheltered and open areas, flowering dogwood *(Cornus florida)*.

Conditions drive choices for understory design toward slow-growing, drought tolerant and acid-loving species such as black haw *(Viburnum prunifolium)*, serviceberry *(Amelanchier arborea)* and witch hazel *(Hamamelis virginiana)* for height, and for low masses, maple-leaf viburnum *(Viburnum acerifolium)*, azaleas such as roseshell *(Rhododendron prinophyllum)* and pinxter-flower *(Rhododendron periclymenoides)*, plus low-bush blueberrries and huckleberries.

In nature, density of the herbaceous layer varies with the shrub cover. While scattered graminoid or herbaceous species persist underneath dense shrubs, better opportunities are found in open patches between shrub clumps.

On sites where leaf litter is well managed, spring gets an early start with ephemerals that are up, bloom and settle in for the season just before the leaf cover is out. While any dry-leaning species will do, the authentic touches of teaberry *(Gaultheria procumbens)* and trailing arbutus *(Epigaea repens)* deserve consideration. For simplicity, wild sarsaparilla *(Aralia nudicaulis)* can be used to dominate the herb layer in large clonal patches. This is an ideal habitat for Pink lady's slipper *(Cypripedium acaule)*, a rare orchid challenging to obtain and grow, but an exquisite trophy on the right site.

Soil acidity and dryness make these kinds of landscapes a problem for lawns, even for "deep shade" hybrid graminoids. The necessary leaf litter restricts lawn to paths and some compromise in sustainability.

Black Gum Variation

When circumstances give dominance of ridgetops or high shoulders in the Ridge and Valley region over to black gum *(Nyssa sylvatica)*, often where there has been a history of repeated fires. While the understory remains similar to dry oak forests, black, red and chestnut oak take a secondary seat to black gum.

In nature, varying combinations of the following occur together: Black gum *(Nyssa sylvatica)*, Black oak *(Quercus velutina)*, Chestnut oak *(Quercus prinus)*, Red maple *(Acer rubrum)*, Red oak *(Quercus rubra)*, Sassafras *(Sassafras albidum)* and Sweet birch *(Betula lenta)*

Authentic touches on the woodland floor should include Blueberry *(Vaccinium spp.)*, Black huckleberry *(Gaylussacia baccata)*, Mountain laurel *(Kalmia latifolia)*, Teaberry *(Gaultheria procumbens)*, Trailing arbutus *(Epigaea repens)*, Wild sarsaparilla *(Aralia nudicaulis)*, Witch-hazel *(Hamamelis virginiana)*, Bracken fern *(Pteridium aquilinum)*, Fibrousroot sedge *(Carex communis)* and Pennsylvania sedge *(Carex pensylvanica)*.

Models for conservation

Few ecological communities model sustainable conservation practices as much as the variety of dry oak communities, found at high elevations throughout most of Pennsylvania.

In dry to xeric habitats, the key to survival is conservation of resources, particularly water, and smoothing out extremes in climate.

All five of the great oak canopy species pour vast amounts of leaf litter onto the forest floor each autumn and with a slow decomposition rate, smother any rival species in mulch. Because the leaves are acidic, they poison potential rivals.

These same leaves hold vast amounts of water on or near the surface, steadily releasing it into the ground. Rainwater passing through the acid litter becomes capable of not only carrying nutrients from a very thin humus layer but also dissolving rock particles to permit the trees to take up all the nutrients they require for survival.

Oaks seem unneighborly, and for good reason. If you're a full grown tree you require about a hundred gallons of water daily just to stay alive; casual sharing — or runoff waste — is not an option and in the context of sustainable landscaping, these huge trees prove an interesting point: leaf litter that very slowly decomposes can hold enormous amounts of water just above the soil surface. When it rains in an oak forest, the first quarter inch of precipitation may never reach the ground — but everything thereafter is carefully stored for future use.

As gardeners, we very often clear the landscape of leaves to prevent the powerful pillars in and around our sanctuary from doing what they are intended to do: snuff out competition and render the soil useless for anything but an oak tree. When we strip the ground bare to protect lawns, all we're doing is damaging the habitat for the trees.

Oaks, however, can be fooled. In cultivated areas, we can harvest the leaves, coarsely shred them, and set half aside. About half the leaves go back onto the beds as mulch for all the plants in the fall, and the remainder goes down in late spring to protect growing plants. The leaves will serve the same function of keeping moisture supplies even, but will decompose a bit faster and improve our soil.

In contrast to chip mulch, which becomes crusty and porous when dry, leaf mulch functions well during dry periods and gives the garden a natural look.

Moss enthusiasts are eager to speak up on this opportunity, and indeed there are species of mosses who do well in acidic, dry habitats. Cushion moss (Leucobryum glaucum) is a good example, but it scuffs and tears easily, making it impossible to rake. On the other hand, haircap moss *(Polytrichum commune)* can be raked clear of litter and stands up better to foot traffic, but goes brown when dormant in dry spells, which means watering to keep green.

Perhaps the most popular of the dry woodland graminoids, Pennsylvania sedge *(Carex pennsylvanica),* remains green even in the worst droughts, spreads via rhizomes, but is tricky to mow below a height of three inches and can be purchased only as plugs, making it pricey to install on a large scale and, as with other dry-site graminoids, tends to limit them to accent use. An alternative for long-term development is to establish a patch of sedge, which spreads through root growth, and draw from it on an ongoing basis to establish larger fields in the landscape.

Five of the more popular ferns appear on these kinds of sites. Two with enormous landscape value to naturalize a woodland floor as an alternative to lawn are hayscented fern (*Dennstaedtia punctilobula*) and the somewhat taller northern bracken fern (*Pteridium aquilinum*), both of which spread via long-running rhizomes and, because they are unpalatable to deer, are seen in vast colonies where deer pressure is high. They roam through the leaf litter and require no care. The common Christmas fern (*Polystichum acrostichoides*) is also well suited to these circumstances but remains in a well-behaved clump.

New York fern (*Thelypteris noveboracensis*) is another long-running colonizer and usually listed in the context of moist habitats, especially in ravines. But it turns up often enough upslope to consider it, as does marginal wood fern (*Dryopteris marginalis*).

Although it resembles a fern, the slowly-spreading sweetfern *(Comptonia peregrina)* does well on edges and in openings and will be ignored by deer as it expands to form a brushy zone about three to four feet high.

As with most of the flowering shrubs, a little extra light is appreciated by wild hydrangea *(Hydrangea arborescens),* an energetic clumping shrub of about six feet that resembles most of the hybrid lacecap hydrangeas and which itself has been hybridized into a number of prized varieties.

But in the dappled shade, few herbaceous perennials are more durable than wood asters, blue and white (*Symphyotrichum cordifolium* and *Eurybia divaricata*) and white snakeroot (*Ageratina altissima*). Asters provide a charming autumnal mist of color and in tough situations grow 18 to 24 inches; given a boost in soil, they can reach five feet and put on an enormous display, but at the cost of flopping under their own weight. Snakeroot, the woodland version of Joe-pye, works from a much sturdier three- to four-foot stem and makes a statement with its sheer mass. All three species are prolific seed producers and in acceptable circumstances will create a formidable display.

Gardeners have love-hate relationships with vines. Unchecked, they roam over everything and make a mess, but when managed can become useful accents and green walls to mask deer fence. Dry oak habitats are good settings for several vines, especially Virginia creeper (*Parthenocissus quinquefolia*), enjoyed for its brilliant fall foliage; summer grape (*Vitis aestivalis*) and roundleaf greenbrier (*Smilax rotunifolia*) for their bright foliage and fruits — as well as cat greenbrier (*Smilax glauca*) in southeastern Pennsylvania. Summer grape is edible fruit.

For authenticity in landscaping, consider liberal use of oak leaf mulch with suggestions of exposed bedrock but also surface stones ranging to the size of boulders. Because soils are shallow and conditions harsh, the logs of fallen trees are also common on the forest floor. Those lucky enough to have a ten or fifteen ton log laying about might consider using it as an element of design; it should soon be covered with a velvety moss surface and create a sheltered pocket for many of the small and delicate herbaceous species to add interest to the edge of a garden path.

Primary trees
    Black oak (*Quercus velutina*)
    Chestnut oak (*Quercus prinus*)
    Northern Red oak (*Quercus rubra*)
    Scarlet oak (*Quercus coccinea*)
    White oak (*Quercus alba*)

Associate trees
    American basswood (*Tilia americana*)
    American beech (*Fagus grandifolia*)
    Black cherry (*Prunus serotina*)
    Black gum (*Nyssa sylvatica*) (east)
    Black locust (*Robinia pseudoacacia*)
    Eastern hemlock (*Tsuga canadensis*)
    Eastern white pine (*Pinus strobus*)
    Hop hornbeam (*Ostrya virginiana*)
    Mockernut hickory (*Carya alba*)
    Pignut hickory (*Carya glabra*)
    Pitch pine (*Pinus rigida*)
    Red hickory (*Carya ovalis*)
    Red maple (*Acer rubrum*)
    Sassafras (*Sassafras albidum*)
    Shagbark hickory (*Carya ovata*)
    Short-leaf pine (*Pinus echinata*)
    Sourwood (*Oxydendrum arboreum*) (west)
    Sugar maple (*Acer saccharum*)
    Striped maple (*Acer pensylvanicum*)
    Sweet birch (*Betula lenta*)
    Tuliptree (*Liriodendron tulipifera*)
    Virginia pine (*Pinus virginiana*)
    White ash (*Fraxinus americana*)

Understory Trees and Shrubs
    Bear oak (*Quercus ilicifolia*)
    Black chokeberry (*Photinia melanocarpa*)

Black huckleberry (*Gaylussacia baccata*)
Black-haw (*Viburnum prunifolium*)
Blue ridge blueberry (*Vaccinium pallidum*)
Deerberry (*Vaccinium stamineum*)
Flowering dogwood (*Cornus florida*)
Lowbush blueberry (*Vaccinium angustifolium*)
Maple-leaved viburnum (*Viburnum acerifolium*)
Mountain holly (*Ilex montana*)
Mountain laurel (*Kalmia latifolia*)
Pinxter-flower (*Rhododendron periclymenoides*)
Roseshell azalea (*Rhododendron prinophyllum*)
Serviceberry (*Amelanchier arborea*)
Sheep laurel (*Kalmia angustifolia*)
Summer grape (*Vitis aestivalis*)
Sweet-fern (*Comptonia perigrina*)
Teaberry (*Gaultheria procumbens*)
Wild hydrangea (*Hydrangea arborescens*)
Witch hazel (*Hamamelis virginiana*)

Forbs

Barren strawberry (*Waldsteinia fragarioides*)
Bastard toadflax (*Comandra umbellata*)
Black snakeroot (*Sanicula trifoliata*)
Blue wood aster (*Symphyotrichum cordifolium*)
Canada mayflower (*Maianthemum canadense*)
Downy false-foxglove (*Aureolaria virginica*)
Downy rattlesnake plantain (*Goodyera pubescens*)
Dwarf cinquefoil (*Potentilla canadensis*)
Dwarf dandelion (*Krigia biflora*)
False solomon's seal (*Maianthemum racemosum*)
Gaywings (*Polygala paucifolia*)
Hairy sunflower (*Helianthus hirsutus*)
Indian cucumber root (*Medeola virginiana*)
Naked flower ticktrefoil (*Desmodium nudiflorum*)
Narrowleaf cowwheat (*Melampyrum lineare*)
Pink lady's slipper (*Cypripedium acaule*)
Princes' pine (*Chimaphila maculata*)
Rattlesnake weed (*Hieracium venosum*)
Rock harlequin (*Corydalis sempervirens*)
Sessile bellwort (*Uvularia sessilifolia*)
Solomon's seal (*Polygonatum biflorum*)
Starflower (*Trientalis borealis*)
Tall rattlesnakeroot (*Prenanthes altissima*)
Teaberry (*Gaultheria procumbens*)
Trailing arbutus (*Epigaea repens*)
Venus' pride (*Houstonia purpurea*)
White snakeroot (*Ageratina altissima*)
White wood aster (*Eurybia divaricata*)
Wild sarsaparilla (*Aralia nudicalis*)
Woman's tobacco (*Antennaria plantaginifolia*)
Woodland sunflower (*Helianthus divaricatus*)
Wreath goldenrod (*Solidago caesia*)
Yellow false foxglove (*Aureolaria laevigata*)

Grasses and Sedges

Cypress panic grass (*Dichanthelium dichotomum*)
Fibrousroot sedge (*Carex communis*)
Nodding fescue (*Festuca subverticillata*)
Rough-leaved ricegrass (*Oryzopsis asperifolia*)
Pennsylvania sedge (*Carex pensylvanica*)
Rosy sedge (*Carex rosea*)
Swann's sedge (*Carex swanii*)
Wavy hairgrass (*Deschampsia flexuosa*)

Ferns

Christmas fern (*Polystichum acrostichoides*)
Hayscented fern (*Dennstaedtia punctilobula*)
Marginal wood fern (*Dryopteris marginalis*)
New York fern (*Thelypteris noveboracensis*)
Northern bracken fern (*Pteridium aquilinum*)
Running clubmoss (*Lycopodium clavatum*)

Vines

Cat greenbrier (*Smilax glauca*) (southeast)
Roundleaf greenbrier (*Smilax rotundifolia*)
Summer grape (*Vitis aestivalis*)
Virginia creeper (*Parthenocissus quinquefolia*)

Barrens, Talus Slopes, Boulderfields

Soils range from thin to nonexistant. Nothing blocks the searing heat of full sun and xeric is an understatement. Scraps of soil lurk in cracks and crevices and woody species, particularly trees, struggle to survive in a true test of sustainability.

They turn up with slight variations around most of the state but have the same underlying characteristics and are models of sustainable landscapes at their most xeric. Yet to rock and alpine garden enthusiasts, these kinds of sites become inviting challenges.

Barrens are often thought of as being at the summit of a hill or ridge, but in fact can be found anywhere as openings in any of the dry, acidic forests, woodlands or shrublands, and therefore ideal features to consider on a xeric to dry site. Talus slopes and boulder fields are along the bases of cliffs, but the habitat descriptions often include the cliff and its ledges as part of the set. These make somewhat better models for rock or alpine gardens, especially if a slope is involved.

Barrens

Thin, coarse and acidic soils — or perhaps none at all — over sandstone but sometimes conglomerate rock are typical of rock outcrops, flat summits, high plateaus and upper slopes that face southeast. There are few, if any, trees; those that do gain a foothold are stunted and perhaps deserve a round of applause for surviving at all.

Note: the Serpentine Barrens in Chester and Lancaster Counties comprise a full range of localized ecology and are dealt with separately elsewhere.

These patches turn up where woody vegetation is blocked or at least slowed because the soil is excessively drained, infertile, droughty, and perhaps fouled by such microclimate as frost pockets but more likely frequent fire. Much of the surface is bare rock.

No matter what the underlying cause, grasses and sedges dominate, and the list of primary species reads like a who's who of durability in adverse circumstances.

With improved soil cover, low heath species can form a shrubland not only on these high elevation sites, about 1,200 feet, but also in areas where climate restricts trees or taller shrubs — for example, in droughty high elevation sites or frost pockets of depressions in level outwash plains or in valley floors. Low, slow growing species, such as blueberries and huckleberries, form a design backbone for a variety herbaceous plants

Where organic soil accumulates in bedrock cracks, scattered small trees are possible. Logical starters for barrens include scrub oak *(Quercus ilicifolia)*, mountain ash *(Sorbus americana)*, dwarf chinkapin oak *(Quercus prinoides)* and pitch pine *(Pinus rigida),* but the tree cover will be less than 10 percent. Around the edges, a wider range of dry-habitat species might take hold as soil conditions improve even more.

For authenticity, position taller shrubs to what would be protected areas and limit herbaceous plans to rock crevices and depressions where soils would accumulate.

Mosses and lichens, like Cladonia spp. and Cladina spp. (reindeer lichens), and Polytrichum spp. (hairy-cap mosses) are abundant on some sites and make for authentic touches in building a barren. Navel lichen *(Umbilicaria spp.)*, also known as rock tripe, turns up, too. It has the advantage of being edible — if you're hungry enough. Also consider dicranum moss *(Dicranum polysetum)*, haircap moss *(Polytrichum commune),* juniper polytrichum moss (Polytrichum juniperinum) and polytrichum moss (*Polytrichum piliferum*).

An interesting exception to the "terrible soil" characteristic of barren sites and one that intrigues ecologists is are the Long Pond Barrens on the Pocono Plateau, which features fine-textured and compact Illinoian till. Less permeable than the more common barren sands, these soils can be seasonally wet in spots but subject to drought in summer. Frequent fire seems to be the historical cause of these barrens, and shallow depressions within them form closed basins and frost pockets that impact the community composition. The unique character of this one small area underlies the "critically imperiled" label it wears.

Depressions and frost pockets on till plains, primarily in the northeast, are seen as factors in localized barrens. For the most part, however, these xeric sites are high elevation summits and cliff-tops that, despite a perhaps poor initial landscaping prognosis, offer intriguing landscape options to prove how sustainable a design can be.

Talus-boulder habitats

The exposed acidic bedrock can be granite, quartzite, sandstone, shale or schist, but weathered sandstone caprock is the usual source of rubble.

Resulting soils are local, shallow, infertile, acidic, coarse sands and gravels with bits of organic and root-rich duff deposits between rocks. Air spaces may be more than three feet below the surface, so any rainfall is whisked away. These same rocks can also harbor moss pads on thin, organic to sandy material developed by weathering wide and flat boulder surfaces.

On cliff faces and vertical outcrops, drought-tolerant species take advantage of thin soil layers that collect on narrow ledges or in bedrock crevices, with successional results dependent on the whims of weather.

The canopy itself will almost be less than 50 percent cover — perhaps as little as 10 to 20 percent — and sparse on herbaceous species but instead rounded out with sturdy shrubs that form thickets. Authenticity in the created landscape emphasizes weathered boulders in fields and slopes covered by coarse to fine, bouldery colluvium, with a mulch of deciduous litter to support woody species.

Landscapes could include incised hollows at slope bottoms, concave niches at the tops of slopes, slide masses and landslide scarps, all of which are xeric. However, cooler high elevations and north-facing slopes can also slow evaporation and increase moisture-holding capabilities of the bouldery substrate. On such surfaces, species that accompany eastern hemlock *(Tsuga canadensis)*, can work well.

Cover can vary widely, but is typically open and occupied by gnarled and widely spaced trees. In addition to stresses caused by soil materials, trees taking root in these habitats are subject to frequent wind and ice storm damage.

Such boulder fields are examples landscapes that evolve from one that cannot support vegetative communities to fully forested mountain slopes with well-developed mineral soils.

Because mosses and lichens often lead the way, rich bryophyte and lichen groupings are essential for authenticity with slope aspect sometimes impacting the exact arrangement. This nonvascular layer should cover up to two-thirds of microhabitats.

Good bryophytes to start with are polytrichum moss (*Polytrichum commune*) and leucorbryum moss (*Leucobryum glaucum*). Best lichens to use are blistered naval lichen (*Lasallia papulosa*), naval lichen (*Umbilicaria mammulata*), Baltimore flavoparmelia lichen (*Flavoparmelia baltimorensis*) and reindeer lichen (*Cladina spp.*)

Organizing a habitat

Talus-boulderfield-cliff habitats are by definition successional, and evolution is as unpredictable as the weather. Cooler surfaces or those where there are small natural springs will be more hospitable and can even support mesic species, even if on a limited basis.

The general rule of succession in these habitats is:

First, bare rock outcrops with no vegetation
Then, outcrops with lichen cover
Then, outcrops with lichen and moss cover
Then, sparse herbaceous cover in crevices and

cracks

Finally, outcrops with stunted woodland or forest cover

Because stages can overlap in time and space, depending on local resources and because of the unpredictability of colonization and establishment by plant species, all five stages should be represented.

Trees will be stunted in growth, typically no more than 30 feet, but tree roots can straddle boulders or even run horizontally over the surface in search of pockets of soil.

Starter List for Barrens

Essential grasses
Pennsylvania sedge (*Carex pensylvanica*)
Wavy hairgrass (*Deschampsia flexuosa*)
Little bluestem (*Schizachyrium scoparium*)
Poverty oat grass (*Danthonia spicata*)

Also consider...
Fibrousroot sedge (Carex communis)
Blackseed ricegrass (*Piptatherum racemosum*)
Mountain ricegrass (*Piptatherum pungens*)
Orange grass (*Hypericum gentianoides*)
Big bluestem (*Andropogon gerardii*)
Arctic reed grass (Calamagrostis coarctata)
Variable sedge (*Carex polymorpha*)
Northern oatgrass (*Danthonia compressa*)
Hay sedge (*Carex argyrantha*)
Blue ridge sedge (*Carex lucorum*)
Reedgrass (*Calamagrostis cinnoides*)
Upland bentgrass (*Agrostis perennans*)

Essential shrubs
Black huckleberry (*Gaylussacia baccata*)
Black chokeberry (*Photinia melanocarpa*)
Low sweet blueberry (*Vaccinium angustifolium*)
Lowbush blueberry (*Vaccinium pallidum*)
Scrub oak (*Quercus ilicifolia*)

Also consider
Bristly dewberry (*Rubus hispidus*)
Mountain laurel (*Kalmia latifolia*)
Sheep laurel (*Kalmia angustifolia*)
Sweetfern (*Comptonia peregrina*)
Teaberry (*Gaultheria procumbens*)

Less common
Blackberry (*Rubus spp.*)
Carolina rose (*Rosa carolina*)
Chokecherry (*Prunus virginiana*)
Dangleberry (*Gaylussacia frondosa*)
Deerberry (*Vaccinium stamineum*)
Downy arrowwood (*Viburnum rafinesquianum*)
Highbush blueberry (*Vaccinium corymbosum*)
Kinnikinnick (*Arctostaphylos uva-ursi*)
Low juneberry (*Amelanchier stolonifera*)
Maleberry (*Lyonia ligustrina*)
Minniebush (*Menziesia pilosa*)
Mountain holly (*Nemopanthus mucronatus*)
Prickly dewberry (*Rubus flagellaris*)
Rhodora (*Rhododendron canadense*)
Round serviceberry (*Amelanchier sanguinea*)
Serviceberry (*Amelanchier arborea*)
Sour-top blueberry (*Vaccinium myrtilloides*)
Trailing arbutus (*Epigaea repens*)
Upland highbush blueberry (*Vaccinium stamineum*)
Velvet-leaf huckleberry (*Vaccinium myrtilloides*)
Witch-hazel (*Hamamelis virginiana*)
Withe-rod viburnum (*Viburnum nudum var. cassinoides*)

Essential forbs
Narrowleaf cowwheat (*Melampyrum lineare*)
Shrubby five fingers (*Sibbaldiopsis tridentata*)
Sand cherry (*Prunus pumila*)
Parasol whitetop (*Doellingeria umbellata*)

Also consider:
Harebell (*Campanula rotundifolia*)
Bastard toadflax (*Comandra umbellata*)
Canada mayflower (*Maianthemum canadense*)
Flypoison (*Amianthium muscitoxicum*)
Pussytoes (*Antennaria plantaginifolia*)
Wild columbine (*Aquilegia canadensis*)

Lyre-leaved rock-cress (*Arabis lyrata*)
Wild sarsaparilla (*Aralia nudicaulis*)
Whorled milkweed (*Asclepias verticillata*)
Clasping aster (*Symphyotrichum patens*)
Hairy alumroot (*Heuchera villosa*)
Rattlesnake-weed (*Hieracium venosum*)
Long-leaved bluets (*Houstonia longifolia*)
Allegheny stonecrop (*Hylotelephium telephioides*)
Dwarf dandelion (*Krigia virginica*)
Bush-clovers (*Lespedeza spp.*)
Wood lily (*Lilium philadelphicum*)
Tree ground pine (*Lycopodium dendroideum*)
Fan clubmoss (*Lycopodium digitatum*)
Whorled yellow loosestrife (*Lysimachia quadrifolia*)
False solomon's seal (*Maianthemum racemosum*)
Appalachian sandwort (*Minuartia glabra*)
Partridgeberry (*Mitchella repens*)
Solomon's seal (*Polygonatum biflorum*)
Climbing false buckwheat (*Polygonum scandens*)
Three-toothed cinquefoil (*Potentilla tridentata*)
Canada goldenrod (*Solidago canadensis*)
Gray goldenrod (*Solidago nemoralis*)
Rand's goldenrod (*Solidago simplex ssp. randii*)
Starflower (*Trientalis borealis*)
Perfoliate belwort (*Uvularia perfoliata*)
Prickly pear (*Opuntia humifusa*)

Ferns
Hayscented fern (*Dennstaedtia punctilobula*)
American climbing fern (*Lygodium palmatum*)
Appalachian polypody (*Polypodium appalachianum*)
Northern bracken fern (*Pteridium aquilinum*)

Essential trees
Pitch pine (*Pinus rigida*)
American mountain ash (*Sorbus americana*)

Also consider...
Gray birch (*Betula populifolia*)
Chestnut oak (*Quercus prinus*)
Northern red oak (*Quercus rubra*)
Black oak (*Quercus velutina*)
Red maple (*Acer rubrum*)
Pignut hickory (*Carya glabra*)
Eastern white pine (*Pinus strobus*)

Less often
Balsam fir (*Abies balsamea*)
Yellow birch (*Betula alleghaniensis*)
Sweet birch (*Betula lenta*)
Paper birch (*Betula papyrifera*)
White ash (*Fraxinus americana*)
Red cedar (*Juniperus virginiana*)
Black gum (*Nyssa sylvatica*)
Hophornbeam (*Ostrya virginiana*)
Red spruce (*Picea rubens*)
Quaking aspen (*Populus tremuloides*)
White oak (*Quercus alba*)
Scarlet oak (*Quercus coccinea*)
Dwarf chinkapin oak (*Quercus prinoides*)
Staghorn sumac (*Rhus typhina*)
Dwarf upland willow (*Salix humilis*)
Sassafras (*Sassafras albidum*)

Starter List for Talus-Boulder Sites
Primary trees
Black gum (*Nyssa sylvatica*)
Chestnut oak (*Quercus prinus*)
Gray birch (*Betula populifolia*)
Northern red oak (*Quercus rubra*)
Sweet birch (*Betula lenta*)
Yellow birch (*Betula alleghaniensis*)

Associate trees
American beech (*Fagus grandifolia*)
Bigtooth aspen (*Populus grandidentata*)
Black oak (*Quercus velutina*)
Eastern hemlock (*Tsuga canadensis*)
Eastern red cedar (*Juniperus virginiana*)
Eastern white pine (*Pinus strobus*)
Mountain maple (*Acer spicatum*)
Paper birch (*Betula papyrifera*)
Pignut hickory (*Carya glabra*)
Pin cherry (*Prunus pensylvanica*)
Pitch pine (*Pinus rigida*)
Red maple (*Acer rubrum*)

Scarlet oak (*Quercus coccinea*)
Striped maple (*Acer pensylvanicum*)
Sugar maple (*Acer saccharum*)
White oak (*Quercus alba*)
Virginia pine (*Pinus virginiana*)
White ash (*Fraxinus americana*)

Shrubs

Allegheny blackberry (*Rubus allegheniensis*)
Black huckleberry (*Gaylussacia baccata*)
Blackberries (*Rubus spp.*)
Blue ridge blueberry (*Vaccinium pallidum*)
Currants (*Ribes spp.*)
Lowbush blueberry (*Vaccinium angustifolium*)
Mapleleaf viburnum (*Viburnum acerifolium*)
Mountain laurel (*Kalmia latifolia*)
Northern dewberrry (*Rubus flagellaris*)
Serviceberry (*Amelanchier arborea*)
Sheep laurel (*Kalmia angustifolia*)
Smooth sumac (*Rhus glabra*)
Witch hazel (*Hamamelis virginiana*)
Winged sumac (*Rhus copallinum*)
Staghorn sumac (*Rhus typhina*)

Herbaceous

Allegheny vine (*Adlumia fungosa*)
American alumroot (*Heuchera americana*)
American bittersweet (*Celastrus scandens*)
Appalachian polypody (*Polypodium appalachianum*)
Atlantic goldenrod (*Solidago arguta*)
Bastard toadflax (*Comandra umbellata*)
Bigleaf aster (*Eurybia macrophylla*)
Blue ridge sedge (*Carex lucorum*)
Bluebell bellflower (*Campanula rotundifolia*)
Blunt lobe cliff fern (*Woodsia obtusa*)
Blunt-lobed woodsia (*Woodsia obtusa*)
Common wood fern (*Dryopteris marginalis*)
Early saxifrage (*Saxifraga virginiensis*)
Eastern prickly pear cactus (*Opuntia humifusa*)
Ebony spleenwort (*Asplenium platyneuron*)
False lily of the valley (*Maianthemum racemosum*)
Fringed black bindweed (*Polygonum cilinode*)
Hairy beardtongue (*Penstemon hirsutus*)
Hayscented fern (*Dennstaedtia punctilobula*)
Little bluestem (*Schizachyrium scoparium*)
Maidenhair spleenwort (*Asplenium trichomanes*)
Mountain spleenwort (*Asplenium montanum*)
Northern bracken fern (*Pteridium aquilinum*)
Pennsylvania sedge (*Carex pensylvanica*)
Poverty oat grass (*Danthonia spicata*)
Purple-flowering raspberry (*Rubus odoratus*)
Robert geranium (*Geranium robertianum*)
Rock harlequin (*Corydalis sempervirens*)
Rock polypody (*Polypodium virginianum*)
Rusty woodsia (*Woodsia ilvensis*)
Slimleaf panic grass (*Dichanthelium linearifolium*)
Swann's sedge (*Carex swanii*)
Upland bentgrass (*Agrostis perennans*)
Upland brittle bladder fern (*Cystopteris tenuis*)
Virginia creeper (*Parthenocissus quinquefolia*)
Walking fern (*Asplenium rhizophyllum*)
Wavy hairgrass (*Deschampsia flexuosa*)
White goldenrod (*Solidago bicolor*)
White wood aster (*Eurybia divaricata*)
Wild indigo (*Baptisia tinctoria*)
Wild sarsaparilla (*Aralia nudicaulis*)
Wreath goldenrod (*Solidago caesia*)

Dry Oak - Hickory Forests

Landscapers interested in a park-like effect should be pleased with dry to mesic sites ideal for oak-hickory combinations. All that's essential are slightly acidic to circumneutral, rich and well drained loams or sandy loams. These are common on upper level slopes and coves – particularly those facing south or east — and broad ridgetops.

An open canopy and a sparse shrub layer are key factors to these types of design. Because natural soils are a bit more alkaline than true dry oak forests, the ericaceous layer — mountain laurel and lowbush blueberries — are absent. This creates an broader opportunity for grasses and sedges that work well in a dryish, low-light situation of the kind found only in small openings, and the list is substantial.

About 20 percent of the woodland canopy should be hickory, the preferred choices being bitternut *(Carya cordiformis)*, pignut *(Carya glabra)* and red *(Carya ovalis)*. Oaks still dominate, but white ash *(Fraxinus americana)* works well, as does sugar maple *(Acer saccharum)*, basswood *(Tilia americana)* and hackberry *(Celtis occidentalis)*. As the canopy becomes more dense on either side of the ridge and valley region, consider adding mockernut hickory *(Carya alba)*, white pine *(Pinus strobus)* and red maple *(Acer rubrum)*.

To build an authentic subcanopy, look first to hop-hornbeam *(Ostrya virginiana)* and then to American hornbeam *(Carpinus caroliniana)* on more mesic sites. Other good options include serviceberry *(Amelanchier arborea)*, flowering dogwood (Cornus florida), witch hazel (Hamamelis virginiana) and maple-leaf viburnum *(Viburnum acerifolium)*.

The strength of a sedge-lawn woodland or forest are in the graminoids at the base, which thrive in the absence of shrubs and such ferns as hayscented *(Dennstaedia punctilobula)* and northern bracken (P*teridium aquilinum*). Within the group, Appalachian sedge *(Carex appalachica)*, with its prostrate, flowing form, is often used in natural designs to suggest flowing water.

Most of the sedges and grasses are drought hardy, low and slow growing. There's a temptation to mow them for the cliché turf look, but any cutting under three inches will harm them and, at that point, it's not worth the bother. The clumpy to spiky textures are what make these attractive, so the better alternative is to enjoy the wilder look from a conventional fescue grass path or attractive shale or, in the southeast, slate pavers.

Bringing some height to the group in mesic shade are eastern bottlebrush grass *(Elymus*

Best for hickory lawns

Appalachian sedge (*Carex appalachica*)
Blue ridge sedge (*Carex lucorum*)
Bosc's panic grass (*Dichanthelium boscii*)
Broad looseflower sedge (*Carex laxiflora*)
Dry spike sedge (*Carex siccata*)
Eastern woodland sedge (*Carex blanda*)
Nodding fescue (*Festuca subverticillata*)
Pennsylvania sedge (*Carex pensylvanica*)
Poverty oat grass (*Danthonia spicata*)
Pretty sedge (*Carex woodii*)
Reflexed sedge (*Carex retroflexa*)
Rosy sedge (*Carex rosea*)
Spreading sedge (*Carex laxiculmis*)
Swann's sedge (*Carex swanii*)
Tapered rosette grass (*Dichanthelium acuminatum*)
Upland bentgrass (*Agrostis perennans*)
Wavy hairgrass (*Deschampsia flexuosa*)

hystrix) and hairy woodland brome (*Bromus pubescens*), while in sunnier and drier positions, little bluestem (*Schizachryium scoparium*) should do well.

Fern and fern ally species tend to be rare in these kinds of habitats, but Christmas fern (*Polystichum acrostichoides*), Ebony spleenwort (*Asplenium platyneuron*) and Marginal wood fern (*Dryopteris marginalis*) are worth considering.

Transition zones

In areas between the oak-heath forests upslope and the more mesic habitats preferred by red oaks and mixed hardwoods downslope, dry woods are dominated by oaks — red, black and white, but a variety of hickories fill out a dense canopy.

This blend is ideal for southern to eastern-facing high to midslopes and steps-in-slope in a lot of broken rock and stone just downslope from siltstone and shale outcrops. Sites can be found on gentle to steep slopes with scattered rocks and boulders on the surface, and can very from extremely stony xeric soils to less rocky, more mesic soils. Soils are well-drained sandy loams over sandstone, shale or siltstone bedrock. These can be found throughout the state except for the southwest.

In nature, these transitional sites often have scattered, small seeps or drainages which will impact the herbaceous layer in the immediate vicinity and, if modeled in the landscape, can create authenticity to a design.

Because of the oaks and the more acidic soils, ericaceous species are ideal but tall shrubs are infrequent. The low shrub layer can trend toward low species like huckleberry *(Gaylussacia baccata)* and Blue Ridge and low-bush blueberries *(Vaccinium pallidum* and *V. angustifolium),* but compared to other oak sites, the cover should be less than 40 percent to be authentic.

There is also a corresponding increase in hayscented fern *(Dennstaedtia punctilobula)* and northern bracken ferns. On north-facing slopes, consider liberal use of rosebay (*Rhododendron maximum*), especially in more mesic situations.

Starter List
Trees
    American basswood (*Tilia americana*)
    American beech (*Fagus grandifolia*)
    Bitternut hickory (*Carya cordiformis*)
    Black gum (*Nyssa sylvatica*)
    Black oak (*Quercus velutina*)
    Chestnut oak (*Quercus prinus*)
    Eastern hemlock (*Tsuga canadensis*)
    Eastern red cedar (*Juniperus virginiana*)
    Eastern white pine (*Pinus strobus*)
    Mockernut hickory (*Carya alba*)
    Pignut hickory (*Carya glabra*)
    Red hickory (*Carya ovalis*)
    Red maple (*Acer rubrum*)
    Red oak (*Quercus rubra*)
    Sassafras (*Sassafras albidum*)
    Scarlet oak (*Quercus coccinea*)
    Shagbark hickory (*Carya ovata*)
    Shellbark hickory (*Carya cordiformis*)
    Striped maple (*Acer pensylvanicum*)
    Sugar maple (*Acer saccharinum*)
    Sweet birch (*Betula lenta*)
    Tuliptree (*Liriodendron tulipifera*)
    White oak (*Quercus alba*)
Shrubs
    Allegheny blackberry (*Rubus allegheniensis*)
    American hazelnut (*Corylus americana*)
    American red raspberry (*Rubus idaeus*)
    Beaked hazelnut (*Corylus cornuta*)
    Black haw (*Viburnum prunifolium*)
    Black huckleberry (*Gaylussacia baccata*)
    Blue ridge blueberry (*Vaccinium pallidum*)
    Common hackberry (*Celtis occidentalis*)
    Deerberry (*Vaccinium stamineum*)
    Arrow-wood (*Viburnum rafinesquianum*)
    Great rhododendron (*Rhododendron maximum*)
    Hackberry (*Celtis occidentalis*)
    Flowering dogwood (*Cornus florida*)
    Highbush blueberry (*Vaccinium corymbosum*)
    Hop hornbeam (*Ostrya virginiana*)
    Hornbeam (*Carpinus caroliniana*)
    Lowbush blueberry (*Vaccinium angustifolium*)

Mapleleaf viburnum (*Viburnum acerifolium*)
Mountain laurel (*Kalmia latifolia*)
Northern dewberry (*Rubus flagellaris*)
Redbud (*Cercis canadensis*)
Serviceberry (*Amelanchier arborea*)
Southern arrow-wood (*Viburnum dentatum*)
Witch hazel (*Hamamelis virginiana*)

Grasses and sedges

Appalachian sedge (*Carex appalachica*)
Blue ridge sedge (*Carex lucorum*)
Bosc's panic grass (*Dichanthelium boscii*)
Broad looseflower sedge (*Carex laxiflora*)
Dry spike sedge (*Carex siccata*)
Eastern bottlebrush grass (*Elymus hystrix*)
Eastern woodland sedge (*Carex blanda*)
Fibrousroot sedge (*Carex communis*)
Hairy woodland brome (*Bromus pubescens*)
Little bluestem (*Schizachryium scoparium*)
Nodding fescue (*Festuca subverticillata*)
Pennsylvania sedge (*Carex pensylvanica*)
Poverty oat grass (*Danthonia spicata*)
Pretty sedge (*Carex woodii*)
Reflexed sedge (*Carex retroflexa*)
Rosy sedge (*Carex rosea*)
Swann's sedge (*Carex swanii*)
Tapered rosette grass (*Dichanthelium acuminatum var. acuminatum*)
Upland bentgrass (*Agrostis perennans*)
Wavy hairgrass (*Deschampsia flexuosa*)

Forbs

Anise scented goldenrod (*Solidago odora*)
Atlantic goldenrod (*Solidago arguta*)
Balsam groundsel (*Packera paupercula*)
Bird foot violet (*Viola pedata*)
Canada mayflower (*Maianthemum canadense*)
Common gypsyweed (*Veronica officinalis*)
Dwarf cinquefoil (*Potentilla canadensis*)
Early goldenrod (*Solidago juncea*)
Early saxifrage (*Saxifraga virginiensis*)
False foxglove (*Aureolaria spp.*)
False solomon's-seal (*Smilacina racemosa*)
Fourleaf milkweed (*Asclepias quadrifolia*)
Hairy solomon's seal (*Polygonatum pubescens*)
Indian cucumber (*Medeola virginiana*)
Late purple aster (*Symphyotrichum patens*)
Long branch frostweed (*Helianthemum canadense*)
Narrowleaf cowwheat (*Melampyrum lineare*)
Panicled leaf ticktrefoil (*Desmodium paniculatum*)
Partridgeberry (*Mitchella repens*)
Perfoliate bellwort (*Uvularia perfoliata*)
Plantain-leaved pussytoes (*Antennaria plantaginifolia*)
Pointed leaf ticktrefoil (*Desmodium glutinosum*)
Prostrate ticktrefoil (*Desmodium rotundifolium*)
Rattlesnake weed (*Hieracium venosum*)
Red baneberry (*Actaea rubra*)
Round lobed hepatica (*Hepatica nobilis var. obtusa*)
Roundleaf ragwort (*Packera obovata*)
Roundleaf yellow violet (*Viola rotundifolia*)
Running clubmoss (*Lycopodium clavatum*)
Sessileleaf bellwort (*Uvularia sessilifolia*)
Sicklepod (*Arabis canadensis*)
Smooth forked nailwort (*Paronychia canadensis*)
Solomon's-seal (*Polygonatum biflorum*)
Spreading sedge (*Carex laxiculmis*)
Starflower (*Trientalis borealis*)
Starry false lily of the valley (*Maianthemum stellatum*)
Striped prince's pine (*Chimaphila maculata*)
Virginia spring beauty (*Claytonia virginica*)
Wavy-leaved aster (*Symphyotrichum undulatum*)
White goldenrod (*Solidago bicolor*)
White rattlesnakeroot (*Prenanthes alba*)
White snakeroot (*Ageratina altissima*)
White wood aster (*Eurybia divaricata*)
Whorled loosestrife (*Lysimachia quadrifolia*)
Whorled yellow loosestrife (*Lysimachia quadrifolia*)
Wild sarsaparilla (*Aralia nudicaulis*)
Wild-oats (*Uvularia sessilifolia*)
Yellow trout lily (*Erythronium americanum*)

Ferns
- Christmas fern (*Polystichum acrostichoides*)
- Ebony spleenwort (*Asplenium platyneuron*)
- Hayscented fern (*Dennstaedtia punctilobula*)
- Marginal wood fern (*Dryopteris marginalis*)
- Northern bracken fern (*Pteridium aquilinum*)
- Northern red oak (*Quercus rubra*)
- White ash (*Fraxinus americana*)

Pine-hardwood variation

On dry to mesic, acidic, south to west-facing slopes in the ridge and valley and Allegheny Mountains region, a rare variant are woodlands dominated by Virginia pine *(Pinus virginiana)* and mixed hardwoods, but blends of white pine *(Pinus strobus)*, red cedar *(Juniperus virginiana)* or table-mountain pine *(Pinus pungens)* are acceptable. Conifers are dominant, though, with oak-hickory associates bringing up the rear.

These, too, are models for rock and alpine gardens, noted for unstable, steep shale slopes, often with exposed bedrock, at elevations between 1,000 and 3,000 feet. Bedrock visible on the surface can range as high as 80 percent. Appropriate sites are on convex slopes, ridge spurs, and cliff tops. Soils should be derived from acidic shale, although some sandstone can be blended in; calcium and magnesium levels should be high and organic matter low. These are dry sites, and available moisture is very scarce.

Designs can range from a sparse shrubland to a locally-dense, almost closed forest canopy. With a closed canopy, oaks and conifers should co-dominate, and the herb layer will be less than 25 percent of the surface.

For authenticity, be sure to include abundant lichens, such as *Cladonia* spp. and *Cladina* spp.

Primary trees
- Virginia pine (*Pinus virginiana*)
- Eastern red cedar (*Juniperus virginiana*)
- Eastern white pine (*Pinus strobus*)
- Table mountain pine (*Pinus pungens*)

Associates
- Black oak (*Quercus velutina*)
- Chestnut oak (*Quercus prinus*)
- Mockernut hickory (*Carya alba*)
- Pignut hickory (*Carya glabra*)
- Post oak (*Quercus stellata*)
- Red oak (*Quercus rubra*)
- Shagbark hickory (*Carya ovata*)
- Red hickory (*Carya ovalis*)
- White ash (*Fraxinus americana*)
- White oak (*Quercus alba*)

Shrubs
- Black huckleberry (*Gaylussacia baccata*)
- Blue ridge blueberry (*Vaccinium pallidum*)
- Deerberry (*Vaccinium stamineum*)
- Dwarf hackberry (*Celtis tenuifolia*)
- Fragrant sumac (*Rhus aromatica*)
- Scrub oak (*Quercus ilicifolia*)
- Serviceberry (*Amelanchier arborea*)
- Winged sumac (*Rhus copallinum*)

Herbaceous
- Alum-root (*Heuchera americana*)
- American false pennyroyal (*Hedeoma pulegioides*)
- Beard-tongue (*Penstemon hirsutus*)
- Blue wood aster (*Symphyotrichum cordifolium*)
- Carolina rose (*Rosa carolina*)
- Climbing false buckwheat (*Polygonum scandens*)
- Common dittany (*Cunila origanoides*)
- Hairy lip fern (*Cheilanthes lanosa*)
- Heartleaf skullcap (*Scutellaria ovata*)
- Little bluestem (*Schizachyrium scoparium*)
- Longleaf summer bluet (*Houstonia longifolia*)
- Mountain nailwort (*Paronychia montana*)
- Northern selaginella (*Selaginella rupestris*)
- Panic-grass (*Panicum linearifolium*)
- Pennsylvania sedge (*Carex pensylvanica*)
- Poverty oat grass (*Danthonia spicata*)
- Prickly pear cactus (*Opuntia humifusa*)
- Purple cliff brake (*Pellaea atropurpurea*)
- Pussy-toes (*Antennaria plantaginifolia*)
- Rattlesnake-weed (*Hieracium venosum*)
- Wavy hairgrass (Deschampsia flexuosa)

CHINKAPIN - RED CEDAR - REDBUD WOODLANDS

Dry to xeric upland slopes on alkaline soils are the domain of Chinkapin oak *(Quercus muehlenbergii)*, red cedar *(Juniperus virginiana)* and eastern redbud *(Cercis canadensis)*, which occur in varying combinations depending on local site conditions.

Like their counterparts in acidic high-elevation sites, they are models of sustainability in very difficult circumstances and ideal for gardens over limestone or dolomite substrates. These are more often found in the southern two-thirds of the state, but can be found anywhere that limestone and dolomite are key factors in the soil, as well as patches of calcareous shales.

Natural sites are bold, dramatic and bleak. On south to southwest-facing slopes that average 20 to 30 degree gradients, sometimes steeper, soils are stony, shallow and dry, circumneutral to slightly alkaline, with high magnesium and calcium levels. They range between 1,000 and 2,600 feet in elevation.

Slopes themselves are convex and display complex, rugged and variable microtopography, sometimes with exposed cliff faces or outcrops that have been undercut by area streams. Similar sites occur on knobs or low hills in linear small patches in the ridge and valley region, except where carbonate substrates are continuously exposed.

Plants often grow on thin-soil ledges and in crevices where organic matter has collected. Where there's depth, a number of tree species take hold, the most common being American basswood *(Tilia americana)*, Black gum *(Nyssa sylvatica)*, and even Chestnut oak *(Quercus prinus)* if the soil pH isn't too high.

Where there's redbud, there's also opportunity for flowering dogwood (Cornus florida), but serviceberry *(Amelanchier arborea)* and witch hazel *(Hamamelis virginiana)* are also admirable in the subcanopy and in open areas such native roses as Carolina rose *(Rosa carolina)* can serve as excellent foundation plants.

These are areas best known for grasses and sedges, but a wide array of flowering perennials turns up in no particular pattern, giving the designer a wide range of dry-site materials to work with.

For authenticity, be sure to include many loose stones of all sizes, including exposed bedrock, on about half the surface.

Red Cedar glades

In sites where conditions are dry enough to limit forest development to small patches on slopes and rocky summits, chinkapin oak declines and red cedar increases — but only barely. These openings are more prairie than woodland.

Most appropriate for south to southwest facing hillsides and outcrops, especially in the Lehigh Valley, the emphasis is more on grassland than woodland, anchored by little bluestem *(Schizachyrium scoparium)* and side-oats gramma *(Bouteloua curtipendula)*. These are ideal habitats for tall grasses — big bluestem, Indian grass, switchgrass and composite dropseed lead the way — but also for lower-growing species such as blackseed rice grass *(Piptatherum racemosum)*, bristle-leaf sedge *(Carex eburna)*, Pennsylvania sedge *(Carex pensylvanica)* and wavy hairgrass *(Danthonia spicata)*.

On open patches of ground, it's possible to go for a tall-grass prairie look or construct a meandering path through specimen plantings of tall grasses with lower growing species and accents of flowering plants.

Most of the forbs for these woodlands work well, but for authenticity, be sure to consider spe-

> ## *Limestone and dolomite*
>
> Dolomite and limestone feature the same color ranges of white-to-gray and white-to-light brown (although other colors such as black, green and red are possible).
>
> About the same hardness, they weather quickly. Both are crushed for use in agriculture — to neutralize acidity in soil — and for construction materials.
>
> Limestone, a sedimentary rock, was formed from skeletal remains of small sea creatures and coral and is essentially calcium carbonate ($CaCO_3$).
>
> Dolomite, also known as "dolomite rock" and "dolostone", is a sedimentary rock formed when lime rich mud exposed to magnesium-rich groundwater that collects in basins to become calcium magnesium carbonate, $CaMg(CO_3)_2$.
>
> Over the course of its evolution, the middle two thirds of the state were at various times a shallow sea or a vast alluvial plain, during which time these sediments were laid down.

cialists like candle anemone (*Anemone cylindrica*), golden ragwort (*Packera aurea*), hoary puccoon (*Lithospermum canescens*), orange-fruit horse gentian (*Triosteum aurantiacum*) and white goldenrod (*Solidago bicolor*).

Trees, especially red cedar, will be stunted and sparse in distribution.

Grassland openings

Even more prairie-like are grasslands where soils are thin or conditions too dry for woody plants to grow, patches of grasslands within woodlands, notably southeastern Pennsylvania, can help create the feel of an open area to buffer the adjacent woodland.

They're less than a couple of acres in size and over calcareous bedrock. The style of the landscape area is prairie, so little bluestem (*Schizachyrium scoparium*) joins the list of go-to species. Others grasses and sedges include all those of the adjacent woodland. A limited number of forbs and a few scattered shrubs round things out. Flowering plants unique to this type of area include:

Bush clovers (*Lespedeza spp.*)
False gromwell (*Onosmodium molle*)
Green milkweed (*Asclepias viridiflora*)
Groundsel (Packera obovata)
Silver-rod goldenrod (*Solidago bicolor*)
Tick-trefoil (*Desmodium spp.*)

Rock and alpine features

Among the naturally-occurring features in these dry, upland calcareous woodlands suggest an opportunity for very authentic landscape design: cliffs, outcrops, and very rocky slopes, particularly in southern Pennsylvania.

The preferred building materials for rock or alpine garden feature is limestone or dolomite in a steep arrangement that creates pockets of soil. In the wild, vegetation is patchy and limited to racks and crevices; if using trees and shrubs they would be on the scrubby side due to the limited soil and moisture. Natural landscapes pick up some shade from adjacent woodlands.

Most of the species for the general type of habitat will work well, but this is an opportunity to landscape with distinctive specialists.

Arborvitae *(Thuja occidentalis)* is an excellent choice for anchor points. Also consider:

Alum-root (*Heuchera americana*)
Bladder fern (*Cystopteris bulbifera*)
Bluebell bellflower (*Campanula rotundifolia*)
Bluntlobe cliff fern (*Woodsia obtusa*)
Brittle bladderfern (*Cystopteris fragilis*)
Early saxifrage (*Saxifraga virginiensis*)
Evergreen wood fern (*Dryopteris marginalis*)
Fernleaf yellow false foxglove (*Aureolaria pedicularia*)
Hairy rock-cress (*Arabis hirsuta*)
Maidenhair spleenwort (*Asplenium trichomanes*)
Nodding onion (*Allium cernuum*)
Purple cliff-brake (*Pellaea atropurpurea*)
Richwoods sedge (*Carex oligocarpa*)
Rusty woodsia (*Woodsia ilvensis*)

Sevenbark (*Hydrangea arborescens*)
Shooting star (*Dodecatheon meadia*)
Side-oats gramma (*Bouteloua curtipendula*)
Smooth rock-cress (*Arabis laevigata*)
Upland brittle bladderfern (*Cystopteris tenuis*)
Virginia creeper (*Parthenocissus quinquefolia*)
White heath aster (*Symphyotrichum ericoides*)

Starter plant list
Primary trees:
Chinkapin oak (*Quercus muehlenbergii*)
Eastern red cedar (*Juniperus virginiana*)
Eastern redbud (*Cercis canadensis*)
Associate trees
American basswood (*Tilia americana*)
Arborvitae (*Thuja occidentalis*)
Black gum (*Nyssa sylvatica*)
Chestnut oak (*Quercus prinus*)
Pignut hickory (*Carya glabra*)
Red cedar (*Juniperus virginiana*)
Red hickory (*Carya ovalis*)
Shagbark hickory (*Carya ovata*)
Slippery elm (*Ulmus rubra*)
Sugar maple (*Acer saccharum*)
Sweet pignut hickory (*Carya ovalis*)
White ash (*Fraxinus americana*)
White oak (*Quercus alba*)
Shrubs
Alternate leaf dogwood (*Cornus alternifolia*)
Black haw (*Viburnum prunifolium*)
Carolina rose (*Rosa carolina*)
Common hackberry (*Celtis occidentalis*)
Arrow-wood (*Viburnum rafinesquianum*)
Dwarf hackberry (*Celtis tenuifolia*)
Flowering dogwood (*Cornus florida*)
Fragrant sumac (*Rhus aromatica*)
Hackberry (*Celtis occidentalis*)
Hop-hornbeam (*Ostrya virginiana*)
Roses (*Rosa spp.*)
Serviceberry (*Amelanchier spp.*)
Shadbush (*Amelanchier spp.*)
Smooth sumac (*Rhus glabra*)
Witch hazel (*Hamamelis virginiana*)
Wild hydrangea (*Hydrangea arborescens*)
Grasses and sedges
Big bluestem (*Andropogon gerardii*)
Black seed rice grass (*Piptatherum racemosum*)
Bosc's panic grass (*Dichanthelium boscii*)
Bottlebrush grass (*Elymus hystrix*)
Bristle leaf sedge (*Carex eburnea*)
Composite dropseed (*Sporobolus compositus*)
Hairy woodland brome (*Bromus pubescens*)
Indian grass (*Sorghastrum nutans*)
Little bluestem (*Schizachyrium scoparium*)
Pennsylvania sedge (*Carex pensylvanica*)
Poverty oat grass (*Danthonia spicata*)
Rock muhly (*Muhlenbergia sobolifera*)
Side-oats gramma (*Bouteloua curtipendula*)
Switch grass (*Panicum virgatum*)
Tall gramma (*Bouteloua curtipendula*)
Wavy hairgrass (*Danthonia spicata*)
Forbs
Alum-root (*Heuchera americana*)
American alumroot (*Heuchera americana*)
American gromwell (*Lithospermum latifolium*)
Aromatic aster (*Symphyotrichum oblongifolium*)
Black rattlesnakeroot (*Sanicula canadensis*)
Bladder fern (*Cystopteris bulbifera*)
Blue virgins bower (*Clematis occidentalis*)
Bluebell bellflower (*Campanula rotundifolia*)
Bluntlobe cliff fern (*Woodsia obtusa*)
Brittle bladderfern (*Cystopteris fragilis*)
Bush clovers (*Lespedeza spp.*)
Candle anemone (*Anemone cylindrica*)
Climbing false buckwheat (*Polygonum scandens*)
Early saxifrage (*Saxifraga virginiensis*)
Eastern prickly pear cactus (*Opuntia humifusa*)
Elm leaf goldenrod (*Solidago ulmifolia*)
Evergreen wood fern (*Dryopteris marginalis*)
False gromwell (*Onosmodium molle*)
Fernleaf yellow false foxglove (*Aureolaria pedicularia*)
Flowering spurge (*Euphorbia corollata*)
Four-leaved milkweed (*Asclepias quadrifolia*)

Golden ragwort (*Packera aurea*)
Green milkweed (*Asclepias viridiflora*)
Groundsel (*Packera obovata*)
Gypsy flower (*Cynoglossum officinale*)
Hairy beardtongue (*Penstemon hirsutus*)
Hairy bedstraw (*Galium pilosum*)
Hairy rock-cress (*Arabis hirsuta*)
Heartleaf skullcap (*Scutellaria ovata*)
Hoary mountainmint (*Pycnanthemum incanum*)
Hoary puccoon (*Lithospermum canescens*)
Late purple aster (*Symphyotrichum patens*)
Licorice bedstraw (*Galium circaezans*)
Longleaf summer bluet (*Houstonia longifolia*)
Lyrate rockcress (*Arabis lyrata*)
Lyre-leaved rock-cress (*Arabis lyrata*)
Maidenhair spleenwort (*Asplenium trichomanes*)
Marbleseed (*Onosmodium spp.*)
Michaux's stitchwort (*Minuartia michauxii*)
Moss phlox (*Phlox subulata*)
Mountain nailwort (*Paronychia montana*)
Needle tip blue-eyed grass (*Sisyrinchium mucronatum*)
Nodding onion (*Allium cernuum*)
Orange-fruit horse gentian (*Triosteum aurantiacum*)
Pennsylvania catchfly (*Silene caroliniana*)
Plantain pussytoes (*Antennaria plantaginifolia*)
Purple cliff-brake (*Pellaea atropurpurea*)
Red columbine (*Aquilegia canadensis*)
Richwoods sedge (*Carex oligocarpa*)
Robin's plantain (*Erigeron pulchellus*)
Roundhead lespedeza (*Lespedeza capitata*)
Roundleaf ragwort (*Packera obovata*)
Rusty woodsia (*Woodsia ilvensis*)
Shooting star (*Dodecatheon meadia*)
Silver-rod goldenrod (*Solidago bicolor*)
Smooth rock-cress (*Arabis laevigata*)
Smooth rockcress (*Arabis laevigata*)
Snowberry (*Symphoricarpos albus*)
Tick-trefoil (*Desmodium spp.*)
Upland brittle bladderfern (*Cystopteris tenuis*)
Violet lespedeza (*Lespedeza violacea*)
Violets (*Viola spp.*)
Virginia anemone (*Anemone virginiana*)
Virginia creeper (*Parthenocissus quinquefolia*)
Virginia saxifrage (*Saxifraga virginiensis*)
Wavy leaf aster (*Symphyotrichum undulatum*)
White goldenrod (*Solidago bicolor*)
White heath aster (*Symphyotrichum ericoides*)
White snakeroot (*Ageratina altissima*)
Whorled milkweed (*Asclepias verticillata*)
Wild columbine (*Aquilegia canadensis*)
Woman's tobacco (*Antennaria plantaginifolia*)
Woodland sunflower (*Helianthus divaricatus*)

Sugar Maple - American Basswood Forest

For natural landscapes, few are more inviting than habitats ideal for sugar maple (*Acer saccharum*), American basswood *(Tilia americana)* and white ash *(Fraxinus americana)*.

These are rich forests, high in calcium and on the mesic end of the scale, stuffed with soils perfect for many herbaceous favorites. Sites are on lower to middle slopes, and steepness is not an issue in nature; the grades are often between 30 and 60 percent in low-mountain topography. Limestone bedrock is most common, but dolomite works just as well on these north to east-facing slopes.

Bedrock outcrops can cover up to half the site, and because this is a low to mid-slope habitat, talus and boulderfields are foundations for landscapes. In addition to gravelly colluvium, good soils are circumneutral to slightly alkaline channery silt loams and loams.

It adds up to an ideal habitat for sugar maple, which can occupy most of the canopy and provide a nutritious leaf litter to the surface.

The most appropriate of the tall shrubs for this type of habitat is American bladdernut *(Staphylea trifolia)*, followed by hophornbeam *(Ostrya virginiana)* and witch hazel *(Hamamelis virginiana)*, but northern spicebush *(Lindera benzoin)* fits in well.

Making up for a sparse short-shrub layer is a rich and varied herbaceous array, a result of quick weathering of carbonate materials and extremely fertile soils. High cover of mosses provides a foothold for many species and a key to design are numerous organic mats and soil pockets.

Primary trees
Sugar maple *(Acer saccharum)*
American basswood *(Tilia americana)*
American beech *(Fagus grandifolia)*
Butternut *(Juglans cinerea)*

Associate trees
Bitternut hickory *(Carya cordiformis)*
Eastern hemlock *(Tsuga canadensis)*
Elm spp. *(Ulmus spp.)*
Oaks *(Quercus spp.)*
Paw-paw *(Asimina triloba)*
Sweet birch *(Betula lenta)*
White ash *(Fraxinus americana)*
Yellow birch *(Betula alleghaniensis)*

Shrubs
American bladdernut *(Staphylea trifolia)*
American filbert *(Corylus americana)*
American witch hazel *(Hamamelis virginiana)*
Beaked hazelnut *(Corylus cornuta)*
Eastern hop-hornbeam *(Ostrya virginiana)*
Hornbeam *(Carpinus caroliniana)*
Mountain laurel *(Kalmia latifolia)*
Northern spicebush *(Lindera benzoin)*
Serviceberry *(Amelanchier arborea)*

Ferns
Blunt-lobed woodsia *(Woodsia obtusa)*
Brittle bladderfern *(Cystopteris fragilis)*
Bulblet bladder fern *(Cystopteris bulbifera)*
Christmas fern *(Polystichum acrostichoides)*
Ebony spleenwort *(Asplenium platyneuron)*
Northern maidenhair fern *(Adiantum pedatum)*
Walking fern *(Asplenium rhizophyllum)*
Wood ferns *(Dryopteris spp.)*

Forbs
Black cohosh *(Actaea racemosa)*
Bloodroot *(Sanguinaria canadensis)*
Bloodroot *(Sanguinaria canadensis)*
Blue cohosh *(Caulophyllum thalictroides)*
Broadleaf enchanter's-nightshade *(Circaea canadensis)*
Canadian wild ginger *(Asarum canadense)*
Dogtooth violet *(Erythronium americanum)*
Doll's eyes *(Actaea pachypoda)*
Early meadow-rue *(Thalictrum dioicum)*

Fernleaf phacelia (*Phacelia bipinnatifida*)
Grape spp. (*Vitis spp.*)
Heart-leafed meehania (*Meehania cordata*)
Jack in the pulpit (*Arisaema triphyllum*)
Leaf-cup (*Polymnia canadensis*)
Liverleaf (*Hepatica nobilis var. acuta*)
Pale jewelweed (*Impatiens pallida*)
Purple-flowering raspberry (*Rubus odoratus*)
Ramp (*Allium tricoccum*)
Red trillium (*Trillium erectum*)
Ricegrass (*Piptatherum racemosum*)
Spikenard (*Aralia racemosa*)
Sweet-cicely (*Osmorhiza claytonii*)
Twoleaf miterwort (*Mitella diphylla*)
Virginia springbeauty (*Claytonia virginica*)
Virginia-creeper (*Parthenocissus quinquefolia*)
White wood aster (*Eurybia divaricata*)
Wild sarsaparilla (*Aralia nudicaulis*)
Wild stonecrop (*Sedum ternatum*)
Wood anemone (*Anemone quinquefolia*)
Zigzag goldenrod (*Solidago flexicaulis*)

Grasses and sedges
Bottlebrush-grass (*Elymus hystrix*)
Broad looseflower sedge (*Carex laxiflora*)
Ribbed sedge (*Carex virescens*)
Sprengel's sedge (*Carex sprengelii*)

Pine – Hemlock - Oak Forests

Found on mid to lower slopes, forests that are a combination of eastern white pine (*Pinus strobus*), eastern hemlock (*Tsuga canadensis*) and hardwoods — primarily oaks — are good illustrations of how systems can range from dry to nearly mesic, depending on specific location.

Conifers comprise at least 25 percent of the cover, perhaps more, and share the canopy with hardwoods. And associate species can vary with the region; for example, Red spruce (*Picea rubens*) is common in the northeast, while tuliptree (*Liriodendron tulipifera*) and sweet birch (*Betula lenta*) more common in the southern Appalachians.

What they have in common is the soils are dry-mesic to mesic, acidic, nutrient-poor, sandy loam to sandy soils, including extremely stony, xeric soils and — on lower elevations — very cobbly sandy loam.

In glaciated areas, they appear in protected ravines and ridges, glacial outwash plains or moraines over shale or sandstone; in unglaciated areas, sites are found on more rolling topography underlain by sandstone. Low elevation sites tend to be flat to gently sloping, while higher sites can be on very steep slopes in gorges and hollows, as well as alluvial terraces.

We tend to think of sturdy oaks like chestnut (*Quercus prinus*) as being rugged and durable, but on sites where soils are coarse, droughty and steep, favoring slower growth, white pine will prevail. Both species would do much better in more mesic conditions. On the other hand, these kinds of forests often evolve from second growth pine on old fields, with hardwood saplings and seedlings in the understory. As the pine matures, the hardwoods can exploit natural openings to form a mixture. However the pines are blown down or cut, the hardwoods take prominence, and the pines become the understory.

This process suggests versatility for landscapes, and something of a challenge in evaluating local conditions. On low productivity sites, such as former pasture land, the options would trend more toward blueberries, huckleberries, sweet fern, teaberry, clubmoss and similar species. Slightly mesic sites open up considerable design opportunity, even for such moisture-lovers as mayapple (*Podophyllum peltatum*) in cool ravines and alluvial areas. But the key factor remains: while precipitation is adequate, the soils are always very well to excessively drained.

Authentic touches include liberal use of stone. On these sites, the forest floor is covered by rocks, boulders and even exposed bedrock, and mosses demonstrate the acidity of the materials. Consider cushion moss (*Leucobryum glaucum*) and common haircap moss (*Polytrichum commune*). The occasional fallen log to suggest windthrow is a plus.

Starting points

Statewide, these landscapes can be created with a number of basic species. White pine (*Pinus strobus*) and/or Eastern hemlock (*Tsuga canadensis*) are essential, and good oak choices would be black (*Quercus velutina*), red (*Quercus rubra*) and white (*Quercus alba*). For secondary hardwood associates, American beech (*Fagus grandifolia*), black cherry (*Prunus serotina*), red maple (*Acer rubrum*), sugar maple (*Acer saccharum*), white ash (*Fraxinus americana*), as well as sweet birch (*Betula lenta*) and yellow birch (*Betula alleghaniensis*).

Strong candidates for the subcanopy and shrub layers would be hop-hornbeam (*Ostrya virginiana*), hornbeam (*Carpinus caroliniana*), mapleleaf viburnum (*Virburnum acerifolium*), mountain laurel (*Kalmia latifolia*), spicebush (*Lindera benzoin) and witch hazel (*Hamamelis virginiana*).

On the herbaceous level, Canada mayflower (*Maianthemum canadense*), false solomon's seal (*Maianthemum racemosum*), partridgeberry (*Mitchella repens*), solomon's seal (*Polygonatum biflorum*), starflower (*Trientalis borealis*), teaberry (*Gaultheria procumbens*) and wild sarsaparilla (*Aralia nudicaulis*) are excellent foundation choices.

Starter Plant list
Primary trees
Eastern hemlock (*Tsuga canadensis*)
Eastern white pine (*Pinus strobus*)
Black oak (*Quercus velutina*)
Northern red oak (*Quercus rubra*)
White oak (*Quercus alba*)

Associate trees
Alternate leaf dogwood (*Cornus alternifolia*)
American basswood (*Tilia americana*)
American beech (*Fagus grandifolia*)
Bigtooth aspen (*Populus grandidentata*)
Bitternut hickory (*Carya cordiformis*)
Black cherry (*Prunus serotina*)
Black gum (*Nyssa sylvatica*)
Chestnut oak (*Quercus prinus*)
Eastern red cedar (*Juniperus virginiana*)
Flowering dogwood (*Cornus florida*)
Gray birch (*Betula populifolia*)
Gray dogwood (*Cornus racemosa*)
Mockernut hickory (*Carya tomentosa*)
Mountain maple (*Acer spicatum*)
Norway spruce (*Picea abies*)
Paper birch (*Betula papyrifera*)
Pin oak (*Quercus palustris*)
Pitch pine (*Pinus rigida*)
Red maple (*Acer rubrum*)
Red spruce (*Picea rubens*)
Sassafras (*Sassafras albidum*)
Scarlet oak (*Quercus coccinea*)
Striped maple (*Acer pensylvanicum*)
Sugar maple (*Acer saccharum*)
Sweet birch (*Betula lenta*)
Tuliptree (*Liriodendron tulipifera*)
White ash (*Fraxinus americana*)
White spruce (*Picea glauca*)
Yellow birch (*Betula alleghaniensis*)

Shrubs
Allegheny blackberry (*Rubus allegheniensis*)
American hazelnut (*Corylus americana*)
Beaked hazel (*Corylus cornuta*)
Black huckleberry (*Gaylussacia baccata*)
Black raspberry (*Rubus occidentalis*)
Black-haw (*Viburnum prunifolium*)
Blue ridge blueberry (*Vaccinium pallidum*)
Deerberry (*Vaccinium stamineum*)
Hop hornbeam (*Ostrya virginiana*)
Hornbeam (*Carpinus caroliniana*)
Lowbush blueberry (*Vaccinium angustifolium*)
Mapleleaf viburnum (*Virburnum acerifolium*)
Mountain laurel (*Kalmia latifolia*)
Pinxter-flower (*Rhododendron periclymenoides*)
Rosebay (*Rhododendron maximum*)
Serviceberry (*Amelanchier arborea*)
Sheep laurel (*Kalmia angustifolia*)
Smooth serviceberry (*Amelanchier laevis*)
Smooth sumac (*Rhus glabra*)
Southern arrow-wood (*Viburnum recognitum*)
Speckled alder (*Alnus incana*)
Spicebush (*Lindera benzoin*)
Winterberry (*Ilex verticillata*)
Witch hazel (*Hamamelis virginiana*)
Witch-hobble (*Viburnum lantanoides*)

Herbaceous
American hog peanut (*Amphicarpaea bracteata*)
Asters (*Eurybia spp.*)
Asters (*Symphyotrichum spp.*)
Bearded shorthusk grass (*Brachyelytrum erectum*)
Blue ridge sedge (*Carex lucorum*)
Canada mayflower (*Maianthemum canadense*)
Christmas fern (*Polystichum acrostichoides*)
Clubmosses (*Lycopodium spp.*)
Common cinquefoil (*Potentilla simplex*)
Downy rattlesnake plantain (*Goodyera pubescens*)

Early bluegrass (*Poa cuspidata*)
False solomon's seal (*Maianthemum racemosum*)
Fibrousroot sedge (*Carex communis*)
Flat-top goldentop (*Euthamia graminifolia*)
Giant goldenrod (*Solidago gigantea*)
Halberdleaf yellow violet (*Viola hastata*)
Hayscented fern (*Dennstaedtia punctilobula*)
Indian cucumber root (*Medeola virginiana*)
Indian cucumber-root (*Medeola virginiana*)
Indian pipe (*Monotropa uniflora*)
Intermediate woodfern (*Dryopteris intermedia*)
Little bluestem (*Schizachyrium scoparium*)
Marginal woodfern (*Dryopteris marginalis*)
Mayapple (*Podophyllum peltatum*)
Nakedflower ticktrefoil (*Desmodium nudiflorum*)
Narrow leaf cowwheat (*Melampyrum lineare*)
New York fern (*Thelypteris noveboracensis*)
Northern bracken fern (*Pteridium aquilinum*)
Partridgeberry (*Mitchella repens*)
Pennsylvania sedge (*Carex pensylvanica*)
Pink lady's slipper (*Cypripedium acaule*)
Pretty sedge (*Carex woodii*)
Purple bedstraw (*Galium latifolium*)
Rattlesnake weed (*Hieracium venosum*)
Rock polypody (*Polypodium virginianum*)
Sessileleaf bellwort (*Uvularia sessilifolia*)
Solomon's seal (*Polygonatum biflorum*)
Spinulose woodfern (*Dryopteris carthusiana*)
Starflower (*Trientalis borealis*)
Striped prince's pine (*Chimaphila maculata*)
Teaberry (*Gaultheria procumbens*)
Venus' pride (*Houstonia purpurea*)
Virginia mountain mint (*Pycnanthemum virginianum*)
Wavy hairgrass (*Deschampsia flexuosa*)
White edge sedge (*Carex debilis*)
White snakeroot (*Ageratina altissima*)
Wild bergamot (*Monarda fistulosa*)
Wild sarsaparilla (*Aralia nudicaulis*)
Woodfern (*Dryopteris spp.*)
Wrinkleleaf goldenrod (*Solidago rugosa*)

Mesic Red Oak Forests

If there had to be a model for classic mesic hardwood forests in Pennsylvania, the midslope group defined by northern red oak (*Quercus rubra*) might well qualify. Because the variations under the canopy are so wide and because the list of plants so long, it offers considerable latitude to the landscaper.

Ideal sites are coves, moist north- and east-facing midslopes and well-drained flats as well as upper floodplain terraces, statewide, although less frequent in the unglaciated Allegheny plateau and the Blue Ridge region.

Soils can be over sandstone, siltstone, limestone, limy shales and conglomerate and tend to be slightly acidic, intermediate fertility and possibly rocky, well drained, but not droughty. They can range form fine sandy loam and loamy sand to very stony silt loams, with pH ranging from 5.6 to 7.3 in most stands, although some areas can be less than 5.5 pH.

In nature, the tree canopy ranges from 80 to more than 100 feet and has cover in excess of 80 percent. Sharing dominance with red oak are red maple (*Acer rubrum*), sweet birch (*Betula lenta*), bitternut hickory (*Carya cordiformis*), pignut hickory (*Carya glabra*) and black oak (*Quercus velutina*), with associates that are a who's who of hardwood trees.

Forming a subcanopy that realistically would have 20 to 40 percent cover and range from 15 to 65 feet we find American hornbeam (*Capinus caroliniana*), flowering dogwood (*Cornus florida*), sweet birch and red maple.

An ideal model would have a tall shrub layer that can vary between 5 and 30 percent total cover in the five to 15 foot range and include witch hazel (*Hamamelis virginiana*), northern spicebush (*Lindera benzoin*) and hop-hornbeam (*Ostrya virginiana*).

The short shrub layer, with a cover ranging from 10 to 30 percent, might well include Blue Ridge blueberry (*Vaccinium pallidum*) and mapleleaf viburnum (*Viburnum acerifolium*) for starters but become quite variable from there.

Ranging from 10 to 50 percent cover, the herbaceous layer is rarely more than three feet and includes a wide array of exceptional landscape species — almost anything goes for shady, mesic sites, especially many decorative ferns. In home landscapes, where cover has either been thinned or an opening created, the possibilities become nearly endless.

Primary trees
- Northern red oak (*Quercus rubra*)
- American basswood (*Tilia americana*)
- American beech (*Fagus grandifolia*)

Secondary trees
- American elm (*Ulmus americana*)
- Bitternut hickory (*Carya cordiformis*)
- Black gum (*Nyssa sylvatica*)
- Black oak (*Quercus velutina*)
- Butternut (*Juglans cinerea*)
- Chestnut oak (*Quercus prinus*)
- Eastern hemlock (*Tsuga canadensis*)
- Eastern red cedar (*Juniperus virginiana*)
- Eastern white pine (*Pinus strobus*)
- Mockernut hickory (*Carya tomentosa*)
- Pignut hickory (*Carya glabra*)
- Red hickory (*Carya ovalis*)
- Red maple (*Acer rubrum*)
- Sassafras (*Sassafras albidum*)
- Scarlet oak (*Quercus coccinea*)
- Shagbark hickory (*Carya ovata*)
- Sugar maple (*Acer saccharum*)
- Sweet birch (*Betula lenta*)
- Tuliptree (*Liriodendron tulipifera*)
- White ash (*Fraxinus americana*)

White oak (*Quercus alba*)
Yellow birch (*Betula alleghaniensis*)

Shrubs

Allegheny serviceberry (*Amelanchier laevis*)
American hazelnut (*Corylus americana*)
American holly (*Ilex opaca*)
American hornbeam (*Carpinus caroliniana*)
Beaked hazelnut (*Corylus cornuta*)
Black huckleberry (*Gaylussacia baccata*)
Blue ridge blueberry (*Vaccinium pallidum*)
Burning bush (*Euonymus atropurpurea*)
Flowering dogwood (*Cornus florida*)
Great rhododendron (*Rhododendron maximum*)
Highbush blueberry (*Vaccinium corymbosum*)
Hop-hornbeam (*Ostrya virginiana*)
Lowbush blueberry (*Vaccinium angustifolium*)
Mapleleaf viburnum (*Viburnum acerifolium*)
Mountain laurel (*Kalmia latifolia*)
Northern Arrowwood (*Viburnum recognitum*)
Northern spicebush (*Lindera benzoin*)
Serviceberry (*Amelanchier arborea*)
Southern arrowwood (*Viburnum dentatum*)
Witch hazel (*Hamamelis virginiana*)
Teaberry (*Gaultheria procumbens*)

Ferns and fern allies

Christmas fern (*Polystichum acrostichoides*)
Club mosses (*Lycopodium spp.*)
Hayscented fern (*Dennstaedtia punctilobula*)
Intermediate woodfern (*Dryopteris intermedia*)
Marginal wood fern (*Dryopteris marginalis*)
New York fern (*Thelypteris noveboracensis*)
Northern bracken fern (*Pteridium aquilinum*)

Grasses and sedges

Bearded shorthusk (*Brachyelytrum erectum*)
Pennsylvania sedge (Carex pensylvanica)
Poverty oat grass (*Danthonia spicata*)
Rosy sedge (*Carex rosea*)
Slender woodland sedge (*Carex digitalis*)
Swann's sedge (*Carex swanii*)
Tapered rosette grass (*Dichanthelium acuminatum*)
Upland bentgrass (*Agrostis perennans*)
Virginia wild rye (*Elymus virginicus*)
Wavy hairgrass (*Deschampsia flexuosa*)

Forbs

Black cohosh (*Actaea racemosa*)
Blue cohosh (*Caulophyllum thalictroides*)
Canada clearweed (*Pilea pumila*)
Canada mayflower (*Maianthemum canadense*)
Common blue violet (*Viola sororia*)
Dogtooth violet (*Erythronium americanum*)
Doll's eyes (*Actaea pachypoda*)
Downy yellow violet (*Viola pubescens*)
False solomon's seal (*Maianthemum racemosum*)
Fragile bedstraw (*Galium triflorum*)
Frost grape (*Vitis riparia*)
Indian cucumber-root (*Medeola virginiana*)
Jack-in-the-pulpit (*Arisaema triphyllum*)
Long branch frostweed (*Helianthemum canadense*)
Mayapple (*Podophyllum peltatum*)
Narrowleaf cow wheat (*Melampyrum lineare*)
Panicled leaf ticktrefoil (*Desmodium paniculatum*)
Partridgeberry (*Mitchella repens*)
Pointed leaf ticktrefoil (*Desmodium glutinosum*)
Rattlesnake weed (*Hieracium venosum*)
Red baneberry (*Actaea rubra*)
Rue anemone (*Thalictrum thalictroides*)
Sessileleaf bellwort (*Uvularia sessilifolia*)
Solomon's seal (*Polygonatum biflorum*)
Starflower (*Trientalis borealis*)
Striped prince's pine (*Chimaphila maculata*)
White goldenrod (*Solidago bicolor*)
White snakeroot (*Ageratina altissima*)
White wood aster (*Eurybia divaricata*)
Wild geranium (*Geranium maculatum*)
Wild sarsaparilla (*Aralia nudicaulis*)
Wild-oats (*Uvularia sessilifolia*)
Wreath goldenrod (Solidago caesia

Northern Hardwood Forest

This very common mid-elevation forest dominates northern Pennsylvania. A combination of American beech (*Fagus grandifolia*), red maple (*Acer rubrum*), sugar maple (*Acer saccharum*) and black cherry (*Prunus serotina*) accounts for half the canopy, with sugar maple the usual dominant, and conifers are scattered if present at all.

Typical habitats are the middle of gentle to somewhat steep slopes facing north or east and below 1,700 feet in elevation.

Because these are mesic forests, there's a lot of rosebay (*Rhododendron maximum*) and witch hazel (*Hamamelis virginiana*), but because the canopy is dense, the overall shrub and herbaceous layers tend to be thin. The more open canopy found at many homesites will allow a much broader range of herbaceous species, with ephemerals extending interest into early spring.

Soils are moderate to deep sandy loam, clay loam or loamy sand, slightly acidic to circumneutral, mesic to wet-mesic and rich in nutrients. This is because of thick sugar maple litter on the forest floor and the calcareous nature of underlying bedrock, mostly limestone, calcareous sandstones, siltstones and shales. Some sites feature channery silt loams and gravelly sand loams with rock outcrops, but always on deep tills.

Good sites are flat to moderately sloping glacial features, including till or moraines in glaciated areas and calcareous rocks, sandstone or shale in unglaciated regions.

On some rocky, higher-elevation sites, dense ferns and other herbs may form a lush understory, known as the "fern-glade variant," an interesting landscape design concept.

High in nitrogen relative to lignin, sugar maple leaf litter soon decomposes and increases the nutrient pool in the soil organic layer. Structure and composition of the forest are maintained by single small tree-fall gaps. Yellow birch grows in mineral soils on "tip-up mounds." These mounds, with the adjacent and more mesic hollow, create microtopography that offers interesting design possibilities. Fallen logs give a more natural look and offer habitats to a variety of mosses, and leaf litter as mulch is an important touch.

For real authenticity, be sure to include broom mosses (*Dicranum spp.*) and white cushion moss (*Leucobryum glaucum*).

Ash, Black cherry variations

Within traditional hardwood forests, a variance featuring sugar maple and white ash (*Fraxinus americana*) appears on ridgetops and slight concavities, between 800 and 2,000 feet in elevation on somewhat enriched and silt loams derived from sedimentary rock parented by clays or other subacid bedrock.

The result is a sparse to moderate shrub cover but a substantial herbaceous cover. But the absence of rich-soil indicators like maidenhair fern (*Adiantum pedatum*), blue cohosh (*Caulophyllum thalictroides*) and basswood (*Tilia americana*) suggest it's not all *that* enriched. Thus the herbaceous layer is filled with semi-rich species that are scarce or absent in most northern hardwood forests, notably doll's eyes (*Actaea pachypoda*), jack-in-the-pulpit (*Arisaema triphyllum*), rattlesnake fern (*Botrychium virginianum*), white wood aster (*Eurybia divaricata*), cinnamon fern (*Osmunda cinnamomea*), interrupted fern (*Osmunda claytoniana*) and foamflower (*Tiarella cordifolia*).

In unglaciated areas, black cherry (*Prunus serotina*) can claim supremacy of the canopy on moderately deep loamy sands and loams that are slightly acidic to circumneutral. These nutrient rich, mesic to wet-mesic soils occur on flat to moderate slopes, sometimes on till and glacial outwash. North-facing slopes are the most common, but aspect is not critical. A thick layer of leaf litter covers the forest floor and the area historically was logged for hardwoods.

These types of forests extend across northern Pennsylvania and down the Allegheny, Appalachian and Blue Ridge Mountains, but with little exception remain similar to other northern hardwood forest communities, giving landscapers a good selection of materials to use in designs.

Primary trees
- American beech (*Fagus grandifolia*)
- Sugar maple (*Acer saccharum*)
- White ash (*Fraxinus americana*)
- Black cherry (*Prunus serotina*)

Secondary trees
- American basswood (*Tilia americana*)
- American elm (*Ulmus americana*)
- Butternut (*Juglans cinerea*)
- Eastern hemlock (*Tsuga canadensis*)
- Eastern white pine (*Pinus strobus*)
- Green ash (*Fraxinus pennsylvanica*)
- Mountain maple (*Acer spicatum*)
- Northern red oak (*Quercus rubra*)
- Paper birch (*Betula papyrifera*)
- Pignut hickory (*Carya glabra*)
- Red elderberry (*Sambucus racemosa*)
- Red maple (*Acer rubrum*)
- Red spruce (*Picea rubens*)
- Striped maple (*Acer pensylvanicum*)
- Sweet birch (*Betula lenta*)
- Tuliptree (*Liriodendron tulipifera*)
- White oak (*Quercus alba*)
- Yellow birch (*Betula alleghaniensis*)

Shrubs and subcanopy
- Allegheny blackberry (*Rubus allegheniensis*)
- Alternate leaf dogwood (*Cornus alternifolia*)
- American hornbeam (*Carpinus caroliniana*)
- Beaked hazelnut (*Corylus cornuta*)
- Blue ridge blueberry (*Vaccinium pallidum*)
- Flowering dogwood (*Cornus florida*)
- Hobblebush (*Viburnum lantanoides*)
- Hop hornbeam (*Ostrya virginiana*)
- Mapleleaf viburnum (*Viburnum acerifolium*)
- Mountain holly (*Ilex prinus*)
- Mountain laurel (*Kalmia latifolia*)
- Northern spicebush (*Lindera benzoin*)
- Rosebay (*Rhododendron maximum*)
- Serviceberry (*Amelanchier arborea*)
- Smooth serviceberry (*Amelanchier laevis*)
- Teaberry (*Gaultheria procumbens*)
- Witch hazel (*Hamamelis virginiana*)
- Witch-hobble (*Viburnum lantanoides*)

Ferns and fern allies
- Christmas fern (*Polystichum acrostichoides*)
- Cinnamon fern (*Osmunda cinnamomea*)
- Hayscented fern (*Dennstaedtia punctilobula*)
- Intermediate woodfern (*Dryopteris intermedia*)
- Interrupted fern (*Osmunda claytoniana*)
- Marginal woodfern (*Dryopteris marginalis*)
- Mountain woodfern (*Dryopteris campyloptera*)
- New York fern (*Thelypteris noveboracensis*)
- Northern bracken fern (*Pteridium aquilinum*)
- Rattlesnake fern (*Botrychium virginianum*)
- Shining clubmoss (*Lycopodium lucidulum*)
- Spinulose woodfern (*Dryopteris carthusiana*)

Grasses and sedges
- American millet grass (*Milium effusum*)
- Appalachian sedge (*Carex appalachica*)
- Bearded shorthusk (*Brachyelytrum erectum*)
- Broadleaf sedge (*Carex platyphylla*)
- Drooping woodreed (*Cinna latifolia*)
- Eastern woodland sedge (*Carex blanda*)
- Longstalk sedge (*Carex pedunculata*)
- Pennsylvania sedge (*Carex pensylvanica*)
- Slender woodland sedge (*Carex digitalis*)
- Spreading sedge (*Carex laxiculmis*)
- White edge sedge (*Carex debilis*)

Forbs
- American fly honeysuckle (*Lonicera canadensis*)
- Blue cohosh (*Caulophyllum thalictroides*)
- Bluebead lily (*Clintonia borealis*)
- Common wood-sorrel (*Oxalis acetosella*)
- Doll's eyes (*Actaea pachypoda*)

Foamflower (*Tiarella cordifolia*)
Indian cucumber (*Medeola virginiana*)
Jack-in-the-pulpit (*Arisaema triphyllum*)
Largeleaf goldenrod (*Solidago macrophylla*)
Mayflower (*Maianthemum canadense*)
Mountain wood sorrel (*Oxalis montana*)
Painted trillium (*Trillium undulatum*)
Partridgeberry (*Mitchella repens*)
Red trillium (*Trillium erectum*)
Roundleaf yellow violet (*Viola rotundifolia*)
Sessileleaf bellwort (*Uvularia sessilifolia*)
Starflower (*Trientalis borealis*)
Striped prince's pine (*Chimaphila maculata*)
Sweet white violet (*Viola blanda*)
Twisted stalk (*Streptopus lanceolatus*)
White wood aster (*Eurybia divaricata*)
Whorled wood aster (*Oclemena acuminata*)
Wild sarsaparilla (*Aralia nudicaulis*)
Wild-oats (*Uvularia sessilifolia*)
Wreath goldenrod (*Solidago caesia*)
Zig-zag goldenrod (Solidago flexicaulis)

Hemlock - Oak Forests

Common in northeastern Pennsylvania, hemlock-oak forests are on acidic, very stony sandy loams. In mid-slope positions facing northeast to northwest and elevations between 500 and 2,500 feet, they favor sheltered sites.

Because the habitat is so xeric, dry-site species dominate the canopy. Some sites are quite literally boulder fields, with up to 60 percent cover by large rocks and good habitats for lichens.

The canopy collection is similar to high elevation dry sites, with associate tree species including sweet birch (*Betula lenta*), scarlet oak (*Quercus coccinea*), northern red oak (*Quercus rubra*), red maple (*Acer rubrum*), black gum (*Nyssa sylvatica*), white pine (*Pinus strobus*), white oak (*Quercus alba*) and sassafras (*Sassafras albidum*). If conditions are good, mockernut hickory (*Carya alba*), pignut hickory (*Carya glabra*), American beech (*Fagus grandifolia*) and tuliptree (*Liriodendron tulipifera*) can also be considered.

The dense hemlock cover constrains shrubs and many herbaceous species, but where there are openings serviceberry (*Amelanchier arborea*) works well, along with witch hazel (*Hamamelis virginiana*) and mountain laurel (*Kalmia latifolia*). Less frequent in nature are rosebay (*Rhododendron maximum*) and maple-leaf viburnum (*Viburnum acerifolium*).

Good choices for low shrubs are huckleberry (*Gaylussacia baccata*) and Blue Ridge blueberry (*Vaccinium pallidum*), while understatement is the theme in the herbaceous layer, where Pinesap (*Monotropa hypopithys*) and Indian pipe (*Monotropa uniflora*) add authentic touches. Sparse and scattered in natural forests, the ground is covered with hemlock and oak litter and very little light.

More open canopies on developed sites can be balanced with selective clearing to enhance the light for the go-to group of xeric species:

Blue wood aster (*Symphyotrichum cordifolium*)
Downy rattlesnake plantain (*Goodyera pubescens*)
Hay scented fern (*Dennstaedtia punctilobula*)
Mayflower (*Maianthemum canadense*)
Partridgeberry (*Mitchella repens*)
Pennsylvania sedge (*Carex pensylvanica*)
Striped prince's pine (*Chimaphila maculata*)
Swan's sedge (*Carex swanii*)
Teaberry (*Gaultheria procumbens*)
Virginia creeper (*Parthenocissus quinquefolia*)
Wavy hairgrass (*Deschampsia flexuosa*)
White wood aster (*Eurybia divaricata*)
Wild sarsaparilla (*Aralia nudicaulis*)

MESIC HEMLOCK - HARDWOOD FORESTS

Mesic coves across much of southern Pennsylvania illustrate how subtle shifts in conditions can cause landscapers to adjust designs and plans — not to mention investigate techniques to broaden the range of species for garden use.

The basic elements are straightforward and encouraging to begin with: cool, sheltered, mesic sites on gentle to steep lower to middle slopes, sometimes on moist flats and along major streams. Offering deep, rich, well-drained, acidic loams and silt loams, these sites will attract many species, but it's the perfect habitat for eastern hemlock (*Tsuga canadensis*).

This is also splendid territory for American beech (*Fagus grandifolia*) and sugar maple (*Acer saccharum*), which share much of the natural canopy. But with a closer look, it's apparent the upper end of these bands tend to be more dry-mesic, while the lower parts of the hill trend toward mesic-moist and richer in nutrients.

All this creates subtle variables in species found in nature and creates options for landscapers. Authentic designs reflect the genuine habitat, but the rich collection found on the downslope end is more than inviting.

Something of middle ground begins with a collection that spans the entire range. In the wild, at least 25 percent of the canopy is hemlock, and the shade and duff factors are important in driving the shrub and herbaceous layers below. Beech and sugar maples contribute important nutrition to the duff layer, and keep the site authentic. Good basic choices for associates include American basswood (*Tilia americana*), northern red oak (*Quercus rubra*), red maple (*Acer rubrum*), sweet birch (*Betula lenta*), tuliptree (*Liriodendron tulipifera*), white ash (*Fraxinus americana*), yellow birch (*Betula alleghaniensis*), and, in western Pennsylvania, cucumber-tree (*Magnolia acuminata*).

On the less mesic end of the spectrum, a wide array of hardwoods, as well as white pine, offer possibilities; on the richer end, shagbark hickory (*Carya ovata*), umbrella magnolia (*Magnolia tripetala*), and yellow buckeye (*Aesculus flava*) are good choices.

These types of sites are attractive ground for reliable tall shrubs such as witch hazel (*Hamamelis virginiana*), rosebay (*Rhododendron maximum*) and northern spicebush (*Lindera benzoin*), and a varied collection of moisture and acidic soil-loving herbaceous plants. Low-moisture lovers tend to congregate at higher positions, while those who bask in moisture gravitate downslope.

There's no shortage of possibilities for landscapers in herbaceous choices. While shrubs tend to dominate at higher elevations and the list of herbaceous species a bit shorter because of it, the opposite is true at lower elevations and the lists includes many popular favorites. Just how far these can go in less moist circumstances depends a great deal on local conditions, but probabilities for success are higher here than in most places. A good starter list would include white wood aster (*Eurybia divaricata*), marginal woodfern (*Dryopteris marginalis*), rattlesnake fern (*Botrychium virginianum*) and Canada mayflower (*Maianthemum canadense*) — especially under hemlocks. Black cohosh (*Actaea racemosa*) and wood geranium (*Geranium maculatum*) do very well in dappled shade, as does white snakeroot (*Ageratina altissima*). Bishop's cap (*Mitella diphylla*) and foamflower (*Tiarella cordifolia*) are strong candidates for masses or edge plantings that can handle less moist but humusy circumstances quite well. Ideal for moist but deeply shaded spots, wild ginger

(*Asarum canadense*) is a sturdy naturalizer.

Those who delight in the delicate beauty of ephemerals will find sharp- and round-leaf hepaticas (*Hepatica nobilis*), bloodroot (*Sanguinaria canadense*), anenomes such as wood anemone (*Anemone quinquefolia*), spring beauty *Claytonia virginica*) and dutchman's breeches (*Dicentra cucullaria*), squirrel corn (*Dicentra canadense*) as welcome harbingers of very early spring. Delicate miniatures like partridgeberry (*Mitchella repens*) add authentic touches to rocky patches.

In flatter ground, consider colonies of mayapple (*Podophyllum peltatum*) and jack-in-the-pulpit (*Arisaema triphyllum*) and clumps of Christmas fern (*Polystichum acrosticoides*), intermediate woodfern (*Dryopteris intermedia*) and marginal woodfern (*Dryopteris marginalis*).

Starter plants
Essential trees
Eastern hemlock (*Tsuga canadensis*)
American beech (*Fagus grandifolia*)
Sugar maple (*Acer saccharum*)
Associate trees
American basswood (*Tilia americana*)
Black cherry (*Prunus serotina*)
Black gum (*Nyssa sylvatica*)
Black oak (*Quercus velutina*)
Chestnut oak (*Quercus prinus*)
Cucumber tree (*Magnolia acuminata*)
Cucumber-tree (*Magnolia acuminata*)
Eastern white pine (*Pinus strobus*)
Hickories (*Carya spp.*)
Hop hornbeam (*Ostrya virginiana*)
Mockernut hickory (*Carya alba*)
Northern red oak (*Quercus rubra*)
Pignut hickory (*Carya glabra*)
Red maple (*Acer rubrum*)
Sassafras (*Sassafras albidum*)
Scarlet oak (*Quercus coccinea*)
Shagbark hickory (*Carya ovata*)
Sweet birch (*Betula lenta*)
Tuliptree (*Liriodendron tulipifera*)
Umbrella magnolia (*Magnolia tripetala*)
White ash (*Fraxinus americana*)
White oak (*Quercus alba*)
Yellow birch (*Betula alleghaniensis*)
Yellow buckeye (*Aesculus flava*)
Shrubs
Allegheny serviceberry (*Amelanchier laevis*)
American hornbeam (*Carpinus caroliniana*)
Bladdernut (*Staphylea trifolia*)
Blue ridge blueberry (*Vaccinium pallidum*)
Eastern prickly gooseberry (*Ribes cynosbati*)
Huckleberry (*Gaylussacia baccata*)
Mapleleaf viburnum (*Viburnum acerifolium*)
Mountain laurel (*Kalmia latifolia*)
Northern spicebush (*Lindera benzoin*)
Pawpaw (*Asimina triloba*)
Rosebay (*Rhododendron maximum*)
Serviceberry (*Amelanchier arborea*)
Southern arrowwood (*Viburnum recognitum*)
Teaberry (*Gaultheria procumbens*)
Wild hydrangea (*Hydrangea arborescens*)
Witch hazel (*Hamamelis virginiana*)
Herbaceous
Bishop's-cap (*Mitella diphylla*)
Black cohosh (*Actaea racemosa*)
Bloodroot (*Sanguinaria canadensis*)
Blue cohosh (*Caulophyllum thalictroides*)
Canada mayflower (*Maianthemum canadense*)
Canadian woodnettle (*Laportea canadensis*)
Christmas fern (*Polystichum acrostichoides*)
Clayton's sweetroot (*Osmorhiza claytonii*)
Cut-leaved toothwort (*Cardamine concatenata*)
Downy rattlesnake plantain (*Goodyera pubescens*)
Dutchman's breeches (*Dicentra cucullaria*)
Feathery false lily of the valley (*Maianthemum racemosum*)
Fernleaf phacelia (*Phacelia bipinnatifida*)
Foamflower (*Tiarella cordifolia*)
Fourleaf yam (*Dioscorea quaternata*)
Grape (*Vitis spp.*)
Hairy solomon's seal (*Polygonatum pubescens*)
Hayscented fern (*Dennstaedtia punctilobula*)
Hepatica (*Hepatica nobilis, var acuta, var*

obtusa)
Intermediate woodfern (*Dryopteris intermedia*)
Jack-in-the-pulpit (*Arisaema triphyllum*)
Lady fern (*Athyrium filix-femina*)
Maidenhair fern (*Adiantum pedatum*)
Marginal woodfern (*Dryopteris marginalis*)
Mayapple (*Podophyllum peltatum*)
Mountain stonecrop (*Sedum ternatum*)
New York fern (*Thelypteris noveboracensis*)
Partridgeberry (*Mitchella repens*)
Pipevine (*Aristolochia macrophylla*)
Plantainleaf sedge (*Carex plantaginea*)
Rattlesnake fern (*Botrychium virginianum*)
Roundleaf greenbrier (*Smilax rotundifolia*)
Roundleaf yellow violet (*Viola rotundifolia*)
Slender woodland sedge (*Carex digitalis*)
Spleenworts (*Asplenium spp.*)
Spring-beauty (*Claytonia virginica*)
Squirrel corn (*Dicentra canadensis*)
Starry false lily of the valley (*Maianthemum racemosum*)
Striped prince's pine (*Chimaphila maculata*)
Swan's sedge (*Carex swanii*)
Sweet white violet (*Viola blanda*)
Trilliums (*Trillium spp.*)
Trout-lily (*Erythronium americanum*)
Virginia creeper (*Parthenocissus quinquefolia*)
Walking fern (*Asplenium rhizophyllum*)
Wavy hairgrass (*Deschampsia flexuosa*)
White snakeroot (*Ageratina altissima*)
White wood aster (*Eurybia divaricata*)
Wild ginger (*Asarum canadense*)
Wild leek (*Allium tricoccum*)
Wild sarsaparilla (*Aralia nudicaulis*)
Wood anemone (*Anemone quinquefolia*)
Wood geranium (*Geranium maculatum*)
Wreath goldenrod (*Solidago caesia*)
Yellow fairybells (*Prosartes lanuginosa*)
Yellow fumewort (*Corydalis flavula*)

Rich hardwood forests

Landscapers faced with a site suitable for a rich hardwood forest are to be envied, for here the soil is in a pH range with a lot of latitude, fertile, mesic, and in the middle to bottoms of slopes on cool, protected spots.

And because of that, the list of species, particularly herbaceous species, is extensive and stuffed with many old favorites.

The canopy itself — dominated by sugar maple (*Acer saccharum*), American basswood (*Tilia americana*) and white ash (*Fraxinus americana*) — produces leaf litter that enriches the soil even further, dismissing the need for artificial amendments.

It's helpful to first consider that in nature, there are subtle variations that impact which ecological bin a site is placed. These may or may not be significant in the context of the back yard garden, depending on just how authentic the design is to be, but there's little doubt that the differences can appear fuzzy.

By far the most widespread in nature are *Sugar Maple – Basswood Forests*, which can be found nearly statewide on rich, rocky and lower slopes involving colluvium from calcareous rock.

Tuliptree – Beech - Maple Forests are common, too, but more downslope, most often on toeslopes, on mesic, circumneutral soils.

Mixed Mesophytic Forests are by definition limited to the Pittsburgh Plateau area of southwestern Pennsylvania. Although they appear very similar to Sugar Maple – Basswood Forests, they are as a rule richer in the herbaceous layer. Colluvial soils are in the 5.5 pH range, but tend toward higher amounts of organic matter.

All differences aside, these types of sites, with substantial collection of mesic, circumneutral herbaceous species just right for them, offer a wide array landscaping options and opportunities.

Sugar Maple - Basswood Forest

A combination of sugar maple (*Acer saccharum*), American basswood (*Tilia americana*) and white ash (*Fraxinius americana*) on rich, rocky slopes are the signature of this extensive group. And because they do well here, the collective preferences of the group give us a good sense of the soil underneath.

Sugar maple is successful in a wide range of circumneutral habitats, but basswood prefers medium moisture and a pH of 6.5 and up. Ash is a moisture lover, and does best in soils below 7.2 pH, but is not shade tolerant. All three prefer good drainage in medium to coarse soils, and need at least 30 to 40 inches for their root systems. Only sugar maple has any degree of drought tolerance. Collectively, they are found in more upland habitats, so companion species with a wetland rating of FACU should fit well.

Rocky colluvium, is a defining feature of good sites, suggesting spots in medium to high positions on footslopes. Ideal material originates from calcium bearing sedimentary, but sometimes meta sedimentary and even igneous rock. Some themes found in nature include:

Steep slopes along rivers or streams, covered with colluvium

Talus slopes or shallow rocky soils over calcareous to circumneutral bedrock, often facing north.

Northwest to east-facing coves, lower slopes and slope bases, involving steep, concave Appalachian slopes

Enriched, concave slopes with mesic to wet-mesic conditions, along slope bottoms where colluvium collects.

Steep east and north-facing, rocky-bottomed

ephemeral and intermittent creeks that feature large quantities of colluvium that has washed down over time.

Soils are mineral materials weathered from calcareous shales and limestones, slightly acidic to moderately, and well drained loam to sandy loams and sand, with a deep water table. Limestone, dolomite, sandstone bedrock is typical. Soils can be bouldery to gravelly, but their moisture-holding and the ability to hold and release plant nutrients are quite high; soils tend to have high to very high calcium levels, high magnesium, and moderately low iron and aluminum.

The surface can feature as much as half the area covered with boulders — a helpful concept in building dramatic garden designs.

The list of canopy associates is broad and varied, sometimes driven by local conditions and circumstance. However, good initial choices include northern red oak (*Quercus rubra*), hop-hornbeam (*Ostrya virginiana*), slippery elm (*Ulmus rubra*), red maple (*Acer rubrum*), yellow birch (*Betula alleghaniensis*), American beech (*Fagus grandifolia*), tuliptree (*Liriodendron tulipifera*), cucumber tree (*Magnolia acuminata*) and black cherry (*Prunus serotina*). All make positive contributions to soil nutrients in leaf litter mulches.

Excellent starting points for a shrub layer, that in nature tends to be on the open side, include alternate-leaf dogwood (*Cornus alternifolia*), witch hazel (*Hamamelis virginiana*), fly-honeysuckle (*Lonicera canadensis*), pinxterbloom azalea (*Rhododendron periclymenoides*), American bladdernut (*Staphylea trifolia*) and mapleleaf viburnum (*Viburnum acerifolium*).

Herbaceous layers tend to be lush and diverse, which gives the landscaper a wide range of design possibilities. Worth investigating as foundations are black cohosh (*Actaea racemosa*), white snakeroot (*Ageratina altissima*), wild geranium (*Geranium maculatum*), while mayapple (*Podophyllum peltatum*), Canada mayflower (*Maianthemum canadense*), foamflower (*Tiarella cordifolia*) and wild ginger (*Asarum canadense*) — ideal for difficult shady spots — are great naturalizers, and the prized white trillium (*Trillium grandiflorum*) calls these sites home.

These types of habitats are delights for fern lovers, with at least a dozen of the more popular species turning up on natural sites. Included are the very big ferns, Goldie's woodfern (*Dryopteris goldiana*) for well behaved in dryish spots to the exhuberant ostrich fern (*Matteuccia struthiopteris*), which needs some room to run but is spectacular in a monotropic patch dissected by a soft humusy walking path. Accent clumpers like Christmas fern (*Polystichum acrostichoides*), marginal wood (*Dryopteris marginalis*) give shape and form to beds of low-growing ephemerals, and the old-fashioned landscape favorite, northern maidenhair (*Adiantum pedatum*) is well-suited for this type of habitat.

Any number of sedges can be used for path margins, but delicate taller grasses like bottlebrush (*Elmyus hystrix*) and bluejoint (*Calamagrostis canadensis*) can add whispy interest to designs.

Mixed Mesophytic Forests

Somewhat similar to Sugar Maple – Basswood Forests, the classic Mixed Mesophytic Forests of southwestern Pennsylvania are sometimes referred to as "cove forests" because, in fact, this is the general place where they're found.

The usual big trees of the canopy are all present: sugar maple (*Acer saccharum*), tuliptree (*Liriodendron tulipifera*), American basswood (*Tilia americana*), American beech (*Fagus grandifolia*), northern red oak (*Quercus rubra*), white ash (*Fraxinus americana*), black cherry (*Prunus serotina*) and more.

The difference, though, is that there's no clear canopy dominant and these sites often also include cucumber tree (*Magnolia acuminata*), Ohio buckeye (*Aesculus glabra*) and yellow buckeye (*Aesculus flava*).

Sites are on deep, very rich soils at lower slope position, which leads to a lush herbaceous layer. Although they can be found along stream on alluvial terraces, sometimes on abandoned river terraces, the ideal natrual site is more often on colluvium of moist, cool, concave slopes, bottoms and in steep ravines. When facing north, sites can range from low to high, but when facing south they tend to be confined to the lower part of the slope.

The colluvium itself is derived from sandstone or shale, which can sometimes be calcareous but most often averages around 5.5 pH and contains substantial amount organic matter. The landscaper's best friend is the leaf litter from the canopy, which continues to enrich the soil; most of the forests have an almost 100 percent annual litter turnover, which only serves to strengthen the shrub and herbaceous layer.

Good basic choices for the shrub layer are the ever-popular northern spicebush (*Lindera benzoin*), witch hazel (*Hamamelis virginiana*), wild hydrangea (*Hydrangea arborescens*) and rosebay (*Rhododendron maximum*), but also worth strong design consideration are bladdernut (*Stapylea trifolia*), paw-paw (*Asimina triloba*), redbud (*Cercis canadensis*) and umbrella magnolia (*Magnolia tripetala*).

Trillium enthusiasts will welcome the opportunity to design with such favorites as white trillium (*Trillium grandiflorum*), purple trillium (*Trillium erectum*), and toadshade (*Trillium sessile*), and it's in this kind of habitat that we find excellent habitat for trout lily (*Erythronium americanum*) and speckled wood lily (*Clintonia umbellulata*). Early spring ground is cheery with a chorus of ephemerals: bloodroot (*Sanguinaria canadensis*), hepaticas (*Hepatica nobilis*), woodland anemone (*Anemone quinquefolia*), squirrel-corn (*Dicentra cucullaria*), Dutchman's breeches (*Dicentra cucullaria*) and bishop's cap (*Mitella diphylla*), to name a few.

Black cohosh (*Actaea racemosa*) provides spectacular summer interest after wild geranium (*Geranium maculatum*) and wild blue phlox (*Phlox divaricata*) have had their day. A number of reliable, well-mannered ferns balance out the landscape.

This is also excellent ground to cultivate a wide range of mosses, including American climacium moss (*Climacium americanum*), anomodon moss (*Anomodon attenuatus, Anomodon rostratus*), aulacomnium moss (*Aulacomnium heterostichum*), brachythecium moss (*Brachythecium oxycladon, Brachythecium plumosum*), ciliate hedwigia moss (*Hedwigia ciliata*), delicate thuidium (*Thuidium delicatulum*), denuded dicranodontium moss (*Dicranodontum denudatum*), dicranum moss (*Dicranum fulvum*), hypnum moss (*Hypnum imponens*), loeskeobryum moss (*Loeskeobryum brevirostre*), Ontario rhodobryum moss (*Rhodobryum ontariense*), plagiomnium moss (*Plagiomnium ciliare*), toothed plagiomnium moss (*Plagiomnium cuspidatum*) and white cushion moss (*Leucobryum glaucum*).

Tuliptree – Beech - Maple forests

On gentle to slightly steep positions from midslope down, notably toeslopes, these hardwood forests take advantage of deep circumneutral and mesic soils.

While the northern Pennsylvania canopy can vary, the key players are almost always tuliptree (*Liriodendron tulipifera*), American beech (*Fagus grandifolia*) and sugar maple (*Acer saccharum*). In the Piedmont and points west, red maple (*Acer rubrum*) joins tuliptree and beech in the canopy. In low-elevation successional stands, the forest can be almost entirely tuliptree.

Good sites are toeslopes, lower coves or areas along small drainages, all where near-surface groundwater is responsible for mesic conditions. Topography is flat to rolling, while in southern areas it can be somewhat dissected. In the north, sites can face almost any point of the compass, but in the south they tend to lean toward facing north to east.

While the soils are fertile and well drained, northern sites will have developed over glacial deposits and southern sites more probable over shale or sandstone as well as very old till or alluvium. Soils are silt loams, loams or sandy loams, occasionally silt.

Other site possibilities occur where disturbance, like farming or logging, has opened the canopy and created conditions suitable for these species. Evidence of past agriculture includes stone walls and drainage ditches, while cut stumps suggest logging.

Statewide, a long list of associates are ready to join in on a good location to grow, giving designers very wide latitude in choices. In stands with recent disturbance, quaking aspen (*Populus tremuloides*) and black locust (*Robinia pseudoacacia*) turn up, but oaks are few to absent.

The tall shrub layer, ranging from five to 15 feet, covers between 20 and 60 percent in nature. Excellent candidates for the subcanopy are American hornbeam (*Carpinus caroliniana*), hop hornbeam (*Ostrya virginiana*), and flowering dogwood (*Cornus florida*), along with witch hazel (*Hamamelis virginiana*) and *Lindera benzoin* (northern spicebush). There's a lot of variety in natural settings, often when recent disturbances are involved, and an open canopy will lead to a more exuberant shrub layer.

The short-shrub layer is less than five feet in height and may vary from 10 to 80 percent cover. A leading candidate for landscapers is *Viburnum acerifolium* (mapleleaf viburnum).

However, the herbaceous layer is the strength of this kind of habitat. While someone limited in scope, they are lush in distribution, especially in colonies of mayapple and ferns. Consider cover of at least 50 percent. Good authentic touches are patches of ephemerals such as bloodroot (*Sanguinaria canadensis*), dutchman's breeches (*Dicentra cucullaria*), and squirrel corn (*Dicentra canadensis*), all of which have naturalizing characteristics.

Vines may be present as creeping plants in the herb or short-shrub layer, but may occasionally reach the lower portion of the canopy: summer grape (*Vitis aestivalis*), Virginia creeper (*Parthenocissus quinquefolia*) and greenbriar (*Smilax rotundifolia*).

Suggested plants for all sites
  Trees
    American beech (*Fagus grandifolia*)
    Red maple (*Acer rubrum*)
    Shagbark hickory (*Carya ovata*)
    Sugar maple (*Acer saccharum*)
    Sweet birch (*Betula lenta*)
    Tuliptree (*Liriodendron tulipifera*)
    White ash (*Fraxinus americana*)
  Shrubs
    American hornbeam (*Carpinus caroliniana*)
    Northern spicebush (*Lindera benzoin*)
    Witch hazel (*Hamamelis virginiana*)
  Herbaceous
    Bloodroot (*Sanguinaria canadensis*)
    Christmas fern (*Polystichum acrostichoides*)
    Dutchman's breeches (*Dicentra cucullaria*)
    Jack-in-the-pulpit (*Arisaema triphyllum*)
    Rattlesnake fern (*Botrychium virginianum*)
    Squirrel corn (*Dicentra canadensis*)
    Virginia creeper (*Parthenocissus quinquefolia*)
    Virginia spring beauty (*Claytonia virginiana*)
    Wild leek (*Allium tricoccum*)

Suggested for Sugar Maple and Mixed Mesophytic sites
  Trees
    American basswood (*Tilia americana*)
    Black cherry (*Prunus serotina*)
    Black walnut (*Juglans nigra*)
    Northern red oak (*Quercus rubra*)
    Pawpaw (*Asimina triloba*)
    White oak (*Quercus alba*)
  Shrubs
    American bladdernut (*Staphylea trifolia*)
    Bishop's-cap (*Mitella diphylla*)
    Wild hydrangea (*Hydrangea arborescens*)
  Herbaceous
    Black cohosh (*Actaea racemosa*)
    Blue cohosh (*Caulophyllum thalictroides*)
    Canadian wood nettle (*Laportea canadensis*)
    Cut-leaved toothwort (*Cardamine concatenata*)
    Eastern waterleaf (*Hydrophyllum virginianum*)
    Liverleaf (*Hepatica nobilis*)
    Marginal woodfern (*Dryopteris marginalis*)
    Northern maidenhair fern (*Adiantum pedatum*)
    Trout-lily (*Erythronium americanum*)
    White trillium (*Trillium grandiflorum*)
    Wild ginger (*Asarum canadense*)
    Wood anemone (*Anemone quinquefolia*)

Suggested for Sugar Maple, Tuliptree

Forests
- **Trees**
  - Yellow birch (*Betula alleghaniensis*)
- **Shrubs**
  - Mapleleaf viburnum (*Viburnum acerifolium*)
  - Hop-hornbeam (*Ostrya virginiana*)
- **Herbaceous**
  - White snakeroot (*Ageratina altissima*)
  - Mayapple (*Podophyllum peltatum*)
  - Canada mayflower (*Maianthemum canadense*)

Suggested for Mixed Mesophytic, Tuliptree Forests
- **Trees**
  - Cucumber tree (*Magnolia acuminata*)
  - Eastern hemlock (*Tsuga canadensis*)

Suggested for Sugar Maple Forests
- **Trees**
  - Bitternut hickory (*Carya cordiformis*)
  - Black maple (*Acer nigrum*)
  - Black oak (*Quercus velutina*)
  - Butternut (*Juglans cinerea*)
  - Chestnut oak (*Quercus prinus*)
  - Chinkapin oak (*Quercus muehlenbergii*)
  - Pignut hickory (*Carya glabra*)
  - Slippery elm (*Ulmus rubra*)
- **Shrubs**
  - Alternate-leaf dogwood (*Cornus alternifolia*)
  - Eastern redbud (*Cercis canadensis*)
  - Roundleaf dogwood (*Cornus rugosa*)
  - Pink azalea (*Rhododendron periclymenoides*)
  - Hobblebush (*Viburnum lantanoides*)
- **Herbaceous**
  - Allegheny vine (*Adlumia fungosa*)
  - American fly honeysuckle (*Lonicera canadensis*)
  - American ginseng (*Panax quinquefolius*)
  - American spikenard (*Aralia racemosa*)
  - Bebb's sedge (*Carex bebbii*)
  - Black cohosh (*Actaea racemosa*)
  - Blackseed ricegrass (*Piptatherum racemosum*)
  - Blue wood aster (*Symphyotrichum cordifolium*)
  - Bluejoint (*Calamagrostis canadensis*)
  - Bottlebrush grass (*Elymus hystrix*)
  - Broad beech fern (*Phegopteris hexagonoptera*)
  - Broad looseflower sedge (*Carex laxiflora*)
  - Broadleaf sedge (*Carex platyphylla*)
  - Bulblet bladder fern (*Cystopteris bulbifera*)
  - Canadian clearweed (*Pilea pumila*)
  - Canadian white violet (*Viola canadensis*)
  - Clayton's sweetroot (*Osmorhiza claytonii*)
  - Common hackberry (*Celtis occidentalis*)
  - Common lady fern (*Athyrium filix-femina*)
  - Common moonseed (*Menispermum canadense*)
  - Davis' sedge (*Carex davisii*)
  - Doll's eyes (*Actaea pachypoda*)
  - Early meadow-rue (*Thalictrum dioicum*)
  - Eastern leatherwood (*Dirca palustris*)
  - Eastern rough sedge (*Carex scabrata*)
  - False lily of the valley (*Maianthemum racemosum*)
  - False solomon's-seal (*Smilacina racemosa*)
  - Goldie's woodfern (*Dryopteris goldiana*)
  - Hepatica species (*Hepatica spp.*)
  - Hitchcock's sedge (*Carex hitchcockiana*)
  - Intermediate woodfern (*Dryopteris intermedia*)
  - Jewelweed (*Impatiens capensis*)
  - Male fern (*Dryopteris filix-mas*)
  - Mellic mannagrass (*Glyceria melicaria*)
  - Merrybells (*Uvularia grandiflora*)
  - Nerveless woodland sedge (*Carex leptonervia*)
  - Ostrich fern (*Matteuccia struthiopteris*)
  - Pale touch me not (*Impatiens pallida*)
  - Plantainleaf sedge (*Carex plantaginea*)
  - Purple flowering raspberry (*Rubus odoratus*)
  - Round lobe hepatica (*Hepatica nobilis var. obtusa*)
  - Roundleaf yellow violet (*Viola rotundifolia*)
  - Showy orchid (*Galearis spectabilis*)
  - Silver false spleenwort (*Deparia acrostichoides*)
  - Smooth rockcress (*Arabis laevigata*)
  - Solomon's seal (*Polygonatum biflorum*)

Sprengel's sedge (*Carex sprengelii*)
Spring-beauty (*Claytonia virginica*)
Summer sedge (*Carex aestivalis*)
Violets (*Viola spp.*)
White wood aster (*Eurybia divaricata*)
Wild geranium (*Geranium maculatum*)
Zig-zag goldenrod (*Solidago flexicaulis*)

Suggested for Mixed Mesophytic sites
  Trees
    Ohio buckeye (*Aesculus glabra*)
    Redbud (*Cercis canadensis*)
    Umbrella magnolia (*Magnolia tripetala*)
  Shrubs
    Rosebay (*Rhododendron maximum*)
  Herbaceous
    Black cohosh (*Actaea racemosa*)
    Blunt leaf waterleaf (*Hydrophyllum canadense*)
    Canadian honewort (*Cryptotaenia canadensis*)
    Canadian white violet (*Viola canadensis*)
    Foamflower (*Tiarella cordifolia*)
    Fragrant bedstraw (*Galium triflorum*)
    Pipevine (*Aristolochia macrophylla*)
    Purple trillium (*Trillium erectum*)
    Sharp-lobed hepatica (*Hepatica nobilis var. acuta*)
    Speckled wood-lily (*Clintonia umbellulata*)
    Summer grape (*Vitis aestivalis var. bicolor*)
    Sweetroot (*Osmorhiza spp.*)
    Toadshade trillium (*Trillium sessile*)
    Wild blue phlox (*Phlox divaricata*)
    Wood geranium (*Geranium maculatum*)
    Woodland stonecrop (*Sedum ternatum*)
    Yellow buckeye (*Aesculus flava*)
    Yellow fairy-bells (*Prosartes lanuginosa*)
    Yellow fumewort (*Corydalis flavula*)

Suggested for Tuliptree sites
  Trees
    Black locust (*Robinia pseudoacacia*)
    Black-gum (*Nyssa sylvatica*)
    Mockernut hickory (*Carya tomentosa*)
    Quaking aspen (*Populus tremuloides*)
    Red oak (*Quercus rubra*)
  Shrubs
    Flowering dogwood (*Cornus florida*)
  Herbaceous
    Dwarf cinquefoil (*Potentilla canadensis*)
    Greenbrier (*Smilax rotundifolia*)
    Hayscented fern (*Dennstaedtia punctilobula*)

PIEDMONT MESOPHYTIC FOREST

The fertile soils, gently rolling surface, moderate climate and extended growing season found in the southeastern corner of Pennsylvania — the Piedmont and Atlantic Coastal Plain — provide rich opportunity for a broad array of native species. Beginning at the northern tip in the Delaware River Valley, extending southwesterly toward South Mountain and then east to the Delaware Bay, this region has volcanic origins, was folded and refolded extensively by tectonic collision, smoothed out by erosion and the recipient of a variety of alluvial and colluvial materials, mostly from the Appalachians but also tremendous flows of meltwater from continental glaciation.

The result toward the north are rich, mesophytic forests with base-rich soils derived from lime sands and mafic rock, perfect ground for American beech (*Fagus grandifolia*) and tuliptree (*Liriodendron tulipifera*) and all their associates. Constant associates for these canopy dominants are Bitternut hickory (*Carya cordiformis*) and Northern red oak (*Quercus rubra*), followed by a long string of others. Elsewhere, the dominance used to shift toward toward Sweet gum (*Liquidambar styraciflua*) and a variety of oaks, but those distinctive habitats have been degraded by urbanization and agriculture.

On the brighter side, a certain amount of research on post-agricultural succession in the Piedmont provides more than helpful direction for natural landscaping enthusiasts in southeastern Pennsylvania. A system dominated by Virginia pine (*Pinus virginiana*) evolves on these sand to silt loams when farmland goes fallow and also arises from cleared or burned over areas. And it's rich with options to give gardeners a substantial palette from which to create impressive designs, considering the breadth of species suitable for specific habitats in the region.

Many of these are similar to the serpentine-barrens systems, also found in the region, and discussed separately. Good choices to start with include:

Trees and shrubs
Allegheny blackberry (*Rubus allegheniensis*)
Black gum (*Nyssa sylvatica*)
Black huckleberry (*Gaylussacia baccata*)
Black oak (*Quercus velutina*)
Blue ridge blueberry (*Vaccinium pallidum*)
Chestnut oak (*Quercus prinus*)
Eastern white pine (*Pinus strobus*)
Hickory (*Carya spp.*)
Mountain laurel (*Kalmia latifolia*)
Pitch pine (*Pinus rigida*)
Red maple (*Acer rubrum*)
Red oak (*Quercus rubra*)
Red pine (*Pinus resinosa*)
Red cedar (*Juniperus virginiana*)
Sassafras (*Sassafras albidum*)
Scarlet oak (*Quercus coccinea*)
Shining sumac (*Rhus copallina*)
Short-leaf pine (*Pinus echinata*)
Sweet birch (*Betula lenta*)
Table-mountain pine (*Pinus pungens*)
Trailing arbutus (*Epigaea repens*)
Upland highbush blueberry (*Vaccinium stamineum*)
Virginia creeper (*Parthenocissus quinquefolia*)
Virginia pine (*Pinus virginiana*)
White ash (*Fraxinus americana*)
White oak (*Quercus alba*)
Wild indigo (*Baptisia tinctoria*)
Wild black cherry (*Prunus serotina*)
Wintergreen (*Gaultheria procumbens*)

Herbaceous and vines
Cleavers (*Galium spp.*)
Common goldstar (*Hypoxis hirsuta*)
Cypress panic grass (*Dichanthelium dicho-*

tomum)
Eastern prickly pear cactus (*Opuntia humifusa*)
Flowering spurge (*Euphorbia corollata*)
Greenbrier (*Smilax spp.*)
Little bluestem (*Schizachyrium scoparium*)
Northern bracken fern (*Pteridium aquilinum*)
Plantain pussytoes (*Antennaria plantaginifolia*)
Poison-ivy (*Toxicodendron radicans*)
Poverty oat grass (*Danthonia spicata*)
Queen devil (*Hieracium gronovii*)
Rattlesnake weed (*Hieracium venosum*)
Stout goldenrod (*Solidago squarrosa*)
Striped prince's pine (*Chimaphila maculata*)
Tick-trefoil (*Desmodium spp.*)
Two-flower dwarf dandelion (*Krigia biflora*)
Violet lespedeza (*Lespedeza violacea*)
Virginia tephrosia (*Tephrosia virginiana*)
White-tinged sedge (*Carex albicans var. albicans*)
Wild sarsaparilla (*Aralia nudicaulis*)

Urban wetland

In a five to six mile wide strip along the Delaware estuary, a palustrine system is marked by vernal pools and wetlands to the southeast and somewhat more varied habitats to the northwest. Urbanization has eliminated much of the natural vegetation outside the Delhaas and Five Mile Woods Preserves. Sweet gum (*Liquidambar styraciflua*) would be the canopy dominant. The area is seasonally flooded by perched groundwater in early spring, but dry by late summer and soils would be acidic sandy or clay loams. Good choices for this unique habitat are:

Trees and shrubs
American holly (*Ilex opaca*)
Black gum (*Nyssa sylvatica*)
Common winterberry (*Ilex verticillata*)
Highbush blueberry (*Vaccinium corymbosum*)
Northern spicebush (*Lindera benzoin*)
Partridgeberry (*Mitchella repens*)
Pin oak (*Quercus palustris*)
Pinxterflower (*Rhododendron periclymenoides*)
Red maple (*Acer rubrum*)
River birch (*Betula nigra*)
Sassafras (*Sassafras albidum*)
Southern arrowwood (*Viburnum dentatum*)
Southern red oak (*Quercus falcata*)
Swamp azalea (*Rhododendron viscosum*)
Swamp chestnut oak (*Quercus michauxii*)
Swamp dewberry (*Rubus hispidus*)
Swamp doghobble (*Leucothoe racemosa*)
Swamp white oak (*Quercus bicolor*)
Sweet gum (*Liquidambar styraciflua*)
Sweet pepperbush (*Clethra alnifolia*)
Sweetbay (*Magnolia virginiana*)
Sweetgum (*Liquidambar styraciflua*)
Willow oak (*Quercus phellos*)

Herbaceous species and vines
Bellwort (*Uvularia sessilifolia*)
Blunt broom sedge (*Carex tribuloides*)
Canada mayflower (*Maianthemum canadense*)
Catbrier (*Smilax glauca*)
Cinnamon fern (*Osmunda cinnamomea*)
Clearweed (*Pilea pumila*)
Common rush (*Juncus effusus*)
False nettle (*Boehmeria cylindrica*)
Fetterbush (*Leucothoe racemosa*)
Greater bladder sedge (*Carex intumescens*)
Greenwhite sedge (*Carex albolutescens*)
Jewelweed (*Impatiens capensis*)
Knotweed (*Polygonum spp.*)
Long's sedge (*Carex longii*)
Netted chain fern (*Woodwardia areolata*)
New York fern (*Thelypteris noveboracensis*)
Poison-ivy (*Toxicodendron radicans*)
Roundleaf greenbrier (*Smilax rotundifolia*)
Royal fern (*Osmunda regalis*)
Sensitive fern (*Onoclea sensibilis*)
Slender woodoats (*Chasmanthium laxum*)
White edge sedge (*Carex debilis var. debilis*)
Woolgrass (*Scirpus cyperinus*)

Serpentine Barrens

Appearing in Chester, Lancaster and Delaware counties, the distinctive "Serpentine Barrens" are actually a range of habitats that blur into one another as local environments shift.

While the list of plants that can handle the unique soils is extensive, the region illustrates one of the dilemmas of native plant landscaping. To remain a pure habitat, soils must remain thin, gravelly, with very few trees — especially pitch pine — and periodically be cleaned out by fire.

Research on the history of fires, charcoal excavation and field observations support the theory of barrens preservation through fire, and both historical accounts and aerial photos demonstrate how rock outcrops plus gravelly, very thin soil has declined. The result is that both woody and herbaceous species invade from the margins to provide shade, cut surface temperatures, add organic matter that leads to soil development and boosts moisture retention. The result is a more temperate environment — still sustainable, but in a different way.

Natural succession hinges on the invasion of Virginia pine *(Pinus virginiana)*, the shade it creates, the evolution of organic matter in soils and transition to more conventional forests. For gardeners, these species — all fine for the region — yield a much broader landscaping palette. The resulting designs meet all the criteria for sustainability and environmental responsibility, but the *original* habitat and its special character fade away, to the dismay of ecologists.

With such disturbance factors as fire and livestock grazing, there's little chance for soil "improvement" — but a genuine opportunity for preservation of unique and somewhat endangered habitats that support a specialized set of plant life. When disturbance is suppressed, the habitats shifts to species that, long term, modify the surface soil to conditions that most would define as satisfactory and conventional. Some say livestock grazing helps and close management of succession in backyard habitats will suffice, but fire remains the best means to preservation and, obviously, the least desired in a suburban setting.

Serpentine outcrops

Serpentine outcrops are found in scattered sites from Quebec south into Alabama, and where they appear present soils that have very low levels of nitrogen, phosphorus, potassium and calcium. To counter this, most gardeners reach for plentiful quantities of conventional fertilizers, the consequence of which is to lose sustainability and risk stream pollution in stormwater runoff. Serpentine soils do, however, have high levels of nickel, chromium and cobalt, as well as high magnesium to calcium ratios.

The outcrops are evidence of what happens when parts of the Earth's crust covered by oceans collide with neighboring tectonic plates and are altered by both water and heat. *Mafic* and *ultramafic* rock, rich in magnesium and iron was formed 490 million years ago from shield volcanos, very much like those found in Hawaii. Everything was fine for 40 million years until the oceanic plate to the east was pushed under the new landmass. A combination of heat, pressure and water deformed the igneous rock, now metamorphic, and laid it up as *serpentinite* outcrops on the continental crust.

Soils of the barrens

Silt loams characteristic of serpentine areas are primarily the Chrome series, but also Aldino, Calvert and Conowingo, which are deeper.

Chrome soils — from weathered serpentine, occur on level to steep convex hillslopes, dry to mesic and well drained with a pH of 6.7, and because of the physical and chemical properties create a prairie-like barrens or pine-savannah.

Aldino soils — from wind-deposited sediments and weathered serpentine, on gentle hillslopes, mesic to moist and moderately to somewhat poorly drained, with a pH of 5.8, and often used for agricultural or residential use.

Conowingo soils — from weathered rock, often serpentine, high in magnesium, on level to sloping, well-dissected uplands of the northern Piedmont Plateau, mesic to moist, moderately well to somewhat poorly drained, with a pH of 5.6.

Calvert soils — from silty material such as alluvium over serpentine residuum, in valley flats and depressions, usually near drainage heads mesic to moist and poorly drained with a pH of 5.2, and very limited range in Delaware County.

Habitat types

Gravel forb communities

Gravel forb communities are found only where very thin soil or gravel lies over serpentine bedrock, mostly on summits and upper slopes and facing south. Soils can be as little as an inch deep. Because they are in full sun, daytime surface temperatures can be high and conditions can often be extremely dry.

Forbs dominate, notably lyre-leaved rock-cress (*Arabis lyrata*), whorled milkweed (*Asclepius verticillata*), serpentine aster (*Symphyotrichum depauperatum*), barrens chickweed (*Cerastium arvense*), moss pink (*Phlox subulata*) and quill fameflower (Phemeranthus teretifolius) are good first choices, but by no means the full extent of the list. With full sun, xeric conditions, and lots of stone, these hold the potential for exceptional rock or alpine gardens.

Appropriate plant species include:

Annual fimbry (*Fimbristylis annua*)
Annulus panic-grass (*Panicum annulum*)
Arrow-feather (*Aristida purpurascens*)
Arrow-leaved violet (*Viola sagittata*)
Barrens chick-weed (*Cerastium arvense var. villosissimum*)
Big bluestem (*Andropogon gerardii*)
Churchmouse three-awn (*Aristida dichotoma*)
Cypress panicgrass (*Panicum dichotomum*)
Few-flowered nutrush (*Scleria pauciflora*)
Gray goldenrod (*Solidago nemoralis*)
Green milkweed. (*Asclepias viridiflora*)
Heller's rosette grass (*Panicum oligosanthes*)
Indian grass (*Sorghastrum nutans*)
Little bluestem (*Schizachyrium scoparium*)
Lyre-leaved rock-cress (*Arabis lyrata*)
Moss-pink (*Phlox subulata ssp. subulata*)
Muhly (*Muhlenbergia mexicana*)
Old-field cinquefoil (*Potentilla canadensis*)
One-sided rush (*Juncus secundus*)
Oundseed panicgrass (*Panicum sphaerocarpon*)
Perennial foxtail (*Setaria geniculata*)
Plain ragwort (*Senecio anonymus*)
Plantain pussytoes (*Antennaria plantaginifolia*)
Poverty grass (*Sporobolus vaginiflorus*)
Prairie dropseed (*Sporobolus heterolepis*)
Prairie rose (*Rosa carolina*)
Prairie senna (*Chamaecrista fasciculata*)
Purple love-grass (*Eragrostis spectabilis*)
Rock sandwort (*Minuartia michauxii*)
Round-leaved fame-flower (*Talinum teretifolium*)
Serpentine aster (*Aster depauperatus*)
Side-oats gramma (*Bouteloua curtipendula*)
Slender knotweed (*Polygonum tenue*)
Slimspike three-awn (*Aristida longispica*)
Small white snakeroot (*Eupatorium aromaticum*)
Sundrops (*Oenothera fruticosa*)
Western panicgrass (*Panicum acuminatum*)
Whorled milkweed (*Asclepias verticillata*)
Whorled milkwort (*Polygala verticillata*)
Yarrow (*Achillea millefolium*)

Grasslands

Serpentine grasslands can be divided into two types: mid to upper slopes rarely facing east and lower to mid slopes commonly facing north.

The first, dominated by Little bluestem (*Schiz-*

achyrium scoparium and Prairie dropseed (*Sporobolus heterolepis*), are most often on slopes between 3 and 6 degrees with very shallow, dry gravelly sands or silt loams. They can sometimes be found on midslopes with 6 to 16-degree slopes, but sites will often include bedrock or bare ground.

The second, dominated by Little bluestem and Indiangrass (*Sorghastrum nutans*), is on shallow silt or clay loams, often less than an inch thick.

Landscapes in either direction should include some Eastern red cedar (*Juniperus virginiana*), Small's ragwort (*Packera anonyma*) and Serpentine aster (*Symphyotrichum depauperatum*). To varying degrees, shining sumac (*Rhus copallina*), smooth sumac (*Rhus glabra*) and black huckleberry (*Gaylussacia baccata*), as well as Big bluestem (*Andropogon gerardii*) are appropriate to round out the landscape.

Authentic touches for the drier habitats would include Lyrate rockcress (*Arabis lyrata*), Field chickweed (*Cerastium arvnense*), roundseed panicgrass (*Dichanthelium sphaerocarpon*), fewflower nutrush (*Scleria pauciflora*) and gray goldenrod (*Solidago nemoralis*).

Lower slope habitats, being a bit more moist, have a wider range of species. Good choices to consider are Common yarrow (*Achillea millefolium*), Lesser snakeroot (*Ageratina aromatica*), Green comet milkweed (*Asclepias viridiflora*), Wavy hairgrass (*Danthonia spicata*), Tufted hairgrass (*Deschampsia cespitosa*), Narrow leaf evening primrose (*Oenothera fruticosa ssp. glauca*), Switch grass (*Panicum virgatum*), Common cinquefoil (*Potentilla simplex*), Marsh bristle grass (*Setaria parviflora*), White heath aster (*Symphyotrichum ericoides*), Calico aster (*Symphyotrichum lateriflorum*), and New York ironweed (*Vernonia noveboracensis*).

Shrublands

As areas evolve with increasing amounts of organic matter and depth of soil, grasslands grade into shrublands that feature an increasing amount of small trees. Although still very much a dense, prairie-like habitat are red cedar (*Juniperus virginiana*), pitch pine (*Pinus rigida*), Virginia pine (*Pinus virginina*) and black locust (*Robinia pseudoacacia*) st up shop, soon to be followed by blackjack oak (*Quercus marilandica*) and post oak (*Quercus stellata*) with some sassafras (*Sassafras albidum*).

On less attractive sites, trees may be sparse. As their numbers approach 25 percent cover, the shrubland degrades into a woodland.

In the meantime, shrub choices for authentic landscapes should include shining sumac (*Rhus copallina*), chinquapin oak (*Quercus prinoides*), smooth sumac (*Rhus glabra*) and black huckleberry (*Gaylussacia baccata*). Most of the grasses and forbs from open sites are just fine, and a good working list for design includes:

    Annual fimbry (*Fimbristylis annua*)
    Arrow-feather (*Aristida purpurascens*)
    Arrowleaf violet (*Viola sagittata*)
    Barrens chickweed (*Cerastium arvense var. uillosissimum*)
    Churchmouse three-awn (*Aristida dichotoma*)
    Creeping phlox (*Phlox subulata ssp. subulata*)
    Early saxifrage (*Saxifraga virginiensis*)
    Few-flowered nut-rush (*Scleria pauciflora*)
    Field chickweed (*Cerastium arvense*)
    Gray goldenrod (*Solidago nemoralis*)
    Green comet milkweed (*Asclepias viridiflora*)
    Heller's rosette grass (*Dichanthelium oligosanthes*)
    Indian grass (*Sorghastrum nutans*)
    Knotroot fox-tail (*Setaria geniculata*)
    Little bluestem (*Schizachyrium scoparium*)
    Lopsided rush (*Juncus secundus*)
    Lyrate rockcress (*Arabis lyrata*)
    Needletip blue-eyed grass (*Sisyrinchium mucronatum*)
    Old-field cinquefoil (*Potentilla canadensis*)
    Palespike lobelia (*Lobelia spicata*)
    Philadelphia panicgrass (*Panicum philadelphicum*)
    Plain ragwort (*Senecio anonymus*)
    Plantain pussytoe (*Antennaria plantaginifolia*)
    Pleatleaf knotweed (*Polygonum tenue*)

Poverty grass (*Sporobolus vaginiflorus*)
Panic-grass (*Panicum depauperatum*)
Prairie dropseed (*Sporobolus heterolepis*)
Purple lovegrass (*Eragrostis spectabilis*)
Quill fameflower (*Talinum teretifolium*)
Roundseed panicgrass (*Dichanthelium sphaerocarpon*)
Satin grass (*Muhlenbergia mexicana*)
Serpentine aster (*Symphyotrichum depauperatum*)
Side-oats gramma (*Bouteloua curtipendula*)
Slimleaf panicgrass (*Dichanthelium linearifolium*)
Slimspike three-awn (*Aristida longispica*)
Small white snakeroot (*Eupatorium aromaticum*)
Smooth sumac (*Rhus glabra*)
Starved panicgrass (*Dichanthelium depauperatum*)
Sundrops (*Oenothera fruticosa*)
Virginia pine (*Pinus virginiana*)
Whitehair rosette grass (*Dichanthelium villosissimum*)
Whorled milkweed (*Asclepias verticillata*)
Whorled milkwort (*Polygala verticillata*)
Yarrow (*Achillea millefolium*)

Forests and woodlands

Further downslope, where soils are deeper, habitats support energetic woodland and forest communities, with slope aspect an important factor in planning a landscape.

Forested areas are dominated by pitch pine *(Pinus rigida)* and Virginia pine *(Pinus virginiana)*, most often with blackjack oak *(Quercus marilandica)* and Post oak *(Quercus stellata)* with a greenbrier *(Smilax spp.)* understory.

Pitch pine - oak forests are found on higher positions of slopes and interfluves, facing south. Soils are silt loams, more than a foot deep, dry to mesic at higher elevations and mesic to moist at lower sites.

Virginia pine - oak forests more often face north, rarely east. At higher elevations, dry gravelly sands and silt loams are typically thin, excessively well drained and commonly with exposed bedrock or bare ground. On mid to lower slopes, soils are mesic to moist silt loams and clay loams more than 20 inches deep, but can be as little as an inch in spots.

Species suitable for either type of forest include:
Black cherry (*Prunus serotina*)
Black gum (*Nyssa sylvatica*)
Black huckleberry (*Gaylussacia baccata*)
Black locust (*Robinia pseudoacacia*)
Blackjack oak (*Quercus marilandica*)
Bracken fern (*Pteridium aquilinum*)
Chinquapin oak (*Quercus prinoides*)
Deerberry (*Vaccinium stamineum*)
Eastern red cedar (*Juniperus virginiana*)
Lowbush blueberry (*Vaccinium pallidum*)
Post oak (*Quercus stellata*)
Red maple (*Acer rubrum*)
Sassafras (*Sassafras albidum*)
Scrub oak (*Quercus ilicifolia*)
Virginia pine (*Pinus virginiana*)
Wild sarsaparilla (*Aralia nudicaulis*)
Distinct to Pitch pine – Oak Forests are:
Allegheny blackberry (*Rubus allegheniensis*)
Black oak (*Quercus velutina*)
Blue sedge (*Carex glaucodea*)
Cat greenbrier (*Smilax glauca*)
Large toothed aspen (*Populus grandidentata*)
Northern bayberry (*Morella pensylvanica*)
Northern spicebush (*Lindera benzoin*)
Pitch pine (*Pinus rigida*)
Poverty oat grass (*Danthonia spicata*)
Red oak (*Quercus rubra*)
Roundleaf greenbrier (*Smilax rotundifolia*)
Southern arrowwood (*Viburnum recognitum*)
Southern red oak (*Quercus falcata*)
White oak (*Quercus alba*)
Winged sumac (*Rhus copallinum*)
Unique to Virginia pine – Oak forests are:
Calico aster (*Symphyotrichum lateriflorum*)
Catbrier (*Smilax glauca*)
Common cinquefoil (*Potentilla simplex*)
Common yarrow (*Achillea millefolium*)
Evening primrose (*Oenothera fruticosa*)
Fewflower nutrush (*Scleria pauciflora*)

Field chickweed (*Cerastium arvense*)
Gray goldenrod (*Solidago nemoralis*)
Green comet milkweed (*Asclepias viridiflora*)
Greenbrier (*Smilax rotundifolia*)
Indian grass (*Sorghastrum nutans*)
Lesser snakeroot (*Ageratina aromatica*)
Little bluestem (*Schizachyrium scoparium*)
Lyrate rockcress (*Arabis lyrata*)
Marsh bristle grass (*Setaria parviflora*)
New York ironweed (*Vernonia noveboracensis*)
Prairie dropseed (*Sporobolus heterolepis*)
Roundseed panicgrass (*Dichanthelium sphaerocarpon*)
Serpentine aster (*Symphyotrichum depauperatum*)
Small's ragwort (*Packera anonyma*)
Switch grass (*Panicum virgatum*)
Tufted hairgrass (*Deschampsia cespitosa*)
Wavy hairgrass (*Danthonia spicata*)
White heath aster (*Symphyotrichum ericoides*)

Seepage wetlands

A distinctive form of wetland appears in serpentine areas at the bases of gentle slopes and adjacent to streams where groundwater saturates the surface for most of the growing season. These are saturated clay loams and muck, derived from the underlying serpentine bedrock and can be fifteen feet or more thick. Groundwater is rich in magnesium and iron, and the habitats are almost entirely grasses. Woody vegetation is limited to occasional trees around the edges, such as red maple *(Acer rubrum)* and hazel alder *(Alnus serrulata)*.

Common plant species include tufted hairgrass (*Deschampsia cespitosa*), rice cutgrass (*Leersia oryzoides*), slender spike-rush (*Eleocharis tenuis*) and deer-tongue grass (*Dichanthelium clandestinum*). Popular favorites are found here, too, including stands of Indian grass (*Sorghastrum nutans*), false foxglove (*Agalinis purpurea*), New York ironweed (*Vernonia noveboracensis*) and spotted joe-pye weed *(Eupatorium perfoliatum)*. Other good choices for this unique habitat would be barrens chickweed *(Cerastium arvense var. uillosissimum)*, satin grass *(Muhlenbergia mexicana)*, false nutsedge *(Cyperus strigosus)*, swamp thistle *(Cirsium muticum)*, native smartweeds *(Polygonum spp.)*, whip-grass (Scleria trigomerata), bugleweed *(Lycopus uniflorus)*, poverty rush *(Juncus tenuis)* and American burnet (Sanguisorba canadensis).

Starter List for Serpentine Soils
Trees
Black cherry (*Prunus serotina*)
Black locust (*Robinia pseudoacacia*)
Black oak (*Quercus velutina*)
Black gum (*Nyssa sylvatica*)
Blackjack oak (*Quercus marilandica*)
Chinquapin oak (*Quercus prinoides*)
Eastern red cedar (*Juniperus virginiana*)
Large-toothed aspen (*Populus grandidentata*)
Pitch pine (*Pinus rigida*)
Post oak *(Quercus stellata)*
Red cedar (*Juniperus virginiana*)
Red maple *(Acer rubrum)*
Red oak *(Quercus rubra)*
Sassafras *(Sassafras albidum)*
Scrub oak *(Quercus ilicifolia)*
Shining sumac *(Rhus copallina)*
Smooth sumac *(Rhus glabra)*
Southern red oak *(Quercus falcata)*
Virginia pine *(Pinus virginiana)*
White oak *(Quercus alba)*
Winged sumac *(Rhus copallinum)*

Shrubs
Allegheny blackberry (*Rubus alleghemensis*)
Black huckleberry (*Gaylussacia baccata*)
Blue ridge blueberry (*Vaccinium pallidum*)
Deerberry (*Vaccinium stamineum*)
Northern bayberry (*Morella pensylvanica*)
Northern spicebush (*Lindera benzoin*)
Prairie rose (*Rosa carolina*)
Southern arrowwood (*Viburnum recognitum*)
Wild sarsaparilla (*Aralia nudicaulis*)

Forbs
Annual fimbry (*Fimbristylis annua*)

Arrow-feather (*Aristida purpurascens*)
Arrowleaf violet (*Viola sagittata*)
Calico aster (*Symphyotrichum lateriflorum*)
Cat greenbrier (*Smilax glauca*)
Common cinquefoil (*Potentilla simplex*)
Common yarrow (*Achillea millefolium*)
Creeping phlox (*Phlox subulata ssp. subulata*)
Early saxifrage (*Saxifraga virginiensis*)
Field chickweed (*Cerastium arvense*)
Gray goldenrod (*Solidago nemoralis*)
Green milkweed (*Asclepias viridiflora*)
Greenbrier (*Smilax rotundifolia*)
Lesser snakeroot (*Ageratina aromatica*)
Lyrate rockcress (*Arabis lyrata*)
Moss-pink (*Phlox subulata ssp. subulata*)
Narrow leaf evening primrose (*Oenothera fruticosa ssp. glauca*)
New York ironweed (*Vernonia noveboracensis*)
Old-field cinquefoil (*Potentilla canadensis*)
Palespike lobelia (*Lobelia spicata*)
Plain ragwort (*Senecio anonymus*)
Plantain pussytoes (*Antennaria plantaginifolia*)
Pleatleaf knotweed (*Polygonum tenue*)
Prairie senna (*Chamaecrista fasciculata*)
Quill fameflower (*Talinum teretifolium*)
Rock sandwort (*Minuartia michauxii*)
Roundleaf greenbrier (*Smilax rotundifolia*)
Serpentine aster (*Symphyotrichum depauperatum*)
Small white snakeroot (*Eupatorium aromaticum*)
Small's ragwort (*Packera anonyma*)
Sundrops (*Oenothera fruticosa*)
White heath aster (*Symphyotrichum ericoides*)
Whorled milkweed (*Asclepias verticillata*)
Whorled milkwort (*Polygala verticillata*)
Yarrow (*Achillea millefolium*)

Grasses and Sedges

Annulus panic-grass (*Panicum annulum*)
Big bluestem (*Andropogon gerardii*)
Blue sedge (*Carex glaucodea*)
Churchmouse three-awn (*Aristida dichotoma*)
Cypress panicgrass (*Dichanthelium dichotomum*)
Deertongue (*Dichanthelium clandestinum*)
Fewflower nutrush (*Scleria pauciflora*)
Heller's rosette grass (*Dichanthelium oligosanthes*)
Indian grass (*Sorghastrum nutans*)
Knotroot fox-tail (*Setaria geniculata*)
Little bluestem (*Schizachyrium scoparium*)
Lopsided rush (*Juncus secundus*)
Marsh bristle grass (*Setaria parviflora*)
Satin grass (*Muhlenbergia mexicana*)
Needletip blue-eyed grass (*Sisyrinchium mucronatum*)
One-sided rush (*Juncus secundus*)
Oundseed panicgrass (*Panicum sphaerocarpon*)
Perennial foxtail (*Setaria geniculata*)
Philadelphia panicgrass (*Panicum philadelphicum*)
Poverty grass (*Sporobolus vaginiflorus*)
Poverty oat grass (*Danthonia spicata*)
Poverty panic-grass (*Panicum depauperatum*)
Poverty rush (*Juncus tenuis*)
Prairie dropseed (*Sporobolus heterolepis*)
Purple love-grass (*Eragrostis spectabilis*)
Rice cutgrass (*Leersia oryzoides*)
Roundseed panicgrass (*Dichanthelium sphaerocarpon*)
Side-oats gramma (*Bouteloua curtipendula*)
Slimleaf panicgrass (*Dichanthelium linearifolium*)
Slimspike three-awn (*Aristida longispica*)
Starved panicgrass (*Dichanthelium depauperatum*)
Switch grass (*Panicum virgatum*)
Tufted hairgrass (*Deschampsia cespitosa*)
Wavy hairgrass (*Danthonia spicata*)
Western panicgrass (*Panicum acuminatum*)
Whitehair rosette grass (*Dichanthelium villosissimum*)

Ferns

Bracken fern (*Pteridium aquilinum*)
Christmas fern (*Polystichum acrostichoides*)

ERIE-ONTARIO LAKE PLAIN

Like the Atlantic Coastal Plain at the diagonally opposite end of the state, this ecoregion is a thin band just a few miles wide but with several distinct land features that create unusual habitats.

Chief among them are very steep and actively eroding bluffs. In stream gorges, groundwater seepages develop just where glacial and glacial-lacustrine deposits encounter underlying eroded sandstone and shale. Along the Lake Erie shore itself, the bluffs are found on the margins of dense, restrictive till and beach deposits of sand and gravel. Bluff communities tend to be open, dominated by a blend of shrubs and herbaceous plants, with some trees. They are always in an active state of succession.

Also found in the lake plain are unique palustrine forests formed around vernal ponds scattered across flat topography, often with hummock and hollow microtopography. Here the water table lingers near the surface for most of the year, providing a good habitat for communities dominated by American elm (*Ulmus americana*), Red ash (*Fraxinus pennsylvanica*), pumpkin ash (*Fraxinus profunda*), and silver maple (*Acer saccharinum*). Less frequent are black gum (*Nyssa sylvatica*), cottonwood (*Populus deltoides*), American basswood (*Tilia americana*), red maple (*Acer rubrum*), and yellow birch (*Betulia alleghaniensis*). Northern spicebush (*Lindera benzoin*) is a dominant shrub, and a variety of sedges and ferns fill out the field.

Distinct grasslands occur in the proximity of the lake shore. Where winter ice scour and wave action impact the sandy to gravelly shoreline, American beachgrass (*Ammophila breviligulata*), sea-rocket (*Cakile edentula*), Canada wild-rye (*Elymus canadensis*), cocklebur (*Xanthium stumarium*) and silverweed (*Potentilla anserina*) tend to dominate the landscape and would be sound choices for the garden. At a safer distance from the beach, the immense sand deposits are more likely covered with Indian grass (*Sorghastrum nutans*), little bluestem (*Schizachyrium scoparium*), and switch grass (*Panicum virgatum*). Other species to consider include Muhlenberg's sedge (*Carex muhlenbergii*) and parachute sedge (Carex tonsa). Shrub and tree cover tends to be less than 25 percent.

On dunes, the regional grasses are joined by bayberry (*Myrica pensylvanica*) and cottonwoods (*Populus deltoides*).

Because the entire zone is adjacent to the northwestern glaciated Allegheny Plateau, most of the plain's succession leads toward species and habitats found next door.

Trees

Alternate-leaved dogwood (*Cornus alternifolia*)
Cottonwood (*Populus deltoides*)
Eastern hemlock (Tsuga canadensis)
Hop-hornbeam (*Ostrya virginiana*)
Hornbeam (*Carpinus caroliniana*)
Red cedar (*Juniperus virginiana*)
Red osier dogwood (*Cornus sericea*)
Red willow (*Cornus amomum*)
Round-leaved dogwood (*Cornus rugosa*)
Speckled alder (*Alnus incana*)
Staghorn sumac (*Rhus typhina*)
Sugar maple (*Acer saccharum*)
Willows (*Salix spp.*)

Shrubs

Shadbush (*Amelanchier arborea*)
Bayberry (*Myrica pensylvanica*)
Bayberry willow (*Salix myricoides*)
Ninebark (*Physocarpus opulifolius*)
Northern spicebush (*Lindera benzoin*)

Prickly wild rose (*Rosa acicularis*)
Purple-flowering raspberry (*Rubus odoratus*)

Grasses and sedges

American beachgrass (*Ammophila breviligulata*)
Bebb's sedge (*Carex bebbii*)
Blackgirdle bulrush (*Scirpus atrocinctus*)
Bluejoint (*Calamagrostis canadensis*)
Broom sedge (*Carex scoparia*)
Bulrush (*Schoenoplectus spp.*)
Fowl mannagrass (*Glyceria striata*)
Golden-fruited sedge (*Carex aureus*)
Little bluestem (*Schizachyrium scoparium*)
Muhlenberg's sedge (*Carex muhlenbergii*)
Panic grass (*Panicum commonsianum*)
Sharp-fruited rush (*Juncus acuminatus*)
Shaved sedge (*Carex tonsa*)
Switchgrass (*Panicum virgatum*)

Forbs, Ferns

Canada goldenrod (*Solidago canadensis*)
Canada wild-rye (*Elymus canadensis*)
Cocklebur (*Xanthium strumarium*)
Common horsetail (*Equisetum arvense*)
Early meadow rue (*Thalictrum dioicum*)
Golden ragwort (*Senecio aureus*)
Grass-of-parnassus (*Parnussia glauca*)
Heart-leaved aster (*Symphiotrichum cordifolium*)
Jack-in-the-pulpit (*Arisaema triphyllum*)
Marginal wood fern (*Dryopteris marginalis*)
Morrow's honeysuckle (*Lonicera morrowii*)
Pale jewelweed (*Impatiens pallida*)
Sea-rocket (*Cakile edentula*)
Seaside spurge (*Chamaesyce polygonifolia*)
Sheep sorrel (*Rumex acetosella*)
Silverweed (*Potentilla anserina*)
Silverweed cinquefoil (*Argentina anserina*)
Southern blue flag (*Iris virginicas*)
Zigzag goldenrod (*Solidago flexicaulis*)

WETLANDS

From an ecological standpoint, the varied landforms we group as wetlands are important and popularly studied. Investigation from almost any perspective reflects that more than half the attention is devoted to these priceless habitats, all of which merit protection, preservation and restoration.

However, very few of us desire to actually live and garden in a wetland. Saturated soils and standing water are not ideal for human use and historically have been forcibly altered to "enhance" the land for agricultural purposes or development. Who wants a marsh when you can have a beach? Who prefers a swamp over a park for youth sports? Who wants that mucky patch of ground when it can be drained, graded and turned into a lawn? And although most of the early communities sprang up along natural transportation routes — rivers and streams — we prefer to construct mammoth levees to keep our collective basements dry.

In an enlightened society, we are happily becoming aware of the function of these complicated and flexible systems and sense the opportunity to *publicly* own them, turn them into preserves and conservation zones, and live in greater harmony with Nature.

Wetlands make difficult backyard landscapes, if only because of the sheer scale and complexity of oftentimes a series of ecosystems that are inter-related and difficult to function out of context. But there's some enormously alluring species of plants that come from wetland communities, and we landscapers delight in pushing the limits of sustainability to add a charmer to our collection.

The overall thrust of our discussion has been *sustainable* landscape design, which implies that we work with plant communities best suited for the xeric to mesic habitats that serve well for residential and commercial development. Those willing to loosen the margins of what's appropriate and develop microhabitats for garden displays are understandably drawn to features that lead to a wetland.

Swamps and marshes come to mind when we picture *wetland*. But these are less common than most habitats that serve the concept. If the presence of an overabundance of water is the standard, then flukes in topography are the general cause and drainage is very often the specific issue.

A popular impression of a *meadow* is a glorious patch of open ground, wall to wall with cheery flowers, probably closer to a moist prairie or savanna, neither of which is natural for Pennsylvania. In fact, a meadow is a wetland, saturated to the point that it's difficult for natural succession to get a foothold and as a consequence a landscape that welcomes native plants dominated by sedges and

> ## *Vernal Pools*
> Found within dry oak forests with open canopies, vernal pools can occur as wetland meadow in shallow depressions that are flooded in spring, most often on saddles between ridges and high plateaus in the Appalachians. They dry out in summer months, permitting herbaceous species to become established in the pool area. Graminoids are the dominants, especially including Northeastern bulrush (*Scirpus ancistrochaetus*). Trees that most often ring the area include White oak (*Quercus alba*), Black gum (*Nyssa sylvatica*) and Red maple (*Acer rubrum*), while common shrubs are Spicebush (*Lindera benzoin*), Winterberry (*Ilex verticillata*) and Swamp dewberry (*Rubus hispidus*). Among the meadow grasses and sedges, Royal fern (*Osmunda regalis*) is a regular.

grasses. Where groundwater is oozing from a calcareous hillside, it becomes a fen; where groundwater emerges from acidic rock such as sandstone and shale, it becomes a seep. And these are mucky *all* the time.

In broad upland areas where a layer of very hard material is near the surface to block drainage, depressions feature soils that have water at or just below the surface for much of the year, typically flooding or ponding in the spring and very slowly drying out later in the season with routine evaporation. In woodlands and forests, similar situations create palustrine zones where standing water can linger for a very long time. Bogs — highly acidic, very limited in plant variety, and often very cold — are the results of glacial scars, and may over long periods of time degrade into depressions.

What we often regard as a wetland — the sites on valley floors known as *riparian* zones and the resulting *floodplain* remain wet only because large volumes of water are passing through rather than stalled or standing still. And whereas many wetlands tend to start wet and finish dry over the course of a growing season, floodplains have the potential of altering moisture levels at any time, depending on precipitation.

The potential for landscaping should be obvious when it comes to developing plant palettes for artificial features such as rain gardens and backyard ponds and streams. Some species are genetically designed for the wet-spring, dry-autumn cycle, and flooding at other times may not be tolerated. They may well be equipped for soils that are poorly drained, which runs counter to the rain garden goal of drying out within 72 hours to avoid mosquitos.

On the other hand, if there's a naturally-occurring wet patch in a corner of the landscape, the ground that never seems to dry out (precluding that lovely lawn scheme), is mucky and ponds up after a rain, well, there's hope. A wide range of species will be more than pleased to help us create a distinctive garden to enjoy.

By their very nature, floodplains tend to be better models for rain gardens, discussed later, but some of the features of a good riparian zone can widen the landscape design potential. Most of Pennsylvania's rivers and streams are stony to bouldery — think rock gardens — or have wide, sandy, and attractively organized plant collections on the margins. In energetic landscapes really pushing the limits of sustainability to create lush habitats, the *backswamp* features, wooded and open, of riparian zones should attract attention.

Let's have a look at possibilities in detail.

Meadows

Most often on alluvial bottomlands statewide, meadows are dominated by grasses and sedges with some habitat-suitable shrubs. The common soil traits are muck over mineral soils and they are subjected to spring flooding but dry by mid to late summer. Flooding is the cause of the open nature of the habitat.

Soils are alluvium from acidic sandstones and shales, but includes poorly-drained clay, clay loam, muck, sandy clay, sandy loam or silty clay and vegetated surfaces are commonly leaf litter, downed wood and standing water. In nature, the precise combination of trees and shrubs depends a great deal on the nature of seasonal flooding and general moisture of the soil. Intense and longer flooding scours the surface of tree seedlings, while more gentle and drier conditions allow species increasingly intolerant of anaerobic conditions to become established.

Trees
  Black gum (*Nyssa sylvatica*)
  Black locust (*Robinia pseudoacacia*)
  Black willow (*Salix nigra*)
  Bog willow (*Salix pedicellaris*)
  Gray alder (*Alnus incana*)
  Gray dogwood (*Cornus racemosa*)
  Green ash (*Fraxinus pennsylvanica*)
  Hazel alder (*Alnus serrulata*)
  Red maple (*Acer rubrum*)
  Red-osier dogwood (*Cornus sericea*)
  Silky dogwood (*Cornus amomum*)
  Swamp dogwood (*Cornus racemosa*)
  White oak (*Quercus alba*)
  Willows (*Salix spp.*)

Shrubs
  Allegheny blackberry (*Rubus allegheniensis*)

Bristly dewberry (*Rubus hispidus*)
Buttonbush (*Cephalanthus occidentalis*)
Highbush blueberry (*Vaccinium corymbosum*)
Leatherleaf (*Chamaedaphne calyculata*)
Meadowsweet (*Spiraea alba*)
Northern arrow-wood (*Viburnum recognitum*)
Southern arrow-wood (*Viburnum dentatum*)
Spicebush (*Lindera benzoin*)
Steeplebush (*Spiraea tomentosa*)
Swamp dewberry (*Rubus hispidus*)
Sweet gale (*Myrica gale*)
White meadowsweet (*Spiraea alba*)
Winterberry (*Ilex verticillata*)

Grasses, Sedges, Rushes

American mannagrass (*Glyceria grandis*)
Awlfruit sedge (*Carex stipata*)
Bailey's sedge (*Carex baileyi*)
Black bulrush (*Scirpus atrovirens*)
Blister sedge (*Carex vesicaria*)
Blunt broom sedge (*Carex tribuloides*)
Broadleaf cattail (*Typha latifolia*)
Broom sedge (*Carex scoparia*)
Bulrush (*Scirpus spp.*)
Bur reed (*Sparganium spp.*)
Canada bluejoint (*Calamagrostis canadensis*)
Canada rush (*Juncus canadensis*)
Common cattail (*Typha latifolia*)
Common rush (*Juncus effusus*)
Corkscrew rush (*Juncus effusus*)
Crested sedge (*Carex cristatella*)
Deertongue (*Dichanthelium clandestinum*)
False hop sedge (*Carex lupuliformis*)
Fowl bluegrass (*Poa palustris*)
Fox sedge (*Carex vulpinoidea*)
Greater bladder sedge (*Carex intumescens*)
Hairgrass (*Agrostis scabra*)
Hairy fruit sedge (*Carex trichocarpa*)
Hairy sedge (*Carex lacustris*)
Hop sedge (*Carex lupulina*)
Longhair sedge (*Carex comosa*)
Mannagrass (*Glyceria acutiflora*)
Needle spike-rush (*Eleocharis acicularis*)
Nodding Sedge (*Carex gynandra*)
Northeastern bulrush (*Scirpus ancistrochaetus*)
Northern long sedge (*Carex folliculata*)
Northwest territory sedge (*Carex utriculata*)
Owl-fruit sedge (*Carex stipata*)
Pale meadowgrass (*Torreyochloa pallida*)
Prickly bog sedge (*Carex atlantica*)
Rattlesnake mannagrass (*Glyceria canadensis*)
Reed canary grass (*Phalaris arundinacea*)
Rice cutgrass (*Leersia oryzoides*)
Rufous bulrush (*Scirpus pendulus*)
Rushes (*Juncus spp.*)
Shallow sedge (*Carex lurida*)
Silvery sedge (*Carex canescens*)
Soft rush (*Juncus effusus*)
Spike-rushes (*Eleocharis spp.*)
Three-way sedge (*Dulichium arundinaceum*)
Trumpet weed (*Eupatoriadelphus fistulosus*)
Tussock sedge (*Carex stricta*)
Upright sedge (*Carex stricta*)
White beak-rush (*Rhynchospora alba*)
Whitegrass (*Leersia virginica*)
Woodland bulrush (*Scirpus expansus*)
Woolgrass (*Scirpus cyperinus*)

Forbs

American water horehound (*Lycopus americanus*)
Arrowhead (*Sagittaria rigida*)
Arrowleaf tearthumb (*Polygonum sagittatum*)
Beggar-ticks (*Bidens spp.*)
Blunt leaf bedstraw (*Galium obtusum*)
Boneset (*Eupatorium perfoliatum*)
Broadleaf arrowhead (*Sagittaria latifolia*)
Bugleweed (*Lycopus uniflorus*)
Calamus (*Acorus calamus*)
Canada goldenrod (*Solidago canadensis*)
Canadian St. John's-wort (*Hypericum canadense*)
Common boneset (*Eupatorium perfoliatum*)
Dotted smartweed (*Persicaria punctata*)
Dwarf St. John's-wort (*Hypericum mutilum*)
Earth loosestrife (*Lysimachia terrestris*)
Fraser's marsh St. John's-wort (*Triadenum fraseri*)

Giant goldenrod (*Solidago gigantea*)
Goldenrods (*Solidago spp.*)
Great blue lobelia (*Lobelia siphilitica*)
Harlequin blue flag (*Iris versicolor*)
Jewelweed (*Impatiens capensis*)
Joe-pye weed (*Eupatorium maculatum*)
Low smartweed (*Persicaria longiseta*)
Marsh bellflower (*Campanula aparinoides*)
Marsh seedbox (*Ludwigia palustris*)
Marsh St. John's-wort (*Triadenum virginicum*)
Monkey flower (*Mimulus ringens*)
New York ironweed (*Vernonia noveboracensis*)
Northern bugleweed (*Lycopus uniflorus*)
Pale St. Johnswort (*Hypericum ellipticum*)
Purple marshlocks (*Comarum palustre*)
Purple stem angelica (*Angelica atropurpurea*)
Smallspike false nettle (*Boehmeria cylindrica*)
Smartweeds (*Persicaria spp.*)
Smartweeds (*Polygonum spp.*)
Spotted trumpet weed (*Eupatorium maculatum*)
Stiff marsh bedstraw (*Galium tinctorium*)
Swamp milkweed (*Asclepias incarnata*)
Swamp smartweed (*Polygonum hydropiperoides*)
Tall meadow-rue (*Thalictrum pubescens*)
Two-headed water starwort (*Callitriche heterophylla*)
Virginia water horehound (*Lycopus virginicus*)
Water parsnip (*Sium suave*)
Wrinkleleaf goldenrod (*Solidago rugosa*)

Ferns
Cinnamon fern (*Osmunda cinnamomea*)
Marsh fern (*Thelypteris palustris*)
Royal fern (*Osmunda regalis*)
Sensitive fern (*Onoclea sensibilis*)
Virginia chain fern (*Woodwardia virginica*)

Freshwater marshes

Cutgrass marshes tend to be found as small patches in alluvial bottomlands, near beaver ponds and on disturbed flats, most commonly on alluvium primarily from acidic sandstones and shales that can include poorly drained clay, clay loam, muck, sandy clay, sandy loam or silty clay, with a pH averaging 4.0. Unvegetated surface is mostly leaf litter, downed wood and standing water.

Trees
Black locust (*Robinia pseudoacacia*)
Black willow (*Salix nigra*)
Gray dogwood (*Cornus racemosa*)
Green ash (*Fraxinus pennsylvanica*)
Red-osier dogwood (*Cornus sericea*)
Silky dogwood (*Cornus amomum*)
Swamp dogwood (*Cornus racemosa*)
Willow (*Salix spp.*)

Shrubs
Allegheny blackberry (*Rubus allegheniensis*)
Arrow-wood (*Viburnum recognitum*)
Bristly dewberry (*Rubus hispidus*)
Buttonbush (*Cephalanthus occidentalis*)
White meadowsweet (*Spiraea alba var. alba*)
Steeplebush (*Spiraea tomentosa*)

Grasses, Sedges, Rushes
Awlfruit sedge (*Carex stipata*)
Bailey's sedge (*Carex baileyi*)
Black bulrush (*Scirpus atrovirens*)
Blister sedge (*Carex vesicaria*)
Bluejoint (*Calamagrostis canadensis*)
Blunt broom sedge (*Carex tribuloides*)
Common cattail (*Typha latifolia*)
Broom sedge (*Carex scoparia*)
Bur reed (*Sparganium spp.*)
Canada bluejoint (*Calamagrostis canadensis var. canadensis*)
Corkscrew rush (*Juncus effusus*)
Crested sedge (*Carex cristatella*)
Deertongue (*Dichanthelium clandestinum*)
Fox sedge (*Carex vulpinoidea*)
Greater bladder sedge (*Carex intumescens*)
Hairy fruit sedge (*Carex trichocarpa*)
Hop sedge (*Carex lupulina*)
Nodding sedge (*Carex gynandra*)
Northern long sedge (*Carex folliculata*)
Pale meadowgrass (*Torreyochloa pallida*)
Rattlesnake grass (*Glyceria canadensis*)

Reed canary grass (*Phalaris arundinacea*)
Rice cutgrass (*Leersia oryzoides*)
Rufous bulrush (*Scirpus pendulus*)
Shallow sedge (*Carex lurida*)
Silvery sedge (*Carex canescens*)
Soft rush (*Juncus effusus*)
Spike-rushes (*Eleocharis spp.*)
Three-way sedge (*Dulichium arundinaceum*)
Tussock sedge (*Carex stricta*)
Woodland bulrush (*Scirpus expansus*)
Woolgrass (*Scirpus cyperinus*)

Ferns
Cinnamon fern (*Osmunda cinnamomea*)
Marsh fern (*Thelypteris palustris*)
Royal fern (*Osmunda regalis*)
Sensitive fern (*Onoclea sensibilis*)
Virginia chain fern (*Woodwardia virginica*)

Forbs
Arrowhead (*Sagittaria rigida*)
Arrowleaf tearthumb (*Polygonum sagittatum*)
Beggar-ticks (*Bidens spp.*)
Boneset (*Eupatorium perfoliatum*)
Broadleaf arrowhead (*Sagittaria latifolia*)
Bugleweed (*Lycopus uniflorus*)
Canada goldenrod (*Solidago canadensis*)
Canadian St. John's-wort (*Hypericum canadense*)
Dwarf St. John's-wort (*Hypericum mutilum*)
Earth loosestrife (*Lysimachia terrestris*)
Giant goldenrod (*Solidago gigantea*)
Goldenrods (*Solidago spp.*)
Great blue lobelia (*Lobelia siphilitica*)
Jewelweed (*Impatiens capensis*)
Joe-pye weed (*Eupatorium maculatum*)
Marsh seedbox (*Ludwigia palustris*)
Marsh St. John's-wort (*Triadenum virginicum*)
Monkey flower (*Mimulus ringens*)
New York ironweed (*Vernonia noveboracensis*)
Northern arrow-wood (*Viburnum recognitum*)
Northern bugleweed (*Lycopus uniflorus*)
Smallspike false nettle (*Boehmeria cylindrica*)
Smartweeds (*Persicaria spp.*)
Smartweeds (*Polygonum spp.*)
Stiff marsh bedstraw (*Galium tinctorium*)
Trumpet weed (*Eupatoriadelphus fistulosus*)
Two-headed water starwort (*Callitriche heterophylla*)
Virginia Marsh St. Johnswort (*Triadenum virginicum*)
Virginia water hore-hound (*Lycopus virginicus*)
Wrinkleleaf goldenrod (*Solidago rugosa*)

Fens

Fens are different than meadows in that they are almost always moist to wet, small and almost always calcareous. Instead of seasonal flooding, springs provide a constant supply of groundwater, mostly from limestone rock and with a pH range of 6.9 to 8.1. In high concentrations, it forms a mucky soil called *marl*.

Fens tend to be an acre or less in size. In the wettest parts, woody vegetation cannot survive, so the woodland opening tends to be dominated by sedges, often quite spongy because of the moisture. Around the edges, where it's more dry, some shrubs and trees can grow.

Depth of organic matter is minimal at the point of water source, but can reach as deep as three feet in collection basins, creating habitats of silt loams to mucky peat. In some, the soil results from mats of rhizomatous sedges over deep peat.

Plants for fens
Trees
Alder (*Alnus spp.*)
Alderleaf buckthorn (*Rhamnus alnifolia*)
Eastern hemlock (*Tsuga canadensis*)
Eastern red cedar (*Juniperus virginiana*)
Gray dogwood (*Cornus racemosa*)
Poison sumac (*Toxicodendron vernix*)
Red-osier dogwood (*Cornus sericea*)
Speckled alder (*Alnus incana spp. rugosa*)
Willows (*Salix spp.*)
Sageleaf willow (*Salix candida*)
Tamarack (*Larix laricina*)

Shrubs

Arrowwood (*Viburnum recognitum*)
Bayberry (*Myrica pensylvanica*)
Bog laurel (*Kalmia polifolia*)
Chokeberries (*Photinia spp.*)
Cranberry (*Vaccinium macrocarpon*)
Dwarf blackberry (*Rubus pubescens*)
Labrador-tea (*Rhododendron groenlandicum*)
Leatherleaf (*Chamaedaphne calyculata var. angustifolia*)
Meadowsweet (*Spiraea alba var. latifolia*)
Ninebark (*Physocarpus opulifolius*)
Rhodora (*Rhododendron canadense*)
Sheep laurel (*Kalmia angustifolia*)
Small cranberry (*Vaccinium oxycoccos*)
Sweet gale (*Myrica gale*)
Velvetleaf berry (*Vaccinium myrtilloides*)
Wintergreen (*Gaultheria procumbens*)

Grasses, Sedges, Rushes
Atlantic sedge (*Carex sterilis*)
Baltic rush (*Juncus articus*)
Bottlebrush sedge (*Carex hystericina*)
Bristly stalked sedge (*Carex leptalea*)
Buxbaum's sedge (*Carex buxbaumii*)
Capillary beak-rush (*Rhynchospora capillacea*)
Coastal mannagrass (*Glyceria obtusa*)
Common horsetail (*Equisetum arvense*)
Dioecious sedge (*Carex sterilis*)
Fowl mannagrass (*Glyceria striata*)
Golden-fruited sedge (*Carex aurea*)
Hairy sedge (*Carex lacustris*)
Inland sedge (*Carex interior*)
Many-fruited sedge (*Carex lasiocarpa*)
Mountain rush (*Juncus balticus*)
Northeastern sedge (*Carex cryptolepis*)
Northern long sedge (*Carex folliculata*)
Northwest Territory sedge (*Carex utriculata*)
Prairie sedge (*Carex prairea*)
Shallow sedge (*Carex lurida*)
Smooth saw grass (*Cladium mariscoides*)
Soft rush (*Juncus effusus*)
Spiked muhly (*Muhlenbergia glomerata*)
Thin-leaved cotton-grass (*Eriophorum viridicarinatum*)
Three seeded sedge (*Carex trisperma*)
Tussock sedge (*Carex stricta*)
Water bulrush (*Schoenoplectus subterminalis*)
Water sedge (*Carex aquatilis*)
White beak rush (*Rhynchospora alba*)
Wood's sedge (*Carex tetanica*)
Wool-grass (*Scirpus cyperinus*)
Yellow sedge (*Carex flava*)

Ferns
Cinnamon fern (*Osmunda cinnamomea*)
Marsh fern (*Thelypteris palustris*)
Royal fern (*Osmunda regalis*)
Sensitive fern (*Onoclea sensibilis*)

Forbs
Blue vervain (*Verbena hastata*)
Bog silvery sedge (*Carex canescens*)
Bog willow herb (*Epilobium leptophyllum*)
Bogbean (*Menyanthes trifoliata*)
Boneset (*Eupatorium perfoliatum*)
Bugleweed (*Lycopus uniflorus*)
Calico aster (*Symphyotrichum lateriflorum*)
Cleavers (*Callum tinctorium*)
Common cattail (*Typha latifolia*)
Flat-leaved bladderwort (*Utricularia intermedia*)
Golden ragwort (*Senecio aureus*)
Grass-of parnassus (*Parnassia glauca*)
Harlequin blue flag (*Iris versicolor*)
Humped bladderwort (*Utricularia gibba*)
Jewelweed (*Impatiens capensis*)
Marsh cinquefoil (*Potentilla palustris*)
Marsh St. John's-wort (*Triadenum virginicum*)
Meadow spikemoss (*Selaginella apoda*)
Mountain-mint (*Pycnanthemum virginianum*)
New York ironweed (*Veronia noveboracensis*)
Northern bog aster (*Symphyotrichum boreale*)
Ontario lobelia (*Lobelia kalmii*)
Parasol whitetop (*Doellingeria umbellata*)
Pitcher-plant (*Sarracenia purpurea*)
Purple-stemmed aster (*Aster puniceus ssp. firmus*)
Shrubby cinquefoil (*Potentilla fruticosa*)

Skunk cabbage (*Symplocarpus foetidus*)
Snakemouth orchid (*Pogonia ophioglossoides*)
Spotted Joe-pye-weed (*Eutrochium maculatum*)
Spreading goldenrod (*Solidago patula*)
Spreading Jacob's-ladder (*Polemonium reptans*)
Starflower (*Smilacina stellata*)
Starry false lily of the valley (*Maianthemum stellatum*)
Stiff marsh bedstraw (*Galium tinctorium*)
Swamp thistle (*Cirsium muticum*)
Swamp verbena (*Verbena hastata*)
Turtlehead (*Chelone glabra*)
Water avens (*Geum rivale*)
Willow-herb (*Epilobium leptophyllum*)
Wood lilies (*Clintonia spp.*)

Seeps

Communities of less than an acre, seeps are found where groundwater comes to the surface in a diffuse flow to saturate soil for most of the growing season. They can be calcareous, but are more often on the acidic side and there's little variance in the population because of it.

Where they are open, graminoids — notably a variety of sedges — will dominate. In more shady situations, broad-leaved plants (forbs) will take command. Either way, herbaceous vegetation is more than 90 percent cover and can reach up to 6 feet in height.

Seeps are found at lower-elevation streamheads and stream border where groundwater emerges and in the drainages of lower slopes, as well as the lower slopes of moraines, in ravines and at the bases of slopes that separate stream terraces in deep valleys cut by glacial melt water. In some cases, a layer of sapric muck can be as deep as three feet, but more often it is less than 15 inches.

The "poor fens" of high flats in western Pennsylvania has water oozing from sandstone and as a result can have pH as low as 3.8. Here, high water tables over shallow bedrock perpetuate the habitat, which often includes hummock and hollow microtopography. If a site has been subjected to logging or fire in the past century, this type of habitat occurs as a successional community. Expect to find a carpet of sphagnum mosses here.

Plants for seeps

Trees and Shrubs
Chokeberries (*Photinia spp.*)
Eastern red cedar (*Juniperus virginiana*)
Highbush blueberry (*Vaccinium corymbosum*)
Northern spicebush (*Lindera benzoin*)
Poison sumac (*Toxicodendron vernix*)
Willow (*Salix spp.*)

Grasses, Sedges, Rushes

Atlantic sedge (*Carex sterilis*)
Bog bluegrass (*Poa paludigena*)
Bog sedge (*Carex atlantica*)
Bristly-stalked sedge (*Carex leptalea*)
Brome-like sedge (*Carex bromoides*)
Capillary beak-rush (*Rhynchospora capillacea*)
Common horse-tail (*Equisetum arvense*)
Cotton-grass (*Eriophorum virginicum*)
Eastern rough sedge (*Carex scabrata*)
Field horsetail (*Equisetum arvense*)
Fowl bluegrass (*Poa palustris*)
Fowl mannagrass (*Glyceria striata*)
Hairy sedge (*Carex lacustris*)
Hairy-fruit sedge (*Carex trichocarpa*)
Horsetails (*Equisetum spp.*)
Limestone sedge (*Carex granularis*)
Long-hair sedge (*Carex comosa*)
Nodding sedge (*Carex gynandra*)
Northern long sedge (*Carex folliculata*)
Prickly bog sedge (*Carex atlantica*)
Rice cutgrass (*Leersia oryzoides*)
Silvery sedge (*Carex canescens*)
Slender mannagrass (*Glyceria melicaria*)
Soft rush (*Juncus effusus*)
Spiked muhly (*Muhlenbergia glomerata*)
Sweet woodreed (*Cinna arundinacea*)
Thin-leaved cotton-grass (*Eriophorum viridicarinatum*)
Three seeded sedge (*Carex trisperma*)
Tussock sedge (*Carex stricta*)
Water horsetail (*Equisetum fluviatile*)

White beak sedge (*Rhynchospora alba*)
White edge sedge (*Carex debilis*)
Wool-grass (*Scirpus cyperinus*)
Yellow sedge (*Carex flava*)

Ferns

Cinnamon fern (*Osmunda cinnamomea*)
Fancy fern (*Dryopteris carthusiana*)
Marsh fern (*Thelypteris palustris*)
New York fern (*Thelypteris noveboracensis*)
Northern bog clubmoss (*Lycopodiella inundata*)
Sensitive fern (*Onoclea sensibilis*)

Herbaceous

Bishop's cap (*Mitella diphylla*)
Bitter cress (*Cardamine bulbosa*)
Blue violet (*Viola sororia*)
Bog goldenrod (*Solidago uliginosa*)
Boneset (*Eupatorium spp.*)
Brook lobelia (*Lobelia kalmii*)
Bulbous bittercress (*Cardamine bulbosa*)
Canada clearweed (*Pilea pumila*)
Canadian woodnettle (*Laportea canadensis*)
Common blue violet (*Viola sororia*)
Enchanter's nightshade (*Circaea alpina*)
False green hellebore (*Veratrum viride*)
Foamflower (*Tiarella cordifolia*)
Fragrant bedstraw (*Galium triflorum*)
Golden ragwort (*Packera aurea*)
Golden saxifrage (*Chrysosplenium americanum*)
Goldthread (*Coptis trifolia*)
Grass-of-parnassus (*Parnassia glauca*)
Hemlock parsley (*Conioselinum chinense*)
Hogpeanut (*Amphicarpaea bracteata*)
Jack-in-the-pulpit (*Arisaema triphyllum*)
Jewelweed (*Impatiens capensis*)
Lettuce saxifrage (*Saxifraga micranthidifolia*)
Marsh blue violet (*Viola cucullata*)
Marsh marigold (*Caltha palustris*)
Marsh pennyroyal (*Hydrocotyle americana*)
Monkey flower (*Mimulus ringens*)
Mountain watercress (*Cardamine rotundifolia*)
New york Ironweed (*Vernonia noveboracensis*)
Partridgeberry (*Mitchella repens*)
Pennsylvania bittercress (*Cardamine pensylvanica*)
Purple avens (*Geum rivale*)
Purpleleaf willowherb (*Epilobium coloratum*)
Purplestem angelica (*Angelica atropurpurea*)
Round-leaved sundew (*Drosera rotundifolia*)
Roundleaf goldenrod (*Solidago patula*)
Skunk cabbage (*Symplocarpus foetidus*)
Small enchanter's nightshade (*Circaea alpina*)
Spreading globeflower (*Trollius laxus*)
Stoneworts (*Chara spp.*)
Swamp aster (*Aster radula*)
Swamp lousewort (*Pedicularis lanceolata*)
Swamp saxifrage (*Saxifraga pensylvanica*)
Sweet bedstraw (*Galium triflorum*)
Thoroughwort (*Eupatorium spp.*)
Touch-me-not (*Impatiens spp.*)
Turtlehead (*Chelone glabra*)
Violets (*Viola spp.*)
Water avens (*Geum rivale*)
Watercress (*Nasturtium officinale*)
White turtlehead (*Chelone glabra*)
Whorled mountainmint (*Pycnanthemum verticillatum*)
Wood nettle (*Laportea canadensis*)
Yellow marsh marigold (*Caltha palustris*)

Bryophytes

Sphagnum spp.
Polytrichum spp.

Shrublands

Wetlands dominated by a combination of shrubs and graminoids are found throughout the state and can range from acidic to calcareous, but share a common trait: seasonal flooding due to a fluctuating water table that rises above the surface in spring and early summer and drops below it in late summer. Sometimes the flooding is defined as "semipermanent." Soils remain saturated as a result.

Typically, the surface layer is muck from decomposing plant matter over organic, but more typically mineral soils. Muck depth can vary and, as a result, impact the specific mix of plants.

These wetlands are common on lake and pond margins and the shallow water along shorelines, closed sand plain basins, small open but isolated basins, wet swales, and along floodplains — often in river system oxbows — and backwater sloughs. Other potential sites include slope bases, notably the zone dividing forest vegetation on the upslope and herbaceous vegetation on the downslope. They also turn up on rocky shoals and bars in riparian areas, as well as marsh borders, red maple wetlands, and within upland forests where water can perch for extended periods and drain very slowly.

The key factor, though, is prolonged saturation resulting from high water tables. Species associated with kind of habitat vary with climate and precise soil conditions and composition.

Trees
- American elder (*Sambucus canadensis*)
- Common elderberry (*Sambucus nigra ssp. canadensis*)
- Hazel alder (*Alnus serrulata*)
- Diamond willow (*Salix eriocephala*)
- Hazel alder (*Alnus serrulata*)
- Red maple (*Acer rubrum*)
- Red-osier dogwood (*Cornus sericea*)
- Silky dogwood (*Cornus amomum*)
- Silky willow (*Salix sericea*)
- Silver maple (*Acer saccharinum*)
- Smooth alder (*Alnus serrulata*)
- Speckled alder (*Alder incana*)
- Swamp dogwood (*Cornus racemosa*)
- White ash (*Fraxinus pennsylvanica*)
- Willows (*Salix spp.*)

Shrubs
- Arrow-wood (*Viburnum recognitum*)
- Buttonbush (*Cephalanthus occidentalis*)
- Chokeberry (*Photinia spp.*)
- Dwarf red blackberry (*Rubus pubescens*)
- Fetterbush (*Leucothoe racemosa*)
- Highbush blueberry (*Vaccinium corymbosum*)
- Inkberry (*Ilex glabra*)
- Leatherleaf (*Chamaedaphne calyculata*)
- Maleberry (*Lyonia ligustrina*)
- Meadowsweet (*Spiraea alba var. latifolia*)
- Ninebark (*Physocarpus opulifolius*)
- Dwarf red blackberry (*Rubus pubescens*)
- Red raspberry (*Rubus idaeus*)
- Serviceberry (*Amelanchier spp.*)
- Sheep laurel (*Kalmia angustifolia*)
- Southern arrow wood (*Viburnum dentatum*)
- Steeplebush (*Spiraea tomentosa*)
- Swamp azalea (*Rhododendron viscosum*)
- Swamp dewberry (*Rubus hispidus*)
- Sweet gale (*Myrica gale*)
- Sweet pepperbush (*Clethra alnifolia*)
- Viburnums (*Viburnum spp.*)
- White meadowsweet (*Spiraea alba*)
- Winterberry (*Ilex verticillata*)

Grasses, Sedges, Rushes
- American bur-reed (*Sparganium americanum*)
- Blister sedge (*Carex vesicaria*)
- Bluejoint (*Calamagrostis canadensis*)
- Cattails (*Typha spp.*)
- Fowl mannagrass (*Glyceria striata*)
- Green bulrush (*Scirpus atrovirens*)
- Hairy sedge (*Carex lacustris*)
- Longhair sedge (*Carex comosa*)
- Parasol whitetop (*Doellingeria umbellata*)
- Prairie sedge (*Carex prairea*)
- Rice cutgrass (*Leersia oryzoides*)
- Rushes (*Juncus spp.*)
- Shallow sedge (*Carex lurida*)
- Slender mannagrass (*Glyceria melicaria*)
- Spike-rushes (*Eleocharis spp.*)
- Three-seeded sedge (*Carex trisperma*)
- Three-way sedge (*Dulichium arundinaceum*)
- Tussock sedge (*Carex stricta*)
- Wool-grass (*Scirpus cyperinus*)

Ferns
- Cinnamon fern (*Osmunda cinnamomea*)
- Marsh fern (*Thelypteris palustris*)
- Royal fern (*Osmunda regalis*)
- Sensitive fern (*Onoclea sensibilis*)

Forbs
- Blue skullcap (*Scutellaria lateriflora*)
- Broadleaf pondweed (*Potamogeton natans*)
- Bugleweed (*Lycopus uniflorus*)

Dotted smartweed (*Polygonum punctatum*)
Hemlock water parsnip (*Sium suave*)
Jewelweed (*Impatiens capensis*)
Lesser duckweed (*Lemna minor*)
Marsh marigold (*Caltha palustris*)
Marsh St. John's-wort (*Triadenum virginicum*)
Mermaid-weed (*Proserpinaca palustris var. crebra*)
Mild water-pepper (*Polygonum hydropiperoides*)
Northern bugleweed (*Lycopus uniflorus*)
Purple stem beggarticks (*Bidens connata*)
Purplestem aster (*Symphyotrichum puniceum*)
Skunk cabbage (*Symplocarpus foetidus*)
Smallspike false nettle (*Boehmeria cylindrica*)
Spatterdock (*Nuphar lutea*)
Spotted Joe pye weed (*Eupatorium maculatum*)
Swamp loosestrife (*Decodon verticillatus*)
Three petal bedstraw (*Galium trifidum*)
Variegated yellow pond lily (*Nuphar variegata*)
Violets (*Viola spp.*)
Virginia chain fern (*Woodwardia virginica*)
Virginia marsh St. John's wort (*Triadenum virginicum*)
Water arum (*Calla palustris*)
Water-willow (*Decodon verticillatus*)
Water smartweed (*Polygonum amphibium*)
White panicle aster (*Symphyotrichum lanceolatum*)

Depressions and Swamps

In areas that either collect water or retain it because of high groundwater levels or "perching" on hard substrates or bedrock, a variety of specialized wetland habitats organize to exploit accumulations of rich silts and organic matter.

They can have foundations of peat or mineral soils rich with organic matter and be found on upland flats, along slow-moving streams, lake margins or as elements of large wetland complexes. Some are primarily herbaceous and may include standing ponds and swamps, while others are dry enough to permit tall-shrub canopies. It's not unusual for some to be vegetation-free in winter through early spring, filling out with plants as water recedes for the season. Prolonged to semi-permanent flooding, however, is the usual circumstance.

Depending on the surrounding soil sources, pH ranges are broad and reflect the neighboring community. Although depressions and swales are often considered models for rain gardens, the issue in artificial habitats becomes speed of complete drainage and periods when soils become too dry to support wetland species.

Depending on specific local conditions, species to consider for these wetland habitats can include:

Common trees
American elder (*Sambucus canadensis*)
Black gum (*Nyssa sylvatica*)
Bog willow (*Salix pedicellaris*)
Gray alder (*Alnus incana*)
Hazel alder (*Alnus serrulata*)
Pin oak (*Quercus palustris*)
Red maple (*Acer rubrum*)
Red-osier dogwood (*Cornus sericea*)
Silky dogwood (*Cornus amomum*)
Silky willow (*Salix sericea*)
Silver maple (*Acer saccharinum*)
Smooth alder (*Alnus serrulata*)
Speckled alder (*Alder incana*)
Swamp dogwood (*Cornus racemosa*)
White ash (*Fraxinus pennsylvanica*)
White oak (*Quercus alba*)
Willows (*Salix spp.*)

Shrubs
Bog rosemary (*Andromeda polifolia*)
Buttonbush (*Cephalanthus occidentalis*)
Common elderberry (*Sambucus nigra ssp. canadensis*)
Cranberry (*Vaccinium macrocarpon*)
Dwarf red blackberry (*Rubus pubescens*)
Highbush blueberry (*Vaccinium corymbosum*)
Leatherleaf (*Chamaedaphne calyculata*)
Maleberry (*Lyonia ligustrina*)
Ninebark (*Physocarpus opulifolius*)
Northern arrow-wood (*Viburnum recog-

nitum)
Red raspberry (*Rubus idaeus*)
Smooth alder (*Alnus serrulata*)
Southern arrow-wood (*Viburnum dentatum*)
Steeplebush (*Spiraea tomentosa*)
Swamp azalea (*Rhododendron viscosum*)
Swamp dogwood (*Cornus racemosa*)
Sweet gale (*Myrica gale*)
Virburnums (*Viburnum spp.*)
Water-willow (*Decodon verticillatus*)
White meadowsweet (*Spiraea alba*)
Winterberry (*Ilex verticillata*)

Grasses and Sedges
American bur-reed (*Sparganium americanum*)
American mannagrass (*Glyceria grandis*)
Awlfruit sedge (*Carex stipata*)
Blister sedge (*Carex vesicaria*)
Bluejoint (*Calamagrostis canadensis*)
Bulrush (*Scirpus atrovirens*)
Bur-reed (*Sparganium spp.*)
Canada rush (*Juncus canadensis*)
Cattails (*Typha spp.*)
Cotton-grass (*Eriophorum vaginatum*)
Creeping spike rush (*Eleocharis palustris*)
False hop sedge (*Carex lupuliformis*)
Few seed sedge (*Carex oligosperma*)
Floating mannagrass (*Glyceria septentrionalis*)
Fowl bluegrass (*Poa palustris*)
Fowl mannagrass (*Glyceria striata*)
Green bulrush (*Scirpus atrovirens*)
Hairgrass (*Agrostis scabra*)
Hairy sedge (*Carex lacustris*)
Hop sedge (*Carex lupulina*)
Longhair sedge (*Carex comosa*)
Mannagrass (*Glyceria acutiflora*)
Mellic mannagrass (*Glyceria melicaria*)
Mud sedge (*Carex limosa*)
Nerveless woodland sedge (*Carex leptonervia*)
Nodding sedge (*Carex gynandra*)
Northeastern bulrush (*Scirpus ancistrochaetus*)
Northern long sedge (*Carex folliculata*)
Northwest territory sedge (*Carex utriculata*)
Pale meadow grass (*Torreyochloa pallida*)
Prairie sedge (*Carex prairea*)
Rattlesnake mannagrass (*Glyceria canadensis*)
Reed canary grass (*Phalaris arundinacea*)
Rice cutgrass (*Leersia oryzoides*)
Shallow sedge (*Carex lurida*)
Short hair sedge (*Carex crinita var. crinita*)
Silvery sedge (*Carex canescens*)
Smooth saw grass (*Cladium mariscoides*)
Tall cottongrass (*Eriophorum angustifolium*)
Tawny cotton-grass (*Eriophorum virginicum*)
Soft rush (*Juncus effusus*)
Soft-stem bulrush (*Schoenoplectus tabernaemontani*)
Three-seeded sedge (*Carex trisperma*)
Three-way sedge (*Dulichium arundinaceum*)
Tussock sedge (*Carex stricta*)
White beak sedge (*Rhynchospora alba*)
Whitegrass (*Leersia virginica*)
Woodland bulrush (*Scirpus expansus*)
Wool-grass (*Scirpus cyperinus*)
Wooly fruit sedge (*Carex lasiocarpa*)

Ferns
Cinnamon fern (*Osmunda cinnamomea*)
Marsh fern (*Thelypteris palustris*)
Royal fern (*Osmunda regalis*)
Sensitive fern (*Onoclea sensibilis*)
Virginia chain fern (*Woodwardia virginica*)

Forbs
American white water lily (*Nymphaea odorata*)
Arrow-arum (*Peltandra virginica*)
Arrowhead (*Sagittaria rigida*)
Beggar-ticks (*Bidens spp.*)
Bladderwort (*Utricularia geminiscapa*)
Blue skullcap (*Scutellaria lateriflora*)
Broadleaf arrowhead (*Sagittaria latifolia*)
Broadleaf pondweed (*Potamogeton natans*)
Bugleweed (*Lycopus uniflorus*)
Bur marigold (*Bidens laevis*)
Calamus (*Acorus calamus*)
Canadian St. John's-wort (*Hypericum canadense*)

Common bladderwort (*Utricularia macrorhiza*)
Coon's tail (*Ceratophyllum demersum*)
Dotted smartweed (*Polygonum punctatum*)
Dwarf St. John's-wort (*Hypericum mutilum*)
Earth loosestrife (*Lysimachia terrestris*)
Flat leaf bladderwort (*Utricularia intermedia*)
Fraser's marsh St. John's-wort (*Triadenum fraseri*)
Golden-club (*Orontium aquaticum*)
Green arrow arum (*Peltandra virginica*)
Harlequin blue flag (*Iris versicolor*)
Hemlock water parsnip (*Sium suave*)
Jewelweed (*Impatiens capensis*)
Lesser duckweed (*Lemna minor*)
Marsh cinquefoil (*Potentilla palustris*)
Marsh marigold (*Caltha palustris*)
Marsh St. John's-wort (*Triadenum virginicum*)
Marsh-purslane (*Ludwigia palustris*)
Mermaid-weed (*Proserpinaca palustris* var. *crebra*)
Mild water-pepper (*Polygonum hydropiperoides*)
Northern bugleweed (*Lycopus uniflorus*)
Pale St. Johns-wort (*Hypericum ellipticum*)
Parasol whitetop (*Doellingeria umbellata*)
Pickerel-weed (*Pontederia cordata*)
Pitcher-plant (*Sarracenia purpurea*)
Purple marshlocks (*Comarum palustre*)
Purple stem beggarticks (*Bidens connata*)
Purplestem aster (*Symphyotrichum puniceum*)
Round-leaved sundew (*Drosera rotundifolia*)
Skunk cabbage (*Symplocarpus foetidus*)
Smallspike false nettle (*Boehmeria cylindrica*)
Smart-weeds (*Polygonum spp.*)
Snakemouth orchid (*Pogonia ophioglossoides*)
Spatterdock (*Nuphar lutea*)
Spike-rushes (*Eleocharis spp*)
Spoon leaf sundew (*Drosera intermedia*)
Spotted joe pye weed (*Eupatorium maculatum*)
Swamp-candles (*Lysimachia terrestris*)
Three petal bedstraw (*Galium trifidum*)
Variegated yellow pond lily (*Nuphar variegata*)
Violets (*Viola spp.*)
Water plantain (*Alisma plantagoaquatica*)
Water knotweed (*Polygonum amphibium*)
Water smartweed (*Polygonum hydropiperoides*)
White panicle aster (*Symphyotrichum lanceolatum*)

Palustrine Wetlands

Most palustrine wetlands — sometimes called woodland swamps — more closely resemble bogs than fens because of high levels of peaty muck as well as acidic conditions, often below pH 5.5. Unlike fens, which rely on seeps for water supply, many palustrine habitats are found in basins and depressions on flat ground not subjected to flooding, but always with groundwater levels at or near the surface. But poor drainage conditions are nonetheless the usual culprits in maintaining these habitats, which tend to be prized by ecologists and get a considerable amount of attention and study.

Perching of water on shallow bedrock or fragipans combined with poorly drained soils compounded by enormous amounts of decaying organic matter are at the core of the habitat, and the acidity of water and material tends to enforce a low pH set of inhabitants. These can vary from nutrient poor to moderately rich, and tend to be organized on otherwise level ground or very gentle slopes adjacent to formal wetlands.

In glaciated areas of the state, compacted till silt and clay deposits can form the fragipan, and they occur at both low and high elevations. Across the state, the compacted clays or near-surface bedrock in flats produce a varied set of habitats governed by canopy cover. Where forest is well established with moisture-loving trees, ground vegetation tends to be sparse and limited to mosses and ferns. More typically, the sheer saturation constrains tree growth and results in luxuriant shrub and herbaceous opportunity. Hummock and hollow microtopography is routine.

Appropriate species vary on the basis of light requirements and relative soil moisture, but a considerable list should get gardeners started:

Trees
- American elm (*Ulmus americana*)
- Balsam fir (*Abies balsamea*)
- Birch (*Betula spp.*)
- Bitternut hickory (*Carya cordiformis*)
- Black ash (*Fraxinus nigra*)
- Black elderberry (*Sambucus canadensis*)
- Black gum (*Nyssa sylvatica*)
- Black spruce (*Picea mariana*)
- Black willow (*Salix nigra*)
- Bur oak (*Quercus macrocarpa*)
- Dogwoods (*Cornus spp.*)
- Eastern hemlock (*Tsuga canadensis*)
- Eastern white pine (*Pinus strobus*)
- Gray alder (*Alnus incana*)
- Gray birch (*Betula populifolia*)
- Green ash (*Fraxinus pennsylvanica*)
- Hazel alder (*Alnus serrulata*)
- Hickories (*Carya spp.*)
- Hornbeam (*Carpinus caroliniana*)
- Mountain ash (*Sorbus americana*)
- Pin oak (*Quercus palustris*)
- Pitch pine (*Pinus rigida*)
- Poison sumac (*Toxicodendron vernix*)
- Quaking aspen (*Populus tremuloides*)
- Red maple (*Acer rubrum*)
- Red spruce (*Picea rubens*)
- River birch (*Betula nigra*)
- Shagbark hickory (*Carya ovata*)
- Silky dogwood (*Cornus amomum*)
- Silky willow (*Salix sericea*)
- Silver maple (*Acer saccharinum*)
- Slippery elm (*Ulmus rubra*)
- Smooth alder (*Alnus serrulata*)
- Speckled alder (*Alnus incana*)
- Striped maple (*Acer pensylvanicum*)
- Sugar maple (*Acer saccharum*)
- Swamp white oak (*Quercus bicolor*)
- Sweet gum (*Liquidambar styraciflua*)
- Tamarack (*Larix laricina*)
- Tuliptree (*Liriodendron tulipifera*)
- White ash (*Fraxinus americana*)
- White oak (*Quercus alba*)
- Yellow birch (*Betula alleghaniensis*)

Shrubs
- Alderleaf buckthorn (*Rhamnus alnifolia*)
- Allegheny blackberry (*Rubus allegheniensis*)
- Allegheny serviceberry (*Amelanchier laevis*)
- Arrow-wood (*Viburnum recognitum*)
- Black chokeberry (*Aronia melanocarpa*)
- Black haw (*Viburnum prunifolium*)
- Black huckleberry (*Gaylussacia baccata*)
- Black raspberry (*Rubus occidentalis*)
- Blueberries (*Vaccinium spp.*)
- Bog laurel (*Kalmia polifolia*)
- Bristly dewberry (*Rubus hispidus*)
- Bunchberry (*Cornus canadensis*)
- Buttonbush (*Cephalanthus occidentalis*)
- Canada yew (*Taxus canadensis*)
- Catberry (*Nemopanthus mucronatus*)
- Common serviceberry (*Amelanchier arborea*)
- Cranberry (*Vaccinium macrocarpon*)
- Creeping snowberry (*Gaultheria hispidula*)
- Dwarf red blackberry (*Rubus pubescens*)
- Great rhododendron (*Rhododendron maximum*)
- Highbush blueberry (*Vaccinium corymbosum*)
- Leatherleaf (*Chamaedaphne calyculata*)
- Leatherwood (*Dirca palustris*)
- Lowbush blueberry (*Vaccinium angustifolium*)
- Maleberry (*Lyonia ligustrina*)
- Meadowsweet (*Spiraea latifolia*)
- Meadowsweet (*Spiraea tomentosa*)
- Mountain holly (*Ilex montana*)
- Mountain laurel (*Kalmia latifolia*)
- Nannyberry (*Viburnum lentago*)
- Northern arrow-wood (*Viburnum recognitum*)
- Northern dewberry (*Rubus flagellaris*)
- Northern spicebush (*Lindera benzoin*)
- Partridgeberry (*Mitchella repens*)
- Possumhaw (*Viburnum nudum var. cassinoides*)
- Red chokeberry (*Photinia pyrifolia*)
- Rhodora (*Rhododendron canadense*)

Sheep laurel (*Kalmia angustifolia*)
Southern arrow-wood (*Viburnum dentatum*)
Swamp azalea (*Rhododendron viscosum*)
Swamp doghobble (*Leucothoe racemosa*)
Swamp rose (*Rosa palustris*)
Sweet pepperbush (*Clethra alnifolia*)
Velvetleaf huckleberry (*Vaccinium myrtilloides*)
White meadowsweet (*Spirea alba var. latifolia*)
Winterberry (*Ilex verticillata*)
Wintergreen (*Gaultheria procumbens*)
Witch hazel (*Hamamelis virginiana*)
Withe-rod viburnum (*Viburnum nudum var. cassinoides*)

Grasses, Sedges, Rushes

Awlfruit sedge (*Carex stipata*)
Blunt broom sedge (*Carex tribuloides*)
Bristly stalked sedge (*Carex leptalea*)
Brome-like sedge (*Carex bromoides*)
Canada bluejoint (*Calamagrostis canadensis*)
Common rush (*Juncus effusus*)
Cotton grass (*Eriophorum spp.*)
Creeping spike-rush (*Eleocharis palustris*)
Drooping sedge (*Carex prasina*)
Eastern rough sedge (*Carex scabrata*)
Eastern woodland sedge (*Carex blanda*)
Fowl mannagrass (*Glyceria striata*)
Fox sedge (*Carex vulpinoidea*)
Fringed sedge (*Carex crinita*)
Greater bladder sedge (*Carex intumescens*)
Green bulrush (*Scirpus atrovirens*)
Hairgrass (*Agrostis scabra*)
Hairy sedge (*Carex lacustris*)
Halberd-leaved tearthumb (*Polygonum arifolium*)
Longhair sedge (*Carex comosa*)
Mannagrass (*Glyceria spp.*)
Melic mannagrass (*Glyceria melicaria*)
Nodding sedge (*Carex gynandra*)
Northern long sedge (*Carex folliculata*)
Rice cutgrass (*Leersia oryzoides*)
Riverbank wild rye (*Elymus riparius*)
Rosy sedge (*Carex rosea*)
Rushes (*Scirpus spp.*)
Shallow sedge (*Carex lurida*)
Silvery sedge (*Carex canescens*)
Soft leaf sedge (*Carex disperma*)
Soft rush (*Juncus effusus*)
Spikerush (*Eleocharis spp.*)
Spreading sedge (*Carex laxiculmis*)
Squarrose sedge (*Carex squarrosa*)
Sweet woodreed (*Cinna arundinacea*)
Tawny cotton-grass (*Eriophorum virginicum*)
Three-seeded sedge (*Carex trisperma*)
Three-way sedge (*Dulichium arundinaceum*)
Tussock cottongrass (*Eriophorum vaginatum var. spissum*)
Tussock sedge (*Carex stricta*)
Upright sedge (*Carex stricta*)
Virginia wild rye (*Elymus virginicus*)
White beak sedge (*Rhynchospora alba*)
White beak-rush (*Rhynchospora alba*)
White edge sedge (*Carex debilis*)
Whitegrass (*Leersia virginica*)
Woodrush (*Luzula spp.*)
Wool grass (*Scirpus cyperinus*)

Ferns

Bog fern (*Thelypteris simulata*)
Cinnamon fern (*Osmunda cinnamomea*)
Crested shield fern (*Dryopteris cristata*)
Hayscented fern (*Dennstaedtia punctilobula*)
Interrupted fern (*Osmunda claytoniana*)
Lady fern (*Athyrium filix-femina*)
Marsh fern (*Thelypteris palustris*)
Mountain woodfern (*Dryopteris campyloptera*)
New York fern (*Thelypteris noveboracensis*)
Northern bracken fern (*Pteridium aquilinum*)
Ostrich fern (*Matteuccia struthiopteris*)
Rare clubmoss (*Lycopodium obscurum*)
Royal fern (*Osmunda regalis*)
Sensitive fern (*Onoclea sensibilis*)
Shining clubmoss (*Huperzia lucidula*)
Virginia chain fern (*Woodwardia virginica*)

Forbs

American globeflower (*Trollius laxus*)
American golden saxifrage (*Chrysosplenium*

americanum)
American water plantain (*Alisma subcordatum*)
Arrow-arum (*Peltandra virginica*)
Arrow-leaf tearthumb (*Polygonum sagittatum*)
Arrowhead (*Sagittaria latifolia*)
Beggar-ticks (*Bidens spp.*)
Blue flag iris (*Iris versicolor*)
Blue mistflower (*Eupatorium coelestinum*)
Blue monkshood (*Aconitum uncinatum*)
Bluebead (*Clintonia borealis*)
Bog goldenrod (*Solidago uliginosa*)
Bog willowherb (*Epilobium leptophyllum*)
Boneset (*Eupatorium perfoliatum*)
Broadleaf arrowhead (*Sagittaria latifolia*)
Brown wide lip orchid (*Liparis liliifolia*)
Bulblet-bearing water hemlock (*Cicuta bulbifera*)
Bulbous bittercress (*Cardamine bulbosa*)
Canada mayflower (*Maianthemum canadense*)
Common cinquefoil (*Potentilla simplex*)
Common marsh bedstraw (*Galium palustre*)
Common moonseed (*Menispermum canadense*)
Ditch stonecrop (*Penthorum sedoides*)
Dwarf ginseng (*Panax trifolius*)
Earth loosestrife (*Lysimachia terrestris*)
False solomon's seal (*Smilacina trifolia*)
Goldthread (*Coptis trifolia*)
Greater purple fringed orchid (*Platanthera grandiflora*)
Green false hellebore (*Veratrum viride*)
Harlequin blue flag (*Iris versicolor*)
Indian strawberry (*Duchesnea indica*)
Jack-in-the-pulpit (*Arisaema triphyllum*)
Jewelweed (*Impatiens spp.*)
King-of-the-meadow (*Thalictrum pubescens*)
Labrador tea (*Ledum groenlandicum*)
Limestone adder's tongue (*Ophioglossum engelmannii*)
Lizard's tail (*Saururus cernuus*)
Marsh blue violet (*Viola cucullata*)
Marsh St. John's-wort (*Triadenum virginicum*)
Mayapple (*Podophyllum peltatum*)
Monkey flower (*Mimulus ringens*)
Mountain bugbane (*Actaea podocarpa*)
Northern bugleweed (*Lycopus uniflorus*)
Pennsylvania bittercress (*Cardamine pensylvanica*)
Pitcher-plant (*Sarracenia purpurea*)
Purple avens (*Geum rivale*)
Purple fringeless orchid (*Platanthera peramoena*)
Purple milkwort (*Polygala sanguinea*)
Purple stem aster (*Symphyotrichum puniceum*)
Purple stem beggerticks (*Bidens connata*)
Quillworts (*Isoetes spp.*)
Robin runaway (*Dalibarda repens*)
Rough bedstraw (*Galium asprellum*)
Roundleaf goldenrod (*Solidago patula*)
Roundleaf greenbrier (*Smilax rotundifolia*)
Roundleaf sundew (*Drosera rotundifolia*)
Seedbox (*Ludwigia alternifolia*)
Showy lady's slipper (*Cypripedium reginae*)
Skunk cabbage (*Symplocarpus foetidus*)
Small enchanter's nightshade (*Circaea alpina*)
Smallspike false nettle (*Boehmeria cylindrica*)
Smooth white violet (*Viola macloskeyi ssp. pallens*)
Southern agrimony (*Agrimonia parviflora*)
Spatulate-leaved sundew (*Drosera intermedia*)
Spotted ladysthumb (*Polygonum persicaria*)
Starflower (*Trientalis borealis*)
Stiff cowbane (*Oxypolis rigidior*)
Swamp loosestrife (*Decodon verticillatus*)
Swamp saxifrage (*Saxifraga pensylvanica*)
Three-leaf false lily-of-the-valley (*Maianthemum trifolium*)
Threeleaf goldthread (*Coptis trifolia*)
Touch-me-not (*Impatiens spp*)
Tuberous grass pink (*Calopogon tuberosus*)
Twinflower (*Linnaea borealis*)
Violet wood sorrel (*Oxalis violacea*)
Violets (*Viola spp.*)

Virginia creeper (*Parthenocissus quinquefolia*)
Virginia springbeauty (*Claytonia virginica*)
Virginia water-horehound (*Lycopus virginicus*)
Water arum (*Calla palustris*)
White turtlehead (*Chelone glabra*)
Whorled milkwort (*Polygala verticillata*)
Whorled wood aster (*Oclemena acuminata*)
Wood anemone (*Anemone quinquefolia*)
Wrinkleleaf goldenrod (*Solidago rugosa*)
Yellow marsh marigold (*Caltha palustris*)

Bogs

Scattered across glaciated areas of Pennsylvania, bogs with some range of variety created specialized wetlands from water running off from adjacent areas and setting up highly acidic, nutrient poor areas that fill from the outside edges inward with dense mats of sphagnum and decomposing plant materials. A key feature is that they are *oligotrophic* – that is, poor in plant nutrients but at deeper levels of very cold water very rich with oxygen. The result is a very slow and methodical decomposition rate and hospitality for a very limited range of plant species. The mat itself remains saturated throughout the year, and most plants on the surface grow less than two feet tall. Where the mat is deep enough, or along the edges, it's possible for Black spruce to take root. Leatherleaf is far and away to most dominant shrub.

Trees and shrubs
Black huckleberry (*Gaylussacia baccata*)
Black spruce (*Picea mariana*)
Bog laurel (*Kalmia polifolia*)
Bog-rosemary (*Andromeda polifolia*)
Cranberry (*Vaccinium macrocarpon*)
Highbush blueberry (*Vaccinium corymbosum*)
Labrador tea (*Ledum groenlandicum*)
Leatherleaf (*Chamaedaphne calyculata*)
Red chokeberry (*Aronia arbutifolia*)
Red maple (*Acer rubrum*)
Sheep laurel (*Kalmia angustifolia*)
Small cranberry (*Vaccinium oxycoccos*)
Swamp azalea (*Rhododendron viscosum*)
Tamarack (*Larix laricina*)

Herbaceous
Brown-fruited rush (*Juncus pelocarpus*)
Cotton-grass (*Eriophorum vaginatum*)
Horned bladderwort (*Utricularia cornuta*)
Pitcher-plant (*Sarracenia purpurea*)
Round-leaved sundew (*Drosera rotundifolia*)
Spatulate-leaved sundew (*Drosera intermedia*)
Tawny cotton-grass (*Eriophorum virginicum*)
Three-seeded sedge (*Carex trisperma*)
White beak-rush (*Rhynchospora alba*)
White-fringed orchid (*Platanthera blephariglottis*)
Yellow-eyed grass (*Xyris prinus*)

Riparian zones and Floodplains

If open and closed upland depressions give us physical models for rain gardens, riparian areas and the floodplains at their bases offer the best functional concepts.

As discussed earlier, depressions collect and either pond or flood seasonally, creating rich habitats for many species in very slow-draining landscapes. The slow draining aspect is a problem for gardens because of the potential for mosquito development after 72 hours of standing water. Yet the appropriate community relies on the humusy to silty qualities of the topography that causes the poor drainage in the first place.

But when we think of riparian systems and the implied floodplains, we see a structure much more appropriate for garden design. Although flooding is more common in the spring as a result of meltwater flow, it can occur at any time with sustained and heavier precipitation. Riparian systems deliver water from one place to another, and streams and rivers "breathe" as a consequence of floodplains.

Rain gardens in the popular context are shallow, artificial depressions in the downslope vicinity of a downspout (and naturally, never above a septic system or within a few feet of the house foundation). And it forms a garden bed that can for a short time handle inundation, so design is a simple matter if an adaptable palette of plants can be organized.

Riparian systems, on the other hand, carry the allure of a much more varied and linear potential. At high elevations, they begin with ephemeral — think now and then, when it rains a lot — streams that created headslopes of many different shapes. As water flow takes on permanent flow in lower elevations, the stream begins to flex erosional muscles and, where it can, creates *alluvial terraces*. Well above the channel, these terraces soon accommodate species that like the proximity of water but don't want to get their feet wet. Lower terraces invite those who don't mind the rare disaster, while down close to the active channel a network of subtle features develop. Along the channel itself we very often find a naturally-created levee. Further away, the bottomland may be an occasionally-flooded grassland or an interesting *backswamp*. If the landscape is impacted by frequent and high velocity flow — such as we find close to the bottom of a downspout — species able to endure *flood scouring* set up shop. Where it flattens out and becomes a more gentle but broader flow, larger herbaceous and shrubs can manage, transitioning at last into floodplain forests.

Elevations, valley shape, soils, volume and velocity are endlessly varied along Pennsylvania's 83,000 miles of streams and rivers, so when we evaluate them for models, our own landscapes are limited only by our sense of aesthetics and the resource we deal with — average annual precipitation that can occur at any time and at any rate, ranging from a hundredth of an inch to substantial downpours.

Riparian systems in nature, like any group of ecosystems, are vast, powerful and way beyond the replication in a backyard garden project. But when we remember that we are *suggesting* rather than modeling, we enjoy distinct advantages.

First, the enormous power of high velocity and prolonged flooding is not an issue; our inundations will be far more friendly and gentle. This implies that our plant selection can come from a much broader array than what Nature can dictate in topographical segments. Drawing from a composite of many researched habitats, we soon assemble an enormous list of species that can handle the gushing torrent from our downspouts. And it can be divided into subsections of more and less frequently listed plants — the former being sure bets and the latter being likely, but perhaps worth double-checking.

Second, our landscaping issues can taken advantage of larger concepts but on a micro scale. We don't require five-ton boulders to construct a matrix of cobbles and silts, and our terraces need not be dozens of feet high and wide. Since our flooding event is by comparison quite minor, we can use much more modest development to make it work but still plant faithfully to Nature's specifications; if we're a bit off for whatever reason, it's not a tragedy.

What we *do* create is a stormwater management system that ranges from very active at the headslope end and benign at the "500-year-flood" end. In landscape design, rills channel water along the desired downhill path, and even they can be managed for effect. To delay dissipation of water into the topsoil, we restrict permeability by lining the rill with increasingly impervious materials at the base, such as tightly-packed soils and stone. A narrow channel and steeper grade will force water to move more quickly, while a broader rill on a gentle slope will cause it to spread out and service a wider area. At the focal point of the rain garden, the traditional closed depression can be terraced and populated with species less tolerant of inundation, often featuring construction of stone for dramatic design. In Nature, the rock found at higher elevation headslopes will tend to be the sharper-edged materials characteristic of recent colluvium and frost-heaved fractured bedrock. In more established alluvial areas, it will be more rounded, as in what is commonly described river stone.

Headslope soils are often richer in organic matter, but not unmanageably so. Often, a blanket of shredded leaves used as mulch will establish the concept quickly and inexpensively. Alluvial soils tend toward finer, more mineral materials, such as silty to sandy loams, even clays that might have been released from stream load.

Channels designated for actual flow can be evolved into a series of obstructions to create the "riffle and pool" concepts of smaller streams or the rocky to sandy margins of wider rivers that themselves often include meandering bars, levees, somewhat silty backswamps and lush bottomlands. Many actual floodplains in gentle systems are closed canopy forests, while others illustrate the enormous variety of riparian plants for full-sun situations.

These are, by definition, constructed landscapes for conservation and aesthetic effect, and in a comprehensive design become useful features for three-dimensional garden rooms. As such, they are microtopography settings that are not sustainable in the broad sense of the term, but positive in the context of preservation of natural resources.

Common characteristics of species found on floodplains is that they are either riparian by nature or adaptable to periodic inundation to some extent. Factors impacting suitability include depth and duration of flooding or velocity.

Plant list for floodplains, rain gardens
Common Trees
American elm (*Ulmus americana*)
American hornbeam (*Carpinus caroliniana*)
American sycamore (*Platanus occidentalis*)
Bitternut hickory (*Carya cordiformis*)
Black walnut (*Juglans nigra*)
Black willow (*Salix nigra*)
Butternut (*Juglans cinerea*)
Eastern cottonwood (*Populus deltoides*)
Green ash (*Fraxinus pennsylvanica*)
Red maple (*Acer rubrum*)
Red osier dogwood (*Cornus sericea*)
River birch (*Betula nigra*)
Silky dogwood (*Conpus amomum*)
Silky willow (*Salix sericea*)
Silver maple (*Acer saccharinum*)
Smooth alder (*Alnus serrulata*)
Speckled alder (*Alder incana*)
Swamp dogwood (*Cornus racemosa*)
Sycamore (*Platanus occidentalis*)
White ash (*Fraxinus americana*)
Less common trees
American basswood (*Tilia americana*)
American beech (*Fagus grandifolia*)
American elder (*Sambucus canadensis*)
American hazelnut (*Corylus americana*)

American hog peanut (*Amphicarpaea bracteata*)
Black ash (*Fraxinus nigra*)
Black cherry (*Prunus serotina*)
Black elderberry (*Sambucus canadensis*)
Black locust (*Robinia pseudoacacia*)
Black maple (*Acer nigrum*)
Box elder (*Acer negundo*)
Coastal plain willow (*Salix caroliniana*)
Common elderberry (*Sambucus nigra* ssp. *canadensis*)
Diamond willow (*Salix eriocephala*)
Eastern hop-hornbeam (*Ostrya virginiana*)
Eastern red cedar (*Juniperus virginiana*)
Elderberry (*Sambucus nigra*)
Gray alder (*Alnus incana*)
Gray dogwood (*Cornus racemosa*)
Hazel alder (*Alnus serrulata*)
Heart-leaved willow (*Salix eriocephala*)
Hornbeam (*Carpinus caroliniana*)
Missouri river willow (*Salix eriocephala*)
Pin oak (*Quercus palustris*)
Quaking aspen (*Populus tremuloides*)
Red elm (*Ulmus rubra*)
Red oak (*Quercus rubra*)
Red spruce (*Picea rubens*)
Red-willow (*Cornus amomum*)
Sandbar willow (*Salix exigua*)
Shining willow (*Salix lucida*)
Slippery elm (*Ulmus rubra*)
Sugar maple (*Acer saccharum*)
Swamp white oak (*Quercus bicolor*)
Tuliptree (*Liriodendron tulipifera*)
Virginia pine (*Prunus virginiana*)

Common shrubs

Highbush blueberry (*Vaccinium corymbosum*)
Ninebark (*Physocarpus opulifolius*)
Northern arrow-wood (*Viburnum recognitum*)
Northern spicebush (*Lindera benzoin*)
Virginia creeper (*Parthenocissus quinquefolia*)
Winterberry (*Ilex verticillata*)

Less common shrubs

Arrow-wood (*Viburnum dentatum*)
Black raspberry (*Rubus occidentalis*)
Bristly dewberry (*Rubus hispidus*)
Buttonbush (*Cephalanthus occidentalis*)
Dwarf red blackberry (*Rubus pubescens*)
Hackberry (*Celtis occidentalis*)
Honeysuckle (*Lonicera spp.*)
Maleberry (*Lyonia ligustrina*)
Nannyberry (*Viburnum lentago*)
Northern bayberry (*Myrica pensylvanica*)
Red chokeberry (*Photinia pyrifolia*)
Red raspberry (*Rubus idaeus*)
Southern arrow wood (*Viburnum dentatum*)
Steeplebush (*Spiraea tomentosa*)
Swamp azalea (*Rhododendron viscosum*)
White meadowsweet (*Spiraea alba*)
Velvetleaf huckleberry (*Vaccinium myrtilloides*)
Virburnums (*Viburnum spp.*)
Virgin's-bower (*Clematis virginiana*)

Common Forbs

Bugleweed (*Lycopus uniflorus*)
Canadian wood nettle (*Laportea canadensis*)
Canada Clearweed (*Pilea pumila*)
Dogtooth violet (*Erythronium americanum*)
Dotted smartweed (*Polygonum punctatum*)
False nettle (*Boehmeria cylindrica*)
Giant goldenrod (*Solidago gigantea*)
Golden ragwort (*Packera aurea*)
Green-dragon (*Arisaema dracontium*)
Indian hemp (*Apocynum cannabinum*)
Jack-in-the-pulpit (*Arisaema triphyllum*)
Jewelweed (*Impatiens capensis*)
Jumpseed (*Polygonum virginianum*)
River grape (*Vitis riparia*)
Skunk cabbage (*Symplocarpus foetidus*)
Smallspike false nettle (*Boehmeria cylindrica*)
Stinging nettle (*Urtica dioica*)
White avens (*Geum canadense*)
White snakeroot (*Ageratina altissima*)
Wingstem (*Verbesina alternifolia*)
Wrinkle-leaf goldenrod (*Solidago rugosa*)
Violets (*Viola spp.*)

Less common forbs

Arrowleaf tearthumb (*Polygonum sagittatum*)

Beggarticks (*Bidens spp.*)
Bloodroot (*Sanguinaria canadensis*)
Blue cohosh (*Caulophyllum thalictroides*)
Blue skullcap (*Scutellaria lateriflora*)
Blue vervain (*Verbena hastata*)
Blue-eyed-mary (*Collinsia verna*)
Blunt leaf waterleaf (*Hydrophyllum canadense*)
Bog goldenrod (*Solidago uliginosa*)
Boneset (*Eupatorium perfoliatum*)
Broadleaf pondweed (*Potamogeton natans*)
Calico aster (*Symphyotrichum lateriflorum*)
Canada goldenrod (*Solidago canadensis*)
Canadian burnet (*Sanguisorba canadensis*)
Canadian honewort (*Cryptotaenia canadensis*)
Cardinal flower (*Lobelia cardinalis*)
Cattails (*Typha spp.*)
Cleavers (*Galium aparine*)
Clustered black snakeroot (*Sanicula odorata*)
Common blue violet (*Viola sororia*)
Common cattail (*Typha latifolia*)
Common smart-weed (*Polygonum hydropipe*)
Common sneezeweed (*Helenium autumnale*)
Common yellow wood-sorrel (*Oxalis stricta*)
Cream violet (*Viola striata*)
Cutleaf coneflower (*Rudbeckia laciniata*)
Dogtooth violet (*Erythronium americanum*)
Earth loosestrife (*Lysimachia terrestris*)
Enchanter's nightshade (*Circaea lutetiana*)
Field mint (*Mentha arvensis*)
Flat-topped white aster (*Doellingeria umbellata*)
Foamflower (*Tiarella cordifolia*)
Frost grape (*Vitis riparia*)
Goldenrods (*Solidago spp.*)
Grass-leaved goldenrod (*Euthamia graminifolia*)
Great nettle (*Urtica dioica*)
Green arrow arum (*Peltandra virginica*)
Ground nut (*Apios americana*)
Halbardleaf tearthumb (*Polygonum arifolium*)
Hemlock water parsnip (*Sium suave*)

Joe-pye-weed (*Eutrochium fistulosum*)
Lesser duckweed (*Lemna minor*)
Little leaf buttercup (*Ranunculus abortivus*)
Long style sweetroot (*Osmorhiza longistylis*)
Marsh marigold (*Caltha palustris*)
Marsh pennywort (*Hydrocotyle americana*)
Marsh pepper knotweed (*Polygonum hydropiper*)
Marsh seedbox (*Ludwigia palustris*)
Marsh St. John's-wort (*Triadenum virginicum*)
Mayapple (*Podophyllum peltatum*)
Mermaid-weed (*Proserpinaca palustris var. crebra*)
Mild water-pepper (*Polygonum hydropiperoides*)
Nodding lady's tresses (*Spiranthes cernua*)
Ontario lobelia (*Lobelia kalmii*)
Pale touch-me-not (*Impatiens pallida*)
Parasol whitetop (*Doellingeria umbellata*)
Pennsylvania smartweed (*Polygonum pensylvanicum*)
Purple pitcher plant (*Sarracenia purpurea*)
Purple stem aster (*Symphyotrichum puniceum var. puniceum*)
Purple stem beggarticks (*Bidens connata*)
Purplestem aster (*Symphyotrichum puniceum*)
Ramp (*Allium tricoccum*)
Roundleaf sundew (*Drosera rotundifolia*)
Shrubby cinquefoil (*Dasiphora fruticosa ssp. floribunda*)
Smooth goldenrod (*Solidago gigantea*)
Spatterdock (*Nuphar lutea*)
Spotted joe pye weed (*Eupatorium maculatum*)
Spotted ladysthumb (*Polygonum persicaria*)
Spotted trumpet weed (*Eupatorium maculatum*)
Squirrel corn (*Dicentra canadensis*)
Stiff marsh bedstraw (*Galium tinctorium*)
Striped cream violet (*Viola striata*)
Swamp loosestrife (*Decodon verticillatus*)
Swamp milkweed (*Asclepias incarnata*)
Swamp smartweed (*Polygonum hydropiperoides*)

Tall meadow-rue (*Thalictrum pubescens*)
Three petal bedstraw (*Galium trifidum*)
Three-lobe beggarticks (*Bidens tripartita*)
Toadshade (*Trillium sessile*)
Touch-me-not (*Impatiens pallida*)
Variegated yellow pond lily (*Nuphar variegata*)
Virginia bluebells (*Mertensia virginica*)
Virginia spring beauty (*Claytonia virginica*)
Virginia waterleaf (*Hydrophyllum virginianum*)
Wakerobin (*Trillium erectum*)
Water knotweed (*Polygonum amphibium*)
Water-willow (*Justicia americana*)
White panicle aster (*Symphyotrichum lanceolatum*)
Wild blue phlox (*Phlox divaricata*)
Wild cucumber (*Echinocystis lobata*)
Wild garlic (*Allium canadense*)
Wild germander (*Teucrium canadense*)
Wild ginger (*Asarum canadense*)
Wild leek (*Allium tricoccum*)
Wood geranium (*Geranium maculatum*)
Wood-nettle (*Laportea canadensis*)
Zigzag goldenrod (*Solidago flexicaulis*)

Common grasses and sedges

Bluejoint (*Calamagrostis canadensis*)
Deertongue grass (*Dichanthelium clandestinum*)
Fowl mannagrass (*Glyceria striata*)
Greater bladder sedge (*Carex intumescens*)
Reed canary grass (*Phalaris arundinacea*)
Rigid sedge (*Carex tetanica*)
Riverbank wild rye (*Elymus riparius*)
Shallow sedge (*Carex lurida*)
Twisted sedge (*Carex torta*)
Virginia wild rye (*Elymus virginicus*)

Less common grasses and sedges

Autumn bent (*Agrostis perennans*)
Awl fruit sedge (*Carex stipata*)
Bald spike-rush (*Eleocharis erythropoda*)
American bur-reed (*Sparganium americanum*)
Bentgrass (*Agrostis spp.*)
Big bluestem (*Andropogon gerardii*)
Blister sedge (*Carex vesicaria*)
Blunt broom sedge (*Carex tribuloides*)
Bottlebrush grass (*Elymus hystrix*)
Bristly-stalked sedge (*Carex leptalea ssp. leptalea*)
Brome-like sedge (*Carex bromoides*)
Broom sedge (*Carex scoparia var. scoparia*)
Bulrush (*Scirpus polyphyllus*)
Carpet bentgrass (*Agrostis stolonifera*)
Common rush (*Juncus effusus*)
Cutgrass (*Leersia virginica*)
Dioecious sedge (*Carex sterilis*)
Fall panic grass (*Panicum dichotomiflorum*)
Field horsetail (*Equisetum arvense*)
Floating mannagrass (*Glyceria septentrionalis*)
Fringed sedge (*Carex crinita*)
Graceful sedge (*Carex gracillima*)
Grass of parnassus (*Parnassia glauca*)
Gray's sedge (*Carex grayi*)
Green bulrush (*Scirpus atrovirens*)
Hairy sedge (*Carex lacustris*)
Hop sedge (*Carex lupulina*)
Inflated narrow-leaf sedge (*Carex grisea*)
Knotted rush (*Juncus nodosus*)
Limp mannagrass (*Glyceria laxa*)
Long beaked sedge (*Carex sprengelii*)
Longhair sedge (*Carex comosa*)
Mellic mannagrass (*Glyceria melicaria*)
Muhly (*Muhlenbergia spp.*)
Needle beak sedge (*Rhynchospora capillacea*)
Nodding fescue (*Festuca subverticillata*)
Nodding sedge (*Carex gynandra*)
Northeastern sedge (*Carex cryptolepis*)
Northern sea oats (*Chasmanthium latifolium*)
Prairie sedge (*Carex prairea*)
Rice cutgrass (*Leersia oryzoides*)
Rattlesnake mannagrass (*Glyceria canadensis*)
Short hair sedge (*Carex crinita var. crinita*)
Slender spike rush (*Eleocharis tenuis*)
Spiked muhly (*Muhlenbergia glomerata*)
Sweet woodreed (*Cinna arundinacea*)
Switchgrass (*Panicum virgatum*)
Three-seeded sedge (*Carex trisperma*)

Three-way sedge (*Dulichium arundinaceum*)
Tufted hairgrass (*Deschampsia caespitosa*)
Tussock sedge (*Carex stricta*)
Upland bentgrass (*Agrostis perennans*)
White beak sedge (*Rhynchospora alba*)
Whitegrass (*Leersia virginica*)
Wiegand's wild rye (*Elymus wiegandii*)
Wool-grass (*Scirpus cyperinus*)
Yellow sedge (*Carex flava*)

Common ferns
Cinnamon fern (*Osmunda cinnamomea*)
Marsh fern (*Thelypteris palustris*)
Ostrich fern (*Matteuccia struthiopteris*)
Royal fern (*Osmunda regalis*)
Sensitive fern (*Onoclea sensibilis*)

Less common ferns
Christmas fern (*Polystichum acrostichoides*)
Crested woodfern (*Dryopteris cristata*)
Lady fern (*Athryium filix-femina*)
Silvery glade fern (*Deparia acrostichoides*)
Virginia chain fern (*Woodwardia virginica*)

LAKES, PONDS, MARSHES

Natural landscapes that feature standing water — lakes, ponds, and very slow moving rivers — host a substantial array of species ranging from small, free-floating aquatics to shrubs and trees all of which share a common trait: they are *hydromorphic*, adaptable to excessively wet conditions for long periods of time.

Although we often think of habitats in the context of the margins around lakes and ponds — *marshes* — they also include depressions where water levels can fluctuate seasonally but never really dry, as well as oxbow ponds, backwater sloughs and margins of slow-moving streams. Those whose property includes a natural pond or lake shore margin will find marsh plants appealing and successful in landscape design.

Soils range from peaty to mineral, but are commonly coated with mucks involving clays and silts with high levels of decomposed organic matter. Some involve calcareous materials, but more often they are over acidic bedrock such as sandstone and, less often, shale. Many smaller, shaded vernal ponds are unvegetated, their bottoms covered by dead leaves and algae, while larger examples can display zones of vegetation directly related to water tolerance. Many are full to part sun habitats.

Trees, on the drier margins:
Black gum (*Nyssa sylvatica*)
Gray alder (*Alnus incana*)
Hazel alder (*Alnus serrulata*)
Pin oak (*Quercus palustris*)
Red maple (*Acer rubrum*)
Red spruce (*Picea rubens*)
Silky dogwood (*Cornus amomum*)
Willows (*Salix spp.*)

Shrubs, on drier margins:
Bristly dewberry (*Rubus hispidus*)
Buttonbush (*Cephalanthus occidentalis*)
Great laurel (*Rhododendron maximum*)
Highbush blueberry (*Vaccinium corymbosum*)
Maleberry (*Lyonia ligustrina*)
Northern wild gooseberry (*Ribes hirtellum*)
Possum-haw (*Viburnum nudum*)
Southern arrow-wood (*Viburnum dentatum*)
Swamp dewberry (*Rubus hispidus*)
Swamp rose (*Rosa palustris*)
Sweet gale (*Myrica gale*)
White meadowsweet (*Spiraea alba*)
Winterberry (*Ilex verticillata*)

Grasses, sedges, rushes
American bur-reed (*Sparganium americanum*)
American mannagrass (*Glyceria grandis*)
Annual wild rice (*Zizania aquatica*)
Awlfruit sedge (*Carex stipata*)
Baltic rush (*Juncus articus var. littoralis*)
Beaked sedge (*Carex rostrata*)
Blister sedge (*Carex vesicaria*)

Bluejoint (*Calamagrostis canadensis*)
Broadfruit bur-reed (*Sparganium eurycarpum*)
Bulrush (*Scirpus spp.*)
Bur-reed (*Sparganium spp.*)
Canada bluegrass (*Poa compressa*)
Canadian rush (*Juncus canadensis*)
Chairmaker's bulrush (*Schoenoplectus americanus*)
Common cattail (*Typha latifolia*)
Common rush (*Juncus effusus*)
Common spikerush (*Eleocharis palustris*)
Fowl bluegrass (*Poa palustris*)
Green bulrush (*Scirpus atrovirens*)
Hairgrass (*Agrostis scabra*)
Hairy sedge (*Carex lacustris*)
Hard stem bulrush (*Schoenoplectus acutus*)
Inland sedge (*Carex interior*)
Knotted rush (*Juncus nodosus*)
Longhair sedge (*Carex comosa*)
Mannagrass (*Glyceria spp.*)
Matted spike-rush (*Eleocharis intermedia*)
Narrow panicle sedge (*Juncus brevicaudatus*)
Narrowleaf cattail (*Typha angustifolia*)
Nerveless woodland sedge (*Carex leptonervia*)
Nodding sedge (*Carex gynandra*)
Northeastern bulrush (*Scirpus ancistrochaetus*)
Northern long sedge (*Carex folliculata*)
Northwest territory sedge (*Carex utriculata*)
Pale meadow grass (*Torreyochloa pallida*)
Panicled bulrush (*Scirpus microcarpus*)
Prairie sedge (*Carex prairea*)
Prickly bog sedge (*Carex atlantica*)
Redtop (*Agrostis gigantea*)
Reed canary grass (*Phalaris arundinacea*)
Rice cutgrass (*Leersia oryzoides*)
River bulrush (*Schoenoplectus fluviatilis*)
Schweinitz's sedge (*Carex schweinitzii*)
Shallow sedge (*Carex lurida*)
Sharp-fruited rush (*Juncus acuminatus*)
Short hair sedge (*Carex crinita var. crinita*)
Silvery sedge (*Carex canescens*)
Soft rush (*Juncus effusus*)
Soft-stem bulrush (*Schoenoplectus tabernaemontani*)
Spike rush (*Eleocharis spp.*)
Tawny cottongrass (*Eriophorum virginicum*)
Three-way sedge (*Dulichium arundinaceum*)
Torrey's bulrush (*Schoenoplectus torreyi*)
Tussock sedge (*Carex stricta*)
Water horsetail (*Equisetum fluviatile*)
Water sedge (*Carex aquatilis*)
Weakstalk bulrush (*Schoenoplectus purshianus*)
White beak sedge (*Rhynchospora alba*)
Winter bentgrass (*Agrostis hyemalis*)
Wood's sedge (*Carex tetanica*)
Woodland rush (*Juncus subcaudatus*)
Wool-grass (*Scirpus cyperinus*)
Wooly fruit sedge (*Carex lasiocarpa*)
Wooly sedge (*Carex pellita*)

Ferns
Cinnamon fern (*Osmunda cinnamomea*)
Marsh fern (*Thelypteris palustris*)
Royal fern (*Osmunda regalis*)
Sensitive fern (*Onoclea sensibilis*)

Forbs
Arrow-arum (*Peltandra virginica*)
Arrow-leaved tearthumb (*Polygonum sagittatum*)
Arrowhead (*Sagittaria rigida*)
Arrowleaf tearthumb (*Polygonum sagittatum*)
Beggar-ticks (*Bidens spp.*)
Bladderwort (*Utricularia geminiscapa*)
Blue flag iris (*Iris versicolor*)
Blue skullcap (*Scutellaria lateriflora*)
Bog willowherb (*Epilobium leptophyllum*)
Boneset (*Eupatorium perfoliatum*)
Broadleaf arrowhead (*Sagittaria latifolia*)
Buckbean (*Menyanthes trifoliata*)
Bugleweed (*Lycopus uniflorus*)
Bur marigold (*Bidens laevis*)
Calamus (*Acorus calamus*)
Canadian St. John's-wort (*Hypericum canadense*)
Canadian waterweed (*Elodea canadensis*)
Clearweed (*Pilea pumila*)

Cleavers (*Galium spp.*)
Climbing hempvine (*Mikania scandens*)
Coast cockspur grass (*Echinochloa walteri*)
Common bladderwort (*Utricularia macrorhiza*)
Common duck meat (*Spirodela polyrrhiza*)
Common duckweed (*Lemna minor*)
Coon's tail (*Ceratophyllum demersum*)
Creeping spike rush (*Eleocharis palustris*)
Crimson-eyed rosemallow (*Hibiscus moscheutos*)
Crowned beggarticks (*Bidens coronata*)
Curly pondweed (*Potamogeton crispusI*)
Dock (*Rumex spp.*)
Dotted smartweed (*Polygonum punctatum*)
Duckweed (*Lemna spp.*)
Dwarf St. John's-wort (*Hypericum mutilum*)
Flat leaf bladderwort (*Utricularia intermedia*)
Fraser's marsh St. John's wort (*Triadenum fraseri*)
Golden-club (*Orontium aquaticum*)
Grass leaf mud plantain (*Heteranthera dubia*)
Great ragweed (*Ambrosia trifida*)
Green arrow arum (*Peltandra virginica*)
Groundnut (*Apios americana*)
Halberd-leaved tearthumb (*Polygonum arifolium*)
Harlequin blueflag (*Iris versicolor*)
Hemlock water parsnip (*Sium suave*)
Hornwort (*Ceratophyllum spp.*)
Inundated clubmoss (*Lycopodiella inundata*)
Jewelweed (*Impatiens capensis*)
Joe-pye weed (*Eupatorium spp.*)
Lesser bladderwort (*Utricularia minor*)
Lesser clearweed (*Pilea fontana*)
Lizard's tail (*Saururus cernuus*)
Long root smartweed (*Polygonum amphibium var. emersum*)
Marsh bellflower (*Campanula aparinoides*)
Marsh seedbox (*Ludwigia palustris*)
Marsh St. John's-wort (*Triadenum virginicum*)
Marsh-purslane (*Ludwigia palustris*)
New York ironweed (*Vernonia noveboracensis*)
Pickerel-weed (*Pontederia cordata*)
Pondweed (*Potamogeton spp.*)
Pondweed (*Stuckenia spp.*)
Purple marshlocks (*Comarum palustre*)
Ribbonleaf pondweed (*Potamogeton epihydrus*)
Scaldweed (*Cuscuta gronovii*)
Skunk cabbage (*Symplocarpus foetidus*)
Smallspike false nettle (*Boehmeria cylindrica*)
Smartweeds (*Polygonum spp.*)
Smooth beggartick (*Bidens laevis*)
Spotted Joe-pye-weed (*Eupatorium maculatum*)
Spotted water hemlock (*Cicuta maculata*)
Sundew (*Drosera spp.*)
Swamp beggar-ticks (*Bidens bidentoides*)
Swamp milkweed (*Asclepias incarnata*)
Swamp smartweed (*Polygonum hydropiperoides*)
Swamp verbena (*Verbena hastata*)
Tearthumb (*Persicaria sagittata*)
Tidalmarsh amaranth (*Amaranthus cannabinus*)
Tufted loosestrife (*Lysimachia thyrsiflora*)
Variegated yellow pond lily (*Nuphar variegata*)
Virginia chain fern (*Woodwardia virginica*)
Wapato (*Sagittaria latifolia*)
Water arum (*Calla palustris*)
Water horehound (*Lycopus americanus*)
Water knotweed (*Polygonum amphibium*)
Water plantain (*Alisma plantagoaquatica*)
Water smartweed (*Polygonum hydropiperoides*)
Water-plantain (*Alisma plantago-aquatica*)
Watershield (*Brasenia schreberi*)
White water lily (*Nymphaea odorata*)
Yellow pond lily (*Nuphar lutea*)

Appendix - Pennsylvania Soils

Abbottstown silt loams

Where they are found: level to slightly concave sloping upland flats, depressions and drainageways, often in valleys and on hillslopes, in the Northern Piedmont.

Characteristics: mesic to moist, about pH 6.0, possibly with somewhat poor drainage, especially in winter months, but generally deep and fertile.

Composition: About 25 percent sand, 55 percent silt, 20 percent clay, with about two percent organic matter in the surface layer, from locally weathered non-calcareous red shale, siltstone, fine-grained sandstone.

Current use: almost entirely for agricultural crops, with wooded areas in mixed hardwoods dominated by hickories and oaks.

Taxonomy: Fine-loamy, mixed, active, mesic Aeric Fragiaqualfs.

Albrights silt loams

Where they are found: nearly level to moderately steep concave lower mountain slopes and ridges, especially footslopes and toeslopes and in U-shaped drainage heads.

Characteristics: dry to mesic, moderately well drained silt loams, often with root-restrictive layers 18 to 32 inches below the surface, with pH ranging from 4.6 to 5.5.

Composition: about 25 percent sand, 53 percent silt, 22 percent clay, with organic matter in the top 12 inches ranging from 1.4 to 2.1 percent, from colluvium or glacial deposits of reddish shale, siltstone and fine-grained sandstone in the Appalachian Ridge and Valley region, the Allegheny Plateau and Mountains and nearby glaciated areas of Pennsylvania.

Current use: about a third cleared, mostly for pasture, with the remainder in hardwood forests dominated by oaks, red maple, white ash and yellow poplar.

Taxonomy: Fine-loamy, mixed, semiactive, mesic Aquic Fragiudalfs.

Alden silt loams

Where they are found: moist to wet upland depressions high in organic matter on nearly flat till plains.

Characteristics: moist to wet, sometimes mucky silt loams that are very poorly drained with a pH of 6.3; although not flooded, they are frequently ponded with groundwater levels at or near the surface from November through June, and as such meet the criteria for hydric soil.

Composition: About 23 percent sand, 53 percent silt, 24 percent clay, with at least 5 percent organic matter that can be found 18 to 40 inches below the surface.

Current use: cleared areas that are drained sometimes used for pasture, but most are woodland with stands of red and silver maple, green and black ash, alder, hemlock, white cedar, willow and elm. Some abandoned agriculture use areas are reverting to wetland herbaceous plants that grow in or near water.

Taxonomy: Fine-loamy, mixed, active, nonacid, mesic Mollic Endoaquepts.

Aldino silt loams

Where they are found: gentle hillslopes in Delaware County.

Characteristics: mesic to moist, somewhat poorly to moderately drained but fertile silt loams with a pH of 5.8.

Composition: about 27 percent sand, 55 percent silt and 18 percent clay. Organic matter in the top

12 inches is about 2.5 percent. They formed in materials from a combination of wind-deposited sediment and weathered serpentine to create an overlying silt mantle. They are not flooded or ponded but the water table can reach 20 inches from December through April.

Current use: agricultural, suitable for a wide variety of crops, and residential. Good choices for canopy trees include Sugar maple (*Acer saccharum*), White ash (*Fraxinus americana*), Yellow poplar (*Liriodendron tulipifera*), Red oak (*Quercus rubra*), White oak (*Quercus alba*), Black oak (*Quercus velutina*) and Pinus virginiana (*Virginia pine*)

Taxonomy: Fine-silty, mixed, active, mesic Typic Fragiudalfs.

Allegheny silt loams

Where they are found: higher stream terraces, foot slopes and alluvial fans in western Pennsylvania. They include the deactivated Holston series of Jefferson County.

Characteristics: moist to wet, deep, well drained, acidic and humus-poor soils with relatively low native fertility, especially in calcium, magnesium and potassium, with a pH of 4.6. Not subject to flooding or ponding, and moisture tends to be concentrated in organic layers at the surface.

Composition: about 29 percent sand, 49 percent silt and 22 percent clay, with about 2 percent organic matter in the top 12 inches, formed in weathered rock found at the bases of steep slopes comprised of acidic sandstone, siltstone and shale.

Current use: when cleared, as pasture or cultivated crop fields, which require either soil amendments or rotation back to forest to regather nutrients. Suitable for many species of plants and historically forested by coniferous and deciduous trees.

Taxonomy: Fine-loamy, mixed, semiactive, mesic Typic Hapludults.

Allenwood silt loams

Where they are found: smooth to slightly convex glaciated valley sides and uplands, as well as terraces and till plains in some areas, in the Ridge and Valley province of eastern Pennsylvania.

Characteristics: mesic to moist, well drained, acidic, silt loams and gravelly silt loams that tend to be relatively low in native fertility (calcium, magnesium, potassium) but ideal for natural forest; soil pH ranges from 4.6 to 5.3.

Composition: about 29 percent sand, 53 percent silt, 18 percent clay, with about 2 percent organic matter in the top 12 inches. Formed in pre-Wisconsin glacial deposits derived from sandstone, shale and siltstone similar to the underlying bedrock. Well-distributed precipitation exceeds evapotranspiration, but moisture tends to be concentrated in organic layers at the surface.

Current use: most in cultivation for hay, small grain and other crops as well as pasture; wooded areas are generally oak-hickory forest.

Taxonomy: Fine-loamy, mixed, semiactive, mesic Typic Hapludults.

Allis silt loams

Where they are found: thin till mantle of glacial lake plains and depressions in ground moraines, primarily in Erie County.

Characteristics: dry to wet, with a pH of 4.8; while flooding and ponding is rare and available moisture tends to be low much of the year, seasonal groundwater levels are high from November to June and many meet the criteria as hydric. Drainage is considered poor with root-restrictive layers at 12 to 30 inches.

Composition: about 21 percent sand, 50 percent silt and 29 percent clay with organic matter ranging from 3.5 to 5 percent and more. Soils formed from till dominated by and usually underlain with acidic shale sometimes interbedded with sandstone and siltstone.

Current use: agricultural uses is primarily for growing hay and pasture; native vegetation is dominated by red maple (*Acer rubrum*), white pine (*Pinus strobus*), white ash (*Fraxinus americana*), hemlock (*Tsuga canadensis*) and American elm (*Ulmus americana*).

Taxonomy: Fine, illitic, acid, mesic Typic Endoaquepts.

Alton loams

Where they are found: level to steep, gravelly glacial outwash deposits on terraces, alluvial fans, kames and remnant beach ridges in diverse locations.

Characteristics: dry to mesic, very deep, well to excessively drained loams and sandy loams, typically stony, with pH beteen 5.3 and 6.1 — decreasing with steepness of slope.

Composition: About 56 percent sand, 36 percent silt and 8 percent clay, with about 2.3 percent organic matter in the top 12 inches, formed from deposits dominated by hard, acidic rock plus material from regolith limestone below 40 inches. Silty lacustrine material can be found in some locations below 40 inches.

Current use: cleared land is used mostly for vegetable and fruit growing, along with general farm crops. Native vegetation is typically dominated by sugar maple (*Acer saccharum*), beech (*Fagus grandifolia*), hemlock (*Tsuga canadensis*), pine (*Pinus spp.*), basswood (*Tilia americana*), hickory (*Carya spp.*) and hophornbeam (*Ostrya virginiana*).

Taxonomy: Loamy-skeletal, mixed, active, mesic Dystric Eutrudepts.

Alvira silt loams

Where they are found: smooth to slightly concave hillslopes of old glaciated uplands in northwestern and east-central Pennsylvania.

Characteristics: dry to mesic, but seasonally moist, poorly drained, deep silt loams and gravelly silt loams with a pH of 4.6; the water table can be at 12 inches from October through May but then tends to become dry.

Composition: about 27 percent sand, 53 percent silt, 20 percent clay with about 1 percent organic matter in the top 12 inches, formed in loamy pre-Wisconsin till from sandstone, shale, siltstone and some quartzite.

Current use: pasture, some cropland and woodlands, with forested areas tending toward mixed hardwoods dominated by yellow poplar (*Liriodendron tulipifera*) and oaks, especially red oak (*Quercus rubra*).

Taxonomy: Fine-loamy, mixed, active, mesic Aeric Fragiaquults.

Amwell silt loams

Where they are found: colluvial locations on lower hillslopes, sometimes extending from the base of steeper slopes onto upland flats and depressions in Bucks County.

Characteristics: mesic to moist, deep to very deep, moderately well to somewhat poorly drained silt loams with high to very high surface runoff, a pH of 6.0 and a zone of saturation at about 20 inches in winter to late spring. Water seepage on top of a fragipan, if present, is common on slopes.

Composition: about 28 percent sand, 55 percent silt and 17 percent clay, with about 3 percent organic matter in the top 12 inches, generally fine loamy colluvium derived from igneous rock in upper horizons and old glacial drift and alluvium weathered from shale or igneous rock below.

Current use: mostly woodland, with common trees being pin oak (*Quercus palustris*), red maple (*Acer rubrum*), elm (*Ulmus spp.*), ash (*Fraxinus spp.*) and red oak (*Quercus rubra*); some cleared areas are used for pasture or cultivated crops.

Taxonomy: Fine-loamy, mixed, active, mesic Aquic Fragiudalfs.

Andover loams

Where they are found: typically in valleys and concave toeslopes and footslopes, but also nearly level to sloping benches, depressions and swales, and most often at the bases of prominent ridges. Stony and gravelly loams can also be found on mountain slopes and valley sides.

Characteristics: dry to mesic but seasonally moist, poorly-drained sandy, gravelly and stony loams, usually on surfaces up to 8 percent grades but occasionally to 15 percent with a fragipan between 18 and 30 inches and seasonal water saturation as high as 3 inches from October through June, with a pH of 5.0 to 5.7 depending on composition.

Composition: widely variable between 38 and 60 percent sand, 17 to 44 percent silt, and 20 to 23 percent clay, with about 1.5 percent organic matter in the top 12 inches; formed in colluvium derived from acidic red and gray sandstone and shale.

Current use: about 30 percent is in cropland and pasture use; woodland dominants are primarily oak-hickory hardwoods — especially red oak (*Quercus rubra*) and yellow poplar (*Liriodendron tulipifera*) with limited stands of white pine and hemlock.

Taxonomy: Fine-loamy, mixed, active, mesic Typic Fragiaquults.

Arendtsville gravelly loams

Where they are found: on dissected upland hillslopes, ranging from gentle to steep, in southeastern Pennsylvania.

Characteristics: dry to mesic, deep, well drained, gravelly loams and silt loams with a typical pH of 5.2

Composition: variable, with gravelly loams composed of about 42 percent sand, 39 percent silt and 19 percent clay, and silt loams composed of 27 percent sand, 54 percent silt and 19 percent clay; soil pH ranges from 5.2 to 5.8 and organic matter in the top 12 inches is typically around 2 percent. Soils formed from weathered rocks created on ancient alluvial fans, built from quartzite, aporhyolite and sandstone in a red, sandy matrix of Triassic residuum loam.

Current use: most cleared land is used for cherry and peach orchards, while native woodland is primarily hardwoods of mixed oak.

Taxonomy: Fine-loamy, mixed, semiactive, mesic Typic Hapludults.

Armagh silt loams

Where they are found: depressions in benches and on broad ridgetops with slopes of less than 8 percent, mostly on the Allegheny Plateau in western Pennsylvania.

Characteristics: mesic to moist, poorly drained silt loams, about 5.0 pH, with a seasonal zone of saturation as high as 3 inches with some ponding from October to June, but usually dry at other times of the year; they generally meet criteria as hydric.

Composition: about 10 to 20 percent sand, 50 to 55 percent silt, and 30 to 33 percent silt, with organic matter ranging up to 2.5 percent, but more commonly around 1 percent, in the top 12 inches; soils formed from weathered acidic gray shale interbedded with some sandstone and siltstone.

Current use: about a third of the land is in cropland or pasture, while the remainder is in woodlands, generally mixed hardwoods dominated by oaks, yellow poplar (*Liriodendron tulipifera*) and red maple (*Acer rubrum*). Soils are suitable for white ash (*Fraxinus americana*) and black cherry (*Prunus serotina*). Poor drainage and stony content comprise the major land use limitations.

Taxonomy: fine, mixed, active, mesic Typic Endoaquults.

Arnot silt loams

Where they are found: valley sides, with slopes ranging from gentle to nearly vertical, in glaciated areas of northeastern Pennsylvania.

Characteristics: dry to mesic, acidic (4.8 pH), excessively well drained, rocky and thin silt loams, often mixed with rock outcrops and frequently categorized as a channery loam.

Composition: variable with 30 to 45 percent sand, 40 to 55 percent silt and 13 percent clay, formed from deposits of Wisconsin-age till derived mostly from acidic shales, siltstones and sandstone, but sometimes including both conglomerate and quartzite. Bedrock is usually at 10 to 20 inches and Arnot soils are often found in elevations between 1,000 and 1,800 feet.

Current use: primarily in forest with limited cleared areas for pasture and hay. Native vegetation is dominated by oak (*Quercus spp.*), beech (*Fagus grandifolia*), black cherry (*Prunus serotina*), sugar maple (*Acer saccharum*), hemlock (*Tsuga canadensis*) and white pine (*Pinus strobus*).

Taxonomy: loamy-skeletal, mixed, active, mesic Lithic Dystrudepts.

Ashton silt loams

Where they are found: alluvial fans and low stream terraces in Juniata and Mifflin Counties.

Characteristics: moist to wet riparian silt loams that are deep, well drained and rarely flooded, about 6.5 pH.

Composition: about 12 percent sand, 68 percent silt and 20 percent clay, with about 2.5 percent organic matter in the top 12 inches, formed in alluvium derived from limestone or partly in weathered limestone.

Current use: nearly all areas for a variety of agricultural crops; native vegetation consists mostly of oaks (*Quercus spp.*), maples (*Acer spp.*), sycamore (*Plantanus spp.*), elms (*Ulmus spp.*), black gum (*Nyssa sylvatica*), yellow poplar (*Liriodendron tulipifera*), hickories (*Carya spp.*), beech (*Fagus spp.*) and ash (*Fraxinus spp.*)

Taxonomy: fine-silty, mixed, active, mesic Mollic Hapludalfs.

Atherton loams

Where they are found: depressions of water-sorted glacial materials in mostly Luzerne and Columbia counties, but also scattered in Lackawanna and Wyoming Counties.

Characteristics: mesic to wet, deep, poorly drained loams and silt loams, high in organic matter, subject to common winter-spring ponding, about 6.2 pH, and classified as hydric.

Composition: about 45 percent sand, 33 percent silt and 22 percent clay, with more than 6 percent organic matter in the top 12 inches, and formed from fine-loamy glaciofluvial deposits derived from sandstone and siltstone.

Current use: where not drained, soils are commonly in woodlots of elm and soft maple, is idle or is pastured. Drained areas are used for growing corn, small grains, hay and pasture. Primary canopy trees include red maple (*Acer rubrum*) and white pine (*Pinus strobus*).

Taxonomic class: fine-loamy, mixed, active, nonacid, mesic Aeric Endoaquepts.

Athol silt loams

Where they are found: nearly level to moderately steep, convex, dissected ridgetops and sideslopes of the northern Piedmont.

Characteristics: dry to mesic, deep, well-drained silt loams and gravelly loams with a range of 5.4 to 6.0 pH.

Composition: about 25 percent sand, 55 percent silt and 20 percent clay, with 2 to 2.5 percent organic matter in the top 12 inches, formed from reddish, calcareous locally weathered conglomerates that included quartz, sandstone, shale and limestone.

Current use: about 85 percent in pasture or cultivated; woodlands consist of hardwoods dominated by oak and hickory. Soils are particularly suited for yellow poplar (*Liriodendron tulipifera*), shortleaf pine (*Pinus echinata*), Virginia pine (*Pinus virginiana*), and red oak (*Quercus rubra*).

Taxonomy: fine-loamy, mixed, active, mesic ultic Hapludalfs.

Atkins silt loams

Where they are found: nearly level to slightly sloping floodplains that are often inundated, on the Allegheny Plateau in western Pennsylvania.

Characteristics: mesic to wet, deep, poorly drained silt loams where groundwater levels are at 6 inches from October through June and within a foot for most of the remaining time, with a pH of 5.0 to 5.3. Ponding is rare, but flooding common, with very slow internal drainage; most of the flooding is caused by shallow standing to slow-moving water on the surface.

Composition: about 22 percent sand, 54 percent silt and 24 percent clay, formed from recent alluvium derived from acid sandstone and shale, washed down from elevations above.

Current uses: commonly used for pasture, but sites have also been filled in and for many years developed for urban use. In their natural state, most are wooded with mixed hardwoods consisting of water-tolerant oaks, red maples, black gum, sweet gum, willow, elm, ash and alder. Aquatic grasses and sedges can also be found.

Taxonomy: fine-loamy, mixed, active, acid, mesic Fluvaquentic Endoaquepts.

Bagtown cobbly loams

Where they are found: gentle to very steep mountain backslopes, footslopes, benches and colluvial fans in south-central Pennsylvania.

Characteristics: mesic to wet, very stony, well drained, generally deep loams with a pH of 5.0.

Composition: about 46 percent sand, 42 percent silt and 12 percent clay, with about 2 percent organic matter in the top 12 inches, primarily from colluvial materials composed of light gray to medium gray quartzite, conglomerate and meta-graywacke. Sandy shales and siltstone can be found on lower footslopes.

Current use: mostly woodland or forest production, with some areas used for pasture and orchards. Spoils are well suited for yellow poplar (*Liriodendron tulipifera*), white oak (*Quercus alba*) and red oak (*Quercus rubra*).

Taxonomy: coarse-loamy, siliceous, semiactive, mesic Oxyaquic Hapludults.

Baile silt loams

Where they are found: upland depressions and footslopes in the northern Piedmont.

Characteristics: mesic to wet, poorly drained, very deep silt loams with groundwater near the surface from November through April and classified as hydric, with a pH of about 5.3.

Composition: about 22 percent sand, 55 percent silt and 33 percent clay, with about 2.5 percent organic matter in the top 12 inches, from local alluvium over residuum from acidic crystalline rock, mostly mica schist, grantized schist and gneiss.

Current use: areas that have been drained are used for some corn, hay, but mostly pasture. Native vegetation includes pin oak (*Quercus palustris*), birch (*Betula spp.*), red maple (*Acer rubrum*) and holly (*Ilex spp.*), with understories featuring laurel (*Kalmia spp.*), and a variety of herbs and sedges.

Taxonomy: fine-loamy, mixed, semiactive, mesic Typic Endoaquults.

Barbour loams

Where they are found: level to convex flood plains, low terraces and alluvial fans, with slopes ranging up to 8 percent, in northern Pennsylvania.

Characteristics: dry to mesic, very well-drained, very deep fine sand, silt and gravelly loams that not ponded but rarely to frequently flooded, with a pH of about 5.3.

Composition: typically 60 to 70 percent sand, with silt and clay about evenly divided for the balance, although loams are more often 45 percent sand, 43 percent silt and 12 percent clay. Organic matter can vary between 2 and 3 percent in the top 12 inches. Soils formed in recent alluvial deposits from regions of acidic, reddish sandstone, shale and siltstone.

Current use: most areas have been cleared for corn, small grains, hay, vegetables and pasture; where woodlots remain, the dominant trees are maple, oak, beech, elm and sycamore. Appropriate species include sugar maple (*Acer saccharum*), red oak (*Quercus rubra*), white ash (*Fraxinus americana*), black walnut (*Juglans nigra*), Yellow poplar (*Liriodendron tulipifera*), White pine (*Pinus strobus*), American sycamore (*Platanus occidentalis*) and black cherry (*Prunus serotina*).

Taxonomy: coarse-loamy over sandy or sandy-skeletal, mixed, active, mesic Fluventic Dystrudepts.

Basher loams

Where they are found: flood plains and low terraces with slopes up to 3 percent in northern and western Pennsylvania.

Characteristics: dry to mesic, moderately well drained and very deep loams and silt loams with a pH generally between 4.8 and 5.3.

Composition: most commonly silt loams with about 32 percent sand, 56 percent silt and 12 percent clay, but sandy loams tend to be about 60 percent sand, 30 percent silt and 10 percent clay. Organic matter ranges from 1.5 to 3 percent, commonly about 2.3 percent, and soils formed in recent alluvial deposits derived from acidic reddish siltstone, shale and sandstone.

Current use: although occasionally to frequently flooded, most have been cleared for a wide range of agricultural crops; woodlots generally include maple, hemlock, oak and white pine. Appropriate species include sugar maple (*Acer saccharum*), red oak (*Quercus rubra*), American basswood (*Tilia americana*), and black walnut (*Juglans nigra*).

Taxonomy: coarse-loamy, mixed, active, mesic Fluvaquentic Dystrudepts.

Bath loams

Where they are found: gentle to steep mountain and ridge hillslopes in the Glaciated Allegheny Plateau on elevations between 800 and 1800 feet above sea level.

Characteristics: dry to mesic, well drained, very deep silt, stony, channery and flaggy loams, commonly with a fragipan at about 30 inches, with a pH of 5.3.

Composition: range of 33 to 44 percent sand, 45 to 55 percent silt and about 12 percent clay, formed in loamy till primarily from gray to brown siltstone, sandstone and shale, but with 2 and more commonly 3 percent organic matter in the top 12 inches.

Current use: while most areas have been cleared to grow general farm crops, woodland areas are typically dominated by northern hardwoods and some white pine. Suitable species include sugar maple (*Acer saccharum*), black cherry (*Prunus serotina*) and red oak (*Quercus rubra*).

Taxonomy: coarse-loamy, mixed, active, mesic Typic Fragiudepts.

Bedington silt loams

Where they are found: nearly level valleys to steep, convex uplands and on sideslopes of ridges and hills in the Ridge and Valley and Piedmont areas of Pennsylvania.

Characteristics: dry to mesic, well-drained, very deep soils formed in residuum weathered from gray, dark brown to olive acidic shale or interbedded shale, siltstone, and fine-grained sandstone, with a pH of about 5.8.

Composition: about 25 percent sand, 53 percent silt and 12 percent clay, with organic matter in the top 12 inches usually at 1.7 percent.

Current use: About 70 percent of the soils are in pasture and cropland - principally corn, small grain and hay - while woodlands are dominated by hickory, oak, yellow-poplar and red maple.

Taxonomy: fine-loamy, mixed, active, mesic Typic Hapludults.

Belmont silt loams

Where they are found: gently sloping to very steep benches and sideslopes in Columbia County.

Characteristics: dry to mesic, well-drained, deep, silt loams with a pH of 5.8; outcrops of bedrock are common on steep slopes, but more typically bedrock is between 40 and 60 inches.

Composition: about 20 percent sand, 55 percent silt and 25 percent clay, with about 1.5 percent organic matter in the top 12 inches, and formed in residuum mostly from limestone, but with some interbedding of sandstone, siltstone and shale.

Current use: About two thirds is cleared and used mostly for pasture, while the remaining acreage is typically mixed hardwoods dominated by red, black and white oak, sugar maple, yellow poplar, white ash, basswood, shagbark hickory, black walnut and black locust.

Taxonomy: Fine-loamy, mixed, active, mesic Typic Hapludalfs.

Beltsville silt loams

Where they are found: upland coastal plain on summits, shoulders and backslopes of broad interstream divides (interfluves and sideslopes) in Delaware and Montgomery counties, generally at elevations of 80 to 380 feet above sea level.

Characteristics: mesic to wet, moderately well drained, very deep silty eolian soils over loamy fluviomarine deposits, with a pH of 5.1.

Composition: about 27 percent sand, 55 percent silt and 18 percent clay, with about 1.3 percent organic matter in the top 12 inches and formed from wind and fluviomarine deposits.

Current use: woodland, cropland and urban development; where wooded, the canopy is dominated by black oak, white oak, pin oak, yellow poplar, sweetgum, red maple, American Holly, beech, and shortleaf and Virginia pine.

Taxonomy: fine-loamy, mixed, semiactive, mesic Typic Fragiudults.

Benson silt loams

Where they are found: on glaciated broad plains, summits and side slopes of hills, ridges, knolls and mounds with slopes ranging up to 70 percent in Monroe County.

Characteristics: dry to mesic, excessively drained shallow silt loams formed in loamy till underlain by limestone or calcareous shale bedrock (10 to 20 inches) with moderate permeability, often with rock outcrops, and a pH of 6.8.

Composition: about 26 percent sand, 54 percent silt and 20 percent clay, with just under 3 percent organic matter in the top 12 inches and formed in glacial deposits.

Current use: generally considered too stony and steep for cultivation and are best used for conservation/wildlife areas. Most areas are wooded and dominated by sugar maple, beech, yellow birch, basswood, red oak, hickory, white ash, white pine, northern white cedar, red cedar, and hemlock.

Taxonomy: loamy-skeletal, mixed, active, mesic Lithic Eutrudepts.

Berks soil series

Where they are found: rounded summits, shoulders, and backslopes of dissected uplands, with slopes ranging up to 80 percent.

Characteristics: mesic to moist, well drained, moderately deep silt loams, often in complexes with other soils, with a pH generally 5.1 to 5.5, but sometimes reaching 5.9.

Composition: typically about 30 percent sand, 55 percent silt and 15 percent clay and usually with 1 to 1.5 percent organic matter in the top 12 inches, formed in residuum weathered from mostly shales interbedded with fine-grained sandstone and siltstone, with moderate to somewhat rapid permeability.

Current use: about 60 percent of Berks soils are in pasture or cropland (corn, wheat, oats, barley, Christmas trees and hay) while the remainder are in woodland or other uses. Native vegetation is mixed, deciduous hardwood forest, well suited for Virginia pine (*Pinus virginiana*), red oak (*Quercus rubra*) and black oak (*Quercus velutina*), yellow birch (*Betula lenta*), white ash (*Fraxinus americana*), black cherry (*Prunus serotina*) and white pine (*Pinus strobus*).

Taxonomy: Loamy-skeletal, mixed, active, mesic Typic Dystrudepts.

Bermudian silt loams

Where they are found: on nearly level floodplains in Adams and York counties.

Characteristics: mesic to moist, well-drained, very deep silt loams that are occasionally flooded, with a pH of 5.3.

Composition: about 26 percent sand, 54 percent silt and 20 percent clay, with less than 2 percent organic matter in the top 12 inches, formed in recent alluvial deposits from weathered upland red and brown shales, sandstone and conglomerate.

Current use: about two-thirds of the soils, considered prime farmland, are in pasture or cultivated, while 25 percent is wooded, consisting mostly of mixed hardwoods, and 10 percent is in non-agricultural use.

Taxonomy: fine-loamy, mixed, active, mesic Fluventic Dystrudepts.

Bethesda loams

Where they are found: on almost level to slightly sloping interfluves, base slopes, head slopes and benches, as well as very steep nose slopes and side slopes (up to 90 percent) in surface mining areas in western Pennsylvania.

Characteristics: dry to mesic, well-drained, very stony and very channery loams of human-modified hills, moderately deep to very deep and well drained; typical pH is 4.6.

Composition: about 25 percent sand, 50 percent silt and 25 percent clay with no organic matter in the surface layers, formed from strip mining operations of Pennsylvanian-age regolith and consisting of partially weathered fine earth and bedrock fragments, typically acidic shales, siltstones, coal and medium to fine-grained sandstone.

Current use: wildlife habitat and recreational areas; most of the reclaimed areas were seeded with grasses and some trees, while some sites are used for hay and pasture. Species appropriate for these sites include white pine (*Pinus strobus*), Virginia pine (*Pinus virginiana*), red oak (*Quercus rubra*), honey locust (*Robinia pseudoacacia*), red maple (*Acer rubrum*), white ash (*Fraxinus americana*), yellow poplar (*Liriodendron tulipifera*), black cherry (*Prunus serotina*),

Taxonomy: loamy-skeletal, mixed, active, acid, mesic Typic Udorthents.

Birdsall silt loams

Where they are found: low areas where the water table is at or close to the surface for most of the year in depressions and drainageways on till uplands and on terraces and depressions of glacial outwash plains in Erie County.

Characteristics: moist to wet, very deep, very poorly drained silt loams on ancient glacial lake beds, with a pH of 6.5. Seasonal zone of saturation is at the surface from October through July, and while not flooded it is frequently ponded, and classified as hydric.

Composition: 9 percent sand, 66 percent silt, 25 percent clay, with up to 6 percent organic matter in the top 12 inches, developed in water-deposited silts and very fine sands.

Current use: water issues require careful conservation measures. These areas are mostly forest with scattered areas in brushy, unimproved pasture; dominant vegetation includes red maple, elm, eastern hemlock, aspen, tamarack, some eastern white pine, alder, willow, sedges, cattails and rushes.

Taxonomy: Coarse-silty, mixed, active, nonacid, mesic Typic Humaquepts.

Birdsboro silt loams

Where they are found: on nearly level to sloping stream terraces and alluvial fans in southeastern Pennsylvania.

Characteristics: mesic to moist, well drained and very deep silt loams, rarely flooded, with a pH of 5.8 to 6.0.

Composition: about 26 percent sand, 54 percent silt and 20 percent clay, with about 1.7 percent organic matter in the top 12 inches, from old alluvial deposits derived from red sandstone, siltstone and shales.

Current use: generally considered to be prime farmland, about two thirds is cultivated or in pasture, 25 percent in non-agricultural uses and the remainder wooded with mixed hardwoods, well suited for yellow poplar (*Liriodendron tulipifera*), Virginia pine (*Pinus virginiana*), shortleaf pine (*Pinus echinata*) and red oak (*Quercus rubra*).

Taxonomy: fine-loamy, mixed, active, mesic Oxyaquic Hapludults.

Blairton silt loams

Where they are found: nearly level to moderately steep slopes, on upland flats, in drainage heads and in depressions, in mostly southeastern Pennsylvania.

Characteristics: dry to mesic, somewhat poorly to moderately well drained silt loams, often stony, deep soils, generally with pH between 4.6 and 5.4.

Composition: about 25 percent sand, 55 percent silt and 20 percent clay, with 2 to 2.5 percent organic matter in the top 12 inches, formed in colluvium and residuum from weathered, non-calcareous gray shale and some sandstone, with moderately slow permeability and lithic bedrock between 20 and 40 inches.

Current use: most areas in pasture or cropland; woodlands tend to be mixed hardwoods, especially suitable for sugar maple (*Acer saccharum*), white ash (*Fraxinus americana*), yellow poplar (*Liriodendron tulipifera*) and red oak (*Quercus rubra*).

Taxonomy: fine-loamy, mixed, active, mesic Aquic Hapludults.

Bogart loams

Where they are found: widely scattered, stratified glacial outwash deposits on plains, beach ridges and terraces between 700 and 1300 feet above sea level, typically on convex low-relief slopes up to 12 percent, in Beaver and Lawrence counties.

Characteristics: dry to mesic, well drained, very deep loams with a pH of about 5.6.

Composition: about 44 percent sand, 41 percent silt and 15 percent clay, with about 2.5 percent organic matter in the top 12 inches, from Wisconsinan age glacial outwash.

Current use: about half the soils are cultivated, principally with hay, oats and corn; about one-fourth is forested, with sugar maple, beech, and oak the dominant species. The remaining one-fourth is used for pasture or for nonagricultural purposes. Soils are well suited for sugar maple (*Acer saccharum*), white ash (*Fraxinus americana*), black walnut (*Juglans nigra*), yellow poplar (*Liriodendron tulipifera*), black cherry (*Prunus serotina*), white oak (*Quercus alba*) and red oak (*Quercus rubra*).

Bowmansville silt loams

Where they are found: nearly level floodplains and valley floors, up to 3 percent slope, in southeastern Pennsylvania.

Characteristics: dry to moist, poorly drained, very deep soils, with water saturation at or near the surface from September through May and a pH of about 5.8. Depending on location, flooding is occasional to frequent and when in complexes with Knauers soils, ponding is common. Soils qualify as hydric.

Composition: about 27 percent sand, 55 percent silt and 18 percent clay, with 2 to 2.5 percent organic matter in the top 12 inches, formed in alluvial deposits primarily from weathered upland materials including red and brown shale and sandstones, as well as dolerite and basalt.

Current use: About two-thirds of the soils are in pasture and the remainder wooded with mixed hardwood trees, particularly pin oak (*Quercus palustris*).

Braceville loams

Where they are found - nearly level to moderately steep (to 25 percent) soils on terraces, beaches, fans, and moraines in glacial outwash areas of northern Pennsylvania.

Characteristics: dry to mesic loams, gravelly loams and silt loams that are moderately well drained, deep but with fragipans between 20 and 32 inches, and with slow permeability, with 5.3 pH.

Composition: widely variable, but generally ranging between 33 and 50 percent sand, 40 to 50 percent silt and the balance in clay, with about 1.5 percent organic matter in the top 12 inches; formed in coarse-loamy glacial outwash consisting of stratified sand, silt and gravel mostly from non-calcareous gray shale and sandstone, but with small amounts of limestone and reddish rock; a thin mantle of silt is possible in some areas.

Current use: most land has been cleared for pasture and crops, while remaining woodlands are dominated by northern hardwoods, such as sugar maple (*Acer saccharum*), white ash (*Fraxinus americana*), yellow poplar (*Liriodendron tulipifera*), black cherry (*Prunus serotina*) and red oak (*Quercus rubra*)

Taxonomy: coarse-loamy, mixed, active, mesic Typic Fragiudepts.

Brandywine loams

Where they are found: nearly level to steep side slopes and elevated ridges in Delaware County

Characteristics: generally dry to mesic loams that are excessively drained, very deep and moderately permeable; very stony loams can be mesic to moist, with a pH of 5.0.

Composition: about 57 percent sand, 30 percent silt and 13 percent clay, with about 1 percent, formed in residuum from gneiss and similar Cambrian and Precambrian rock.

Current use: primarily pasture or agricultural crops, but large areas are in non-farm use or idle. Native vegetation consists mostly of black oak (*Quercus velutina*), yellow poplar (*Liriodendron tulipifera*), dogwood (*Cornus florida*), Virginia pine (*Pinus virginiana*) and shortleaf pine (*Pinus echinata*).

Taxonomy: sandy-skeletal, mixed, mesic Typic Dystrudepts.

Brecknock soil series

Where they are found: nearly level to very steep convex slopes (up to 60 percent) of upland hills and low ridges.

Characteristics: Runoff is slow to very rapid; bedrock is generally 40 to 60 inches and erosion is a conservation concern on steep slopes.

Current use: About 55 percent of Brecknock soils are in pasture or cropland and 5 percent is non-agricultural use; the remainder is wooded, mostly mixed hardwoods. Primary canopy trees include *Pinus echinata, Pinus virginiana* and *Quercus rubra*.

General description: well drained, deep soils

formed from weathered residuum of metamorphosed red shale and sandstone (porcelanite).

Taxonomy: fine-loamy, mixed, superactive, mesic Ultic Hapludalfs.

Brinkerton silt loams

Where they are found: concave footslopes, depressions, lower hillslopes and around drainageways in western and southeastern Pennsylvania.

Characteristics: mesic to wet, often hydric, poorly drained and very deep fine silt loams with a pH typically about 5.3 but can range up to 5.9. Seasonal zones of saturation can reach 3 inches from October through May.

Composition: generally 10 but up to 20 percent sand, about 65 percent silt and the balance as clay, with around 2 percent organic matter in the top 12 inches and formed in colluvium derived from acidic gray shale and siltstone.

Current use: Most of the areas are woodlands composed of mixed hardwoods dominated by northern red oak (Quercus rubra), sugar maple (Acer saccharum) and black cherry (Prunus serotina), with some hemlock (Tsuga canadensis) and white pine (Pinus strobus). Areas that have been cleared are primarily pasture.

Taxonomy: fine-silty, mixed, superactive, mesic Typic Fragiaqualfs.

Brooke silty clay loam

Where they are found: On ridges, ridge saddles and rounded knolls in Greene and Washington counties.

Characteristics: dry to mesic, well drained and moderately deep silty clay loams with slow permeability and very plastic and sticky subsoils, with a 6.7 pH.

Composition: about 16 percent sand, 49 percent silt and 35 percent clay, with about 4 percent organic matter in the top 12 inches and formed in residuum weathered from limestone or interbedded calcareous shales and limestones.

Current use: primarily pasture (particularly bluegrass) with alfalfa hay on gentle slopes. Black locust trees are frequent in pastures, and native vegetation is mixed hardwoods, including sugar maple (Acer saccharum), white ash (Fraxinus americana), black walnut (Juglans nigra), yellow poplar (Liriodendron tulipifera), white oak (Quercus alba), red oak (Quercus rubra) and black locust (Robinia pseudoacacia)

Taxonomy: fine, mixed, active, mesic Mollic Hapludalfs.

Brownsburg silt loams

Where they are found: summits and backslopes of hills in Bucks County.

Characteristics: mesic to moist, well-drained, deep silt loams with a pH of 6.0.

Composition: about 30 percent sand, 56 percent silt and 14 percent clay, with about 2.5 percent organic matter in the top 12 inches, formed in a shallow mantle of loess and underlying residuum of red metamorphic shale and sandstone.

Current use: about 40 percent in cropland and another 30 percent in pasture; the remainder is in woodland or idle reverting to woodland, dominated by mixed hardwoods, especially yellow poplar (Liriodendron tulipifera) and red oak (Quercus rubra).

Taxonomy: Coarse-loamy, mixed, active, mesic Typic Hapludalfs

Buchanan loams

Where they are found: nearly level to very steep terraces and concave sections of mountain footslopes, mostly in the Appalachians and on the eastern Allegheny plateau.

Characteristics: mesic to moist, poorly to well drained, deep loams often described as channery, stony, silty, and gravelly, with a typical pH of 4.6 to 4.8, but can be as high as 5.1.

Composition: between 35 and 40 percent sand, 40 and 45 percent silt and the balance in clay, with about 1 percent organic matter in the top 12 inches and formed in colluvium on mountain footslopes, sideslopes and in valleys from acidic sandstone, quartzite, shale and siltstone.

Current use: mostly woodland, dominated by mixed hardwoods such as oak (Quercus spp.), maple (Acer spp.) and ash (Fraxinus spp.); a few areas have been cleared and are used for row crops, small grains and pasture. Soils are also considered suitable for yellow poplar (*Liriodendron tulipifera*), American beech (*Fagus grandifolia*), black cherry (*Prunus serotina*), white pine (*Pinus strobus*), and Virginia pine (*Pinus virginiana*).

Taxonomy: Fine-loamy, mixed, semiactive, mesic Aquic Fragiudults.

Buckingham silt loams

Where they are found: along drainageways and headslopes on concave toeslopes and depressions in Montgomery, Bucks and Lehigh counties.

Characteristics: dry to mesic, somewhat poorly drained, very deep silt loams, with a typical pH of 6.1. Listed as hydric when in complexes with other soils, where seasonal zones of saturation are at or near the surface from November to May, are sometimes flooded and often ponded.

General description: somewhat poorly drained, very deep silt loams formed in colluvium of weathered gray and red metamorphic shale, sandstone and siltstone.

Current use: about 30 percent in pasture or hayland and 20 percent in cropland; the remaining 50 percent are woodland or idle reverting to woodland, composed mainly of mixed hardwoods, including: red maple (*Acer rubrum*), sugar maple (*Acer saccharum*), white ash (*Fraxinus americana*), yellow poplar (*Liriodendron tulipifera*) and red oak (*Quercus rubra*).

Taxonomy: Fine-loamy, mixed, active, mesic Aeric Fragiaqualfs.

Bucks silt loams

Where they are found: upland divides and rolling slopes in Lancaster and Lebanon counties.

Characteristics: mesic to moist, well drained and deep upland silt loams with a pH of 5.2.

Composition: about 23 percent sand, 54 percent silt and 23 percent clay, with 1.3 percent organic matter in the top 12 inches and formed in a layer of silt over locally-weathered generally red shale, but also brownish shale and some layers of siltstone and fine-grained sandstone.

Current use: most of the soils - historically mixed oak (*Quercus spp.*), yellow poplar (*Liriodendron tulipifera*), ash (*Fraxinus spp.*) and hickory (*Carya spp.*) - have been cleared for a wide variety of crops, pasture and nursery plants.

Taxonomy: fine-loamy, mixed, active, mesic Typic Hapludults.

Cadosia channery loams

Where they are found: relatively steep headslopes in hollows and lower side slopes - generally 15 to 70 percent - on valley sides and ridges in Potter County.

Characteristics: mesic to moist, well drained, very deep channery loams with a pH of 5.3.

Composition: about 45 percent sand, 43 percent silt and 12 percent clay, with about 2 percent organic matter in the top 12 inches, formed in till and colluvium from shale, siltstone and sandstone, mostly on glaciated uplands between 1,000 and 1,800 feet above sea level.

Current uses: mostly wooded, with the canopy dominated by sugar maple (*Acer saccharum*), beech (*Fagus grandifolia*), white ash (*Fraxinus americana*), black cherry (*Prunus serotina*), northern red oak (*Quercus rubra*), eastern white pine (*Pinus strobus*) and hemlock (*Tsuga canadensis*).

Taxonomy: loamy-skeletal, mixed, active, mesic Typic Dystrudepts.

Califon loams

Where they are found: upland flats or concave slopes up to 15 percent in the northern Piedmont in southeastern Pennsylvania, generally between 200 and 1,100 feet above sea level.

Characteristics: moist to wet, deep, moderately well to somewhat poorly drained loams with a pH of about 5.3.

Composition: about 42 percent sand, 40 percent silt and 18 percent clay, with about 2.5 percent organic matter in the top 12 inches, formed mostly on driftless landscapes - but also in old till - in colluvium from granitic gneiss. A seasonal zone of precipitation can be between 3 and 18 inches from November to April and fragipans around 20 inches, resulting in significant drainage issues in some locations.

Current use: mostly for pasture, hay and woodland comprised of red maple (*Acer rubrum*), pin oak (*Quercus palustris*), yellow poplar (*Liriodendron tulipifera*) and elm (*Ulmus spp*). Other appropriate species include white ash (*Fraxinus americana*), white oak (*Quercus alba*), red oak (*Quercus rubra*) and black oak (*Quercus velutina*).

Taxonomy: fine-loamy, mixed, active, mesic Typic Fragiudults.

Calvert silt loams

Where it is found: scattered in on valley flats and depressions, usually near drainage heads, with less than 5 percent slopes in Delaware County (less than 20 acres and considered inactive by NRCS).

Characteristics: mesic to moist poorly drained silt loams with a pH of 5.2 and a seasonal zone of water saturation at less than a foot from November to April.

Composition: about 21 percent sand, 55 percent silt and 24 percent clay, with about 2 percent organic matter in the top 12 inches, formed from silty material, likely alluvium over residuum from serpentine or similar rocks.

Current use: unknown, but appropriate canopy species include red maple (*Acer rubrum*), American holly (*Ilex opaca*) and pin oak (*Quercus palustris*)

Taxonomy: fine-silty, mixed, mesic Typic Fragiaqualfs.

Calvin loams

Where they are found: hillslopes, side slopes ranging up to 80 percent and summits of ridges.

Characteristics: dry to mesic, well drained and moderately deep, usually channery to shaly silt loams, with a pH of about 5.4.

Composition: about 28 percent sand, 53 percent silt and 19 percent clay, with about 1.3 percent organic matter in the top 12 inches, formed from residuum of red, non-calcareous shale, sandstone and siltstone with rapid permeability

Current use: with favorable topography, pasture and cropland but sometimes idle; steep and stony slopes are mostly woodland composed of mixed hardwoods, dominated by oaks (*Quercus spp.*) and with some maple (*Acer spp.*) and Virginia pine (*Pinus virginiana*).

Taxonomy: loamy-skeletal, mixed, active, mesic Typic Dystrudepts

Cambridge silt loams

Where they are found: convex knolls, summits, shoulders and sideslopes on till plains and moraines with slopes up to 25 percent in Crawford County.

Characteristics: mesic to moist, well drained, very deep silt loams with a pH of 4.6.

Composition: about 25 percent sand, 53 percent silt and 22 percent clay, with about 2 percent organic matter in the top 12 inches, formed in low-lime Wisconsinan till dominated by acidic sandstone, shale and siltstone and including a minor limestone component, often with a fragipan that can be shallow to moderately deep; permeability is moderate above the fragipan.

Current use: mostly cropland, hayland, pasture and woodlands, with abandoned cultivated areas reverting to trees and brush; native vegetation is primarily hardwoods dominated by sugar maple (*Acer saccharum*), beech (*Fagus grandifolia*), red oak (*Quercus rubra*), and white oak (*Quercus alba*).

Taxonomy: coarse-loamy, mixed, superactive, mesic Oxyaquic Fragiudalfs.

Canadice silt loams

Where they are found: on Wisconsinan-age lake plains, broad concave flats, depressions, valley floors and slackwater terraces, with slopes of less than 3 percent.

Characteristics: mesic to wet, poorly drained but very deep silt and silty clay loams with slow permeability and high organic content, a pH of about 5.7, with water near the surface from December through June and classified as hydric. Brief ponding is common during periods of heavy rain and spring snowmelt.

Composition: about 19 percent sand, 53 percent silt and 28 percent clay, with organic matter in the top 12 inches ranging from 5 to 7 percent and formed in glacial lake sediments underlain by till.

Current use: 30 percent pasture, 30 percent cropland and the remainder in farm woodlots or idle; original vegetation was mixed hardwoods, especially red maple (*Acer rubrum*) and white pine (*Pinus strobus*).

Taxonomy: fine, illitic, mesic Typic Endoaqualfs.

Caneadea silt loams

Where they are found: level to steep convex slopes on glacial lake plains and ancient lake beds, slackwater terraces and valley floors of depressional landscapes.

Characteristics: mesic to moist, somewhat poorly drained, very deep silt loams with very slow permeability, with intermittent perched water table is 6 to 12 inches between November to May and a pH of 6.0.

Composition: about 18 percent sand, 53 percent silt and 29 percent clay, with about 2 percent organic matter in the top 12 inches, formed in calcareous, clayey Wisconsin age glaciolacustrine sediments, generally 570 to 1,300 feet above sea level.

Current use: Primary soil use is pasture or woodland, but some are used for such crops as corn, small grains and hay. Native vegetation was mixed hardwood forest, dominated by oaks (*Quercus* spp.), sugar maple (*Acer saccharum*), beech (*Fagus grandifolia*) and hickory (*Carya* spp.), but also suitable for white ash (*Fraxinus americana*), black cherry (*Prunus serotina*), red maple (*Acer rubrum*) and slippery elm (*Ulmus rubra*). Primary canopy trees:

Taxonomy: fine, illitic, mesic Aeric Endoaqualfs.

Canfield silt loams

Where they are found: Interfluves, headslopes, nose slopes and sideslopes on till plains and moraines in northwestern Pennsylvania.

Characteristics: mesic to moist, moderately well drained, deep silt loams, often with a fragipan between 15 and 30 inches, and a pH typically about 5.8.

Composition: about 29 percent sand, 54 percent silt and 17 percent clay, with about 2 percent organic matter in the top 12 inches, formed in low-lime Wisconsinan age till, frequently with a thin loess mantle.

Current use: most areas cultivated, principally for grains and hay, while steeper slopes are used for pasture or woodland; normal vegetation is mixed hardwoods, including sugar maple (*Acer saccharum*), beech (*Fagus grandifolia*), white ash (*Fraxinus americana*), American sycamore (*Platanus occidentalis*), white oak (*Quercus alba*), red oak (*Quercus rubra*), white pine (*Pinus strobus*) and slippery elm (*Ulmus rubra*).

Taxonomy: fine-loamy, mixed, active, mesic Aquic Fragiudalfs.

Captina silt loams

Where they are found: generally in gently sloping uplands and old stream terraces, more commonly in the Ozark Highlands but reported in a small area of Dauphin County (about 300 acres).

Characteristics: mesic to moist, moderately well drained, very deep silt loam with slow permeability and a pH of 5.3.

Composition: about 25 percent sand, 54 percent silt and 21 percent clay, with about 2.5 percent organic matter in the top 12 inches and formed in a thin mantle of silty material and underlying old aluvium weathered from limestone, cherty limestone and dolomite or siltstone.

Current use: Primary uses are pasture and hay, but also cultivated for some vegetable crops. Native vegetation was hardwood forest, particularly white ash (*Fraxinus americana*), black walnut (*Juglans nigra*), yellow poplar (*Liriodendron tulipifera*), white pine (*Pinus strobus*) and Virginia pine (*Pinus virginiana*).

Taxonomy: fine-silty, siliceous, active, mesic, Typic Fragiudults.

Carbo silty clay loams

Where they are found: gentle to very steep upland valleys and ridges in the Appalachian Ridges and Valleys in Franklin and Fulton counties.

Characteristics: dry to mesic, well drained, slowly permeable and moderately deep silty clay loams with a pH of 6.7.

Composition: about 16 percent sand, 47 percent silt and 37 percent clay, with about 1.5 percent organic matter in the top 12 inches, formed from weathered limestone bedrock, sometimes interbedded with shale, generally between 600 and 2,500 feet above sea level.

Current use: cleared areas for cropland or pasture and forested areas dominated by northern red oak (*Quercus rubra*), yellow poplar (*Liriodendron tulipifera*), hickory (*Carya spp.*), maple (*Acer spp.*), black walnut (*Juglans nigra*), locust (*Robinia spp.*), eastern red cedar (*Juniperus virginiana*), and Virginia pine (*Pinus virginiana*).

Taxonomy: very-fine, mixed, active, mesic Typic Hapludalfs.

Carlisle silt loams

Where they are found: depressions within glacial lake plains, ground moraines, flood plains, outwash plains and swamps on slopes less than 2 percent.

Characteristics: moist to wet, very poorly drained, very deep muck and silt loam, sometimes flooded but frequently ponded, with a zone of saturation at the surface from September through June, and considered hydric.

Composition: generally more than 85 percent organic matter, although silt loams can include 54 percent silt, 31 percent sand and 15 percent clay, with about 30 percent organic matter, formed from herbaceous and woody organic materials.

Current use: Many of these areas have been drained and for both pasture and a variety of truck crops and sod production; remaining areas are woodland or cut-over woodland. Typical canopy trees include elm (*Ulmus spp.*), white ash (*Fraxinus americana*), red maple (*Acer rubrum*), willow (*Salix spp.*), tamarack (*Larix laricina*), quaking aspen (*Populus tremuloides*), and alder (*Alnus spp.*).

Taxonomy: euic, mesic Typic Haplosaprists.

Carrollton channery silt loams

Where they are found: dissected valley sides, bedrock-controlled benches, and convex ridgetops with slopes ranging from 3 to 50 percent, in unglaciated areas of Forest and Warren counties.

Characteristics: dry to mesic, well drained, moderately deep channery silt loams, with bedrock between 20 and 40 inches and a pH of 5.3.

Composition: 26 percent sand, 52 percent silt and 22 percent clay, with about 1 percent organic matter in the top 12 inches, formed in residuum weathered from interbedded fine-grained sandstone, siltstone and shale

Current use: while some areas are used for pasture and cropland, most is native woodland composed of mixed hardwoods dominated by sugar maple (*Acer saccharum*), northern red oak (*Quercus rubra*), white oak (*Quercus alba*), black cherry (*Prunus serotina*) and beech (*Fagus grandifolia*). Many areas cleared for crop production are idle and reverting to brush and trees.

Taxonomy: fine-loamy, mixed, active, frigid Typic Hapludults.

Castile gravelly silt loam

Where they are found: level to somewhat undulating glacial outwash plains, valley trains and associated eskers, kames and water-deposited areas of moraines in McKean County

Characteristics: dry to mesic, moderately well drained, very deep gravelly silt loam with a pH of 5.3.

Composition: about 34 percent sand, 52 percent silt and 14 percent clay, with more than 3 percent organic matter in the top 12 inches, formed in water-sorted gravelly and sandy material high in gray sandstone, siltstone and shale, with smaller amounts of limestone and igneous erratics.

Current use: most areas are cleared and used for hay, small grains and corn, as well as some vegetable crops. Woodlots are dominated by red maple (*Acer rubrum*), sugar maple (*Acer saccharum*), American beech (*Fagus grandifolia*), hemlock (*Tsuga canadensis*), ash (*Fraxinus spp.*), white pine (*Pinus strobus*) and cherry (*Prunus spp.*) to the north, but oak (*Quercus spp.*) and hickory (*Carya spp.*) dominate further south.

Taxonomy: loamy-skeletal, mixed, active, mesic Aquic Dystrudepts.

Catden muck

Where they are found: Nationally, in swamps, lake plain depressions, outwash plains, kettles, moraines and flood plains; in Northampton County, the sites are on kettles, formed in glaciate periods when massive blocks of buried ice melted.

Characteristics: moist to wet; more than 90 percent herbaceous and woody organic materials form a very poorly drained, very deep muck not flooded but often ponded and has a zone of water saturation at or near the surface year-round except for July and August and therefore considered hydric.

Composition: More than 90 percent organic matter.

Current use: most areas are used for wildlife, or are in woodland. Common vegetation is red maple (*Acer rubrum*), skunk cabbage, marsh fern, and sphagnum moss.

Taxonomy: euic, mesic Typic Haplosaprists.

Catoctin channery silt loams

Where it is found: nearly level to steep ridges and sideslopes in the northern Piedmont and Blue Ridge Mountains.

Characteristics: dry to mesic, well-drained, moderately deep channery silt loams with rapid permeability over bedrock at 20 to 40 inches and a pH of 5.8.

Composition: about 29 percent sand, 56 percent silt and 15 percent clay, with about 1 percent organic matter in the top 12 inches, formed from material weathered mostly from greenstone and other dark colored rock.

Current use: cleared areas are primarily for pasture, but most of the soils are in forest dominated by red oak (*Quercus rubra*), white oak (*Quercus alba*), yellow poplar (*Liriodendron tulipifera*), ash (*Fraxinus spp.*), hickory (*Carya spp.*), walnut (*Juglans nigra*), locust (*Robinia spp.*), redbud (*Cercis canadensis*) and red cedar (*Juniperus virginiana*), but also suitable for shortleaf pine (*Pinus echinata*), Virginia pine (*Pinus virginiana*) and black oak (*Quercus velutina*).

Taxonomy: loamy-skeletal, mixed, superactive, mesic Ruptic-Alfic Eutrudepts.

Cavode silt loams

Where they are found: broad, level to somewhat steep ridgetops, sideslopes and benches in western Pennsylvania.

Characteristics: mesic to moist, somewhat poorly drained, deep upland silt loams with moderate to slow permeability, with a pH of 5.0. Seasonal zones of water saturation can be less than 15 inches from October through May.

Composition: about 17 percent sand, 56 percent silt and 27 percent clay, with about 2.5 percent organic matter in the top 12 inches, and formed in residuum of weathered gray and yellow acidic shale, often interbedded with siltstone and sandstone.

Current use: About two-thirds cleared for cropland or pasture; wooded areas tend to be mixed hardwoods dominated by oaks (*Quercus spp.*), red maple (*Acer rubrum*) and yellow poplar (*Liriodendron tulipifera*).

Taxonomy: fine, mixed, active, mesic Aeric Endoaquults.

Cedarcreek channery loams

Where they are found: level to gently sloping benches and hillslopes, as well as steep outslopes in strip mining areas of western Pennsylvania.

Characteristics: dry to mesic, well drained, very deep and very stony partially weathered fine earth and bedrock fragments with a pH of 4.6.

Composition: about 37 percent sand, 45 percent silt and 18 percent clay, with little or no organic matter in the top 12 inches, formed from bedrock crushed by machinery, mainly acidic sandstone and siltstone with small amounts of shale and coal formed in acidic regolith and deposited from surface coal mining.

Current use: emphasizes reclamation of surface mined land and vegetation commonly includes grasses, legumes, black locust, white pine, autumn olive, and other plants commonly used in surface mine reclamation. Some areas are used for pasture, hay crops, or orchards, others are planted to white pine (*Pinus strobus*) and red oak (*Quercus rubra*), and still others have established stands of naturally seeded yellow poplar (*Liriodendron tulipifera*), black birch (*Betula nigra*), black locust (*Robinia pseudoacacia*), and sycamore (*Platanus occidentalis*).

Taxonomy: Loamy-skeletal, mixed, active, acid, mesic Typic Udorthents.

Ceres channery silt loams

Where they are found: nearly level to very steep uplands between 1,800 and 2,400 feet above sea level in McKean County.

Characteristics: dry to mesic, well drained, deep channery silt loams with moderate permeability and a pH of 4.7.

Composition: about 23 percent sand, 54 percent silt and 23 percent clay with about 1.3 percent organic matter in the top 12 inches formed in either residuum of red shale, siltstone and sandstone or, along ice margins, a thin layer of glacial till or loess over red residuum.

Current use: gentler slopes cleared and used for pasture or hayland, but some are idle and reverting to forest. Steeper slopes tend to be forested, mainly mixed oaks (*Quercus spp.*), sugar maple (*Acer saccharum*), red maple (*Acer rubrum*), birch (*Betula spp.*), beech (*Fagus grandifolia*), white ash (*Fraxinus americana*) and black cherry (*Prunus serotina*).

Taxonomy: fine-loamy, mixed, semiactive, frigid Typic Hapludults.

Chagrin loams

Where it is found: on floodplains that receive alluvium from upland areas of shale, siltstone, sandstone, limestone and low-lime glacial drift, usually in areas of Wisconsinan Age glaciation, but sometimes in unglaciated valleys, gernerally western Pennsylvania but also reported in York County.

Characteristics: mesic to moist, well drained, moderately permeable and deep silt and sandy loams that are occasionally flooded with a pH of 6.5.

Composition: sandy loams are about 66 percent sand, 20 percent silt and the balance in clay; silt loams are about 27 percent sand, 55 percent silt and the balance in clay. All have about 3 percent organic matter in the top 12 inches and were formed in flood plain alluvium, with slopes ranging up to 3 percent.

Current use: Most areas in woodland and pasture, though some have been cleared for cropland. Native vegetation is hardwood forest composed of hickory (*Carya spp.*), beech (*Fagus grandifolia*), sugar maple (*Acer saccharum*), sycamore (*Plantanus occidentalis*) and ash (*Fraxinus spp.*). Also suitable are black walnut (*Juglans nigra*), yellow poplar (*Liriodendron tulipifera*), black cherry (*Prunus serotina*), white oak (*Quercus alba*) and red oak (*Quercus rubra*).

Taxonomy: fine-loamy, mixed, active, mesic Dystric Fluventic Eutrudepts.

Chalfont silt loams

Where they are found: nearly level to sloping uplands in southeastern Pennsylvania.

Characteristics: mesic to moist, somewhat poorly drained but deep silt loams with a pH of 6.2.

Composition: about 11 percent sand, 70 percent sit and 19 percent clay, with between 2 and 2.5 percent organic matter in the top 12 inches, formed in a loess mantle overlying residuum of sandstone and shale.

Current use: Most cleared and used for cropland, hay and pasture; wooded areas tend toward mixed hardwoods, primarily oaks (*Quercus spp.*) and yellow poplar (*Liriodendron tulipifera*).

Taxonomy: fine-silty, mixed, active, mesic Aquic Fragiudalfs.

Chavies loams

Where they are found: long, narrow to broad, nearly level to steep stream terraces where flooding is rare to never.

Characteristics: mesic to moist, well drained and very deep sandy and silt loams with rapid permeability and pH ranging from 5.6 to 5.9.

Composition: sandy loams are about 62 percent sand, 25 percent silt and the balance in clay; silt loams are about 35 percent sand, 50 percent silt and the balance in clay. All have about 2 percent organic matter in the top 12 inches and were formed in mixed alluvium mostly from soils of acidic shale, siltstone and sandstone origin.

Current use: Almost all the soil is used for a wide variety of crops, but where native vegetation persists hickory (*Carya spp.*), beech (*Fagus grandifolia*), birch (*Betula spp.*), maple (*Acer spp.*), elm (*Ulmus spp.*), yellow poplar (*Liriodendron tulipifera*), sycamore (*Platanus occidentalis*), black gums (*Nyssa sylvatica*), hemlock (*Tsuga canadensis*), white oak (*Quercus alba*), red oak (*Quercus rubra*) and some pines (*Pinus spp.*) are found.

Taxonomy: coarse-loamy, mixed, active, mesic Ultic Hapludalfs.

Chenango loams

Where they are found: water-sorted material on outwash plains, eskers, kames, terraces and alluvial fans.

Characteristics: dry to mesic, well to excessively drained very deep gravelly and silt loams with a pH of 5.3.

Composition: varies widely; sand ranges from 34 to 68 percent and silt from 19 to 54 percent, with about 12 percent clay and 1.5 to 3.5 percent organic matter in the top 12 inches. Soils formed in water-sorted loamy and gravelly drift - as well as some alluvial deposits - from gray sandstone, siltstone and shale, with lesser amounts from limestone and igneous rock.

Current use: Most gentle slope areas cleared for a variety of agricultural use, and steeper areas are cleared for pasture and hay. Woodlots include sugar maple (*Acer saccharum*), red maple (*Acer rubrum*), American beech (*Fagus grandifolia*), ash (*Fraxinus spp.*), eastern hemlock (*Tsuga canadensis*), and eastern white pine (*Pinus strobus*) in northernmost areas, with oak (*Quercus spp.*) and hickory (*Carya spp.*) more common in the southern end of the range.

Taxonomy: loamy-skeletal, mixed, superactive, mesic Typic Dystrudepts.

Chester silt loams

Where they are found: upper slopes and upland divides in the northern Piedmont Plateau.

Characteristics: mesic to moist, well drained, deep and usually silt loams with a pH of about 5.3.

Composition: typically about 26 percent sand, 54 percent silt and 20 percent clay, with about 1.5 percent organic matter in the top 12 inches and formed from weathered micaceous schist.

Current use: mostly agriculture use, including pasture; native vegetation is red oak (*Quercus rubra*), white oak (*Quercus alba*), yellow poplar (*Liriodendron tulipifera*), and hickory (*Carya spp.*). Also appropriate are Virginia pine (*Pinus virginiana*), shortleaf pine (*Pinus echinata*); black oak (*Quercus velutina*) and southern red oak (*Quercus falcata*).

Taxonomy: fine-loamy, mixed, semiactive, mesic Typic Hapludults.

Chewacla silt loams

Where it is found: floodplains of Piedmont and Coastal Plain river valleys in Delaware County.

Characteristics: mesic to wet, somewhat poorly drained, very deep silt loam, frequently flooded, with a pH of 5.4.

Composition: about 25 percent sand, 54 percent silt and 21 percent clay, with about 2.5 percent organic matter in the top 12 inches, formed from alluvium.

Current use: most areas cultivated for corn and small grain, but where wooded, the canopy is dominated by yellow poplar (*Liriodendron tulipifera*), sweetgum (*Liquidambar styraciflua*), water oak (*Quercus nigra*), eastern cottonwood (*Populus deltoides*), green ash (*Fraxinus pennsylvanica*), blackgum (*Nyssa sylvatica*), red maple (*Acer rubrum*), willow oak (*Quercus phellos*), and American sycamore (*Platanus occidentalis*). Loblolly pine (*Pinus taeda*) is in some areas less frequently flooded. Common understory plants include river birch (*Betula nigra*), hackberry (*Celtis occidentalis*), greenbrier (*Smilax rotundifolia*), American holly (*Ilex opaca*), black willow (*Salix nigra*), sourwood (Oxydendrum spp.), and eastern hophornbeam (*Ostrya virginiana*).

Taxonomy: fine-loamy, mixed, active, thermic Fluvaquentic Dystrudepts.

Chili loams

Where they are found: outwash plains and terraces, kames and beach ridges in Beaver,

Lawrence and Mercer counties.

Characteristics: mesic to moist, well drained, very deep silt loams with moderate permeability and a pH of about 5.7.

Composition: silt loams are about 32 percent sand and 56 percent silt, while the loiams are about 42 percent sand and 40 percent silt, with the balance in clay. Organic matter is about 1.5 to 2 percent in the top 12 inches, and soils were formed in mostly non-calcareous sandstone and limestone Wisconsinan Age outwash deposits, usually with a substantial amount of quartz gravel and commonly covered with silt.

Current use: areas with slopes less than 12 percent are usually cleared and used for agriculture, while steeper areas are wooded, usually dominated by oaks (*Quercus spp.*) and hickories (*Carya spp.*); native vegetation was deciduous hardwood forest, including sugar maple (*Acer saccharum*), white ash (*Fraxinus americana*), black walnut (*Juglans nigra*), yellow poplar (*Liriodendron tulipifera*) and black cherry (*Prunus serotina*).

Taxonomy: fine-loamy, mixed, active, mesic Typic Hapludalfs.

Chippewa silt loams

Where it is found: nearly level depressions with concave surface shapes in till deposits of glaciated areas. (Note: this series includes the inactive Ellery soil series.)

Characteristics: mesic to wet, poorly drained, very deep silt loams with a dense fragipan between 10 and 24 inches and a pH of 5.5; zone of water saturation is at or near the surface in spring, but ponding is possible and the soils are categorized as hydric.

Composition: about 25 percent sand, 54 percent silt and 21 percent clay, with more than 4 percent organic matter in the top 12 inches and developed from till deposits dominated by siltstone, shale and sandstone rock fragments

Current use: most areas are forested, with cleared areas in pasture or reverting to woodland. Natural vegetation includes silver maple (*Acer saccharinum*), red maple (*Acer rubrum*), black ash (*Fraxinus nigra*), white ash (*Fraxinus americana*), swamp elm (*Ulmus americana*), hemlock (*Tsuga canadensis*) and northern white cedar (*Thuja occidentalis*).

Taxonomy: fine-loamy, mixed, active, mesic Typic Fragiaquepts.

Chrome silt loams

Where they are found: level to steep convex hillslopes in Chester and Delaware counties.

Characteristics: dry to mesic, well drained, moderately deep silt and silty clay loams with a pH of 6.7, generally unfavorable to many plant species and resulting in prairie-pine ecosystems described as barrens.

Composition: about 15 percent sand, 50 percent silt and 35 percent clay, with about 1.3 percent organic matter in the top 12 inches, formed in residuum of weathered serpentine.

Current use: about 90 percent are either woodland or pasture, with 10 percent cultivated; the physical and chemical properties of serpentine soils (low water capacity, stoniness, shallowness and high levels of magnesium and iron, nickel, chromium and cobalt, coupled with low levels of calcium and silica) create a prairie-pine ecosystem described as "barrens" or pine-savannah.

Taxonomy: fine, mixed, superactive, mesic Typic Hapludalfs.

Clarksburg silt loams

Where they are found: nearly level valley flats to concave, somewhat steep hillslopes.

Characteristics: mesic to moist, moderately well drained, deep silt loams with a pH of 5.8.

Composition: about 25 percent sand, 55 percent silt and 20 percent clay, with about 1.5 percent organic matter in the top 12 inches and developed in a regolith of colluvium or residuum (sometimes glacial till) weathered from limestone, both calcareous and noncalcareous shale, and limestone.

Current use: About 30 percent of the land is in mixed hardwoods dominated by oaks (*Quercus spp.*), hickory (*Carya spp.*) and locust (*Robinia pseudoacacia*), while most has been cleared and is used for general farm crops and pasture.

Taxonomy: fine-loamy, mixed, superactive,

mesic Oxyaquic Fragiudalfs.

Clearbrook channery silt loam

Where they are found: nearly level to moderately steep uplands, generally along stream heads and in depressions, in Franklin County

Characteristics: dry to mesic, somewhat poorly drained, moderately deep channery silt loam with a pH of 5.5 and slow permeability.

Composition: about 23 percent sand, 53 percent silt and 24 percent clay, with less than 1 percent organic matter in the top 12 inches and formed in residuum from weathered acidic gray sandstone and shale.

Current use: mostly cleared and used for pasture; suitable canopy species include yellow poplar (*Liriodendron tulipifera*) and red oak (*Quercus rubra*).

Taxonomy: Loamy-skeletal, mixed, active, mesic Aeric Epiaquults.

Clymer loams

Where they are found: upland ridges and hills, and on sideslopes, typically up to 15 percent but can range to 80 percent, in the Allegheny plateau and ridge and valley areas of Pennsylvania (Note: this series includes the inactive Fleetwood sandy loams of Carbon County; very stony loams have been assigned to Dekalb.)

Characteristics: dry to mesic, well drained, deep and often stony or channery silt loams with moderate permeability and a pH of about 4.7.

Composition: varies between 30 and 55 percent sand, 35 and 40 percent silt and the balance in clay, generally with about 2 percent organic matter in the top 12 inches and formed in residuum mostly from sandstone, but with some siltstone and shale.

Current use: Most areas are forested, primarily oaks (Quercus spp.), maples (Acer spp.), some white pine (Pinus strobus) and Virginia pine (Pinus virginiana); cleared areas are used for cropland or pasture.

Taxonomy: Coarse-loamy, siliceous, active, mesic Typic Hapludults.

Codorus silt loams

Where they are found: nearly level slopes of floodplains in southeastern Pennsylvania.

Characteristics: mesic to moist, moderately well drained to somewhat poorly drained, very deep silt loams with a pH of 5.3 and while occasionally flooded is not considered hydric.

Composition: about 27 percent sand, 53 percent silt and 20 percent clay, with about 3 percent organic matter in the top 12 inches and formed in recently deposited alluvium parented by weathered metamorphic and crystalline upland rock, notably schist, gneiss, phyllite and others.

Current use: about 75 percent in pasture or cropland, and about 20 percent are wooded, mostly mixed hardwoods; 5 percent are in non-agricultural uses. Primary canopy trees include sugar maple (*Acer saccharum*), white ash (*Fraxinus americana*), yellow poplar (*Liriodendron tulipifera*), black walnut (*Juglans nigra*), white pine (*Pinus strobus*) and red oak (*Quercus rubra*)

Taxonomy: fine-loamy, mixed, active, mesic Fluvaquentic Dystrudepts.

Cokesbury silt loams

Where they are found: concave footslope and toeslope positions of headslopes, along waterways, in upland depressions or in bands along the base of steeper slopes.

Characteristics: mesic to moist, poorly drained, very deep silt loams with a pH of 5.3.

Composition: about 39 percent sand, 40 percent silt and 21 percent clay, formed either in old till or on northern Piedmont driftless landscapes in granitic gneiss colluvium.

Current use: primarily for woodland or unimproved pasture, and some urban areas in Chester County; native vegetation is dominated by pin oak (*Quercus palustris*), elm (*Ulmus spp.*) and maple (*Acer spp.*)

Taxonomy: fine-loamy, mixed, active, mesic Typic Fragiaquults.

Collamer soil series

Where they are found: glacial lake plains and till plains that have a thick covering of lake sediments, with slopes up to 25 percent, in a complex with Williamson soils, in Erie County. (Note: this series now includes the former Berrien soil series.)

Characteristics: mesic to moist, moderately well drained, very deep fine sandy and silt loams with a pH of 5.3.

Composition: in a 50-50 mix with Williamson loams; sandy loams are about 50 percent sand and 40 percent silt, while silt loams are about 21 percent sand and 68 percent silt, with the remainder in clay and with about 3 percent organic matter in the top 12 inches. The complex formed in calcareous lake laid silt and other fine sand deposits.

Current use: Most areas have been cleared and are used for a wide range of agriculture; woodlots include sugar maple (*Acer saccharum*), red oak (*Quercus rubra*), black cherry (*Prunus serotina*), basswood (*Tilia americana*), hickory (*Carya spp.*) and other hardwoods.

Taxonomy: Fine-silty, mixed, semiactive, mesic Glossaquic Hapludalfs.

Colonie soil series

Where they are found: appears nationally in Wisconsinan Age lake plains, including summits, shoulders, back and foot slopes as well as dunes, outwash plains, deltas and beach ridges; in Erie County, scattered sites are on beach ridges and lake plains. (Note: this series now includes the inactive Ottawa Soil Series.)

Characteristics: dry to mesic, well to excessively drained, deep loamy fine sand with a pH of 5.0.

Composition: about 83 percent sand, 15 percent silt and 2 percent clay, with about 1.4 percent organic matter in the top 12 inches and formed in glaciofluvial, glaciolacustrine or eolian deposits that are dominated by fine to very fine sand, typically between 95 and 900 feet above sea level.

Current use: mostly is cultivated, but large areas are idle and grass-covered and woodlots include sugar maple (*Acer saccharum*), red oak (*Quercus rubra*) and other hardwoods including white oak (*Quercus alba*) and black oak (*Quercus velutina*), along with some red pine (*Pinus resinosa*).

Taxonomy: mixed, mesic Lamellic Udipsamments.

Comly silt loams

Where they are found: nearly level to moderately steep, concave upland drainageways, broad flats and footslopes.

Characteristics: mesic to moist, moderately well drained, very deep, mostly silt loams with a typical pH of 5.8, a fragipan between 20 and 35 inches and a seasonal zone of saturation at less than 6 inches from November to March.

Composition: 21 to 25 percent sand, about 54 percent silt and the balance in clay, with about 1.6 percent organic matter in the top 12 inches and formed in colluvium, residuum or materials that were altered by periglacial or glacial activity.

Current use: almost all in cropland or pasture as well as some non-farm use; the 10 percent in woodland are mixed hardwoods, including as oak (*Quercus spp.*), hickory (*Carya spp.*) and yellow poplar (*Liriodendron tulipifera*); also appropriate are sugar maple (*Acer saccharum*), white ash (*Fraxinus americana*) and quaking aspen (*Populus tremuloides*).

Taxonomy: fine-loamy, mixed, active, mesic Oxyaquic Fragiudalfs.

Comus silt loams

Where they are found: floodplains in Chester, Delaware and Lancaster counties.

Characteristics: mesic to wet, well drained, very deep silt loams that are occasionally flooded with a pH of 5.3.

Composition: about 32 percent sand, 56 percent silt and 12 percent clay, with about 3 percent organic matter in the top 12 inches, formed from alluvium containing large amounts of mica.

Current use: Most are cultivated or used as pasture; native vegetation is northern red oak (*Quercus rubra*), yellow poplar (*Liriodendron tulipifera*), red maple (Acer rubrum) and black walnut (*Juglans nigra*).

Taxonomy: Coarse-loamy, mixed, active, mesic Fluventic Dystrudepts.

Conestoga silt loams

Where they are found: level to moderately steep upland hillslopes on the northern Piedmont Plateau.

Characteristics: mesic to moist, well drained, very deep silt loams with a pH of 6.2.

Composition: about 25 percent sand, 54 percent silt, and 21 percent clay, with about 2 percent organic matter in the top 12 inches, formed in residuum from calcareous schist and micaceous limestone.

Current use: Mostly cultivated for a variety of field crops, and extensive acreage is being converted to non-farm use. Woodlands tend toward mixed oak (*Quercus spp.*), hickory (*Carya spp.*) and yellow poplar (*Liriodendron tulipifera*).

Taxonomy: fine-loamy, mixed, active, mesic Typic Hapludalfs.

Congaree silt loams

Where they are found: floodplains in Delaware County. (Also listed as Comus soil series.)

Characteristics: mesic to moist, well drained, deep and moderately permeable silt loams, with a pH of 5.3 and occasional brief flooding in winter and spring.

Composition: about 32 percent sand, 56 percent silt and 12 percent clay, with about 3 percent organic matter in the top 12 inches and formed in alluvium, two to six feet thick, derived from gneiss and granite and sometimes mica schist.

Current use: mostly cleared for a variety of pasture and cropland; native vegetation includes oak (*Quercus spp.*), hickory (*Carya spp.*), black gum (*Nyssa sylvatica*), yellow poplar (*Liriodendron tulipifera*) and loblolly pine (*Pinus taeda*).

Taxonomy: fine-loamy, mixed, active, nonacid, thermic Oxyaquic Udifluvents.

Conneaut silt loam

Where they are found: broad convex flats, depressions, short side slopes along drainageways and on slight rises of Wisconsinan Age lake plains.

Characteristics: moist to wet, poorly to somewhat poorly drained silt loam, with a pH of 4.9 and an intermittent perched seasonal high water table at 6 to 12 inches between November and May.

Composition: about 7 percent sand, 72 percent silt and 21 percent clay, with about 2.5 percent organic matter in the top 12 inches and formed in loess or silty glaciolacustrine sediments and underlying low-lime till, with moderately slow permeability. Soil was modified and leveled by wave action during the period of glacial lakes.

Current use: Most areas are in woodland or are former cropland reverting to woodland, generally deciduous forest, including red maple (*Acer rubrum*), green ash (*Fraxinus pennsylvanica*), eastern cottonwood (*Populus deltoides*), black cherry (*Prunus serotina*), swamp white oak (*Quercus bicolor*) and pin oak (*Quercus palustris*). Urban development is increasing and some land is used for pasture.

Taxonomy: fine-silty, mixed, active, nonacid, mesic Aeric Epiaquepts.

Conotton loams

Where they are found: treads and risers on glacial lake and outwash plains and stream terraces, as well as side slopes and interfluves of beach ridges, eskers and kames, with slopes up to 50 percent.

Characteristics: dry to mesic, well drained, very deep and generally gravelly and coarse-sandy loams with a pH of 5.6.

Composition: usually about 68 percent sand, 20 percent silt and 12 percent clay, but sand can be as low as 41 percent and silt as high as 42 percent in some areas. Organic matter is about 1.25 percent in the top 12 inches, and soils formed in Wisconsinan Age stratified gravel and sand outwash deposits.

Current use: where slopes are less than 12 percent, land has been cleared and used for general farming, mostly grain crops; steeper slopes are often in woodland or pasture. Native vegetation includes deciduous hardwoods, primarily oaks (*Quercus spp.*) and hickory (*Carya spp.*), as well as red maple (*Acer rubrum*), yellow poplar (*Liriodendron tulipifera*), black cherry (*Prunus serotina*) and white ash (*Fraxinus americana*).

Taxonomy: loamy-skeletal, mixed, active, mesic Typic Hapludalfs.

Conowingo silt loams

Where they are found: level to sloping, well-dissected uplands of the northern Piedmont Plateau.

Characteristics: mesic to moist, moderately well to somewhat poorly drained, deep silt loams with a pH of 5.6.

Composition: about 20 percent sand, 55 percent silt and 25 percent clay, with about 1.6 percent organic matter in the top 12 inches and formed from weathered rock high in magnesium, typically serpentine.

Current use: Many areas are used for corn, small grains, soybeans and pasture. Large areas are idle or in residential developments. Native vegetation includes scrub hardwoods, mostly oaks (*Quercus spp.*), with some shortleaf pine (*Pinus echinata*) and Virginia pine (*Pinus virginiana*).

Taxonomy: Fine-loamy, magnesic, mesic Aquic Hapludalfs.

Cookport loams

Where they are found: moderately steep side slopes and broad, nearly level to gently sloping ridgetops in the unglaciated Allegheny Plateau.

Characteristics: mesic to moist, moderately well drained, deep loams, with moderate permeability and often with a fragipan between 15 and 30 inches and a pH of 4.8 to 5.0.

Composition: about 41 percent sand, 38 percent silt and 21 percent clay, with 2 to 2.5 percent organic matter in the top 12 inches and formed in residuum of mostly weathered interbedded sandstone and siltstone, but also some shale.

Current use: mostly forested, dominated by oaks (*Quercus spp.*), black cherry (*Prunus serotina*), red maple (*Acer rubrum*), sugar maple (*Acer saccharum*), white ash (*Fraxinus americana*) and yellow poplar (*Liriodendron tulipifera*). Cleared areas are used for corn, small grain, hay or pasture.

Taxonomy: fine-loamy, mixed, active, mesic Aquic Fragiudults.

Covegap cobbly sandy loams

Where they are found: upland fan terraces near major ridge gaps on convex to concave toeslopes in Franklin County.

Characteristics: mesic to moist, well drained, very deep cobbly sandy loams with moderate permeability and a pH of 5.8.

Composition: about 66 percent sand, 19 percent silt and 15 percent clay, with about 3 percent organic matter in the top 12 inches and formed in colluvium from siltstone, sandstone and shale deposited over limestone.

Current use: About a third of the soils are in pasture, a third in cropland or hayland, 10 percent in orchards and 20 percent in woodland composed of mixed hardwoods, especially white ash (*Fraxinus americana*), black walnut (*Juglans nigra*) and red oak (*Quercus rubra*).

Taxonomy: loamy-skeletal, mixed, subactive, mesic Typic Paleudults.

Craigsville gravelly loams

Where they are found: level to gently sloping first bottoms along major streams and tributaries.

Characteristics: dry to mesic, well-drained, very deep gravelly loams with rapid permeability, rarely to occasionally flooded, with a pH of 5.0 to 5.2 and often in a complex with Wyoming, Barbour and Buchanan soils.

Composition: about 46 to 66 percent sand, 23 to 37 percent silt and the balance in clay, with less than 2 percent organic matter in the top 12 inches and formed in coarse-textured alluvium washed from sandy and gravelly uplands weathered from acidic sandstone and quartzite.

Current use: more than half these soils are forested, typically yellow-poplar (*Liriodendron tulipifera*), white pine (*Pinus strobus*), northern red oak (*Quercus rubra*), white oak (*Quercus alba*), red maple (*Acer rubrum*), sugar maple (*Acer saccharum*), Virginia pine (*Pinus virginiana*); American sycamore (*Platanus occidentalis*) and black walnut (*Juglans nigra*); the remainder are used for pasture and such crops as hay, small grain and corn.

Taxonomy: loamy-skeletal, mixed, superactive, mesic Fluventic Dystrudepts.

Croton silt loams

Where they are found: level to sloping upland flats or depressions in the Triassic shale and sandstone belt of Pennsylvania.

Characteristics: mesic to moist, poorly drained, deep silt loams with moderate permeability, often with a fragipan between 15 and 25 inches, and a pH of 5.1 to 5.7. Because of seasonal zones of saturation reaching 3 inches from November through May and occasional ponding, the soils are classified as hydric. Excess water often lingers above the fragipan in late winter and early spring, but is either used or evaporated by summer.

Composition: about 7 percent sand, 65 to 70 percent silt and the balance in clay, with about 2.5 to 4 percent organic matter in the top 12 inches and formed from medium-texture materials mostly over fine-grained silty sandstones, argillites siltstones or red shale. Some upper soil horizons formed in a thin silt layer deposited either by water or wind.

Current use: Native vegetation is dominated by pin oak (*Quercus palustris*), white oak (*Quercus alba*), swamp white oak (*Quercus bicolor*), white ash (*Fraxinus americana*), beech (*Fagus grandifolia*) and red maple (*Acer rubrum*); cleared areas are typically pasture, hayland or idle.

Taxonomy: fine-silty, mixed, active, mesic Typic Fragiaqualfs.

Culleoka silt loams

Where they are found: narrow crests of ridges and steep upland hillsides.

Characteristics: dry to mesic, well drained, moderately deep silt loams with a pH of 6.4 and moderate to rapid permeability.

Composition: about 26 percent sand, 52 percent silt and 22 percent clay, with more than 2 percent organic matter in the top 12 inches, formed in colluvium or residuum from interbedded limestone, shale, siltstone and fine-grained sandstone.

Current use: cleared areas for pasture, hay, some tobacco and grains; native forest is typically composed of red oak (*Quercus rubra*), white oak (*Quercus alba*), black oak (*Quercus velutina*), red maple (*Acer rubrum*), sugar maple (*Acer saccharum*), black walnut (*Juglans nigra*), white ash (*Fraxinus americana*), hickory (*Carya spp.*), beech (*Fagus grandifolia*), elm (*Ulmus spp.*), hackberry (*Celtis spp.*), locust (*Robinia spp.*), Kentucky coffeetree (*Gymnocladus dioicus*), redbud (*Cercis canadensis*), dogwood (*Cornus spp.*), and red cedar (*Juniperus virginiana*).

Taxonomy: Fine-loamy, mixed, active, mesic Ultic Hapludalfs.

Dalton soil series

Where they are found: level to sloping footslopes along valley sides and sometimes on flats or slight depressions in moraine-covered areas in Erie County.

Characteristics: dry to mesic, somewhat poorly drained, very deep silt loam with a pH of 5.3 and moderate permeability above a dense fragipan at 12 to 22 inches, but slow in and below it.

Composition: about 14 percent sand, 72 percent silt and 14 percent clay, with about 2 percent organic matter in the top 12 inches, formed in a loamy till with a silty lacustrine mantle above siltstone, sandstone and shale.

Current use: mostly cleared and is used for pasture or grain crops, but some areas are idle. Woodlots include sugar maple (*Acer sacchrum*), American beech (*Fagus grandifolia*), red oak (*Quercus rubra*), hemlock (*Tsuga canadensis*) and other northern hardwoods.

Taxonomy: coarse-silty, mixed, active, mesic Aeric Fragiaquepts.

Darien silt loams

Where they are found: on convex flats, summits, shoulders, back slopes and slight rises on moraines, drumlins and till plains in Erie County and forms a complex with Platea silt loam.

Characteristics: mesic to moist, somewhat poorly drained but deep silt loams with moderately slow permeability and a seasonal zone of water saturation is at 9 inches from October through June and a pH of 5.2.

Composition: about 20 percent sand, 55 percent silt and 25 percent clay, with more than 5 percent organic matter in the top 12 inches, formed in Wisconsinan age till.

Current use: mostly for hay and grain crops, but many areas are idle and reverting back to woodland. Native vegetation was sugar maple (*Acer saccharum*), red maple (*Acer rubrum*), red oak (*Quercus rubra*), black cherry (*Prunus serotina*), hemlock (*Tsuga canadensis*) and white pine (*Pinus strobus*), but white ash (*Fraxinus americana*), eastern cottonwood (*Populus deltoides*), swamp white oak (*Quercus bicolor*) and pin oak (*Quercus palustris*) are also suitable.

Taxonomy: fine-loamy, mixed, active, mesic Aeric Endoaqualfs

Dekalb loams

Where they are found: level to very steep ridges and uplands, with slopes typically convex and with gradients up to 80 percent. *Note: this series includes the inactive Fleetwood stony loams of Carbon County.*

Characteristics: dry to mesic, excessively drained, moderately deep loams, especially channery loams, with rapid permeability, depth to lithic bedrock between 20 and 72 inches and a typical pH of 5.0, but can go as low as 4.1.

Composition: ranges from about 45 to 67 percent sand, 20 to 40 percent silt and generally about 14 percent clay with about 2 percent organic matter in the top 12 inches, formed from residuum of gray and brown acidic sandstone in areas interbedded with shale and graywacke.

Current use: mostly in forests composed of mixed oaks, especially red oak (Quercus rubra), chestnut oak (Quercus prinus), maple (Acer spp.), some white pine (Pinus strobus) and hemlock (Tsuga canadensis). Small areas have been cleared for cultivation and pasture.

Taxonomy: loamy-skeletal, siliceous, active, mesic Typic Dystrudepts.

Delaware fine sandy loams

Where they are found: low to middle terraces along major rivers and creeks.

Characteristics: mesic to moist, well drained, deep fine sandy loams that are rarely flooded, with moderate internal drainage and high permeability, and a pH of 6.2.

Composition: 63 to 69 percent sand, 23 to 29 percent silt and less than 10 percent clay, with 2.5 to 3 percent organic matter in the top 12 inches, formed in postglacial alluvium, principally from areas of sandstone, siltstone and shale.

Current use: mostly for a variety of agricultural crops; the few that are wooded are dominated by maples (*Acer spp.*), American beech (*Fagus grandifolia*), cottonwood (*Populus deltoides*), red oak (*Quercus rubra*), American sycamore (*Plantanus occidentalis*), American basswood (*Tilia americana*) or ash (*Fraxinus spp.*).

Taxonomy: coarse-loamy, mixed, active, mesic Typic Dystrudepts.

Deposit gravelly loam

Where they are found: nearly level areas of alluvial fans or low stream terraces, in valleys along high-gradient streams, in Cumberland and Franklin counties.

Characteristics: dry to mesic, moderately well drained, deep gravelly loams that are frequently flooded, with a pH of 5.6.

Composition: about 60 percent sand, 30 percent silt and 10 percent clay, with 2.5 percent organic matter in the top 12 inches and 7 percent organic matter surface horizon, formed in alluvium overlying alluvial fan or glaciofluvial deposits containing shale, siltstone and sandstone.

Current use: mostly used for hay, corn or pasture, others are mixed hardwood forest composed of sugar maple (*Acer saccharum*), black cherry (*Prunus serotina*), red maple (*Acer rubrum*), white ash (*Fraxinus americana*) and willows (*Salix spp.*).

Taxonomy: loamy-skeletal, mixed, active, mesic Fluvaquentic Dystrudepts.

Dormont silt loams

Where they are found: backslopes and hill summits in southwestern Pennsylvania.

Characteristics: moist to wet, moderately well drained, deep silt loams with slow permeability and a pH of 6.6.

Composition: about 26 percent sand, 54 percent loam and 20 percent clay, with 3 percent organic matter in the top 12 inches formed in residuum and colluvium from non-acidic siltstone and shale with some thin beds of sandstone and limestone.

Current use: on gentler slopes, mostly cleared and farmed, pasture or idle. Wooded areas are dominated by mixed oaks, especially red oak (*Quercus rubra*), red maple (*Acer rubrum*), sugar maple (*Acer saccharum*), white ash (*Fraxinus americana*) and yellow-poplar (*Liriodendron tulipifera*).

Taxonomy: fine-loamy, mixed, superactive, mesic Oxyaquic Hapludalfs.

Downsville gravelly loams

Where they are found: very high old stream terraces, about 100 to 250 feet above the active floodplain, with topography that is typically hilly and rolling, but can be undulating and steep, in Franklin County.

Characteristics: mesic to moist, well drained, moderately permeable gravelly loams with a pH of 6.0.

Composition: about 44 percent sand, 41 percent silt and 15 percent clay, with less than 2 percent organic matter in the top 12 inches, and formed in unconsolidated material or old alluvium composed of sandstone, shale, chert and limestone, including limestone rock outcrops and sink holes.

Current use: While most of the soil is cultivated for a variety of crops, some areas are left open for wildlife habitat with forests generally composed of oak (*Quercus spp.*), hickory (*Carya spp.*), maple (*Acer spp.*), yellow poplar (*Liriodendron tulipifera*), walnut (*Juglans nigra*), locust (*Robinia pseudoacacia*), and white pine (*Pinus strobus*).

Taxonomy: loamy-skeletal, mixed, active, mesic Typic Paleudults.

Doylestown silt loams

Where they are found: level to gently sloping concave upland depressions drainageways in the Northern Piedmont and Northern Coastal Plain.

Characteristics: dry to mesic, poorly drained, deep silt loams with slow permeability, a pH of 5.8, a fragipan at 15 to 25 inches and a seasonal zone of saturation is at 3 inches from September through May; classified as hydric.

Composition: about 7 percent sand, 68 percent silt and 25 percent clay, with about 1.6 percent organic matter in the top 12 inches and formed from eolian deposits over a variety of materials weathered from sandstone, shale, limestone, schist and gneiss.

Current use: About half the soils are in cropland and the remainder in woodland, pasture or non-farm use. Forest areas are dominated by water-tolerant mixed hardwoods, such as pin oak (*Quercus palustris*).

Taxonomy: fine-silty, mixed, active, mesic Typic Fragiaqualfs.

Drifton loams

Inactive; now part of the Buchanan Series.

Dryrun soil series

Where they are found: alluvial flats and slightly concave fans and fan terraces at the base of mountain streams flowing onto valley floors in Franklin County.

Characteristics: mesic to moist, moderately well drained, moderately permeable and very deep gravelly loam with a pH of 6.4.

Composition: about 41 percent sand, 39 percent silt and 10 percent clay, with about 2.5 percent organic matter in the top 12 inches and formed in alluvial material from surrounding mountains covering limestone residuum.

Current use: most in pasture and cropland; appropriate woodland species include white ash (*Fraxinus americana*), black walnut (*Juglans nigra*), yellow poplar (*Liriodendron tulipifera*), white pine (*Pinus strobus*) and red oak (*Quercus rubra*).

Taxonomy: loamy-skeletal, mixed, active, mesic Aquic Hapludults.

Duffield silt loams

Where they are found: nearly level to steep hillsides.

Characteristics: mesic to moist, well drained, deep silt loams with moderate permeability, often in complexes with Ryder soils and with a pH of about 6.6.

Composition: about 25 percent sand, 53 percent silt and 12 percent clay, with about 2.5 percent organic matter in the top 12 inches and formed in residuum from impure limestone.

Current use: about 90 percent is cultivated for general farm crops; woodlands are composed of mixed oak, especially red oak (*Quercus rubra*) and also yellow poplar (*Liriodendron tulipifera*)

Taxonomy: fine-loamy, mixed, active, mesic Ultic Hapludalfs.

Duncannon loams

Where they are found: level to moderately steep uplands and terraces

Characteristics: mesic to moist, well drained, deep and silt loams, sandy loams and loams with moderate permeability and a pH of 5.6.

Composition: loams are about 36 percent sand and 49 percent silt; sandy loams are 62 percent sand and 23 percent silt; silt loams are about 14 percent sand and 70 percent silt, all with the balance in clay and all with between 2.5 and 3 percent organic matter in the top 12 inches. Soils formed from silty to fine sandy loam material, probably eolian, overlying residuum including shale, limestone, sandstone, schist, and stream and glacial deposits.

Current use: mostly cleared for use as cropland, hayland and pasture; woodlands are mixed hardwoods composed mostly of upland oaks, especially red oak (*Quercus rubra*), yellow poplar (*Liriodendron tulipifera*) and ash (*Fraxinus spp.*).

Taxonomy: coarse-silty, mixed, active, mesic Ultic Hapludalfs.

Dunning soil series

Where they are found: floodplains with slack water and fine-textured alluvium.

Characteristics: moist to wet, very poorly drained, slowly permeable deep silty loams, classified as hydric, with a pH of 6.7, frequently flooded and occasionally ponded.

Composition: about 18 to 23 percent sand and 45 to 52 percent silt, with the balance in clay and about six percent organic matter in the top 12 inches, formed in alluvium washed from limestone hillsides.

Current use: where drained and cleared, a variety of agricultural crops; native forest is composed of water-tolerant hardwoods including red maple (*Acer rubrum*), sycamore (*Platanus occidentalis*), gums (*Nyssa sylvatica* and *Liquidambar styraciflua*), boxelder (*Acer negundo*), willow (*Salix spp.*), pin oak (*Quercus palustris*), swamp white oak (*Quercus bicolor*), and cottonwood (*Populus deltoides*), interspersed with glades of cane, grass, and sedge.

Taxonomy: Fine, mixed, active, mesic Fluvaquentic Endoaquolls.

Edgemere loams

Where it is found: along drainageways and structural benches below seep areas.

Characteristics: dry to mesic, poorly drained, very deep stony loam, with moderate permeability above a fragipan between 15 and 25 inches, with a pH of 4.8.

Composition: about 45 percent sand, 43 percent silt and 12 percent clay, with about 3.6 percent organic matter in the top 12 inches and formed in till mostly from shale and sandstone areas.

Current use: mostly wooded and used for timber; scattered areas were once cleared for use as pasture, but the stony character of the soils precludes agricultural use.

Taxonomy: loamy-skeletal, mixed, superactive, mesic Typic Fragiaquepts.

Edgemont loams

Where they are found: nearly level to very steep ridge and mountain slopes.

Characteristics: dry to mesic, well drained, deep channery and very stony loams with high permeability and a pH ranging from 4.2 to 5.6, increasing as slopes become more gentle.

Composition: 43 to 54 percent sand and 35 to 42 percent silt with the balance in clay and about 2 percent organic matter in the top 12 inches, formed in residuum from metaquartzite, quartz schist, quartz conglomerate and quartzite.

Current use: mostly mixed hardwood forest dominated by yellow poplar (*Liriodendron tulipifera*), ash (*Fraxinus spp.*) and red oak (*Quercus rubra*); some areas have been cleared and are used for cropland and pasture and a portion of the areas are urbanized.

Taxonomy: fine-loamy, mixed, active, mesic Typic Hapludults.

Edom silt loams

Where they are found: gently sloping to dissected steep hillslopes.

Characteristics: dry to mesic, well drained, deep silt and silty clay loams with slow to moderate permeability and a pH of 6.5. It often appears in complexes, most notably with Klinesville and Weikert soils.

Composition: about 20 percent sand, 52 percent silt and 28 percent clay, although silty clay loams have about 40 percent silt and 40 percent clay; organic matter in the top 12 inches is about 1.7 percent and soils formed in residuum of interbedded shaly or platy limestone and calcareous shale

Current use: mostly cleared for a variety of agricultural crops, with wooded areas generally mixed hardwoods dominated by oaks (*Quercus spp.*).

Taxonomy: fine, illitic, mesic Typic Hapludalfs.

Eldred soil series

Where they are found: level to steep hillsides, valley sides and ridgetops in McKean County.

Characteristics: mesic to moist, moderately well drained, very deep silt loam with moderate permeability and a pH of 5.3.

Composition: about 20 percent sand, 51 percent silt and 29 percent clay, with about 1 percent organic matter in the top 12 inches and formed in residuum of weathered interbedded siltstone, shale and fine-grained sandstone.

Current use: cleared areas are used for grain and hay crops as well as pasture, and abandoned idle land is currently in second-growth hardwood forest. Native vegetation is mixed hardwood, dominated by northern red oak (*Quercus rubra*), white oak (*Quercus alba*), black cherry (*Prunus serotina*), sugar maple (*Acer saccharum*), beech (*Fagus grandifolia*) and white pine (*Pinus strobus*).

Taxonomy: Fine-loamy, mixed, semiactive, frigid Aquic Hapludults.

Elk soil series

Where they are found: high stream terraces in Lancaster and York counties.

Characteristics: mesic to moist, well drained, deep and moderately permeable silt loams with a pH of 5.5.

Composition: about 11 percent sand, 69 percent silt and 20 percent clay, with up to 2.2 percent organic matter in the top 12 inches and formed in residuum from limestone, shale, siltstone, sandstone and sometimes loess.

Current use: mostly agricultural for corn, tobacco, small grains, soybeans and hayland or pasture. Native vegetation is dominated by oaks (*Quercus spp.*), elms (*Ulmus spp.*), walnut (*Juglans nigra*), hickory (*Carya spp.*), ash (*Fraxinus spp.*), but also suitable for red maple (*Acer rubrum*), sycamore (*Platanus occidentalis*), yellow poplar (*Liriodendron tulipifera*), hackberry (*Celtis occidentalis*) and sweet gum (*Liquidambar styraciflua*).

Taxonomy: fine-silty, mixed, active, mesic Ultic Hapludalfs.

Elkins silt loam

Where they are found: floodplains with slopes under 3 percent in primarily in Fayette County.

Characteristics: Mesic to moist, poorly drained, deep silt loams with slow permeability, with a pH of 4.3, that are occasionally flooded, have a seasonal zone of saturation at less than 12 inches from November through June and are classified as hydric. The series often appears as minor elements with other soils series.

Composition: about 7 percent sand, 68 percent silt and 25 percent clay with about 2.2 percent organic matter in the top 12 inches, formed in acidic alluvium washed from upland soils parented by sandstone, siltstone and shale with slopes up to 3

percent.

Current use: where drained, cleared and used mostly for pasture or hayland. Where ponded, these soils are in marsh grasses and sedges. Native vegetation is water tolerant hardwoods such as yellow poplar (*Liriodendron tulipifera*), pin oak (*Quercus palustris*) and black willow (*Salix nigra*).

Taxonomy: fine-silty, mixed, superactive, acid, mesic Fluvaquentic Endoaquepts.

Elko silt loams

Where they are found: level to steeply sloped broad ridgetops, upland depressions and upper side slopes between 1,800 and 3,000 feet above sea level in unglaciated areas of the Appalachian Plateau.

Characteristics: dry to mesic, moderately well drained, deep silt loams with moderate permeability above a fragipan between 18 and 30 inches and a pH of 4.4.

Composition: about 26 percent sand, 52 percent silt and 22 percent clay and less than 3 percent organic matter in the top 12 inches, formed in the residuum of interbedded weathered fine-grained sandstone, siltstone and shale

Current use: a few small areas are used for agriculture, mostly hayland and pasture, and abandoned land is in native grasses and shrubs with second-growth hardwoods. Native vegetation is mixed hardwoods, including sugar maple (*Acer saccharum*), northern red oak (*Quercus rubra*), black cherry (*Prunus serotina*), striped maple (Acer pensylvanicum), beech (*Fagus grandifolia*) and white pine (*Pinus serotina*).

Taxonomy: fine-loamy, mixed, semiactive, frigid Aquic Fragiudults.

Ellery silt loams

Inactive; see Chippewa series.

Elliber loams

Where they are found: sideslopes and summits of secondary ridges, especially the narrow to broad ridges of the Onodaga and Old Port formations of the Appalachian Ridge and Valley region.

Characteristics: mesic to moist, well drained, deep cherty, channery and silt loams with a pH of 4.6 and moderate permeability.

Composition: about 30 percent sand, 55 percent silt and 18 percent clay, with loams containing about 40 percent sand and 45 percent silt. Organic matter in the top 12 inches ranges from 1 to 2 percent and soils were formed in residuum of weathered calcareous shale, silty chert, siliceous siltstone and cherty limestone, with some areas influenced by either colluvial or glacial action.

Current use: about a third of the soils are cultivated, especially in orchards; the remainder is forested with mixed hardwoods, including yellow poplar (Liriodendron tulipifera) and red oak (Quercus rubra).

Taxonomy: loamy-skeletal, mixed, semiactive, mesic Typic Hapludults.

Elnora loamy fine sands

Where they are found: relict longshore bars and beach ridges of Wisconsinan age glacial lake plains and associated deltas on the Erie and Ontario Lake Plain.

Characteristics: dry to mesic, moderately well drained, very deep loamy fine sand with a pH of 5.4.

Composition: about 79 percent sand, 16 percent silt and 5 percent clay, with about 3 percent organic matter in the top 12 inches, and formed in windblown or water-sorted very fine sand

Current use: most areas are used for a wide range of agriculture; native vegetation is composed of sugar maple (*Acer saccharum*), northern red oak (*Quercus rubra*), white ash (*Fraxinus americana*), black cherry (*Prunus serotina*), beech (*Fagus grandifolia*), hemlock (*Tsuga canadensis*), and white pine (*Pinus strobus*).

Taxonomy: mixed, mesic Aquic Udipsamments.

Empeyville sandy loams

Where it is found: Till plains in Monroe County.

Characreristics: dry to mesic, moderately well drained, very deep ston sandy loams with a fragipan between 14 and 22 inches and a pH of 5.5.

Composition: about 77 percent sand, 13 percent silt and 10 percent clay, with about 2 percent organic matter in the top 12 inches, formed in loamy till derived mostly from acidic siltstone, sandstone and shale

Current use: mostly forested, with small logging operations and a few areas of hayland or pasture. Forests are dominated by northern red oak (*Quercus rubra*), eastern white pine (*Pinus strobus*), paper birch (*Betula papyrifera*), American beech (*Fagus grandifolia*), eastern hemlock (*Tsuga canadensis*) and sugar maple (*Acer saccharum*).

Taxonomy: coarse-loamy, isotic, frigid Aquic Fragiorthods.

Erie silt loams

Where they are found: footslopes, concave lower valley slopes and broad divides in ground moraines of the Glaciated Allegheny Plateau.

Characteristics: dry to mesic, somewhat poorly drained, deep silt loams with moderate permeability, a fragipan between 18 and 28 inches, and a pH of 5.6.

Composition: about 26 percent sand, 53 percent silt and 21 percent clay, with about 2.6 percent organic matter in the top 12 inches and formed in Wisconsinan Age till parented by sandstone, siltstone, shale and some limestone.

Current use: While some acreage is used for forage crops and pasture associated with dairy farms, most is idle. Woodlots typically include sugar maple (*Acer saccharum*), white ash (*Fraxinus americana*), black cherry (*Prunus serotina*), red oak (*Quercus rubra*), white pine (*Pinus strobus*), and hemlock (*Tsuga canadensis*).

Taxonomy: fine-loamy, mixed, active, mesic Aeric Fragiaquepts.

Ernest loams

Where they are found: upland footslopes, hillslopes, head slopes and base slopes.

Characteristics: mesic to moist, well to poorly drained, deep silt and stony loams with moderately low permeability, a fragipan between 20 and 36 inches, and a pH of about 5.2.

Composition: about 25 percent sand, 54 percent silt and 21 percent clay, with about 2.5 percent organic matter in the top 12 inches and formed in colluvium derived from acidic fine-grained sandstone, siltstone and shale.

Current use: mostly cleared for cropland and pasture; woodlands consist of some white pine (*Pinus strobus*) and hemlock (*Tsuga canadensis*) but mostly mixed hardwoods, including red maple (*Acer rubrum*), sugar maple (*Acer saccharum*), white ash (*Fraxinus americana*), yellow poplar (*Liriodendron tulipifera*), red oak (*Quercus rubra*), black walnut (*Juglans nigra*) and black cherry (*Prunus serotina*).

Taxonomy: fine-loamy, mixed, superactive, mesic Aquic Fragiudults.

Evendale cherty silt loams

Where they are found: nearly level to sloping concave footslopes in the Ridge and Valley sections of Pennsylvania.

Characteristics: mesic to moist, somewhat poorly drained, deep cherty silt loam with slow permeability and a pH of about 5.9.

Composition: about 18 percent sand, 52 percent silt and 29 percent clay, with about 1.5 percent organic matter in the top 12 inches and formed in fine to moderately fine textured glacially influenced materials or colluvium derived from limestone containing chert, usually overlying shale or residuum from shaly limestone and shale.

Current use: mostly agricultural, including pasture, hay and row crops; wooded areas are mixed hardwoods, especially red oak (*Quercus rubra*) and yellow poplar (*Liriodendron tulipifera*).

Taxonomy: Fine, mixed, semiactive, mesic Aquultic Hapludalfs.

Fairplay soil series

Where they are found: nearly level active floodplains and heads of limestone springs where water discharge is high in calcium carbonate, in Cumberland and Franklin counties.

Characteristics: moist to wet, very poorly drained and very deep marl, with slow permeability and pH of 7.5 that is frequently flooded, frequently ponded, with a zone of saturation near the surface from October through May and classified as hydric.

Composition: about 24 percent sand, 52 percent silt and 24 percent clay, with 4 percent organic matter in the top 12 inches, formed in alluvial, calcareous marl sediments on slopes of less than 3 percent.

Current use: sometimes used for pasture or agricultural crops, but mostly for wetland wildlife habitat; primary canopy trees include red maple (*Acer rubrum*), silver maple (*Acer saccharinum*), white ash (*Fraxinus americana*), green ash (*Fraxinus pennsylvanica*), pin oak (*Quercus palustris*) and black willow (*Salix nigra*).

Taxonomy: fine-loamy, carbonatic, mesic Fluvaquentic Endoaquolls.

Fairpoint series

Where they are found: very steep sideslopes, benches and nearly level ridgetops of regolith from surface mine operations.

Characteristics: dry to mesic, well drained, deep channery loams with slow permeability and a pH of about 6.5.

Composition: about 22 percent sand, 49 percent silt and 29 percent clay, with negligible organic matter in the top 12 inches, formed in surface mining operation regolith ranging from acidic to neutral, generally from calcareous shale, fine and medium grained sandstone, siltstone and coal.

Current use: Mostly recreation and wildlife, with many areas supporting volunteer deciduous trees and others seeded for hay or pasture. Primary canopy trees suitable for these sites include white pine (*Pinus strobus*), black cherry (*Prunus serotina*), red oak (*Quercus rubra*) and black locust (*Robinia pseudoacacia*).

Taxonomy: Loamy-skeletal, mixed, active, nonacid, mesic Typic Udorthents.

Fitchville silt loams

Where they are found: shoulders and summits of lake plains and on treads and terraces in glaciolacustrine sediments typically at elevations between 720 and 1,200 feet above sea level.

Characteristics: mesic to moist, somewhat poorly drained, very deep silt loams with moderate permeability, with a pH of 5.9.

Composition: about 11 percent sand, 67 percent silt, and 22 percent clay, with about 2.2 percent organic matter in the top 12 inches, formed in stratified glaciolacustrine sediments, derived mostly from shales and sandstones, on lake plains and slackwater terraces of the Wisconsinan age.

Current use: Mostly cleared, primarily for pasture but also cultivated crops. In wooded areas, dominant species are sugar maple (*Acer saccharum*), beech (*Fagus grandifolia*), red oak (*Quercus rubra*), pin oak (*Quercus palustris*), elm (*Ulmus spp.*) and hickory (*Carya spp.*).

Taxonomy: fine-silty, mixed, superactive, mesic Aeric Endoaqualfs.

Fleetwood loams

Inactive; see Clymer for sandy loams and Dekalb for very stony loams.

Fountainville silt loams

Where they are found: along broad drainageways and drain heads on backslopes and summits in Bucks County.

Characteristics: mesic to moist, moderately well drained deep silt loams with moderate permeability above a fragipan between 20 and 40 inches and a pH of 6.1.

Composition: about 12 percent sand, 70 percent silt and 18 percent clay, with about 2 percent organic matter in the top 12 inches and formed in a thin coating of loess over residuum weathered from brown to red siltstone and shale.

Current use: about 40 percent of the area is in cropland, 25 percent in hayland or pasture and 35 percent in woodland or idle and reverting to woodland of generally mixed hardwoods, especially red oak (*Quercus rubra*) and yellow poplar (*Liriodendron tulipifera*).

Taxonomy: fine-silty, mixed, active, mesic Oxyaquic Fragiudalfs.

Frankstown channery silt loams

Where they are found: on gentle to steeply sloping uplands in limestone valleys in Fulton

County.

Characteristics: mesic to moist, well drained deep channery silt loams with moderate permeability with a pH of about 5.6.

Composition: about 20 percent sand, 54 percent silt and 26 percent clay, with about 2 percent organic matter in the top 12 inches and formed in residuum from siliceous limestone interbedded with limy shale and siltstone.

Current use: where cleared, for pasture, hayland and some crops; native vegetation is forest dominated by oaks (*Quercus spp.*), ash (*Fraxinus spp.*), hickory (*Carya spp.*), elm (*Ulmus spp.*), maple (*Acer spp.*), black walnut (*Juglans nigra*) and flowering dogwood (*Cornus florida*).

Taxonomy: Fine-loamy, mixed, semiactive, mesic Typic Hapludults.

Fredon loams

Where they are found: terraces just above the lowest depressions and stream floodplains of outwash terraces and outwash plains in Butler and Erie counties.

Characteristics: mesic to moist, poorly drained, very deep loams with high permeability, hydric classification and pH ranging between 5.4 and 6.5. A seasonal zone of water saturation is at 6 inches from October through June.

Composition: about 48 percent sand, 38 percent silt and 24 percent clay, with 5 to 6 percent organic matter in the top 12 inches, formed in glaciofluvial materials parented by slate, shale, sandstone, limestone and small amounts of granitic gneiss.

Current use: cleared areas in cropland or pasture; natural woodland vegetation is dominated by red maple (*Acer rubrum*), elm (*Ulmus spp.*), willow (*Salix spp.*), ash (*Fraxinus spp.*) and some sedges and wetland plants.

Taxonomy: Coarse-loamy over sandy or sandy-skeletal, mixed, active, nonacid, mesic Aeric Endoaquepts.

Freetown mucky peat

Where they are found: bogs on lake, outwash and till plains and moraines, with slopes less than 1 percent.

Characteristics: moist to wet, very poorly drained, very deep organic mucky peats of more than 50 inches of highly decomposed organic material in bogs that can vary from small enclosed depressions to several hundred acres in size, especially in Pike County. Soils are about 75 percent organic material, pH 4.5, and are frequently ponded, especially in winter and early spring.

Composition: about 75 percent organic matter.

Current use: mostly forested, but some acreage has been cleared for truck crops, primarily cranberries. Woodlands are dominated by red maple (*Acer rubrum*), American elm (*Ulmus americana*), green ash (*Fraxinus pennsylvanica*), eastern hemlock (*Tsuga canadensis*), Atlantic white cedar (*Chamaecyparis thyoides*), balsam fir (*Abies balsamea*), buttonbush (*Cephalanthus occidentalis*), winterberry (*Ilex verticillata*), swamp azalea (*Rhododendron viscosum*), and leatherleaf (*Chamaedaphne calyculata*).

Taxonomy: Dysic, mesic Typic Haplosaprists

Frenchtown silt loams

Where they are found: broad flat areas, base slopes, depressions and along natural drainageways on till plains.

Characteristics: mesic to moist, poorly drained, very deep silt loams with a pH of 5.3 and moderate permeability above a fragipan between 15 and 30 inches, occasionally ponded with a seasonal zone of water saturation at or near the surface between October and May, and classified as hydric.

Composition: about 25 percent sand, 52 percent silt and 23 percent clay, and about 2 percent organic matter in the top 12 inches, formed in Wisconsinan till of principally siltstone and sandstone, sometimes covered with a thin layer of loess.

Current uses: mostly divided between cropland, pasture, cropland reverting to forest and forest, with natural vegetation dominated by elm (*Ulmus spp.*), white ash (*Fraxinus americana*), red maple (*Acer rubrum*), swamp white oak (*Quercus bicolor*), eastern cottonwood (*Populus deltoides*), and pin oak (*Quercus palustris*).

Taxonomy: Fine-loamy, mixed, active, mesic Typic Fragiaqualfs.

Funkstown silt loams

Where they are found: head slope positions and upland draws in Franklin and Fulton counties.

Characteristics: mesic to moist, moderately well drained, deep and moderately permeable and frequently flooded silt loams with a pH of 7.0.

Composition: about 27 percent sand, 54 percent silt and 19 percent clay with about 3 percent organic matter in the top 12 inches and formed from alluvial and colluvial materials washed down from adjacent uplands and covering limestone residuum.

Current use: Mostly for pasture or crops; in urban areas, they are found in open space or along waterways. Among appropriate canopy species are yellow poplar (*Liriodendron tulipifera*) and red oak (*Quercus rubra*).

Taxonomy: fine-loamy, mixed, active, mesic Oxyaquic Hapludalfs.

Gageville soil series

Where they are found: footslopes, back slopes and shoulders of dissected Wisconsinan Age end and ground moraines and till plains in Erie County.

Characteristics: mesic to moist, moderately well drained, very deep and somewhat slowly permeable silt loams with a pH of 4.8.

Composition: about 31 percent sand, 55 percent silt and 14 percent clay with about 2.6 percent organic matter in the top 12 inches and formed in low-lime, loamy till.

Current use: Most areas are wooded, with original vegetation described as deciduous forest, usually composed of sugar maple (*Acer saccharum*), white ash (*Fraxinus americana*), black walnut (*Juglans nigra*), yellow poplar (*Liriodendron tulipifera*), black cherry (*Prunus serotina*), white oak (*Quercus alba*) and red oak (*Quercus rubra*).

Taxonomy: fine-loamy, mixed, semiactive, mesic Oxyaquic Hapludalfs.

Gaila silt loams

Where they are found: level to very steep summits and shoulders of ridges in Chester County.

Characteristics: mesic to moist, well drained, very deep silt loams with moderately high permeability and a pH of 5.3.

Composition: about 38 percent sand, 42 percent silt and 20 percent clay, with less than 1 percent organic matter in the top 12 inches, formed in residuum of quartz muscovite and mica schist.

Current use: about 90 percent in oak-hickory and pine forest, especially shortleaf pine (*Pinus echinata*) and Virginia pine (*Pinus virginiana*), with limited areas used mostly for hayland and pasture, as well as residential or non-farm development.

Taxonomy: Fine-loamy, mixed, active, mesic Inceptic Hapludults.

Gibraltar silt loams

Where they are found: valley flats, hills and levees of floodplains in southeastern Pennsylvania impacted by coal washings.

Characteristics: mesic to moist well drained, very deep silt loams with high permeability, rarely flooded, with a pH of 6.1.

Composition: about 34 percent sand, 58 percent silt and 8 percent clay with less than 2 percent organic matter in the top 12 inches and formed in recent alluvium derived from coal washings deposited over alluvium composed of reddish sandstone, shale and siltstone, with high permeability.

Current use: Some areas in cropland or hayland, but most are in woodland and used for timber production from mixed hardwoods, especially yellow poplar (*Liriodendron tulipifera*) and red oak (*Quercus rubra*).

Taxonomy: coarse-loamy, mixed, active, nonacid, mesic Mollic Udifluvents.

Gilpin silt loams

Where they are found: level to very steep convex dissected uplands, often hillslopes and in complexes with other soils, in the Allegheny Plateau.

Characteristics: dry to mesic, moderately

deep, well drained silt loams, sometimes channery and stony, with moderate permeability and a pH of 4.6 to 5.5.

Composition: about 25 percent sand, 52 percent silt and 23 percent clay with less than 2 percent organic matter in the top 12 inches and formed from nearly horizontally-interbedded brown and gray acidic siltstone, shale and some sandstone.

Current use: mostly for cropland and pasture, but also mixed hardwood forests dominate by oaks (*Quercus spp.*) and suitable for white pine (*Pinus strobus*), shortleaf pine (*Pinus echinata*), Virginia pine (*Pinus virginiana*), black cherry (*Prunus serotina*), sugar maple (*Acer saccharum*), red maple (*Acer rubrum*).

Taxonomy: fine-loamy, mixed, active, mesic Typic Hapludults.

Ginat silt loams

Where they are found: flats and closed depressions on stream terraces.

Characteristics: mesic to moist, poorly drained, deep silt loams with moderate permeability and a pH ranging from 4.6 (Clarion county) to 5.9. A seasonal zone of water saturation is between 6 and 15 inches from November through May, but soils are neither flooded or ponded.

Composition: about 10 percent sand, 55 percent silt and 25 percent clay, with less than 2 percent organic matter in the top 12 inches and formed in silty alluvium over loamy and clayey, silty slackwater alluvium with slopes of less than 1 percent.

Current use: corn and soybean production with some hay, pasture and brushy idle pasture. A few areas are in woodland; native vegetation is mixed hardwood forest, including red maple (*Acer rubrum*), ash (*Fraxinus spp.*), sweet gum (*Liquidambar styraciflua*), white oak (*Quercus alba*) and pin oak (*Quercus palustris*).

Taxonomy: fine-silty, mixed, active, mesic Typic Endoaqualfs.

Gladstone gravelly loams

Where they are found: rolling foothills and upland divides.

Characteristics: mesic to moist, well drained, very deep soils with high permeability and a pH of 5.3 to 6.0.

Composition: about 40 percent sand, 40 percent silt and 20 percent clay, with about 2.5 percent organic matter in the top 12 inches and formed in residuum and colluvium from granitic gneiss; in some areas, weathering of granitic gneiss regolith appears to have been highly weathered, possibly by ancient periglacial or glacial activity.

Current use: most of the non-stony areas for a variety of agricultural crops and some of the gently sloping area are urban development. Stony surface areas tend to be woodlands dominated by yellow poplar (*Liriodendron tulipifera*), upland oaks such as white oak (*Quercus alba*) and red oak (*Quercus rubra*), ash (*Fraxinus spp.*) and hickory (*Carya spp.*).

Taxonomy: fine-loamy, mixed, active, mesic Typic Hapludults.

Glenelg silt loams

Where they are found: nearly level to very steep well dissected uplands in the northern Piedmont Plateau and Blue Ridge.

Characteristics: mesic to moist, well drained, very deep, highly permeable and mostly channery silt and silt loams with a pH of 5.4.

Composition: about 24 percent sand, 54 percent silt and 22 percent clay, with about 1.5 percent organic matter in the top 12 inches and formed in residuum of micaceous schist.

Current use: mostly for a variety of agricultural crops and pasture; native vegetation is red oak (*Quercus rubra*), white oak (*Quercus alba*), black oak (*Quercus velutina*), hickory (*Carya spp.*), red maple (*Acer rubrum*), shortleaf pine (*Pinus echinata*), Virginia pine (*Pinus virginiana*) and yellow poplar (*Liriodendron tulipifera*).

Taxonomy: fine-loamy, mixed, semiactive, mesic Typic Hapludults.

Gleneyre silt loams

Where they are found: nearly level fluvial lacustrine deposits on floodplains of glacial lakebeds in Pike and Wayne counties.

Characteristics: moist to wet, very poorly

drained, very deep coarse-silty loams, with a pH of 5.9, in complexes with Kimbles soils that are frequently flooded, frequently ponded, have a seasonal zone of saturation at or near the surface throughout the year and are considered hydric.

Composition: about 6 percent sand, 84 percent silt and 10 percent clay, with about 11 percent organic matter in the top 12 inches, formed in postglacial lacustrine deposits

Current use: most areas are covered with hummocks of sedges and reeds; trees include red maple (*Acer rubrum*), pin oak (*Quercus palustris*) and hemlock (*Tsuga canadensis*).

Taxonomy: Coarse-silty over sandy or sandy-skeletal, mixed, active, nonacid, mesic Typic Fluvaquents.

Glenford silt loams

Where they are found: side slopes, shoulders and summits on lake plains and treads and risers on stream terraces and outwash plains.

Characteristics: mesic to moist, moderately well drained, very deep silt loams with moderate permeability with a pH ranging from 5.2 to 5.8.

Composition: about 11 percent sand, 66 percent silt and 23 percent clay with 1.5 to 3 percent organic matter in the top 12 inches and formed in stratified Wisconsinan Age glaciolacustrine or stream sediments from materials dominated by sandstone and shale.

Current use: mostly cleared for cropland and pasture, and areas in urban areas are non-agricultural use. Native vegetation was deciduous forest including sugar maple (*Acer saccharum*), white ash (*Fraxinus americana*), yellow poplar (*Liriodendron tulipifera*), black cherry (*Prunus serotina*), white oak (*Quercus alba*) and red oak (*Quercus rubra*).

Taxonomy: fine-silty, mixed, superactive, mesic Aquic Hapludalfs.

Glenville silt loams

Where they are found: level to sloping upland flats, footslopes or near drainageway heads.

Characteristics: mesic to moist, moderately well to somewhat poorly drained, very deep mostly silt loams with moderate permeability, sometimes a fragipan between 15 and 30 inches, and a pH of about 5.8.

Composition: about 28 percent sand, 55 percent silt and 17 percent clay, with about 2.4 percent organic matter in the top 12 inches and formed in residuum and colluvium impacted by soil creep from weathered micaceous schist, gneiss, phyllite and other acidic crystalline rock.

Current use: Mostly in agricultural use for crops and pasture, and large areas are near urban development. Native vegetation is mixed hardwoods, such as sugar maple (*Acer saccharum*), white ash (*Fraxinus americana*), yellow poplar (*Liriodendron tulipifera*) and red oak (*Quercus rubra*).

Taxonomy: fine-loamy, mixed, active, mesic Aquic Fragiudults.

Gresham silt loams

Where they are found: till plains on moraines in Butler County.

Characteristics: mesic to moist, poorly drained, deep silt loams with slow permeability and a fragipan between 15 and 26 inches and a pH of 4.9.

Composition: about 24 percent sand, 54 percent silt and 22 percent clay, with about two percent organic matter in the top 12 inches, formed in low-lime Illinoian till with many sandstone and shale fragments and a silty mantle of loess up to 16 inches thick in some areas.

Current use: mostly pasture or cropland; wooded areas are mixed hardwoods, including sugar maple (*Acer saccharum*), white ash (*Fraxinus americana*), yellow poplar (*Liriodendron tulipifera*), black cherry (*Prunus serotina*), white oak (*Quercus alba*), pin oak (*Quercus palustris*) and red oak (*Quercus rubra*).

Taxonomy: fine-loamy, mixed, active, mesic Aeric Fragiaqualfs.

Guernsey loams

Where they are found: sideslopes and benches of dissected uplands.

Characteristics: mesic to moist, moderately well drained silt and silty clay loams with moderately slow to slow permeability, a pH of 5.8 and often in complexes with other soils. Springs and hillside seeps are frequent, and slope creep and slippage is common.

Composition: about 18 percent sand, 53 percent silt and 29 percent clay, with about 1.5 percent organic matter in the top 12 inches and formed in residuum and colluvium from interbedded shale, siltstone and limestone

Current use: mostly agricultural, especially pasture; some areas remain forested and original vegetation was hardwood forest, including sugar maple (*Acer saccharum*), white ash (*Fraxinus americana*), yellow poplar (*Liriodendron tulipifera*), black cherry (*Prunus serotina*) white oak (*Quercus alba*) and red oak (*Quercus rubra*).

Taxonomy: fine, mixed, superactive, mesic Aquic Hapludalfs.

Hagerstown loams

Where they are found: floors of valleys and adjacent hillsides.

Characteristics: mesic to moist, well drained, deep silt and silty clay loams with moderate permeability, with a typical pH of 5.6, but can be as high as 6.3. Hagerstown soils are often found in complexes involving Carbo, Opequon and rock outcrops.

Composition: 22 to 25 percent sand and 43 to 50 percent silt with the balance in clay; among silty clay loams, sand is about 23 percent, silt 37 percent and clay 40 percent. Organic matter ranges from 1.3 to 2.5 percent in the top 12 inches, and soils formed in residuum of fairly pure, hard gray limestone.

Current use: Mostly used for a variety of crops and pastures, with large areas in non-farm use. Native vegetation is mixed hardwoods, including black walnut (*Juglans nigra*), yellow poplar (*Liriodendron tulipifera*), red oak (*Quercus rubra*), Virginia pine (*Pinus virginiana*), white oak (*Quercus alba*), hickory (*Carya spp.*) and basswood (*Tilia americana*).

Taxonomy: Fine, mixed, semiactive, mesic Typic Hapludalfs

Halsey silt loams

Where they are found: shallow depressions on generally level terraces and floodplain steps, and sometimes in seepage areas of steeper sloping terraces of glaciofluvial landforms.

Characteristics: mesic to moist, very poorly drained, deep silt loams, with high permeability, often ponded and considered hydric, with a pH of 6.5. When on low terraces they are subject to occasional flooding, but seasonal zone of water saturation can be at or just under the surface from October through June. Inadequate outlets are usually responsible for slow surface drainage.

Composition: 30 to 43 percent sand, 40 to 56 percent silt and about 16 percent clay, with organic matter ranging from 2.2 to 4 percent in the top 12 inches and formed in glacial outwash of mostly slate, shale, quartz and sandstone, sometimes with minor quantities of limestone, granite, gneiss

Current use: mostly wooded; natural vegetation includes red maple (*Acer rubrum*), elm (*Ulmus spp.*), ash (*Fraxinus spp.*), willow (*Salix spp.*), river birch (*Betula nigra*), white oak (*Quercus alba*), swamp white oak (*Quercus bicolor*), sedges, and rushes. Some small cleared and drained areas are used as pasture or cropland.

Taxonomy: Coarse-loamy over sandy or sandy-skeletal, mixed, active, nonacid, mesic Typic Humaquepts.

Hanover silt loams

Where they are found: till-covered sandstone hills, till plains and moraines.

Characteristics: mesic to moist, well drained, deep mostly silt loams with moderate permeability above a fragipan at 17 to 30 inches and a pH of about 5.4.

Composition: about 26 percent sand, 54 percent silt and 20 percent clay, with about 1.6 percent organic matter in the top 12 inches and formed in Illinoian age till often with a veneer of loess that can be up to 16 inches thick in some areas.

Current use: mostly for pasture and cropland; steeper slopes are in woodlands, often including sugar maple (*Acer saccharum*), beech (*Fagus*

grandifolia), white ash (*Fraxinus americana*), pitch pine (*Pinus resinosa*), white pine (*Pinus strobus*), sycamore (*Platanus occidentalis*), white oak (*Quercus alba*), red oak (*Quercus rubra*) and slippery elm (*Ulmus rubra*).

Taxonomy: Fine-loamy, mixed, semiactive, mesic Typic Fragiudults.

Harbor sandy loams

Where they are found: low beach ridges, offshore bars and deltas, including rises, convex flats, knolls, shoulders and backslopes, of Wisconsinan-age lake plains.

Characteristics: mesic to moist, moderately well drained, very deep fine sandy loams with a pH of 5.4.

Composition: about 69 percent sand, 22 percent silt and 9 percent clay, with about 4 percent organic matter in the top 12 inches and formed in sandy glaciolacustrine sediments, typically dominated by quartz from non-calcareous sandstones or granitic rock in the underlying low-lime till. During the glacial lake period, the till was leveled and altered by the action of waves, so a thin line of stone is often found at the contact point of lake sediments and the till.

Current use: Soils are used for nursery stock and orchards as well as corn and hay production; native vegetation was mixed hardwoods, including red maple (*Acer rubrum*), green ash (*Fraxinus pennsylvanica*), quaking aspen (*Populus tremuloides*), bur oak (*Quercus macrocarpa*), red oak (*Quercus rubra*), black oak (*Quercus velutina*) and slippery elm (*Ulmus rubra*).

Taxonomy: Coarse-loamy, mixed, active, mesic Aquic Hapludalfs.

Hartleton channery silt loams

Where they are found: sideslopes and convex uplands.

Characteristics: dry to mesic, well drained, deep channery silt loams with moderate permeability and a pH of about 5.0.

Composition: about 25 percent sand, 55 percent silt and 20 percent clay, with less than 2 percent organic matter in the top 12 inches, formed in frost-churned materials or till primarily from brown sandstone and olive brown shale.

Current use: woodlands are dominated by red oak (*Quercus rubra*), chestnut oak (*Quercus prinus*), white pine (*Pinus strobus*) and Virginia pine (*Pinus virginiana*), and cleared areas are used for pasture, orchards and other crops.

Taxonomy: Loamy-skeletal, mixed, active, mesic Typic Hapludults.

Hatboro silt loams

Where they are found: nearly level floodplains and valley floors.

Characteristics: mesic to moist, poorly drained, deep silt loams with a pH of 5.9, that are occasionally to frequently flooded and sometimes ponded; a seasonal zone of water saturation can reach the surface, or be just below it, all year and organic content and permeability is high.

Composition: about 28 percent sand, 55 percent silt and 17 percent clay, with about 2.4 percent organic matter in the top 12 inches and formed from alluvium mostly from schist, gneiss and other crystalline and metamorphic rock.

Current use: about half in pasture, 35 percent in woodland, and the remainder in cropland. Woodlands are mixed hardwoods, including red maple (*Acer rubrum*), sycamore (*Platanus occidentalis*) and pin oak (*Quercus palustris*).

Taxonomy: fine-loamy, mixed, active, nonacid, mesic Fluvaquentic Endoaquepts.

Haven silt loams

Where they are found: level to moderately sloping outwash plains, terraces, valley trains, and water-sorted moraine deposits in Crawford County.

Characteristics: dry to mesic, well drained, very deep silt loams with high permeability, with a pH of 5.3.

Composition: about 31 percent sand, 58 percent silt and 11 percent clay, with about 2.75 percent organic matter in the top 12 inches and formed from 18 to 36 inches of loamy materials sorted by water and low in gravel over stratified gravel and sand.

Current use: Mostly cleared for a variety of

agricultural crops and urban development. Typical woodland trees include black oak (*Quercus velutina*), white oak (*Quercus alba*), northern red oak (*Quercus rubra*), maple (*Acer spp.*), red pine (*Pinus resinosa*) and beech (*Fagus grandifolia*).

Taxonomy: coarse-loamy over sandy or sandy-skeletal, mixed, active, mesic Typic Dystrudepts.

Hazleton loams

Where they are found: upper third of backslopes, shoulders and summits, typically convex and with gradients up to 80 percent.

Characteristics: dry to mesic, well drained, deep, mostly channery and very stony loams with a typical pH of 4.6 and often in complexes with associated soils including Clymer, Dekalb and Gilpin.

Composition: about 57 percent sand, 34 percent silt and 9 percent clay, often with 2.5 percent organic matter in the top 12 inches, but can be less than 1 percent, and developed in the residuum of acidic gray, brown or red sandstone.

Current use: mostly forest composed of red maple (*Acer rubrum*), red oak (*Quercus rubra*), chestnut oak (*Quercus prinus*), cherry (*Prunus spp.*) and some conifers. A few areas have been cleared for cropland, but more commonly used as pasture.

Taxonomy: Loamy-skeletal, siliceous, active, mesic Typic Dystrudepts.

Henrietta marsh

Where they are found: lake outwash and till plains and glacial drainageways; in Erie County it occurs in fresh water marshes and bogs.

Characteristics: moist to wet, very poorly drained, deep soil with moderate permeability, frequently ponded and a zone of saturation is at or near the surface throughout the year and classified as hydric,

Composition: more than 53 percent organic matter, with no data on sand, silt, clay, formed in organic materials less than 16 inches thick over loamy and sandy sediments.

Current use: nationally, most of the soils are used for cropland, with some small areas for pasture and woodland; in Pennsylvania, the hydric soil is unsuitable for agriculture and potential canopy trees include red maple (*Acer rubrum*), sweet birch (*Betula lenta*), ash (*Fraxinus americana*), green ash (*Fraxinus pennsylvanica*), swamp white oak (*Quercus bicolor*), pin oak (*Quercus palustris*), eastern white cedar (*Thuja occidentalis*) and basswood (*Tilia americana*).

Taxonomy: coarse-loamy, mixed, superactive, nonacid, mesic Histic Humaquepts.

Highfield silt loams

Where they are found: slopes up to 50 percent, mountain crests and intermountain valleys in the South Mountain area.

Characteristics: dry to mesic, well drained, deep, mostly channery and very stony silt loams with moderate permeability and a pH between 5.4 and 5.8, often in complexes with Catoctin loams.

Composition: about 30 percent sand, 54 percent silt and 16 percent clay, with less than 2 percent organic matter in the top 12 inches, formed in residuum of metabasalt, metarhyolite, metaandesite, greenstone schist and other light-colored rock.

Current use: about half the area is cleared for general farm crops and orchards, while wooded areas are dominated by mixed hardwoods, especially red oak (*Quercus rubra*) and black oak (*Quercus velutina*), including yellow poplar (*Liriodendron tulipifera*).

Taxonomy: coarse-loamy, mixed, active, mesic Ultic Hapludalfs.

Hollinger silt loams

Where they are found: level to steep dissected uplands in the northern Piedmont.

Characteristics: mesic to moist, well drained, deep silt loams with a pH of 6.5.

Composition: about 29 percent sand, 54 percent silt and 17 percent clay, with about 2 percent organic matter in the top 12 inches and formed in residuum with high permeability of micaceous limestone, phyllite and calcareous schist.

Current use: almost all cultivated for a variety of agricultural crops, but a small amount is in woodland composed of mixed oak (*Quercus spp.*), hickory (*Carya spp.*), Virginia pine (*Pinus virginiana*) and yellow poplar (*Liriodendron tulipifera*).

Taxonomy: fine-loamy, mixed, active, mesic Typic Hapludalfs.

Holly silt loams

Where they are found: slight depressions, backswamps and broad flat areas of floodplains. *Note: this series now includes the inactive Papakating Soil Series (Carbon County)*

Characteristics: mesic to moist, poorly drained, deep mostly silt loams with moderately high permeability, frequently flooded and rarely to often ponded, and with a zone of saturation at or just below the surface, usually in winter to spring but year-round in some areas. Soils are classified as hydric and have a pH between 6.3 and 6.5.

Composition: typically about 25 percent sand, 53 percent silt and 22 percent clay, with about 3 percent organic matter in the top 12 inches and and formed in the alluvium from upland areas of noncalcareous sandstone and shale as well as low-lime drift.

Current use: while some areas have been cleared and used for pasture or cultivation, most areas used for wetland wildlife habitat; native vegetation is silver maple (*Acer saccharinum*), box elder (*Acer negundo*), willow (*Salix spp.*), swamp white oak (*Quercus bicolor*), pin oak (*Quercus palustris*) and other trees that are tolerant of wet sites.

Taxonomy: Fine-loamy, mixed, active, nonacid, mesic Fluvaquentic Endoaquepts.

Holston silt loams

Where they are found: level to moderately steep (up to 25 percent) intermediate and high stream terraces above floodplains, as well as benches and footslopes in Clarion County. Inactive; see Allegheny series.

Hornell silt loams

Where they are found: small area of level to steep bedrock-controlled upland slopes in Erie County.

Characteristics: dry to mesic, poorly drained, deep silt loams with slow permeability, but with a seasonal zone of water saturation is at 9 inches from October through June, and a pH between 5.1 and 5.9.

Composition: about 6 percent sand, 65 percent silt and 30 percent clay, with 4 percent organic matter in the top 12 inches and formed in till generally 20 to 40 inches deep over acidic shale or siltstone. Some of the mantle can include weathered shale bedrock residuum.

Current use: cleared areas are used for a number of agricultural crops, while native vegetation includes red maple (*Acer rubrum*), sugar maple (*Acer saccharum*), white ash (*Fraxinus americana*), eastern hemlock (*Tsuga canadensis*), black cherry (*Prunus serotina*), red oak (*Quercus rubra*) and eastern white pine (*Pinus strobus*).

Taxonomy: Fine, illitic, acid, mesic Aeric Endoaquepts.

Howard silt loams

Where they are found: outwash terraces in Erie County; elsewhere, level to rolling outwash plains and valley trains as well as rolling to very steep eskers, kames and terrace faces.

Characteristics: dry to mesic, well to excessively drained, very deep gravelly silt loams with high permeability with a pH of 6.2.

Composition: about 35 percent sand, 53 percent silt and 12 percent clay, with about 3 percent organic matter in the top 12 inches and formed in glacial outwash deposits that include substantial amounts of limestone rock fragments, along with a variety of sedimentary and igneous origin rock fragments.

Current use: Mostly cleared for a variety of agricultural crops, but steep areas are either pasture or woodland composed of sugar maple (*Acer saccharum*), beech (*Fagus grandifolia*), red oak (*Quercus rubra*), white ash (*Fraxinus americana*), black cherry (*Prunus serotina*) and white pine (*Pinus strobus*).

Taxonomy: loamy-skeletal, mixed, active, mesic Glossic Hapludalfs.

Howell loams

Where they are found: nearly level to steep uplands in the Atlantic Coastal Plain and in a complex with urban land in Philadelphia County.

Characteristics: mesic to moist, well drained, deep loams formed from fine, unconsolidated sediments that contain small amounts of diatomaceous earth or glauconite; no pH or compositional data.

Current use: non-farm purposes; native vegetation would include mixed hardwoods, such as yellow poplar (*Liriodendron tulipifera*) and white oak (*Quercus alba*) and some Virginia pine (*Pinus virginiana*).

Taxonomy: fine, mixed, semiactive, mesic Typic Hapludults.

Hublersburg silt loams

Where they are found: level to steep convex upland slopes

Characteristics: mesic to moist, well drained, very deep silt and cherty silt loams with moderate permeability and a pH of about 5.0 in silt loams and 5.8 in cherty silt loams.

Composition: about 23 percent sand, 51 percent silt and 24 percent clay, with about 2.5 percent organic matter in the top 12 inches and formed in residuum of weathered cherty limestone.

Current use: mostly cultivated or in pasture, with about 5 percent in non-agricultural use and 15 percent in mixed hardwood forest dominated by sugar maple (*Acer saccharum*), white ash (*Fraxinus americana*) and red oak (*Quercus rubra*).

Taxonomy: clayey, illitic, mesic Typic Hapludults.

Huntington silt loams

Where they are found: on toeslopes of river valley floodplains.

Characteristics: mesic to moist, well drained, very deep silt loams with high permeability, occasionally flooded, with a pH of 6.7.

Composition: about 7 percent sand, 69 percent silt and 24 percent clay, with more than 4 percent organic matter in the top 12 inches and formed in alluvium washed from sandstone, shale and limestone.

Current use: Mostly in crops or pasture; in woodland, mixed hardwoods dominate, especially red oak (*Quercus rubra*) and yellow poplar (*Liriodendron tulipifera*).

Taxonomy: fine-silty, mixed, active, mesic Fluventic Hapludolls.

Hustontown soil series

Where they are found: valley flats and sides, including headslopes, U-shaped drainageways and colluvial fans, as well as concave footslopes and toe slopes of dissected uplands.

Characteristics: mesic to moist, moderately well drained, deep mostly channery silt loam and silt loams with moderate permeability and a fragipan between 18 and 32 inches, with a pH of 5.5.

Composition: about 26 percent sand, 53 percent silt and 21 percent clay, with about 1.7 percent organic matter in the top 12 inches and formed in colluvium parented by acidic red shale, siltstone and sandstone.

Current use: evenly divided between agricultural use as cropland and pasture and woodlands of mixed hardwoods dominated by red maple (*Acer rubrum*), white ash (*Fraxinus americana*), yellow poplar (*Liriodendron tulipifera*) and red oak (*Quercus rubra*).

Taxonomy: Fine-loamy, mixed, active, mesic Oxyaquic Fragiudalfs.

Itmann channery loams

Where they are found: level to gently sloping benches, gently to strongly sloping hillslopes and steep outslopes of waste materials from deep-mined coal

Characteristics: dry to mesic, excessively drained, very deep soils with rapid permeability with a pH of 4.6.

Composition: about 46 percent sand, 44 percent silt and 10 percent clay, with no organic matter in the top 12 inches and formed in the acidic regolith of waste materials from deep coal mining, generally a mix of partly weathered fine earth and bedrock fragments consisting of acidic carboliths with traces of sandstone, siltstone and shale. The materials are from bedrock crushed by machinery before weathering.

Current use: usually barren or may support sparse populations of grasses, annuals and some hardwoods, including black birch (*Betula nigra*), sycamore, (*Plantanus occidentalis*), yellow-poplar (*Liriodendron tulipifera*) and black oak (*Quercus velutina*). Reclamation areas typically support grasses, legumes, black locust (*Robinia pseudoacacia*) and other reclamation plant materials. Primary canopy trees:

Taxonomy: Loamy-skeletal, mixed, semiactive, acid, mesic Typic Udorthents

Ivory silty clay loams

Where they are found: level to moderately steep hillsides, benches and upland ridgetops in unglaciated areas of the Appalachian Plateau.

Characteristics: mesic to moist, poorly drained, deep silty clay loams with a pH of 4.8.

Composition: about 23 percent sand, 55 percent silt and 22 percent clay, with about 3 percent organic matter in the top 12 inches and formed in residuum derived from local shale, fine-grained sandstone and siltstone and relatively high in organic matter.

Current use: cleared areas for agriculture, while forested areas include red oak (*Quercus rubra*), white oak (*Quercus alba*), sugar maple (*Acer saccharum*), beech, (*Fagus grandifolia*), hemlock (*Tsuga canadensis*), and white pine (*Pinus strobus*).

Taxonomy: fine, mixed, subactive, frigid Aeric Endoaquults.

Jimtown loams

Where they are found: outwash and stream terraces, outwash plains and beach ridges.

Characteristics: mesic to moist, somewhat poorly drained, deep loams with slow permeability with a pH of 5.8.

Composition: about 43 percent sand, 39 percent silt and 18 percent clay, with about 2 percent organic matter in the top 12 inches and formed in Wisconsinan Age stratified outwash deposits.

Current use: mostly for a a variety of agricultural crops and woodland dominated by such mixed hardwoods as elm (*Ulmus spp.*), sugar maple (*Acer saccharum*), white ash (*Fraxinus americana*), beech (*Fagus grandifolia*), yellow poplar (*Liriodendron tulipifera*), black cherry (*Prunus serotina*), white oak (*Quercus alba*) and red oak (*Quercus rubra*).

Taxonomy: fine-loamy, mixed, superactive, mesic Aeric Endoaqualfs.

Joanna loams

Where they are found: gently sloping to very steep, convex hillslopes in Triassic areas of the Piedmont.

Characteristics: mesic to moist, well drained, deep loams with high permeability with a pH between 5.1 and 5.5.

Composition: about 41 percent sand, 40 percent silt and 19 percent clay, with about 2 percent organic matter in the top 12 inches and formed in residuum from interbedded red sandstone and Triassic Age conglomerate that includes some quartz.

Current use: gently sloping areas cultivated, especially for grain and hay crops; steeper and stony areas are for pasture and forest. Native vegetation is of the oak-hickory forest type, including Virginia pine (*Pinus virginiana*).

Taxonomy: fine-loamy, mixed, active, mesic Typic Hapludults.

Jugtown silt loams

Where they are found: on nearly level floodplains in Ridge and Valley limestone valleys.

Characteristics: mesic to moist, moderately well drained, deep silt loams with moderate permeability and occasionally to frequently flooded, with a pH of 6.7.

Composition: about 29 percent sand, 53 percent silt and 17 percent clay, with about 3 percent organic matter in the top 12 inches and formed in alluvium parented by calcareous shale, limestone and sandstone.

Current use: about half in cropland, 40 percent in pasture or hayland and 10 percent in mixed hardwood forest that includes sugar maple (*Acer*

saccharum), white ash (*Fraxinus americana*), yellow poplar (*Liriodendron tulipifera*), black cherry (*Prunus serotina*), white oak (*Quercus alba*) and red oak (*Quercus rubra*).

Taxonomy: fine-loamy, mixed, active, mesic Aquic Hapludalfs.

Kanona silt loams

Where they are found: sides and broad tops of glaciated hills and till plains.

Characteristics: dry to mesic, poorly drained, deep silt and silty clay loams, with moderate permeability and a pH of 6.1.

Composition: about 23 percent sand, 51 percent silt and 26 percent clay with about 3.5 percent organic matter in the top 12 inches and formed in fine textured supraglacial till containing substantial amounts of soft shale and some siltstone.

Current use: Very little used for croplands and small areas are used for pasture and hay; most is either in, or idle and reverting to, native woodland that typically includes red maple (*Acer rubrum*), sugar maple (*Acer saccharum*), black cherry (*Prunus serotina*), white ash (*Fraxinus americana*), red oak (*Quercus rubra*) and white pine (*Pinus strobus*).

Taxonomy: fine, illitic, nonacid, mesic Aeric Endoaquepts.

Kedron silt loams

Where they are found: nearly level to moderately steep slopes in Luzerne, Monroe and Schuylkill counties.

Characteristics: mesic to moist, moderately well to poorly drained, deep mostly stony and channery loams with slow permeability, a fragipan between 20 and 32 inches, and a pH between 4.6 and 5.2.

Composition: about 22 percent sand, 55 percent silt and 13 percent clay, with about 2.5 percent organic matter in the top 12 inches and formed in either till or colluvium from reddish shale, fine-grained sandstone and siltstone.

Current use: about 30 percent in pasture and some cropland, but mostlhy forested with mixed hardwoods, including red maple (*Acer rubrum*), sugar maple (*Acer saccharum*), white ash (*Fraxinus americana*), yellow poplar (*Liriodendron tulipifera*) and red oak (*Quercus rubra*).

Taxonomy: fine-loamy, mixed, active, mesic Aquic Fragiudults.

Keene silt loams

Where they are found: benches, hills and ridgetops of unglaciated, dissected uplands in the western and central Allegheny Plateau on interfluves and head slopes, side slopes, nose slopes and base slopes.

Characteristics: mesic to moist, moderately well drained, deep silt loams with moderate permeability and a pH of 5.9.

Composition: about 11 percent and, 69 percent silt and 20 percent clay with 2 percent organic matter in the top 12 inches and formed in a 36-inch deep mantle of silty residuum from Pennsylvanian acidic shale, siltstone, coal underclay, and some limestone on uplands.

Current use: Mostly agricultural croplands, with sloping areas often in pasture or hayland; woodlands are dominated by deciduous hardwood forest that includes sugar maple (*Acer saccharum*), white ash (*Fraxinus americana*), black walnut (*Juglans nigra*), yellow poplar (*Liriodendron tulipifera*), black cherry (*Prunus serotina*), white oak (*Quercus alba*) and red oak (*Quercus rubra*).

Taxonomy: fine-silty, mixed, superactive, mesic Aquic Hapludalfs.

Kensington silt loams

Where they are found: sideslopes, nose slopes, head slopesand interfluves of till plains.

Characteristics: mesic to moist, moderately well drained, deep silt loams with moderate permeability and a pH of 5.9.

Composition: about 26 percent sand, 54 percent silt, and 20 percent clay with about 2.4 percent organic matter in the top 12 inches and formed in a combination of loess, Illinoian or Wisconsinan age tills and residuum of underlying fine-grained sandstone or siltstone and Pennsylvanian age shale from till plains.

Current use: mostly pasture and grain crops;

remaining woodlands are dominated by red maple (*Acer rubrum*), sugar maple (*Acer saccharum*), white ash (*Fraxinus americana*), white oak (*Quercus alba*), red oak (*Quercus rubra*), hickory (*Carya spp.*), yellow poplar (*Liriodendron tulipifera*) and black cherry (*Prunus serotina*).

Taxonomy: fine-loamy, mixed, active, mesic Aquic Hapludults

Kimbles soil series

Where they are found: nearly flat alluvial fans, stream dikes and stream entrances of meandering streams within glacial lakebeds.

Characteristics: mesic to moist, poorly drained, deep lacustrine soils with slow permeability and a pH of 5.9 and appear in complexes with Gleneyre soils, are frequently flooded and ponded, meet hydric criteria, and have a zone of saturation at or just below the surface at least from October through June, sometimes year round.

Composition: about 6 percent sand, 84 percent silt and 10 percent clay, with about 11 percent organic matter in the top 12 inches and formed in sandy to silty fluvial deposits from nearby glaciolacustrine sediments.

Current use: Mostly covered with either hemlocks (*Tsuga canadensis*) or dense stands of highbush blueberries, rhododendron, tamarack (*Larix laricina*), black spruce (*Picea mariana*), and reeds and sedges; also suitable for swamp white oak (*Quercus bicolor*) and pin oak (*Quercus palustris*).

Taxonomy: coarse-silty over sandy or sandy-skeletal, mixed, active, nonacid, mesic Typic Endoaquepts.

Kingsville loamy fine sand

Where they are found: depressions and concave flats on deltas and offshore bars of Wisconsinan age lake plains.

Characteristics: mesic to wet, very poorly drained, deep soils with rapid permeability that are frequently ponded with a seasonal zone of water saturation at near the surface year-round.

Composition: about 84 percent sand, 9 percent silt and 7 percent clay with 4 percent organic matter in the top 12 inches and formed in glaciolacustrine sediments.

Current use: A small amount in cropland, pasture and nurseries, but most is woodland or former cropland reverting to woodland. Native vegetation is primarily swampy forest consisting of elm (*Ulmus spp.*), green ash (*Fraxinus pennsylvanica*), red maple (*Acer rubrum*), pin oak (*Quercus palustris*), swamp white oak (*Quercus bicolor*), yellow birch (*Betula alleghaniensis*) and yellow poplar (*Liriodendron tulipifera*).

Taxonomy: mixed, mesic Mollic Psammaquents.

Kinzua channery silt loams

Where they are found: level to steep valley sides and hillsides and ridgetops in unglaciated areas of the Appalachian Plateau.

Characteristics: mesic to moist, well drained, very deep channery silt loams with moderate permeability and a pH of 5.3.

Composition: about 26 percent sand, 52 percent silt and 22 percent clay, with about 1.7 percent organic matter in the top 12 inches and formed in weathered colluvium or residuum of interbedded fine-grained sandstone, siltstone and shale.

Current use: cleared areas are primarily pasture, hayland and grain crops, while abandoned idle land is in second-growth hardwoods. Native vegetation is mixed hardwoods, principally red oak (*Quercus rubra*), white oak (*Quercus alba*), sugar maple (*Acer saccharum*), beech (*Fagus grandifolia*) and white pine (*Pinus strobus*). Other appropriate species include black cherry (*Prunus serotina*) and white ash (*Fraxinus americana*).

Taxonomy: fine-loamy, mixed, active, frigid Typic Hapludults.

Klinesville silt loams

Where they are found: gently to very steeply sloping convex hillslopes on dissected ridges and valley sides.

Characteristics: dry to mesic, excessively drained, shallow, channery and shaly silt loams with high permeability and a pH of 5.3.

Composition: about 30 percent sand, 55 percent silt and 15 percent clay, with less than 1 percent organic matter in the top 12 inches and formed in residuum of reddish shale mixed with some slate, fine-grained sandstone and siltstone.

Current use: mostly as pasture or forest, although less-sloping areas are occasionally used for tilled crops and hayland. Forests are dominated by chestnut oak (*Quercus prinus*), black oak (*Quercus velutina*), red oak (*Quercus rubra*) and Virginia pine (*Pinus virginiana*).

Taxonomy: loamy-skeletal, mixed, active, mesic Lithic Dystrudepts.

Knauers silt loams

Where they are found: on slight depressions in backwater positions of poorly drained floodplains, typically in complexes with Bowmansville silt loams.

Characteristics: mesic to moist, poorly drained, very deep silt loams that are occasionally flooded and often ponded, with seasonal zones of saturation at or near the surface much of the year, and is usually classified as hydric, with a pH of 6.0.

Composition: about 28 percent sand, 55 percent silt and 17 percent clay, with about 2 percent organic matter in the top 12 inches and formed in recent alluvial deposits generally derived from shales and sandstones.

Current use: About two thirds in pasture, while wooded areas are predominately mixed hardwoods, dominated by pin oak (*Quercus palustris*).

Taxonomy: fine-loamy over sandy or sandy-skeletal, mixed, active, nonacid, mesic Typic Fluvaquents.

Kreamer silt loams

Where they are found: nearly level to slightly sloping concave valley floors and hillsides in the Ridge and Valley sections of Pennsylvania (18,000 acres).

Characteristics: mesic to moist, moderately well drained, deep silt loams with moderately slow permeability and a pH of 5.9.

Composition: about 30 percent sand, 53 percent silt and 17 percent clay, with about 1.3 percent organic matter in the top 12 inches and formed in generally fine-textured colluvium or drift derived from limestone and cherty limestone.

Current use: mostly cultivated for general farm crops; wooded areas are typically mixed hardwoods that can include yellow poplar (*Liriodendron tulipifera*), red oak (*Quercus rubra*), hickory (*Carya spp.*), black walnut (*Juglans nigra*) and elm (*Ulmus spp.*)

Taxonomy: fine, illitic, mesic Aquic Hapludults.

Lackawanna loams

Where they are found: nearly level to steep glaciated hillslopes and ridges of the Allegheny Plateau at elevations ranging from 750 to 1,800 feet above sea level.

Characteristics: mesic to moist, well drained, very deep channery and very stony loams with moderate permeability, often with a fragipan between 17 and 36 inches, sometimes occurring in a complex with Oquaga channery loams and with a pH of about 5.0.

Composition: about 44 percent sand, 40 percent silt and 16 percent clay, with about 1.5 to 2.8 percent organic matter in the top 12 inches and formed in till from materials parented by shale, siltstone and reddish-colored sandstones.

Current use: Level to gently sloped areas have been cleared and are used for pasture, hayland and some crops, while others are idle and significant acreage has reverted to woodland or brush. Forests are dominated by sugar maple (*Acer saccharum*), American beech (*Fagus grandifolia*), red oak (*Quercus rubra*), white pine (*Pinus strobus*) and birch (*Betula spp.*).

Taxonomy: coarse-loamy, mixed, active, mesic Typic Fragiudepts.

Laidig loams

Where they are found: lower to middle slope benches and footslopes.

Characteristics: dry to mesic, well drained, very deep gravelly, stony and channery loams often with a fragipan between 30 and 50 inches, with moderate permeability and a typical pH of 4.6 to 4.8.

Composition: about 41 percent sand, 38 percent silt and 21 percent clay, with generally less than 2 percent organic matter in the top 12 inches (possibly none) and formed in at least six feet of colluvium parented by acidic gray sandstone, some shale and siltstone above a fragipan at 30 to 50 inches.

Current use: limited acreage cleared for pasture and cropland but most areas forested and dominated by red oak (*Quercus rubra*), white (*Quercus alba*) and chestnut oak (*Quercus prinus*), sugar maple (*Acer saccharum*), beech (*Fagus grandifolia*) and hemlock (*Tsuga canadensis*). Other appropriate species include white ash (*Fraxinus americana*), yellow poplar (*Liriodendron tulipifera*), white pine (*Pinus strobus*), black cherry (*Prunus serotina*), black locust (*Robinia pseudoacacia*), scarlet oak (*Quercus coccinea*), and black oak (*Quercus velutina*), hickory (*Carya spp.*)

Taxonomy: fine-loamy, siliceous, active, mesic Typic Fragiudults.

Lakin loamy fine sands

Where they are found: primarily risers and terrace treads on the leeward side of major rivers.

Characteristics: dry to mesic, excessively drained, deep loamy fine sand with rapid permeability and not subjected to flooding or ponding, with a pH of 5.3.

Composition: about 79 percent sand, 16 percent silt and 4 percent clay, with about 1 percent organic matter in the top 12 inches and formed in coarse-textured alluvium.

Current use: small acreage for specialty crops, but most in forages or pasture; wooded areas are hardwoods dominated by locust (*Robinia pseudoacacia*), sassafras (*Sassafras albidum*), oak (*Quercus spp.*), elm (*Ulmus spp.*), maple (*Acer spp.*), birch (*Betula spp.*) and paw-paw (*Asimina triloba*).

Taxonomy: mixed, mesic Lamellic Udipsamments.

Lamington silt loams

Where they are found: nearly level and stream terraces in the Northern Piedmont.

Characteristics: mesic to moist, poorly drained, very deep silt loams on stream terraces that, in Pennsylvania, are not subject to flooding or ponding, but because a seasonal zone of saturation can be at 3 inches from November through March are classified as hydric, with a pH of about 5.7, and with permeability ranging from low to high.

Composition: about 25 percent sand, 54 percent silt and 21 percent clay, with about 2 percent organic matter in the top 12 inches and formed in old sediments mostly parented by red and gray Triassic sandstone and shale.

Current use: Mostly cleared for cropland and pasture; native vegetation was mixed hardwoods dominated by oaks, especially pin oak (*Quercus palustris*).

Taxonomy: fine-loamy, mixed, semiactive, mesic Typic Fragiaquults.

Langford silt loams

Where they are found: convex to planar hillsides, including drumlins, and summits in the Ontario and Erie Lake Plain and glaciated Allegheny Plateau from 1,100 to 1,800 feet above sea level.

Characteristics: dry to mesic, moderately well drained, deep silt loams, with a fragipan between 21 and 36 inches, and moderate permeabilty above the fragipan, with a pH of 6.2.

Composition: about 30 percent sand, 55 percent silt and 15 percent clay, with about 4.5 percent organic matter in the top 12 inches and formed in loamy till derived from shale, sandstone, siltstone and some limestone.

Current use: Many areas cleared for pasture, hayland and grain crops, but a substantial amount is idle; woodlots include sugar maple (*Acer saccharum*), beech (*Fagus grandifolia*), black cherry (*Prunus serotina*), red oak (*Quercus rubra*), white pine (*Pinus strobus*), white ash (*Fraxinus americana*) and hemlock (*Tsuga canadensis*).

Taxonomy: fine-loamy, mixed, active, mesic Typic Fragiudepts.

Lansdale loams

Where they are found: hillsides of rolling uplands in the Northern Piedmont.

Characteristics: mesic to moist, well drained, deep soils with high permeability and a pH between 5.1 and 5.9, but mostly 5.2.

Composition: about 46 percent sand, 43 percent silt and 11 percent clay, with about 2.6 percent organic matter in the top 12 inches and formed in residuum weathered from varying combinations of sandstone and conglomerate.

Current use: extensively for a variety of agricultural crops and urban development; native vegetation is mixed hardwoods, primarily oaks (*Quercus spp.*), hickories (*Carya spp.*), yellow poplar (*Liriodendron tulipifera*), shortleaf pine (*Pinus echinata*) and Virginia pine (*Pinus virginiana*).

Taxonomy: Coarse-loamy, mixed, active, mesic Typic Hapludults.

Lantz silt loams

Where they are found: upland depressions, drainage heads and intermittent, small drainageways within the Blue Ridge and its footslopes.

Characteristics: mesic to moist, very poorly drained, deep silt loams with slow permeability and a pH of 6.1.

Composition: about 26 percent sand, 53 percent silt and 21 percent clay with about 4.5 percent organic matter in the top 12 inches and formed in residuum and colluvium from meta-igneous and metamorphic rock, possibly influenced by local alluvium.

Current use: some for pasture, but mostly in native vegetation consisting of maple (*Acer spp.*), hornbeam (*Carpinus spp.*), alder (*Alnus spp.*), willow (*Salix spp.*), sedge and other wetland species.

Taxonomy: Fine-loamy, mixed, active, mesic Mollic Endoaqualfs.

Lawrenceville silt loams

Where they are found: nearly level to sloping terraces and uplands.

Characteristics: mesic to moist, moderately well drained, deep silt loams with a pH of about 6.1, often with a fragipan in the 24 to 38 inch range.

Composition: about 14 percent sand, 69 percent silt and 17 percent clay, with about 3 percent organic matter in the top 12 inches and formed in silty materials covering a variety of consolidated and unconsolidated deposits.

Current use: mostly cleared to grow a variety of agricultural crops; woodlands are typically oak-hickory mixed hardwoods, notably yellow poplar (*Liriodendron tulipifera*) and red oak (*Quercus rubra*).

Taxonomy: Fine-silty, mixed, active, mesic Oxyaquic Fragiudalfs.

Leck Kill silt loams

Where they are found: level to very steep and usually convex upland slopes.

Characteristics: mesic to moist, well drained, deep typically channery loams with a pH of 5.9.

Composition: about 27 percent sand, 55 percent silt and 18 percent clay, with less than 2 percent organic matter in the top 12 inches and formed in mostly residuum but also till weathered from red shale, sandstone and siltstone.

Current use: more gentle slopes often cleared for cropland, but some are now idle and reverting to forest. Steeper areas are predominantly pasture or forest, which is composed principally of cherry (*Prunus serotina*), beech (*Fagus grandifolia*), birch (*Betula spp.*), red maple (*Acer rubrum*), sugar maple (*Acer saccharum*) and mixed oaks, especially red oak (*Quercus rubra*).

Taxonomy: fine-loamy, mixed, semiactive, mesic Typic Hapludults.

Leetonia loams

Where they are found: narrow ridge crests and long sideslopes in mountainous topography above 1,800 feet.

Characteristics: dry to mesic, well drained, deep, stony loamy sand and sandy loams with moderate permeability and a pH of 4.3.

Composition: about 83 to 92 percent sand, 9 percent silt and the balance in clay, with less than 2 percent organic matter in the top 12 inches and formed in the highly siliceous residuum of sandstones, quartzites and conglomerates.

Current use: mostly mixed forest composed of chestnut oak (*Quercus prinus*), white oak (*Quercus alba*), black oak (*Quercus velutina*), maple

(*Acer spp.*), dogwood (*Cornus spp.*), white pine (*Pinus strobus*), table mountain pine (*Pinus pungens*), pitch pine (*Pinus rigida*) and Virginia pine (*Pinus virginiana*).

Taxonomy: Sandy-skeletal, siliceous, mesic Entic Haplorthods.

Legore silt loams

Where they are found: level to steep slopes on dikes of intruded igneous rock in the Northern Piedmont.

Characteristics: mesic to moist, well drained, deep silt and channery silt loams with high permeability and a pH of about 5.7

Composition: about 23 percent sand, 52 percent silt and 25 percent clay, with less than 2 percent organic matter in the top 12 inches and formed from weathered diabase, diorite and related rock.

Current use: mostly for pasture, orchards and general cropland; native vegetation is mixed hardwoods dominated by oaks (*Quercus spp.*), hickory (*Carya spp.*) and black locust (*Robinia pseudoacacia*) along with some shortleaf pine (*Pinus echinata*) and Virginia pine (*Pinus virginiana*).

Taxonomy: Fine-loamy, mixed, active, mesic Ultic Hapludalfs.

Lehew loams

Where they are found: nearly level to steep ridges and mountain side slopes.

Characteristics: dry to mesic, well drained, moderately deep loams with moderately rapid permeability and a pH of about 5.3.

Composition: about 50 percent sand, 40 percent silt and 10 percent clay, with about 2 percent organic matter in the top 12 inches (declining as slopes steepen) and formed in materials parented by interbedded reddish sandstone, shale and siltstone.

Current use: Mainly mixed hardwood forests on steeper slopes, while gentle slopes are cropland and orchards. Virginia pine (*Pinus virginiana*) is often seen on abandoned fields; other common species include white pine (*Pinus strobus*) and red oak (*Quercus rubra*).

Taxonomy: loamy-skeletal, siliceous, semiactive, mesic Typic Dystrudepts.

Lehigh silt loams

Where they are found: nearly level to steep low ridges and hills in the Triassic basins of the Northern Piedmont.

Characteristics: dry to mesic, moderately well to somewhat poorly drained, deep silt loams with low permeability and a pH of 5.9.

Composition: about 27 percent sand, 55 percent silt and 18 percent clay, with less than 2 percent organic matter in the top 12 inches and formed in residuum from metamorphosed shale and sandstone (porcelanite), which typically occurs in bands separating areas of diabase and red Triassic sandstone and shale.

Current use: about 68 percent pasture and cropland, 10 percent non-farm to urban and 22 percent woodlands dominated by upland oaks, especially red oak (*Quercus rubra*) and often including red maple (*Acer rubrum*), sugar maple (*Acer saccharum*), white ash (*Fraxinus americana*) and yellow poplar (*Liriodendron tulipifera*).

Taxonomy: fine-loamy, mixed, superactive, mesic Aquic Hapludalfs.

Letort silt loams

Where they are found: nearly level to moderately steep Northern Piedmont uplands.

Characteristics: mesic to moist, well drained, deep silt loams with moderate permeability and a pH of 5.9.

Composition: about 25 percent sand, 54 percent silt, and 21 percent clay, with about 2 percent organic matter in the top 12 inches and formed in the residuum of interbedded micaceous limestone, schist and graphite phyllite.

Current use: mostly cultivated with a variety of crops, although extensive acreage is being converted to non-farm use. Small acreage in woodlots is composed of mixed oak, especially red oak (*Quercus rubra*), hickory (*Carya spp.*) and yellow poplar (*Liriodendron tulipifera*).

Taxonomy: Fine-loamy, mixed, superactive, mesic Typic Hapludalfs.

Lewisberry sandy loams

Where they are found: gently to steeply sloping ridges and hills in the Northern Piedmont.

Characteristics: dry to mesic, well drained, deep sandy and often very stony loams with moderately rapid permeability and a pH of 5.3.

Composition: about 66 percent sand, 23 percent silt and 11 percent clay, with about 2 percent organic matter in the top 12 inches and formed in somewhat coarse-textured residuum of reddish and weakly-cemented conglomerate and sandstone.

Current use: About 40 percent cleared for general farm crops and the remainder is in woodlands composed of mixed hardwoods, predominantly oaks, especially red oak (Quercus rubra), as well as yellow poplar (Liriodendron tulipifera), shortleaf pine (Pinus echinata) and Virginia pine (Pinus virginiana).

Taxonomy: Coarse-loamy, mixed, semiactive, mesic Ultic Hapludalfs.

Library silt loams

Where they are found: benches, footslopes, backslopes and ridgetops.

Characteristics: mesic to moist, somewhat poorly drained, deep silt and silty clay loams with slow permeability and a pH of 6.0.

Composition: about 16 percent sand, 58 percent silt and 26 percent clay, although silty clay loams have much less sand and about 36 percent clay; organic matter in the top 12 inches is about 2.8 percent and soils formed in residuum from thin-bedded, impure limestone and calcareous shales

Current use: mostly pasture and hayfields, although some are idle; woodlands are composed of mixed hardwoods such as red maple (Acer rubrum), sugar maple (Acer saccharum), white ash (Fraxinus americana), yellow poplar (Liriodendron tulipifera) and red oak (Quercus rubra).

Taxonomy: fine, mixed, active, mesic Aeric Endoaqualfs.

Lickdale silt loams

Where they are found: slight depressions and upland flats with slopes less than 5 percent.

Characteristics: mesic to moist, poorly drained, deep silt loams with low permeability and a pH of 5.3; because of a seasonal zone of water saturation typically at or just below the surface from November through June, the soils meet hydric criteria.

Composition: about 9 percent sand, 68 percent silt and 23 percent clay, with between 3 and 12 percent organic matter in the top 12 inches and formed in the residuum of acidic shales and sandstones, along with occasional local alluvium.

Current use: although some artificially drained areas are used for pasture and corn, most areas are native vegetation composed of typical wetland hardwoods - including willows (Salix spp.), alders (Alnus spp.), pin oak (Quercus palustris) and red maple (Acer rubrum) - with ground cover chiefly of herbs and sedges.

Taxonomy: Fine-loamy over sandy or sandy-skeletal, mixed, active, acid, mesic Humic Endoaquepts.

Linden loams

Where they are found: nearly level floodplains subjected to stream overflow.

Characteristics: mesic to moist, well drained, deep loams and silt loams, with moderately rapid permeability, rarely to occasionally flooded (except in Lycoming County, which is frequently flooded), with a pH of 5.8.

Composition: typically about 45 percent sand, 41 percent silt and 14 percent clay, although sand to silt ratios can vary, and about 2 percent organic matter in the top 12 inches. Soils formed in alluvial sediments washed from nearby uplands underlain by red and brown shales, some conglomerate and sandstones.

Current use: Mostly cleared for pasture and cropland; woodlands are typically mixed hardwoods that often include sugar maple (Acer saccharum), white ash (Fraxinus americana), black walnut (Juglans nigra), yellow poplar (Liriodendron tulipifera), white pine (Pinus strobus), black cherry (Prunus serotina) and red oak (Quercus rubra).

Taxonomy: coarse-loamy, mixed, active, mesic Fluventic Dystrudepts.

Lindside silt loams

Where they are found: floodplains and toeslopes.

Characteristics: mesic to moist, moderately well drained, deep silt loams with moderate permeability that are occasionally to frequently flooded, with a pH of 6.5 to 7.0.

Composition: about 11 percent sand, 68 percent silt and 21 percent silt, with about 3 percent organic matter in the top 12 inches and formed in alluvium from limestone uplands.

Current use: mostly cleared for pasture and croplands; where wooded, mixed hardwoods dominate, including red maple (*Acer rubrum*), white ash (*Fraxinus americana*), black walnut (*Juglans nigra*), yellow poplar (*Liriodendron tulipifera*), white oak (*Quercus alba*) and red oak (*Quercus rubra*).

Taxonomy: Fine-silty, mixed, active, mesic Fluvaquentic Eutrudepts.

Litz silt loams

Where they are found: long, slightly convex sideslopes and narrow convex ridges.

Characteristics: dry to mesic, well drained, moderately deep silt loams and shaly silt loams with moderate permeability and a pH of about 5.0.

Composition: about 25 percent sand, 55 percent silt and 20 percent clay, with less than 1 percent organic matter in the top 12 inches and formed in residuum from leached calcareous shale with some widely spaced, thin strata of limestone. About 20 to 25 percent of the parent rock is shale and 10 to 25 percent of parent rock is calcareous.

Current use: mostly cleared for pasture, with small areas for grain crops and hay; native vegetation includes oaks, especially red oak (*Quercus rubra*), yellow poplar (*Liriodendron tulipifera*), hickory (*Carya spp.*), locust (*Robinia pseudoacacia*), shortleaf pine (*Pinus echinata*) and Virginia pine (*Pinus virginiana*).

Taxonomy: Loamy-skeletal, mixed, active, mesic Ruptic-Ultic Dystrudepts.

Lobdell silt loams

Where they are found: nearly level floodplains, usually in areas of Wisconsinan or Illinoian glaciation but also in some unglaciated valleys.

Characteristics: mesic to moist, moderately well drained, deep silt loams with moderate permeability and a pH of 6.2. They are typically occasionally and briefly flooded, with the exception of Bedford County (frequently flooded) and high bottom loams in Erie County (not flooded).

Composition: typically about 26 percent sand, 53 percent silt and 11 percent clay, but sand-silt ratios can vary; organic matter in the top 12 inches varies between 1.6 and 2 percent. Soils were formed in recent loamy alluvium from upland areas of shale, sandstone and low lime glacial drift.

Current use: some areas in cropland and pasture; woodlands are dominated by beech (*Fagus grandifolia*), white ash (*Fraxinus americana*), elm (*Ulmus spp.*), sugar maple (*Acer saccharum*), white oak (*Quercus alba*), red oak (*Quercus rubra*) and sycamore (*Plantanus occidentalis*).

Taxonomy: fine-loamy, mixed, active, mesic Fluvaquentic Eutrudepts.

Lordstown loams

Where they are found: nearly level to very steep hillsides and hilltops in bedrock-controlled dissected uplands, mostly in the glaciated Allegheny Plateau.

Characteristics: dry to mesic, well drained, deep channery, stony and silt loams, with moderate permeability and a pH of 5.4.

Composition: about 45 percent sand, 41 percent silt and 14 percent clay, with less than 2 percent organic matter in the top 12 inches and formed in frost-churned (cryoturbated) materials and till parented by sandstone and siltstone.

Current use: areas cleared for pasture or hayland are mostly idle or reverting to woodland or brush. Very limited acreage is in corn and small grains, although potatoes are locally grown on undulating to sloping areas. Reforested areas typically include red pine (*Pinus resinosa*), sugar maple (*Acer saccharum*), white ash (*Fraxinus americana*) and red oak (*Quercus rubra*).

Taxonomy: coarse-loamy, mixed, active, mesic Typic Dystrudepts.

Loudonville gravelly silt loams

Where they are found: glacial hills and outwash terraces.

Characteristics: dry to mesic, well drained, moderately deep gravelly silt loams with a pH of 5.3.

Composition: about 25 percent sand, 53 percent silt and 22 percent clay, with about 1 percent organic matter in the top 12 inches and formed in medium textured loamy till from either the Wisconsinan or Illinoian age, sometimes with a loess mantle of less than 14 inches, and underlain by siltstone or sandstone within a depth of 20 to 40 inches.

Current use: most areas cleared for cultivated crops, pasture or orchards (especially near Lake Erie) and many other areas in non-agricultural use. Native vegetation was hardwood forest, principally white oak (*Quercus alba*), red oak (*Quercus rubra*), black oak (*Quercus velutina*), hickory (*Carya spp.*) with smaller amounts of white ash (*Fraxinus americana*) and sugar maple (*Acer saccharum*).

Taxonomy: fine-loamy, mixed, active, mesic Ultic Hapludalfs.

Lowell silty clay loams

Where they are found: benches, footslopes, sideslopes (up to 65 percent) and ridgetops.

Characteristics: mesic to moist, well drained, deep silty clay loams with moderately slow permeability and a pH of 6.7.

Composition: about 20 percent sand, 49 percent silt and 31 percent clay, with about 2 percent organic matter in the top 12 inches and formed in residuum of limestone interbedded with thin layers of shales and coated with as much as 18 inches of loess or soil creep of residuum from either limestone or interbedded shale, siltstone and limestone.

Current use: Mostly cleared for pasture and cropland, but native forest includes upland oaks, especially red oak (*Quercus rubra*), walnut (*Juglans nigra*), hickory (*Carya spp.*), white ash (*Fraxinus americana*), hackberry (*Celtis spp.*), redbud (*Cercis canadensis*), black locust (*Robinia pseudoacacia*) and red cedar (*Juniperus virginiana*) as dominant species.

Taxonomy: fine, mixed, active, mesic Typic Hapludalfs.

Luray silt loams

Where they are found: level areas and slight depressions of lake plains, terraces, outwash plains and some till plains in Mercer County.

Characteristics: mesic to moist, poorly drained, deep silt and silty clay loams with moderately slow permeability and a pH of 5.3 and in a complex with Frenchtown silt loams. With a seasonal zone of saturation at or near the surface from November through June and frequent ponding, the soil is classified as hydric.

Composition: about 26 percent sand, 52 percent silt and 22 percent clay, with about 2 percent organic matter in the top 12 inches and formed in either silty lacustrine material or slackwater sediments of Wisconsinan age that area frequently ponded and with a seasonal zone of saturation at or near the surface from November through June.

Current use: More than half the soils are cultivated with a variety of crops; some areas are in pasture while others are wooded. Native vegetation is swamp grasses and sedges as well as deciduous swamp forest, often including such species as red maple (*Acer rubrum*), green ash (*Fraxinus pennsylvanica*), eastern cottonwood (*Populus deltoides*), swamp white oak (*Quercus bicolor*) and pin oak (*Quercus palustris*).

Taxonomy: Fine-silty, mixed, superactive, mesic Typic Argiaquolls.

Macove silt loams

Where they are found: nearly level to steep mountain benches and footslopes in a complex with Gilpin loams.

Characteristics: dry to mesic, well drained and very deep silt loams with moderately rapid permeability and a pH of 5.0.

Composition: between 20 and 28 percent sand, and 49 to 53 percent silt, with the balance in clay and about 1.3 percent organic matter in the top 12 inches, formed in colluvium from acidic fine grain sandstone, shale and siltstone in the adjacent uplands.

Current use: some for pasture, but mostly native vegetation of mixed hardwoods and pines (*Pinus spp.*), including red maple (*Acer rubrum*), white oak (*Quercus alba*) and red oak (*Quercus rubra*).

Taxonomy: Loamy-skeletal, mixed, active, mesic Typic Hapludults.

Mahoning silt loams

Where they are found: Wisconsinan age till plains

Characteristics: mesic to moist, somewhat poorly drained, deep, silt loams with slow permeability and a pH of 6.0

Composition: about 18 percent sand, 53 percent silt and 29 percent clay, with about 2 percent organic matter in the top 12 inches and formed in low-lime till mostly from siltstone and shale, with minor amounts of limestone and some crystalline erratics.

Current use: mostly under cultivation or in pasture, but a considerable acreage remains wooded with white oak (*Quercus alba*), pin oak (*Quercus palustris*), sugar maple (*Acer saccharum*), red maple (*Acer rubrum*), yellow poplar (*Liriodendron tulipifera*), white ash (*Fraxinus americana*) and beech (*Fagus grandifolia*) the dominant species.

Taxonomy: Fine, illitic, mesic Aeric Epiaqualfs.

Mandy channery silt loams

Where they are found: nearly level to very steep broad ridgetops and upper slopes of mountains above 1,800 feet in McKean County.

Characteristics: dry to mesic, well drained, moderately deep channery silt loams with moderate permeability and a pH of 4.8.

Composition: about 30 percent sand, 56 percent silt and 14 percent clay with less than 1 percent organic matter in the top 12 inches and formed in residuum from interbedded acidic shale and siltstone with inclusions of sandstone.

Current use: Forested, with native vegetation including American beech (*Fagus grandifolia*), red maple (*Acer rubrum*), yellow birch (*Betula lenta*), black cherry (*Prunus serotina*), striped maple (*Acer pensylvanicum*), red spruce (*Picea rubens*), aspen (*Populus spp.*) and eastern hemlock (*Tsuga canadensis*). Heath barrens feature huckleberry (*Gaylussacia spp.*), blueberry (*Vaccinium spp.*), mountain laurel (*Kalmia latifolia*), great rhododendron (*Rhododenron maximum*), roseshell azalea (*Rhododendron prinophyllum*) and flame azalea (*Rhododendron calendulaceum*)

Taxonomy: loamy-skeletal, mixed, active, frigid Typic Dystrudepts.

Manlius loams

Where they are found: nearly level to steep bedrock-controlled landforms in the Glaciated Allegheny Plateau.

Characteristics: dry to mesic, well to excessively drained, somewhat shallow and mostly channery loams with a pH of 4.8.

Composition: 32 to 39 percent sand and 48 to 56 percent silt, with about 12 percent clay and about 2 percent organic matter in the top 12 inches and formed in thin till or frost-disturbed material derived almost entirely from local shale, although some erratic gravel and stones have been observed.

Current use: some less-steep areas are used for silage corn, hay and oats, and grapes, and unimproved pasture and idle land are common in cleared areas. Most steep areas are in woodlots that have been deeply incised by erosion and tend to be dominated by northern hardwoods such as sugar maple (*Acer saccharum*) and beech (*Fagus grandifolia*) as well as some hemlock (*Tsuga canadensis*) and white pine (*Pinus strobus*).

Taxonomy: loamy-skeletal, mixed, active, mesic Typic Dystrudepts.

Manor loams

Where they are found: backslopes, shoulders and summits of hills in the Northern Piedmont.

Characteristics: mesic to moist, well drained, very deep mostly loams that can be channery or stony, with a pH of about 5.1.

Composition: about 43 percent sand, 40 percent silt and 17 percent clay, with about 1.3 percent organic matter in the top 12 inches and formed in residuum from micaceous schist.

Current use: mostly cropland, pasture and urban development; woodlands consist of of black oak (*Quercus velutina*), chestnut oak (*Quercus prinus*), red oak (*Quercus rubra*), white oak (*Quercus alba*), hickory (*Carya spp.*), yellow poplar (*Liriodendron tulipifera*), red maple (*Acer rubrum*), shortleaf pine (*Pinus echinata*) and Virginia pine (*Pinus virginiana*). Also suitable are black gum (*Nyssa sylvatica*) and southern red oak (*Quercus falcata*).

Taxonomy: coarse-loamy, micaceous, mesic Typic Dystrudepts.

Mardin loams

Where they are found: backslopes, shoulders and broad summits of glaciated hills generally between 800 and 1,800 feet above sea level.

Characteristics: dry to mesic, moderately well drained, deep channery, stony or gravelly silt loams and loams with a dense fragipan between 14 and 26 inches below the surface and a pH of about 5.1.

Composition: silt loams about 32 percent sand and 55 percent silt, while loams are 44 percent and 40 percent silt, with the balance in clay, and about 2 percent organic matter in the top 12 inches, all formed in loamy till.

Current use: although most areas are cleared for pasture and such crops as silage corn, small grains and hay, a significant acreage is idle or reverting to brush or trees. Woodlots typically include sugar maple (*Acer saccharum*), beech (*Fagus grandifolia*), white ash (*Fraxinus americana*), black cherry (*Prunus serotina*), hemlock (*Tsuga canadensis*) and sometimes red oak (*Quercus rubra*) and white pine (*Pinus strobus*).

Taxonomy: coarse-loamy, mixed, active, mesic Typic Fragiudepts.

Markes silt loams

Where they are found: nearly level to slightluy sloping upland depressions, mostly in the Ridge and Valley province.

Characteristics: seasonally wet, poorly drained, somewhat shallow silt loams with a pH of about 5.8. Bedrock is typically between 20 and 40 inches and a seasonal zone of saturation is at 3 inches from September through May, hence the soils meet hydric criteria.

Composition: about 22 percent sand, 53 percent silt and 25 percent clay, with less than 2 percent organic matter in the top 12 inches and formed from residuum of gray shale.

Current use: mostly cleared for pasture and cropland; woodland areas are typically mixed hardwoods strongly dominated by oaks, notably red oak (*Quercus rubra*) and red maple (*Acer rubrum*).

Taxonomy: Loamy-skeletal, mixed, active, mesic Typic Endoaqualfs.

Marsh soils

Where they are found: gently sloping hillslopes on the Northern Coastal Plain in Philadelphia County totaling about 400 acres.

Characteristics: mesic to wet, very poorly drained, moderately deep soils that are frequently flooded, with water saturation at the surface year round and organic content in the surface horizon at 55 percent and a moderately saline horizon within 30 inches of the soil surface; no pH data.

Composition: more than 57 percent organic matter with no data on sand, silt or clay content; formed in colluvium or residuum of interbedded sandy limestone, shale and siltstone on slopes less than 1 percent.

Taxonomy: Fine-loamy, mixed, semiactive, thermic Ultic Hapludalfs.

Matapeake silt loams

Where they are found: upland interfluves and side slopes of the Atlantic Coastal Plain in Bucks County, between 5 and 125 feet above sea level.

Characteristics: mesic to moist, well drained, very deep silt loams with a pH of about 5.5.

Composition: about 19 percent sand, 69 percent silt and 12 percent clay with about 1.3 percent organic matter in the top 12 inches and formed in silty eolian sediments over coarser fluvial or marine sediments.

Current uses: almost all cultivated, typically for corn, soybeans and small grains and a small amount of the acreage is irrigated. Native vegetation is dominated by oaks, especially white oak (*Quercus alba*); some cutover areas have Virginia pine (*Pinus virginiana*), loblolly pine (*Pinus taeda*) or shortleaf pine (*Pinus echinata*).

Taxonomy: Fine-silty, mixed, semiactive, mesic Typic Hapludults.

Matewan channery loams

Where they are found: strongly sloping to very steep, usually convex nose slopes, upper sideslopes and ridgetops.

Characteristics: dry to mesic, well drained, moderately deep channery loams with bedrock at 20 to 40 inches and a pH of 6.1.

Composition: about 44 percent sand, 41 percent silt and 15 percent clay, with about 3 percent organic matter in the top 12 inches and formed in residuum of gray and brown acidic sandstone, sometimes interbedded with shale and siltstone.

Current use: mostly forests of mixed hardwoods, primarily oaks (*Quercus spp.*), hickory (*Carya spp.*) and maple (*Acer spp.*), but some areas have been cleared for cropland, pasture or hayland.

Taxonomy: loamy-skeletal, mixed, active, mesic Typic Dystrudepts.

Mattapex silt loams

Where they are found: swales, flats, depressions and marine terraces on nearly level surfaces in the Atlantic Coastal Plain.

Characteristics: mesic to moist, moderately well drained, deep silt loams with a pH of 5.8.

Composition: about 13 percent sand, 71 percent silt and 16 percent clay with less than 2 percent organic matter in the top 12 inches, formed in silty eolian deposits over fluviomarine sediments.

Current use: both cropland and woodland, including white oak (*Quercus alba*), scarlet oak (*Quercus coccinea*), loblolly pine (*Pinus taeda*), red maple (*Acer rubrum*), yellow poplar (*Liriodendron tulipifera*), sweet gum (*Liquidambar styraciflua*), sassafras (*Sassafras albidum*), dogwood (*Cornus spp.*), greenbrier (*Smilax spp.*) and American holly (*Ilex opaca*).

Taxonomy: fine-silty, mixed, active, mesic Aquic Hapludults.

Maurertown silt loams

Where they are found: floodplains of slackwater areas and low stream terraces along both streams and intermittent drainageways, with slope gradients up to 2 percent.

Characteristics: mesic to moist, poorly drained, deep silt loams with very slow permeability that are frequently flooded and ponded, with seasonal zone of saturation at or near the surface from November through June and classified as hydric, with a pH of 6.0.

Composition: about 14 percent sand, 51 percent silt and 35 percent clay, with less than 2 percent organic matter in the top 12 inches and formed in clayey alluvial deposits.

Current use: Most areas in pasture; native vegetation is primarily red maple (*Acer rubrum*), sweet gum (*Liquidambar styraciflua*), pin oak (*Quercus palustris*) and yellow-poplar (*Liriodendron tulipifera*).

Taxonomy: fine, mixed, semiactive, mesic Typic Endoaqualfs.

Mechanicsburg silt loams

Where they are found: plane to convex nose slopes, head slopes, sideslopes and upland interfluves.

Characteristics: mesic to moist, well drained deep silt loams with a pH of 5.8.

Composition: about 30 percent sand, 50 percent silt and 20 percent clay, with less than 2 percent organic matter in the top 12 inches and formed in Wisconsinan or Illinoian age till, generally two to three feet thick and composed of materials weathered from acidic underlying fractured fine-grained sandstone or siltstone.

Current use: most gentle slopes cultivated for a variety of crops, while more sloping areas are in woodland and wildlife habitat. Natural vegetation includes sugar maple (*Acer saccharum*), white oak (*Quercus alba*), red oak (*Quercus rubra*), hickory (*Carya spp.*), white ash (*Fraxinus americana*), black walnut (*Juglans nigra*), black cherry (*Prunus serotina*) and hickory (*Carya spp.*)

Taxonomy: Fine-loamy, mixed, active, mesic Ultic Hapludalfs.

Meckesville loams

Where they are found: lower and middle concave sideslopes of dissected uplands.

Characteristics: mesic to moist, well drained, deep silt, channery and gravelly loams with a fragipan between 25 and 48 inches and a pH between typically 4.6 and a high of 5.3.

Composition: widely varied; silt loams are about 22 percent sand, 54 percent silt, while stony loams are 41 percent sand and 37 percent silt, but stony silt loams are 25 percent sand and 55 percent silt. Organic matter in the top 12 inches is less than 2 percent and soils were formed in glacial till, colluvium or materials impacted by frost action from red sandstone, shale and siltstone.

Current use: about 70 percent in woodland and 30 percent in pasture, cropland or idle. Forested areas area dominated by oak (*Quercus spp.*), maple (*Acer spp.*) and ash (*Fraxinus spp.*) with some hickory (*Carya spp.*).

Taxonomy: fine-loamy, mixed, active, mesic Typic Fragiudults.

Melvin silt loams

Where they are found: level to depressed areas of floodplains and in upland depressions.

Characteristics: moist to wet, poorly drained, deep silt loams and silt clay loams occasionally to frequently flooded and rarely to occasionally ponded and with moderate permeability a pH of about 6.7 and seasonal zones of saturation near the surface from December to May.

Composition: about 13 percent sand and 70 percent silt with about 17 percent clay, but silty clay loams have less than 7 percent sand and more than 30 percent clay. Organic matter in the top 12 inches ranges from less than 1 percent to as much as 3 percent in complexes with Newark soils, and the loams were formed in silty alluvium derived from limestone, shale, siltstone, sandstone and loess.

Current use: mostly pasture or woodland, but when drained are sometimes used for croplands. Many areas are used for wetland wildlife habitats. Native vegetation includes water-tolerant hardwoods such as pin oak (*Quercus palustris*), swamp white oak (*Quercus bicolor*), American sycamore (*Platanus occidentalis*), black willow (*Salix nigra*), alder (*Alnus spp.*), sweet gum (*Liquidambar styraciflua*), black gum (*Nyssa sylvatica*), red maple (*Acer rubrum*), box elder (*Acer negundo*) and cottonwood (*Populus deltoides*).

Taxonomy: Fine-silty, mixed, active, nonacid, mesic Fluvaquentic Endoaquepts.

Mertz silt loams

Where they are found: gently to steeply sloping middle and upper parts of chert ridges.

Characteristics: mesic to moist, well drained, deep channery and cherty silt loam with moderate permeability and a pH of 6.2.

Composition: about 27 percent sand, 54 percent silt and 19 percent clay, with about 2 percent organic matter in the top 12 inches and formed in colluvial or glacially-influenced materials derived from limestone and containing a range of chert fragments.

Current use: mostly cleared and cultivated for general farm crops; wooded areas are typically mixed hardwoods, such as yellow poplar (*Liriodendron tulipifera*), Virginia pine (*Pinus virginiana*) and red oak (*Quercus rubra*).

Taxonomy: loamy-skeletal, mixed, semiactive, mesic Typic Hapludults.

Middlebury silt loams

Where they are found: nearly level floodplains, second bottomlands and some alluvial fans with high water tables.

Characteristics: mesic to moist, moderately well drained, deep and mostly silt loams with moderate permeability that are occasionally flooded, and have a pH of about 6.0; a seasonal zone of water saturation is at 15 inches from November through May.

Composition: about 32 percent sand, 56 percent silt and 12 percent clay — notable exceptions being sandy loams where the sand-silt ratio is about

63:25 — with 3.5 to 5 percent organic matter in the top 12 inches and formed in recent alluvium from areas of sandstone and shale with some lime-bearing material.

Current use: Mostly cleared for pasture and cropland, including nursery crops. Wooded areas are dominated by yellow poplar (*Liriodendron tulipifera*), willow (*Salix spp.*), elm (*Ulmus spp.*), red oak (*Quercus rubra*), sycamore (*Platanus occidentalis*) and sugar maple (*Acer saccharum*).

Taxonomy: coarse-loamy, mixed, superactive, mesic Fluvaquentic Eutrudepts.

Mill silt loams

Where they are found: depressions, broad flats and drainageways on till plains and moraines between 720 and 1,200 feet.

Characteristics: mesic to moist, poorly drained, deep silt loams with slow permeability that are frequently ponded, have a seasonal zone of water saturation at the surface from October through June and meet the criteria as hydric, with a pH of about 5.8.

Composition: about 26 percent sand, 53 percent silt and 21 percent clay, with about 4 percent organic matter in the top 12 inches and formed in low-lime, Wisconsinan age till that has been influenced by clayey shale and limestone.

Current use: cropland when drained, hayland and woodland; the natural vegetation is hardwood forest, often composed of red maple (*Acer rubrum*), sugar maple (*Acer saccharum*), white ash (*Fraxinus americana*), yellow poplar (*Liriodendron tulipifera*), eastern cottonwood (*Populus deltoides*), black cherry (*Prunus serotina*), swamp white oak (*Quercus bicolor*) and pin oak (*Quercus palustris*).

Taxonomy: Fine-loamy, mixed, superactive, nonacid, mesic Aeric Epiaquepts.

Millheim silt loams

Where they are found: nearly level to moderately steep convex upland slopes.

Characteristics: dry to mesic, well drained, deep silt loams with moderate permeability and a pH of 5.4.

Composition: about 20 percent sand, 51 percent silt and 29 percent clay, with about 1.6 percent organic matter in the top 12 inches and formed in residuum of dark-colored, calcareous and carbonaceous shales interbedded with some limestone.

Current use: about 70 percent in cropland, with the remainder in pasture, non-farm use and woodland composed mostly of mixed hardwoods such as yellow poplar (*Liriodendron tulipifera*) and red oak (*Quercus rubra*).

Taxonomy: fine, illitic, mesic Typic Hapludalfs.

Miner silt loams

Where they are found: shallow depressions and narrow drainageways on till plains and lake plains modified by lake action, typically between 700 and 910 feet above sea level.

Characteristics: mesic to moist, poorly drained, deep silt loams with slow permeability that are frequently ponded, have a seasonal zone of saturation at the surface from November through June and classified as hydric, with a pH of 6.6.

Composition: about 15 percent sand, 51 percent silt and 34 percent clay, with about 2 percent organic matter in the top 12 inches and formed in low-lime till, mostly from acidic shales, on lake and till plains with slopes less than 2 percent.

Current use: Cleared areas are used for a variety of crops, hay and pasture; areas adjacent to urban areas are typically in non-agricultural use. Much acreage remains in woodland in which elm (*Ulmus spp.*), red maple (*Acer rubrum*) and green ash (*Fraxinus pennsylvanica*) are common; other species include eastern cottonwood (*Populus deltoides*), black cherry (*Prunus serotina*), swamp white oak (*Quercus bicolor*) and pin oak (*Quercus palustris*).

Taxonomy: Fine, illitic, mesic Mollic Epiaqualfs.

Monongahela silt loams

Where they are found: stream terraces of old alluvium.

Characteristics: mesic to moist, moderately well drained, deep silt loams, not flooded or ponded, with moderate permeability above a fragipan at 18 to 30 inches and a pH of about 5.0 to 5.5.

Composition: about 26 percent sand, 55 percent silt and 19 percent clay, with about 2.5 percent organic matter in the top 12 inches and formed in old alluvium that came from acidic sandstone and shale.

Current use: Mostly cleared of original hardwood forest for pasture, cultivated crops and urban development; forest species would include red maple (*Acer rubrum*), white ash (*Fraxinus americana*), black walnut (*Juglans nigra*), yellow poplar (*Liriodendron tulipifera*), white pine (*Pinus strobus*), Virginia pine (*Pinus virginiana*), red oak (*Quercus rubra*) and black cherry (*Prunus serotina*).

Taxonomy: fine-loamy, mixed, semiactive, mesic Typic Fragiudults.

Montalto silt loams

Where they are found: backslopes, shoulders and summits of hills in the northern Piedmont.

Characteristics: mesic to moist, well drained, moderately permeable, deep channery and very stony silt loams with a pH of 5.6.

Composition: about 17 percent sand, 52 percent silt and 31 percent clay with about 1 percent organic matter in the top 12 inches and formed in residuum weathered from gabbro rock.

Current use: primarily used for croplands and pastures; where wooded, native vegetation includes: hickory (*Carya spp.*), beech (*Fagus grandifolia*), yellow poplar (*Liriodendron tulipifera*), black oak (*Quercus velutina*), black locust (*Robinia pseudoacacia*), black walnut (*Juglans nigra*), white pine (*Pinus strobus*) and Virginia pine (*Pinus virginiana*).

Taxonomy: fine, mixed, semiactive, mesic Ultic Hapludalfs.

Montevallo channery silt loams

Where they are found: gently to steeply sloping valley sides and narrow ridgetops in Carbon County.

Characteristics: dry to mesic, well drained, shallow but moderately permeable channery silt loams with a pH of 5.3. Depth to bedrock is 10 to 20 inches.

Composition: about 27 percent sand, 55 percent silt and 18 percent clay with about 1.2 percent organic matter in the top 12 inches and formed in residuum of siltstones and silty shales that may contain some sandstone.

Current use: mostly forest; native trees include hickory (*Carya spp.*), red oak (*Quercus rubra*), white oak (*Quercus alba*), blackjack oak (*Quercus marilandica*), shortleaf pine (*Pinus echinata*), Virginia pine (*Pinus virginiana*).

Taxonomy: loamy-skeletal, mixed, subactive, thermic, shallow Typic Dystrudepts.

Morris loams

Where they are found: slightly concave uplands and till plains.

Characteristics: dry to mesic, poorly drained, deep channery loams, channery silt loams, flaggy loams and very stony loams with moderate permeability above a dense fragipan between 11 and 22 inches and a pH of about 5.3.

Composition: Varies, with loams about 44 percent sand and 41 percent silt and silt loams about 27 percent sand and 54 percent silt, with the balance in clay. Organic matter for all is about 3 percent in the top 12 inches, and all were formed in till derived from reddish sandstone, siltstone and shale.

Current use: Although many areas were cleared for pasture, hayland and some cropland, much is now idle. Woodlands are dominated by red maple (*Acer rubrum*), elm (*Ulmus spp.*), hemlock (*Tsuga canadensis*), black ash (*Fraxinus nigra*), sugar maple (*Acer saccharum*), white pine (*Pinus strobus*) and oaks, especially red oak (*Quercus rubra*).

Taxonomy: coarse-loamy, mixed, active, mesic Aeric Fragiaquepts.

Morrison sandy loams

Where they are found: nearly level to very steep valley sides.

Characteristics: mesic to moist, well drained,

deep mostly channery and gravelly sandy loams with moderate to rapid permeability and a pH of about 4.6.

Composition: about 68 percent sand, 18 percent silt and 14 percent clay, with about 2 percent organic matter in the top 12 inches and formed in residuum of noncalcareous sandstone.

Current use: about 25 percent cleared for general farm crops; wooded areas are mixed oak with some pine (*Pinus spp.*), including red oak (*Quercus rubra*), yellow poplar (*Liriodendron tulipifera*), red maple (*Acer rubrum*), sugar maple (*Acer saccharum*), and hickory (*Carya spp.*).

Taxonomy: Fine-loamy, mixed, active, mesic Ultic Hapludalfs.

Mt. Airy loams

Where they are found: on strongly dissected uplands of the inner Piedmont Plateau, in complexes with Manor loams.

Characteristics: dry to mesic, excessively drained, moderately permeable loams with moderately rapid permeability and a pH of 5.3.

Composition: between 30 and 35 percent sand, 43 and 48 percent silt and 21 percent clay, with about 1.5 percent organic matter in the top 12 inches and formed in the residuum of micaceous crystalline rocks.

Current use: mostly cleared for pasture, orchards and cropland, with numerous small wooded areas that attract urban and suburban development. Natural vegetation is mixed hardwoods, dominated by black oak (*Quercus velutina*), chestnut oak (*Quercus prinus*), hickory (*Carya spp.*), yellow poplar (*Liriodendron tulipifera*), and red maple (*Acer rubrum*), with an understory or dogwood (*Cornus spp.*), holly (*Ilex spp.*), and huckleberry (*Gaylussacia spp.*), and some areas with laurel (*Kalmia spp.*) and azalea (*Rhododendron spp.*).

Taxonomy: loamy-skeletal, micaceous, mesic Typic Dystrudepts.

Mount Lucas silt loams

Where they are found: steep concave lower slopes and nearly level upland flats.

Characteristics: mesic to moist, moderately well to somewhat poorly drained deep silt loams with slow permeability and a pH of 5.9.

Composition: about 30 percent sand, 51 percent silt and 19 percent clay, with about 1.5 to 2 percent organic matter in the top 12 inches and formed in weathered diabase or other dark-colored rocks.

Current use: About half the area cleared for general farm crops; woodlands are oak-hickory mixed hardwoods, often including yellow poplar (*Liriodendron tulipifera*), Virginia pine (*Pinus virginiana*) and red oak (*Quercus rubra*).

Taxonomy: fine-loamy, mixed, superactive, mesic Aquic Hapludalfs.

Mt. Zion silt loams

Where they are found: smooth to convex footslopes and backslopes.

Characteristics: mesic to moist, moderately well drained, moderately permeable deep gravelly silt loams with moderate permeability and a pH of 5.6. As much as 10 percent of the surface can be covered with stones and boulders.

Composition: about 14 percent sand, 71 percent silt and 15 percent clay, with about 1.8 percent organic matter in the top 12 inches and formed in residuum and colluvium of weathered metabasalt and metarhyolite.

Current use: Many areas have been cleared for pasture and general crops; native vegetation is mixed hardwoods, including yellow poplar (*Liriodendron tulipifera*) and red oak (*Quercus rubra*).

Taxonomy: coarse-loamy, mixed, active, mesic Oxyaquic Hapludalfs.

Murrill silt loams

Where they are found: benches, fans, footslopes and lower backslopes.

Characteristics: mesic to moist, well drained, deep mostly gravelly silt loams with moderate permeability a typical pH of 5.3 but can range as high as 6.0.

Composition: about 27 percent sand, 55 percent silt and 18 percent clay, with about 2 percent organic matter in the top 12 inches and formed in colluvium from acidic sandstones and shales, with some limestone or highly calcareous shales over residuum of limestone. Sinkholes in karst topography are common.

Current use: mostly cleared for use as pastures, orchards and cropland; woodlands contain mostly hickory (*Carya spp.*), yellow poplar (*Liriodendron tulipifera*), dogwood (*Cornus spp.*), white ash (*Fraxinus americana*), elm (*Ulmus spp.*) and beech (*Fagus grandifolia*), along with black walnut (*Juglans nigra*), white pine (*Pinus strobus*), northern red oak (*Quercus rubra*).

Taxonomy: Fine-loamy, mixed, semiactive, mesic Typic Hapludults.

Myersville silt loams

Where they are found: nearly level to very steep mountainside slopes.

Characteristics: dry to mesic, well drained, deep silt loams with moderate permeability and a pH of 5.3.

Composition: about 31 percent sand, 57 percent silt and 12 percent clay with about 2 percent organic matter in the top 12 inches and formed in residuum of basic crystalline rocks, especially greenstone schist.

Current use: Cleared areas for orchards, pasture, hayland and row crops while wooded areas are dominated by white oak (*Quercus alba*), red oak (*Quercus rubra*) and black oak (*Quercus velutina*), hickory (*Carya spp.*), yellow poplar (*Liriodendron tulipifera*), dogwood (*Cornus spp.*), red maple (*Acer rubrum*), walnut (*Juglans nigra*) and Virginia pine (*Pinus virginiana*).

Taxonomy: fine-loamy, mixed, active, mesic Ultic Hapludalfs.

Nanticoke silt loams

Where they are found: tidal and mud flats and floodplains in the Atlantic Coastal Plain and generally less than 3 feet above sea level

Characteristics: moist to wet, frequently flooded and ponded, poorly drained deep silt loams with low permeability, a seasonal zone of saturation at the surface year-round, classified as hydric, with a pH of 6.5.

Composition: about 19 percent sand, 68 percent silt and 13 percent clay, with more than 5 percent organic matter in the top 12 inches and formed from silty estuarine sediments.

Current use: Primary uses are wetland wildlife habitat, with the dominant vegetation including Spatterdock (*Nuphar luteum*), arrow-arum (*Peltandra virginica*), arrowhead (*Sagittaria spp.*), and pickerelweed (*Pontederia cordata*).

Taxonomy: Fine-silty, mixed, active, nonacid, mesic Typic Hydraquents.

Natalie Series

Inactive; see Buchanan series

Neshaminy silt loams

Where they are found: nearly level to very steep upland slopes.

Characteristics: mesic to moist, well drained, deep soils with rapid permeability and a pH of 5.4.

Composition: about 30 percent sand, 54 percent silt and 16 percent clay with about 3.7 percent organic matter in the top 12 inches and formed in weathered diabase and other dark-colored rock.

Current use: Less steep or less stony areas cleared for pasture, hay and cropland, as well as urban and suburban development. Stony, steep areas are mostly woodland of mixed hardwoods dominated by hickories (*Carya spp.*) and oaks (*Quercus spp.*).

Taxonomy: fine-loamy, mixed, superactive, mesic Ultic Hapludalfs.

Newark silt loams

Where they are found: upland depressions and nearly level floodplains.

Characteristics: mesic to moist, somewhat poorly drained, deep and occasionally to frequently flooded and sometimes ponded silt loams with moderate permeability and a pH of 6.7.

Composition: about 12 percent sand, 68 percent silt and 20 percent clay with about 2 percent organic matter in the top 12 inches and formed in mixed alluvium of shale, siltstone, sandstone, limestone and loess, with slopes up to 3 percent.

Current use: Most areas for a variety of cropland and pasture; woodlands are dominated by bottomland hardwoods, especially water-tolerant oaks such as red oak (*Quercus rubra*) pin oak (*Quercus palustris*) and Shumard's oak (*Quercus shumardii*), maples (*Acer spp.*), elms (*Ulmus spp.*), sycamore (*Plantanus occidentalis*), yellow poplar (*Liriodendron tulipifera*), willow (*Salix spp.*), shagbark hickory (*Carya ovata*), green ash (*Fraxinus pennsylvanica*), reeds and rushes.

Taxonomy: fine-silty, mixed, active, nonacid, mesic Fluventic Endoaquepts.

Nockamixon silt loams

Where they are found: convex footslopes and lower side slopes of northern Piedmont hills.

Characteristics: mesic to moist, somewhat poorly drained, deep silt loams with moderate permeability and a pH of 5.8.

Composition: about 26 percent sand, 54 percent silt and 20 percent clay with about 2 percent organic matter in the top 12 inches and formed in colluvium from non-acid gray metamorphic shale, sandstone and siltstone residuum with a fragipan at 16 to 30 inches on steeper slopes.

Current use: About 15 percent for cropland and 20 percent for pasture or hayland; the remaining 65 percent are either in woodland or idle and reverting to woodland, typically mixed hardwoods such as red maple (Acer rubrum), sugar maple (Acer saccharum), white ash (Fraxinus americana), yellow poplar (Liriodendron tulipifera) and red oak (Quercus rubra).

Taxonomy: fine-loamy, mixed, active, mesic Aquic Fragiudalfs.

Nolin silt loams

Where they are found: nearly level floodplains, concave depressions that receive runoff from adjacent hillsides, and natural levees of major rivers and streams.

Characteristics: mesic to moist, well drained, deep silt loams with moderate permeability that are occasionally flooded and a pH of 7.3.

Composition: about 7 percent sand, 70 percent silt and 23 percent clay, with about 3 percent organic matter in the top 12 inches and formed in alluvium from sandstones, siltstones, shales, limestones and loess.

Current use: Mostly for a variety of crops; forested areas tend to consist of such bottomland hardwoods as river birch (*Betula nigra*), yellow poplar (*Liriodendron tulipifera*), sycamore (*Plantanus occidentalis*), elm (*Ulmus spp.*), willow (*Salix spp.*), box elder (*Acer negundo*), oak (*Quercus spp.*), hickory (*Carya spp.*) and red maple (*Acer rubrum*).

Taxonomy: fine-silty, mixed, active, mesic Dystric Fluventic Eutrudepts.

Nollville channery silt loams

Where they are found: gently to moderately sloping, low relief, convex and typically long and narrow ridges that usually have a north-south orientation in the Appalachian Ridge and Valley province.

Characteristics: mesic to moist, well drained, deep and moderately permeable channery silt loams with pH ranging from 6.2 to 6.8 and typically in complexes with Ryder or Wurno soils.

Composition: about 24 percent sand, 54 percent silt and 22 percent clay, with generally less than 2 percent organic matter in the top 12 inches and formed in residuum of limestone and limy shale.

Current use: mostly cleared for pasture, cropland and orchards, with a small acreage in mixed hardwood forest that often includes yellow poplar (*Liriodendron tulipifera*) and red oak (*Quercus rubra*).

Taxonomy: Fine-loamy, mixed, semiactive, mesic Typic Hapludalfs.

Nolo loams

Where they are found: nearly level to strongly sloping plateaus and broad ridgetops.

Characteristics: mesic to moist, poorly drained, deep loams with slow permeability with some ponding, a seasonal zone of water saturation is at 3 inches during from September through June, classified as hydric and with a pH of about 4.3.

Composition: about 43 percent sand, 41 percent silt and 16 percent clay, with about 1.5 to 3 percent organic matter in the top 12 inches and formed in residuum from acidic, brownish-gray sandstone mixed with some shale and siltstone.

Current use: About 90 percent in mixed hardwood forest dominated by red maple (*Acer rubrum*), red oak (*Quercus rubra*), pin oak (*Quercus palustris*), swamp white oak (*Quercus bicolor*), hickory (*Carya spp.*), black gum (*Nyssa sylvatica*), and some hemlock (*Tsuga canadensis*) and white pine (*Pinus strobus*).

Taxonomy: Fine-loamy, mixed, superactive, mesic Typic Fragiaquults.

Norwich silt loams

Where they are found: seeps, depressions and low-relief till plains.

Characteristics: dry to mesic, poorly drained, deep and occasionally ponded silt loams with slow permeability, a fragipan between 10 and 22 inches, a seasonal zone of saturation at or near the surface from November through May and classified as hydric.

Composition: about 25 percent sand and 54 percent silt, with about 21 percent clay, although sand content can be higher in very stony or channery silt loams, and about 3 percent organic matter in the top 12 inches; formed in till high in reddish sandstone, siltstone and shale.

Current use: Most areas are forested, idle or used for pasture, with red maple (*Acer rubrum*), ash (*Fraxinus spp.*), elm (*Ulmus spp.*), alder (*Alnus spp.*) and hemlock (*Tsuga canadensis*) common in woodlands.

Taxonomy: fine-loamy, mixed, active, mesic Typic Fragiaquepts.

Oatlands silt loams

Where they are found: sideslopes and ridges in the northern Piedmont, in complexes with Athol silt loams.

Characteristics: mesic to moist, well drained, moderately deep silt loams with moderate permeability and a pH of about 6.0.

Composition: about 25 percent sand, 54 percent silt and 21 percent clay, with about 2 percent organic matter in the top 12 inches and formed in residuum of Triassic-Jurassic interbedded conglomerates and sandstone.

Current use: most of the soils are cleared and used for cropland, hayland and pasture, as well as residential and commercial development. A few small areas are in native oak-hickory forest.

Taxonomy: fine-loamy, mixed, active, mesic Ultic Hapludalfs.

Onoville silt loams

Where they are found: footslopes, lower hillsides, benches, and summits of ridges and hills in unglaciated areas of the Appalachian Plateau at elevations above 1,800 feet.

Characteristics: dry to mesic, moderately well drained, deep silt loams with moderate permeability above a fragipan between 16 and 36 inches and a pH of 5.0.

Composition: about 16 percent sand, 60 percent silt and 24 percent clay, with about 3.5 percent organic matter in the top 12 inches formed in residuum or colluvium of interbedded shale, siltstone and fine-grained sandstone.

Current use: More gentle slopes often cleared for pasture and some cropland; abandoned idle land is in second growth hardwoods. Native vegetation is mixed hardwoods dominated by red oak (*Quercus rubra*), white oaks (*Quercus alba*), sugar maple (*Acer saccharum*), beech (*Fagus grandifolia*), white ash (*Fraxinus americana*), black cherry (*Prunus serotina*) and white pine (*Pinus strobus*).

Taxonomy: fine-loamy, mixed, subactive, frigid Aquic Fragiudults.

Opequon silty clay loams

Where they are found: backslopes, shoulders and summits of mountains, hills and valley sides, including karst valleys, commonly with rock outcrops and with gradients up to 100 percent.

Characteristics: dry to mesic, well drained, shallow mostly silty clay loams with moderate to slow permeability and a pH of 6.5; bedrock is between 12 and 20 inches.

Composition: generally between 6 and 11 percent sand, 48 percent silt and the balance in clay with about 1.3 percent organic matter in the top 12 inches and formed in residuum from relatively pure limestone or dolomite, which in some areas may contain chert.

Current use: Mostly in permanent pasture, and in non-rocky areas may be used for cropland. Where wooded, native vegetation is mostly mixed oaks, especially red oak (*Quercus rubra*) and white oak (*Quercus alba*), with cedars, notably eastern red cedar (*Juniperus virginiana*) common in unmanaged pasture and abandoned fields.

Taxonomy: clayey, mixed, active, mesic Lithic Hapludalfs.

Oquaga loams

Where they are found: level to very steep hillslopes.

Characteristics: dry to mesic, excessively drained, moderately deep mostly channery but also flaggy and very stony loams with moderate permeability with a pH of 4.8, and often in complexes with Lordstown, Arnot and Lackawanna loams.

Composition: about 43 percent sand, 40 percent silt and 17 percent clay, with about 1.7 percent organic matter in the top 12 inches and formed in a thin mantle of reddish till, with lithology dominated by the local and underlying reddish sandstone, siltstone and shale.

Current use: mostly forested or used for unimproved pasture, while some crops are grown on more gentle slopes. Native vegetation includes sugar maple (*Acer saccharum*), beech (*Fagus grandifolia*), white pine (*Pinus strobus*), white ash (*Fraxinus americana*), hemlock (*Tsuga canadensis*), red oak (*Quercus rubra*), chestnut oak (*Quercus prinus*) and white oak (*Quercus alba*).

Taxonomy: loamy-skeletal, mixed, superactive, mesic Typic Dystrudepts.

Orrville silt loams

Where they are found: steps on floodplains in or bordering areas of Wisconsinan or Illinoian glaciation.

Characteristics: mesic to moist, poorly drained, deep silt loams with moderate permeability that are occasionally to frequently flooded and have a pH of about 6.2.

Composition: about 26 percent sand, 54 percent silt and 20 percent clay, with about 3 percent organic matter in the top 12 inches and formed in loamy alluvium from upland areas of low-lime drift and from areas of sandstone, siltstone, limestone and shale.

Current use: Varies with flooding frequency and accessibility; areas in wider valleys are often in croplands, while narrow areas and those dissected by old stream channels tend to be in permanent pasture or woodland, which was originally deciduous forest, including sugar maple (*Acer saccharum*), white ash (*Fraxinus americana*), yellow poplar (*Liriodendron tulipifera*), black cherry (*Prunus serotina*), white oak (*Quercus alba*), pin oak (*Quercus palustris*) and red oak (*Quercus rubra*).

Taxonomy: fine-loamy, mixed, active, nonacid, mesic Fluventic Endoaquepts.

Otego silt loams

Where they are found: on floodplain steps near till plateaus and glacial outwash terraces.

Characteristics: mesic to moist, moderately well drained, deep, frequently flooded silt loams with moderate permeability and a pH of 5.3.

Composition: about 21 percent sand, 68 percent silt and 11 percent clay, with about 2.5 percent organic matter in the top 12 inches and formed in post-glacial alluvium mostly of materials from sandstone, siltstone and shale.

Current use: mostly cleared for a variety of crops, hay and pasture, but some areas have reverted to woodland or brush. Native vegetation includes sugar maple (*Acer saccharum*), white ash (*Fraxinus americana*), willows (*Salix spp.*) and yellow poplar (*Liriodendron tulipifera*). Brushy areas often contain dogwoods (*Cornus spp.*), willows (*Salix spp.*), spiraea (*Spiraea spp.*) and hawthorn (thorn apple) (*Crataegus spp.*).

Taxonomy: coarse-silty, mixed, superactive, mesic Fluvaquentic Dystrudepts.

Othello silt loams

Where they are found: swales, drainageways and depressions on the Atlantic Coastal Plain.

Characteristics: mesic to moist, poorly

drained, very deep silt loams with slow permeability and a pH of 5.6; with a seasonal zone of water saturation at 6 inches from January through May, the soils meet hydric criteria.

Composition: about 10 percent sand, 68 percent silt and 22 percent clay, with about 1 percent organic matter in the top 12 inches and formed from silty eolian deposits, glaciofluvial or fluviomarine sediments.

Current use: Some in cropland or pasture, but most are forested with such wetland hardwoods as sweet gum (*Liquidambar styraciflua*), black gum (*Nyssa sylvatica*), red maple (*Acer rubrum*), white oak (*Quercus alba*), swamp white oak (*Quercus bicolor*), pin oak (*Quercus palustris*) and loblolly pine (*Quercus taeda*). Understory species include black gum, sweet pepperbush (*Clethra alnifolia*), greenbrier (*Smilax rotundifolia*), American holly (*Ilex opaca*) and highbush blueberry (*Vaccinium corymbosum*).

Taxonomy: fine-silty, mixed, active, mesic Typic Endoaquults.

Otisville sandy loams

Where they are found: widely scattered on long narrow ridges, sideslopes, shoulders and summits of terraces, eskers, kames on outwash plains and beaches and offshore bars on lake plains.

Characteristics: dry to mesic, excessively drained, deep sandy loams with rapid permeability and a pH of 5.2, found in complexes with Tyner loams.

Composition: about 78 percent sand, 16 percent silt and 16 percent clay with less than 1 percent organic matter in the top 12 inches and formed in Wisconsinan age outwash reworked as gravelly beach deposits.

Current use: pasture, cropland and orchards. Woodlots are typically dominated by oak-hickory associations at the southern limit of the series while sugar maple and American beech are prominent near the northern limit and common species include sugar maple (*Acer saccharum*), white pine (*Pinus strobus*), white oak (*Quercus alba*), red oak (*Quercus rubra*) and black oak (*Quercus velutina*).

Taxonomy: Sandy-skeletal, mixed, mesic Typic Udorthents.

Ottawa series

Deactivated and merged with Colonie loams.

Painesville sandy loams

Where they are found: slight rises or broad convex flats on lake plains.

Characteristics: mesic to moist, poorly drained, deep fine sandy loams with slow permeability, a pH of 5.0 and seasonal zone of saturation at about 9 inches from October through June.

Composition: 69 percent sand, 22 percent silt and 9 percent clay with about 3 percent organic matter in the top 12 inches and formed in glaciolacustrine sediments and the underlying till on Wisconsinan age lake plains.

Current use: mostly woodland or abandoned cropland reverting to woodland, but some areas are used for nursery crops, pasture and hayland, with urban development increasing. Native vegetation is hardwood forest, including red maple (*Acer rubrum*), sugar maple (*Acer saccharum*), white ash (*Fraxinus americana*), yellow poplar (*Liriodendron tulipifera*), black cherry (*Prunus serotina*), white oak (*Quercus alba*), pin oak (*Quercus palustris*) and red oak (*Quercus rubra*).

Taxonomy: Coarse-loamy, mixed, active, nonacid, mesic Aeric Epiaquepts.

Painesville sandy loams

Where they are found: slight rises or broad convex flats on lake plains.

Characteristics: mesic to moist, poorly drained, deep fine sandy loams with slow permeability, a pH of 5.0 and seasonal zone of saturation at about 9 inches from October through June.

Composition: 69 percent sand, 22 percent silt and 9 percent clay with about 3 percent organic matter in the top 12 inches and formed in glaciolacustrine sediments and the underlying till on Wisconsinan age lake plains.

Current use: mostly woodland or abandoned cropland reverting to woodland, but some areas are used for nursery crops, pasture and hayland, with urban development increasing. Native vegetation is hardwood forest, including red maple (*Acer rubrum*), sugar maple (*Acer saccharum*), white ash (*Fraxinus americana*), yellow poplar (*Liriodendron tulipifera*), black cherry (*Prunus serotina*), white oak (*Quercus alba*), pin oak (*Quercus palustris*) and red oak (*Quercus rubra*).

Taxonomy: Coarse-loamy, mixed, active, nonacid, mesic Aeric Epiaquepts.

Palms mucky loams

Where they are found: closed depressions on floodplain backswamps, hillside seeps, and lake, till and outwash plains and moraines.

Characteristics: mesic to moist, poorly drained, deep mucks with slow to moderate permeability in organic matter above the loam and moderate to slow in the loam; no pH data. Frequently ponded and with a seasonal zone of water saturation is at the surface from November through May, the soils are classified as hydric.

Composition: between 45 and 60 percent sand and 30 to 40 percent silt, with the balance clay and about 87 percent organic matter in the top 12 inches, formed in herbaceous organic materials between 16 and 51 inches thick and underlying loamy deposits.

Current use: mostly marshy vegetation that includes grasses, reeds and sedges as well as alder (*Alnus spp.*), aspen (*Populus tremuloides*), willow (*Salix spp.*) and dogwood (*Cornus spp.*). Other appropriate species include red maple (*Acer rubrum*), black ash (*Fraxinus nigra*), sweet gum (*Liquidambar styraciflua*) and white cedar (Thuga occidentalis). Drained areas are used for pasture and some truck crops.

Taxonomy: loamy, mixed, euic, mesic Terric Haplosaprists.

Papakating series

Deactivated; see Holly loams.

Parker gravelly loams

Where they are found: gentle to steep slopes of ridges and hills in the northern Piedmont.

Characteristics: dry to mesic, excessively drained, deep gravelly loams with rapid permeability and a pH of about 5.7.

Composition: about 53 percent sand, 30 percent silt and 17 percent clay, with about 2 percent organic matter in the top 12 inches and formed in residuum parented by granitic gneiss bedrock.

Current use: About half cleared for cropland, and most cleared areas are idle and in various stages of second-growth forest dominated by dogwood (*Cornus spp.*) and red cedar (*Juniperus virginiana*). In areas not repeatedly logged, forests are generally oak-hickory, including white oak (*Quercus alba*), scarlet oak (*Quercus coccinea*), chestnut oak (*Quercus prinus*) and black oak (*Quercus velutina*).

Taxonomy: loamy-skeletal, mixed, semiactive, mesic Typic Dystrudepts.

Paupack mucky peat

Where they are found: till plains, moraines, lake plains or behind glacially-blocked drainageways.

Characteristics: mesic to moist, poorly drained, moderately deep organic material over gravelly alluvium, typically ponded year-round and classified as hydric; no pH data.

Composition: no soil data, but organic matter and formed in organic materials of highly decomposed woody plants in glacially-blocked drainage patterns, shallow lakes and ponds that range from 5 to 100 or more acres.

Current use: Most areas are wooded with hemlocks (*Tsuga canadensis*), black spruce (*Picea mariana*), white pine (*Pinus strobus*), high bush blueberry (*Vaccinium corymbosum*), tamarack (*Larix laricina*), and rhododendron (*Rhododendron maximum*).

Taxonomy: Loamy-skeletal, mixed, dysic, mesic Terric Haplosaprists.

Pecktonville silt loams

Where they are found: convex slopes on upland ridges.

Characteristics: mesic to moist, well drained, deep, slowly permeable gravelly silt loams with a pH of 5.3; rock outcrops and sink holes are common.

Composition: about 26 percent sand, 53 percent silt and 21 percent clay, with about 3 percent organic matter in the top 12 inches and formed in residuum from primarily limestone, interbedded with shale, chert and sandstone.

Current use: most areas cleared for pasture or cropland; woodlands are dominated by oak-hickory forests, including chestnut oak (*Quercs prinus*) and red oak (*Quercus rubra*).

Taxonomy: fine, mixed, active, mesic Typic Paleudults.

Pekin silt loams

Where they are found: stream terrace risers and treads, and floodplain steps.

Characteristics: mesic to moist, well drained, deep silt loams with a fragipan that are rarely, if ever, flooded or ponded, with moderate permeability and a pH of 6.2.

Composition: about 10 percent sand, 67 percent silt and 23 percent clay, with about 1.4 percent organic matter in the top 12 inches and formed in mixed silty alluvium and loess.

Current use: mostly cleared for cropland and pasture; forested areas are mixed hardwoods, including sugar maple (*Acer saccharum*), yellow poplar (*Liriodendron tulipifera*), Virginia pine (*Pinus virginiana*) and white oak (*Quercus alba*).

Taxonomy: fine-silty, mixed, active, mesic Aquic Fragiudults.

Penargyl channery silt loams

Where they are found: gently sloping to moderate backslopes, shoulders and summits from 200 to 1,200 feet above sea level.

Characteristics: mesic to moist, well drained, deep channery silt loam with moderate permeability and a pH of 5.9.

Composition: about 27 percent sand, 54 percent silt and 19 percent clay, with about 2 percent organic matter in the top 12 inches and formed in till derived from igneous, metamorphic and sedimentary rock overlying residuum of acidic brown shale, commonly on sloping ground moraine.

Current use: mostly cleared for cropland; forested areas are dominated by upland oaks such as red oak (*Quercus rubra*), maple (*Acer spp.*), beech (*Fagus grandifolia*) and birch (*Betula spp.*).

Taxonomy: fine-loamy, mixed, active, mesic Typic Hapludults.

Penlaw silt loams

Where they are found: on nearly level to sloping concave areas such as swales, depressions and hills.

Characteristics: mesic to moist, somewhat poorly drained, deep soils with moderate permeability and a pH of 6.5, with a fragipan between 15 and 30 inches

Composition: about 11 percent sand, 68 percent silt and 21 percent clay, with about 2.5 percent organic matter in the top 12 inches and formed in colluvium mostly from limestone but with some sandstone and shale.

Current use: almost all cleared and used for pasture and cropland; wooded areas tend to be mixed hardwoods dominated by oak and hickory, including red maple (*Acer rubrum*), sugar maple (*Acer saccharum*), white ash (*Fraxinus americana*), yellow poplar (*Liriodendron tulipifera*), red oak (*Quercus rubra*) and pin oak (*Quercus palustris*).

Taxonomy: fine-silty, mixed, semiactive, mesic Aquic Fragiudalfs.

Penn silt loams

Where they are found: nearly level to steep and moderately dissected uplands in the Northern Piedmont.

Characteristics: dry to mesic, well drained, moderately deep soils with moderate permeability and a pH of about 5.9.

Composition: about 27 percent sand, 55 percent silt and 13 percent clay, with about 1.4 percent organic matter in the top 12 inches and formed in residuum of fine-grained sandstone, siltstone and noncalcareous reddish shale, generally of Triassic age.

Current use: About 75 percent cleared for rotational cropland; woodlands are typically mixed hardwood forest dominated by oaks, including yellow poplar (*Liriodendron tulipifera*), loblolly pine

(*Pinus echinata*), Virginia pine (*Pinus virginiana*) and red oak (*Quercus rubra*).

Taxonomy: fine-loamy, mixed, superactive, mesic Ultic Hapludalfs.

Pennval silt loams

Where they are found: footslopes of prominent valley ridges in Clinton County.

Characteristics: mesic to moist, well drained, deep silt loams with moderate permeability and a pH of 5.2.

Composition: 22 percent sand, 57 percent silt and 21 percent clay with about 1 percent organic matter in the top 12 inches and formed in colluvium from interbedded siltstone and shale or sandstone.

Current use: forested with mixed hardwoods, including yellow poplar (*Liriodendron tulipifera*) and red oak (*Quercus rubra*).

Taxonomy: fine-loamy, mixed, active, mesic Typic Hapludults.

Pequea silt loams

Where they are found: upland hillslopes in the Northern Piedmont.

Characteristics: dry to mesic, well drained, deep silt loams with moderate to rapid permeability and a pH of 6.7.

Composition: about 32 percent sand, 53 percent silt and 15 percent clay, with about 2 percent organic matter in the top 12 inches and formed in residuum from schist, graphitic phyllite and micaceous limestone.

Current use: evenly divided between cropland, pasture and woodland that consist of mixed hardwoods dominated by red oak (*Quercus rubra*), black oak (*Quercus velutina*), hickory (*Carya spp.*), poplar (*Liriodendron tulipifera*) and Virginia pine (*Pinus virginiana*).

Taxonomy: coarse-loamy, mixed, active, mesic Typic Eutrudepts.

Phelps gravelly silt loams

Where they are found: level to gently sloping or slightly depressed regions of glacial outwash terraces.

Characteristics: dry to mesic, moderately well drained, deep gravelly silt loams with slow permeability and a pH of 6.5.

Composition: about 31 percent sand, 47 percent silt and 22 percent clay, with about 3 percent organic matter in the top 12 inches and formed in glacial outwash covered by two to three feet of silty or loamy material overlying calcareous, stratified gravel and sand in most locations.

Current use: Mostly cleared and used for pasture, hayland and cropland; native vegetation was sugar maple (*Acer saccharum*), white ash (*Fraxinus americana*), oak (*Quercus spp.*), other hardwoods and some pine (*Pinus strobus*) and hemlock (*Tsuga canadensis*).

Taxonomy: fine-loamy over sandy or sandy-skeletal, mixed, active, mesic Glossaquic Hapludalfs.

Philo loams

Where they are found: nearly level floodplains.

Characteristics: mesic to moist, moderately well drained, deep, mostly silt loams with moderate to moderately rapid permeability that is occasionally flooded because of stream overflow, with a pH of 5.3 to 5.9.

Composition: among silt loams, about 30 percent sand, 56 percent silt and 14 percent clay, while loams are more commonly about 58 percent sand and about 29 percent silt. Organic matter is about 2 percent in the top 12 inches and the soils formed in recent alluvium washed mainly from soils derived from sandstone and shale.

Current use: mostly cleared and used for pasture or cropland; original vegetation was mixed, water tolerant hardwoods such as white ash (*Fraxinus americana*), yellow poplar (*Liriodendron tulipifera*), white oak (*Quercus alba*), red oak (*Quercus rubra*), black oak (*Quercus velutina*) and red maple (*Acer rubrum*).

Taxonomy: Coarse-loamy, mixed, active, mesic Fluvaquentic Dystrudepts.

Platea silt loams

Where they are found: sideslopes, shoulders and summits on till plains and moraines.

Characteristics: mesic to moist, somewhat poorly drained, deep silt loams with slow permeability, a fragipan between 18 and 26 inches and pH of 4.8.

Composition: about 10 percent sand, 67 percent silt and 23 percent clay, with about 1.4 percent organic matter in the top 12 inches and formed in low-lime Wisconsinan age till that has been influenced by clayey siltstone.

Current use: mostly for pasture, hayland and cropland, with some woodlands. Native vegetation is hardwood forest, dominated by beech (*Fagus grandifolia*), sugar maple (*Acer saccharum*), ironwood (*Carpinus caroliniana*), wild cherry (*Prunus spp.*), basswood (*Tilia americana*), slippery elm (*Ulmus rubra*), white ash (*Fraxinus americana*), red maple (*Acer rubrum*) and red oak (*Quercus rubra*).

Taxonomy: fine-silty, mixed, active, mesic Aeric Fragiaqualfs.

Pocono gravelly sandy loams

Where they are found: gently sloping to steep uplands in the east-central Pennsylvania anthracite coal region in Luzerne County.

Characteristics: dry to mesic, well drained, deep gravelly sandy loams with moderate permeability and a pH of 4.6; most are considered extremely stony.

Composition: about 54 percent sand, 33 percent silt, and 13 percent clay, with about 1.25 percent organic matter in the top 12 inches and formed in residuum or till derived from acidic sandstone and conglomerate.

Current use: mostly woodlands composed of chestnut oak (*Quercus prinus*), black oak (*Quercus velutina*), aspen (*Populus tremuloides*), birch (*Betula spp.*), pitch pine (*Pinus rigida*), blueberry (*Vaccinium spp.*), mountain laurel (*Kalmia latifolia*) and ferns.

Taxonomy: loamy-skeletal, siliceous, mesic Typic Hapludults.

Pope loams

Where they are found: nearly level floodplains.

Characteristics: mesic to moist, well drained, deep loams, sandy loams and silt loams that are generally occasionally flooded, although some rarely are and others frequently are, with moderate permeability and a pH generally between 4.6 and 4.8.

Composition: sandy loams about 66 percent sand and 21 percent silt, loams about 52 percent sand and 36 percent silt and silt loams between 35 and 55 percent sand and 35 and 55 percent silt, all with the balance in clay and generally less than 1 percent organic matter in the top 12 inches. Soils formed from alluvium of acidic sandstone, siltstone and shale.

Current use: Much of the soils are cleared and used for cropland, pasture and hayland; native vegetation in woodlands is mixed deciduous hardwoods, principally yellow poplar (*Liriodendron tulipifera*), white oak (*Quercus alba*), river birch (*Betula nigra*), sycamore (*Plantanus occidentalis*), beech (*Fagus grandifolia*), bitternut hickory (*Carya cordiformis*), black gum (*Nyssa sylvatica*), red oak (*Quercus rubra*), basswood (*Tilia americana*) and hemlock (*Tsuga canadensis*).

Taxonomy: Coarse-loamy, mixed, active, mesic Fluventic Dystrudepts.

Portville silty clay loams

Where they are found: nearly level to sloping upland footslopes, benches and uplands in the unglaciated Appalachian Plateau of Pennsylvania.

Characteristics: dry to mesic, somewhat poorly drained, deep silty clay loams with a fragipan between 12 and 36 inches, slow permeability and a pH of 4.8.

Composition: about 19 percent sand, 52 percent silt and 29 percent clay, with about 3.5 percent organic matter in the top 12 inches and formed in colluvium weathered from interbedded shale, fine-grained sandstone and siltstone.

Current use: cleared areas are used for pasture and hayland with limited cropland; forests are mixed hardwoods, typically sugar maple (*Acer saccharum*), white ash (*Fraxinus americana*), beech (*Fagus grandifolia*), hemlock (*Tsuga canadensis*), red oak (*Quercus rubra*), black cherry (*Prunus* serotina) and eastern white pine (*Pinus strobus*).

Taxonomy: fine-loamy, mixed, active, mesic Aeric Fragiaqualfs.

Potomac gravelly loams

Where they are found: nearly level floodplains.

Characteristics: dry to mesic, excessively drained, deep gravelly loams with moderate permeability and a pH of 6.2, frequently flooded.

Composition: about 83 percent sand, 12 percent silt and 15 percent clay, with less than 1 percent organic matter in the top 12 inches and formed in coarse-textured, mixed alluvium washed form upland soils derived from sandstone, siltstone, shale and some limestone; often a major component in riverwash materials.

Current use: about half cleared for pasture or hayland; many areas are idle and reverting to woody vegetation; native vegetation was mixed hardwoods, such as black walnut (*Juglans nigra*), sycamore (*Platanus occidentalis*), white oak (*Quercus alba*), red oak (*Quercus rubra*), red cedar (*Juniperus virginina*) and white pine (*Pinus strobus*).

Taxonomy: Sandy-skeletal, mixed, mesic Typic Udifluvents.

Purdy silt loams

Where they are found: nearly level to gently sloping terraces.

Characteristics: mesic to moist, poorly to very poorly drained deep silt loams with very slow permeability and a pH of about 5.1, with a seasonal zone of water saturation is at the surface from November through May, occasionally to frequently ponded but not flooded and meet hydric criteria.

Composition: about 18 percent clay, 53 percent silt and 29 percent clay, with about 2 percent organic matter in the top 12 inches and formed in massive silty clay with occasional layers of coarser material in slackwater-deposited alluvial materials.

Current use: mostly cleared for pasture, while forests are dominated by oaks, particularly pin oak (*Quercus palustris*), red maple (*Acer rubrum*), beech (*Fagus grandifolia*) and hickory (*Carya spp.*) and suitable for sweet gum (*Liquidambar styraciflua*), yellow poplar (*Liriodendron tulipifera*), Virginia pine (*Pinus virginiana*) and loblolly pine (*Pinus echinata*).

Taxonomy: Fine, mixed, active, mesic Typic Endoaquults.

Rainsboro silt loams

Where they are found: treads and risers on high stream terraces in areas of or related to Illinoian glaciation.

Characteristics: mesic to moist, moderately well drained, deep silt loams with a fragipan between 22 and 34 inches, slow permeability and a pH of 5.7.

Composition: about 10 percent sand, 68 percent silt and 22 percent clay, with about 1.4 percent organic matter in the top 12 inches and formed in loess, old alluvium and underlying Illinoisan outwash deposits.

Current use: mostly cleared for cropland and a few areas are in pasture or mixed, deciduous hardwood forest that include sugar maple (*Acer saccharum*), white ash (*Fraxinus americana*), black walnut (*Juglans nigra*), yellow poplar (*Liriodendron tulipifera*), black cherry (*Prunus serotina*), white oak (*Quercus alba*) and red oak (*Quercus rubra*).

Taxonomy: fine-silty, mixed, superactive, mesic Oxyaquic Fragiudalfs.

Ramsey sandy loams

Where they are found: upper side slopes and summits of hills and mountains, locally in complexes with Dekalb loams.

Characteristics: dry to mesic, excessively drained, shallow sandy loams and rapid permeability and a pH of 5.0; rock outcrops are common and bedrock is 10 to 20 inches below the surface.

Composition: about 66 percent sand, 19 percent silt and 15 percent clay, with about 2 percent organic matter in the top 12 inches formed in residuum (occasionally colluvium) from quartzite or sandstone.

Current use: most areas are forested with mixed hardwood and pine; some has been cleared for pasture.

Taxonomy: loamy, siliceous, subactive, mesic Lithic Dystrudepts.

Raritan silt loams

Where they are found: nearly level to strongly sloping stream terraces, usually above current overflow.

Characteristics: mesic to moist, moderately well to somewhat poorly drained, deep silt loams with moderate permeability and a pH of 6.0.

Composition: about 30 percent sand, 51 percent silt and 19 percent clay, with about 2.4 percent organic matterin the top 12 inches and formed in sediments of reddish, noncalcareous shale, sandstone and siltstone uplands.

Current use: mostly cleared for cropland, with a substantial amount of acreage in urban-industrial use. Woodlands are mixed hardwoods, dominated by oaks, often including yellow poplar (*Liriodendron tulipifera*), loblolly pine (*Pinus echinata*) and Virginia pine (*Pinus virginiana*).

Taxonomy: fine-loamy, mixed, active, mesic Aquic Fragiudults.

Ravenna silt loams

Where they are found: at or near the lowest landscape positions of Wisconsinan age till plains.

Characteristics: mesic to moist, poorly drained, deep silt loams. with moderate permeability above a fragipan at 14 to 30 inches, a seasonal zone of water saturation at 12 inches from November through June and a pH of about 5.6.

Composition: about 26 percent sand, 54 percent silt and 21 percent clay, with about 1.4 percent organic matter in the top 12 inches and formed in Wisconsinan age till, often with a thin loess mantle or other silty material.

Current use: mostly cropland, with some pasture and woodland consisting of deciduous forest dominated by sugar maple (*Acer saccharum*), beech (*Fagus grandifolia*) and red oak (*Quercus rubra*). Other species include pin oak (*Quercus palustris*), black oak (*Quercus velutina*), white ash (*Fraxinus americana*) and yellow poplar (*Liriodendron tulipifera*).

Taxonomy: fine-loamy, mixed, active, mesic Aeric Fragiaqualfs.

Ravenrock silt loams

Where they are found: tread-riser backslopes and footslopes in the Blue Ridge Mountains.

Characteristics: mesic to moist, well drained, deep and slowly permeable soils with a pH of about 5.5 and in complexes with Rorhersville or Highfield-Rock soils.

Composition: about 29 percent sand, 53 percent silt and 18 percent clay, with about 2.2 percent organic matter in the top 12 inches and formed in colluvium and creep from metarhyolite or greenstone (chloritic metabasalt).

Current use: timber production, recreation, wildlife habitat, water supply and some home sites, with native vegetation dominated by northern red oak (*Quercus rubra*), yellow poplar (*Liriodendron tulipifera*), black gum (*Nyssa sylvatica*), ash (*Fraxinus spp.*), red maple (*Acer rubrum*), shagbark hickory (*Carya ovata*), and yellow birch (Betula alleghaniensis) and understory vegetation including spice bush (*Lindera benzoin*), witch hazel (*Hamamelis virginiana*), viburnum (*Viburnum spp.*), and dogwood (*Cornus spp.*).

Taxonomy: loamy-skeletal, mixed, active, mesic Ultic Hapludalfs.

Rayne silt loams

Where they are found: hillsides and ridgetops in the Allegheny Plateau.

Characteristics: mesic to moist, well drained, deep silt loams with moderate permeability a pH of 5.0, sometimes in complexes with Gilpin soils.

Composition: about 26 percent sand, 54 percent silt and 20 percent clay, with about 1.6 percent organic matter in the top 12 inches and formed in residuum of interbedded siltstone, shale and fine-grained sandstone

Current use: About cleared for cropland, hayland and pasture, and abandoned land is in second-growth pines and hardwoods. Oak-dominated forests of mixed hardwoods cover about 25 percent and include red oak (*Quercus rubra*), yellow poplar (*Liriodendron tulipifera*), loblolly pine (*Pinus echinata*), white pine (*Pinus strobus*) and

Virginia pine (*Pinus virginiana*).

Taxonomy: fine-loamy, mixed, active, mesic Typic Hapludults.

Readington silt loams

Where they are found: nearly level to sloping concave hillsides, upland flats, stream heads and drainageways in the Northern Piedmont.

Characteristics: mesic to moist, moderately well drained, deep silt loams with moderate permeability, a fragipan between 20 and 36 inches and a pH of about 5.8.

Composition: about 26 percent sand, 54 percent silt and 20 percent clay, with about 1.4 percent organic matter in the top 12 inches and formed in medium-textured residuum primarily from reddish, noncalcareous shale, fine-grained sandstone and siltstone.

Current use: Nearly 90 percent in cropland, with wooded areas dominated by mixed oak-hickory hardwoods that include red oak (*Quercus rubra*), Virginia pine (*Pinus virginiana*), shortleaf pine (*Pinus echinata*) and yellow poplar (*Liriodendron tulipifera*).

Taxonomy: fine-loamy, mixed, active, mesic Oxyaquic Fragiudalfs.

Reaville silt loams

Where they are found: interfluves with very minor dissection in the Northern Piedmont.

Characteristics: dry to mesic, moderately well to somewhat poorly drained deep silt loams with rapid permeability and a pH of 5.8.

Composition: about 25 percent sand, 55 percent silt and 20 percent clay, with about 1.8 percent organic matter in the top 12 inches and formed in the residuum of red Triassic, interbedded fine-grained sandstone, siltstone and shale.

Current use: mostly cleared for a variety of cropland and pasture, and some areas are used for urban development. Native vegetation was mixed hardwoods, dominated by oaks, notably red oak (*Quercus rubra*) and also including Virginia pine (*Pinus virginiana*).

Taxonomy: Fine-loamy, mixed, active, mesic Aquic Hapludalfs.

Red Hook loams

Where they are found: convex flats and slight rises on outwash plains as well as treads of outwash and stream terraces.

Characteristics: mesic to moist, somewhat poorly drained, deep loams and silt loams with slow permeability that are rarely, if ever, flooded with the exception of some in Mercer County that are frequently flooded and with a pH of about 6.0. A seasonal zone of water saturation is at 12 inches from December through May.

Composition: varies between 30 to 55 percent sand and 32 to 53 percent silt with the balance in clay and about 5 percent organic matter in the top 12 inches, formed in Wisconsinan age glaciofluvial deposits with relatively high amounts of organic matter, mostly outwash.

Current use: mostly cleared for pasture, hayland and some cropland, while woodlots are generally dominated by elm (*Ulmus spp.*), red maple (*Acer rubrum*), sugar maple (*Acer saccharum*), hemlock (*Tsuga canadensis*) and ash (*Fraxinus spp.*), with some white pine (*Pinus strobus*), river birch (*Betula nigra*), beech (*Fagus grandifolia*), white oak (*Quercus alba*) and swamp white oak (*Quercus bicolor*).

Taxonomy: coarse-loamy, mixed, superactive, nonacid, mesic Aeric Endoaquepts.

Rexford loams

Where they are found: nearly level to strongly sloping stream and glacial outwash terraces and water-sorted moraines.

Characteristics: dry to mesic, poorly drained, deep silt loams, gravelly loams and silt loams with slow permeability, a fragipan at 15 to 24 inches and a pH of about 5.5. A seasonal zone of water saturation is at 16 inches from October through May.

Composition: loams are between 44 and 52 percent sand and 33 to 35 percent silt; silt loams are about 30 percent sand and 55 percent silt, all with about 15 percent clay and all with about 3 percent organic matter in the top 12 inches and formed in water-sorted materials mostly from gray shales and sandstones.

Current use: mostly cleared for pasture, hayland and some grain crops; smaller areas are in mixed northern hardwood forest that include sugar maple (*Acer saccharum*), white ash (*Fraxinus americana*), black cherry (*Prunus serotina*) and red oak (*Quercus rubra*).

Taxonomy: coarse-loamy, mixed, active, mesic Aeric Fragiaquepts.

Rimer fine sandy loams

Where they are found: nearly level convex lake plain and till plain surfaces in the Lake Erie Glaciated Plateau.

Characteristics: dry to mesic, somewhat poorly drained, deep fine sandy loams with rapid permeability and a pH of 6.2. A seasonal zone of water saturation is at 10 inches from January through April.

Composition: about 90 percent sand, 3 percent silt and 7 percent clay with less than 1 percent organic matter in the top 12 inches and formed in a combination of glaciolacustrine deposits and underlying till.

Current use: Mostly cultivated for a variety of crops; small areas in pasture or woodlands composed of such mixed hardwoods as beech (*Fagus grandifolia*), elm (*Ulmus spp.*), hickory (*Carya spp.*), maple (*Acer spp.*) and oaks (*Quercus spp.*).

Taxonomy: loamy, mixed, active, mesic Aquic Arenic Hapludalfs.

Riverhead sandy loams

Where they are found: nearly level to steep outwash plains, beaches, valley trains and water-sorted moraines.

Characteristics: dry to mesic, well drained, deep sandy loams with moderate permeability and a pH of 4.8.

Composition: about 69 percent sand, 25 percent silt and 6 percent clay, with about 2.5 percent organic matter in the top 12 inches and developed in 20 to 40 inches of water-sorted sandy loam or fine sandy loam fairly low in gravel content and over stratified sand and grave.

Current use: Mostly cleared and used for cropland and suburban development. Native vegetation includes red oak (Quercus rubra), white oak (Quercus alba) and black oak (Quercus velutina), American beech (Fagus grandifolia) and sugar maple (Acer saccharum), with some white pine (Pinus strobus) and black cherry (Prunus serotina).

Taxonomy: coarse-loamy, mixed, active, mesic Typic Dystrudepts.

Rohrersville silt loams

Where they are found: lower footslopes, drainage heads and intermittent drainageways and concave upland flats in the Northern Blue Ridge.

Characteristics: mesic to moist, somewhat poorly drained, deep silt loams with slow permeability, a fragipan between 20 and 35 inches and a pH of 5.1 to 5.8. A seasonal zone of water saturation is at 15 inches from November through March.

Composition: between 18 and 23 percent sand, about 55 percent silt and the balance in clay with about 2 percent organic matter in the top 12 inches and formed in local alluvial and colluvial materials over residuum from metaigneous (metamorphic rock formed from igneous rock) rock, especially metaandesite and metabasalt.

Current use: mostly pasture and cropland; forested areas are dominated by wetland hardwoods as elm (*Ulmus spp.*), maple (*Acer spp.*), willow (*Salix spp.*), and alders (*Alnus spp.*), with a ground cover chiefly of sedges.

Taxonomy: fine-loamy, mixed, superactive, mesic Fragiaquic Hapludalfs.

Rowland silt loams

Where they are found: relatively narrow flood plains in the Northern Piedmont and Northern Coastal Plain.

Characteristics: mesic to moist, moderately well to somewhat poorly drained silt loams with slow permeability and a pH of 5.3 to 6.3 but commonly 5.8 that are occasionally to frequently flooded.

Composition: about 30 percent sand, 55 percent silt and 15 percent clay, with about 3 percent organic matter in the top 12 inches and formed in alluvial sediments washed from nearby gently sloping to sloping uplands underlain mostly with sandstone, red to brown shale and conglomerate.

Current use: mostly cleared for cropland or pasture; wooded areas are mixed hardwoods, often including yellow poplar (*Liriodendron tulipifera*) and red oak (*Quercus rubra*).

Taxonomy: fine-loamy, mixed, superactive, mesic Fluvaquentic Dystrudepts.

Rushtown silt loams

Where they are found: long and narrow, gently to steeply sloping, linear and concave footslopes and lower backslopes in the Northern Appalachian Ridges and Valleys.

Characteristics: dry to mesic, excessively drained, deep shaly silt loams with rapid permeability and a pH of 5.3.

Composition: about 26 percent sand, 54 percent silt and 20 percent clay, with less than 2 percent organic matter in the top 12 inches and formed in colluvium of shale and siltstone fragments.

Current use: Some areas cleared for pasture and limited cropland, but borrow pits are very common because these soils are a popular source for secondary road base materials. Forested areas are mixed hardwoods, mostly oak-pine, including chestnut oak (*Quercus prinus*), red oak (*Quercus rubra*), black oak (*Quercus velutina*), white pine (*Pinus strobus*) and Virginia pine (*Pinus virginiana*).

Taxonomy: loamy-skeletal over fragmental, mixed, active, mesic Typic Dystrudepts.

Ryder silt loams

Where they are found: convex slopes on dissected hills and valley sides, often in complexes with Duffield and Nollville soils.

Characteristics: dry to mesic, well drained, moderately deep mostly channery silt loams with moderate permeability and a pH of about 6.2.

Composition: about 25 percent sand, 55 percent clay and 15 percent silt with about 1.5 percent organic matter in the top 12 inches and formed in the residuum of thinly bedded shaly limestone.

Current use: Mostly in cropland, with about 20 percent in woodlands, pasture or non-farm use; wooded areas are mixed hardwoods that often include white ash (*Fraxinus americana*), yellow poplar (*Liriodendron tulipifera*), white pine (*Pinus strobus*) and red oak (*Quercus rubra*).

Taxonomy: fine-loamy, mixed, semiactive, mesic Ultic Hapludalfs.

Sassafras loams

Where they are found: sideslopes and summits of hills in the Atlantic coastal plain, between 35 and 330 feet above sea level.

Characteristics: mesic to moist, well drained, deep loams with moderate permeability and a pH of 5.2.

Composition: about 46 percent sand, 44 percent silt and 11 percent clay, with about 1.2 percent organic matter in the top 12 inches and formed in sandy marine and old alluvial sediments.

Current use: Mostly pastures, cropland, orchards, a wide variety of non-farm uses and some woodlands, composed mostly of mixed upland hardwoods with some shortleaf pine (*Pinus echinata*) and Virginia pine (*Pinus virginiana*).

Taxonomy: fine-loamy, siliceous, semiactive, mesic Typic Hapludults.

Scio silt loams

Where they are found: terraces or old alluvial fans, but also on lake plains and beds, outwash plains and lacustrine mantled uplands.

Characteristics: mesic to moist, moderately well drained, deep mostly silt loams with slow permeability and a pH of 5.3.

Composition: about 22 percent sand, 70 percent silt and 8 percent clay, with about 4 percent organic matter in the top 12 inches and formed in lacustrine, alluvial or eolian sediments dominated by very fine sand and silt, with a gravel content of less than 5 percent and may be 40 inches deep over loamy, sandy or gravelly material.

Current use: Mostly cleared for a variety of crops; native vegetation consists of northern red oak (*Quercus rubra*), white ash (*Fraxinus americana*), sugar maple (*Acer saccharum*), black cherry (*Prunus serotina*), eastern hemlock (*Tsuga canadensis*) and eastern white pine (*Pinus strobus*).

Taxonomy: coarse-silty, mixed, active, mesic

Aquic Dystrudepts.

Sciotoville silt loams

Where they are found: stream terraces, especially along the Ohio River and its tributaries.

Characteristics: mesic to moist, moderately well drained, deep silt loams with moderate permeability, a pH of 6.0 and a fragipan between 18 and 38 inches. Sand and gravel deposits are typically found between 7 and 10 feet.

Composition: about 14 percent sand, 70 percent silt and 16 percent clay, with about 2 percent organic matter in the top 12 inches and formed in old silty, acidic alluvium with some minor amounts of alluvium from shale and micaceous limestone mixed with some quartzite.

Current use: Mostly cultivated, with steeper areas in pasture or woodland consisting of hardwood forest that can include red maple (*Acer rubrum*), sugar maple (*Acer saccharum*), white ash (*Fraxinus americana*), yellow poplar (*Liriodendron tulipifera*), black cherry (*Prunus serotina*) and red oak (*Quercus rubra*).

Taxonomy: fine-silty, mixed, active, mesic Aquic Fragiudalfs.

Sebring silt loams

Where they are found: broad flats and depressions of slackwater terraces and lake plains.

Characteristics: mesic to moist, poorly drained, deep silt loams with slow permeability and a pH between 5.0 and 5.6. Because of a seasonal zone of saturation at or near the surface from October through June, the soils are frequently ponded and classified as hydric.

Composition: about 8 percent sand, 67 percent silt and 25 percent clay, with about 3 percent organic matter in the top 12 inches and formed in stratified Wisconsinan age glaciolacustrine sediments.

Current use: although mostly cleared, agricultural use is limited to pasture because of wetness. In wooded areas, pin oak (*Quercus palustris*) and swamp oak (*Quercus bicolor*) dominate; other species can include red maple (*Acer rubrum*), green ash (*Fraxinus pennsylvanica*), eastern cottonwood (*Populus deltoides*), and black cherry (*Prunus serotina*).

Taxonomy: fine-silty, mixed, superactive, mesic Typic Endoaqualfs.

Sewell channery sandy loams

Where they are found: nearly level to gently sloping benches, gently to strongly sloping hillslopes and steep outslopes, in connection with surface coal mining.

Characteristics: dry to mesic, well drained, deep channery sandy loams with rapid permeability and a pH of 4.6

Composition: about 57 percent sand, 30 percent silt and 13 percent clay, with less than 1 percent organic matter in the top 12 inches, formed in acidic fine earth and bedrock fragments crushed by machinery of mostly brown and gray acidic sandstone, siltstone, shale and coal, from the surface mining of coal, generally on summits.

Current use: surface mine reclamation, dominated by grasses, legumes, black locust and other species common to reclamation. Some areas have established stands of yellow poplar (*Liriodendron tulipifera*), sourwood (*Oxydendrum arboreum*), red maple (*Acer rubrum*), white pine (*Pinus strobus*), black locust (*Robinia pseudoacacia*), sycamore (*Plantanus occidentalis*) and oaks (*Quercus spp.*), while others are used for pasture and cropland.

Taxonomy: loamy-skeletal, mixed, semiactive, acid, mesic Typic Udorthents.

Sheffield silt loams

Where they are found: large flats and depressions on till plains.

Characteristics: mesic to moist, poorly drained, deep silt loams with slow permeability, a fragipan between 15 and 30 inches, a seasonal zone of saturation as at the surface from December through May, resulting in occasional ponding, and a classification as hydric.

Composition: about 8 percent sand, 67 percent silt and 25 percent clay, with about 3 percent organic matter in the top 12 inches and formed in mostly low-lime glacial till influenced by clayey shale and siltstone.

Current use: divided between cropland where adequately drained, pasture, and idle land. Native vegetation includes elm (*Ulmus spp.*), ash (*Fraxinus spp.*), red maple (*Acer rubrum*), sugar maple (*Acer saccharum*), eastern cottonwood (*Populus deltoides*), swamp white oak (*Quercus bicolor*) and pin oak (*Quercus palustris*).

Taxonomy: fine-silty, mixed, active, mesic Typic Fragiaqualfs.

Shelmadine silt loams

Where they are found: stream heads, drainageways, upland flats and depressions with gradients up to 15 percent in glaciated and glaciated fringe areas.

Characteristics: dry to mesic, poorly drained, deep silt loams with slow permeability and a pH of 4.6, with a fragipan at 15 to 30 inches, a seasonal zone of water saturation is at 3 inches from November through June and classified as hydric.

Composition: about 26 percent sand, 55 percent silt and 19 percent clay, with about 1.3 percent organic matter in the top 12 inches and formed in pre-Wisconsinan age glacial or periglacial materials from shale, siltstone and sandstone.

Current use: about 40 percent cleared for pasture and cropland; wooded areas are primarily mixed northern hardwood forest, often including black cherry (*Prunus serotina*) and red oak (*Quercus rubra*).

Taxonomy: fine-loamy, mixed, semiactive, mesic Typic Fragiaquults.

Shelocta silt loams

Where they are found: mostly concave, gently sloping to steep benches, footslopes and mountainsides on the Allegheny Plateau.

Characteristics: mesic to moist, well drained, deep and moderately permeable silt loams with a pH of 5.2.

Composition: about 27 percent sand, 53 percent silt and 20 percent clay, with about 2.2 percent organic matter in the top 12 inches and formed in a mix of colluvium and residuum from sandstone, siltstone and shale.

Current use: About 25 percent cleared for pasture and cropland, and 75 percent is in mixed hardwood forest composed mostly of oaks, especially white oak (*Quercus alba*) and scarlet oak (*Quercus coccinea*), gum (*Nyssa sylvatica* and *Liquidambar styraciflua*), red maple (*Acer rubrum*), yellow poplar (*Liriodendron tulipifera*), cucumbertree (*Magnolia acuminata*), shortleaf pine (*Pinus echinata*) and hemlock (*Tsuga canadensis*).

Taxonomy: fine-loamy, mixed, active, mesic Typic Hapludults.

Shohola loams

Where they are found: drainageways and structural benches below seep areas.

Characteristics: dry to mesic, somewhat poorly drained, deep loams in complexes with Edgemere (hydric) soils, with a fragipan between 18 and 30 inches, moderate permeability and a pH of 4.7.

Composition: about 45 percent sand, 43 percent silt and 12 percent clay, with less than 1 percent organic matter in the top 12 inches and formed in loamy till, primarily from shale and sandstone areas.

Current use: mostly wooded and used for timber; a few areas were at one time cleared for pasture.

Taxonomy: loamy-skeletal, mixed, active, mesic Aeric Fragiaquepts.

Shongo silt loams

Where they are found: concave footslopes, lower hillsides, benches and saddles in the Eastern Allegheny Plateau.

Characteristics: dry to mesic, poorly drained, deep silt loams with moderate permeability, a fragipan at 16 to 30 inches and a pII of 5.2.

Composition: about 16 percent sand, 57 percent silt and 27 percent clay, with about 3 percent organic matter in the top 12 inches and formed in colluvium from interbedded fine-grained sandstone, siltstone and shale.

Current use: cleared areas for pasture and hayland, but most are reverting back to woodland; native vegetation is mixed hardwood forest dominated by sugar maple (*Acer saccharum*), white ash (*Fraxinus americana*), beech (*Fagus grandifolia*), hemlock (*Tsuga canadensis*), and eastern white pine (*Pinus strobus*), along with some black cherry (*Prunus serotina*) and red oak (*Quercus rubra*).

Taxonomy: fine-loamy, mixed, active, frigid Aeric Fragiaqualfs.

Sideling gravelly loams

Where they are found: footslopes and colluvial fans below sandstone-capped ridges in the Northern Appalachian Ridges and Valleys.

Characteristics: mesic to moist, moderately well drained, deep, mostly gravelly loams with slow permeability and a pH of 5.3.

Composition: about 40 percent sand, 37 percent silt and 13 percent clay, with less than 1 percent organic matter in the top 12 inches and formed in colluvium of acidic sandstone over shale residuum.

Current use: Mostly in oak-hickory forest, but some gentler slopes are used for pasture and orchards.

Taxonomy: fine-loamy, siliceous, semiactive, mesic Oxyaquic Hapludults.

Skidmore gravelly loams

Where they are found: on relatively narrow and occasionally inundated floodplains in the Central Allegheny Plateau.

Characteristics: dry to mesic, well to excessively drained, deep gravelly loam with moderately rapid permeability that are occasionally flooded with a pH of 6.7.

Composition: about 40 percent sand, 48 percent silt and 12 percent clay, with about 2 percent organic matter in the top 12 inches and formed in cobbly, channery or gravelly alluvium derived mostly from Mississippian-aged sandstone, siltstone and limestone.

Current use: Most areas are used for pasture and hayland; native forests are composed mostly of white oak (*Quercus alba*), red oak (*Quercus rubra*), yellow poplar (*Liriodendron tulipifera*), sycamore (*Platanus occidentalis*), birch (*Betula spp.*), beech (*Fagus grandifolia*), and hickory (*Carya spp.*), and can include some black walnut (*Juglans nigra*), sweet gum (*Liquidambar styraciflua*) and eastern cottonwood (*Populus deltoides*).

Taxonomy: loamy-skeletal, mixed, semiactive, mesic Dystric Fluventic Eutrudepts.

Skytop flaggy sandy loam

Where they are found: gentle to steep upper side slopes and high exposed ridgetops above 1,800 feet in elevation in Pike County.

Characteristics: dry to mesic, well drained, deep mostly flaggy sandy loams with rapid permeability and a pH of 4.7.

Composition: about 67 percent sand, 29 percent silt and 4 percent clay with about 1.8 percent organic matter in the top 12 inches and formed in sandy till mostly from gray to brown quartzite, sandstone and conglomerate over hard sandstone bedrock-controlled topography.

Current use: Almost entirely forested with such northern hardwoods as white oak (*Quercus alba*), chestnut oak (*Quercus prinus*), maple (*Acer spp.*), beech (*Fagus grandifolia*) and birch (*Betula spp.*)

Taxonomy: loamy-skeletal, siliceous, active, frigid Typic Dystrudepts.

Sloan silt loams

Where they are found: floodplains or in streamside depressions on the Allegheny Plateau.

Characteristics: mesic to moist, very poorly drained, deep silt and silty clay loams with moderate to somewhat slow permeability, a pH between 5.3 and 7.0 (lower in channery silt loams), a seasonal zone of water saturation between 3 and 6 inches from November through June and classified as hydric.

Composition: between 18 and 32 percent sand, 52 to 56 percent silt and the balance in clay, with about 4 percent organic matter in the top 12 inches and formed in loamy alluvium mostly from soils formed in Wisconsinan age loamy calcareous drift.

Current use: mostly artificially drained for cropland, while other floodplain areas on smaller streams are used for pasture or woodland consisting of deciduous forest dominated by elm (*Ulmus spp.*), sycamore (*Platanus occidentalis*), silver maple (*Acer saccharinum*) and willow (*Salix spp.*); other species can include red maple (*Acer rubrum*), green ash (*Fraxinus pennsylvanica*), eastern cottonwood (*Populus deltoides*), swamp white oak (*Quercus bicolor*) and pin oak (*Quercus palustris*).

Taxonomy: fine-loamy, mixed, superactive, mesic Fluvaquentic Endoaquolls.

Solon channery silt loams

Where they are found: till plains and sideslopes of till plain ridges and valley sides in the Glaciated Allegheny Plateau.

Characteristics: dry to mesic, well drained, deep channery silt loams with moderate permeability and a pH of 5.3.

Composition: about 32 percent sand, 56 percent silt and 12 percent clay, with about 3.7 percent organic matter in the top 12 inches and formed in till and colluvium from siltstone, sandstone and shale.

Current use: Mostly forested with sugar maple (*Acer saccharum*), beech (*Fagus grandifolia*), white ash (*Fraxinus americana*), black cherry (*Prunus serotina*), northern red oak (*Quercus rubra*), eastern white pine (*Pinus strobus*) and hemlock (*Tsuga canadensis*).

Taxonomy: loamy skeletal, mixed, active, mesic Typic Dystrudepts.

Stanhope silt loams

Where they are found: flood plain steps with gradients in the Lake Erie Glaciated Plateau.

Characteristics: mesic to moist, poorly drained, deep silt loams with moderate to slow permeability, that are frequently but briefly flooded, classified as hydric, have a seasonal zone of water saturation is at 5 inches from October through June and a pH of 5.1.

Composition: about 10 percent sand, 68 percent silt and 22 percent and about 3 percent organic matter in the top 12 inches, formed in alluvium parented by low-lime till and lacustrine sediments and relatively high organic matter.

Current use: mostly deciduous forest that can include sugar maple (*Acer saccharum*), white ash (*Fraxinus americana*), yellow poplar (*Liriodendron tulipifera*), black cherry (*Prunus serotina*), white oak (*Quercus alba*), pin oak (*Quercus palustris*) and red oak (*Quercus rubra*).

Taxonomy: fine-silty, mixed, active, nonacid, mesic Fluvaquentic Endoaquepts.

Steff loams

Where they are found: nearly level floodplains in the Western Allegheny Plateau.

Characteristics: mesic to moist, moderately well drained, deep and moderately permeable loams that are occasionally to frequently flooded, with a pH of about 5.5.

Composition: mostly about 26 percent sand, 54 percent silt and 20 percent clay with about 1 percent organic matter in the top 12 inches, but high bottom soils found on low terraces are more commonly 12 percent sand, 70 percent silt and 18 percent clay and organic matter is about 2.5 percent. All were formed in alluvium derived from acidic sandstones, siltstones, shales and loess. Soils are occasionally to frequently flooded.

Current use: Mostly pasture and cropland; native vegetation is mixed hardwoods composed of river birch (*Betula nigra*), sycamore (*Platanus occidentalis*), willow (*Salix spp.*), water-tolerant oaks (*Quercus spp.*), yellow poplar (*Liriodendron tulipifera*), shagbark hickory (*Carya ovata*) and red maple (*Acer rubrum*), with some sugar maple (*Acer saccharum*), sweet gum (*Liquidambar styraciflua*) and black gum (*Nyssa sylvatica*).

Taxonomy: fine-silty, mixed, active, mesic Fluvaquentic Dystrudepts.

Steinsburg loams

Where they are found: gentle to steep upland slopes in the Northern Piedmont.

Characteristics: dry to mesic, well drained, deep channery sandy and gravelly loams with moderately rapid permeability and a pH of about 5.3.

Composition: channery sandy loams are about 66 percent sand and 20 percent silt while gravelly loams are about 52 percent sand and 34 percent silt, all with about 14 percent clay and less than 2 percent organic matter in the top 12 inches, formed in the residuum of weakly cemented acidic sandstone, arkosic sandstone and conglomerate.

Current use: About 75 percent in cropland or pasture; woodland areas are dominated by oak (*Quercus spp.*), maple (*Acer spp.*) and ash (*Fraxinus spp.*), with some Virginia pine (*Pinus virginiana*) and yellow poplar (*Liriodendron tulipifera*).

Taxonomy: coarse-loamy, mixed, active, mesic Typic Dystrudepts.

Suncook loamy sands

Where they are found: nearly level flood plains in the Glaciated Allegheny Plateau.

Characteristics: dry to mesic, excessively drained, deep loamy sands with rapid permeability, a pH of 5.5, and are occasionally to frequently flooded; most flooding ranges from annually to once per decade and generally does not occur during the growing season.

Composition: about 84 percent sand, 14 percent silt and 2 percent clay, with about 3 percent organic matter in the top 12 inches and formed in alluvial deposits mostly from quartzite, schist, gneiss and granite.

Current use: mostly wooded or in brushy, unimproved pasture, while some areas have been cleared for pasture, hayland and scattered croplands. Common trees include sycamore (*Platanus occidentalis*), aspen (*Populus tremuloides*), white oak (*Quercus alba*), black oak (*Quercus velutina*), red maple (*Acer rubrum*), white pine (*Pinus strobus*) and ironwood (*Carpinus caroliniana*); understory species include bayberry (*Myrica gale*), ground cedar (*Lycopodium spp.*), lowbush blueberry (*Vaccinium spp.*), pipsisswea (Chimaphila umbellata) and hairy-cap moss (Polytrichum commune).

Taxonomy: mixed, mesic Typic Udipsamments.

Swanpond silt clay loams

Where they are found: slightly concave to slightly convex gentle slopes in broad, topographically low upland areas in the Great Valley area

Characteristics: mesic to moist, moderately well drained, deep and slowly permeable silt clay loams with a pH of 6.5 and often in complexes with Edom soils.

Composition: about 20 percents sand, 42 percent silt, and 38 percent clay, with about 1 percent organic matter in the top 12 inches and formed in residuum of Ordovician and Cambrian limestone bedrock.

Current use: mostly cleared for cropland, hayland and pasture, and some are used for urban development. A small acreage is in woodland consisting of mixed hardwoods, often including yellow poplar (*Liriodendron tulipifera*) and red oak (*Quercus rubra*).

Taxonomy: very-fine, mixed, active, mesic Vertic Paleudalfs.

Swartswood loams

Where they are found: nearly level to very steep upland slopes.

Characteristics: dry to mesic, well drained, deep channery and stony loams with rapid permeability, surface boulders and stones common in most wooded areas, a fragipan between 22 and 36 inches and a pH of 4.6.

Composition: between 44 and 65 percent sand, 20 and 40 percent silt and about 15 percent clay, with less than 2 percent organic matter in the top 12 inches with the exception of complexes with Wurtsboro soils (7 percent organic matter), and formed in till parented mostly from gray and brown quartzite, conglomerate and sandstone.

Current use: Mostly woodland dominated by northern hardwoods such as maple (*Acer spp.*), beech (*Fagus grandifolia*) and birch (*Betula spp.*) with some ash (*Fraxinus americana*) and red oak (*Quercus rubra*); some non-stony areas are partly cleared for cultivation.

Taxonomy: coarse-loamy, mixed, active, mesic Typic Fragiudepts.

Teegarden silt loams

Where they are found: till plains on the Lake Erie Glaciated Plateau.

Characteristics: mesic to moist, moderately

well drained, deep silt loams with moderate permeability, a fragipan between 18 and 30 inches, and a pH of about 5.9.

Composition: about 27 percent sand, 55 percent silt and 18 percent clay, with about 2 percent organic matter in the top 12 inches and formed in loess, till from Illinoisan or early Wisconsinan ages, and residuum from underlying Pennsylvanian age fine-grained sandstone, shale and siltstone.

Current use: Mostly cleared for cropland and pasture; a few areas in woodland are mixed hardwood forest composed mostly of white oak (*Quercus alba*), red oak (*Quercus rubra*), hickory (*Carya spp.*) and sugar maple (*Acer saccharum*); other species may include beech (*Fagus grandifolia*), white ash (*Fraxinus americana*), sycamore (*Platanus occidentalis*) and slippery elm (*Ulmus rubra*).

Taxonomy: fine-loamy, mixed, active, mesic Aquic Fragiudalfs.

Thorndale silt loams

Where they are found: shallow depressions and drainageways in southern Pennsylvania.

Characteristics: mesic to moist, poorly drained, deep silt loams with varied permeability, a pH of 6.2, a seasonal zone of water saturation is at 3 inches from September through May and hence classified as hydric.

Composition: about 11 percent sand, 65 percent silt and 24 percent clay, with about 2 percent organic matter in the top 12 inches and formed in medium-textured colluvium derived from calcareous shale, limestone and siltstone.

Current use: mostly cleared used for pasture; those that have been drained are used for cropland. Woodland species include red maple (*Acer rubrum*), ash (*Fraxinus spp.*), sycamore (*Platanus occidentalis*), black cherry (*Prunus serotina*), pin oak (*Quercus palustris*) and red oak (*Quercus rubra*).

Taxonomy: fine-silty, mixed, active, mesic Typic Fragiaqualfs.

Thurmont gravelly loams

Where they are found: footslopes, colluvial fans, benches and stream terraces.

Characteristics: mesic to moist, well drained, deep gravelly loams with moderate permeability and a pH of 5.0.

Composition: about 43 percent sand, 39 percent silt and 18 percent clay, with about 1 percent organic matter in the top 12 inches and formed in colluvial and alluvial materials from a variety of metamorphic rocks.

Current use: about 25 percent cleared for cropland and pasture; forest vegetation is composed of white oak (*Quercus alba*), black oak (*Quercus velutina*), hickory (*Carya spp.*), wild cherry (*Prunus spp.*), beech (*Fagus grandifolia*), yellow poplar (*Liriodendron tulipifera*), black gum (*Nyssa sylvatica*), Virginia pine (*Pinus virginiana*), dogwood (*Cornus florida*) and elm (*Ulmus spp.*).

Taxonomy: fine-loamy, mixed, active, mesic Oxyaquic Hapludults.

Tilsit silt loams

Where they are found: ridgetops with slopes of up to 15 percent on the Allegheny Plateau.

Characteristics: mesic to moist, moderately well drained, deep and slowly permeable silt loams with a pH of 4.8 and a fragipan between 18 and 28 inches.

Composition: about 14 percent sand, 67 percent silt and 19 percent clay, with about 1.4 percent organic matter in the top 12 inches and formed in silty residuum from acidic siltstone or fine-grained sandstone that may be interbedded with soft shale.

Current use: About half used for cropland and pasture and the remainder is idle or in woodland, with native vegetation dominated by white oak (*Quercus alba*), scarlet oak (*Quercus coccinea*), black oak (*Quercus velutina*), southern red oak (*Quercus falcata*), hickory (*Carya spp.*), Virginia pine (*Pinus virginiana*), shortleaf pine (*Pinus echinata*), pitch pine (*Pinus rigida*), red maple (*Acer rubrum*), black gum (*Nyssa sylvatica*), yellow poplar (*Liriodendron tulipifera*), dogwood (*Cornus florida*), beech (*Fagus grandifolia*), ironwood (*Carpinus caroliniana*), persimmon (*Diospyros virginiana*) and sassafras (*Sassafras albidum*).

Taxonomy: fine-silty, mixed, semiactive, mesic Typic Fragiudults.

Timberville silt loams

Where they are found: colluvial fans, low areas adjacent to upland drainageways and the concave areas at drainageway heads.

Characteristics: mesic to moist, well drained, deep silt loams with moderate permeability and a pH of 6.0; subject to rare short-duration flooding between April and October.

Composition: about 30 percent sand, 54 percent silt and 16 percent clay with about 2 percent organic matter in the top 12 inches and formed in alluvial and colluvial materials derived from limestone with interbedded sandstone.

Current use: mostly cleared for cropland and pasture; the remaining woodland is forested with mixed hardwoods, oftn including red oak (*Quercus rubra*), yellow poplar (*Liriodendron tulipifera*) and black walnut (*Juglans nigra*).

Taxonomy: fine, mixed, active, mesic Typic Hapludults.

Tioga loams

Where they are found: higher floodplain positions with gradients less than 3 percent.

Characteristics: mesic to moist, well drained, deep, occasionally flooded silt loams, gravelly loams and fine sandy loams with moderate permeability and a pH of about 6.2.

Composition: sandy loams are about 68 percent sand and 21 percent silt; gravelly loams are about 45 percent sand and 44 percent silt; silt loams are about 33 percent sand and 56 percent silt; all are about 11 percent clay and have between 1.4 and 4 percent organic matter in the top 12 inches and were and formed in alluvium mostly from shale, siltstone and sandstone areas.

Current use: Mostly cleared for cropland; woodlots contain ash (*Fraxinus spp.*), maple (*Acer spp.*), red oak (*Quercus rubra*) and elm (*Ulmus spp.*), and are generally suitable for yellow poplar (*Liriodendron tulipifera*), hackberry (*Celtis occidentalis*), black walnut (*Juglans nigra*), sycamore (*Platanus occidentalis*), and pin oak (*Quercus palustris*).

Taxonomy: coarse-loamy, mixed, superactive, mesic Dystric Fluventic Eutrudepts.

Titusville silt loams

Where they are found: glaciated benches at the foot of steeper slopes, interfluves and hillsides in the Lake Erie Glaciated Plateau.

Characteristics: mesic to moist, moderately well drained, deep silt loams with a pH of about 5.0, slow permeability, a fragipan between 16 and 28 inches a seasonal zone of water saturation is at 18 inches during from November through May.

Composition: about 25 percent sand, 54 percent silt and 21 percent clay with about 1.6 percent organic matter in the top 12 inches and formed in weathered Illinoian till, mostly of sandstone and shale materials, with a mantle of loess as much as 16 inches thick.

Current use: About half cleared for cropland and pasture, although many area are now idle. Woodlands are mixed hardwoods, primarily hickory (*Carya spp.*), white oak (*Quercus alba*), red oak (*Quercus rubra*), and sugar maple (*Acer saccharum*), with some beech (*Fagus grandifolia*), sycamore (*Platanus occidentalis*), white ash (*Fraxinus americana*) and slippery elm (*Ulmus rubra*).

Taxonomy: fine-loamy, mixed, active, mesic Aquic Fragiudalfs.

Towhee silt loams

Where they are found: upland flats and depressions in the Northern Piedmont.

Characteristics: mesic to moist, poorly drained, deep silt loams with varied permeability, a fragipan between 20 and 30 inches, and a pH of 6.7. With a seasonal zone of saturation at or near the surface from September through June, the soils are classified as hydric.

Composition: about 26 percent sand, 55 percent silt and 19 percent clay, with about 3 percent organic matter in the top 12 inches and formed in colluvium from diorite, gabbro or diabase.

Current use: Mostly woodland with water-tolerant tree species, such as sugar maple (*Acer saccharum*), white ash (*Fraxinus americana*), yellow poplar (*Liriodendron tulipifera*) and red oak (*Quercus rubra*) and a few areas are cleared for pasture and cropland.

Taxonomy: fine-loamy, mixed, superactive, mesic Typic Fragiaqualfs.

Trego gravelly silt loams

Where they are found: nearly level to slightly concave colluvial footslopes and alluvial fans.

Characteristics: mesic to moist, moderately well drained, deep and slowly permeable gravelly silt loams, often with a fragipan between 20 and 30 inches and a pH of 5.0 to 5.6.

Composition: about 37 percent sand, 46 percent silt and 17 percent clay, with about 3 percent organic matter in the top 12 inches and formed in acidic alluvium with colluvial influences from metamorphic crystalline rocks.

Current use: cropland, pasture and forest production; native vegetation is mixed hardwood forest, often including yellow poplar (*Liriodendron tulipifera*) and red oak (*Quercus rubra*).

Taxonomy: fine-loamy, mixed, active, mesic Fragiaquic Hapludults.

Trumbull silt loams

Where they are found: gently sloping and depressional areas of till plains in the Lake Erie Glaciated Plateau.

Characteristics: mesic to moist, poorly drained, deep, hydric silt loams with slow to very slow permeability and a pH of 5.5 that have a seasonal zone of saturation at or near the surface from November through June and can be ponded.

Composition: about 24 percent sand, 47 percent silt and 28 percent clay, with about 3 percent organic matter in the top 12 inches and formed in low-lime glacial till.

Current use: mostly cleared for cropland, but many areas are used for pasture or woodland and are no longer cultivated, and many others are in non-agricultural and urban use. Dominant woodland species are elm (*Ulmus spp.*), red maple (*Acer rubrum*), pin oak (*Quercus palustris*), and green ash (*Fraxinus pennsylvanica*); others can include eastern cottonwood (*Populus deltoides*), black cherry (*Prunus serotina*), swamp white oak (*Quercus bicolor*) and red oak (*Quercus rubra*).

Taxonomy: fine, illitic, mesic Typic Epiaqualfs.

Tughill loams

Where they are found: level to slightly sloping gradients, but more commonly low-lying or depressional areas, partially blocked drainageways and beaver-impounded streams on till plains, generally in complexes with Lickdale soils.

Characteristics: dry to mesic but very poorly drained, deep loams, stony loams and silt loams with a pH of 4.8 and rapid permeability. Although not flooded or ponded, a seasonal zone of water saturation is at 3 inches from November through June and the soils are classified as hydric. Surface stones or boulders from glacial melt fluvial scour are on the surface in some areas.

Composition: 32 to 45 percent sand, 45 to 56 percent silt and 22 percent clay, with about 12 percent organic matter in the top 12 inches and formed in till dominated by somewhat coarsely textured materials from either sandstone, siltstone and shale or from acidic siliceous rocks with organic matter in the surface horizon.

Current use: Mostly forested with red maple (*Acer rubrum*), hemlock (*Tsuga canadensis*), fir (*Abies balsamea*), spruce (*Picea rubens*), elm (*Ulmus spp.*) and yellow poplar (*Liriodendron tulipifera*), with some areas idle or used for unimproved pasture.

Taxonomy: Loamy-skeletal, mixed, active, nonacid, frigid Typic Endoaquepts.

Tunkhannock gravelly loams

Where they are found: nearly level to very steep valley trains, kames and outwash terraces between 800 and 1,800 feet above sea level.

Characteristics: dry to mesic, well drained, deep gravelly loams with rapid permeability and a pH of 4.8.

Composition: about 45 to 51 percent sand, 34 to 41 percent silt and 15 percent clay, with about 2 percent organic matter in the top 12 inches and formed in water-sorted glacial materials parented by reddish sandstone, siltstone and shale.

Current use: gently-sloping areas cleared for cropland, while forested areas are dominated by black cherry (*Prunus serotina*), red maple (*Acer rubrum*), sugar maple (*Acer saccharum*), beech (*Fagus grandifolia*), white ash (*Fraxinus americana*), oak (*Quercus spp.*), hemlock (*Tsuga canadensis*) and white pine (*Pinus strobus*).

Taxonomy: Loamy-skeletal, mixed, superactive, mesic Typic Dystrudepts.

Tygart silt loams

Where they are found: stream terraces not subject to over-bank flooding on the Allegheny Plateau.

Characteristics: mesic to moist, poorly drained, deep silt loams, with slow permeability and a pH of 5.1. A seasonal zone of water saturation is at 12 inches from December through May.

Composition: about 23 percent sand, 51 percent silt and 26 percent clay, with about 2 percent organic matter in the top 12 inches and formed in clayey slackwater alluvium washed from uplands of mixed sedimentary materials.

Current use: mostly cleared for pasture and cropland; natural vegetation is mostly mixed hardwoods, often including red maple (*Acer rubrum*), white ash (*Fraxinus americana*), yellow poplar (*Liriodendron tulipifera*), red oak (*Quercus rubra*) and black oak (*Quercus velutina*).

Taxonomy: fine, mixed, semiactive, mesic Aeric Endoaquults.

Tyler silt loams

Where they are found: High Illinoian-age terraces and dissected valley fill in depressions between 600 and 800 feet above sea level.

Characteristics: mesic to moist, somewhat poorly drained, deep silt loams with moderately slow permeability above a fragipan at 18 to 32 inches, a seasonal zone of water saturation is at 7 inches from November through May, and a pH of about 5.3.

Composition: about 11 percent sand, 67 percent silt and 22 percent clay, with more than 2 percent organic matter in the top 12 inches and formed in silty alluvium with a mantle of loess.

Current use: mostly cleared for cropland, hayland and pasture; in remaining woodlands, the native vegetation is mixed deciduous hardwood forest including sugar maple (*Acer saccharum*), beech (*Fagus grandifolia*), white ash (*Fraxinus americana*), yellow poplar (*Liriodendron tulipifera*), sycamore (*Platanus occidentalis*), white oak (*Quercus alba*), red oak (*Quercus rubra*), slippery elm (*Ulmus rubra*) and red maple (*Acer rubrum*).

Taxonomy: fine-silty, mixed, active, mesic Aeric Fragiaquults.

Tyner sandy loams

Where they are found: outwash plains and terraces and the beaches and offshore bars of lake plains from the Wisconsinan age, generally 570 to 1,020 feet above sea level, in the Lake Erie Glaciated Plateau.

Characteristics: mesic to moist, excessively drained, deep sandy loams with rapid permeability, in a complex with Otisville soils, with a pH of 5.2.

Composition: about 78 percent sand, 16 percent silt and 7 percent clay, with less than 1 percent organic matter in the top 12 inches and formed in sandy glacial outwash.

Current use: cleared for a variety of crops and often irrigated; some areas are in woodlands consisting mostly of deciduous forest that can include white oak (*Quercus alba*), red oak (*Quercus rubra*), quaking aspen (*Populus tremuloides*), white pine (*Pinus strobus*), red pine (*Pinus resinosa*) and jack pine (*Pinus banksiana*).

Taxonomy: Mixed, mesic Typic Udipsamments.

Unadilla loams

Where they are found: rolling lacustrine plains, old alluvial terrace deposits and outwash terraces.

Characteristics: mesic to moist, well drained, deep fine sandy and silt loams with rapid permeability and a pH of 5.3.

Composition: sandy loams are about 45 percent sand, 45 percent silt and 10 percent clay; silt loams range from 21 to 35 percent sand and 56 to 68 percent silt with the remainder in clay. Between 2 and 4 percent organic matter is found in the top 12 inches and the soils were formed in old alluvial deposits or silty, lacustrine sediments in water or wind-deposited materials high in coarse silt and very fine sand, usually less than 5 feet thick and underlain by sand and gravel or in some places, till.

Current use: mostly cleared for a variety of crops. In woodlots, sugar maple (*Acer saccharum*), American beech (*Fagus grandifolia*), red oak (*Quercus rubra*) and some hickory (*Carya spp.*) are dominant, with some white ash (*Fraxinus americana*), black cherry (*Prunus serotina*) and white pine (*Pinus strobus*).

Taxonomy: coarse-silty, mixed, active, mesic Typic Dystrudepts

Ungers stony loams

Where they are found: gentle to steep convex slopes in the Ridge and Valley Province.

Characteristics: mesic to moist, well drained, deep stony loams with moderate permeability and a pH of about 4.8.

Composition: about 48 percent sand, 35 percent silt and 17 percent clay, with about 1 percent organic matter in the top 12 inches and formed in residuum of red sandstone and some shale.

Current use: Most gentle slopes cleared for cropland while steeper areas are used for pasture and forest; native vegetation is oak-hickory forest, including red oak (*Quercus rubra*), white oak (*Quercus alba*), hickory (*Carya spp.*), red maple (*Acer rubrum*), white pine (*Pinus strobus*) and Virginia pine (*Pinus virginiana*).

Taxonomy: fine-loamy, mixed, semiactive, mesic Typic Hapludults.

Upshur loams

Where they are found: ridgetops, benches and hillsides on the Allegheny Plateau.

Characteristics: mesic to moist, well drained, deep, slowly permeable silty clay, and in complexes as silt loams with a pH of about 6.2 and often in complexes with Gilpin silt loams.

Composition: about 7 percent sand, 51 percent silt and 42 percent clay; in complexes with Gilpin silt loams, sand is around 25 percent, silt 52 percent and clay 23 percent. Soils generally have around 1.5 percent organic matter in the top 12 inches and were formed in residuum from clay shales that are sometimes interbedded with thin layers of siltstone.

Current use: Many areas, cleared for pasture and cropland, have reverted to woodlands in which such mixed hardwoods as white oak (*Quercus alba*), red oak (*Quercus rubra*), hickory (*Carya spp.*) and yellow poplar (*Liriodendron tulipifera*) are dominant species along with some white pine (*Pinus strobus*) and Virginia pine (*Pinus virginiana*).

Taxonomy: fine, mixed, superactive, mesic Typic Hapludalfs.

Urbana silt loams

Where they are found: nearly level to moderate slopes on northern Piedmont and Northern Coastal Plain uplands.

Characteristics: mesic to moist, well to somewhat poorly drained, deep silt loams with slow permeability and a pH of 5.8

Composition: about 29 percent sand, 55 percent silt and 16 percent clay, with about 1.7 percent organic matter in the top 12 inches and formed in residuum of actinolite, sericite and related fine-grained schistose rocks that are comparatively high in bases.

Current use: mostly urban development, pasture and cropland, with some native vegetation of black oak (*Quercus velutina*), yellow poplar (*Liriodendron tulipifera*), hickory (*Carya spp.*), dogwood (*Cornus florida*) and Virginia pine (*Pinus virginiana*).

Taxonomy: Fine-loamy, mixed, active, mesic Aquic Fragiudalfs.

Valois gravelly silt loams

Where they are found: gentle to steep complex slopes of end or lateral moraines and terraces, especially along lower valley sides, in the Glaciated Allegheny Plateau usually between 600 and 1,800

feet above sea level.

Characteristics: mesic to moist, well drained, deep mostly gravelly silt loams with moderate to rapid permeability and a pH of 4.8. Landforms are covered with materials impacted by frost or till, and the till itself is usually calcareous at depths over 12 feet. Subsurface stratification is often weak because of fluvial sorting.

Composition: 32 to 45 percent sand and 43 to 55 percent silt, with about 12 percent clay and 2.8 percent organic matter in the top 12 inches and formed in till dominated by sandstone and either siltstone or shale with some slate or phyllite and often have a small component of materials from calcareous rocks.

Current use: Most nearly level to rolling areas cleared for pasture, hayland and some cropland; woodlots are typically dominated by American beech (*Fagus grandifolia*), sugar maple (*Acer saccharum*), red oak (*Quercus rubra*) and other hardwoods.

Taxonomy: coarse-loamy, mixed, superactive, mesic Typic Dystrudepts.

Vandergrift silt loams

Where they are found: footslopes, benches, hillsides and hilltops on the Central and Western Allegheny Plateau.

Characteristics: mesic to moist, moderately well to somewhat poorly drained, deep mostly silt loams with slow permeability, a pH of 5.6 and often in complexes with Ernest, Gilpin, Guernsey, Cavode and Wharton soils.

Composition: about 17 percent sand, 51 percent silt and 32 percent clay, with about 2.4 percent organic matter in the top 12 inches and formed in residuum of interbedded calcareous and noncalcareous gray and red shales, siltstone and some limestone,

Current use: cleared and in cropland, urban use or idle; woodlands are dominated by hickory (*Carya* spp.), red oak (*Quercus rubra*), red maple (*Acer rubrum*), sugar maple (*Acer saccharum*), yellow poplar (*Liriodendron tulipifera*) and walnut (*Juglans nigra*), with some white ash (*Fraxinus americana*) and black cherry (*Prunus serotina*).

Taxonomy: fine, mixed, superactive, mesic Aquic Hapludalfs.

Vanderlip loamy sands

Where they are found: nearly level to very steep sideslopes (and ridgetops in the Appalachian Ridge and Valley province.

Characteristics: dry to mesic, excessively drained, deep mostly loamy sands with rapid permeability and a pH of 5.3.

Composition: about 84 percent sand, 9 percent silt and 7 percent clay, with about 1.25 percent organic matter in the top 12 inches and formed in residuum of nonacidic and weakly to moderately cemented sandstones.

Current use: Mostly mixed hardwood forest dominated by oaks, especially red oak (*Quercus rubra*) and black oak (*Quercus velutina*), with some white pine (*Pinus strobus*) and Virginia pine (*Pinus virginiana*).

Taxonomy: Mesic, coated Lamellic Quartzipsamments.

Varilla sandy loams

Where they are found: lower slopes of hills and mountains.

Characteristics: dry to mesic, somewhat excessively drained, deep sandy loams with moderately rapid permeability and a pH of 5.0; locally in a complex with Laidig soils.

Composition: about 64 percent sand, 28 percent silt and 8 percent clay with about 1.7 percent organic matter in the top 12 inches and formed in loamy, stony colluvium or residuum of mostly sandstone.

Current use: Mostly second-growth forest dominated by eastern hemlock (*Tsuga canadensis*), white oak (*Quercus alba*), yellow poplar (*Liriodendron tulipifera*), chestnut oak (*Quercus prinus*), American beech (*Fagus grandifolia*), scarlet oak (*Quercus coccinea*), pitch pine (*Pinus rigida*), Virginia pine (*Pinus virginiana*) and hickory (*Carya* spp.), with secondary amounts of red maple (*Acer rubrum*), northern red oak (*Quercus rubra*), black oak (*Quercus velutina*), black gum (*Nyssa sylvatica*), sourwood (*Oxydendrum arboreum*) and black cherry (*Prunus serotina*). More gently sloping areas are used for pasture and urban development.

Taxonomy: Loamy-skeletal, siliceous, semi-active, mesic Typic Dystrudepts.

Venango silt loams

Where they are found: convex flats, slight rises, low summits, shoulders and sideslopes of till plains and moraines.

Characteristics: mesic tom moist, somewhat poorly drained, deep silt loams with moderate permeability, a fragipan between 16 and 30 inches and a pH of 4.8.

Composition: about 27 percent sand, 54 percent silt and 19 percent clay, with about 2.4 percent organic matter in the top 12 inches and formed in Wisconsinan age till influenced by sandstone, siltstone and shale, with some limestone.

Current use: Mostly cropland, pasture and hayland, but many areas are reverting to trees and brush. Woodlands are dominated by beech (*Fagus grandifolia*), sugar maple (*Acer saccharum*), black cherry (*Prunus serotina*) and red maple (*Acer rubrum*), but white ash (*Fraxinus americana*), sycamore (*Platanus occidentalis*), red oak (*Quercus rubra*), white oak (*Quercus alba*) and slippery elm (*Ulmus rubra*) may be found.

Taxonomy: fine-loamy, mixed, active, mesic Acric Fragiaqualfs.

Volusia silt loams

Where they are found: gentle to steep concave to planer slopes on lower valley sides and on broad divides of maturely dissected glaciated plateaus, generally 1,200 and 1,800 feet above sea level.

Characteristics: dry to mesic, somewhat poorly drained, deep channery and very stony silt loams with a dense fragipan at 10 to 22 inches, rapid permeability and a pH of 5.5.

Composition: about 25 percent sand, 53 percent silt and 22 percent clay with about 3 percent organic matter in the top 12 inches and formed in firm basal till derived from sandstone, siltstone and brittle shale or slate, sometimes underlain by lacustrine materials.

Current use: mostly cleared for pasture, hayland and silage crops, but some are now idle with a cover of brush and forbs. Woodlots contain sugar maple (*Acer saccharum*), red maple (*Acer rubrum*), American beech (*Fagus grandifolia*), hemlock (*Tsuga canadensis*) with some white ash (*Fraxinus americana*) and red oak (*Quercus rubra*).

Taxonomy: fine-loamy, mixed, active, mesic Aeric Fragiaquepts.

Wallington loams

Where they are found: level to gently sloping lake plains and silt-covered uplands in the Lake Erie Glaciated Plateau.

Characteristics: mesic to moist, somewhat poorly drained, deep fine sandy and silt loams with moderate permeability over a fragipan at 12 to 24 inches and a pH of 5.7.

Composition: sandy loams are about 61 percent sand and 28 percent silt, while silt loams are about 34 percent sand and 55 percent silt, all with about 11 percent clay and 2.75 percent organic matter in the top 12 inches, formed in water-sorted or wind-sorted silt and very fine sand.

Current use: cleared areas for pasture, hayland and a variety of croplands, especially where artificially drained. Woodlots include red maple (*Acer rubrum*), sugar maple (*Acer saccharum*), white ash (*Fraxinus americana*), hemlock (*Tsuga canadensis*) and elm (*Ulmus spp.*)

Taxonomy: coarse-silty, mixed, active, mesic Aeric Fragiaquepts.

Warners silt loams

Where they are found: depressions, nearly level floodplains, hillside seepage areas and lake margins.

Characteristics: hydric, moist to wet, very poorly drained, deep silt loams with slow permeability that are frequently flooded and ponded, with a seasonal zone of saturation at the surface from November through June and a pH of 7.0

Composition: about 7 percent sand, 67 percent silt and 26 percent clay, with 6 percent organic matter in the top 12 inches, formed in mixed mineralogy materials overlying marl, either impregnated with calcium carbonate or having marl within the soil, typically from springs flowing from limestone rock.

Current use: where cleared and drained, for pasture and cropland. Wettest areas feature such hydrophytic vegetation as sedges and cattails, while woodlands are dominated by elm (*Ulmus spp.*), red maple (*Acer rubrum*), willow (*Salix spp.*), and shrubs tolerant of wet sites.

Taxonomy: Fine-silty, carbonatic, mesic Fluvaquentic Endoaquolls.

Washington silt loams

Where they are found: nearly level to steep pre-Wisconsinan till plains within limestone valleys, often with many shallow and closed depressions.

Characteristics: mesic to moist, well drained, deep silt loams with moderate permeability and a pH of 6.5.

Composition: about 25 percent sand, 50 percent silt and 25 percent clay, with about 2.4 percent organic matter in the top 12 inches and formed in pre-Wisconsinan age drift or colluvium from mostly granitic gneiss and limestone, usually overlying limestone bedrock.

Current use: Almost all of the soils are cleared for a variety of agricultural crops and pasture. Appropriate woodland species include red oak (*Quercus rubra*), white ash (*Fraxinus americana*) and yellow-poplar (*Liriodendron tulipifera*).

Taxonomy: fine-loamy, mixed, semiactive, mesic Ultic Hapludalfs.

Wasnot sandy loams

Where they are found: gentle to steep slopes of upper side slopes and high ridgetops in the Glaciated Allegheny Plateau and Catskill Mountains.

Characteristics: dry to mesic, somewhat excessively drained, shallow very flaggy sandy loams with very rapid permeability, bedrock at 10 to 20 inches and and a pH of 4.8.

Composition: about 67 percent sand, 29 percent silt and 4 percent clay, with about 3 percent organic matter in the top 12 inches and formed in till mostly from gray to brown quartzite, conglomerate and sandstone over hard sandstone bedrock-controlled topography.

Current use: Soils are almost entirely northern hardwood forest dominated by chestnut oak (*Quercus prinus*), white oak (*Quercus alba*), red maple (*Acer rubrum*), beech (*Fagus grandifolia*) and birch (*Betula spp.*), with some pitch pine (*Pinus rigida*).

Taxonomy: Loamy-skeletal, siliceous, active, frigid Lithic Dystrudepts.

Watchung silt loams

Where they are found: nearly level to gently sloping depressions and hills in the northern Piedmont.

Characteristics: mesic to moist, poorly drained, deep mostly hydric silt loams with slow permeability, a seasonal zone of water saturation is at 6 inches from December through June and a pH of about 5.7.

Composition: about 24 percent sand, 53 percent silt and 23 percent clay, with about 1.7 percent organic matter in the top 12 inches and formed in residuum of diorite, diabase and gabbro.

Current use: Although some areas are used for pasture and corn, most is native vegetation such as northern red oak (*Quercus rubra*), pin oak (*Quercus palustris*), willows (*Salix spp.*), box elder (*Acer negundo*), sedges, ironweed (*Veronia altissima*) and Joe-pye-weed (*Eutrochium purpureum*).

Taxonomy: fine, smectitic, mesic Typic Albaqualfs.

Watson silt loams

Where they are found: nearly level to moderately steep glaciated sections of the Northern Appalachian Ridges and Valleys

Characteristics: mesic to moist, moderately well drained, deep mostly silt loams with slow permeability with a pH of about 5.0.

Composition: about 24 percent sand, 54 percent silt and 12 percent clay, with about 1.5 percent organic matter in the top 12 inches and formed in loamy pre-Wisconsin till derived from sandstone, siltstone and shale similar to that of underlying rock.

Current use: mostly cleared for cropland;

wooded areas are mixed hardwoods, including sugar maple (*Acer saccharum*), yellow poplar (*Liriodendron tulipifera*) and red oak (*Quercus rubra*).

Taxonomy: fine-loamy, mixed, active, mesic Typic Fragiudults.

Wauseon sandy loams

Where they are found: lake plains and deltas of late Wisconsinan age in the Lake Erie Glaciated Plateau.

Characteristics: mesic to moist, poorly drained, deep hydric sandy loams with a pH of 6.2, moderately rapid permeability and a seasonal zone of water saturation at 9 inches from January through April.

Composition: about 84 percent sand, 7 percent silt and 9 percent clay, with about 1.4 percent organic matter in the top 12 inches and formed in sandy and loamy glaciolacustrine sediments and the underlying till.

Current use: Mostly cropland, but undrained areas host primarily marsh vegetation including deciduous swamp forests of swamp white oak (*Quercus bicolor*), red maple (*Acer rubrum*), slippery elm (*Ulmus rubra*), basswood (*Tilia americana*) and sycamore (*Platanus occidentalis*).

Taxonomy: coarse-loamy over clayey, mixed over illitic, superactive, mesic Typic Epiaquolls.

Wayland silt loams

Where they are found: nearly level or depressed areas of floodplains mostly in areas immediately adjacent to Wisconsin glaciation.

Characteristics: mesic to moist, poorly drained, deep silt and silty clay loams that are frequently flooded and ponded, with slow permeability, a seasonal zone of water saturation is the surface from November through June in many areas, classified as hydric and have a pH of about 6.6.

Composition: about 9 percent sand, 65 percent silt and 26 percent clay, although sand-clay ratios can vary, with about 3.5 percent organic matter in the top 12 inches and formed in recent alluvium in low or slackwater floodplain areas of streams receiving upland runoff containing some calcareous drift.

Current use: although some areas have been cleared and drained for pasture or cropland, most are in native vegetation such as red maple (*Acer rubrum*), alder (*Alnus spp.*), willow (*Salix spp.*) and other species tolerant of wet sites.

Taxonomy: fine-silty, mixed, active, nonacid, mesic Fluvaquentic Endoaquepts.

Wehadkee silt loams

Where they are found: on floodplains along streams that drain from the mountains and piedmont in the Northern Piedmont and Northern Coastal Plain.

Characteristics: mesic to moist, poorly drained, deep silt loams with moderate permeability, frequent flooding, a seasonal zone of water saturation is at 3 inches from October through May, and a pH of about 5.9.

Composition: about 28 percent sand, 55 percent silt and 17 percent clay, with about 2.4 percent organic matter in the top 12 inches and formed in loamy sediments washed from soils parented by schist, granite, gneiss, phyllite and other metamorphic and igneous rocks.

Current use: Mostly forested with water-tolerant hardwoods including sweetgum (*Liquidambar styraciflua*), blackgum (*Nyssa sylvatica*), willow (*Salix spp.*), oak (*Quercus spp.*), yellow poplar (*Liriodendron tulipifera*), hickory (*Carya spp.*), beech (*Fagus grandifolia*) and elm (*Ulmus spp.*). Areas that have been drained are used for pasture and some cropland.

Taxonomy: fine-loamy, mixed, active, nonacid, thermic Fluvaquentic Endoaquepts.

Weikert soil series

Where they are found: gentle to very steep convex dissected uplands, sometimes in complexes with Gilpin, Culleoka, Hartleton, Klinesville and Berks soils.

Characteristics: dry to mesic, well drained, shallow, mostly shaly, flaggy, stony and silt loams with moderately rapid permeability and a pH of 5.3.

Composition: about 26 percent sand, 53 percent silt and 21 percent clay, with about 1.3 percent organic matter in the top 12 inches and formed in residuum of interbedded fine-grained sandstone, siltstone and interbedded gray and brown acidic shale.

Current use: mostly cleared for cropland or pasture, with some idle; forested areas are mixed deciduous hardwoods, often including red oak (*Quercus rubra*), black oak (*Quercus velutina*), red maple (*Acer rubrum*) and black locust (*Robinia pseudoacacia*), with some Virginia pine (*Pinus virginiana*) and white pine (*Pinus strobus*).

Taxonomy: loamy-skeletal, mixed, active, mesic Lithic Dystrudepts.

Weinbach silt loams

Where they are found: nearly level to gently sloping terraces on the Allegheny Plateau.

Characteristics: mesic to moist, somewhat poorly drained, deep and very slowly permeable silt loams with a fragipan at 20 to 30 inches and a pH of 5.8. A seasonal zone of water saturation is at 10 inches from November through May.

Composition: about 11 percent sand, 68 percent silt and 21 percent clay, with about 1.75 percent organic matter in the top 12 inches and formed in old acidic alluvium composed of stratified silty clay loam, sand and loam with some sand in underlying materials, derived mainly from quartzite, sandstone and shale. Some areas may include components of glacial drift and some loess.

Current use: mostly cleared for cropland, while a small portion is in permanent pasture, idle or forested with mixed hardwoods, often including sugar maple (*Acer saccharum*), ash (*Fraxinus spp.*), yellow poplar (*Liriodendron tulipifera*), Prunus serotina (*black cherry*), white oak (*Quercus alba*) and red oak (*Quercus rubra*).

Taxonomy: fine-silty, mixed, active, mesic Aeric Fragiaqualfs.

Wellsboro silt loams

Where they are found: nearly level to steep slopes on the glaciated Allegheny Plateau.

Characteristics: dry to mesic, moderately well to somewhat poorly drained, deep flaggy, stony, channery and silt loams with moderate permeability, a pH of about 5.1, often with a fragipan at 14 to 26 inches and typically with a seasonal zone of saturation around 15 inches in March and April.

Composition: about 43 percent sand, 39 percent silt and 18 percent clay, with about 2 percent organic matter in the top 12 inches and formed in firm till derived from reddish sandstone, shale and siltstone.

Current use: Many areas cleared for pasture and cropland, although some are now idle. Woodlots include sugar maple (*Acer saccharum*), American beech (*Fagus grandifolia*), red oak (*Quercus rubra*) and white pine (*Pinus strobus*).

Taxonomy: coarse-loamy, mixed, active, mesic Typic Fragiudepts.

Wellston silt loams

Where they are found: nearly level to steep slopes on uplands, especially ridgetops in the Allegheny Plateau.

Characteristics: mesic to moist, well drained, deep silt loams with moderate permeability and a pH of 5.4.

Composition: about 11 percent sand, 67 percent silt and 22 percent clay, with about 1.6 percent organic matter in the top 12 inches and formed from silty material in loess or siltstone, or sandstone and siltstone, or a combination of those materials to depths of up to 40 inches, overlying acidic sandstone and siltstone with occasional strata of shale.

Current use: about half cleared for cropland and the remainder is in pasture and woodland, with native vegetation including white oak (*Quercus alba*), red oak (*Quercus rubra*), hickory (*Carya spp.*), dogwood (*Cornus spp.*), yellow poplar (*Liriodendron tulipifera*), shortleaf pine (*Pinus echinata*) and black cherry (*Prunus serotina*), with some sugar maple (*Acer saccharum*), white ash (*Fraxinus americana*), black walnut (*Juglans nigra*) and Virginia pine (*Pinus virginiana*).

Taxonomy: fine-silty, mixed, active, mesic Ultic Hapludalfs.

Westmoreland silt loams

Where they are found: noseslopes, headslopes, hillsides and interfluves of dissected uplands.

Characteristics: mesic to moist, well drained, moderately permeable, deep silt loams with a pH between 5.3 and 5.6.

Composition: about 22 percent sand, 55 percent silt and 23 percent clay, with about 1.6 percent organic matter in the top 12 inches and formed in colluvium and residuum from interbedded sandstone, siltstone and limestone.

Current use: cropland, pasture and woodlands composed of mixed hardwoods dominated by oak, especially red oak (*Quercus rubra*) and maple (*Acer spp.*), along with some yellow poplar (*Liriodendron tulipifera*) and white pine (*Pinus strobus*).

Taxonomy: fine-loamy, mixed, active, mesic Ultic Hapludalfs.

Weverton flaggy loams

Where they are found: ridges and backslopes of the Northern Blue Ridge.

Characteristics: dry to mesic, well drained, deep flaggy loams with moderate permeability and a pH of 5.0.

Composition: about 41 percent sand, 40 percent silt and 19 percent clay, with less than 1 percent organic matter in the top 12 inches and formed from a combination of slope creep and residuum of interbedded quartzite, quartz muscovite schist and phyllite.

Current use: Except for a few small recreational areas and home gardens and lawns, the soils are mixed hardwoods dominated by chestnut oak (*Quercus prinus*) with some Virginia pine (*Pinus virginiana*) and red oak (*Quercus rubra*).

Taxonomy: Loamy-skeletal, mixed, semiactive, mesic Typic Hapludults.

Wharton silt loams

Where they are found: nearly level to steep slopes on uplands on the Allegheny Plateau.

Characteristics: mesic to moist, moderately well drained, deep, mostly silt loams with slow permeability and a pH between 4.8 and 5.3, sometimes in complexes with Gilpin, Vandergrift and Cookport soils and urban land.

Composition: about 22 percent sand, 56 percent silt and 22 percent clay, generally with between 1 and 2 percent organic matter in the top 12 inches and formed in the residuum of interbedded fine-grained sandstone, siltstone and clay shales.

Current use: More gently sloped areas mostly cleared for pasture and cropland; steeper slopes are forested with mixed hardwoods, often including red maple (*Acer rubrum*), yellow poplar (*Liriodendron tulipifera*), red oak (*Quercus rubra*), sugar maple (*Acer saccharum*), white ash (*Fraxinus americana*), black cherry (*Prunus serotina*).

Taxonomy: fine-loamy, mixed, active, mesic Aquic Hapludults.

Wheeling silt loams

Where they are found: stream and outwash terraces.

Characteristics: mesic to moist, well drained, deep silt loams and gravelly loams with moderate permeability and a pH of 5.8.

Composition: about 30 percent sand, 52 percent silt and 18 percent clay, with about 1.6 percent organic matter in the top 12 inches and formed in loamy to silty alluvial materials on river terraces that are rarely to never flooded.

Current use: many areas for residential and cropland with woodlands, mostly on steeper slopes, generally dominated by oaks (*Quercus spp.*), hickory (*Carya spp.*), maple (*Acer spp.*) and walnut (*Juglans nigra*).

Taxonomy: fine-loamy, mixed, active, mesic Ultic Hapludalfs.

Wick silt loams

Where they are found: floodplain steps and floodplains in the Lake Erie Glaciated Plateau.

Characteristics: mesic to moist, poorly drained, deep silt loams with slow to moderate permeability that are frequently flooded, have a seasonal zone of water saturation at or near the surface year round, meet hydric criteria and have a pH of 5.5.

Composition: about 10 percent sand, 69 percent silt and 21 percent clay, with about 5.2 percent organic matter in the top 12 inches and formed in silty alluvium primarily from Wisconsinan age till.

Current use: generally for woodland, some pasture and nature preserves; natural vegetation is deciduous forest, often including red maple (*Acer rubrum*), green ash (*Fraxinus pennsylvanica*), eastern cottonwood (*Populus deltoides*), black cherry (*Prunus serotina*), swamp white oak (*Quercus bicolor*) and pin oak (*Quercus palustris*).

Taxonomy: fine-silty, mixed, superactive, nonacid, mesic Fluvaquentic Endoaquepts.

Williamson loams

Where they are found: on lake plains in the Lake Erie Glaciated Plateau in complexes with Collamer soils.

Characteristics: mesic to moist, moderately well drained, deep fine sandy and silt loams with moderate permeability above a fragipan between 22 and 30 inches and a pH of 5.3.

Composition: in sandy loams, about 48 percent sand and 40 percent silt with 12 percent clay; in silt loams, about 21 percent sand and 68 percent silt and 11 percent clay, all with about 3 percent organic matter in the top 12 inches and formed in very fine sandy or silty lacustrine or eolian deposits.

Current use: mostly cleared for cropland and some pasture; woodlots are composed of sugar maple (*Acer saccharum*), red oak (*Quercus rubra*), beech (*Fagus grandifolia*), hop hornbeam (*Ostrya virginiana*), black ash (*Fraxinus nigra*) and some white pine (*Pinus strobus*).

Taxonomy: Coarse-silty, mixed, active, mesic Typic Fragiudepts.

Wiltshire silt loams

Where they are found: level to slightly concave footslopes, upland depressions, flats and edges of drainage swales in the Northern Appalachian Ridges and Valleys.

Characteristics: mesic to moist, moderately drained, deep silt loams with slow permeability and a pH of 5.8.

Composition: about 27 percent sand, 54 percent silt and 19 percent clay, with about 2 percent organic matter in the top 12 inches and formed in colluvium of micaceous schist, greenstone schist and phyllite over residuum of low-grade marble.

Current use: mostly urban, with some in pasture or cropland. Wooded areas often include red oak (*Quercus rubra*) and yellow poplar (*Liriodendron tulipifera*).

Taxonomy: fine-loamy, mixed, semiactive, mesic Oxyaquic Fragiudalfs.

Woodstown loams

Where they are found: upland marine and old stream terraces at elevations ranging from 5 to 120 feet in the Northern Piedmont and Northern Coastal Plain.

Characteristics: mesic to moist, moderately well drained, deep and moderately permeable loams with a pH of 5.8.

Composition: about 40 percent sand, 43 percent silt and 17 percent clay, with about 2.5 percent organic matter in the top 12 inches and formed from old alluvial and sandy marine sediments.

Current use: mostly cropland and pasture, while native vegetation includes oak (*Quercus spp.*) and other hardwoods along with some Virginia pine (*Pinus virginiana*) and loblolly pine (*Pinus taeda*).

Taxonomy: Fine-loamy, mixed, active, mesic Aquic Hapludults.

Wooster silt loams

Where they are found: Wisconsinan age convex slopes on till plains and moraines.

Characteristics: mesic to moist, well drained, deep gravelly and channery silt loams with moderate permeability, a fragipan between 18 and 36 inches and a pH of about 5.3.

Composition: about 31 percent sand, 54 percent silt and 15 percent lcay, with 2 to 4 percent organic matter in the top 12 inches and formed in low-lime till, often with a mantle of loess up to 16 inches thick.

Current use: Most areas with slopes under 18 percent are cleared for pasture, hayland and grain crops, but substantial areas are used for woodland, particularly recreational use and wildlife habitats; forests are dominated by sugar maple (*Acer saccharum*), oak (*Quercus spp.*) and hickory (*Carya spp.*), which can include beech (*Fagus grandifolia*), white ash (*Fraxinus americana*), yellow poplar (*Liriodendron tulipifera*), sycamore (*Platanus occidentalis*), white oak (*Quercus alba*), red oak (*Quercus rubra*), slippery elm (*Ulmus rubra*), basswood (*Tilia americana*) and black cherry (*Prunus serotina*).

Taxonomy: Fine-loamy, mixed, active, mesic Oxyaquic Fragiudalfs.

Worsham silt loams

Where they are found: concave to convex slopes in depressions, drain heads, slope bases and upland flats in the Northern Piedmont.

Characteristics: mesic to moist, poorly drained, deep, hydric silt loams with very slow permeability and a pH of 5.2. Although not ponded or flooded, a seasonal zone of water saturation is at 3 inches from November through April.

Composition: about 25 percent sand, 51 percent silt and 24 percent clay, with about 2 percent organic matter in the top 12 inches and formed from alluvium parented by granite, gneiss or schist.

Current use: mostly woodland or pasture, with limited cropland. Native vegetation is sweetgum (*Liquidambar styraciflua*), blackgum (*Nyssa sylvatica*), willow oak (*Quercus phellos*), pin oak (*Quercus palustris*), alder (*Alnus spp.*), elm (*Ulmus spp.*), some pine (*Pinus spp.*) and other water-tolerant species.

Taxonomy: fine, mixed, active, thermic Typic Endoaquults.

Worth sandy loams

Where they are found: nearly level to steep landforms on till plains at elevations of 1,000 to 2,000 feet in the Glaciated Allegheny Plateau and Catskill Mountains.

Characteristics: dry to mesic, well drained, deep stony sandy loams with moderate permeability, a fragipan between 18 and 36 inches and a pH of 5.1.

Composition: about 68 percent sand, 21 percent silt and 11 percent clay, with about 3.4 percent organic matter in the top 12 inches and formed in till derived from shale, siltstone and sandstone, which might have a thin silty mantle of eolian material.

Current use: Mostly forested, with some hayland or pasture. Common woodland species include northern red oak (*Quercus rubra*), eastern white pine (*Pinus strobus*), paper birch (*Betula papyrifera*), American beech (*Fagus grandifolia*), eastern hemlock (*Tsuga canadensis*), and red pine (*Pinus resinosa*).

Taxonomy: Coarse-loamy, isotic, frigid Typic Fragiorthods.

Wurno channery silt loams

Where they are found: sideslopes and smooth ridges in the Northern Appalachian Ridges and Valleys in complexes with Nollville soils.

Characteristics: dry to mesic, well drained, moderately deep channery silt loams with moderate permeability and a pH of about 6.7. (Nollville soils are mesic to moist).

Composition: about 25 percent sand, 54 percent silt and 21 percent clay, with less than 1 to about 2 percent organic matter in the top 12 inches and formed from interbedded limestone and shale.

Current use: Mostly cleared for pasture and cropland; a few acres are wooded and can include Virginia pine (*Pinus virginiana*) and scarlet oak (*Quercus coccinea*).

Taxonomy: Loamy-skeletal, mixed, semiactive, mesic Dystric Eutrudepts.

Wurtsboro loams

Where they are found: level to moderately steep slopes in glaciated uplands.

Characteristics: mesic to moist, moderately well drained to somewhat poorly drained, deep, moderately permeable and mostly very stony and fine sandy loams with a fragipan at 17 to 28 inches and a pH of 4.6.

Composition: about 44 percent sand, 41 percent silt and 15 percent clay, with about 1.5 percent organic matter in the top 12 inches and formed in till parented by acidic gray and brown quartzite, conglomerate and sandstone.

Current use: almost entirely wooded, with native vegetation dominated by maple (*Acer spp.*), beech (*Fagus grandifolia*) and birch (*Betula spp.*)

with some red oak (*Quercus rubra*).

Taxonomy: Coarse-loamy, mixed, active, mesic Typic Fragiudepts.

Wyalusing loams

Where they are found: alluvial floodplain deposits along streams with gradients below 5 percent.

Characteristics: mesic to moist, poorly drained, deep, hydric, fine sandy and silt loams, with rapid permeability and frequent flooding. A seasonal zone of water saturation is at 3 inches from September through June.

Composition: fine sandy loams are 68 percent sand, 17 percent silt and 15 percent clay with about 2 percent organic matter in the top 12 inches; silt loams are 42 percent sand, 44 percent silt and 14 percent clay, with 3.5 percent organic matter in the top 12 inches. All were formed in alluvial deposits with underground seepage from surrounding uplands and base flow from nearby streams and uplands

Current use: Mostly pasture or idle, with wooded areas dominated by beech (*Fagus grandifolia*), maple (*Acer spp.*) and elm (*Ulmus spp.*).

Taxonomy: Coarse-loamy over sandy or sandy-skeletal, mixed, active, nonacid, mesic Fluvaquentic Endoaquepts.

Wyoming sandy loams

Where they are found: nearly level to steep slopes on outwash terraces, valley trains, kames, eskers and moraines.

Characteristics: dry to mesic, somewhat excessively drained, deep mostly sandy loams with rapid permeability and a pH of about 4.8.

Composition: about 67 percent sand, 21 percent silt and 12 percent clay with about 2 percent organic matter in the top 12 inches and formed in gravelly, water-sorted material from gray and red sandstone, shale and siltstone.

Current use: Most gentle slopes cleared for cropland and some are being urbanized; wooded areas include maple (*Acer spp.*), beech (*Fagus grandifolia*), ash (*Fraxinus spp.*), oak (*Quercus spp.*), hemlock (*Tsuga canadensis*) and white pine (*Pinus strobus*).

Taxonomy: Loamy-skeletal, mixed, active, mesic Typic Dystrudepts.

Zipp silt loams

Where they are found: level or slight depressions of lake plains, floodplain steps and broad, slightly concave lacustrine terraces.

Characteristics: mesic to moist, poorly drained, deep silt loams with slow permeability that are frequently flooded, have a seasonal zone of water saturation is at 9 inches from September through May, are classified as hydric and have a pH of 5.8.

Composition: about 26 percent sand, 56 percent silt and 18 percent clay with about 2 percent organic matter in the top 12 inches and formed in fine-textured lacustrine or slackwater sediments with slopes of less than 1 percent.

Current use: mostly drained and used for pasture, hayland and cropland; wooded areas are composed of mixed deciduous forest, often including pin oak (*Quercus palustris*)

Taxonomy: Fine, mixed, active, nonacid, mesic Typic Endoaquepts.

Zoar silt loams

Where they are found: level to strongly sloping terraces on the Appalachian Plateau.

Characteristics: mesic to moist, moderately well drained, deep silt loams with slow permeability and a pH of 5.0.

Composition: about 25 percent sand, 53 percent silt, and 22 percent clay, with about 2.5 percent organic matter in the top 12 inches and formed in acidic, clayey, lacustrine or slackwater sediments.

Current use: mostly for cropland, pasture or urban development. Appropriate tree species include red maple (*Acer rubrum*), white pine (*Pinus strobus*), white oak (*Quercus alba*), red oak (*Quercus rubra*), and black oak (*Quercus velutina*).

Taxonomy: Fine, mixed, semiactive, mesic Aquic Hapludults.

APPENDIX - PENNSYLVANIA NATIVE PLANTS

Calamagrostis porteri (Porter's reedgrass) [perennial graminoid] — open dry to mesic woodlands and edges in the Ridge and Valley section, especially south-central Pennsylvania. *Callitriche heterophylla* (Water-starwort) [perennial forb] — statewide aquatic in slow streams and ponds and on muddy shorelines, OBL. Prefers medium to fine textured soils with a pH of 5.2 to 6.8 in full to part sun.

Acalypha deamii (Three-seeded mercury) [annual forb] — uncommon to rare in bottomland woodlands and edges, usually in riparian areas; reported only in a wooded hollow in Allegheny County. Grows 6 to 30 inches with greenish late-summer flowers in dappled sunlight to medium shade on mesic to moist sandy or gravelly loam. Prefers areas subjected to spring flooding with alluvial soils.

Acalypha gracilens (Slender mercury) [annual forb] — rocky open woodlands and glades, prairies, shaly slopes and low meadows, southeast. Grows 1 to 3 feet with greenish-white flowers from spring to fall in dry to moist sandy loams in sun to part shade.

Acalypha rhomboidea (Three-seeded mercury) [annual forb] — statewide, especially southeast, in moist prairies and fields, openings in or lightly shaded areas of floodplain forests, limestone glades, stream banks, seeps and disturbed ground, FACU-. Grows 6 to 24 inches with green flowers in summer; prefers full sun to light shade and dry to mesic fertile, loamy soil, but can tolerate gravelly or clay soils.

Acalypha virginica (Three-seeded mercury) [annual forb] — disturbed, rocky woodlands, bluffs and borders, thickets, prairies, fields and wet meadows, partially shaded, gravelly seeps, stream banks, FACU-, mostly southeast but also scattered southwest. Somewhat drought tolerant, prefers soil pH above 5.9, intolerant of anaerobic conditions, and a minimum soil depth of six inches. Grows 1 to 3 feet with red flowers in summer in acidic, well-drained, mesic to moist fertile loams in part shade.

Box elder (Acer negundo)

Acer negundo (Box-elder) [tree] — moist sites along lakes and streams, on floodplains and in low-lying wet places, FAC+. Mostly southeast and southwest; scattered elsewhere. Grows 30 to 50 feet in all orders and textures of soils from gravel to clay with a pH of at least 5.0; prefers well-drained deep, sandy loam, loam, or clay loam soils with a medium to rocky texture and a pH of 6.5 to 7.5. Moderate tolerance for anaerobic conditions and quite tolerant of limestone soils; requires a minimum of 40 inches of soil and is shade and drought tolerant.

Acer pensylvanicum (Moosewood) [tree] — moist, acid soils in deep valleys and on cool, moist, shaded, north-facing slopes, FACU. Statewide, except scattered southeast. Grows to 45 feet; small forest openings and under thinned overstories in part shade; prefers cool, moist well-drained loam, especially alfisols and mollisols at least 28 inches deep with a pH of 4.7 to 6.5; low anaerobic and limestone tolerance, but somewhat shade tolerant.

Acer saccharinum (Silver maple) [tree] — streamside communities and lake fringes, and occasionally in swamps, gullies, and small depressions of slow drainage, FACW. Statewide, especially southeast. Grows 50 to 80 feet in average, medium to wet soils at least 32 inches deep, preferably inceptisols and mollisols, in full sun to part shade. Prefers moist soils and has a high tolerance for anaerobic conditions, but good in poor, dry soils but with low drought tolerance; pH range 4.5 to 7.3, but prefers pH above 5.5 and accepts some shade.

Acer saccharum (Sugar maple) [tree] — statewide in rich, mesic woods and drier upland woods, on level areas or in coves, ravines and other sheltered locations on adjacent lower especially north-facing slopes. Often associated with stream terraces, stream banks, valleys, canyons, ravines, and wooded natural levees; occasionally found on dry rocky hillsides, FACU. Grows to 80 feet in wide variety of soils, at least 40 inches deep, derived from shale, limestone and sandstone, typically alfisols and mollisols, but prefers deep, moist, fertile, well-drained sandy to silty loam; also associated with alluvial or calcareous soils. Intolerant of drought and flooded soils and grows poorly on dry, shallow soils; pH 3.7 to 7.3 but prefers pH ranges 5.5 to 7.3.

Acer spicatum (Mountain maple) [tree/shrub] — statewide in cool woods where the climate is humid and precipitation is year-round, including flats, bogs, and along streams with a distinct preference for medium-textured soils, but also can occur on drier and well-drained acidic soils such as talus slopes and cliff faces, FACU-. Grows to 35 feet; sun to part shade in moist cool acidic soil as low as pH 4.8 and a minimum of 32 inches in depth.

Aconitum reclinatum (White monkshood) [perennial forb] — Shaded ravines of woods in mountains and upper Piedmont. Rare in southwestern Pennsylvania and is listed as endangered. To 3 feet with white flowers in summer.

Aconitum uncinatum (Blue monkshood) [perennial forb] — rare in rich, wet areas near streams and springs and low woods; occasionally in less mesic woods and clearings. Generally found in southwestern counties. Grows to 4 feet, violet-purple flowers in spring, in part shade in moist, calcareous fertile soil. Does well in open woodlands; may be ignored by rabbits and deer.

Acorus americanus (Sweet flag) [perennial forb] — Very rare emergent semi-aquatic in silty soil in shallows, ponds, marshes and quiet water less than 20 inches deep. Scattered northwest and listed as endangered. Grows to 6 feet, yellow to brown flowers in late spring on fine-textured moist to wet soils (pH range of 5.6 to 7.2) in full sun to part shade. A vigorous spreader in wet soils and works well for retaining soil at the edge of a stream or pond.

Actaea pachypoda (Dolls-eyes) [perennial forb] — statewide in rich, open upland woods and thickets. Grows 12 to 30 inches with white flowers in late spring in part shade to shade in moist sandy humusy loam, pH 5 to 6.

Actaea podocarpa (American bugbane) [perennial forb] — Mostly southwest in rich coves and rich northern hardwood forests. Grows to about 30 inches in a clump with flower stems 5 to 6 feet bearing bottlebrush-like, branched racemes to 20

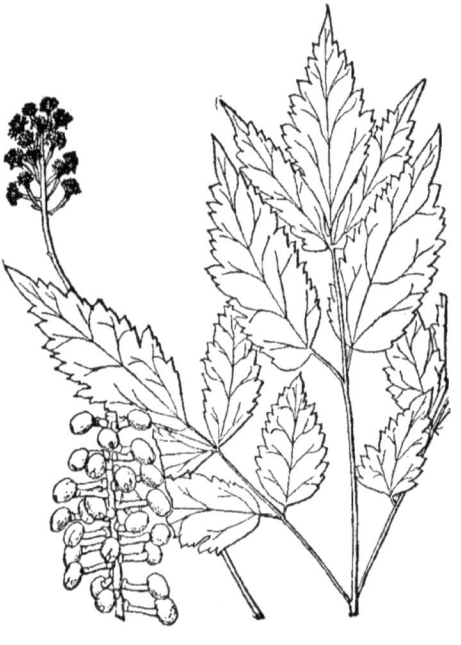

Doll's Eyes (*Actaea pachypoda*)

inches long of fluffy, creamy white flowers in summer. Prefers humusy, moisture-retentive soils in part shade to shade, sheltered from strong winds. Foliage scorches if too dry.

Actaea racemosa (Black cohosh, black snakeroot) [perennial forb] — rich moist woods, wooded slopes, ravines, along riverbanks and thickets, statewide. Grows 3 to 8 feet, white flowers on tall racemes in early summer, similar to *A. podocarpa*, which blooms earlier. Part shade to shade in moist rich humus, pH 5 to 7.

Actaea rubra (Red baneberry) [perennial forb] — mostly northest and northwest in upland hardwood and mixed-wood forest habitats on fresh or moist, fine-textured mineral soils. Grows 12 to 30 inches with white flowers in late spring; part sun to open shade in moist humus rich loam, pH 5 to 6.

Adiantum aleuticum (Aleutian maidenhair) [fern/ally] — rare on shaded banks, serpentine barrens, talus slopes, wooded ravines. Fronds 12 to 24 inches; rhizome: clump-forming. Grow in part shade to shade in a moist humusy loam over serpentine rock.

Adiantum pedatum (Northern maidenhair) [fern/ally] — rich, deciduous woodlands, often on humus-covered talus slopes and lime soils, mesic to slightly moist; low drought and anaerobic tolerances, but needs high fertility in soil. Fronds 12 to 30 inches; rhizome: short creeping. Grow in part shade to shade in moist, sandy organic loam at least 10 inches deep, pH 4.6 to 6.6; avoid fine-textured soils. A favorite of landscapers and found at many garden centers.

Adlumia fungosa (Allegheny vine) [biennial vine] — scattered statewide in moist coves, ledges and alluvial slopes, rocky woodlands and thickets. Grows to 10 feet with white to pink flowers in summer, prefers rocky, well drained loams in part shade.

Adlumia fungosa (Allegheny-vine) [perennial vine] — moist coves, rocky woods, ledges, alluvial slopes, and thickets; statewide. Climbing, to 10 feet. White flowers, summer to fall. Grow in part shade to shade in moist humusy loam.

Aeschynomene virginica (Sensitive joint-vetch) [annual forb] — rare in Atlantic Coastal Plain fresh water intertidal marshes, OBL. Grows to six feet with yellow-red flowers in summer and fall. freshwater intertidal marshes OBL; Philadelphia and Delaware Counties. To six feet with yellow-red flowers in summer and fall; mucky, sandy or gravelly soils with twice-daily tides far enoiugh upstream so the water is nearly fresh or barely brackish; among very few species correct for such tidal inundation.

Aesculus glabra (Ohio buckeye) [tree] — Bottomlands and moist stream banks, 60 to 80 feet, FACU+; mostly southwest and southeast. Average, well-drained soils in full sun to part shade; prefers fertile and moist soil, with a preference to medium to fine textured soils at least 36 inches deep with a pH of at least 5.0; intolerant of anaerobic conditions.

Agalinis auriculata (Eared false-foxglove) [annual forb] — serpentine barrens, woodland openings and meadows, floodplains and fields in Bucks and Montgomery counties; endangered. Grows to 30 inches in full sun to part shade in dry to mesic soils; parasitic on roots of other plants.

Agalinis decemloba (Blue Ridge false-foxglove) [annual forb] — serpentine barrens; reported in southern Lancaster County, extirpated. FACU. Grows to about two feet with lavender flowers in summer. on dry, serpentine soils.

Agalinis paupercula (Small-flowered false-foxglove) [annual forb] — very rare in northwest and southeastern Pennsylvania in damp, open places such as sandy ground and pond shores, FACW+ and listed as endangered. Parasitic on roots of varioius plants, grows 1 to 3 feet with pink flowers in late summer to fall in moist, sandy loams in sun.

Agalinis purpurea (False-foxglove) [annual forb] — moist, sandy prairies and fields, serpentine barrens, rocky shorelines, sandy open woodlands and some boggy areas, widely scattered statewide but most concentrated on Atlantic Coastal Plain; FAW- and parasitic on roots of many species. Grows 3 to 6 feet in sun to part sun on well drained sandy soils with many showy white, red or purple flowers in late summer and useful along paths.

Agalinis tenuifolia (Slender false-foxglove) [annual forb] — scattered statewide but concentrated in the far southeast and southwest in dry to mesic fields, prairies and open woodlands, as well as mesic to moist meadows, glades, thicketes, low flats and field edges, FAC. Prefers slightly disturbed habitats with loose, friable, slightly acidic and moist infertile soil containing silt and sand in sun to part shade. Adapts to rocky dry soils; does best when a host plant is nearby.

Agastache nepetoides (Yellow giant hyssop) [perennial forb] — generally upland moist, rich, open woodland areas, thickets and woodland borders, FACU. Mostly southern, especially southeast. Grows 3 to 5 feet, greenish-yellow flowers in late summer; full sun in moist rich loam.

Agastache scrophulariifolia (Purple giant hyssop) [perennial forb] — moist woods and thickets; statewide, except northern tier, especially southeast. Grows 3 to 5 feet, purple flowers in late summer; sun to part shade in moist rich humus, pH 6 to 7. Shade tolerant, but prefers sun.

Ageratina altissima (White snakeroot) [perennial forb] — rich rocky woods, at the base of cliffs and rock outcrops, and in thickets and fields, FACU-; statewide. Grows 12 to 60 inches, white flowers in summer and fall; average, medium to wet, well-drained soils in full sun to part shade. Prefers part shade in moist, humusy soils, pH 6 to 7.

Ageratina aromatica (Small-leaved whitesnakeroot) [perennial forb] — Rare in pine-oak and oak-hickory upland woodlands, sand ridges and burned pinelands, mostly southeast. Grows to 4 feet in sun to part shade with white flowers in late summer; prefers sandy, well drained soil. AKA *Eupatorium aromaticum*.

Agrimonia microcarpa (Small-fruited agrimony) [perennial forb] — Woodlands, mostly Piedmont. Grows 18-24 inches with late summer yellow flowers in full sun, slightly acidic to circumneutral soils.

Agrimonia parviflora (Southern agrimony) [perennial forb] — moist to wet woods and thickets, FAC; statewide except scattered north. Grows up to 45 inches, yellow flowers in late summer; part shade to shade in moist sandy loam.

Agrimonia pubescens (Downy agrimony) [perennial forb] — Rocky woodlands and woods edges, generally rich slopes, mostly southern Pennsylvania. Grows 18 to 30 inches with yellow flowers in late summer to fall in sun to part sun and dry to mesic loamy soil.

Agrimonia rostellata (Woodland agrimony) [perennial forb] — Fields, thickets, woodlands scattered throughout Pennsylvania (FACU). Grows up to 30 inches in partial sun to light shade, in mesic to dry-mesic soil containing loam, clay-loam, glacial till, or rocky material with pH from 4.5 to 7.0; yellow flowers in spring.

Agrimonia striata (Roadside agrimony) [perennial forb] — moist upland woods and thickets, FACU-; statewide except southern tier. Grows up to 36 inches, yellow flowers in late summer; part shade to shade in moist sandy loam, pH 5 to 6.

Agrostis hyemalis (Hairgrass or Winter bentgrass) [perennial graminoid] — dry or moist soil in woods and fields, bogs, meadows, and along roadsides, FAC. Mostly southeast far west; scattered elsewhere. A short-lived perennial that grows 12 to 32 inches in sun to part shade in dry to moist sandy loam at least pH 5.5 and 8 inches deep, with a preference to acidic soils; tolerates anaerobic conditions.

Agrostis perennans (Autumn bentgrass) [perennial graminoid] — woods, thickets, open areas, swamps, swales, sphagnum bogs and on stream banks, FACU; statewide. Grows 20 to 40 inches; part sun to part shade in mesic to wet, acidic, silty and clay loams at least 8 inches deep, between 5.5 and 7.5 pH. Tolerates anaerobic conditions but not drought.

Agrostis scabra (Fly-away grass) [perennial graminoid] — meadows, shrublands, woodlands, marshes, and stream and lake margins, FAC; statewide, especially northeast. Grows 12 to 32 inches; sun to part sun in dry to moist medium to fine-textured loams with a minimum pH of 6.0 and depth of 12 inches. Low drought and anaerobic tolerance.

Aletris farinosa (Colic-root, True unicorn root) [perennial forb] — Rare in moist bogs, dry to mesic prairies, and dry, upland woods and thickets; FAC. Scattered statewide, most concentrated in southeastern counties (Piedmont, Atlantic Coastal Plain); endangered. Grows 2 to 3.5 feet in full sun to part shade in humusy moist soil with white flowers in late spring to mid-summer.

Alisma subcordatum (Broad-leaved water-plantain) [perennial forb] — aquatic; shallow ponds, stream margins, marshes, and ditches, OBL; statewide. Grows 12 to 36 inches, pink to white flowers in summer; sun to part sun in medium to fine textured silty loam between 5.0 and 7.0 pH, in ponds and pond edges. Intolerant of shade or drought; does well in anaerobic situations.

Alisma triviale (Broad-leaved water-plantain) [perennial forb] — Rare in shallow, muddy marshes, ditches, ponds and stream margins; OBL. Mostly western counties; endangered. Grows 2 to 3 feet in full to part sun in boggy soils, wet pond margins or in shallow water. Whorls of white flowers in summer.

Allium canadense (Wild onion) [perennial forb] — upland glades, bluffs, open woods, prairies and disturbed sites, FACU; statewide except for the highest elevations on the Allegheny Plateau. Grows 8 to 12 inches, pink to white flowers in early summer; full sun to part shade in moist rich loam, pH 6.5 to 7.

Allium cernuum (Nodding onion) [perennial forb] — moist soils in cool mountainous regions. Mostly southwest, scattered elsewhere. White flowers in spring. Grow in well-drained soil, especially sandy loams in full sun to light shade; does best in full sun with light afternoon shade and will naturalize by self-seeding and bulb offsets.

Allium tricoccum (Ramp) [perennial forb] — moist ground in rich upland woods, depressions, streamside bluffs, and colluvial slopes, FACU+; statewide except for the Central Appalachians. Grows up to 20 inches, white flowers in spring; deciduous shade (needs sun in early spring) in rich moist mesic loam, pH 6.8 to 7.2.

Alnus incana ssp. *rugosa* (Speckled alder) [shrub] — moist lowlands, frequently along streams and lakes; common in swamps and the older zones of bogs; statewide, except southeast, FACW. Shrub to 20 feet; sun to part shade in moist to wet rich loams of all textures, minimum 24 inches, between 5.0 and 7.0 pH; high tolerance for anaerobic conditions, but none for drought; somewhat tolerant of shade.

Alnus serrulata (Smooth alder or Hazel alder) [shrub] — stream banks, ditches, edges of sloughs, swampy fields and bogs, and lakeshores, OBL. Statewide, especially southeast, except north. Shrub to 20 feet; sun to shade in moist to wet circumneutral fine sandy loams, peats and mucks, 5.0 to 7.0 pH and at least 24 inches deep. Very flood and anaerobic tolerant, but no drought tolerance. Alders fix nitrogen and thus serve as nutrient-giving pioneers in reclamation projects.

Wild Onion (*Allium canadense*)

Alnus viridis ssp. *crispa* (Mountain alder) [shrub] — very rare as isolated individuals or in thickets adjacent to lakeshores, streams, bogs; on sandy to gravelly slopes and flats or cool, rocky wooded slopes; FAC; widely scattered and endangered. Typically 6 to 12 feet on rocky, dry, acidic but cool sites with medium-fertility soils of all textures at least 20 inches deep in full sun to shade; high anaerobic and low drought tolerances; pH 4.8 to 7.0.

Alopecurus aequalis (Short-awned foxtail) [perennial graminoid] — widely scattered throughout Pennsylvania in moist meadows and swamps and lakeshores, especially on disturbed sites, OBL. Grows 9 to 18 inches in full to part sun in moist to wet, even mucky, soils rich with decaying organic matter; tolerates shallow standing water for up to two months during the growing season.

Alopecurus carolinianus (Carolina foxtail) [annual graminoid] — wet meadows and wetland edges in the Atlantic Coastal Plain and Piedmont; FACW. Possibly native to midwest, southeastern US. To about 10 inches in sun, mesic to moist sandy loams.

Amaranthus cannabinus (Salt-marsh water-hemp) [annual forb] — rare on the the uppermost areas of freshwater intertidal marshes of the Atlantic Coastal Plain, OBL. Pink flowers in late summer to fall with a preference for coastal salt or brackish marshes, slough edges, tidal riverbanks and flats.

Amaranthus pumilus (Seabeach amaranth) [annual forb] — Reported only in Philadelphia County and of conservation concern, possibly extirpated. Grows to about 18 inches on maritime sandudnes and beaches, primarily on foredunes, coastal islands and non-eroding beaches where it acts as "sand binder."

Ambrosia artemisiifolia (Common ragweed) [annual forb] — Considered invasive and noxious, the common cause of hay fever because of copious fine yellow pollen release from male plants. Statewide in dry fields, meadows, disturbed sites and waste ground. Grows 1 to 3 feet in a wide range of soils with flowers in summer, in sun to part shade; prefers slightly dry conditions.

Ambrosia psilostachya (Western ragweed) [perennial forb] — Dry to mesic grasslands, savannas, meadows, sandy woodlands and widespread in waste places, roadsides, railroads, overgrazed rangeland, and other disturbed places; FACU-. Grows up to 2 feet with whitish-green flowers in late summer and autumn, in sun to part shade in dry sandy soils.

Ambrosia trifida (Giant ragweed) [annual forb] — Considered invasive and noxious, a common cause of hay fever. Statewide, but especially east of the Allegheny front, in mesic to moist fields, prairies, meadows and disturbed ground, to seven feet or more in full sun to light shade with a preference for fertile, mesic, loamy soils, flowering in late summer to fall.

Amelanchier arborea (Shadbush) [tree/shrub] — swampy lowlands, dry open woodlands and sandy bluffs, rocky ridges, forest edges and fields, FAC-; statewide. Grows to 48 feet with white flowers in early spring on well-drained, medium to coarse, mesic to moist, moderately fertile loams at least 20 inches deep in sun to part shade. Somewhat anaerobic and drought tolerant, but intolerant of limestone soils; prefers soil pH from 4.8 to 7.9 and is shade tolerant.

Amelanchier bartramiana (Mountain juneberry) [tree/shrub] — widely scattered in northern Pennsylvania swamps, sphagnum bogs and peaty thickets; FAC and listed as endangered. Grows to 10 feet with white flowers in spring; prefers mesic to moist loams ranging from acidic to circumneutral, less than pH 6.8, in sun to light shade. Good for sunny edges or dappled shade. AKA *Amelanchier oligocarpa*.

Amelanchier canadensis (Shadbush) [tree/shrub] — moist upland woods and edges, bogs, and swamps, FAC. Mostly southeast, scattered elsewhere. Shrub or small tree growing to 20 feet on average, medium, well-drained, coarse to fine-tex-

Giant ragweed (*Ambrosia trifida*)

tured soils at least 20 inches deep with a pH of 5.5 to 7.5 in full sun to part shade. Tolerant of a somewhat wide range of soils and moderately tolerant of anaerobic conditions, drought and limestone soils. Often confused in the nursery trade with *A. arborea*. White flowers in spring.

Amelanchier humilis (Low juneberry) [tree/shrub] — dry open ground, rocky bluffs and lakeshores, FACU. Widely scattered, especially Allegheny Mountains. Shrub to 20 feet; sun to part shade in dry acidic sandy loam. White flowers in spring.

Amelanchier laevis (Allegheny serviceberry, or smooth serviceberry) [tree/shrub] — thickets, open woods, sheltered slopes, roadside banks and wood margins; statewide. Shrub or small tree to 45 feet with white flowers in spring; grows in full sun to part shade in average, mesic sandy loams. Tolerant of a wide range of soils, but prefers moist, well-drained, medium to coarse-textured loams at least 30 inches deep and with a pH of 4.8 to 7.0. Intolerant of anaerobic conditions or drought, but somewhat tolerant of limestone soils.

Amelanchier obovalis (Coastal juneberry) [shrub] — scattered in southeastern Pennsylvania in thickets and on peaty barrens; FACU. Grows 3 to 4 feet with white flowers in early spring, followed by edible red berries in early summer. Tolerant of a wide range of soils at least 24 inches deep, but intolerant of shade, anaerobic conditions or drought. Works well in masses with other large perennials.

Amelanchier stolonifera (Low juneberry) [tree/shrub] — woods, old fields, fence rows and barrens, FACU; statewide, especially northern end of Central Appalachians. Colonizing shrub to 6 feet; full sun to part shade in mesic to moist, well-drained soil in full sun to part shade. Tolerant of a wide range of soils. White flowers in spring.

Amianthium muscitoxicum (Fly-poison) [perennial forb] — Mesic to moist wooded slopes, meadows, savannas and barrens and bogs, generally in sandy or peaty soils (FAC), mostly northern Ridge and Valley, Piedmont. Grows 1 to 3 feet, with whitish-green flowers in late spring, in part shade in slightly acidic rich loams; tolerates seasonal flooding.

Ammannia coccinea (Tooth cup) [annual forb] — muddy pond shores and river flats, limestone quarries and grassy areas prone to occasional flooding, scattered southeast and listed as endangered, OBL. Grows to less than 12 inches with purple flowers in summer in full sun on moist to wet muddy soils; seeds germinate better if temporarily submerged in water, then left in the muddy soil. Tolerates disturbed wetlands.

Ammophila breviligulata (American beachgrass) [perennial graminoid] — Very rare on beaches and sand dunes on the Atlantic coast and along the Great Lakes; considered important in stabilizing dunes; Atlantic Coastal Plain and the Erie and Ontario Lake Plain. Grows 1 to 3 feet in full sun, dry to mesic conditions and on very sandy soil with a minimum depth of 20 inches and a pH between 5.8 and 7.8; intolerant of fine-textured soils, shade and anaerobic conditions. Quite tolerant of limestone soils, and moderately drought tolerant.

Amorpha fruticosa (False-indigo) [tree/shrub] — open woods, pond and stream edges, gravel bars in floodplains, roadsides, thickets, FACW; mostly southeast, scattered southwest. Grows 6 to 12 feet with violet to purple flowers in late spring. Grow in sun to part shade in moist sandy to clayey loams.

Amphicarpaea bracteata (Hog peanut) [perennial vine] — Mesic to wet woods, thickets, floodplains, low wooded areas and slopes along streams but also seeps and damp sandy meadows and prairies, usually in alluvium, statewide, FAC. Twining vine 3 to 6 feet, with pink to white flowers in late summer to early autumn with a preference for full sun to light shade and mesic to moist sandy loams.

Anaphalis margaritacea (Pearly everlasting) [perennial forb] — dry, sandy or gravelly soil of fields, woods, edges and roadsides; statewide, mostly north and east. Grows 1 to 3 feet, white flowers in late summer; average, medium, well-drained soil in full sun to part shade. Prefers full sun and somewhat dry, sandy conditions.

Andromeda polifolia var glaucophylla (Bog rosemary) [tree/shrub] — rare on moist to wet acidic peaty ground, OBL; mostly northeast, scattered northwest. Grows to 18 inches in part sun to part shade in acidic moist organic peats, sands and mucks. Pinkish-white flowers in spring.

Andropogon gerardii (Big bluestem) [perennial graminoid] — stream banks, roadsides, moist meadows, and prairies, FAC-; statewide. Grows 3 to 10 feet in sun to part sun in average, dry to medium, well to drained soils in full sun; prefers dry, infertile soil ranging from coarse to fine with a pH between 6.0 and 7.5 and a minimum depth of 20 inches. Prefers somewhat sterile soils that can be limestone-based and tolerates anaerobic conditions; intolerant of shade.

Andropogon glomeratus (Bushy bluestem) [perennial graminoid] — Moist meadows, swales and swamps, FACW+. Mostly southeast, especially Piedmont and Coastal Plain. Grows 2 to 5 feet, in full sun, in a wide range of moist to wet, relatively sterile soils with a pH between 5.0 and 6.3 at least 12 inches deep; poor drainage is helpful. Highly adaptable to anaerobic conditions, but intolerant of limestone soils, drought and shade.

Andropogon gyrans (Elliott's beardgrass) [perennial graminoid] — dry to moist open woodlands and fields, extreme southeastern Pennsylvania.

Andropogon virginicus (Broom sedge or bluestem) [perennial graminoid] — old fields, hillsides, and waste grounds, FACU; statewide except Allegheny Mountains and Northern Unglaciated Allegheny Plateau. Grows 20 to 60 inches in sun to part sun in dry to moist sandy to medium loams with a depth of 14 inches and pH between 4.9 and 7.0; avoid coarse-textured soils. Tolerant of limestone-based soils and drought tolerant, but intolerant of anaerobic conditions and shade.

Anemone canadensis (Canada anemone) [perennial forb] — moist thickets and open woodlands, meadows and wet prairies, clearings and the shores of lakes and streams; occasionally in swampy areas, mostly northwest, FACW. Grows 12 to18 inches with white flowers in early summer. Best in moist, humusy but well-drained soils in part shade; tolerates full sun. A very aggressive spreader (rhizomes and seed), ideal for naturalizing large areas, but a favorite browse of deer.

Anemone cylindrica (Thimbleweed) [perennial forb] — rare in dry open woods, prairies, pastures, roadsides. Listed as endangered in Pennsylvania. Grows 12 to 24 inches in sun to part shade in dry, rocky soils.

Anemone quinquefolia (Wood anemone) [perennial forb] — moist upland open woods and thickets, banks and shady roadsides, FACU; statewide. Grows 4 to 8 inches, white flowers in spring; part shade to shade in damp to moist rich loam, pH 5 to 6.

Anemone virginiana (Virginia anemone) [perennial forb] — upland rocky and dry open woods, slopes, thickets and prairies; statewide. Grows up to 12 inches, greenish-white flowers in early summer, followed by attractive seed pods that persist into fall; sun to part shade in dry to moist sandy loam.

Angelica atropurpurea (Purple-stemmed angelica) [perennial forb] — swamps, moist meadows, stream banks and wet woods, OBL; statewide except for higher elevations on the Allegheny Plateau and the central Appalachian ridges and valleys. Grows 3 to 10 feet, white flowers in summer; full sun to dappled shade in medium to wet soils.

Angelica triquinata (Filmy angelica) [perennial forb] — Floodplains, especially mountain stream banks, and wet woodlands (UPL), generally along the Allegheny Front. Grows 2 to 4 feet with white to greenish flowers in fall in mesic to moist humusy loam in sun to part shade; flowers are poisonous and can cause bees to appear intoxicated.

Angelica venenosa (Hairy angelica) [perennial forb] — dry to moist open woods, roadsides, banks, serpentine barrens and old fields; statewide, mostly south. Grows up to 6 feet, white flowers in midsummer; full sun to part shade in dry, sandy to gravelly loamy or sandy loams with decaying organic matter, generally circumneutral. Tolerates temporary standing water.

Antennaria howellii ssp. canadensis (Howell's pussytoe) [perennial forb] — Statewide in dry woodlands on slopes, ridges and cliffs, as well as along roadsides. Grows 1 to 3 feet with white flowers in spring, full sun on dry, sandy loams.

Antennaria neglecta (Overlooked pussytoe) [perennial forb] — mesic to dry prairies, slopes of upland open woodlands, dry meadows in woodland areas, savannas, shale glades, eroded clay banks, pastures, abandoned fields, and roadsides; mostly southeast. Grows up to 6 inches with brown/gray flowers in spring; sun to part sun in dry to moist clay loam, pH 5.5 to 7.5.

Antennaria parlinii (Parlin's pussytoe) [perennial forb] — open woods and fields; statewide, especially southeast (Piedmont). Grows up to 8 inches with white flowers in spring in sun to part sun in dry, sandy, well drained loam.

Antennaria plantaginifolia (Plantain-leaved pussytoe) [perennial forb] — dry open woods, pastures, fields, rocky barrens; statewide, especially Central Appalachians and Piedmont. Grows up to about 10 inches, white flowers in spring in sun to part sun in dry, sandy, well drained loam, pH 4 to 7.

Antennaria solitaria (Solitary pussytoe) [perennial forb] — Dry woodlands in southwestern Pennsylvania; endangered. Grows up to 10 inches with whitish flowers in spring in dry to mesic loams in part sun to part shade. Spreads by runners and can be used as a groundcover, especially on dry, shady slopes; avoid mulching.

Antennaria virginica (Shale-barren pussytoe) [perennial forb] — Dry, shaly barrens in the Allegheny Mountains (south-central counties) where it roots into rock crevices to form thick mats. Spreads slowly by runners to form silvery mats in dry, partly shady, poor soil, an ideal ground cover for such sites, including rock gardens. Prefers sun to part sun with southern to western exposure; blooms in spring on 15 inch stalks.

Apios americana (Ground-nut) [perennial vine] — moist to wet woods and floodplains, statewide; FACW. Twining, to 10 feet; pink flowers in summer. Sun to part shade in mesic to moist loam, any texture, with a pH range of 6.0 to 7.5 and moderate fertility. High anaerobic, shade and limestone soil tolerance, but intolerant of drought.

Aplectrum hyemale (Puttyroot) [perennial forb] — rich moist woods and bottomlands, FAC. Mostly southeast (Piedmont), scattered elsewhere. Grows 12 to 24 inches, purple flowers in early summer; part shade to shade in moist rich humus.

Apocynum androsaemifolium (Pink dogbane) [perennial forb] — well-drained upland forest sites, open hillsides and ridges, especially on dry, fresh, sandy and coarse loamy soils; statewide. Also found in clearings and fields, along forest margins, on roadsides and disturbed ground. Grows 8 to 32 inches, pink flowers in early summer; sun to part shade in dry, sandy loam, pH 5 to 6.

Indian hemp (Apocynum cannabinum)

Apocynum cannabinum (Indian hemp) [perennial forb] — upland open woods, pastures, waste ground, disturbed sites, wooded slopes, on roadsides and along railroads, FACU; statewide. Grows up to 5 feet with pink flowers in early summer; sun to part sun in dry to moist moderately fertile sandy loam, all textures, ranging in pH from 4.5 to 7.0 and a minimum of 12 inches deep. Moderately tolerant of anaerobic conditions, drought, shade and limestone-based soils.

Aquilegia canadensis (American columbine) [perennial forb] — statewide on open, steep, rocky wooded bluffs of streams and stream banks, wooded slopes of deep ravines, limestone bluffs and ledges, borders and clearings in deciduous or mixed woods or thickets, FAC. Grows up to 32 inches with yellow and red flowers in late spring in sun to part shade in average well-drained soil, pH 5 to 7. Prefers rich, moist soils in light to moderate shade, with pH of 6 to 7.

Arabis canadensis (Sicklepod) [biennial forb] — thinly wooded rocky banks, uplands and slopes, shaded cliffs, bluffs and sand dunes, areas along woodland paths, mostly southern Pennsylvania and scattered north. Grows 1 to 3 feet with whitish-green flowers in late spring to early summer in part sun to light shade and dry to mesic rocky or sandy soils; occasional wildfires are beneficial.

Arabis glabra (Towercress) [perennial forb] — fields, open woods, ledges, usually in dry soil. Pennsylvania distribution includes most eastern, northern and southwestern counties. Grows 16 to 40 inches, greenish-white flowers in late spring; part sun to shade in dry to moist rocky clay loam.

Arabis laevigata var. burkii (Smooth rockcress) [biennial forb] — mesic woodlands and ravines near streams and, dry slopes, bluffs and cliffs, typically on hilly sites dominated by deciduous trees, generally in the Appalachians, especially toward the south. Grows to about 42 inches with white flowers in spring in part sun to part shade on dry to mesic rocky loams.

Arabis lyrata (Lyre-leaved rockcress) [biennial forb] — statewide on serpentine barrens and dry, rocky outcrops and slopes, more common in the southeast, FACU statewide. Grows to 3 feet with white flowers in spring on dry to mesic gravelly or sandy loams.

Arabis missouriensis (Missouri rockcress) [annual forb] — rocky wooded slopes and ridges, including pine forests on sterile sand and gravel outwash plains, scattered in eastern Pennsylvania and listed as endangered. Grows to about 25 inches with white flowers in spring on rocky to sandy dry, acidic soils in part shade.

Aralia hispida (Bristly sarsaparilla) [perennial forb] — Statewide, but mostly northeast along roadsides and both dry woodlands and moist coves. Grows 1 to 3 feet with whitish-green flowers in summer in dry to moist sandy loams in full sun to shade; very drought tolerant.

Aralia nudicaulis (Wild sarsaparilla) [perennial forb] — dry, upland open woods and thickets with thin soil, FACU; statewide. Grows 12 to 36 inches, greenish flowers in spring; part sun to shade in dry to moist rich humus of all textures and moderate fertility, pH 5.0 to 7.2. Shade, drought and limestone-soil tolerant, but intolerant of anaerobic conditions and requires 10 inch soil depth.

Wild sarsaparilla (Aralia nudicaulis)

Aralia racemosa (Spikenard) [perennial forb] — statewide in rich wooded slopes, ravines, moist ledges and bluffs. Grows up to 6 feet with greenish flowers in early summer; part sun to part shade in moist rich humus.

Aralia spinosa (Devil's walking stick) [tree/shrub] — upland and low woods, thickets, stream edges, palustrine wetlands and savannas, FAC. Statewide, especially west. Grows to 32 feet; sun to part sun in well-drained fertile to poor soils of all textures, ranging from pH 4.8 to 6.6; prefers sites with fertile, deep, acidic, sandy peat soils at least 32 inches deep. Low anaerobic but high limestone tolerance. Aggressive spreader via suckers; intolerant of shade.

Arctostaphylos uva-ursi ssp. coactilis (Bearberry or kinnikinnick) [tree/shrub] — very rare in dry nutrient-poor soils, often in open pine forests during intermediate succession. Rang is scattered northeast and northwest, but listed as extirpated. Prostrate stems to about 6 inches high in sun to shade in dry to mesic uncompacted or loose rocky or sandy acidic soil, but not fine textured soils, with a pH ranging from 5.5 to 8.0. Intolerant of fertilizer and anaerobic conditions, but very drought tolerant and low fertility and moisture requirements. Pinkish white flowers in early spring.

Arethusa bulbosa ssp. leptoclados (Dragon's-mouth, swamp pink) [perennial forb] — Scattered in sphagnum bogs, fens, sedge meadows and coniferous swamps, with a preference for acidic, sandy, moist meadows. (OBL); endangered. Grows 3 to 14 inches with pinkish flowers in late spring; a native orchid in full to part sun.

Arisaema dracontium (Green-dragon) [perennial forb] — Wet to mesic deciduous woodlands, thickets, and bottoms; FACW. Scattered statewide, especially southeast. Grows 1 to 3 feet with green-brown flowers in late spring, similar to Jack-in-the-Pulpit. Prefers constantly moist soil rich in organic matter; does poorly in clay soils. Grows well in moist conditions along streams or ponds; part sun to part shade. Goes dormant in summer. Roots contain calcium oxalate and are poisonous in an uncooked state; handle roots and seed pods with great care.

Arisaema triphyllum (Jack-in-the-pulpit) [perennial forb] — moist low woods, swamps, bogs and floodplains, FACW-; statewide. Grows up to 36 inches, with the familiar greenish flowers in spring; part shade to full shade in constantly moist soil rich in organic matter at least 8 inches deep, pH 4.8 to 7, with a preference of 5.0 to 6.0. Avoid fine textured soils; low drought but moderate anaerobic tolerance and high fertility requirements. Roots contain calcium oxalate and are poisonous in an uncooked state; handle roots and seed pods with great care; gloves are suggested.

Aristida dichotoma (Povertygrass) [annual graminoid] — scattered statewide in clearings, sandy fields, granite outcrops and pine woodlands, UPL. Two varieties: *dichotoma* in the Applachians and eastward and *curtissii* more to the western part of the state. Grows to about two feet in sun to part sun in dry, sandy, sterile, acidic soils.

Aristida longespica (Slender threeawn) [annual graminoid] — sandy fields and clearing in pine and oak woodlands, UPL. Two varieties: *geniculata* is scattered in Northampton, Chester and Delaware counties, while *longespica* has a broader range in southeastern Pennsylvania. Grows to about 24 inches in dry, sterile, sandy, acidic soils in full to part sun.

Aristida oligantha (Prairie threeawn) [annual graminoid] — scattered south, mostly southeast, in gravel and sand prairies, glades, and overgrazed pastures and waste areas. Grows 1 to 3 feet in full sun on dry, sandy, calcareous or tight clayey soils; has value in soil erosion protection in loose-soil areas but no value as forage and seeds can create difficulties in sheep wool and with the eyes of sheep and cattle.

Aristida purpurascens (Arrow-feather) [perennial graminoid] — Rare in glades, fields, and pine savannas in sandy or clay soils, FAC. Southeast, especially Piedmont. Grows 15 to 30 inches in dry, sandy soils in full sun, but tolerates some shade.

Aristolochia macrophylla (Dutchman's pipe) [perennial vine] — rare on rugged rocky slopes and in rich, often dissected, upland forests; scattered southwest. Grows 20 to 30 feet in rich, well drained, moist soil in full sun to part shade; does not tolerate dry soils. To control growth, cut back in late winter.

Aristolochia serpentaria (Virginia snakeroot) [perennial forb] — rich, rocky upland woods, thickets, ravines and slopes, UPL; mostly south. Grows up to 20 inches, greenish-white flowers in spring; part shade to shade in dry to moist sandy loam.

Arnica acaulis (Leopard's-bane) [perennial forb] — Sandy pine woods and clearings, often in damp soils, chiefly on Atlantic Coastal Plain and in serpentine barrens. Grows 1 to 3 feet with yellow flowers in late spring in part shade in mesic to moist sandy soils.

Arnoglossum atriplicifolium (Pale Indian plantain) [perennial forb] — open woods, fields and on moist banks; statewide except northern tier. Grows up to 9 feet, yellow flowers in late summer and early fall; sun to part shade in dry to moist sandy loam, pH 4 to 5.5. AKA *Cacalia atriplicifolia*.

Arnoglossum reniforme (Great Indian-plantain) [perennial forb] — wet to mesic prairies and savannas. Scattered southwest and southeast. White flowers in summer; grows to 8 feet. Grow in full sun in moist, rich well-drained loam. AKA *Cacalia muhlenbergii*.

Aruncus dioicus (Goat's-beard, bride's feathers) [perennial forb] — moist, rich woods in mountainous areas, FACU; mostly southwest. White flowers in late spring; grows to 4 to 6 feet, open habit. Grow in part shade in rich, medium to wet well-drained soils; tolerates flooding. Often found in better garden centers.

Asarum canadense (Wild ginger) [perennial forb] — statewide in the understory of mesic to moist upland deciduous forests (rarely coniferous). Grows 6 to 12 inches with brownish-purple flowers in early spring; part shade to full shade in moist humus, pH 4 to 7. Slowly spreads by very shallow rhizomes to form large colonies; wilts if soil becomes too dry and burns in part sun. Not related to the culinary spice, but has been used as a substitute, hence the name.

Asclepias amplexicaulis (Blunt-leaved milkweed) [perennial forb] — dry fields and upland open woods, usually in sandy soil, nostly east and in the Central Appalachians. Grows 12 to 36 inches with greenish-pink flowers in summer in sun to part sun in dry, sandy loam.

Asclepias exaltata (Poke milkweed) [perennial forb] — statewide in rich upland woods and woods edges, FACU. Grows 12 to 32 inches with greenish-purple flowers in early summer; part shade to shade in dry to moist sandy loam, pH 5.5 to 7.

Asclepias incarnata (Swamp milkweed) [perennial forb] — floodplains and wet meadows, OBL; statewide. Grows up to 5 feet, pink-rose flowers in early summer; full to part sun in constantly moist, medium to fine-textured, rich loam with moderate fertility and a pH of 5.0 to 8.0, at least 16 inches deep. Very tolerant of anaerobic conditions and intolerant of drought or shady sites.

Asclepias quadrifolia (Four-leaved milkweed) [perennial forb] — dry woodlands and along roadsides, statewide. Grows up to 24 inches in sun to shade in dry to mesic, well drained, circumneutral soils; produces white-pink flowers in early summer.

Asclepias rubra (Red milkweed) [perennial forb] — Sphagnum bogs, marshy areas and pine barrens in the Piedmont, OBL. Grows 1 to 3 feet with pink-reddish flowers in spring in moist to wet, slightly acidic soils in sun to part shade.

Asclepias syriaca (Common milkweed) [perennial forb] — statewide in dry, upland woods edges fields and prairies. Host species for monarch butterflies. Grows 3 to 6 feet, very fragrant purple-whitish flowers in early summer; prefers sun to part sun in dry sandy loam, pH 4 to 7.

Asclepias tuberosa (Butterfly weed) [perennial forb] — dry fields, roadsides and shale barrens; statewide especially south. Grows 12 to 30 inches with orange-yellow flowers in early summer in sun to part shade. Prefers dry to medium wet, well drained sandy loam with low fertility, pH 4.5 to 6.8 and a minimum depth of 16 inches. Avoid anaerobic conditions; high drought tolerance and adaptable to limestone-based soils.

Asclepias variegata (White milkweed) [perennial forb] — upland dry or rocky woods, sandy open ground, ravine bottoms, low woods, slopes, ridges and along roadsides, FACU, endangered. Mostly southeast; grows up to 36 inches with white to pinkish flowers in early summer; sun to part shade in dry sandy loam.

Asclepias verticillata (Whorled milkweed) [perennial forb] — open woods, dry slopes, serpentine barrens on dry rocky sandy soil, mostly southeast. Grows 8 to 20 inches with white-greenish flowers in summer, sun to part sun, in sandy loam, pH 4.8 to 6.8.

Asclepias viridiflora (Green milkweed) [perennial forb] — dry rocky slopes, serpentine barrens, rocky prairies, glades; mostly south, especially southeast. Grows 12 to 32 inches with greenish flowers in summer in sun to part sun on dry, sandy loam.

Asimina triloba (Pawpaw) [tree/shrub] — Ravine slopes, stream banks and floodplains with deep, rich, moist soils ranging from sandy to loamy but not fine-textured. Grows 10 to 40 feet, FACU+; statewide except northern Allegheny plateaus. Average medium to wet soils but prefers acidic, fertile, moist soil at least 20 inches deep ranging from a pH of 4.7 to 7.2. Low anaerobic and drought tolerance; prefers sun to part shade, but becomes leggy in shade.

Asplenium montanum (Mountain spleenwort) [fern/ally] — statewide, but more common south, in moist, shady crevices of sandstone and other acidic rock on cliff, balds, ledges and ridges; erect rhizome, occasional branching.

Asplenium platyneuron (Ebony spleenwort) [fern/ally] — forest floor or on rocks, often invading masonry and disturbed dry to mesic soils. Fronds 8 to 18 inches; rhizome: short creeping to ascending. Grow in part shade to shade in dry to moist sandy clay loam, pH 5 to 7.5.

Asplenium resiliens (Black-stemmed spleenwort) [fern/ally] — rare on limestone cliffs and in sinkholes on calcareous rock, especially south-central areas and endangered. Fronds: several inches; rhizomes: erect. Grow in moist humusy soil over limestone rocks in part shade.

Asplenium ruta-muraria (Wall rue spleenwort) [fern/ally] — southern Pennsylvania from the Appalachians east in shaded calcareous, especially limestones and shales, ledges, cliffs, talus and boulders.

Asplenium trichomanes (Maidenhair spleenwort) [fern/ally] — acidic rocks such as sandstone, basalt, and granite, very rarely on calcareous rocks; not usually found in the northwest. Fronds 4 to 7 inches; rhizome: short creeping to ascending. Grow in part shade to shade in dry to moist rocky, humusy loam, pH 4 to 7.5. *Asplenium trichomanes ssp. quadrivalens* (Appressed maidenhair spleenwort) is found calcareous rocks, such as limestone and dolomite while *ssp. trichomanes* (Maidenhair spleenwort) grows in neutral to moderately acidic rocks, such as sandstone, granite and basalt.

Asplenium x ebenoides (Scott's spleenwort) [fern/ally] — widely scattered southeast; sterile hybrid of *Asplenium platyneuron × rhizophyllum,* and only present when both parents are found on shaded crevices of limestone or sandstone.

Athyrium filix-femina (Lady fern) [fern/ally] — wooded valleys along streams, on rich wooded slopes and on floors of ravines, swamps, moist meadows and thickets. Fronds 12 to 24 inches; rhizome: erect or ascending in clumps. Grow in part sun to part shade in mesic to moist, moderately fertile, rich sandy loam at least 12 inches deep and with a pH 4.5 to 7.0; avoid coarse or medium textured soils. Low anaerobic or drought tolerances. Available at many garden centers.

Atriplex prostrata (Halberd-leaved orach) [annual forb] — statewide in beaches, salt marshes, and low moist areas in both brackish and rich soils. Possibly introduced; grows up to 40 inches with greenish-white flowers in late summer; grow in moist to wet fertile well-drained loams.

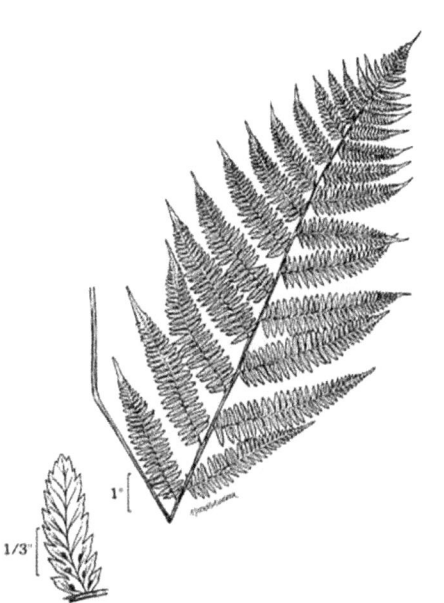

Lady fern (Athyrium filix-femina)

Aureolaria flava (False foxglove) [perennial forb] — parasitic on the roots of especially white oak (Quercus alba). Two varieties: *flava* (Smooth false-foxglove) is found statewide, especially southeast in dry, rocky, thickets and woodlands; *macrantha* (Yellow false-foxglove) is scattered in the Allegheny Plateau and prefers more mesic loamy soils. Grows to 40 inches in light to medium shade with yellow flowers in June; prefers dry to mesic loamy soils.

Aureolaria laevigata (False-foxglove) [perennial forb] — parasitic on the roots of especially white oak (Quercus alba); on the Allegheny plateau in dry, rocky, thickets and woodlands. Grows to 30 inches in part shade to shade in oak forests, with yellow flowers in summer.

Aureolaria pedicularia (Cut-leaf false-foxglove) [annual forb] — – Sandy, dry, open woodlands, edges and thickets, especially the Appalachians and southwest, almost always including oaks, preferably *Quercus velutina* (black oak) as a host plant. Grows to 40 inches with yellow flowers in late summer, with a preference for full sun and dry to mesic sandy soils with oaks nearby

Aureolaria virginica (Downy false-foxglove) [perennial forb] — dry open deciduous woods; statewide, especially southeast. Grows 20 to 60

inches, yellow flowers in late summer; part shade to shade in dry sandy loam, pH 4 to 6.

Baccharis halimifolia (Groundsel-tree) [tree/shrub] — mostly southeast and rare in marshes (including salt), beaches and other sandy places and disturbed sites such as wet fields and roadsides, FACW. Grows up to 10 feet with white flowers in late summer on circumneutral, mesic to wet, gravels to fine sands; wet sandy loams in sun to part shade, at least 20 inches deep, are preferred with pH from 5.5 to 7.8. High anaerobic but low drought and limestone tolerances, and shade is somewhat tolerated.

Baptisia australis (Blue false-indigo) [perennial forb] — Mostly western Pennsylvania in edges of woods, prairies and limestone glades in circumneutral soils. Grows 36 to 48 inches with late spring purple flowers in well drained, dry to medium circumneutral soils in full sun (best) to part shade. Drought and poor-soil tolerant.

Baptisia tinctoria (Wild indigo) [perennial forb] — dry, open woods and clearings in sandy soil; statewide except north central and northeastern counties. Grows up to 36 inches, yellow flowers in summer; sun to part shade in dry to moist medium to coarse-textured sandy loam, a minimum of 16 inches deep, with a pH of 5.8 to 7. Although it prefers low-fertility, acidic soils, limestone-based soils and drought are well tolerated. Avoid anaerobic conditions.

Bartonia paniculata (Screwstem) [annual forb] — acidic seeps and fens, wet woodlands including bogs, sphagnum pond margins, OBL, mostly southeastern Pennsylvania. Grows to 15 inches with yellowish flowers in late summer to fall, part sun to part shade, in decomposing organic matter.

Downy false-foxglove (Aureolaria virginica)

Bartonia virginica (Bartonia, yellow screwstem) [annual forb] — sphagnum bogs, moist to wet meadows, conifer swamps and peaty swales, FACW, scattered statewide. Grows 4 to 16 inches in sun to part shade in moist to wet, acidic peaty and humusy soils with white to yellow flowers in late summer.

Betula alleghaniensis (Yellow birch) [tree] — statewide on stream banks, swampy woods, and rich, moist, forested slopes, FAC. Grows to 100 feet; well-drained fertile loams and moderately well-drained sandy loams at least 30 inches deep, especially inceptisols and alfisols of all textures, with a pH range of 4.0 to 8.0. Intolerant of anaerobic and limestone-soil conditions.

Betula lenta (Sweet birch) [tree] — statewide on rich, moist, cool forests, especially on protected slopes, to rockier, more exposed sites especially on inceptisols and ultisols, FACU. Grows to 80 feet; part shade to shade in dry to moist slightly acidic rich, moist, well drained soil, medium to coarse textured and at least 28 inches deep. Preference is to soils with a pH between 4.5 and 6.5, but accepts pH as low as 3.0 and as high as 6.8; intolerant of shade. Moderate anaerobic tolerance, but none for limestone-based soils and drought.

Betula nigra (River birch) [tree] — mostly southeast on alluvial, often clay, soils on lowlands, floodplains, stream banks, and lake margins. Typically on sandbars and new land near streams, inside natural levees or fronts. Sometimes found on scattered upland sites, FACW. Grows to 100 feet in alluvial clay soils at least 20 inches deep in full sun to part sun with high soil moisture, with a strong preference for entisols and tolerates coarse-textured soils. Soil can be well or poorly drained as long as it is at or near field capacity year round. Can grow in highly acidic (pH less than 4.0) soils, but prefers 4.5 to 6.5 and is intolerant of shade.

Betula papyrifera (Paper birch) [tree/shrub] — moist open upland forests, especially on rocky slopes, and sometimes in swampy woods, FACU. Mostly northeast and scattered elsewhere. Grows to 100 feet in sun to part sun in moist mineral-organic soil, especially inceptisols and entisols at least 24 inches deep with pH between 4.2 and 7.4, but prefers cooler north to northeast facing slopes with slow drainage and little competition and pH between 5.0 and 6.5. Low tolerance for anaerobic, limestone soils and drought.

Bidens beckii (Beck's water-marigold) [perennial forb] — still or slow-moving waters in usually calcareous lakes and swamps, widely scattered in glaciated areas and listed as endangered in Pennsylvania.

Bidens bidentoides (Swamp beggar-ticks) [annual forb] — on the Atlantic Coastal Plain on stream banks, estuaries, tidal shores, sandy bogs and mud flats, FACW+, listed as threatened. Grows to 3 feet with white-yellow flowers in late summer and autumn on moist to wet, sandy to muddy soils in sun to part sun.

Bidens bipinnata (Spanish needles) [annual forb] — — across southern Pennsylvania, especially southeast, in mesic rocky woodlands, shale barrens and fallow fields and roadside banks, south, especially southeast. Grows to 60 inches with white to yellow flowers in late summer to autumn in part sun to dappled shade in fertile, mesic to moist loams.

Bidens cernua (Bur-marigold) [annual forb] — Swamps, seeps, bogs, marshes, river and pond edges, soggy meadows in floodplains, including both quality and degraded wetlands, statewide, OBL. Grows 6 to 36 inches, with yellow flowers in late summer; prefers full to part sun, mesic to wet, circumneutral somewhat fertile mucky clay, loam and sandy soils at least 8 inches deep with a pH between 5.1 and 7.0. Tolerates some shade, but not drought and can handle some anaerobic conditions.

Bidens connata (purplestem beggar-ticks) [annual forb] — statewide, especially southeast, in marshes, stream banks, swamps, bogs, moist meadows and in muddy areas of seasonal wetlands, FACW+. Grows 1 to 4 feet with yellow flowers in late summer to fall in full sun to part shade on moist to wet loams, silty loams and clay loams at least 8 inches deep with a pH of 5.2 to 7.1

Bidens discoidea (Small beggar-ticks) [annual forb] — swamps, low riparian areas, lake and pond shores, bogs, vernal ponds, limestone sinkholes, FACW, scattered south-central and east but more common in the northeast. Grows 12 to 30 inches, yellow summertime flowers, in full to part sun on moist to wet circumneutral loam soils high in decaying organic matter, with a pH of 5.1 to 7.1 and at least 8 inches deep; tolerates brief standing water.

Bidens frondosa (Devil's beggar-ticks) [annual forb] — moist meadows and openings near woodlands, floodplains, thickets, ponds and lakes, as well as swamps, marshes and seeps, statewide but less common far northwest; FACW. Grows 1 to 3 feet with yellow flowers in late summer. in full sun to light shade, in organic, moist fertile soils of medium to coarse texture ranging in pH from 5.2 to 7.2 and at least 8 inches deep; a strong preference for disturbed sites and occasional flooding and low tolerance for drought.

Bidens laevis (Showy bur-marigold) [annual forb] — marshes, wet meadows, stream and pond edges, OBL, mostly southeast. Grows 1 to 3 feet with yellow flowers in late summer into autumn in sun to part shade on moist to wet sandy to clayey loams 8 inches deep ranging in pH from 5.0 to 7.0. Moderate anaerobic but low drought tolerance.

Bidens tripartita (Beggar-ticks) [annual forb] — statewwide in wet fields, marshes, stream banks and pond edges, FACW. Grows 6 to 60 inches with yellow flowers in late summer to autumn in sun to part sun in moist to wet sandy, loamy or clayey soils, such as bog gardens, at least 8 inches deep with a pH range of 5.0 to 7.2. Moderate anaerobic, but low drought, tolerance.

Bidens vulgata (Beggar-ticks) [annual forb] — statewide in moist woodlands including edges and path margins, thickets, floodplain meadows and riverbanks, swamps, marshes and seasonal wetlands.

Grows 1 to 3 feet with yellow flowers in late summer in full sun to light shade, in moist to wet loam or silt loam, with fertility impacting size.

Blephilia ciliata (Wood-mint) [perennial forb] — Swamps, thin woods, meadows, limestone bluffs, woodland slopes and calcareous hillsides. Mostly west (Western Glaciated and Southern Allegheny Plateaus). Grows 9 to 18 inches, lavender flowers in summer; prefers average, dry to mesic, circumneutral, well-drained soils in full sun to part shade.

Blephilia hirsuta (Wood-mint) [perennial forb] — Mesic to moist woodlands, especially along paths, borders and openings and in limestone glades, scattered statwide but mostly southwest, FACU-. Grows 2 to 4 feet with white-blue flowers in summer, with a preference for part sun to light shade, moist to mesic rich, loamy circumneutral to limestone-based soil with decaying leaf mold.

Boehmeria cylindrica (False nettle) [perennial forb] — deciduous moist alluvial woodlands and stream edges, bogs, wet meadows, marshes and swamps (FACW+). Two varieties: *cylindrica* is found statewide while *drummondiana* is more scattered except for the southeast. Grows 2 to 3 feet with white flowers in late summer in light shade on rich, loamy soils at leat 14 inches deep, with a pH of 5.1 to 7.0. Shade tolerant, but avoid coarse-textured, limestone-based or droughty soils.

Boltonia asteroides (Aster-like boltonia) [perennial forb] — very rare and endangered in moist to wet, gravelly to sandy rocky shores and river beds in full to part sun; FACW. Observed in Dauphin, York and Lancaster counties. Grow in well-drained, medium soils, toward dryer and less fertile soils. Rich moist soils will result in plants that tend to flop and need support; poor dry soils will result in shorter plants with smaller flowers. Grows to about 80 inches in all but fine-textured soils with a pH of 5.3 to 7.0 at least 12 inches deep. Low drought tolerance, but accepts anaerobic conditions.

Botrychium dissectum (Cut-leaved grape-fern) [fern/ally] — statewide in moderately acidic soils in a wide range of habitats from moist open woodlands to meadows and barrens; can also grow in relatively deep forest; FAC. Grows in part sun to part shade in dry to mesic rocky loams.

Botrychium lanceolatum ssp. angustisegmentum (Triangle moonwort) [fern/ally] — statewide, but concentrated north in moist, cool humus-rich woodlands and hummocks; FACW. Grow in medium to fine textured, moderatelu fertile soils at least 10 inches deep, with a pH of 4.4 to 6.0, in part shade to shade. Intolerant of drought and limestone-based soils.

Botrychium matricariifolium (Daisy-leaved moonwort) [fern/ally] — statewide except south central in subacidic to circumneutral soils of humus-rich, moist secondary growth woodlands and edges. Grows to about 12 inches in part sun to part shade on mesic to moist slightly acidic loams high in decomposing matter, often in secondary growth forests and woodlands.

Botrychium multifidum (Leathery grape fern) [fern/ally] — scattered far east, especially northeast, and west on moist, subacidic soils in meadows, barrens and thickets; FACU. Grow in sun to part shade in rich, mesic sites. AKA *Sceptridium multifidum*.

Botrychium oneidense (Blunt-lobed grape fern) [fern/ally] — scattered statewide except far southeast in acidic, moist, woodlands and shady swamps, FAC. Prefers rich, moist to wet soils less than pH 6.8 in sun to part shade; grows to about 12 inches. Adaptable to wetlands.

Botrychium simplex (Least moonwort) [fern/ally] — scattered east and northwest in subacidic to circumneutral soils of moist woodlands, marshes, bogs, swamps, dry fields and barrens; FACU. Grows up to an inch in height in sun to part sun.

Botrychium virginianum (Rattlesnake fern) [fern/ally] — moist shaded forests, wooded slopes and shrubby second growth, rare or absent in arid regions. Fronds 6 to 20 inches, rhizome: erect, subterranean. Grow in part shade to shade in mesic to slightly dry rich sandy loam, pH 5.6 to 6.9, at least 10 inches deep. Avoid very coarse or very fine textured soils; intolerant of drought and anaerobic conditions, as well as limestone-based soils.

Bouteloua curtipendula (Side-oats grama) [perennial graminoid] — rare in prairies, fields, forest openings, open rocky slopes; widely scattered. Clump-forming; grows to 3 feet in dry to medium moisture average soils in full sun; tolerates many soils from well-drained sandy loams to heavy clays.

Brachyelytrum erectum (Bearded shorthusk) [perennial graminoid] — moist to dry deciduous woods and thickets, occasionally over limestone bedrock; statewide. Grows 20 to 40 inches; part shade, in mesic soil containing loam, sandy loam, or some rocky material.

Brasenia schreberi (Purple wendock) [perennial forb] — aquatic; ponds, lakes, and sluggish streams, with pink to yellow flowers in summer; ponds with intermediate to low nutrient values, OBL. Mostly northeast (Northern Glaciated Allegheny Plateau), scattered elsewhere. Grow in full sun to part shade in still to slow moving standing water.

Brickellia eupatorioides var. eupatorioides (False boneset) [perennial forb] — rocky, dry slopes, especially limestone, and shale barrens, scattered in southern Pennsylvania. Grows 1 to 3 feet in full sun to part shade on poor sandy to gravelly, often circumneutral and alluvial, soils with white flowers in late summer.

Bearded shorthusk (*Brachyelytrum erectum*)

Bromus altissimus (Bromegrass) [perennial graminoid] — shaded or open woods, along stream banks, and on alluvial plains and slopes, FACW; statewide. AKA *Bromus latigumus*; part sun to part shade in moist, sandy loam.

Bromus ciliatus (Fringed brome) [perennial graminoid] — damp meadows, thickets, woods and stream banks, FACW. Mostly northeast, scattered elsewhere. Grows 24 to 60 inches; sun to part shade in somewhat sterile sandy loam at least 16 inches deep with a pH range of 5.5 to 7.5. Prefers coarse or fine soils, including limestone-based soils, but not those with medium texture and intolerant of both anaerobic and drought conditions.

Bromus kalmii (Bromegrass) [perennial graminoid] — sandy, gravelly, or limestone soils in open woods and calcareous fens, FACU. Scattered statewide, mostly east. Grows 20 to 40 inches in part sun to part shade in dry to moist somewhat sterile rocky, sandy loam at least 8 inches deep with a pH of 5.7 to 7.0. Avoid fine-textured soils and anaerobic conditions, but limestone-based soils are tolerated.

Bromus pubescens (Canada brome) [perennial graminoid] — Statewide in shaded, moist, often upland deciduous woodlands and savannas, especially along rivers, but also common in thickets, woodland borders and swamp edges and rarely in open areas. Grows 24 to 60 inches in part sun to part shade on mesic to moist sandy to silt loams.

Bulbostylis capillaris (Sandrush) [annual graminoid] — statewide on sandy savannas and prairies, calcarous outcrops and sandy waste ground FACU. Grows less than 12 inches with flowering in late summer to fall in dry to moist sandy loams in full to part sun.

Cakile edentula (American sea-rocket) [annual forb] — Coastal areas of Lake Erie and Atlantic Coastal Plain on sandy beaches, but sometimes gravelly to rocky shorelines. Grows 6 to 20 inches with white flowers, spring to fall, in full sun on very sandy dry to mesic soils, but tolerates wetland conditions.

Calamagrostis canadensis (Canada bluejoint) [perennial graminoid] — wet sedge meadows and prairies, bogs, fens, swales and swamps; two varieties, canadensis (more common) and macouniana, FACW; statewide. Grows 24 to 60 inches; sun to part sun in rich moist to wet loam, and tolerates temporary standing water.

Calamagrostis porteri (Porter's reedgrass) [perennial graminoid] — open dry to mesic woodlands and edges in the Ridge and Valley section, especially south-central Pennsylvania. Callitriche heterophylla (Water-starwort) [perennial forb] — statewide aquatic in slow streams and ponds and on muddy shorelines, OBL. Prefers medium to fine textured soils with a pH of 5.2 to 6.8 in full to part sun.

Callitriche palustris (Water-starwort) [perennial forb] — statewide aquatic in swamps, ponds, bottoms of streams and along muddy shorelines, OBL. Grows in a wide range of soils with a pH from 5.2 to 6.8 in full to part sun.

Callitriche terrestris (Water-starwort) [annual forb] — semi-aquatic in pond edges and stream margins, but also damp woods, and gravelly seeps, FACW, both southwest and southeast. Grows less than 12 inches in mesic to moist, well drained soils in part sun to part shade on water feature edges. Prefers compacted soil containing clay, till or rocky material. Greenish flowers from late spring to midsummer.

Calopogon tuberosus (Grass-pink) [perennial forb] — bogs, fens and wet meadows, pine and oak savannas, grasslands and swales, FACW+; mostly east, scattered elsewhere. Grows 12 to 30 inches with pink-purple and yellow flowers in summer; sun to part sun in wet, rich sandy acidic loam.

Caltha palustris (Marsh marigold) [perennial forb] — wet woods, stream banks, muddy meadows, OBL; statewide. Grows up to about 15 inches with yellow to white flowers in spring and early summer; sun to part shade in wet, muddy humus rich loam.

Calycanthus floridus var. laevigatus (Carolina allspice) [tree/shrub] — rare in deciduous and mixed woodlands, along streams and rivers, and woodland margins, FACU+; widely scattered statewide. Grows 6 to 10 feet, reddish-purple flowers in early summer; full sun to part shade in well-drained, medium moisture, average soil; prefers rich loams, and will grow taller in shade than in sun. Tends to sucker and will form colonies in the wild. A variety, var. floridus is introduced and has escaped cultivation, southwest.

Calystegia sepium (Hedge bindweed) [perennial vine] — Herbaceous vine in woodland edges, fields, waste ground (FAC-). Grows to 10 feet with morning-glory-like white to pink flowers in full to part sun, mesic to moist, gravelly to sandy soils.

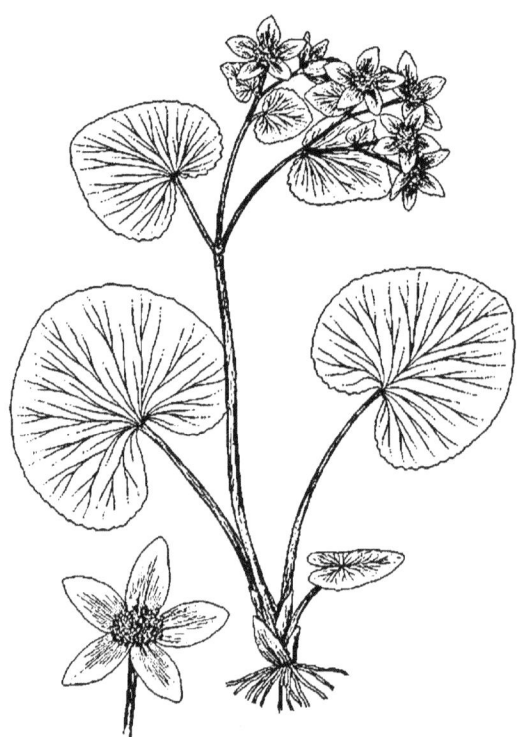

Marsh marigold (Caltha palustris)

Calystegia silvatica ssp. fraterniflora (Bindweed) [perennial vine] — scattered statewide on stream banks, fields, roadsides and moist waste ground; reputed to be an aggressive spreader with morning-glory-like white to pink flowers and possibly introduced.

Calystegia spithamaea ssp. spithamaea (Low bindweed) – [perennial vine] — Herbaceous vine on shale barrens, dry slopes and open ground such as gravel, hill and upland sand prairies, rocky woodlands and limestone glades, mostly southern Pennsylvania. Relatively short-growing, with white to pink flowers in late spring to early summer; spreads by rhizomes. Grow in full sun in dry sandy to rocky soils; presence indicates a high-quality prairie.

Camassia scilloides (Wild hyacinth, Atlantic camas) [perennial forb] — very rare in mesic to moist prairies and meadows as well as open weeds; FAC. Mostly southwestern counties and listed as endangered. Grows 1 to 2 feet with white flowers in spring; prefers moderately fertile, moist but well-drained limestone-based sandy loam at least 10 inches deep, but adapts to soil with a pH ranging from 4.2 to 6.5. Avoid coarse-textured soils and anaerobic and droughty conditions. Green in spring only, then dormant for the year.

Campanula americanum (Tall bellflower) [annual forb] — Stream banks, moist woodlands, rocky wooded slopes, statewide except northern tier, but concentrated in the southern two-thirds of the state, FAC-. Grows 3-6 feet with showy blue flowers in summer and often used to naturalize in the garden in masses. Prefers light shade to part sun (especially afternoons) in rich, well-drained, mesic to moist, loamy soils, and an even moisture supply.

Campanula aparinoides (Marsh bellflower) [perennial forb] — swamps, seeps and moist shores, mostly eastern Pennsylvania, OBL. Grows 18 to 24 inches with pale blue flowers in summer; full to part sun in mesic to moist rich soil of all textures, a minimum depth of 8 inches, and a pH range of 6.0 to 7.5.

Campanula rotundifolia (Harebell) [perennial forb] — dry, rocky upland slopes, prairies, savannas in association with Black Oak, rocky stream edges, bluffs and cliffs, often in crevices of dolomite, limestone or sandstone, FACU. Mostly east and scattered throughout the Central Appalachians. Grows up to 6 feet with blue flowers in summer in sun to shade on dry to mesic, rocky, sandy often shallow loam, pH 5 to 7. In the wild, an indicator of high quality habitat.

Camptosorus rhizophyllus (Walking fern) [fern/ally] — shaded, usually moss-covered boulders and ledges, usually on limestone or other basic rocks, but occasionally on sandstone or other acidic rocks, rarely on fallen tree trunks; not so common in the northwest. Fronds 4 to 10 inches; rhizome: ascending. Grow in part shade to shade in dry to moist calcareous loam, pH 6.5 to 7.5.

Cardamine angustata (Toothwort) [perennial forb] — Moist woodlands and thickets on ridges and bottomlands, especially floodplains, shady ravines, streambeds (FACU). Grows 12 to 18 inches with white flowers in spring; prefers rich mesic to moist bottomland soils high in organic matter.

Cardamine bulbosa (Bittercress) [perennial forb] — Wet ground including shallow water, floodplains, stream banks, marshes, swamps and meadows, OBL, statewide except extreme north central counties. Prefers moderately fertile medium to fine textured soils in part sun to shade, at least 10 inches deep with a pH range of 5.0 to 6.8. Intolerant of drought, but suitable for occasionally anaerobic conditions.

Cardamine concatenata (Toothwort) [perennial forb] — Rich, mesic woodlands, including rocky banks and floodplains, especially moist areas with leaf litter, statewide except extreme north central counties; OBL. Grows 12 to 18 inches with white flowers in spring in full sun to part shade in rich, mesic to moist bottomland soils.

Cardamine diphylla (Crinkleroot toothwort) [perennial forb] — rich woods and floodplains, FACU; mostly north and west on the Allegheny plateau. Grows up to 12 inches with white flowers in spring in sun to part shade on moist to wet humus-rich loam.

Cardamine douglassii (Purplecress) [perennial forb] — Rich woodlands with calcareous springs, low wooded valleys, mesic bottomland forests, rocky hillsides, floodplains, bog seepages, generally western Pennsylvania; OBL. Grows 4-12 inches with white-lavender flowers in mid-spring, preferring dappled sunlight under deciduous trees in fertile loams with substantial leaf mold, especially where limestone is near the surface. Among the species most vulnerable to the spread of *Alliaria petiolata* (garlic mustard).

Cardamine maxima (Large toothwort) [perennial forb] — Very rare in rich woods, shady ravines, ledges steep forested slopes and moist alluvial bottoms and banks. Scattered, mostly central to west. Grows 1 to 3 feet with purple flowers in spring; prefers part shade to shade in rich, humusy soil.

Cardamine parviflora var. arenicola (Small-flowered bittercress) [annual forb] — stream banks, rocky crests, ledges and outcrops, dry woods and meadows, glades, limestone barrens, edges of swamps and marshes, floodplains, FACU, generally southern Pennsylvania. Grows 6 to 15 inches with white flowers in spring on dry to moist loams, sandy loams, including rocky material. Prefers full sun to light shade.

Cardamine pensylvanica (Pennsylvania bittercress) [Annual/Biennial Forb] — statewide in mesic to wet deciduous woodlands, especially floodplains and bottomlands, shady seeps and springs, swamps, low riparian areas, lake margins and stream edges, OBL. Grows to 30 inches with white flowers in part sun to part shade on moist to wet loams and sandy loams high in decaying organic matter.

Cardamine pratensis (Cuckoo-flower) [perennial forb] — swamps, wet meadows and alluvial woods, OBL. Scattered north and east. Grows 8 to 20 inches with white to pink flowers in spring in full sun to part shade on cool, mesic to moist soils.

Cardamine rotundifolia (Mountain watercress) [perennial forb] — stream edges and banks, springs and seepage areas, swamps and low woodlands, including wet, rocky areas; statewide except northeast, OBL. Prefers somewhat acidic sites in part sun to part shade in a wide range of moist to wet soils, including standing water. Ideal for ponds and bog gardens; leaves are edible.

Carex adusta (Crowded sedge) [perennial graminoid] — acidic, sandy, dry soils along shores and in open woods and clearings; reported only in Northampton County and listed as extirpated.

Carex aestivalis (Summer sedge) [perennial graminoid] — scattered statewide, but mostly north, in dry to mesic forests, including seepage slopes, and mountain meadows.

Carex aestivalis x gracillima (Sedge) [perennial graminoid] — widely scattered statewide on wooded slopes, mostly eastern Pennsylvania; a naturally-occurring hybrid.

Carex aggregata (Glomerate sedge) [perennial graminoid] — prefers calcareous soils in meadows, thickets and moist open forests in southern Pennsylvania, especially Piedmont, FACU.

Carex alata (Broad-winged sedge) [perennial graminoid] — Rare in sedge meadows, bog margins, swampy woods, often on hummocks; reported on both acidic and calcareous soils, OBL. Mostly northwest. Grows 1.5 to 2 feet in full sun to part shade; prefers peaty, moist to wet soils and may go dormant in summer if soil is not consistently moist. Good for water or bog gardens, or in wet soils adjacent to streams and ponds.

Carex albicans var. albicans (Whitetinge sedge) [perennial graminoid] — prefers acidic, dry sandstone and granitic soils but also found in calcareous regions, statewide, under deciduous and cedar trees on wooded slopes and clearings, especially on sandstone ridges, statewide, especially southeast.

Carex albolutescens (Greenwhite sedge) [perennial graminoid] — statewide, especially east, except northern tier counties in acidic swamps, low moist to wet woodland, thickets and meadows; FACW.

Carex albursina (White bear sedge) [perennial graminoid] — On steep slopes and around limestone escarpments in moist beech-maple and mixed deciduous forests; occasionally under oaks or oak-hickory; UPL. Scattered statewide. Grows 12 inches in light to medium shade and moist to slightly dry sites with some organic matter and some protection from wind.

Carex amphibola (Eastern narrowleaf sedge) [perennial graminoid] — statewide, especially southeast, in dry to mesic upland deciduous forests and meadows; prefers acidic floodplain loams and slopes above streams. Grows 8 to 12 inches in part shade to shade.

Carex annectens (Yellowfruit sedge) [perennial graminoid] — dry to moist, often calcareous soils in open habitats and wet meadows, FACW; statewide. Grows 16 to 40 inches; sun to part sun in dry to moist sandy loam.

Carex appalachica (Appalachian sedge) [perennial graminoid] — dry to mesic deciduous or mixed forests, usually on sandy or rocky soils. Mostly east, scattered elsewhere except Central Appalachians. Grows 8 to 24 inches; part sun to part shade in dry to moist rocky sandy loam; an excellent species to suggest flowing water on slopes.

Carex aquatilis (Water sedge) [perennial graminoid] — Rare in shallow water along shores and in marshes, commonly over neutral to calcareous substrates, OBL. Widely scattered statewide. Grows 1 to 3 feet in sun to part shade, typically in wet soil to standing water; good for wetland restoration projects.

Carex argyrantha (Hay sedge) [perennial graminoid] — dry and rocky (especially sandstone) woods and clearings; statewide. Grows 12 to 40 inches; part shade to shade in dry rocky sandy loam.

Carex atherodes (Awned sedge) [perennial graminoid] — Rare in wet prairies and meadows, marshes, wet thickets, and open sites near streams, ponds and lakes, sometimes in water up to 20 inches deep, OBL. Widely scattered statewide; endangered. Grows 12 to 40 inches in sun to part shade in rich, consistently moist to wet sites.

Carex atlantica ssp. capillacea (Prickly bog sedge) [perennial graminoid] — swamps, bogs, and along shores, OBL; mostly southeast (Piedmont), scattered elsewhere. Grows 4 to 40 inches; part sun to part shade in moist silty loam.

Carex aurea (Golden-fruited sedge) [perennial graminoid] — Rare in open to shaded moist habitats, typically meadows and seepage slopes and most often on calcareous soils, FACW. Mostly northwest (Erie and Ontario Lake Plain); endangered. Grows up to 20 inches and prefers part shade and moist alkaline soils.

Carex backii (Back's sedge) [perennial graminoid] — over calcareous to acidic substrates on rocky, dry, open to shaded slopes, ridges and barrens, typically in hardwood, mixed or coniferous forests including pine plantations; reported only in northern Lackawanna County in rocky woods at the base of a sandstone ledge and listed as extirpated in Pennsylvania.

Carex baileyi (Bailey's sedge) [perennial graminoid] — sandy, peaty, or gravelly pond, lake, and stream shores, meadows, swamps, seeps, ditches, usually in acidic soils, OBL; statewide except southeast (Central Appalachians and Piedmont). Grows 8 to 28 inches; part sun to part shade in moist to wet, rich, silty loam.

Carex barrattii (Barratt's sedge) [perennial graminoid] — prefers soils over acidic substrata in bogs, swamps and wet woods, OBL; reported only in Delaware County and listed as extirpated in Pennsylvania and of concern nationally.

Carex bebbii (Bebb's sedge) [perennial graminoid] — rare in wet places with calcareous or neutral soils, gravelly lakeshores, stream banks, meadows and forest seeps, OBL; northwest (Erie and Ontario Lake Plain) and east (Hudson Valley Section). Grows 8 to 32 inches; sun to part shade in moist rich loam.

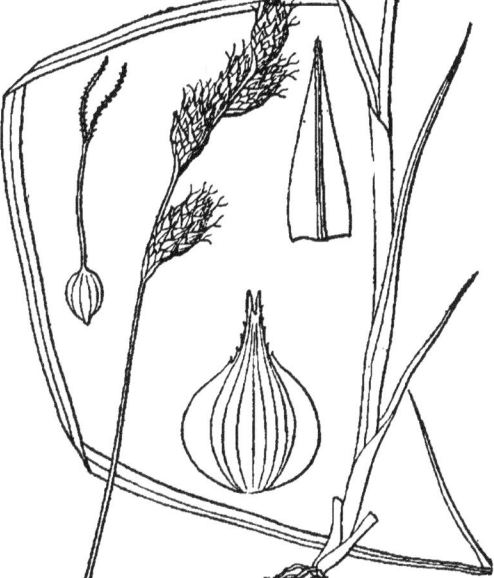

Bicknell's sedge (Carex bicknellii)

Carex bicknellii (Bicknell's sedge) [perennial graminoid] — rare in dry woods, thickets, fields and barrens. Mostly east (Piedmont, Delaware River Valley). Grows 12 to 48 inches; sun to part shade in dry to mesic sandy loam.

Carex blanda (Eastern woodland sedge) [perennial graminoid] — swamps, bottomlands and mesic to dry woods, including lawns, roadsides and stream banks, FAC; statewide, mostly southeast (Piedmont and Central Appalachians). Grows 6 to 24 inches; sun to part shade in dry to mesic rich sandy loam.

Carex brevior (Sedge) [perennial graminoid] — prairies, meadows, open woods, dry road banks, often in calcareous or neutral soils. Mostly southeast (Piedmont). Grows 12 to 40 inches; sun to part shade in dry to mesic rich sandy loam.

Carex bromoides (Brome-like sedge) [perennial graminoid] — wet hardwood forests, wooded floodplains and swamps, occasionally wet meadows and marsh edges, FACW; statewide. Grows 10 to 32 inches; part sun to part shade in moist, rich humusy loam.

Carex brunnescens (Brownish sedge) [perennial graminoid] — prefers moist, temporarily dry areas on thin peaty soils in thickets, woodlands, rocky slopes and heaths, FACW, generally northern Pennsylvania.

Carex bullata (Bull Sedge) [perennial graminoid] — prefers acidic soils in open swamp forests and seeps, bogs and boggy meadows, peat to sand ponds and lakeshores, OBL; widely scattered, mostly southeastern Pennsylvania and listed as endangered.

Carex bushii (Bush's Sedge) [perennial graminoid] — dry to moist upland woods, thickets, and fields, FACW. Mostly southeast (Piedmont, Central Appalachians); scattered elsewhere. Grows 10 to 36 inches; medium to moist soils in full sun to part shade.

Carex buxbaumii (Bauxbaum's sedge) [perennial graminoid] — calcareous swamps, swales, wet meadows, marshes, and fens, OBL. Mostly southeast (Piedmont); widely scattered elsewhere. Grows 10 to 40 inches; sun to part sun in moist to wet silty loam, circumneutral soils.

Carex canescens var. canescens (Bog silvery sedge) [perennial graminoid] — prefers wet and generally acidic habitats such as sphagnum bogs, swamps, marshes, meadows, shorelines and coniferous forests and meadows, OBL; scattered statewide but especially north. Grows 6 to 24 inches, sun to part shade. Two varieties: *canescens* (Bog silvery sedge) and *disjuncta* (Silvery sedge).

Carex careyana (Carey's sedge) [perennial graminoid] — widely scattered in western Pennsylvania in calcareous, moist, rich deciduous to conifer-deciduous forest, mostly on slopes; prefers limestone escarpments and adjacent rocky woodlands, washes, sinks and cave entrances and is listed as endangered in Pennsylvania.

Carex caroliniana (Carolina sedge) [perennial graminoid] — across southern Pennsylvania, especially Piedmont and coastal plain, in meadows, fields, thickets and moist woodlands; FACU. Grows to about 30 inches in a wide variety of soils, especially suitable for mesic to wet flatwoods, prairies, swamps and seeps in sun to part sun.

Carex cephaloidea (Thinleaf sedge) [perennial graminoid] — neutral to basic soils on dry to moist deciduous to mixed forests and edges and meadows, especially on stream banks, scattered statewide but mostly east; FAC+. Grows to 24 inches in part sun to shade.

Carex cephalophora (Oval-leaf sedge) [perennial graminoid] — Statewide in dry to wet, sandy or rocky deciduous or mixed forests, thickets, savannas, woodland borders and meadows in

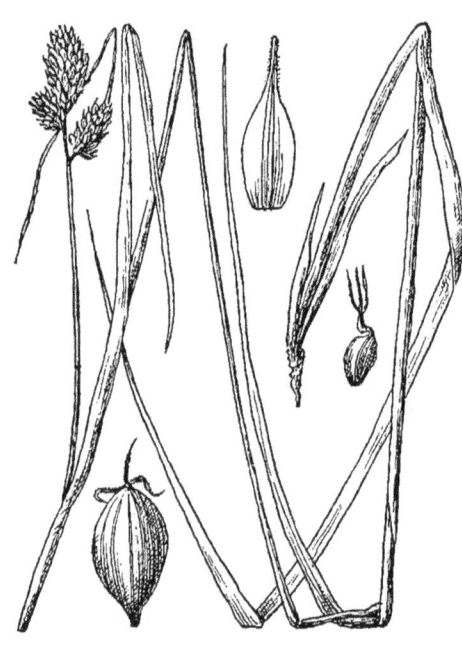

Bush's Sedge (*Carex bushii*)

wooded areas, old fields and pastures and can invade lawns, FACU; statewide. Grows 12 to 24 inches in sun to part shade on a wide range of loams at least 8 inches deep, with a pH range of 4.8 to 7.0, prefers disturbed sites, especially where there is occasional mowing. Avoid fine textured soils and anaerobic conditions but does tolerate drought.

Carex chordorrhiza (Creeping sedge) [perennial graminoid] — reported from a single site in a Tioga county sphagnum bog and listed as extirpated in Pennsylvania; prefers bogs, fens, sedge marshes and floating mats along lakeshores, typically in very wet sites and sometimes in shallow water; OBL.

Carex collinsii (Collin's sedge) [perennial graminoid] — most often on moist to wet sites under *Chamaecyparis thyoides* (Atlantic white cedar) or *Picea mariana* (Black spruce) in shaded seeps and sphagnum bogs; northeastern Pennsylvania along margins of glaciated areas and listed as endangered.

Carex communis var. communis (Fibrousroot sedge) [perennial graminoid] — common statewide in rich to poor, dry to moist well-drained soils in partial shade of mixed deciduous-coniferous and deciduous forests and woodlands, especially in clearings, on slopes and ledges and crevices of bluffs.

Carex comosa (Longhair sedge) [perennial graminoid] — swamps and wet thickets, stream, pond and lake shores, depressions in wet meadows, marshes, often in shallow water or on emergent stumps, floating logs, and floating mats of vegetation, OBL; mostly northwest, northeast and southeast. Grows 20 to 48 inches; sun to part sun in wet, silty, loam at least 8 inches deep with a pH range of 4.6 to 7.5 (but preferring acidic sites) and sometimes standing water. Avoid coarse-textured soils and droughty conditions.

Carex conjuncta (Soft fox sedge) [perennial graminoid] — Openings in floodplain forests, seasonally wet meadows, swales, thickets and upper borders of tidal marshes, FACW. Scattered statewide, but most common in the southeast. Grows up to 3 feet in full sun to light shade in moist, fertile, loamy soils.

Carex conoidea (Open field sedge) [perennial graminoid] — moist meadows and prairies, shores of lakes, ponds, and rivers, usually in acidic sands or loams, FACU; mostly southeast, scattered elsewhere. Grows 5 to 30 inches; sun to part sun in moist, rich organic loam.

Carex crawfordii (Crawford's sedge) [perennial graminoid] — Rare in standing water, moist to wet sites and open, sandy, somewhat dry disturbed areas, FAC. Scattered north (northern Allegheny plateaus) endangered. Grows 10 to 20 inches in sun to part sun in wet to mesic, well-drained soils.

Carex crinita var. (Fringed sedge) [perennial graminoid] — Wet meadows, marshes, bogs, floodplain forests, swamps and edges of streams, lakes and ponds, OBL. Two varieties; *crinita,* relatively common statewide, especially southeast, and *brevicrinis,* rare on widely scattered sites and listed as endangered. Grows 3 to 4 feet in moist to wet, well-drained rich soils, especially silty, organic loams, in sun to part shade; prefers part shade.

Carex cristatella (Crested sedge) [perennial graminoid] — moist to wet meadows, marshes, thickets, stream banks, and ditches, FACW. Mostly southeast, scattered elsewhere. Grows 12 to 40 inches; sun to part sun in moist to wet silty organic loam.

Carex cryptolepis (Northeastern sedge) [perennial graminoid] — scattered in glaciated areas especially on shorelines and meadows, and listed as threatened in Pennsylvania; reports vary with some describing acidic, sandy and organic soils but not lime-rich, while others suggest wet, calcareous sites.

Carex cumulata (Clustered sedge) [perennial graminoid] — northeastern Pennsylvania in wet to preferably dry and acidic rocky, gravelly or sandy soils, often in acidic woodlands and thickets as well as drying peat bogs where it usually appears with Polytrichum mosses; alluvium and abandoned railroad sites are mentioned.

Carex davisii (Davis' sedge) [perennial graminoid] — southeastern Pennsylvania, especially along the Delaware River and in Montgomery County, most commonly in rich, deciduous floodplain forests, along streams and on wooded ravine slopes, fields, meadows an thickets, often with calcareous soil; FAC-. Grows 18 to 36 inches in part sun to part shade in rich humusy loam.

Carex debilis (White edge sedge) [perennial graminoid] — statewide in wetland areas such as deciduous floodplain forests, swamps, bogs, wet woodlands and edges, stream banks, meadows and wet prairies, typically in acidic soils, FAC. Three varieties: *rudgei,* the most common, is concentrated in the northeast; *debilis* is generally found in the southeast, while *pubera* is most often in the southern end of the Ridge and Valley region. Grows to about 24 inches in part sun to part shade on soils at least 8 inches deep with a pH of between 4.6 and 6.6. Low fertility requirements, but intolerant of limestone and fine-textured soils; adaptable to anaerobic conditions.

Carex deweyana var. deweyana (Dewey sedge)

[perennial graminoid] — wet to dry forests and forest edges, FACU. Northern tier, especially glaciated plateau areas. Grows 8 to 40 inches in part sun to part shade in rich rocky loam.

Carex diandra (Lesser panicled sedge) [perennial graminoid] — rare on bog hummocks and pond margins, OBL. Extreme northeast and northwest (glaciated plateaus). Grows 12 to 30 inches in sun to part sun on pond edges in wet, organic loam of any texture, at least 8 inches deep, with a pH between 5.0 and 7.2. High anaerobic and low fertility requirements; avoid droughty conditions.

Carex digitalis var. *digitalis* (Slender woodland sedge) [perennial graminoid] — common statewide, especially east in mixed mesic to dry-mesic soils of deciduous and mixed deciduous-coniferous forests, UPL. Grows to about 18 inches in part sun to part shade in mesic to moist, well-drained loams.

Carex disperma (Soft-leaved sedge) [perennial graminoid] — scattered in northern Pennsylvania, especially in glaciated areas, in bogs, wet meadows, swamps and swampy woodlands, especially with rhododendron and conifers, FACW+. Grows in sun to part shade in medium to fine-textured, moderately fertile, mesic to moist loams at least 8 inches deep and with a pH of 4.5 to 6.5. Adaptable to anaerobic conditions, but not to drought or limestone-based soils.

Carex echinata var. echinata (Prickly sedge) [perennial graminoid] — bogs, swamps, peaty or sandy shores of streams or lakes, wet meadows, usually in acidic soils, OBL; mostly east, scattered elsewhere. Grows 4 to 36 inches; sun to part sun in moist to wet, moderately fertile, silty loam at least 8 inches deep with a pH between 5.6 and 7.2. Avoid droughty conditions and coarse-textured soils.

Carex emmonsii (Emmons' sedge) [perennial graminoid] — prefers mesic to moist rich slope soils in part shade of deciduous woodlands, but in Pennsylvania is reported on drier, acidic, sandy loam under mixed deciduous-pine woods; scatted statewide, but concentrated in southeast and aka *Carex albicans var. emmonsii.*

Carex emoryi (Sedge) [perennial graminoid] — stream banks, swales, marshes, seepy areas, wet meadows and fens, OBL. Scattered statewide. Grows 12 to 40 inches; sun to part shade in moist to wet rich sandy loam. Especially useful for restoration of wetlands, stormwater projects and soil retention.

Carex festucacea (Fescue sedge) [perennial graminoid] — Scattered statewide, mostly southeast, in moist to wet or seasonally wet open woodlands and poorly drained fields and thickets; FAC. Grows to about 30 inches in mesic to moist soils in sun to part sun.

Carex flava (Yellow sedge) [perennial graminoid] — moist to wet habitats, such as open meadows, fens, partially shaded shrub peaty wetlands and swamps, on lime to rich soils, OBL; mostly northeast and northwest. Grows 4 to 32 inches; sun to part sun in moist to wet rich loam.

Carex foenea (Fernald's hay sedge) [perennial graminoid] — very widely scattered in northern Pennsylvania in usually dry, but sometimes moist, acidic sands and gravels on grasslands and in open woods as well as open, disturbed sites; listed as endangered.

Carex folliculata (Northern long sedge) [perennial graminoid] — wet forests, bogs, seeps, wet meadows, marsh edges, stream banks, lakeshores, in acidic, sandy, or peaty soils, OBL; statewide. Grows 12 to 48 inches; part sun to shade in moist to wet rich humusy soils.

Carex formosa (Handsome sedge) [perennial graminoid] — usually calcareous soils in dry to mesic forests and ravines and moist meadows; reported only in Centre County and listed as endangered in Pennsylvania.

Carex frankii (Frank's sedge) [perennial graminoid] — moist to wet meadows and woodlands, stream banks, ditches, low marshy ground, often calcareous, OBL; mostly south. Grows up to 2 feet with leaves up to 1/3 inch wide in full sun (preferred) to part shade in a wet to moist, moderately fertile, silty to loamy soil at least 9 inches deep with a pH of 5.9 to 7.2; temporary flooding is tolerated, making it ideal for erosion control and rain gardens. Avoid coarse textured soils and droughty conditions.

Carex garberi (Elk sedge) [perennial graminoid] — calcareous gravels and sandy swales in fens, meadows and especially along shorelines in Erie County; FACW and listed as endangered in Pennsylvania.

Carex geyeri (Geyer's sedge) [perennial graminoid] — rare in dry mountain and subalpine grasslands, burned areas and open conifer woodlands, common in the western U.S. but isolated in central Pennsylvania and consequently technically listed as endangered. Grows 6 to 12 inches on well-drained, somewhat sterile, rocky, gravelly or sandy soils at least 10 inches deep, with a pH of 6.0 to 7.7, in sun to part sun. Avoid coarse-textured soils and anaerobic conditions.

Carex glaucodea (Blue sedge) [perennial graminoid] — mesic to wet deciduous forests or seasonally moist prairies, usually in clays or loams; mostly southeast (Piedmont), scattered southwest and northeast. Grows 4 to 20 inches; part sun to part shade in clayey to sandy loams.

Carex gracilescens (Slender looseflower sedge) [perennial graminoid] — prefers limestone or chalk on clay or marl soils in moist to dry deciduous or mixed coniferous-deciduous forests and edges in partial shade often on steep slopes, as well as stream bottoms, statewide but especially southeast.

Carex gracillima (Graceful sedge) [perennial graminoid] — mesic to dry deciduous forests, including edges and openings, mixed conifer to hardwood forests, coniferous swamps, thickets, meadows, and along roadsides, FACU; statewide. Grows 8 to 40 inches; part shade in moderately-fertile, medium to fine-textured, dry to mesic sandy loam at least 8 inches deep with a pH of 4.7 to 6.9.

Limestone Meadow Sedge
(Carex granularis)

Avoid limestone soils and droughty conditions.

Carex granularis (Limestone meadow sedge) [perennial graminoid] — meadows, fens, glades, or shores, moist woods, and bottomland swamps, especially along streams usually in clayey or sandy to clay soils, FACW+. Throughout Pennsylvania, except northern tier counties. Two varieties, *granularis* and *haleana* (mostly southeast). Grows 8 to 36 inches; part sun to part shade in moist to wet, fertile, silty loam at least 8 inches deep with a pH range of 6.0 to 7.2; avoid coarse-textured soils and droughty conditions.

Carex grayi (Gray's sedge) [perennial graminoid] — wet to mesic deciduous forests and openings, typically on fine alluvial or lacustrine deposits, and river bottoms, FACW+. Mostly southeast (Piedmont); scattered statewide. Grows 18 to 30 inches in fertile, moist soil in full sun, especially at or near water; tolerates light shade. Prefers medium to fine-textured soils at least 8 inches deep, with a pH between 5.7 and 7.2. Tolerates anaerobic conditions, but not drought.

Carex grisea (Inflated narrow-leaf sedge, Wood gray sedge) [perennial graminoid] — statewide in dry to moist, preferably mesic, sandy and calcium rich soils in deciduous forests and opening, especially alluvium on floodplains, especially southeast; FAC. Grows 8 to 30 inches; sun to part shade in rich moist organic loam.

Carex gynandra (Nodding sedge) [perennial graminoid] — swamps, floodplain forests, wet meadows, marshes, bogs, stream edges, margins of lakes and ponds and roadside ditches, OBL; statewide. Grows 30 to 60 inches; part sun to part shade in moist to wet silty loam.

Carex haydenii (Cloud sedge) [perennial graminoid] — widely scattered in swamps, moist prairies, bogs and fens, sandy floodplains and wet meadows of the Ridge and Valley and northern Piedmont, OBL. Grows 12 to 24 inches in full sun on moist to wet, sandy soils; tolerates brief standing water.

Carex hirsutella (Fuzzy wuzzy sedge) [perennial graminoid] — meadows and dry to mesic upland woodland, slopes, savannas, glades, meadows and abandoned fields in neutral to basic soils; statewide. Woodland sites are often dominated by oaks. Grows 10 to 30 inches; sun to part shade in dry to mesic, somewhat sterile, sandy loam that usually includes rocky material or clay.

Carex hirtifolia (Hairy sedge, Pubescent sedge) [perennial graminoid] — dry to mesic to thickets, forested slopes, occasionally lowland forests; mostly southeast and scattered elsewhere. Grows 12 to 32 inches; part sun to part shade in mesic to dry soil containing loam, clay to loam, or some rocky material. Above average tolerance of dry conditions.

Carex hitchcockiana (Hitchcock's sedge) [perennial graminoid] — mostly southern Ridge and Valley and Piedmont regions in often rocky and mesic deciduous forests with diversity in vascular plant communities, preferably on calcium-rich loams just above streams, including serpentine barrens and dry woodlands.

Carex hyalinolepis (Shoreline sedge) [perennial graminoid] — Very rare along streams, lakes and ponds and in swamps and wet meadows, often on clay soils with seasonal saturation, OBL. Extreme southeast (Atlantic Coastal Plain). Grows up to 4 feet in full to part sun on moist to wet clay to silt loams.

Nodding sedge (*Carex gynandra*)

Carex hystericina (Bottlebrush sedge) [perennial graminoid] — swamps, moist meadows and fens, seeps and edges of lakes, ponds and streams, mostly in calcareous soils, OBL. Mostly southeast (Piedmont, Central Appalachians) and northwest (Western Glaciated Allegheny Plateau). Grows 8 to 40 inches; sun to part sun in moist to wet rich silty loam.

Carex interior (Inland sedge) [perennial graminoid] — wet meadows and prairies, fens, swamps, river and lake shores, seeps; usually in calcareous soils, OBL. Scattered statewide, especially northwest, southeast. Grows 8 to 40 inches in sun to part sun on moist to wet, rich, silty, moderately fertile loams at least 8 inches deep and with a pH range of 5.4 to 7.2. Avoid coarse-textured soils and droughty conditions.

Carex intumescens (Great bladder sedge) [perennial graminoid] — dry to wet forests and openings, thickets, and wet meadows, FACW+; statewide. Grows 6 to 32 inches in part shade to shade on dry to mesic, fertile acidic humusy loams, typically medium to fine-textured, at least 8 inches deep and with a pH between 4.8 and 6.9. Tolerant of anaerobic conditions, but not drought.

Carex jamesii (Sedge) [perennial graminoid] — rich mesic floodplains, slopes, ravines and hardwood forests, typically on lime-rich substrates; UPL; mostly south. Grows 2 to 4 inches on wet to mesic, circumneutral to slightly alkaline, soils.

Carex lacustris (Hairy sedge) [perennial graminoid] — swamps, wet thickets and floodplain woodlands, wet dolomite prairies and swales, sandy marsh edges, sedge meadows, fens and shores of lakes, ponds and streams, OBL; scattered statewide except southwest. Grows 10 to 50 inches; sun to part sun in moist to wet silty loam containing mud, silt or calcareous sand. Prefers medium to fine-textured soils with moderate fertility, a minimum of 12 inches deep, and a pH between 5.6 and 6.8. Tolerates seasonal flooding, but not drought.

Carex laevivaginata (Smoothsheath sedge) [perennial graminoid] — Preferably calcareous soils that are seasonally saturated to inundated in swamps, marshes, tidal marsh edges or alluvial bottomlands, statewide except north central and northeast; OBL. Grows to 30 inches in sun to part shade.

Carex lasiocarpa (Wooly fruit sedge) [perennial graminoid] — wet meadows, stream banks, fens and bogs, lakeshores, especially in very wet sites and sometimes forming floating mats, OBL; mostly northeast and scattered elsewhere. Grows 10 to 50 inches; sun to part sun in moist to wet silty or peaty loam.

Carex laxiculmis var. laxiculmis (Spreading sedge) [perennial graminoid] — wet, low, deciduous or mixed deciduous and evergreen forests; stream edges and springs, and seeps, especially on clay soils; statewide. Grows 4 to 40 inches; part shade to shade in mesic to moist humusy sandy loam.

Carex laxiflora (Broad looseflower sedge) [perennial graminoid] — higher elevations of dry to moist deciduous or mixed deciduous to evergreen forests, FACU; statewide. Grows 5 to 25 inches; part shade to shade in mesic to moist humusy sandy loam.

Carex leavenworthii (Leavenworth's sedge) [perennial graminoid] — widely scattered, mostly southeast, in dry fields, meadows, clearings, pastures, open woodlands, forest edges and disturbed sites; easily confused with *Carex cephalophora*.

Carex leptalea (Bristlystalked sedge) [perennial graminoid] — statewide except far southwest in mossy to wet woods, conifer bogs and swamps, meadows, fens, swales, stream banks and lake shores, as well as shaded damp rock ledges and marshy fields; OBL. Grows to 30 inches in sun to part shade on moist to wet, medium to fine-textured soils at least 8 inches deep with a pH between 4.8 and 6.9. Tolerant of shade and anaerobic conditions, but not drought or limestone-based soils.

Carex leptonervia (Nerveless woodland sedge) [perennial graminoid] — moist to wet forests across northern Pennsylvania and along the Allegheny front at generally higher elevations, scattered elsewhere; FACW. Grows to about 12 inches in medium to fine-textured, moderately fertile, mesic to moist soils at least 8 inches deep with a pH of 5.0 to 6.8. Avoid droughty conditions and limestone-based soils.

Carex limosa (Mud sedge) [perennial graminoid] — typically on sphagnum bog mats and hummocks, but also wet meadows and shorelines, mostly northeast but also scattered northwest; OBL. Grows to about 20 inches in coarse to medium textured, relatively sterile but mesic to moist soils at least 8 inches deep with a pH range of 4.8 to 7.5. Good for anaerobic conditions, but intolerant of drought and shade.

Carex longii (Long's sedge) [perennial graminoid] — scattered in eastern Pennsylvania on wet to seasonally wet sandy soils of open thickets and woodlands, fields, pond margins and sometimes bogs; OBL. Grows to about 3 feet in mesic to wet, well-drained loams in sun to part sun.

Carex lucorum (Blue Ridge sedge) [perennial graminoid] — statewide on preferably sandy, acidic, well-drained dry to mesic soils in open pine and oak woodlands, sometimes on slopes and cleared areas. Grows to about 24 inches in dry to mesic, sandy loams.

Carex lupuliformis (False hop sedge) [perennial graminoid] — rare in calcareous marshes, wet woods, sometimes in shallow water, FACW; scattered statewide. Grows 20 to 48 inches; full sun to part shade in silty rich soils continually moist to wet.

Carex lupulina (Hop sedge) [perennial graminoid] — wet mixed to deciduous swampy forests and openings and wet meadows, OBL; statewide. Grows 10 to 50 inches in part sun to part shade in medium to fine textured, moist to wet, moderately fertile silty loam at least 18 inches deep and with a pH between 6.2 and 7.0. Moderately tolerant of anaerobic conditions and limestone soils, but intolerant of drought.

Carex lurida (Shallow sedge) [perennial graminoid] — pond, lake and stream shores, marshes and wet meadows, seeps and swampy forests, usually in sandy acidic soils, OBL; statewide. Grows 10 to 50 inches; sun to part sun in moist to wet moderately rich silty loam of all textures, at least 16 inches deep, and with a pH of 4.9 to 6.8. Moderately tolerant of shade, anaerobic conditions and limestone soils; avoid droughty conditions.

Carex meadii (Mead's sedge) [perennial graminoid] — Calcareous, often over diabase, prairies, wet sedge meadows, fens, moist depressions, open woodlands and cedar and limestone glades, generally in the lower Piedmont; FAC. Grows 6 to 15 inches in full to part sun on dry to mesic loams and clay loams, including rocky, calcareous soils. Adaptable and relatively easy to grow.

Carex mesochorea (Midland sedge) [perennial graminoid] — dry open woodlands and grasslands, including such disturbed ground as roadside banks, railroads and fallow fields, widely scattered but mostly southeast; FACU. Can reach 3 feet in sun to part sun on dry to mesic, well drained, sandy loams.

Carex mitchelliana (Mitchell's sedge) [perennial graminoid] — lake, pond and stream margins, wet meadows, swamps, floodplain forests; reported only in Crawford County and listed as endangered and critically imperiled in Pennsylvania. Grows 18 to 40 inches in sun to part sun in mesic to wet soils.

Carex molesta (Troublesome sedge) [perennial graminoid] — dry to wet, frequently heavy, calcareous soils in dry to mesic prairies, open woodlands, thickets, swamps, depressions, bottomlands and seasonally-degraded wetlands, especially in disturbed habitats. Mostly southeast and scattered elsewhere. Grows 15 to 30 inches in sun to part sun on dry to wet, clayey to silty loam. Adaptable to all moist to wet soil textures with a depth of at least 10 inches and a pH between 4.9 and 7.0. Intolerant of shade but somewhat tolerant of droughty conditions.

Carex muehlenbergii (Muehlenberg's sedge) [perennial graminoid] — sandy, dry savannas and fields, dunes, rocky upland woodlands open forests; mostly east, scattered elsewhere. Grows 10 to 40 inches; sun to part sun in dry to mesic sandy loam.

Carex nigromarginata (Black edge sedge) [perennial graminoid] — dry, acidic rocky soils in woodlands, thickets and forest clearings in part shade of mixed deciduous-pine forests or full sun along clearing edges, frequently found on stream banks, southeastern Pennsylvania, especially Piedmont; UPL. Grows to 12 inches in sun to part sun in dry to mesic, well drained sandy loams.

Carex normalis (Greater straw sedge) [perennial graminoid] — generally wet woods, thickets, meadows and along roadsides, FACU; statewide. Grows 2 to 3 feet in sun to part shade on mesic to moist sandy clay loam and ideal for rain gardens.

Carex novae-angliae (New England sedge) [perennial graminoid] — across northern Pennsylvania in mixed deciduous forests, sometimes under hemlock-spruce canopies, but more often under Sugar Maple (*Acer saccharum*), American Beech (*Fagus grandifolia*), or American Basswood (*Tilia americana*); typical sites include mesic woodlands and slopes above streams or along limestone bluffs, as well as savannas and mesic prairies, especially lower positions on hills; FACU. Grows to about 20 inches in mesic to moist loams, part sun to part shade.

Carex oligocarpa (Richwoods sedge) [perennial graminoid] — prefers calcium-rich loams on rocky mesic to dry to mesic deciduous forests above streams, mostly in the Ridge and Valley and Piedmont. Grows to 20 inches in part sun to part shade in mesic, loamy soils high in decaying organic material.

Carex oligosperma (Few-seeded sedge) [perennial graminoid] — prefers acidic sandy to peaty soils in sphagnum-dominated bogs and poor fens as well as open swamps, marshes, lake shores and riverbanks, northeastern Pennsylvania plus Centre County; OBL. Grows 12 to 30 inches in sun to part sun on moist to wet, humusy loams.

Carex ormostachya (Spike sedge) [perennial graminoid] — prefers sandy gravels in moist to dry forests and shale barrens, widely scattered but mostly northern Pennsylvania; grows to about 15 inches in dry to mesic, well drained loams, sun to part shade.

Carex pallescens (Pale sedge) [perennial graminoid] — Mostly northern Pennsylvania, especially northeast, in moist, peaty meadows, fields and clearings, cedar forestss and open woodlands and borders of beech-maple forests.

Carex pauciflora (Few-flowered sedge) [perennial graminoid] — prefers open mats of sphagnum bogs and acidic peats, occasionally in part shade of conifers, OBL; northeastern Pennsylvania as well as northwestern Warren County. Grows to about 6 inches in moist to wet, acidic, humusy soils.

Carex paupercula (Bog sedge) [perennial graminoid] — bogs and boggy woodlands, fens, and marshes, typically associated with sphagnum; scattered north, but especially northwestern Monroe County, OBL; aka *Carex magellanica subsp. irrigua*.

Carex pedunculata (Longstalk sedge) [perennial graminoid] — rich, rocky, wooded slopes or swampy woods. Scattered statewide except southwest and southeast. Grows 2 to 12 inches; part shade to shade in moist to dry sandy loams.

Carex pellita (Woolly sedge) [perennial graminoid] — swamps, moist meadows, and along shores of lakes and ponds, OBL. Mostly southeast (Piedmont); scattered elsewhere. Grows 12 to 40 inches in full to part sun on moist to wet rich loams.

Carex pensylvanica (Pennsylvania sedge, oak sedge) [perennial graminoid] — well drained, acidic but mineral-rich sandy, rocky, and loamy soils in deciduous forests, edges and openings; statewide. Grows 4 to 16 inches; part shade to shade in dry to mesic sandy rocky loam. A popular edge plant and ground cover that colonizes by rhizomes and is very drought tolerant. Ideal for woodland sedge lawns and resembles grasses, but should not be mowed shorter than several inches.

Carex planispicata (Flat-spiked sedge) [perennial graminoid] — along the Allegheny front and across the eastern Piedmont in dry to moist but preferably mesic deciduous forests, commonly on lower-slope loams adjacent to streams and on upper portions of flood plains.

Carex plantaginea (Plantain sedge) [perennial graminoid] — rich, moist, deciduous or mixed deciduous to evergreen forests, on slopes along streams or along edges of moist depressions. Mostly north and southwest; scattered elsewhere. Grows 8 to 24 inches; part shade in consistently moist organic loams.

Carex platyphylla (Broad-leaf sedge) [perennial graminoid] — rocky or gravelly slopes in rich, moist deciduous forests, usually on limestone, shale, or calcareous metamorphic rocks, often on clay soils; statewide. Grows 6 to 16 inches; part sun to shade in moist, rich sandy humus.

Carex polymorpha (Variable sedge) [perennial graminoid] — thin sandy to peaty soils in open woodlands and barrens, scattered east but concentrated on the Pocono Plateau and of general conservation concern; FACU and listed as endangered in Pennsylvania. Grows on medium to coarse-textured, relatively sterile soils a minimum of 10 inches deep and with a pH between 4.8 and 6.8. Avoid anaerobic conditions and limestone-based soils. Moderate drought tolerance.

Carex prairea (Prairie sedge) [perennial graminoid] — rare in calcareous fens, swamps, marshy shore lines, sedge meadows, FACW; widely scattered, mostly northwest. Grows 20 to 40 inches; sun to part sun in moist rich silty loam.

Carex prasina (Drooping sedge) [perennial graminoid] — statewide in rich, mesic and especially swampy to boggy deciduous forests, often on stream banks or in seepage areas, including moist low ground associated with fens and springs; OBL. Grows 12 to 30 inches in part sun to shade on me-

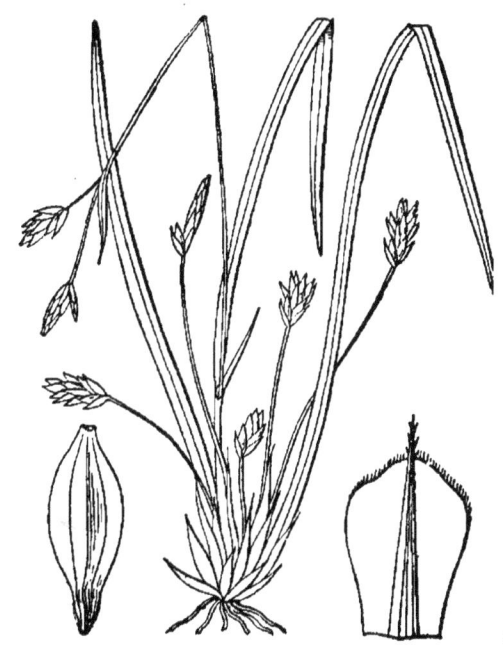

Longstalk sedge (*Carex pedunculata*)

dium to fine textured moist to wet soils with a pH range of 4.8 to 6.8 and at least 8 inches deep. Avoid droughty conditions or limestone-based soils.

Carex projecta (Necklace sedge) [perennial graminoid] — moist to wet meadows, low spots in deciduous and mixed forests, thickets, stream banks and lake shores, FACW; statewide. Grows 20 to 30 inches in part sun to part shade on moist to wet, medium to fine-textured, moderately rich soils at least 8 inches deep with a pH between 4.8 and 7.0. Intolerant of drought or limestone-based soils,

Carex pseudocyperus (Cyperus-like sedge) [perennial graminoid] — wet thickets; shores of lakes, streams and ponds; marshes, wet meadows, sometimes in shallow water or on floating mats of vegetation or logs or on emergent stumps, OBL; mostly northwest and listed as endangered. Grows 2 to 3 feet in full sun on very wet soil, including standing water.

Carex radiata (Eastern star sedge) [perennial graminoid] — wet to mesic mixed and deciduous forests, ravines and seep edges in usually seasonally wet areas; statewide. Grows 10 to 30 inches in part sun to part shade on mesic to wet to mesic loam; prefers dappled shade to medium shade and loamy soils rich in organice matter. Soil must never dry out.

Carex retroflexa (Reflexed sedge) [perennial graminoid] — statewide, especially in Ridge and Valley and Piedmont, in dry, rocky deciduous woodlands, forest openings and thickets. Grows to 25 inches in part sun to part shade on dry to mesic, well drained loams.

Carex retrorsa (Backward sedge) [perennial graminoid] — widely scattered in northern counties and in Ridge and Valley in swamps, wet thickets, stream banks, marshes, sedge meadows and

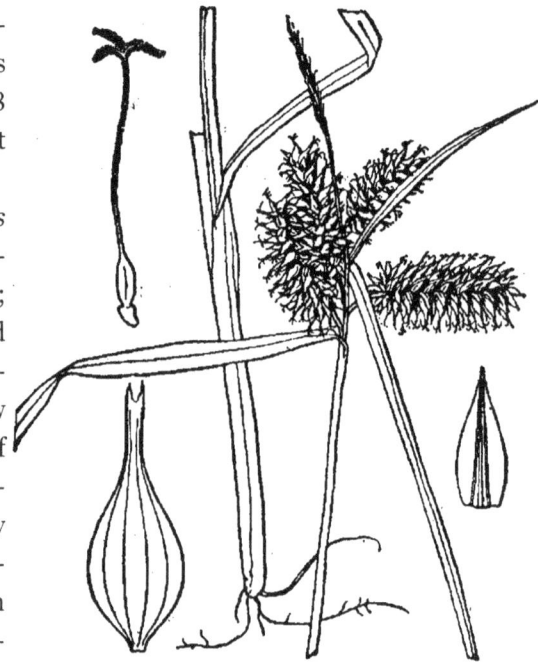

Backward sedge (*Carex retrorsa*)

shorelines of ponds and lakes; FACW+ and listed as endangered in Pennsylvania. Grows 12 to 36 inches; shade to part shade in moist to wet organic loam.

Carex richardsonii (Richardson's sedge) [perennial graminoid] — reported only in Chester county on an open and seasonally wet serpentine barrens; prefers vernally moist open woodlands, alvars, floodplain margins, prairies and outcrops; UPL. Grows to 12 inches in sun to part sun.

Carex rosea (Rosy sedge) [perennial graminoid] — dry and mesic deciduous and mixed forests; statewide. Grows 10 to 35 inches; part sun to shade in dry to mesic sandy loam, a popular ground cover in dry to mesic sites in shady areas.

Carex sartwellii (Sartwell's sedge) [perennial graminoid] — reported only on scattered northwestern glaciated areas in swamps; prefers fens, wet prairies, sedge meadows, marshes, shorelines of lakes, ponds and streams and open, wet thickets, OBL; often found in shallow water and listed as extirpated in Pennsylvania. Grows 18 to 40 inches in sun to part shade.

Carex scabrata (Eastern rough sedge) [perennial graminoid] — on calcareous, circumneutral or acidic soils, statewide, in moist to wet deciduous woodlands, seepage slopes, ravine bottoms, creek margins and less frequently in bogs, swamps and wet clearings; OBL. Grows in medium to fine-textured soils at least 10 inches deep with a pH of 4.7 to 6.8; tolerates shade and anaerobic conditions, but not drought or limestone based soils.

Carex schweinitzii (Schweinitz' sedge) [perennial graminoid] — widely scattered in the Ridge and Valley region and prefers open to lightly shaded, highly calcareous soils in marshes, cold streams, springheads and seeps, fen margins and seepy lake, pond and stream edges; OBL and listed as threatened in Pennsylvania. Grows 8 to 20 inches in part sun to part shade.

Carex scoparia (Broom sedge) [perennial graminoid] — dry to wet open habitats such as gravelly seeps and fens, pond and stream margins, marshes and wet prairies, often on sandy, acidic soils, FACW; statewide. Grows 10 to 40 inches; sun to part sun in moist to wet and varying quality soils containing mud, sand or gravel.

Carex seorsa (Weak stellate sedge) [perennial graminoid] — scattered in northwestern and southeastern Pennsylvania in wet woodlands and swamps; prefers sandy to peaty acidic soils in hardwood area or especially cedar swamps; FACW. Grows to about two feet in moist to wet humusy loams, part sun to part shade.

Carex shortiana (Short's sedge) [perennial graminoid] — thickets and swampy woodlands, thickets and borders, moist prairies (especially along rivers and swales), open spring-fed meadows, seeps and fens, prairie swales, pond margins, and wooded areas of toe slopes, mostly south central and southwest and often in calcareous soils. Grows 12 inches in full to part sun in somewhat fertile, moist, medium to fine-textured soils at least 8 inches deep and with a pH between 4.7 and 6.9. High anaerobic but no drought tolerance.

Carex siccata (Sedge) [perennial graminoid] — widely scattered in open, sandy woodlands in mostly eastern Pennsylvania; prefers sandy oak, oak-pine or pine forests and savannas, dry prairies, sandy fields, rock outcrops and alpine to subalpine meadows, FAC+.

Carex sparganioides (Bur reed sedge) [perennial graminoid] — Statewide in mesic to moist deciduous and mixed forests, FACU; statewide. Grows 15 to 40 inches; part sun to part shade in dry to moist fertile, humusy loam at least 10 inches deep with a pH between 5.0 and 6.8. Avoid coarse or fine textured soils and those composed of limestone materials; low drought tolerance, but somewhat adaptable to anaerobic conditions.

Carex sprengelii (Sprengli's sedge) [perennial graminoid] — dry to mesic hardwood and mixed conifer forests and openings, floodplain forests and riverbanks, lakeshores, limestone river bluffs, frequent on calcareous soils, FACU; mostly in the Delaware River Valley. Grows 10 to 40 inches; sun to part shade in dry to mesic rich sandy and alluvial loam.

Carex squarrosa (Squarrose sedge) [perennial graminoid] — wet bottomland woodlands, swamps, gravelly seeps, forest edges and sedge meadows, FACW. Mostly southeast (Piedmont), scattered south. Grows 18 to 24 inches in full sun to part shade; prefers moist to wet, moderately fertile, loamy soils containing silt, sand or gravel at least 8 inches deep with a pH between 5.6 and 7.3. Tolerates temporary shallow standing water, making it ideal for rain gardens. Avoid coarse-textured soils and droughty conditions.

Carex sterilis (Atlantic sedge) [perennial graminoid] — white to cedar swamps, wet calcareous prairies, fens and meadows, calcareous seeps, lake and river shores, and wet sunny limestone outcrops, OBL; mostly southeast, widely scattered elsewhere. Grows 1 to 3 inches; full sun to part sun in wet to moist circumneutral sandy loams.

Carex stipata var. stipata (Owl fruit sedge) [perennial graminoid] — soils that are periodically saturated or inundated in wet meadows, swamps, marshes, and alluvial bottomlands; statewide. Grows 15 to 40 inches; sun to part sun in moist to wet, rich, silty and alluvial loam at least 8 inches deep with a pH range of 4.9 to 7.9. Shade and anaerobic tolerant; avoid coarse textured soils.

Carex straminea (Eastern straw sedge) [perennial graminoid] — scattered statewide except northern tier counties in marshy shores, swamps and swales; OBL. Grows to about 25 inches in medium to fine textured soils at least 8 inches deep with a pH range of 4.7 to 6.9. Prefers moderately fertile sandy to peaty acidic soils; avoid coarse-textured and limestone-based soils but tolerant of anaerobic conditions and shade.

Carex striatula (Lined sedge) [perennial graminoid] — mostly southern Pennsylvania, especially Piedmont, in rich, dry to moist, deciduous to mixed woodlands, including moist ravine slopes. Grows to about 18 inches in part sun to part shade.

Carex stricta (Tussock sedge or Upright sedge) [perennial graminoid] — lake shores, bogs, marshes and wet meadows, OBL. Mostly southeast (Piedmont), scattered elsewhere. Grows 6 to 44 inches; sun to part sun in moist to wet rich silty or alluvial loam of any texture, at least 18 inches deep and with a pH range of 3.5 to 7.0. Tolerant of shade and anaerobic conditions, but not droughty habitats.

Carex styloflexa (Bent sedge) [perennial graminoid] — prefers sandy, wet, acidic soils in deciduous to mixed woodlands near springs and seeps and small stream margins in southeastern Pennsylvania; FACW-. Grows 12 to 30 inches in part sun to shade.

Carex swanii (Swann's sedge) [perennial graminoid] — Statewide in mesic to dry rocky upland woodlands and slopes as well as savannas and scrublands, often where oaks form a light canopy, FACU. Grows 10 to 20 inches in sun to part shade on dry to mesic sandy loam with some decaying matter and where ground vegetation is somewhat sparse. Because it is somewhat showy, it's popular as a ground cover, specimen display, or naturalizing.

Carex tenera var. tenera (Quill sedge) [perennial graminoid] — moist to dry meadows and open woodlands and edges, savannas, swamps, moist prairies, disturbed meadows, FAC. Scattered statewide except southwest. Grows 10 to 35 inches in part sun to part shade on mesic to wet, moderately fertile, clay to silt loam at least 8 inches deep with a pH range of 4.9 to 7.0. Avoid coarse textured soils. Tolerant of anaerobic conditions, shade, and drought.

Carex tonsa var. rugosperma (Parachute sedge) [perennial graminoid] — prefers dry, sandy acidic soils in open, often rocky, meadows, ridges, heathlands, savannas and edges of pine, oak and poplar woodlands; reported only in Chester County.

Carex torta (Twisted sedge) [perennial graminoid] — Statewide on stream banks, stream beds and floodplains, especially on smaller tributaries of major rivers often subjected to flooding with high velocity and ice scour; FACW. Grows to about 24 inches in medium to coarse textured, somewhat sterile, soils at least 8 inches deep with a pH range of 5.0 to 7.0. Tolerant of shade and anaerobic conditions, but not drought or limestone-based soils.

Carex tribuloides var. tribuloides (Blunt broom sedge) [perennial graminoid] — Statewide in open floodplain forests, moist to wet grasslands, ditches, stream banks and wet thickets; FACW+. Grows 20 to 40 inches in sun to part shade on wet to moist, gravelly, sandy, peaty or loamy soils, but prefers medium to fine-textured, moderately fertile, soils at least 8 inches deep with a pH range of 4.8 to 7.0. Tolerant of shade and anaerobic conditions, but not drought or limestone-based soils.

Carex trichocarpa (Hairy fruit sedge) [perennial graminoid] — wet thickets and meadows, near streams and rivers, and in openings in bottomlands, OBL; statewide except southwest. Grows 20 to 50 inches in sun to part sun on moist to wet, moderately fertile loam at least 10 inches deep with a pH range of 5.7 to 7.0. Somewhat tolerant of shade, but not drought.

Carex trisperma (Threeseeded sedge) [perennial graminoid] — Mostly glaciated areas of northern Pennsylvania and scattered in the Appalachians in wet woodlands, swamps and bogs, especially sphagnum; OBL. Grows in medium to fine textured, somewhat sterile, soils at least 8 inches deep and with a pH between 4.5 and 6.8, sun to shade. No drought or limestone soil tolerance.

Carex tuckermanii (Tuckerman's sedge) [perennial graminoid] — rare in deciduous swamp forests, thickets, often along streams or pond shores and wet meadows, OBL; mostly northwest. Grows 16 to 40 inches in sun to part shade on moist to wet silty loam.

Carex typhina (Cat-tail sedge) [perennial graminoid] — rare in calcareous wet woods, swales and swamps, FACW+. Scattered statewide and listed as endangered. Grows 12 inches in full sun to part shade in medium to fine-textured, moist to wet soils at least 8 inches deep and from pH 5.7 to 7.0. Tolerant of anaerobic conditions, but not drought or coarse-textured soils.

Carex umbellata (Parasol sedge) [perennial graminoid] — statewide, but especially southeast, on dry to mesic, calcareous to circumneutral, sandy to clayey soils in rocky fields, pastures and tall-grass prairies and open mixed to deciduous woodlands; also found on barrens including serpentine and basalt, bluffs, dunes, glades, ridges and slopes. Grows to about 10 inches in dry to mesic, well drained loams in full sun to part sun; good option for rock gardens because of its size.

Carex utriculata (Northwest territory sedge) [perennial graminoid] — pond and lake shorelines, swamps, marshes, meadows, fens, bogs and wet thickets, OBL. Mostly northeast (Northern Glaciated Allegheny Plateau); scattered elsewhere except southwest. Grows 16 to 40 inches; sun to part sun in moist rich loam.

Carex vesicaria (Blister sedge) [perennial graminoid] — stream, pond and lake shores; marshes, bogs, wet meadows, low wet areas in forests, wet thickets and swamps, frequently on sites inundated in spring and dry during summer, OBL; scattered statewide. Grows to 3 feet inches; sun to part sun in moist to wet, moderately fertile, sandy loam of all textures, including anaerobic conditions, at least 8 inches deep and with a pH of 4.5 to 7.5. Moderate shade tolerance, but none for drought.

Carex vestita (Velvet sedge) [perennial graminoid] — generally eastern Pennsylvania in dry to moist, sandy and acidic soils in gravelly meadows, open woodlands and sandy-peaty barrens.

Carex virescens (Ribbed sedge) [perennial graminoid] — deciduous forests and banks ranging from mesic to dry; statewide, especially southeast (Piedmont). Grows 15 to 40 inches; part sun to part shade in mesic to dry sandy loam.

Carex vulpinoidea var. vulpinoidea (Fox sedge) [perennial graminoid] — Statewide in marshes, ditches and wet meadows periodically inundated or saturated, openings in floodplain woodlands, soggy thickets, river bottom prairies, meadows, seeps and swales, as well as low areas near ponds; OBL; Grows 16 to 40 inches; sun to part shade in moist to wet, somewhat fertile, silty loam at least 16 inches deep with a pH range of 6.8 to 8.9; popular for rain gardens. Avoid coarse-textured soils; not drought tolerant.

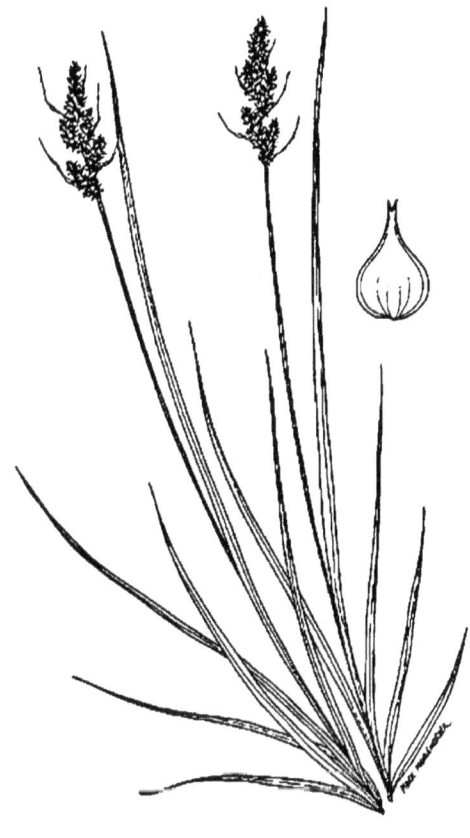

Fox sedge (*Carex vulpinoidea*)

Carex wiegandii (Wiegand's sedge) [perennial graminoid] — reported only in McKean and Elk Counties in sphagnum swamp openings; prefers bogs, openings in acidic conifer, mixed or alder swamps and acidic, sandy to peaty, wet meadows; OBL and listed as threatened in Pennsylvania.

Carex willdenowii (Willdenow's sedge) [perennial graminoid] — Generally southeastern Pennsylvania (Ridge and Valley, Piedmont) on acid, dry mesic soils in open, oak-dominated woodlands, typically on rocky slopes and ridges; UPL.

Carex woodii (Pretty sedge) [perennial graminoid] — dry, calcareous woodland slopes; UPL. Mostly southwest (Southern Allegheny Plateau, Allegheny Mountains); scattered west. Grows 6 to 12 inches in average to dry circumneutral soils, part sun to shade; a good choice for no-mow lawn.

Carpinus caroliniana (Hornbeam) - [tree] rich, deciduous forests along stream banks, on flood plains, and on moist hillsides, FAC; statewide. Deciduous tree to 30 feet; average, medium moisture soil in part shade to full shade. Prefers coarse to medium textured, moderately fertile, mesic to moist, organically rich soils at least 20 inches deep, with a pH range of 4.0 to 7.4. Low tolerance to drought, anaerobic conditions and limestone soils. Tolerant of shade.

Carya cordiformis (Bitternut hickory) - [tree] river flood plains, well-drained hillsides and limestone glades, FACU+; statewide. Deciduous tree to 100 feet; mesic to moist rich, loamy or gravelly soil of all textures with a pH range of 4.8 to 7.4. Tolerant of drought and limestone soils, but intolerant of shade and anaerobic conditions; requires 120-day growing season and a minimum soil depth of 50 inches.

Carya glabra (Pignut hickory) - [tree] deep flood plains, well-drained sandy soils, rolling hills and slopes, dry rocky soils, or thin soils on edge of granite outcrops, FACU-; statewide except north. Deciduous tree to 100 feet; prefers light, well-drained, coarse to medium textured, loamy soils derived from a variety of sedimentary or metamorphic parent material, in full sun to part shade, between 4.8 and 7.3 pH with a minimum soil depth of 50 inches. Drought and limestone soil tolerance, but intolerant of anaerobic conditions.

Carya laciniosa (Shellbark hickory) - [tree] moist, rich bottomlands and slopes, especially along creeks and in cedar glades. FAC; mostly southeast. Deciduous tree to 100 feet in full sun on moist coarse to medium textured fertile, mesic to moist soils with a pH range of 5.0 to 6.6 and a minimum depth of 60 inches. Requires a 150 day growing season; tolerant of shade and limestone-based soils, but not drought or anaerobic conditions.

Carya ovata (Shagbark hickory) - [tree] wet bottomlands, rocky hillsides, and limestone outcrops, FACU; statewide. Deciduous tree to 100 feet; humusy, rich, mesic to moist, well-drained loams in full sun to part shade. Adaptable to all soil textures with a pH range of 4.0 to 7.3 at least 48 inches deep. Moderately shade and drought tolerant, but intolerant of anaerobic sites.

Carya tomentosa (Mockernut hickory) - [tree/shrub] moist rocky open woods and slopes; less common on alluvial bottomlands; statewide except north. Deciduous tree to 100 feet; adaptable to a wide variety of soil textures; prefers finely textured, organic sandy mesic to moist, moderately fertile loams at least 50 inches deep between 4.7 and 6.9 pH. Requires a 160 day growing season; somewhat tolerant of drought and shade, but intolerant of anaerobic conditions. AKA *Carya alba*.

Castanea dentata (American chestnut) - [tree] rich deciduous and mixed forests, particularly with oak; statewide. Tree to 20 feet; moist, well-drained medium textured loams in full sun with a pH between 5.5 and 6.6. Intolerant of coarse and fine textured soils, anaerobic conditions, shade and limestone-based soils. Needs a 150-day growing season. Formerly very common and a forest dominant — grew to 115 feet — before dieback due to chestnut blight. Rarely lives longer than 15 to 20 years, although an energetic breeding program hopes to reverse a declining trend.

Castanea pumila (Chinquapin) - [tree/shrub] dry to moist slopes in open woodlands and forest understory as well as dry to wet sandy barrens. Mostly southeast. Deciduous tree to 10 to 30 feet in well drained, coarse to medium textured, somewhat sterile, soils with a pH between 4.5 and 6.6, at least 20 inches deep. Requires a 150-day growing season and is intolerant of anaerobic conditions and limestone-based soils, but highly tolerant of drought and adaptable to shade; prefers full sun to part shade.

Castilleja coccinea (Indian paintbrush) [biennial forb] — Moist meadows and open woodlands,

Bitternut hickory (*Carya cordiformis*)

rocky glades, stream banks and thickets, widely scattered, generally south, but most concentrated in the Piedmont, FAC. Grows 12 to 18 inches with red flowers in summer, semi-parasitic, especially Schizachyrium, Penstemon and/or Sisyrinchium spp. Prefers full sun to part sun, in mesic to moist, medium-textured, well-drained soils; somewhat challenging to grow from seed and transplanting is usually fatal. Requires soils with a pH range of 4.9 to 6.8 at least 8 inches deep. Accepts low fertility soils, but not anaerobic or droughty conditions.

Caulophyllum thalictroides (Blue cohosh) - [perennial forb] moist rich deciduous and mixed forests; statewide except limestone substrates in the Central Appalachians. Grows 12 to 30 inches, greenish yellow/purple flowers in spring to summer; shady woodland areas in rich, fertile, medium-textured, mesic soils that do not dry out; pH 4.5 to 7.0 at least 16 inches deep. Intolerant of anaerobic sites, limestone-based soils and drought.

Ceanothus americanus (New Jersey tea) - [shrub] dry open plains and prairie-like areas, on sandy or rocky soils in woodland clearings, edges and slopes, on riverbanks or lake shores; statewide. Deciduous shrub to 3 feet; sun to part shade in dry to mesic, coarse to medium textured, sandy, rocky loam with a pH between 4.3 and 6.5 at least 14 inches deep. White flowers in late spring; high drought tolerance and low moisture use, but intolerant of anaerobic conditions.

Celastrus scandens (American bittersweet) - [perennial vine] dry fields, rocky ledges, woods, hedgerows, statewide; FACU-. Dioecious, twining, to 12-16 feet, greenish-white flowers in spring to early summer. Grow in moderately fertile soils of all textures with regular moisture in full sun; suckers at the roots to form large colonies and can strangle trees and shrubs if left unchecked. Moderately drought and limestone-soil tolerance, but high moisture use in soils at least 18 inches deep with a pH range of 5.0 to 7.5. Intolerant of anaerobic conditions.

Celtis occidentalis (Dogberry, Common Hackberry) - [tree] rich moist soil along streams, on flood plains and rocky wooded hillsides and woodlands, FACU; mostly southeast, scattered elsewhere. Deciduous tree to 60 feet in moderately fertile soils of all textures with a pH range of 6.0 to 7.8 at least 36 inches deep; prefers mesic to moist, organically rich, well-drained soils in full sun and a 120-day growing season. Tolerates part shade, wind, many urban pollutants and a wide range of soil conditions, including drought and wet, dry and poor soils. Somewhat tolerant of anaerobic conditions, limestone-based soils.

Celtis tenuifolia (Dwarf hackberry) - [tree/shrub] shale banks and slopes along streams in open woods, dry wooded hillsides and limestone bluffs; mostly southeast (Central Appalachians, Piedmont). Shrub or small tree grows to 15 feet; sun to part shade in mesic to moist humusy, sandy loam.

Cenchrus longispinus (Sandbur) [annual graminoid] — sandy prairies, savannas, fields and waste ground, scattered west and more common southeast. Grows to 30 inches in full to part sun on dry-mesic, open sandy soil, especially with a history of disturbance, and because it has a weedy appearance is often considered a nuisance.

Cephalanthus occidentalis (Buttonbush) - [shrub] swamps, bogs, lake margins and low wet ground, OBL; statewide except north. Deciduous shrug to 10 feet; sun to part shade in moist, humusy soils of all textures in full sun to part shade. Grows well in wet soils, including flood conditions and shallow standing water. Adapts to a wide range of soils, except dry, with pH range of 4.7 to 8.6 at least 14 inches deep. Medium drought and limestone soil tolerance.

Cerastium arvense ssp. arvense (Serpentine barrens chickweed) - [perennial forb] Dry, rocky slopes and sandy fields; also common in lawns, cemeteries, roadsides, riverbanks, old pastures, mostly southeast (UPL). White flowers in late spring to early summer; grows 12 to 18 inches in dry, typically well-drained sandy soil in full to part sun.

Cerastium nutans (Nodding chickweed) [annual forb] — statewide on wooded floodplains and stream banks, gravel bars, meadows, shores and boggy sites, FAC. Grows 4 to 16 inches with white flowers in late spring to early summer in full sun to part shade on all soils in mesic to moist conditions. In nature, it prefers sites where there is disturbance by action of water and alluvial soils that include gravel deposits.

Ceratophyllum demersum (Coontail) - [perennial forb] aquatic; quiet waters of lakes and ponds, rivers, streams, swamps, generally submerged, sometimes free floating, OBL; mostly northwest and southeast, scattered elsewhere. Flowers early summer, fruit in late summer; silty garden ponds ranging from fresh to slightly brackish. Adaptable to all soil textures with a pH range between 6.0 and 8.6, somewhat shade tolerant.

Ceratophyllum echinatum (Hornwort) - [perennial forb] aquatic found in lakes and ponds and swamps, mostly northeastern Pennsylvania (OBL). No cultivation data; may be very difficult to obtain from commercial sources.

Cercis canadensis (Redbud) - [tree] woodlands and stream banks that are neither excessively wet or dry or strongly acidic, 20 to 30 feet. Has a natural preference for, and can be used as an indicator of, alkaline soils. FACU-; mostly south, especially Southern Allegheny Plateau and Piedmont. Well-drained, mesic to moist, medium to fine textured soil in full sun to light shade with a pH between 5.0 and 7.9 at least 24 inches deep with a growing season of at least 170 days. Low fertility and moisture requirements; intolerant of anaerobic conditions. Popular for its dramatic display of pink flowers in spring.

Chaerophyllum procumbens (Slender chervil) [annual forb] — low, open bottomlands, woodlands and borders, thickets, rocky glades, FACW, generally in the southern third of Pennsylvania. Grows 6 to 18 inches with white flowers in late spring to early summer in mesic to moist, fertile, loamy soil in part sun.

Chamaecrista fasciculata (Partridge-pea, golden cassia) [annual forb] — Riverbanks, serpentine barrens, sandy flats, sandy prairies and fields, waste ground, FACU, mostly southern Pennsylvania. Easy to grow, nitrogen fixing, 1 to 3 feet with yellow flowers from mid-summer to fall, in sun to part shade. Prefers dry to mesic, deep, sandy, well-drained, coarse to medium textured loamy soils at least 14 inches deep, moderately fertile with a pH between 5.5 and 7.5 and often used in wildflower meadows and borders. Intolerant of anaerobic conditions but tolerates shade and some drought.

Chamaecrista nictitans (Wild sensitive-plant) [annual forb] — open woodlands, thickets and prairies as well as wet or dry shorelines in the southern two-thirds of the state, especially the southeast, FACU-. Grows less than 12 inches with yellow flowers in summer on sandy soils in sun.

Chamaecyparis thyoides (Atlantic white-cedar) - [tree] bogs and swamps, especially sphagnum, along the Atlantic and Gulf coasts, primarily coastal plain; scattered inland, OBL; scattered in southeast and southwest. Grows 35 to 50 feet in wet, acidic, sandy, coarse to medium textured, moderately fertile soils at least 16 inches deep with a pH between 3.5 and 6.3. Prefers sun to part sun and tolerates anaerobic conditions although moisture use is low. Potential for hedging. Intolerant of limestone-based soils and drought.

Chamaedaphne calyculata var. angustifolia (Leatherleaf) - [shrub] bogs and acidic wetlands, especially at higher elevations. OBL; mostly northeast (Northern Glaciated Allegheny Plateau) and northwest (Western Glaciated Allegheny Plateau, Erie and Ontario Lake Plain). Deciduous shrub to 5 feet; sun to part shade in acidic, peaty, moist to wet soils of any texture with a pH between 5.0 and 6.0 and at least 8 inches deep. Low anaerobic and limestone soil tolerances but high moisture and low fertility requirements. White flowers in spring.

Chamaelirium luteum (Devil's bit or Fairywand) - [perennial forb] dry to wet open woods, clearings, barrens in humus-rich soil; FAC; mostly southeast (Piedmont) and scattered elsewhere. Grows to 40 inches, white to yellow flowers in late spring; sun to part shade in dry, rich sandy loam, pH 5 to 7.

Chamaesyce vermiculata (Hairy spurge) [annual forb] — statewide on fields and prairies, common along walkways and roadsides. Grows 1 to 3 feet with white-red flowers in summer into fall on dry to mesic soils of all types.

Chamerion angustifolium ssp. circumvagum

(Fireweed) - [perennial forb] mesic woods, edges and recent clearings in open sandy ground; usually a pioneer species after forest fires, FAC; statewide. Grows 3 to 6 feet with purple-pink flowers in summer; disturbed moderately fertile sandy loam of all textures with a pH between 4.8 and 7.0 and at least 10 inches deep. High anaerobic tolerance and moisture use, intolerant of drought; grow in full sun to part shade; forms dense clumps and spreads aggressively.

Chasmanthium latifolium (Northern sea-oats or Indian wood oats) - [perennial graminoid] rare in rich alluvial woods or rocky slopes along streams and on moist bluffs and stream banks, FACU; scattered in south. Grows 20 to 40 inches in part sun to part shade; prefers in mesic to moist, low fertility sandy loam of any texture, pH 5 to 7.0 at least 10 inches deep. Moderately tolerant of anaerobic conditions and drought; can grow in shade but prefers part sun for good appearance.

Chasmanthium laxum (Slender sea-oats) - [perennial graminoid] sandy, moist soils, FAC. Mostly southeast (Atlantic Coastal Plain); endangered. Grows 1 to 3 feet in full sun to part shade on mesic to moist pebbly to sandy loam of any texture with a pH between 4.5 and 7.0 at least 10 inches deep; moderately drought and anaerobic tolerant and low fertility needs.

Cheilanthes lanosa (Hairy lip fern) - [fern/ally] rocky slopes and ledges, on a variety of substrates including limestone and granite; especially east. Fronds 6 to 16 inches; rhizome: short creeping. Grow in part sun to shade in dry sandy loam, pH 5 to 6.

Chelone glabra (White turtlehead) - [perennial forb] wet open woods, swamps and stream banks, OBL; statewide. Grows 20 to 30 inches, white to pinkish flowers in summer; sun to part shade in moist rich loam, but prefers full sun, pH 5.5 to 7.

White turtlehead (Chelone glabra)

Chenopodium album var. missouriense (Missouri lamb's quarters) [annual forb] — statewide, but less common in northern tier, on disturbed ground including cropland, gardens, weedy meadows and construction sites; uncommon in high quality natural areas. Possibly introduced. Grows 1 to 6 feet with white flowers in summer on mesic, fertile soils in sun to part sun. Aggressive spreader and seeds can remain viable for 40 years, so it's best to destroy plants before seeding.

Chenopodium bushianum (Pigweed) [annual forb] — statewide in woodlands and stream banks but common on cultivated, disturbed and waste ground with yellow flowers in fall. Grows in sun to part shade on a wide range of soils.

Chenopodium capitatum var. capitatum (Indian-paint) [annual forb] — Old fields, open woodlands and clearings, thickets, meadows, but especially burned areas, very widely scsttered statewide. Grows 8 to 24 inches with red flowers in late summer to fall, often after wildfires, in dry to mesic, light sandy soils.

Chenopodium foggii (Goosefoot) [annual forb] — dry prairies, meadows, fields and shaly slopes and rocky woodlands, mostly northeastern Pennsylvania; endangered. Grows 1 to 3 feet with yellow flowers in late summer in part shade to shade in sandy soil.

Chenopodium simplex (Maple-leaved goosefoot) [annual forb] — statewide on rocky woodlands, including edges, openings and glades, thinly wooded bluffs and ledges, thickets and recently logged or burned woodlands. Grows 6 to 48 inches in sun to part shade with greeenish flowers from late spring into fall. Pefers dappled sunlight to part shade in dry to mesic soils, with fertility driving plant size. One of the less weedy of the Chenopodium spp.

Chenopodium standleyanum (Woodland goosefoot) [annual forb] — dry open woodlands and borders, thickets, rocky bluffs and disturbed ground, mostly southeast. Grows to 48 inches depending conditions in dry to mesic loams, clay loams or stony loas in part sun to part shade.

Chimaphila maculata (Striped prince's pine) - [tree/shrub] moist woodlands in undisturbed organic litter of leaves and especially conifer needles; mostly southeast (Piedmont, Central Appalachians), scattered west. Subshrub, 4 to 12 inches; part shade to shade in dry, acidic sandy loam with leaf or needle litter, pH 4 to 5. White flowers in late summer.

Chimaphila umbellata ssp. cisatlantica (Pipsisswea, or prince's pine) - [tree/shrub] upland woods and barrens; statewide except north (Northern Unglaciated Allegheny Plateau). Subshrub 4 to 12 inches; part shade to shade in dry, acidic, coarse to medium textured sandy loam with a pH between 5.4 and 7.4 at least 8 inches deep. White or pink flowers in late summer. Low moisture requirement and moderate drought tolerance, but intolerant of anaerobic conditions and limestone-based soils.

Chionanthus virginicus (Fringe-tree) - [tree] bluffs, thickets, damp woods, 10 to 35 feet, FAC+. Mostly southeast; widely scattered elsewhere. Grow in well-drained, average moisture soil in full sun to part shade; prefers mesic to moist, fertile, coarse to medium textured soils with a pH between 4.5 and 6.5 at least 20 inches deep. Needs a 145-day growing season. Shade and somewhat drought tolerant with high moisture and fertility needs, but low anaerobic tolerance. Rarely requires pruning. Tolerant of urban pollution.

Chrysogonum virginianum (Green-and-gold) - [perennial forb] Very rare in moist to dry woodlands and forests, clearings and edges, especially over limestone. South-central; endangered. Grows 3 to 6 inches and spreads via rhizomes to form an attractive ground cover. Yellow flowers from March into July, but will continue to bloom with moisture into the fall. Grow in part sun to full shade in average soils, but prefers moist, rich organic soil.

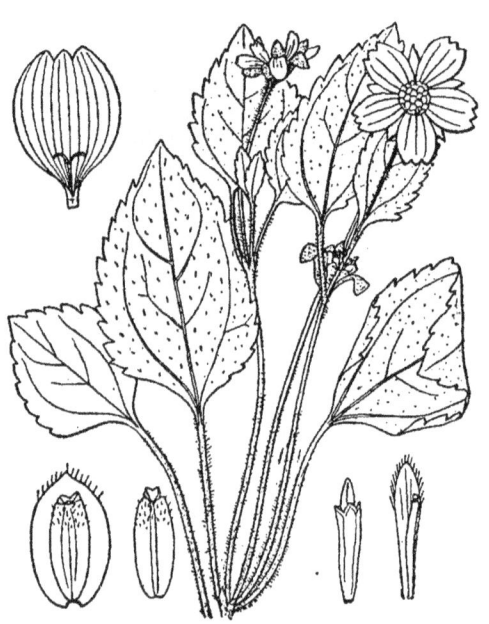

Green-and-gold (Chrysogonum virginianum)

Chrysopsis mariana (Golden aster) - [perennial forb] Rare in open areas of pine and oak woodlands, scrub, natural rock outcrops, fields and roadside embankments; UPL. Mostly southeast; endangered. Grows up to 12 inches, yellow flowers in late summer on open to partly shaded, disturbed clay to sandy soils.

Chrysosplenium americanum (Golden saxifrage) - [perennial forb] Marshy ground including streamsides, seeps, springs, and wet to swampy woods (OBL), statewide.

Cicuta bulbifera (Water-hemlock) - [perennial forb] Wet, bottomland woodlands, marshes, swales and swampy meadows, mostly eastern and northwestern Pennsylvania. (OBL).

Cicuta maculata var. maculata (Beaver-poison or water hemlock) - [perennial forb] swamps, marshes, wet meadows, stream banks and ditches, OBL; statewide. Grows up to 8 inches, white flowers in summer; moist to wet silty organic loam in sun to part sun. All parts highly toxic and may be fatal if eaten.

Cinna arundinacea (Wood reedgrass) - [perennial graminoid] moist woodlands and swamps, depressions, along streams, and in floodplains and upland woods; less frequent in wet meadows, marshes, and disturbed sites, FACU; statewide. Grows 40 to 60 inches in part sun to part shade in moist to wet, moderately fertile, humusy loam of any texture at least 16 inches deep, with a pH between 4.0 and 8.5. Somewhat tolerant of anaerobic conditions and limestone-based soils; low moisture requirement and drought tolerance

Cinna latifolia (Drooping woodreed) - [perennial graminoid] bogs, moist woodlands and shorelines, generally northern Pennsylvania as well as along the Allegheny Front; FACW. Grows 2 to 4 feet in sun to part shade on mesic to wet, moderately soil of any texture with with a pH of 4.7 to 7.0 at least 10 inches deep. Moderate shade tolerance, but low drought and limestone soil adaptability.

Circaea lutetiana ssp. canadensis (Enchanter's-nightshade) - [perennial forb] Scattered on the Allegheny Plateau along stream banks and woodlands in cool, rocky areas. Grows 9 to 24 inches with bluish-white flowers in summer; grow in dappled shade to part shade in mesic to moist, rich, circumneutral, loamy soil with much organic matter.

Cirsium discolor (Field thistle) - [perennial forb] Tall grass prairies and deciduous woodlands, especially openings, as well as disturbed sites (UPL); statewide, but mostly Piedmont and Coastal Plain. Grows 2 to 8 feet with purple flowers in summer, full sun in dry to mesic loamy soils.

Cirsium muticum (Swamp thistle) - [perennial forb] swamps, bogs, stream banks and wet meadows, OBL; statewide. Grows 3 to 6 feet, purple flowers in summer; sun to part sun in moist to wet rich loam.

Cirsium pumilum (Pasture thistle) - [perennial forb] Statewide in dry woodlands, pastures and fields, shaly hillsides and sandy floodplains, along roadsides. Grows 12 to 24 inches in open, dry, generally sandy soils lacking taller competition and generally in areas where fires are common. Grow in part sun to part shade.

Cladium mariscoides (Twig-rush) - [perennial graminoid] widely scattered statewide but most concentrated in northern Wayne County in open, acidic to alkaline wetlands, including marshes, floating bog mats and shallow lake margins, OBL; listed as endangered in Pennsylvania.

Claytonia caroliniana (Carolina spring beauty) - [perennial forb] moist, rocky upland wooded slopes, open woods and thickets, FACU; north and west (Allegheny plateaus). Grows 6 to 12 inches, white to pinkish flowers in spring; part sun to part shade in moist to wet rich loams, pH 5 to 6.

Claytonia virginica (Spring beauty) - [perennial forb] moist woods and meadows, often on alluvial soils, FACU; statewide. Grows 6 to 12 inches, white to pinkish flowers in spring; sun to part shade in moist, medium to fine textured loam.

Clematis occidentalis (Purple clematis) - [perennial vine] rare in open woods, banks, gravelly embankments, rocky woods, slopes and cliffs, mostly southeast (Piedmont). Climbing or trailing woody vine to 10 feet; violet flowers in late spring. Grow in part shade to shade in circumneutral mesic sandy to rocky soils.

Clematis viorna (Leather-flower) - [perennial vine] rare on stream banks and wooded cliffs and thickets, scattered south; endangered. Grows to 35 feet with red to purple flowers in early summer; grow in moist, rich, well drained loam.

Clematis virginiana (Virgin's-bower) - [perennial vine] stream edges, wet roadsides, fencerows, and other moist, disturbed, wooded or open sites, statewide; FAC. Climbing or trailing woody vine to 15 feet. White flowers in summer. Grow in sun to shade; prefers mesic to moist, medium to fine textured, moderately fertile soils in part shade at least 14 inches deep, with a pH range of 5.0 to 6.8. Intolerant of limestone-based soils and anaerobic conditions, but moderately tolerant of drought.

Clethra acuminata (Mountain pepperbush) - [shrub] very rare in deciduous, rocky forests Appalachian slopes, bluffs and ravines, typically on moist sites often near high-elevation streams; scattered southwest (Southern Allegheny Plateau) and endangered. Grows 12 to 20 feet in part shade on acidic, rocky soils, usually moist but can adapt to dryer circumstances. White flowers in mid-summer.

Clethra alnifolia (Sweet pepperbush) - [shrub] low wet woods, bogs and acidic swamps in moderately to poorly drained sites, FAC+; mostly east, especially Atlantic Coastal Plain. Deciduous shrub, 6 to 12 feet; average, medium to wet, well-drained, coarse to medium textured, moderately fertile soil in full sun to part shade. Adaptive to a wide range of soil, moisture and light conditions. Prefers part shade and consistently moist, acidic soils with a pH 4.5 to 7.0 at least 16 inches deep. Tolerates shade, but blooms better in part sun. Low drought and limestone soil tolerance, but moderately accepting of anaerobic conditions. White flowers in summer.

Clinopodium arkansanum (Calamint) - [perennial forb] moist dolomite alvars, open flats and bald knobs, fens, limestone glades and bluffs, and wet prairies and meadows, as well as stream gravel bars; FACU. Northwest (Erie and Ontario Lake Plain). Grows 2 to 8 inches in mats with white to purple flowers from June through late September. Prefers neutral to slightly alkaline, mesic and well-drained soils in full sun, but tolerates light shade. AKA Calamintha arkansana.

Clintonia borealis (Blue bead lily) - [perennial forb] shady, cool moist woods and thickets, mostly in the mountains, FAC; statewide except southeast (Piedmont). Grows up to 16 inches, yellow flowers in late spring, fruit a blue berry in summer; part shade to shade in mesic to moist, medium to fine-textured, moderately fertile, humusy loam at least 8 inches deep with a pH 5.0 to 6.8. Low anaerobic and drought tolerance, but adaptable to limestone-based soils.

Clintonia umbellulata (Speckled wood-lily) - [perennial forb] Rich hardwood forests, especially in coves, ravines, and banks. Mostly west (Western Glaciated and Southern Allegheny plateaus).Grows 1 to 3 feet, white flowers in late spring; prefers acidic, humus-rich (peaty) soils in damp, cool, part shade to shade, and serves as a good groundcover for shady sites. Short-creeping underground stems form dense patches.

Clitoria mariana (Butterfly pea) - [perennial vine] rare in dry, open thickets and open ground, scattered southeast (Piedmont); endangered. Grows 3 to 4 feet in well drained, sandy soils in full to part sun.

Coeloglossum viride var. virescens (Frog orchid) - [perennial forb] Scattered, mostly in Ridge and Valley moist to wet forests, prairies, meadows, thickets and bogs (FACU). Grows up to 30 inches from basal leaves, with reddish-brown flowers in late spring to early summer; grow in part sun to part shade in humus-rich, mesic to wet, acidic woodland soils with plenty of leaf litter.

Collinsia verna (Blue-eyed-Mary) [annual forb] — mesic to moist woodlands, especially lower slopes of river valleys and thickets, especially in the Piedmont. Grows 4-12 inches with white-blue flowers in spring in part shade to shade in mesic to moist, rich loamy soils. Moisture impacts plant size. Tolerates minor disturbance but serves as an indicator of high quality woodlands.

Collinsonia canadensis (Horse balm) - [perennial forb] moist rich woods and on wooded floodplains and ravines, often on limestone substrates, FAC+; statewide. Grows to 48 inches, yellow flowers in summer; part shade to shade in dry to moist organic loam, pH 6 to 7.

Comandra umbellata (Bastard toadflax) - [perennial forb] statewide in dry oak forests (parasitic on roots of oaks) (FACU). Grows up to 12 inches in full to part sun, dry to mesic acidic to circumneutral often sandy to rocky loams, with white flowers in late spring.

Comarum palustre (Marsh cinquefoil) - [perennial forb] emergent aquatic; swamps, bogs and peaty lake margins, OBL. Northeast (Northern Glaciated Allegheny Plateau) and northwest (Western Glaciated Allegheny Plateau and Erie and Ontario Lake Plain). Grows 8 to 24 inches, red-purple flowers in summer; full sun in mucky, peaty soil along pond edges. AKA Potentilla palustris.

Commelina erecta (Erect dayflower) - [perennial forb] Very rare in hummocks, shale barrens, sand dunes and rocky woods including scrub oak and pine woodlands, as well as roadsides and railroad rights of way. Only one southeastern site reported and now believed to be extirpated. Grows in typically prostrate style on stems up to 3 feet long that lie on the ground, with blue and white flowers that last just one day from May to October in part shade on dry, sandy soils.

Commelina virginica (Virginia dayflower) -

[perennial forb] Swamps, river and stream banks, ditches, and bottomlands, shade or full sun; considered extirpated in Pennsylvania; reported only in Philadelphia and Lancaster Counties.

Comptonia peregrina (Sweet-fern) - [shrub] dry, sterile, sandy to rocky soils in pinelands or pine barrens, clearings, or woodlot edges; statewide, but scattered west. Shrub to 3 feet; sun to part shade in average, medium, well-drained soil in full sun to part shade. Prefers sandy, acidic loams, but tolerates coarse to medium textured soils at least 14 inches deep with a pH of 4.0 to 7.0. Spreads to form colonies. Tolerates very dry conditions and wind, drought and requires very little moisture and soil fertility. Low tolerance for limestone-based soils and none for anaerobic conditions. Difficult to transplant after established.

Conioselinum chinense (Hemlock-parsley) - [perennial forb] Rich, moist woodlands and stream banks; FACW; endangered. Grows 12 to 24 inches in moist to wet, humus-rich soils in full sun to part sun; white flowers.

Conoclinium coelestinum (Mistflower) - [perennial forb] along streams, in low woods and woods margins, wet meadows, ditches. FAC. Mostly south, especially Piedmont and Southern Allegheny Plateau. Pale blue flowers in late summer. Grow in well-drained, medium to fine textured, mesic to moist, moderately fertile soils at least 14 inches deep and with a pH of 5.5 to 7.5, in full sun to part shade; prefers full sun. Moderate drought tolerance, but none for anerobic conditions. Aggressive spreader through rhizomes and will form large colonies. Cut back in summer for denser habit. AKA *Eupatorium coelestinum*.

Conopholis americana (Squaw-root) - [perennial forb] rich oak or beech woods, where it is parasitic on oaks; mostly south, scattered elsewhere. Grows up to 6 inches, pale brown to yellowish flowers in late spring; part shade to shade in dry to moist sandy loam, pH 4 to 6.

Conyza canadensis var. canadensis (Horseweed) [annual/biennial forb] — dry fields, upland prairies and weedy meadows plus a wide range of disturbed to waste ground, statewide, UPL. Grows 1 to 7 feet with white flowers in full sun with a preference for dry to mesic, fertile, loamy soil, but tolerates gravelly conditions.

Coptis trifolia ssp. groenlandica (Goldthread) - [perennial forb] rich, damp, mossy woods bogs and swamps, often associated with hemlock and mosses, FACW; mostly north, scattered elsewhere. Grows 6 to 8 inches, white flowers in early spring; shade in moist, acidic, humusy loam, pH 4 to 5.

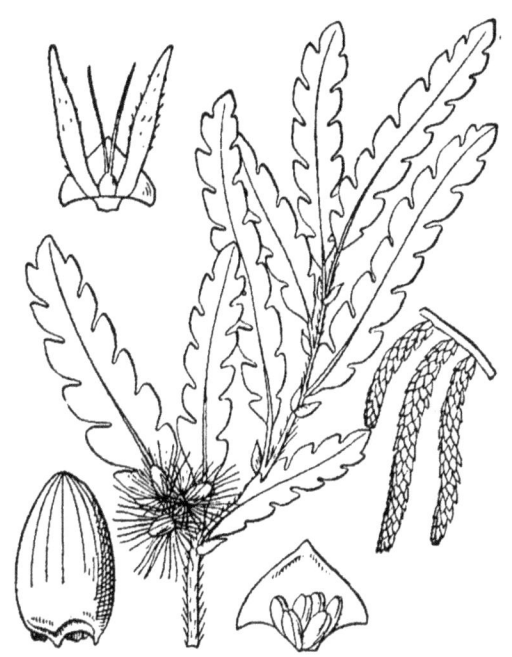

Sweet-fern (Comptonia peregrina)

Corallorhiza maculata (Spotted coralroot) - [perennial forb] Statewide in moist to dry woodlands and conifer plantations, especially in light soils with little other herbaceous cover (FACU). Grows about a foot in leaf litter on mesic sites in part shade.

Corallorhiza odontorhiza (Autumn coralroot) - [perennial forb] Rich, moist to dry mixed and conifer woodlands, mostly Piedmont. Grows about a foot in leaf litter on mesic sites in part shade.

Corallorhiza trifida (Early coralroot) - [perennial forb] Scattered statewide in moist woodlands, upland swamps and bogs (FACW). Grows up to 12 inches with whitish-green flowers in early summer; grow in rich, humusy forest loam in part shade to shade.

Corallorhiza wisteriana (Wister's coralroot) - [perennial forb] Rocky, wooded slopes, usually on limestone and generally richer soils than other coral roots, mostly Piedmont and Coastal Plain. Grows about 12 inches with white-brownish flowers in spring to summer; prefers rich, humusy woodland loams in part shade to shade.

Cornus alternifolia (Alternate-leaved dogwood) - [tree/shrub] moist woodlands, forest margins, stream and swamp borders, and near deep canyon bottoms; statewide. Deciduous shrub or small tree to 25 feet; sun to part shade in sandy, well-drained, moderate-texture, moderately fertile soils at least 20 inches deep with a ph of 4.8 to 7.3. Tolerant of shade, but not anaerobic conditions, drought or limestone soils. White flowers in late spring.

Cornus amomum ssp. amomum (Red willow or Kinnikinik) - [tree/shrub] swamps, stream banks, moist woods, fields and thickets, FACW; statewide. Deciduous shrub to 10 feet. Two local subspecies: *amomum* and *obliqua*; part shade to shade in moist to wet acidic sandy loam of any texture with a pH range of 5.0 to 7.0 at least 16 inches deep. Moderate anaerobic tolerance, but none for droiught or limestone soils. White flowers in late spring.

Cornus canadensis (Bunchberry) - [perennial forb, subshrub] cool, damp woods, bogs and swamp edges, FAC-. Mostly north; scattered south. Grows 4 to 8 inches, white flowers late spring and fruit in late summer; part shade to shade in moist, rich, humusy medium textured soils at least 10 inches deep, with a pH of 5. to 6.9. Intolerant of anaerobic conditions, drought and limestone-based soils; high moisture and moderate fertility requirements.

Cornus florida (Flowering dogwood) - [tree] mesic deciduous woods, on floodplains, slopes, bluffs, and in ravines, FACU; statewide, but scattered north. Tree to 30 feet; varied soils with a pH between 4.8 to 7.7, from moist, deep soils to light-textured, well-drained upland soils; prefers coarse to medium-textured acidic soils at least 18 inches deep. Intolerant of anaerobic conditions, drought, or limestone-based soils, but okay with shade. White flowers in spring, found in many garden centers.

Cornus racemosa (Silky dogwood) - [shrub] swampy meadows, moist old fields, thickets, FAC-; statewide. Grows 3 to 10 feet in sun to part shade in mesic, medium to fine textured, moderately fertile sandy loam at least 16 inches deep with a pH range of 4.8 to 7.4. Tolerates wide range of soil conditions, including both moist and somewhat dry soils, with moderate drought tolerance, and city air pollution. Intolerant of anaerobic conditions and has potential for hedge use. White flowers in spring.

Cornus rugosa (Round-leaved dogwood) - [tree/shrub] well-drained rocky woods and cliffs; statewide, especially east. Shrub or small tree, 3 to 12 feet; part shade to shade in dry to mesic, coarse to medium textured, moderately fertile, sandy loam with a pH range of 6.4 to 7.8 and at least 18 inches deep. Intolerant of anaerobic conditions and not a good choices for hedges, but with low moisture needs is a good candidate for droughty sites. White flowers in spring.

Cornus sericea (Red-osier dogwood) - [tree/shrub] stream banks, swamps, moist fields, thickets, FACW+; mostly northwest; scattered elsewhere. Shrub to 10 feet; sun to part sun in moist, well-drained soil of any texture with a pH range of 4.8 to 7.5 and at least 20 inches deep. Adaptable to a wide range of soil and climatic conditions, with high anaerobic tolerance and low fertility requirements, but high moisture needs and intolerance to drought and limestone-based soils. White flowers in spring. AKA *Cornus stolonifera*.

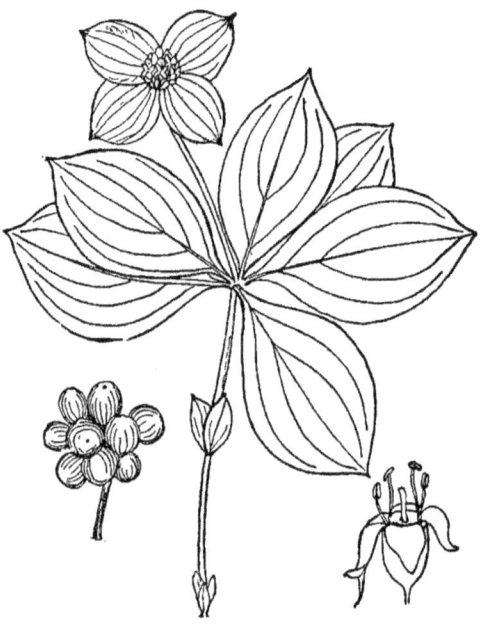

Bunchberry (Cornus canadensis)

Corydalis sempervirens (Rock harlequin) - [perennial forb] dry rocky woods, woodland outcrops and open areas on poor gravelly soil; statewide. Grows 12 to 30 inches, pinkish-white to purple flowers in late spring to early fall; sun to part shade in dry sandy loam, pH 5 to 6.

Corylus americana (American filbert) - [shrub] moist to dry open woods, thickets, hillsides, roadsides, fencerows, and waste places, FACU-; statewide. Grows to 15 feet but more commonly about 10 feet in medium to fine textured, well-drained, moderately fertile soil with a pH between 5.0 and 7.0 at least 20 inches deep. Moderately tolerant of drought and limestone-based soils with slight potential for hedging. Prefers full sun to part sun and is intolerant of anaerobic conditions; forms thickets if suckers are not removed. White flowers in early spring.

Corylus cornuta (Beaked hazelnut) - [shrub] moist to dry roadsides, woodland edges, thickets, fencerows, sometimes as an understory in open woodlands, FACU-; statewide, mostly east, scattered west. Shrub to 15 feet; full sun to part shade in medium-textured, organically rich, mesic, well-drained soils with a pH range of 4.8 to 7.5 at least 16 inches deep. Tolerates hedging, shade, average garden and limestone based soils, but not unamended heavy clays or anaerobic conditions. Yellow flowers in early spring.

Crassula aquatica (Water-pigmyweed) [annual forb] — aquatic found in fresh water and intertidal marshes such as vernal pools, brackish mudflats, pond and stream margins, OBL and listed as extirpated. Grows to about three inches with white-green flowers from spring into fall.

Crataegus chrysocarpa (Fireberry hawthorn) - [tree/shrub] rocky pastures, open woodlands and edges. Large shrub or small tree to 25 feet; sun to part sun in mesic to moist sandy loam; drought tolerant. White flowers in early summer. AKA *Crataegus rotundifolia*.

Crataegus chrysocarpa var. chrysocarpa (Red-fruited hawthorn) - [tree/shrub] open woods, fields, roadsides and stream banks; statewide, especially southeast, except northeast. Shrub or small tree to 32 feet; sun to part sun in mesic to moist well drained sandy loam. Tolerates a wide range of soils as long as drainage is good, light shade and some drought, and many urban pollutants. White flowers in late spring. Also known as *Crataegus coccinea*.

Crataegus crus-galli (Cockspur hawthorn) - [tree/shrub] woods, meadows, roadsides, thickets, especially in dry or rocky places, and slopes of low hills in rich soils, FACU; mostly southeast; scattered elsewhere except north. Large shrub or small tree grows to 32 feet; sun to part sun in mesic to moist well drained sandy loam of all textures, at least 24 inches deep and with a pH erange of 4.5 to 7.2. Tolerates a wide range of well drained soils, infertile soils, light shade, some drought and many urban pollutants, but not anaerobic conditions. Low moisture requirements support adaptability to drought. White to pink flowers in late spring.

Crataegus dilatata (Broadleaf hawthorn) - [tree/shrub] thickets and calcareous hills, including pastures; scattered sites in the northern Allegheny Mountains. Grows to 20 feet in moist to wet soils in full sun to part shade.

Crataegus flabellata (Fanleaf hawthorn) - [tree/shrub] statewide in open woodlands, fencerows, abandoned fields and roadsides. Grows to 20 feet in mesic to slightly dry generally circumneutral sandy or silt loams that are well drained; grow in part sun to part shade.

Crataegus intricata (Biltmore hawthorn) - [tree/shrub] southern Pennsylvania in woodlands, pastures, thickets and barrens. Grows to 10 feet in part sun to part shade, prefers well-drained mesic to moist circumneutral soils and is drought hardy.

Crataegus mollis (Downy hawthorn) - [tree/shrub] fields, roadsides, alluvial thickets, woodland edges, FACU; scattered southeast and northwest. Grows 35 to 75 feet in dry to moist soils in full sun to part shade. Avoid planting near red cedar (rust blight); susceptible to gypsy moth.

Crataegus pruinosa (Frosted hawthorn) - [tree/shrub] statewide, especially southeast, in open woods and thickets. Grows 10 to 20 feet with white flowers in spring; prefers full to part sun in mesic to slightly dry well-drained loamy soils.

Crataegus punctata (Dotted hawthorn) -

[tree/shrub] open hardwood and conifer-hardwood forests; statewide. Large shrub or small tree to 40 feet; sun to shade in dry to moist circumneutral ordinary loams. White, pink, yellow flowers in late spring.

Crataegus succulenta (Long-spined hawthorn) - [tree/shrub] woodland edges and thickets, pastures, rocky bluffs; scattered statewide, especially southeast and central; grows to about 20 feet. Prefers dry sandy or rocky soils in part sun to dappled shade.

Crotalaria sagittalis (Rattlebox) [annual forb] — sandy and gravelly prairies, savannas, rocky glades, fallow fields and openings in upland woodlands, generally southeast. Grows 6 to 12 inches with yellow flowers in late summer into autumn, with a preference for full to part sun in dry to mesic barren soils with sand, gravel and clay, especially with a history of disturbance and no competition.

Croton capitatus (Hogwort) [annual forb] — widely scattered in prairies, glades, fields and disturbed ground in southern Pennsylvania with white flowers in summer. Prefers dry, sandy loams in full sun and serves as an important food source for quail and doves.

Crotonopsis elliptica (Elliptical rushfoil) [annual forb] — found in rocky, open woods and glades; reported in the Atlantic Coastal Plain but listed as extirpated. Grows to about 2 feet in dry to mesic, acidic sandy soils in part sun to part shade.

Cryptogramma stelleri (Slender rockbrake) - [fern/ally] scattered in north central Pennsylvania in sheltered, cool, moist calcareous cliffs, ledges and ravines, often in coniferous forests; listed as endangered.

Cryptotaenia canadensis (Honewort) - [perennial forb] moist woods, wooded stream banks, seeps; FAC; statewide. Grows 10 to 30 inches, white flowers late spring to early summer; part shade in moist, sandy loam.

Cunila origanoides (Common dittany) - [perennial forb] dry open woods, shaly slopes, and serpentine barrens. Mostly southeast; scattered southwest; part sun to part shade in dry, sandy rocky loam.

Cuphea viscosissima (Blue waxweed) [annual forb] — dry open banks and fields in southern Pennsylvania, FAC-. Grows 9 to 18 inches with purple to purplish red flowers in late summer to fall, in dry to mesic moderately fertile, well-drained loams in full to part sun. Tolerates dry conditions.

Cuscuta campestris (golden dodder) [annual vine] — open woodlands and glades, fields and prairies, rocky barrens and thickets, mostly southeast, especially Atlantic Coastal Plain. Parasitic plant with white flowers in summer to fall and popular with hummingbirds and butterflies; dry to mesic soils in part sun to part shade.

Cuscuta cephalanthi (Buttonbush dodder) [Annual Vine] — widely scattered in floodplain woodlands, swamps, soggy thickets along lakes, streams and rivers, marshes, and wet prairies. Parasitic; grows to several feet with white to yellow flowers in late summer to fall in part sun in moist to wet sand, silt, loam or muck. Can weaken host plant and cannot survive without appropriate host, including asters (*Aster* spp.), buttonbush (*Cephalanthus occidentalis*), bugleweed (*Lycopus* spp.), false nettle (*Boehmeria cylindrica*), water willow (*Justicia americana*), goldenrods (*Solidago* spp.), and horsetails (*Equisetum* spp.).

Cuscuta compacta (Dodder) [annual vine] — stream banks and moist thickets, southeastern Pennsylvania; a twining parasitic with white flowers in late summer to fall on shrubs and herbaceous plants in mesic to moist, sandy loams, part sun to part shade.

Cuscuta coryli (Hazel dodder) [annual vine] — widely scattered statewide in dry, rocky woodlands and slopes; a twining parasitic with white flowers in late summer to fall on shrubs and herbaceous plants in dry to mesic loams and sandy loams, part sun to part shade.

Cuscuta gronovii var. gronovii (Common dodder) [annual vine] — statewide parasitic in low wet woodlands, moist thickets and riverbanks on a variety of shrubs and herbaceous species. Two varieties: *gronovii* is found statewide, while *latiflora* is scattered in the southeast. Twining growth to several feet with white flowers on orange-yellow stems that bloom in late summer to fall.

Cuscuta pentagona (Field dodder) [annual

vine] — parasitic in fields, prairies, savannas, thickets, riverbanks and neglected gardens, mostly southeast. Requires suitable host plants, i.e., *Baptisia, Lespedeza, Desmodium, Trifolium, Ceoanthus, Rubus, Impatiens*, and *Euphorbia* spp. and is a major pest of clover, alfalfa and sugar beet fields. Grows to several feet with white flowers in late summer and prefers dry, sandy soils in full to part sun of any quality.

Cuscuta polygonorum (Smartweed dodder) [annual vine] — widely scattered parasitic on especially *Polygonum* spp. in wet prairies and meadows, soggy riverside thickets, fens and sandy marshes. Aggressive spreader that grows to several feet with the appearance of a mass of tangled orange-yellow string, in part sun to part shade in silty and sandy loams high in organic matter, including standing water. White flowers in late summer to fall.

Cymophyllus fraserianus (Fraser's sedge) - [perennial graminoid] reported in Somerset County on mesic to wet mesic shaded slopes and stream banks in rich, typically rocky deciduous, mixed and hemlock forests; listed as endangered in Pennsylvania. Grows 8 to 18 inches in part shade to shade.

Cynanchum laeve (Smooth sallow-wort, honeyvine) - [perennial vine] reported only in Chester and Lancaster counties on river banks; FAC and listed as endangered in Pennsylvania.

Cynoglossum virginianum (Wild comfrey) - [perennial forb] Rich open woodlands and slopes, mostly southern Pennsylvania, especially Piedmont. Grows 24 to 36 inches in full sun to part shade with bluish-white flowers in late spring to early summer; considered a noxious weed in some parts of the U.S.

Cynoglossum virginianum var. boreale (Northern hound's-tongue) [perennial forb] — rich woodlands including slopes, ravines, ridges, thickets and bottomlands, generally northeast. Grows to about 9 inches with small lavender to blue flowers in late spring, sun to part shade, in mesic to moist loams. AKA Cynoglossum boreale.

Cyperus acuminatus (Short-pointed flatsedge) [annual graminoid] — sandy shores and damp disturbed soils in the Atlantic Coastal Plain; OBL. Grows to about 18 inches in full to part sun in moist to wet, medium to fine-textured sandy loams at leat 6 inches deep with a pH erange of 4.9 to 6.8. High tolerance for anaerobic conditions, but none for drought or limestone-based soils.

Cyperus bipartitus (Slender flat sedge) [annual graminoid] — statewide in seeps, swamps, sedge meadows, low-lying areas near lakes and streams and lakes including shorelines, sand and gravel bars and muddy islands, FACW+. Grows to about 10 inches in full to part sun in moist to wet circumneutral sandy, gravelly, mucky or rocky moderately fertile soils with a pH range of 4.5 to 6.5 at least 14 inches deep, with a high tolerance for flooding and wave action but none for drought or shade.

Cyperus compressus (Poorland sedge) [annual graminoid] — sandy waste ground in the Atlantic Coastal Plain, FAC+. Grows to 12 inches in sun to part sun on disturbed mesic, coarse to medium textured sandy loams with a pH of 5.0 to 6.5 at least 8 inches deep. Moderate anaerobic and limestone tolerance, but low fertility requirements and adaptability to droughty conditions.

Cyperus dentatus (Toothed flatsedge) - [perennial graminoid] moist sandy, peaty or gravelly shorelines of rivers, FACW+, in north central and eastern Pennsylvania, especially along the Delaware River. Grows to 20 inches in sun to part shade.

Cyperus diandrus (Umbrella sedge) [annual graminoid] — wet emergent shorelines, bogs, and

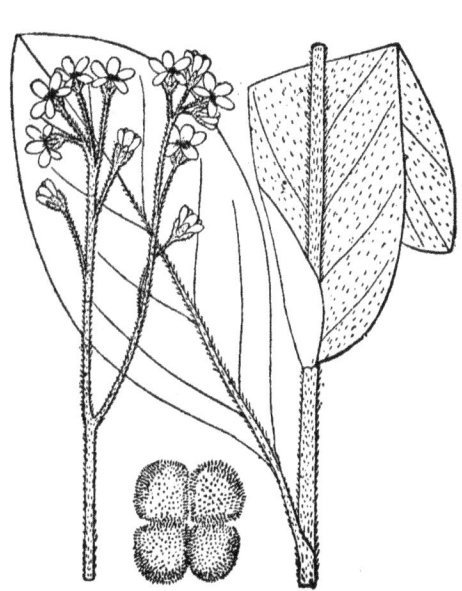

Wild comfrey (Cynoglossum virginianum)

marshes and wet shores, FACW, listed as endangered, widely scattered east. Grows to 12 inches in sandy, peaty, or slightly brackish undisturbed soils in full to part sun.

Cyperus engelmannii (Engelmann's flatsedge) [annual graminoid] — tidal mudflats, emergent marshes and shorelines in the northwest and far southeast, FACW. Grows to 36 inches in full sun on moist to wet sandy loams.

Cyperus erythrorhizos (Redroot flatsedge) [annual graminoid] — river banks, swamps, emergent shorelines and other wet ground, mostly southeast and northwest, FACW+. Grows to about 36 inches in moist to wet alluvial, lacustrine and coastal coarse to medium textured soils at least 10 inches deep and with a pH range of 5.0 to 6.5, full to part sun, well-drained. Moderately tolerant of anaerobic conditions, drought and limestone soils.

Cyperus esculentus (Yellow nutsedge) - [perennial graminoid] low areas of upland prairies and fields, stream edges and pond margins, FACU; statewide. Grows 12 to 40 inches; sun to part sun in moist, rich sandy loams of any texture at least 14 inches deep with a pH of 5.0 to 7.0. Low moisture use and anaerobic tolerance, but adaptable to droughty conditions and limestone soil.

Cyperus filicinus (Fern sedge) [annual graminoid] — swales between dunes and along upper edges of tidal marshes, sometimes emergent shorelines and island ditches, Atlantic Coastal Plain, FACW. Grows to 18 inches in sun to part sun on moist to wet sandy soils.

Cyperus flavescens (Yellow flatsedge) - [annual graminoid] damp to moist open and often disturbed soil in fields and ditches, OBL; grows to about 2 feet. Widely scattered in most of Pennsylvania, but concentrated in the southeast in full to part sun.

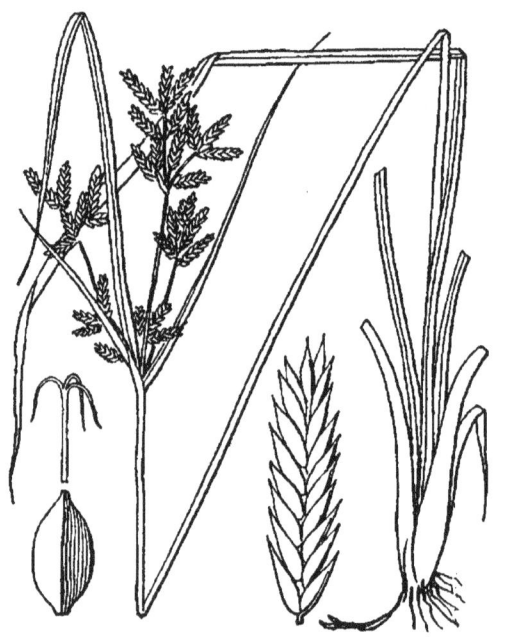

Toothed flatsedge (Cyperus dentatus)

Prefers coarse to medium texture, moderately fertile, mesic to moist soils with a pH range of 5.0 to 7.0 and a depth of at least 8 inches. Somewhat tolerant of anaerobic conditions and limestone soils, but not drought or shade.

Cyperus houghtonii (Houghton's flatsedge) - [perennial graminoid] widely scattered in dry, sandy soil on sand bars and river banks, dunes, lakeshores, and opening in sandy woodlands, often among Pinus banksiana (Jack pine); listed as endangered in Pennsylvania. Grows to 20 inches in sun to part sun.

Cyperus lancastriensis (Manyflower flatsedge) - [perennial graminoid] southeastern Pennsylvania, especially Atlantic Coastal Plain, in mesic to dry-mesic soils, usually in open woodlands, dry fields, riverbanks and floodplains; FACU. Grows 36 inches in sun to part sun on coarse to medium textured, moderately fertile soils with a pH from 5.0 to 7.0 and at least 12 inches deep. Low drought and anaerobic tolerance.

Cyperus lupulinus (Great Plains flatsedge) - [perennial graminoid] statewide, but more common toward the southeast in well drained and usually dry soils of fields, prairies, open woodlands and disturbed sites; UPL.

Cyperus odoratus (Fragrant flatsedge) [annual graminoid] — In the Atlantic Coastal Plain on emergent shorelines, moist meadows, wet sand and gravel flats; FACW. Grows 1 to 3 feet in full to part sun on moist to wet coarse to medium textured soils with a pH of 5.0 to 8.3 and at least 8 inches deep, that are in a wet shoreline or clearing.

Cyperus plukenetii (Plukenet's flatsedge) - [perennial graminoid] very rare on dry sand hills, xeric upland woods, roadside banks.

Cyperus polystachyos (Many-spiked flatsedge)

[annual graminoid] — Found in swales between dunes, tidal river banks and shorelines in the Atlantic Coastal Plain, FACW, but reported as extirpated. Grows to about 18 inches in full to part sun on moist to wet sandy soils.

Cyperus refractus (Reflexed flatsedge) - [perennial graminoid] southern Piedmont and Atlantic Coastal Plain in dry, sandy riverbanks, pastures and woodlands; FACU+ and listed as endangered in Pennsylvania; often confused with C. strigosus, which has shorter anthers. Grows 10 to 30 inches in sun to part sun.

Cyperus retrofractus (Rough flatsedge) - [perennial graminoid] very rare in dry sandy to clayey soils in disturbed sites such as roadsides and pastures.

Cyperus retrorsus (Retrorse flatsedge) - [perennial graminoid] widely scattered in southeastern Pennsylvania on moist to dry sandy soils in thickets and open woodlands; FAC- and listed as endangered in Pennsylvania.

Cyperus schweinitzii (Schweinitz's flatsedge) - [perennial graminoid] rare in sandy openings in woods, sand dunes, sand bars and along stream banks and lake shores, FACU; mostly southeast (Piedmont). Grows up to 12 inches in full sun on dry, very sandy soil.

Cyperus squarrosus (Bearded flatsedge) [annual graminoid] — low riparian areas and floodplains, swampy woodlands, stream margins, sedge meadows, sandstone depressions and glades, and moist fields, FACW+, generally east and especially in the Delaware River valley. Grows to 6 inches in full to part sun in moist to wet sandy, thin or mucky soil.

Cyperus strigosus (False nutsedge) - [perennial graminoid] common statewide in damp to moist woodlands, swamps, fields, stream banks and lake and pond shorelines, often as a garden weed; FACW. Grows 10 to 15 inches in sun to part shade in medium to fine textured, moderately fertile soils with a pH range of 6.4 to 7.0 and at least 16 inches deep. Moderately tolerant of anaerobic conditions and limestone soils, but intolerant of drought and shade.

Cypripedium acaule (Pink lady's slipper) - [perennial forb] dry to wet acidic upland forests, bogs, and brushy barrens; FACU; statewide. Grows 6 to 16 inches, pink flowers late spring; part shade to shade in well mulched, dry to moist sandy acidic loam, pH 4 to 5. Very difficult to transplant because of long, thin root system and soil preferences; tends to be quite pricey and with virtually no guarantees.

Cypripedium candidum (Small white lady's-slipper) - [perennial forb] Very rare in wet to mesic prairies and meadows, fens and very rarely in open wooded sites; OBL. Believed to be extirpated. Grows 6 to 16 inches in calcareous, wet to moist soils rich in organic matter in sun to part sun, with white flowers in late spring.

Cypripedium parviflorum var. parviflorum (Lesser yellow lady's slipper) - [perennial forb] dry deciduous and deciduous-hemlock forests, usually on slopes, FAC+. Scattered statewide, endangered. Grows 8 to 30 inches, yellow flowers in spring; part shade to shade in rich dry to moist acidic sandy loam.

Cypripedium parviflorum var. pubescens (Large yellow lady's slipper) - [perennial forb] moist, rich, rocky woods and slopes, bogs and swamps, FAC+; statewide, endangered. Grows 8 to 30 inches, yellow flowers, spring; sun to part shade in moist to wet silty loam, pH 5 to 7, but prefers 6.5 to 7.

Cypripedium reginae (Large white lady's slipper) - [perennial forb] very rare in hardwood and coniferous fen forests and meadows, hillside seeps, fen and moist meadows, wet prairies and seeping cliffs. FACW; mostly northwest (Western Glaciated Allegheny Plateau) and widely scattered in Central Appalachians. Largest and most showy of the native orchids, with white and pink flowers in late spring to early summer. Grow in full sun to part shade in moist to wet rich, circumneutral soils.

Cystopteris bulbifera (Bublet bladder fern) - [fern/ally] typically moist calcareous cliffs, but also grows on rock in dense woods and occasionally occurs terrestrially in northern swamps. Less common in far west. Fronds 18 to 36 inches; rhizome: short creeping. Grow in part shade to shade in mesic to moist calcareous loam, pH 6.5 to 7.5.

Cystopteris fragilis (Fragile fern) - [fern/ally] commonly on cliff faces and in thin alkaline soil over rock. Fronds 5 to 16 inches; rhizome: compact. Grow in part shade to shade in mesic to slightly dry humusy loams.

Cystopteris laurentiana (Laurentian bladder fern) - [fern/ally] very rare and widely scattered statewide in cracks of ledges and cliffs, usually on calcareous substrates. Fronds to 18 inches; rhizome: short creeping, grow in part sun to shade in dry sandy loam in circumneutral soils.

Cystopteris protrusa (Protruding bladder fern) - [fern/ally] generally southern Pennsylvania in humus-rich, moist, circumneutral, alluvial soils in deciduous flats.

Cystopteris tenuis (Fragile fern) - [fern/ally] statewide, most often on shaded, cool rock crevices, cliff faces and talus slopes with neutral to subacid soils, but sometimes on forest floors.

Dalibarda repens (Dewdrop) — [perennial forb] cool, mossy woodlands, bogs and peat barrens, generally along the Allegheny front and into northern Pennsylvania, especially in the northern Ridge and Valley, FAC. Grows 2 to 5 inches with white flowers in summer, part shade to shade in moist to wet rich, humusy woodland soil.

Danthonia spicata (Poverty grass) — [perennial graminoid] dry rocky, sandy, or mineral soils, usually in open sunny places; statewide. Grows 8 to 24 inches; sun to part shade in dry to mesic sandy loam.

Dasiphora fruticosa (Shrubby cinquefoil) — [shrub] very rare in calcareous swamps and endangered in Pennsylvania; FACW. Typically grows in moisture retentive soils in swamps and moist rocky areas. Scattered sites in the Lehigh Valley. Grows 3 to 4 feet in full sun with yellow flowers in summer; prefers moderately fertile, dry to mesic soil of any texture with a pH range of 5.0 to 8.0 at least 18 inches deep. Intolerant of anaerobic conditions and drought. AKA Dasiphora floribunda.

Decodon verticillatus (Swamp loosestrife) — [perennial forb] shallow waters of lakes, bogs and swamps (OBL), mostly northeast and northwest Pennsylvania. Grows in full sun to part sun in moderately fertile soils of any texture, at least 10 inches deep and with a pH range of 4.9 to 8.6. No drought tolerance.

Delphinium exaltatum (Tall Larkspur) — [perennial forb] very rare on rocky slopes of barrens and open deciduous woods, usually on calcareous substrates as well as shale, mostly southwestern counties (Southern Allegheny Plateau, Allegheny Mountains); endangered. Grows 4 to 6 feet, blue flowers in summer in full sun to part sun. Prefers fertile, mesic well-drained circumneutral soils perhaps with some afternoon shade.

Delphinium tricorne (Dwarf larkspur) — [perennial forb] Rare on thin, deciduous forest slopes, moist ravines, thicket edges, partially shaded cliffs along streams and moist prairies, mostly southwest (Southern Allegheny Plateau); UPL. Grows 8 to 18 inches in rocky to loamy soils ranging from slightly dry to mesic; prefers light dappled shade or part sun. Dark purple flowers in early spring.

Dennstaedtia punctilobula (Hay scented fern) — [fern/ally] rocky slopes, meadows, woods, stream banks, and roadsides, in acid soils. Fronds 15 to 30 inches, rhizome: very long-creeping. Grow in sun to part shade in dry, well drained sandy and acidic loam, pH 4 to 6. A design advantage is that it forms vast colonies, because it is unpalatable to deer, making it a very easy, no-maintenance groundcover.

Deparia acrostichoides (Silvery glade fern) — [fern/ally] along stream edges, river banks and damp woods, often on shaly slopes. Fronds to 40 inches; rhizome: short creeping. Grow in part sun to shade in mesic to moist acidic sandy loam, pH 5 to 7 but prefers 5 to 5.7.

Deschampsia cespitosa (Tufted hairgrass) — [perennial graminoid] widely scattered but most reported in the Piedmont in moist thickets, sandy shorelines and serpentine barrens; other habitats include river sands and gravels and wet meadows, FACW. Grows 2 to 3 feet in part shade; prefers moist, organically rich, well drained soils of any texture and medium fertility with a pH range of 4.8 to 7/2 at least 14 inches deep. Intolerant of shade, drought and limestone-based soils, but adapts well to anaerobic conditions despite low moisture requirements.

Deschampsia flexuosa (Common hairgrass) — [perennial graminoid] dry and generally rocky slopes and in woods and thickets, often on disturbed sites; mostly east, south central. Grows 12 to 40 inches; part sun to part shade in dry to mesic, coarse to medium textured, somewhat sterile, sandy loam with a pH range of 4.8 to 6.8 at least 8 inches deep. Tolerant of shade and droughty conditions, but not anaerobic sites.

Desmodium canadense (Showy tick-trefoil) — [perennial forb] dry open woods and fields, FAC; mostly east and west, scattered center. Grows 20 to 40 inches, blue to violet flowers late summer; sun to part shade in dry to moist sandy loam.

Desmodium ciliare (Tick-clover) — [perennial forb] sandy dry woodlands and edges, mostly Piedmont, scattered in Ridge and Valley. Grows up to 3 feet with purple flowers in late summer in coarse to medium textured well drained soils in part sun to part shade.

Desmodium cuspidatum (Tick-clover) — [perennial forb] rocky, rich woodlands and banks, throughout but especially eastern Pennsylvania. Grows up to 3 feet with dark pink flowers in late summer in dry to mesic sandy loams in part shade to shade.

Desmodium glutinosum (Sticky tick-clover) — [perennial forb] dry to moist rich woods; statewide except for limestone substrates counties in the Central Appalachians. Grows 12 to 36 inches, with pink to purple flowers in summer; part shade to shade in moist, rich loam.

Desmodium humifusum (Eastern trailing tick-trefoil) — [perennial vine] rare across central Pennsylvania in dry, sandy woodlands. Grows to 6 feet with prostrate branches that bear purple flowers in summer. Prefers part sun to part shade in sandy soils from sandstone or chert.

Desmodium laevigatum (Smooth tick-clover) — [perennial forb] along roads and in sandy, dry woodlands, mostly Piedmont. Grows to 36 inches with pink to purple flowers in summer; prefers part shade to shade in mesic, rocky loams.

Desmodium marilandicum (Maryland tick-clover) — [perennial forb] dry upland woodlands and fields, mostly Piedmont. Grows to 36 inches with pink to purple flowers in summer; prefers part shade to shade in mesic, sandy loams.

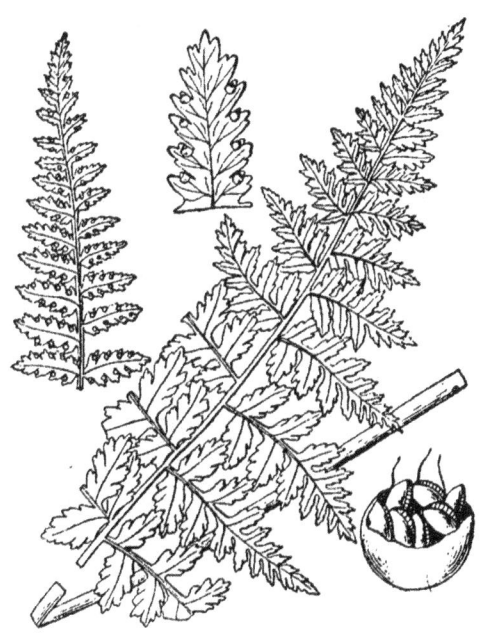

Hayscented fern (Dennstaedtia punctiobula)

Desmodium nudiflorum (Naked-flowered tick-trefoil) — [perennial forb] rich deciduous woodlands and edges, statewide. Grows 4 to 12 inches with pink flowers in mid to late summer; grow in part shade to shade in mesic, moderately acidic soils composed of sand, rocky material or loam with organic matter; root system fixes nitrogen into the soil.

Desmodium nuttallii (Nuttall's tick-trefoil) — [perennial forb] edges of open woodlands, scattered in southeastern Pennsylvania. Grows 1 to 3 feet with lavender flowers in summer; prefers mesic soils in part shade to shade.

Desmodium obtusum (Tick-trefoil) — [perennial forb] scattered on sandy, dry soils of woodlands and edges, mostly southeast. Grows 30 to 36 inches in dry to mesic sandy to rocky soil in part sun with lavender flowers in summer.

Desmodium paniculatum (Tick-trefoil) — [perennial forb] clearings and edges of moist or dry upland woods, UPL; statewide except north-central (Northern Unglaciated Allegheny Plateau). Grows 12 to 36 inches, violet to purple flowers, late summer; sun to part shade in dry to moist, medium to fine textured, somewhat sterile soils with a pH range of 6.0 to 7.0 and at least six inches deep. Intolerant of anaerobic conditions, but with low moisture and fertility requirements a good choice for droughty conditions.

Desmodium perplexum (Perplexed tick-trefoil) — [perennial forb] statewide except northern tier counties (especially southeast) in open woodlands ranging from dry to moist. Grows 2 to 5 feet in somewhat sterile, slightly dry to mesic loams, clay-loams or rocky soils of any texture with a pH range of 5.6 to 7.0 and at least 12 inches deep. Somewhat adaptable to anaerobic conditions, but not limestone-based soils or drought; purple flowers in summer.

Desmodium rotundifolium (Round-leaved tick-trefoil) — [perennial forb] open dry woodlands, throughout, especially southeast. Trailing herbaceous vine to 36 inches with purple flowers in summer; grow in humusy dry sandy soils in part shade to shade.

Desmodium sessilifolium (Sessile-leaved tick-trefoil) — [perennial forb] very rare in rocky open woodland, limestone glades, dry sandy savannas, prairies; believed to be extirpated. Grows 18 to 36 inches in full sun to part sun in dry, sandy soil; tolerates loamy or rocky soils. Purple flowers in summer.

Desmodium viridiflorum (Velvety tick-trefoil) — [perennial forb] rare in southeastern Pennsylvania on dry, open sites. Grows to 6 feet with purple flowers in summer; prefers dry, sandy soils in part sun to part shade.

Dicentra canadensis (Squirrel corn) — [perennial forb] deciduous woods, often among rock outcrops, in rich loam soils; scattered statewide except limestone-substrate Central Appalachians. Grows up to 10 inches, white flowers in early spring; part shade to shade in moist, rich sandy loam, pH 6 to 7.

Dicentra cucullaria (Dutchman's breeches) — [perennial forb] deciduous woods and clearings, in rich loam soils; statewide. Grows to 10 inches, white flowers in early spring; part shade to shade in dry to moist, rich sandy loam, pH 6 to 7.

Dicentra eximia (Wild bleeding heart, fringed bleeding heart) — [perennial forb] very rare in rich woods and on cliffs; prefers damp woods with oak mulch; widely scattered sites northeast and southwest; endangered. Grows 10 to 15 inches, pink to purple flowers in early spring; part shade to shade in dry to moist rich loam. pH 4 to 7 but prefers 4.5 to 5.5.

Dichanthelium acuminatum (Wooly panic grass) — [perennial graminoid] statewide in dry woodland slopes and clearings, savannas, disturbed woodland meadows, mesic to dry prairies, bluffs and sandstone glades, FAC. Grows to 2 feet in full sun to light shade, dry to mesic loam, clay loam, rocky or sandy loams; does not compete well against taller herbaceous species.

Dichanthelium boreale (northern panicgrass) — [perennial graminoid] widely scattered, but especially northeast in fens, bogs, wet meadows and open woodlands; FACU.

Round-leaved tick-trefoil (Desmodium rotundifolium)

Dichanthelium boscii (Bosc's panicgrass) — [perennial graminoid] generally Ridge and Valley and Piedmont in dry woodlands, stream and river banks and on grassy slopes. Grows 12 to 30 inches in part sun to shade in dry to mesic rocky soil.

Dichanthelium clandestinum (Deertongue grass) — [perennial graminoid] statewide in sandy, damp to moist soils of woodlands and forest edges and clearings, thickets and on stream banks; FAC+. Grows 18 to 48 inches in part sun in mesic well drained soils of any texture with a pH range of 4.0 to 7.5 at least 16 inches deep. Intolerant of shade, anaerobic conditions and limestone-based soils. Low fertility and moisture use make it adaptable to droughty conditons.

Dichanthelium commutatum ssp. ashei (Variable Panic grass) — [perennial graminoid] Two subspecies in Pennsylvania: ssp. ashei, reported only in Berks County in dry, open woodlands and *ssp. commutatum*, statewide, but concentrated toward the southeast on rocky slopes and barrens and in dry to wet open woodlands. Prefers coarse to medium textured, somewhat sterile, soils in sun to part sun with a pH range of 4.0 to 6.5 at least 4 inches deep. Low moisture and fertility requirements make it adaptable to droughty conditionns but not anaerobic sites.

Dichanthelium depauperatum (Starved panic grass) — [perennial graminoid] statewide except northern tier counties, especially east, often on sandy, dry soils in open woodlands, serpentine barrens and open, disturbed areas.

Dichanthelium dichotomum (Cyprus panic grass) — [perennial graminoid] statewide on dry sandy, clayey or rocky ground especially in woodlands, but more typically in moist to wet marshes, bogs, swamps, lake and pond margins and low woods, FAC.

Dichanthelium latifolium (Broadleaf rosette grass) — [perennial graminoid] statewide in rich, usually open, deciduous woodlands, along shores and in thickets, FACU-. Grows 24 to 36 inches in part sun to part shade in coarse to medium textured, somewhat sterile soils at least 4 inches deep with a pH range of 4.0 to 6.5. Moderately drought and limestone-soil tolerant but not for anaerobic sites.

Dichanthelium leibergii (Leiberg's panic grass) — [perennial graminoid] very rare on limestone outcrops and sandy woodlands, FACU. Reported only in Centre County and believed to be extirpated. Grows 1 to 2 feet in sandy, calcareous soils in sun to part sun; AKA *Panicum leibergii*.

Dichanthelium linearifolium (Panic grass) — [perennial graminoid] statewide in dry, sandy soils of open woodlands, fields and rock outcrops.

Dichanthelium meridionale (Matting rosette grass) — [perennial graminoid] scattered statewide, especially east, in dry, sandy soil.

Dichanthelium oligosanthes (Heller's rosette grass) — [perennial graminoid] loamy, clayey soil of thickets, especially along the Delaware River, FACU. Mostly southeast; widely scattered elsewhere. Grows 10 to 30 inches; part sun in dry to moist clay loam. AKA *Panicum oligosanthes var. oligosanthes*.

Dichanthelium ovale var. addisonii (Cloaked panicgrass) — [perennial graminoid] reported only in Philadelphia County in dry, sandy, open ground or rocky woodland borders, sand barrens, dunes and prairies. Grow in sun to part shade in coarse to medium textured soils at least four inches deep and with a pH of 4.0 to 6.5. Intolerant of anaerobic conditions, the low moisture and fertility needs make it a good candidate for droughty conditions; aka *Dichanthelium commonsianum var. commonsianum*.

Dichanthelium scabriusculum (Fernald's panic grass) — [perennial graminoid] southeastern Pennsylvania on sandy, wet, open sites such as lake and pond shores, stream banks, bogs and swamps; OBL. Grows to about 24 inches in sun to part sun on mesic, somewhat sterile, soils of any texture with a depth of 4 inches and a pH range of 4.0 to 7.0. Intolerant of anaerobic conditions and drought, but requires a growing season of 200 days.

Dichanthelium scoparium (Velvety panic grass) — [perennial graminoid] sandy, moist meadows and open disturbed areas, scattered in southeastern Pennsylvania, especially Atlantic Coastal Plain, FACW. Grow in sun to shade in coarse to medium textured soils with a pH range of 4.5 to 7.5 at least 6 inches deep. Highly tolerant of limestone-based soils, but not anaerobic conditions or drought.

Dichanthelium sphaerocarpon (Panic grass) — [perennial graminoid] dry, sandy to rocky soils in woodlands, thickets and fields, scattered statewide, especially east.

Dichanthelium spretum (Eaton's rosette grass) — [perennial graminoid] reported only in waste ground along a railroad track in southern Bucks County; listed as extirpated in Pennsylvania.

Dichanthelium xanthophysum (Slender panic grass) — [perennial graminoid] northeastern counties on dry, sandy or rocky soils in open oak, pine or aspen woodlands.

Diervilla lonicera (Bush-honeysuckle) — [tree/shrub] typically on exposed rocky sites with dry to mesic well-drained soil; statewide. Shrub to 4 feet; part shade to shade in dry, rocky slightly acidic loam. Drought tolerant, but not anaerobic conditions. Prefers coarse to medium textured soils with moderate fertility and a pH range of 4.8 to 7.0, at least 16 inches deep.. Red, orange, yellow and purple flowers in summer.

Digitaria cognata (Fall witchgrass) — [perennial graminoid] dry, sandy soils in the Ontario and Erie Lake Plain and Atlantic and Coastal Plain; aka Leptoloma cognatum.

Digitaria filiformis (Slender crabgrass) [annual graminoid] — serpentine barrens, southeastern Pennsylvania; grows to 36 inches in sun on dry open sites, especially serpentine soils.

Digitaria serotina (Dwarf crabgrass) [annual graminoid] — Atlantic coastal plain on disturbed soils, FAC; grows to about 12 inches in sun on dry, sandy loams.

Diodia teres (Rough buttonweed) [annual forb] — upland, sandy, hilly prairies, rocky glades, and riparian gravel bars, FACU; scattered south, mostly southeast. Grows 6 to 12 inches with white to purple flowers in late summer in full sun on dry, poor soils with an abundance of sand, gravel or compacted clay; intolerant of taller competition but drought tolerant.

Dioscorea quaternata (Fourleaf yam) — [perennial vine] Rich, rocky woods, thickets, talus slopes, mostly south-central and southwest; FACU. Grow in moist, sandy loams in sun to part shade.

Dioscorea villosa (Wild yam) — [perennial vine] woods, thickets, rocky slopes; FAC+; statewide. Twining vine to 15 feet; greenish-yellow flowers, early summer. Grow in part shade to shade in dry to moist rocky loam.

Diospyros virginiana (Persimmon) — [tree] open woods, floodplains and old fields, seasonally flooded bottomlands, dry ridgetops and abandoned agricultural land, FAC; mostly southeast; scattered southwest. Deciduous tree to 50 feet; dry to medium, well-drained soils in full sun to part shade. Wide range of soil tolerance, but prefers moist, moderately fertile sandy soils of any texture with a pH range of 4.7 and 7.5 at least 36 inches deep. Drought tolerant, but not suitable for anaerobic conditions or limestone-based soils. Blooms late spring, edible fruit in the fall.

Diphasiastrum digitatum (Deep-rooted running-pine) — [fern/ally] acidic to subacidic soils of open woodlands, thickets, coniferous and hardwood forests and shrubby to open fields that are mesic to slightly dry. Grows to about four inches, especially in disturbed areas and coniferous forest, where it makes a dense carpet in shaded areas. Mowing significantly stunts growth, and it can take months to recover fully. Easily transplanted if kept damp while out of the ground and quickly installed into a good habitat.

Diphasiastrum tristachyum (Deep-rooted running-pine) — [fern/ally] sterile, acidic soils in open coniferous forests and oak forests, sandy barrens and clearings; not quite as common in central counties. Stems 6 to 12 inches; rhizome: short creeping. Grow in part shade to shade in moist acidic humusy loam. Easier to obtain than *Diphasiastrum digitatum*.

Diplazium pycnocarpon (Narrow-leaved glade fern) — [fern/ally] wooded glades and alluvial thickets, neutral soil, but not in ridge and valley provinces, FAC. Less common in highest elevations. Fronds 18 to 40 inches; rhizome: short creeping. Grow in part shade in moist organic circumneutral garden loam.

Dirca palustris (Leatherwood) — [shrub] rich deciduous woods and thickets, FAC; scattered southwest. Shrub to 5 feet; full sun in moist, deep soils; prefers wet sites; pale yellow flowers in early spring.

Disporum lanuginosum (Yellow mandarin) — [perennial forb] Rich moist, deciduous woodlands and coves, mostly west. Grows 1 to 3 feet, greenish-white bell-shaped flowers in spring; prefers humus rich, moist, acidic soil in part shade to shade of deciduous trees. AKA Prosartes lanuginosa.

Distichlis spicata (Seashore saltgrass) — [perennial graminoid] Very rare in brackish marshes and coastal salt flats and adjacent forests and desert scrub habitats, often in dense monotypic stands as clonal colonies, FACW+; mostly southeast. Grows up to 12 inches in full sun, prefers wet, calcareous and saline soils that are medium to fine textured, with at pH range above 6.4 and at least 2 inches deep. Intolerant of shade and moderately adaptable to drought.

Dodecatheon meadia (Shooting-star) — [perennial forb] rare in wet to dry prairies and moist open rocky woods and rocky slopes. FACU; endangered. Widely scattered, mostly southeast. Grows 12 to 15 inches, with white, pink and rarely purple flowers in spring; medium, well-drained (especially sandy) soils in sun to shade. Prefers moist, calcareous, humusy soils in sun to part shade that are coarse to medium textured, range in pH from 4.5 to 7.5, and at least 12 inches deep. Intolerant of poor wet soils, especially in winter.

Doellingeria umbellata (Flat topped white aster) — [perennial forb] moist woods, fields and floodplains, FACW; statewide. Grows 3 to 6 feet, white flowers in late summer to early fall; sun to part shade in moist to wet sandy loam, pH 5 to 6.

Draba reptans (Carolina draba) [annual forb] — found on rocky, open ground such as pastures and prairies, rock outcrops and glades; reported only in Lancaster County and listed as extirpated. Grows 2 to 10 inches with white flowers in spring on dry, rocky, sandy loams in sun to part sun.

Dracocephalum parviflorum (Dragonhead) [annual/biennial forb] — widely scattered in dry fields, open woodlands, trail edges and waste ground in southern Pennsylvania, FACU. Grows 6-32 inches with pink to pale violet flowers in summer in gravelly soils, with a preference to disturbed, slightly moist soils, in sun to part sun.

Drosera intermedia (Spatulate-leaved sundew) — [perennial forb] open peat and along edges of bogs and glacial lakes, OBL; northeast (Northern Glaciated Allegheny Plateau), scattered southeast. Aquatic carnivore; grows 3 to 10 inches, with white flowers; full sun in pond margins in moist to wet rich peaty loam.

Drosera rotundifolia (Round-leaved sundew) — [perennial forb] sphagnum bogs and peaty edges of bogs, OBL; statewide, especially northeast. Grows 3 to 10 inches, white to pink flowers. Aquatic carnivore; grow in full sun in pond margins in moist to wet rich peaty loam.

Shooting-star (*Dodecatheon meadia*)

Dryopteris carthusiana (Spinose wood fern) — [fern/ally] swampy woods, moist wooded slopes, stream banks, and conifer plantations. Fronds 12 to 36 inches; rhizome: ascending crown. Grow in part sun to shade in mesic to moist organic loam.

Dryopteris celsa (Log fern) — [fern/ally] rare on seepage slopes, hammocks and on logs in swamps; best in southeast. Fronds to 50 inches; rhizomes: medium to short creeping. Grow in average, mesic to wet soils in part shade to full shade. Prefers acidic, humusy, moist to wet soils in high shade, sheltered from wind.

Dryopteris clintoniana (Clinton's wood fern) — [fern/ally] deep humus in swampy woods, especially maple swamps. Prefers wet mucky woods, thickets, ideal for the northeast. Fronds 24 to 48 inches; rhizome: short creeping. Grow in part shade to shade in moist to wet rich silty loam, pH 4 to 6.

Dryopteris cristata (Crested shield fern) — [fern/ally] swamps, swampy woods, or open shrubby wetlands; prefers wet mucky woods, thickets. Fronds 12 to 36 inches, rhizome: short creeping. Grow in part shade to shade in moist to slightly wet rich, silty loam, with a pH 3.5 to 6.5 and is at least 12 inches deep. Prefers medium to fine textured soils and is quite tolerant of limestone-based soils, anaerobic conditions and shade, but intolerant of drought. Low fertility but high moisture requirements.

Dryopteris goldiana (Goldie's wood fern) —

[fern/ally] dense, moist woods, especially ravines, limey seeps, or at the edge of swamps, in deep humus. A big, dramatic clumping fern ideal for the southeast, but suitable anywhere. Fronds 36 to 48 inches, rhizome: short creeping. Grow in part shade to shade in mesic to moist, rich, circumneutral, humusy loam, pH 4 to 7.

Dryopteris intermedia (Evergreen wood fern) — [fern/ally] moist rocky woods, especially hemlock hardwoods, ravines, and edges of swamps, FACU; statewide. Fronds 18 to 36 inches. Rhizome: erect crown. Grow in part shade to shade in moist organic loam, pH 4.5 to 7.5.

Dryopteris intermedia x marginalis (Hybrid wood-fern) — [fern/ally] very rare and widely scattered eastern Pennsylvania hybrid between *D. intermedia* and *D. marginalis* in moist, rocky woodlands, especially hemlock-hardwoods, ravines and swamp edges.

Dryopteris marginalis (Marginal wood fern) — [fern/ally] rocky, wooded slopes and ravines, edges of woods, stream banks and road banks, and rock walls. Fronds 18 to 30 inches, rhizome: erect crown. Grow in part sun to shade in mesic to slightly dry rich sandy loam, pH 5 to 6; available at many garden centers.

Dryopteris x boottii (Boott's hybrid wood fern) — [fern/ally] statewide in subacidic soils of swamps and moist woodland edges; a hybrid of *D. cristata* and *D. intermedia*.

Dryopteris x dowellii (Dowell's wood-fern) — [fern/ally] scattered northeast in swamps and wet thickets; a hybrid of *D. clintoniana* and *D. intermedia*.

Dryopteris x pittsfordensis (Pittsford wood-fern) — [fern/ally] rare in east central Pennsylvania in wet woodlands; a hybrid of *D. carthusiana* and *D. marginalis*.

Dryopteris x slossonae (Boot's hybrid wood fern) — [fern/ally] widely scattered statewide, mostly Piedmont, in springheads, swampy woods and on stream banks; a hybrid of *D. cristata* and *D. marginalis*.

Dryopteris x triploidea (Triploid hybrid wood fern) — [fern/ally] statewide in moist woodlands, thickets and swamps; a hybrid of *D. carthusiana* and *D. intermedia*.

Dryopteris x uliginosa (Braun's wood fern) — [fern/ally] widely scattered statewide in thickets, swamps and moist woodlands; a hybrid of *D. carthusiana* and *D. cristata*.

Dulichium arundinaceum (Three-way sedge) — [perennial graminoid] open wet places, lake and pond margins, marshes, swamps, bogs and stream shores, OBL; statewide. Can reach 40 inches; part shade in moist to moderately fertile, moist to wet sandy to clay loam of any texture with a pH ranging from 4.7 to 7.5 and at least 18 inches deep. Low drought tolerance, but adaptable to anaerobic conditions and limestone soils

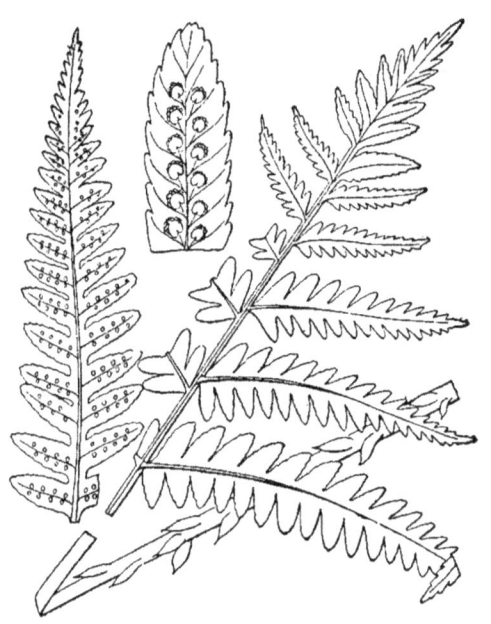

Goldie's wood fern (*Dryopteris goldiana*)

Echinacea laevigata (Appalachian coneflower, smooth coneflower) — [perennial forb] Very rare in open woods, barrens, clearcuts, dry limestone bluffs and fields; believe to be extirpated. Grows up to 4 feet, purple flowers in summer in sunny, well-drained sites rich in calcium and magnesium with low competition (the reason it has historically been rare).

Echinochloa muricata (Barnyard-grass) [annual graminoid] — statewide on low areas along ponds and rivers, including floodplain woodlands, as well as swamps and marshes marshes, swamps, in addition to vacant lots, gardens and moist waste areas. FACW+. Grows 3 to 6 feet in part to full sun on moist to wet, fertile, loamy to silty soils. Prefers degraded wetlands and disturbed areas and has a low drought tolerance.

Echinochloa walteri (Walter's barnyard-grass) [annual graminoid] — Atlantic Coastal plain mudflats and tidal marshes, FACW+ and listed as endangered. Grows to 7 feet in mesic to wet sandy to mucky soils in full sun.

Echinocystis lobata (Prickly cucumber) — [perennial vine] moist alluvial soil on stream banks and woods edges; FAC, statewide. Annual vine with 16-20 foot stems; white flowers in summer. Grow in sun to part sun in moist sandy loam. Inedible fruit.

Echinocystis lobata (Prickly cucumber) [annual vine] — statewide on woodland edges and stream banks in moist alluvial soils, FAC, with white flowers in late summer into fall. Grows 15 to 20 feet in sun to part sun in moist to mesic soils.

Eclipta prostrata (Yerba-de-tajo) [annual forb] — — moist bottomlands, wet shorelines and rocky river banks, FAC, scattered south but especially southeast, as well as along Lake Erie. Grows 1 to 3 feet, blooming in summer in wet, often ruderial muddy soils.

Elatine americana (American waterwort) [annual forb] — aquatic, found on muddy tidal shores and in tidal pools on the Atlantic Coastal Plain, OBL and listed as extirpated.

Elatine minima (Small waterwort) [annual forb] — aquatic in shallow water of northern lakes and along muddy tidal shores, OBL, generally northeast especially Wayne and Pike Counties.

Eleocharis acicularis (Needle spike-rush) — [perennial graminoid] bare, wet soil or in lakes, ponds, vernal pools, meadows, springs and disturbed places, OBL; statewide. Can reach 3 feet; sun to part sun in shallow ponds and pools. Prefers medium to fine textured, moderately fertile, soils at least 14 inches deep with a pH range of 4.5 to 7.0; intolerant of shade, drought and limestone soils.

Eleocharis compressa var. compressa (Flat-stemmed spike-rush) — [perennial graminoid] very rare in damp calcareous soil to shallow water of seasonally wet seeps, grasslands, meadows, barrens, glades, fens, ditches, depressions, as well as river banks; OBL and listed as endangered in Pennsylvania. Grows to 18 inches in sun to part sun in coarse to medium textured soils with a pH range of 5.4 to 7.0 and at least 8 inches deep. Tolerant of anaerobic conditons and limestone soils, but intolerant of shade and drought.

Eleocharis elliptica (Slender spike-rush) — [perennial graminoid] very widely scattered, mostly northwest, wet, calcareous and sandy shorelines, fens, meadows, prairies, flats and swales, FACW+ and listed as endangered in Pennsylvania. Grows up to 36 inches in sun to part sun.

Eleocharis engelmannii (Spike-rush) [annual graminoid] — generally southeastern Pennsylvania in freshwater shorelines, marshes and vernal pools, FACW+. Grows to about 15 inches, full sun, sandy to muddy moist to wet soils.

Eleocharis erythropoda (Bald spike-rush) — [perennial graminoid] non-calcareous or calcareous fresh or brackish shores, marshes, wet meadows, fens, stream banks and swales, OBL; statewide, especially southeast. Can reach 3 feet; full sun in wet to mesic sandy loam, prefers pH of 7 to 8.

Eleocharis flavescens var. olivacea (Capitate spike-rush) — [perennial graminoid] prefers exposed peat at wet pond margins, bogs, stream banks, marshes, moist meadows and swamps; aka *Eleocharis olivacea*, OBL and listed as rare in Pennsylvania, occurring in eastern counties, especially glaciated northeast, and along Lake Erie. Grows to 16 inches in sun to part shade.

Eleocharis geniculata (Canada spikesedge) [annual graminoid] — shorelines and marshes of lakes and lagoons as well as mud flats and salt marshes. Grows less than 12 inches in sun to part sun in sandy to mucky soils. AKA *Eleocharis caribaea*.

Eleocharis intermedia (Matted spike-rush) [annual graminoid] — widely scaattered, mostly east, along streams, lake shores, tidal meadows, calcareous swamps and bogs, FACW+ and listed as threatened. Grows to about 15 inches in sun to part sun in moist to wet circumneutral muddy soils.

Eleocharis microcarpa (Smallfruit spikerush) [annual graminoid] — clearings in pine woodlands and depressions in black gum forests, as well as lakeshores; OBL; rare in southwestern

Pennsylvania. Grows about 15 inches in sun to part sun, sandy to silt loams.

Eleocharis obtusa var. obtusa (Blunt spike-rush) [annual graminoid] — Two varieties: *obtusa,* statewide in fens, marshes, sedge meadows, lake and pond shores, low riparian areas and other areas prone to seasonal flooding, and *peasi in* freshwater shorelines and marshes, tidal mudflats in the Atlantic Coastal Plain and listed as endangered. Both varieties OBL and grow about 18 inches in full sun, in moist to wet, mucky to muddy soils. Anaerobic conditions are tolerated, but not cat tails (*Typha* spp.). No preference on soil texture or pH, but soil should be at least 10 inches deep; avoid droughty conditions.

Eleocharis palustris (Creeping spike-rush) — [perennial graminoid] large colonies at lake and stream margins, bogs, swamps and marshy swales; statewide, especially east. Can reach 50 inches; sun to part sun in ponds, rain gardens and retention basins up to 40 inches deep; can be inundated for up to 4 months. Grow in coarse to medium textured, moderately fertile soils with a pH between 4.0 and 8.0, at least 14 inches deep; intolerant of shade and drought.

Eleocharis parvula (Dwarf spike-rush) — [perennial graminoid] brackish or saline tidal marshes, shores, swamps, ponds, mud flats and ditches, OBL; mostly southeast, endangered. Grows up to 12 inches in full sun; commonly sold as a saline aquarium plant. No preference on soil texture and fertility can be low; intolerant of limestone based soils, shade and drought; prefers pH from 6.0 to 8.0, at least 10 inches deep.

Eleocharis pauciflora var. fernaldii (Fewflower spikerush) — [perennial graminoid] prefers wet calcareous sand in fens, meadows, seeps and near springs; OBL and listed as endangered in Pennsylvania.

Eleocharis quadrangulata (Four-angled spike-rush) — [perennial graminoid] rare in shallow waters of lake and pond edges, swamps, marshes, OBL; mostly southeast and west, endangered. Grows to 3 feet in sun to part sun in low-fertility silty loams in or adjacent to standing water. Adapts to any texture, prefers pH between 5.8 and 7.2 and depth of at least 8 inches. Intolerant of shade, drought and limestone-based soils.

Eleocharis robbinsii (Robbins' spike-rush) — [perennial graminoid] sandy to peaty soils in shallows of freshwater lakes and ponds in the glaciated northeast, OBL and listed as threatened in Pennsylvania.

Eleocharis rostellata (Beaked spike-rush) — [perennial graminoid] rare in very wet calcareous fens, springs and shores, OBL; scattered west, endangered. Grows 1 to 3 feet in sun to part sun on somewhat nutrient-poor alkaline silt loams of any texture with a pH between 6.0 and 8.0 and at least 10 inches deep. Adaptable to anaerobic conditions and limestone-based soils, but intolerant of drought and shade.

Eleocharis tenuis var. tenuis (Slender spike-rush) — [perennial graminoid] statewide except northern tier counties in swamps, bogs, wet woodlands and moist lake and pond shorelines; FACW+. Adapts to soils of any texture and anaerobic conditions, but intolerant of shade, drought and limestone-based soils; prefers moderately fertile, moist to wet soils at least 14 inches deep with a pH between 6.2 and 7.0.

Eleocharis tuberculosa (Long-tubercled spike-rush) — [perennial graminoid] reported only in a sphagnum bog in southern Montgomery County and listed as extirpated in Pennsylvania; prefers wet soils in freshwater ponds, lakes, streams, meadows and grasslands, and bogs. Grows to 30 inches in full sun to part shade.

Elephantopus carolinianus (Elephant's foot) — [perennial forb] Rare in open pine and mixed forests, typically with sandy soils, as well as serpentine barrens, mostly extreme southeastern counties ; FACU. Grows 2 to 3 feet on dry to mesic, moderately fertile sandy soils of any texture with a pH of 5.0 to 7.2 at least 10 inches deep; sun to part sun with white to lavender flowers in late summer, often used as a ground cover in dry, difficult areas. Avoid anaerobic conditions and shade

Ellisia nyctelea (Waterpod) [annual forb] — deciduous, especially rich alluvial, woodlands, and shady banks along major rivers, FACU, mostly southeastern Pennsylvania and listed as threatened.

Grows 6 to 18 inches with pale blue spring to early summer flowers in dry to moist fertile loams with much organic matter; prefers part sun to part shade areas with scant ground vegetation resulting from overhead shade or recent disturbance.

Elodea canadensis (Ditch-moss) — [perennial forb] aquatic, free floating in shallow, mostly calcareous waters of ponds, lakes, creeks and rivers, OBL; statewide. Flowers in summer; grow in fine-textured soil, with a pH of 4.8 to 7.2, at the base of shallow ponds. Intolerant of shade or drought, but prefers limestone habitats.

Elodea nuttallii (Waterweed) — [perennial forb] aquatic found in shallow water of streams, lakes, ponds and tidal mud flats, statewide, but especially eastern Pennsylvania.

Elymus canadensis var. *canadensis* (Canada wild-rye) — [perennial graminoid] alluvial shores and thickets, especially near larger rivers and tributaries, FACU+; statewide, especially southeast (Delaware River Valley). Can reach 36 inches; sun to part sun in in moderately fertile, alluvial loam of any texture with a pH between 5.0 and 7.9 with a depth of at least 16 inches. Moderate drought tolerance and moisture use, adaptable to limestone soils and shade, but intolerant of anaerobic conditions.

Elymus hystrix (Bottlebrush grass) — [perennial graminoid] dry to moist soils in open woods and thickets, especially on base to rich slopes and small stream terraces; statewide. Grows 24 to 36 inches; part sun to part shade in moist loam.

Elymus riparius (Riverbank wild-rye) — [perennial graminoid] moist, generally alluvial and often sandy soils in woods and thickets, usually along larger streams and occasionally along upland ditches, FACW; statewide. Grows 40 to 60 inches; part sun to part shade in mesic to moist alluvial sandy loam of any texture with a pH between 4.5 and 7.2 and a depth of 10 inches. Tolerant of shade, limestone soils and anaerobic conditions but not drought.

Elymus villosus (Wild rye) — [perennial graminoid] moist to moderately dry, generally rocky soils in woods and thickets, especially in calcareous or other base to rich soils; also frequent on drier, sandy soils or damper, alluvial soils in glaciated regions, FACU-; statewide. Grows 20 to 40 inches; part sun to part shade in dry to moist sandy or alluvial loam.

Elymus virginicus (Virginia wild rye) — [perennial graminoid] moist-damp or rather dry soil, mostly on bottomland or fertile uplands, in open woods, thickets, tall forbs, or weedy sites, FACW-; statewide. Grows 20 to 50 inches; part sun to part shade in sandy, moderately fertile, organic loam of any texture, pH 5.0 to 7.0 and at least 16 inches deep. Tolerant of shade, anaerobic conditions, limestone soils and drought.

Elephant's Foot (*Elephantopus carolinianus*)

Epifagus virginiana (Beechdrops) [annual forb] — statewide in forests where *Fagus grandifolia* (American beach) and *Acer saccharum* (sugar maple) codominate. Grows 4 to 20 inches with pink flowers in late summer to fall on mesic soils in part sun to part shade. Parasitic on beech roots, without which it cannot survive.

Epigaea repens (Trailing-arbutus) — [shrub] moist to xeric pine or deciduous forests, clearings and edges, in sandy, rocky, or peaty soil; borders and banks; statewide. Creeping subshrub, about 6 inches, with white-pink flowers in early spring; part sun to part shade in dry sandy rocky acid loam. Can be difficult to transplant.

Epilobium ciliatum (Willow-herb) — [perennial forb] wet rocks and moist, springy soils, statewide but especially northern Pennsylvania (FAC-). Grows 4 to 18 inches with white-purple flowers in late summer to autumn in part shade to shade in mesic wooded slopes dominated by American beech and sugar maple.

Epilobium coloratum (Purple-leaved willow-herb) — [perennial forb] moist fields, shores and floodplains, OBL; statewide. Grows up to 3 feet, pink to white flowers in late summer; sun to part sun in rich, moist sandy loam.

Epilobium leptophyllum (Willow-herb) — [perennial forb] Boggy pastures and marshes, scattered throughout but especially northeast (OBL). Grows to 3 feet with white flowers in summer in full sun on mesic to wet open ground such as meadows and fens in soils that are medium to fine textured with a pH between 4.5 and 6.5 and at least 10 inches deep. High anaerobic tolerance, but none for drought.

Epilobium palustre (Marsh willow-herb) — [perennial forb] woodland swamps and bogs, northeastern Pennsylvania (OBL). Grows to 16 inches on mesic to moist, slightly acidic to circumneutral sandy loams and silt loams that are well drained; part sun to part shade, with white-pink flowers in summer.

Equisetum arvense (Field horsetail) — [fern/ally] moist roadsides, riverbanks, fields, marshes, pastures, and tundra. Stems 8 to 18 inches, rhizome: long creeping. Grow in sun to part sun in mesic to moist rich sandy loam of any texture with a pH between 4.0 and 7.0 and is at least 6 inches deep. Moderate tolerance for anaerobic conditions, but none for drought; high moisture requirements and moderate shade adaptability.

Equisetum fluviatile (Water horsetail) — [fern/ally] standing water; in ponds, ditches, marshes, swales, edges of rivers and lakes. Mostly northeast (Northern Glaciated Allegheny Plateau); scattered elsewhere. Stems 24 to 26 inches; rhizome: short creeping. Grow in sun to part sun in ponds and pond edges or frequently inundated or poorly drained low area with a base of silty loam with a pH between 4.5 and 6.0 at least 6 inches deep. Intolerant of shade and drought, but adaptable to anaerobic conditions and limestone-based soils.

Equisetum hyemale var. affine (Scouring-rush) — [fern/ally] riverbanks, lakeshores and woodlands; moist sandy and gravelly slopes; stream banks, embankments and roadsides. Ideal for southern and western areas. Stems 14 to 48 inches; rhizome: creeping. Grow in sun to part shade in rich moist to wet sandy loam. Can be difficult to control because of deep rhizomes.

Equisetum sylvaticum (Woodland horsetail) — [fern/ally] moist open woods and wet meadows. Less common in the southwest. Stems 10 to 30 inches. Rhizome: creeping. Grow in sun to part shade in moist to wet sandy clay to silt loam of any texture at least 6 inches deep with a pH range of 4.0 to 6.5. Moderately adaptable to anaerobic conditions, but excellent for drought because of its low moisture and fertility needs.

Equisetum variegatum (Variegated horsetail) — [fern/ally] Ontario and Erie Lake Plain in damp to wet circumneutral to alkaline soils on stream banks, flats, woodlands and lakeshores, FACW.

Equisetum x ferrissi (Intermediate scouring-rush) — [fern/ally] widely scattered east and west in moist, clayey to sandy circumneutral soils on riverbanks, prairies and moist lakeshores.

Equisetum x litorale (Shore horsetail) — [fern/ally] widely scattered but mostly along Delaware River; prefers moist stream banks and wet meadows.

Riverbank wild-rye (Elymus riparius)

Eragrostis capillaris (Lacegrass) [annual graminoid] — statewide except the northern tier on dry, sandy riverbanks and floodplains, usually in assocaition with *Pinus, Quercus, Carya* species and *Liquidambar styraciflua*. Grows to 18 inches in dry, sandy soil.

Eragrostis frankii (Sandbar lovegrass) [annual graminoid] — scattered statewide in moist meadows, stream edges and sandbars and forest openings, FACW, usually in association with *Pinus, Quercus* and *Acer* species and *Fagus grandiflora*. Grows to 18 inches in mesic to moist sandy loams in part sun to part shade.

Eragrostis hypnoides (Creeping lovegrass) [annual graminoid] — statewide on sandy to muddy lake and river shores and mudflats, OBL. Grows to eight inches in moist to wet sandy to clayey loams of any texture, a minimum depth of 6 inches, and a pH range of 4.5 to 8.5. Intolerant of shade and drought, but okay with anaerobic condition and limestone soils.

Eragrostis pectinacea (Carolina lovegrass) [annual graminoid] — woodland openings, meadows, prairies, FAC, statewide but more common in the Appalachians and eastward; grows to 3 feet in mesic sandy loams, especially on disturbed sites.

Eragrostis spectabilis (Purple lovegrass) — [perennial graminoid] dry sandy fields, woods margins, roadsides, usually in sandy to clay loam soils; UPL. Mostly east; widely scattered west. Grows 12 to 24 inches; sun to part sun in dry to moist, coarse to medium textured sandy to clay loams at least 4 inches deep with a pH between 4.0 and 7.5. Intolerant of shade and anaerobic conditions, but excellent in drought.

Erechtites hieraciifolius (American burnweed) [annual forb] — Fields and thickets, woodland clearings and disturbed ground, FACU. Grows 1 to 9 feet in mesic to moist loams in full to part sun with white flowers in late summer to early autumn.

Erigenia bulbosa (Harbinger-of-spring) — [perennial forb] spring heads, seeps in upland slopes, mostly southwestern Pennsylvania, but also Piedmont. Grows 3 to 10 inches with white flowers in spring; grow in part sun to paart shade in deciduous woodlands on mesic to moist, rich loamy soil that includes rotting organic matter.

Erigeron annuus (Eastern daisy fleabane) [annual forb] — statewide in dry to moist prairies and fields, disturbed open woodlands and waste ground; FACU. Grows 2 to 4 feet with white flowers in late summer in dry to mesic soils in full to part sun. Can spread aggressively and size is related to fertility and moisture.

Erigeron philadelphicus (Daisy fleabane) — [perennial forb] openings and margins of upland woods, marsh and stream edges, fields, roadsides, lawns, and other open, disturbed sites, FACU; statewide. Grows 8 to 40 inches, with white-pale lavender flowers in early summer; part sun in medium to fine-textured mesic to dry sandy loam at least 10 inches deep with a pH between 4.8 and 7.8. Low tolerance for drought and anaerobic conditions, moderate with shade.

Erigeron pulchellus (Robin's plantain) — [perennial forb] bottomland, especially along creeks; ravines, swamp edges, dry to moist woods, slopes and woodland edges, prairies and meadows, FACU; statewide. Grows to 8 feet, blue to pink-white flowers from late spring through summer; part shade in moist, rich, sandy loams.

Erigeron strigosus var. *strigosus* (Prairie fleabane) [annual forb] — statewide in prairies and savannas, limestone glades and woodland edges; FACU+. Grows 1 to 3 feet with white flowers in spring in full to part sun on circumneutral, dry to mesic, moderately fertile, soils of any texture, often containing clay or gravel, with a pH between 4.8 and 7.2, at least 10 inches deep. Moderate drought but no anaerobic tolerance.

Eriocaulon aquaticum (Seven-angle pipewort) — [perennial forb] aquatic in shallow water and on the sandy or peaty shores of northeastern Pennsylvania lakes, ponds and bogs.

Eriocaulon decangulare (Ten-angle pipewort) — [perennial forb] Moist to wet sands or peats of shores, pine savannas, ditches, edges of cypress domes or savanna (OBL); reported only at a glacial lake in Wayne County and listed as extirpated. Grows in coarse to medium textured, moderately fertile, soils with a pH of 4.0 to 7.6 at least 18 inches deep. Adaptable to anaerobic and drought conditions.

Eriocaulon parkeri (Parkers's pipewort) — [perennial forb] aquatic in muddy tidal flats and brackish marshes; reported only in the Atlantic Coastal plain and listed as extirpated in Pennsylvania (OBL).

Eriophorum gracile (Slender cotton-grass) — [perennial graminoid] scattered statewide but concentrated in the southern Lehigh Valley on generally peaty, acidic soils in wet meadows, bogs, shorelines and marshes; OBL and listed as endangered in Pennsylvania. No cultivation data; may be difficult to find commercially.

Eriophorum tenellum (Rough cotton-grass) — [perennial graminoid] widely scattered but generally glaciated northeast in bogs on wet, peaty substrates; OBL and listed as endangered in Pennsylvania.

Eriophorum vaginatum (Cotton-grass) — [perennial graminoid] sphagnum bogs and swamps in glaciated areas, especially northeast, on peaty soils; found in bogs, meadows, swales, tundra, OBL.

Eriophorum virginicum (Tawny cotton-grass) — [perennial graminoid] bogs and peaty meadows and swamps, OBL. Statewide, scattered in southwest. Grows 1 to 4 feet; full sun in wet, rich silty soil of any texture with a pH range of 3.8 to 6.5 and a depth of at least 14 inches. Intolerant of shade, drought and limestone-based soils, somewhat okay with anaerobic conditions.

Eriophorum viridicarinatum (Thin-leaved cotton-grass) — [perennial graminoid] mostly northwestern glaciated areas, but also northern Lehigh Valley in swamps, wet meadows, fens, bogs, marshes and wet woodlands; OBL and listed as threatened in Pennsylvania.

Eryngium aquaticum (Marsh eryngo, rattlesnake master) — [perennial forb] Very rare in river swamps, marshes, pine wetlands, pond banks and gravelly shores, mostly Atlantic Coastal Plain, believed to be extirpated; OBL. Biennial that grows 3 to 6 feet, with greenish flowers in summer, in part sun to part shade in wet, somewhat acidic soils.

Erythronium albidum (White trout-lily) — [perennial forb] Rare in mesic floodplains and bottomlands, upland forests and woodlands, typically silt to clay loams, mostly southern counties, especially Southern Allegheny Plateau; FACU. Grows 6 to 12 inches, white-yellow flowers in spring to form extensive colonies in part shade to shade in acidic, moist, humusy soils; easiest to grow from corms rather than seed.

Erythronium americanum (Yellow trout lily) — [perennial forb] open deciduous moist woods and rich slopes with deep humus-rich loam; statewide. Grows up to 8 inches, yellow flowers in spring; part shade in dry to moist sandy loam, pH 5 to 7.

Euonymus obovatus (Running strawberry-bush) — [tree/shrub] rich, dry to damp woodlands, thickets and slopes; mostly northwest. Grows 1 to 3 feet in rich, moist soils in part shade to shade; greenish-purple flowers in early summer.

Eupatorium album (White-bracted eupatorium) — [perennial forb] Dry, open or wooded sites, especially sandy pinelands and serpentine barrens on the Atlantic Coastal Plain and listed as extirpated in Pennsylvania. Grows 18 to 40 inches in dry sandy, somewhat acidic soils in full sun with white flowers in late summer to early fall.

Eupatorium altissimum (Tall eupatorium, tall boneset) — [perennial forb] Dry rocky slopes, thickets, clearings, openings in upland forests, limestone glades, abandoned fields, favors disturbed areas to form large colonies, mostly south; FACU. Grows to 4 feet in full to part sun with mesic to dry conditions, circumneutral to alkaline in loam, clay or gravel soils; white flowers in late summer.

Eupatorium fistulosum (Trumpet weed) — [perennial forb] mesic to moist fields, meadows and thickets, FACW; statewide. Grows up to 10 feet, pink-purple flowers in late summer and fall; sun to part sun in moist, rich sandy loam, pH 5.5 to 7.

Eupatorium maculatum (Spotted Joe-pye-weed, spotted trumpetweed) — [perennial forb] floodplains, thickets and swamps, FACW. Mostly north (Western and Northern Glaciated and Northern Unglaciated Allegheny plateaus), scattered elsewhere. Grows up to 6 feet, purple flowers late summer; sun to part sun in mesic to moist, moderately fertile, medium to fine textured silty clay loam, pH 5.5 to 7.0 at least 16 inches deep. Some shade and anaerobic tolerance, but none for drought.

Eupatorium perfoliatum (Boneset) — [perennial forb] flood plains, bogs, swamps and wet meadows, FACW+; statewide. Grows up to 5 feet, white flowers in late summer and fall; sun to part sun in moist to wet rich loam.

Eupatorium pilosum (Ragged eupatorium) — [perennial forb] Moist, low ground such as pond margins, sphagnum bogs or sandy-peaty openings in rocky woods on generally sandy soils in the Piedmont and Atlantic Coastal Plain, FACW. Grows 12 to 24 inches with white flowers in summer; grow in full to part sun in mesic to moist sandy to silt loams, especially near water features.

Eupatorium purpureum (Joe-pye-weed) — [perennial forb] mesic to moist open woods and fields, FAC; statewide. Grows up to 6 feet, pink to purple flowers in late summer and fall; sun to part shade in moist to wet rich sandy loam.

Eupatorium sessilifolium (Upland eupatorium) — [perennial forb] dry wooded slopes and roadsides; statewide except for glaciated plateaus. Grows 24 to 60 inches, white flowers in summer and fall; sun to part shade in dry, rocky sandy loam.

Euphorbia commutata (Wood spurge) [annual forb] — rich calcareous forests, open woodlands, ravines, streambanks and slopes over limestone and rock outcrops, scattered south central to southwest and along Lake Erie. Grows 4 to 12 inches with greenish flowers in spring on mesic to moist calcareous soils in part sun to part shade.

Euphorbia corollata (Flowering spurge) — [perennial forb] dry open woods and shale barrens, fields and sandy waste ground. Southern and western counties in Pennsylvania; scattered elsewhere. Grows up to 3 feet, white flowers in late summer; full sun in dry to mesic sandy loam.

Euphorbia dentata (Toothed spurge) [annual forb] — upland prairies and thickets, wooded slopes, limestone glades, floodplains and waste ground, scattered in southern Pennsylvania. Grows 1 to 3 feet with white-green flowers from spring to fall in dry to mesic poor soils containing much clay, sand and gravel in full sun. AKA *Poinsettia dentata*.

Yellow trout lily (*Erythronium americanum*)

Euphorbia maculata (Spotted spurge, spotted sandmat) [annual forb] — statewide in glades and dry sand prairies, as well as disturbed ground, FACU-. Grows up to six inches in a sprawling manner, with tiny cream flowers in summer, on dry sandy, gravelly or rocky soils in full to part sun; prefers compacted and disturbed soils. AKA *Chamaesyce maculata*.

Euphorbia nutans (Eyebane) [annual forb] — statewide on sandy, clayey and gravel fields and prairies, thickets, woodland openings and disturbed sites. Grows 3 to 18 inches with tiny flowers in midsummer in full sun on dry, poor soils; drought tolerant, but susceptible to conventional herbicides and lawn mowing. AKA *Chamaesyce nutans*.

Euphorbia obtusata (Blunt-leaved spurge) [annual forb] — found in low woods, thickets, alluvial gravel bars and sandy ground, often along creeks and river banks, reported along the Allegheny Front but considered extirpated, FACU-. Grows 8 to 14 inches in sandy, gravelly loams, mesic to moist; AKA *Euphorbia spathulata*.

Euphorbia polygonifolia (Seaside spurge) [annual forb] — dunes and sand plains in the vicinity of Lake Erie; FACU and listed as threatened. Grows less than a foot in a sprawling habit with yellow flowers in summer to fall. Prefers full sun in dry to mesic very sandy loams; vulnerable to coastal development and trampling by people on beaches.

AKA *Chamaesyce polygonifolia*.

Euphorbia purpurea (Glade spurge) — [perennial forb] Very rare in rich, cool, stream valleys, seeps, swamps in the Appalachians and Piedmont, especially in circumneutral to calcareous soils; FAC, endangered. Grows to 3 feet, purplish flowers in spring in part shade to shade.

Eurybia divaricata (White wood aster) — [perennial forb] dry to mesic, deciduous and mixed deciduous woods, edges and clearings; statewide. Grows 10 to 35 inches, with white flowers in autumn; part shade to shade in dry to moist, sandy loam, pH 5 to 7.

Eurybia macrophylla (Bigleaf aster) — [perennial forb] moist, often rocky upland woodlands; statewide. Grows 10 to 35 inches, white flowers in autumn; sun to part shade in dry to moist medium to fine textured sand loam, pH 4.9 to 6.9, at least 10 inches deep. Tolerant of shade and limestone soils, but not drought or anaerobic conditions.

Eurybia radula (Rough aster) — [perennial forb] Wet meadows, fens, sphagnum bogs, creek and lake shores, openings of boggy woods, especially wet spruce or tamarack forests. Scattered south, mostly southeast, Pennsylvania (OBL). Grows 1 to 3 feet in mesic to wet soils in part sun to shade, with blue-ish to white flowers in late summer.

Eurybia schreberi (Schreber's aster) — [perennial forb] Statewide in mesic to damp deciduous mixed forests, thickets on slopes and stream banks. Grows 1 to 4 feet with white flowers in late summer; prefers mesic to moist, well drained sandy to silt loams in part sun to part shade.

Eurybia spectabilis (Showy aster) — [perennial forb] generally sandy but sometimes dry clay soils in woodlands, especially oak-pine woodlands, as well as pine barrens, peat bogs, woods edges, rock outcrops, fields and clearings; Atlantic Coastal Plain, listed as endangered in Pennsylvania. Grows 1 to 2 feet in sun to part shade in dry sandy loams; purple flowers in late summer.

Euthamia graminifolia (Grass-leaved goldenrod) — [perennial forb] moist fields, roadsides, ditches and shores, FACU+; statewide. Two varieties: graminifolia and nuttalli. Grows up to 5 feet, yellow flowers in late summer and fall; sun to part sun in dry to moist sandy loam.

Fagus grandifolia (American beech) — [tree] rich deciduous and mixed-conifer forests, FACU; statewide. Deciduous tree to 80 feet; coarse to medium textured, deep, rich, moist but well-drained soils with a pH of 4.1 to 7.2 and a minimum depth of 32 inches, in full sun to part shade. Intolerant of wet, poorly drained soils, anaerobic conditions and limestone-based soils, but highly adaptable to drought. Often forms thickets or colonies by suckering from the shallow roots.

Joe-pye-weed (Eupatorium purpureum)

Fallopia cilinodis (Fringed bindweed) — [perennial vine] statewide, mostly north in dry woodlands and thickets, and on rocky slopes and roadsides.

Fallopia scandens (Climbing false-buckwheat) — [perennial vine] Twining herbaceous climbing vine found statewide in rocky, dry thickets, banks and woodlands, statewide; FAC. Grows up to 20 feet with whitish-green flowers in part sun; prefers rocky to gravelly, well drained soils, especially on woodland edges and in the vicinity of water.

Festuca paradoxa (Cluster fescue) — [perennial graminoid] very rare in prairies, open woods, thickets, and low open ground, FAC. Scattered statewide, endangered. Grows to 4 feet in wet, wet-mesic and mesic soils in sun to part sun.

Festuca subverticillata (Nodding fescue) — [perennial graminoid] moist to dry deciduous or mixed forests with organic rocky soils, FACU; statewide. Grows 24 to 48 inches; sun to part sun in moist, organic, rocky, sandy loam with a pH of 5.5 to 7.2 in at least 10 inches of soil. Intolerant of anaerobic conditions, limestone-based soils and drought.

Filipendula rubra (Queen-of-the-prairie) — [perennial forb] moist meadows, thickets and roadsides, FACW. Scattered statewide. Grows 3 to 6 feet, pink flowers in early summer; average, medium to wet, well-drained soil in full sun to part shade. Prefers consistently moist, fertile, humusy soils.

Fimbristylis annua (Annual fimbry) [annual graminoid] — savannas, fields, especially near shallow temporary pools in outcrops, mostly southeast, FACW- and listed as threatened. Grows 2 to 15 inches in mesic to moist loams in sun to part sun.

Fimbristylis autumnalis (Slender fimbry) [annual graminoid] — seeps, savannas, stream and banks, pond shores and moist meadows, FACW+, scattered statewide except northeast and more common southeast. Grows to 10 inches in moist to wet sandy, silty or clay loams as well as peats

Fimbristylis puberula (Hairy fimbry) — [perennial forb] sands, moist clays and sandy peats in prairies, savannas, glades and pinelands; reported only in Lancaster county on a swamp edge, listed as extirpated. Grows to 25 inches with reddish flowers in early summer; grow in full to part sun on mesic to moist sandy to silt loams.

Floerkea proserpinacoides (False-mermaid) [annual forb] — statewide in high quality woodlands, often on floodplains and sometimes seeps, FAC. Grows to 12 inches with greenish flowers in mid to late spring in dappled sunlight to light shade with consistently moist loamy or silt loam soils. Threatened by aggressive spreading of the invasive *Alliaria petiolata* (garlic mustard), for which this is also an ideal habitat.

Fragaria vesca spp. americana (Woodland strawberry) — [perennial forb] deciduous wooded slopes; scattered statewide. Grows 6 to 8 inches, white flowers in spring and fruit in early summer; part shade to shade in moist sandy loam.

Fragaria virginiana spp. virginiana (Wild strawberry) — [perennial forb] dry to moist open woodlands and clearings, typically in disturbed areas, FACU; statewide. Grows 6 to 8 inches, white flowers in spring and fruit in early summer; part sun to part shade in dry to moist sandy loam.

Frasera caroliniensis (American columbo) — [perennial forb] rare on dry slopes, abandoned fields and open woods; mostly northwest. Grows to 8 feet with green-brown-purple flowers in summer. Prefers part sun to part shade in well drained, moist, peaty acidic soils. AKA *Swertia caroliniensis*.

Fraxinus americana (White ash) — [tree] middle, moderately-moist slopes and dry, cold ridges and mountaintops, FACU; statewide. Two varieties: *americana* (most common) and *biltmoreana* (southeast, Piedmont, Central Appalachians). Deciduous tree to 80 feet; deep, well-drained, mesic to moist, coarse to medium textured, very fertile soils with a pH range of 4.7 to 7.5, a minimum of 40 inches deep. Low drought and anaerobic condition tolerance. Intolerant of shade and usually found with other hardwoods.

Fraxinus nigra (Black ash) — [tree] deciduous, coniferous, and mixed lowland forests, poorly drained swamps, bogs, gullies, depressions, valley flats, and stream and lake shores, FACW; statewide, especially southeast. Deciduous tree to 80 feet; moist to wet, coarse to medium textured, moderately fertile, mineral or organic soils with a pH of 4.4 to 8.2 at least 40 inches deep. Intolerant of shade and drought and somewhat adaptable to anaerobic conditions.

Fraxinus pennsylvanica (Green ash) — [tree] riparian areas such as floodplains and swamps, but is also in sites that periodically experience drought, FACW; mostly southeast, scattered elsewhere. Deciduous tree to 80 feet in fertile, clay, silt, and/or loam soils that range from poorly to well drained; prefers constantly moist, humusy, well-drained soils in full sun. Accepts all soil textures with a pH between 4.7 and 8.1 and a minimum depth of 40 inches. Moderately adaptable to anaerobic conditions, drought and limestone-based soils

Galactia regularis (Eastern milk-pea) — [perennial vine] reported only in Philadelphia and Lancaster counties on dry, sandy soil and listed as extirpated. Red to pink flowers in summer.

Galactia volubilis (Downy milk-pea) — [perennial vine] reported only in Berks and Philadelphia counties in dry thickets and edges; FAC+ and listed as extirpated. Pink flowers in summer.

Galearis spectabilis (Showy orchis) — [perennial forb] moist, calcareous woodlands, thickets, and old fields; statewide, especially southeast (Piedmont). Grows 4 to 8 inches, pink to purple flowers in spring; part shade to shade in moist rich loam, pH 5 to 6.

Galium aparine (Bedstraw) [annual forb/vine] — statewide, especially below northern tier, on stream banks, wooded slopes and woodlands, FACU. Grows low and spreading with green flowers in early spring in shade on moist, acidic, medium to fine textured, fertile soil at least 4 inches deep with a pH of 5.4 to 7.2. Shade tolerant, but not drought or anaerobic conditions and is often considered a noxious weed.

Galium asprellum (Rough bedstraw) — [perennial forb] Statewide, sprawling over and clinging to other plants in wet thickets, cedar swamps, borders of rivers and streams, marshes and wet meadows; clearings and disturbed moist ground, OBL. Grows 2 to 6 feet, generally prostrate, with white flowers in summer; grow in part shade to shade in mesic to moist, humusy loams with a pH between 5.0 and 7.0 at least 14 inches deep. Shade tolerant, but not anaerobic conditions.

Galium boreale (Northern bedstraw) — [perennial forb] upland rocky woods, slopes, wet fields, fens, roadside banks, FACU; statewide, especially in Central Appalachians and Piedmont regions. Grows 1 to 3 feet, white flowers in late summer; average, medium, well-drained soils in part shade. Prefers moist soils with a pH of 5.0 to 7.2 at least 6 inches deep, where it will often spread by creeping roots and self-seeding. No anaerobic tolerance.

Galium circaezans (Wild licorice) — [perennial forb] Rich forests, ranging from dry oak-hickory to rich beech-maple (rarely in swampy or coniferous sites), UPL. Grows 9 to 24 inches with white flowers in summer; grow in part sun to part shade in dry to mesic, loamy to rocky soil that includes such decaying organic matter as leaves.

Galium concinnum (Shining bedstraw) — [perennial forb] Deciduous forests, including beech-maple and oak-hickory; banks, floodplain forests along streams, mostly southern and western Pennsylvania, UPL. Grows 4 to 20 inches on weak stems with white flowers in early summer; prefers dappled to medium shade in a mesic to dry, loamy to rocky soil with decaying matter such as leaf litter. Drought tolerant, makes a good ground cover underneath trees.

Black ash (Fraxinus nigra)

Galium labradoricum (Bog bedstraw) — [perennial forb] Very rare in fens, bogs, swamps, sedge meadows, and marshy ground along streams and lakes; OBL, endangered in Pennsylvania. Grows 4 to 16 inches with white flowers in early summer; grow in moist to wet, rich loams in sun to part shade, especially in wetland areas.

Galium lanceolatum (Wild licorice) — [perennial forb] Statewide in deciduous forests (beech-maple more often than oak-hickory or northern hemlock-hardwoods). No cultivation data; may be very difficult to obtain from commercial sources.

Grows up to 2 feet with white flowers in early summer; prefers dappled to medium shade in a mesic to dry, loamy to rocky soil with decaying matter such as leaf litter.

Galium latifolium (Purple bedstraw) — [perennial forb] Rare in woodlands, rocky slopes and along roadsides, mostly south central Pennsylvania; listed as endangered. Grows up to 2 feet with greenish flowers in summer in dry to mesic well drained soils in part sun to part shade.

Galium obtusum (Cleavers) — [perennial forb] Scattered in swamps, bogs and wet woods, mostly Piedmont, Ridge and Valley, northwestern Allegheny Plateau, FACW+. Grows less than 2 inches with many branches to give it a bushy appearance. White flowers in late spring to early summer; grow in full sun to part shade in moist to wet soils high in organic matter with a pH of 4.6 to 7.0 at least 8 inches deep; does not like to dry out. Tolerant of shade and anaerobic conditions but not drought.

Galium palustre (Ditch bedstraw) — [perennial forb] Scattered in marshes and on stream banks, mostly northern Pennsylvania (OBL). Grows 4 to 20 inches with white flowers in early summer; prefers mesic to moist rich loams in full to part sun.

Galium pilosum (Bedstraw) — [perennial forb] Open sandy, dry ground, often in old fields and on shale barrens, mostly southern Pennsylvania. Grows up to 18 inches with white flowers in early summer; prefers dappled to medium shade in a mesic to dry, loamy to rocky soil with decaying matter such as leaf litter.

Galium tinctorium (Bedstraw) — [perennial forb] Statewide on wooded stream banks and floodplains, as well as moist, wooded slopes; OBL. Grows up to 3 inches in full to part sun in mesic to moist, rich loams, clay loams, sand and gravel of any texture with a pH between 4.6 and 7.0 at least 8 inches deep; tolerates brief standing water but not drought.

Galium trifidum (Cleavers) — [perennial forb] Rare in thickets and moist woodlands, especially northern Pennsylvania, FACW+. Grows 6 to 20 inches with white flowers in summer; prefers full sun in moist to wet rich loams of any texture with a pH range of 4.6 to 8.0 at least 8 inches deep. No drought tolerance, but adapts to anaerobic conditions and some shade.

Gaultheria hispidula (Creeping snowberry) — [shrub] rare in wet woods and swamps and bogs on hummocks and tree stumps, FACW; mostly northeast, scattered north central and northwest. Creeping shrub to 6 inches; part shade to shade in moist to wet cold humusy to peaty acidic soils of any texture with a depth of at least 12 inches, pH 4.0 to 6.0. White flowers in spring.

Gaultheria procumbens (Teaberry) — [shrub] oak woods or under evergreens; moist sites but tolerates moisture conditions ranging from dry to poorly drained, FACU; statewide. Creeping subshrub spreads from rhizomes; 4 to 8 inches with white flowers in spring; part shade to shade in coarse to medium textured, dry to mesic to moist sandy, well-drained organic loam. Prefers pH 4.5 to 6.5. Intolerant of anaerobic conditions, but well adapted for drought.

Gaylussacia baccata (Black huckleberry) — [shrub] dry to mesic acidic woods and thickets, often among oaks, FACU; statewide except north-central. Shrub to 3 feet with white to pink flowers in early summer and fruit in late summer; part shade to shade in mesic to moist sandy organic loam at least 14 inches deep, of any texture, pH 4.0 to 6.5. Low fertility and moisture requirements, and intolerant of anaerobic conditions.

Gaylussacia frondosa (Dangleberry) — [shrub] dry to mesic acidic oak woods and thickets, FAC; mostly southeast, scattered elsewhere. Grows to 6 feet, with white to pink flowers in early summer and fruit in late summer; part shade to shade in dry to mesic, coarse textured, sandy organic loam, pH 3.8 to 5.5. Drought and shade tolerant but not anaerobic conditions or limestone soils.

Gentiana alba (Yellowish gentian) — [perennial forb] Rare on wooded hillsides, limestone glades, rocky bluffs; FACU, scattered statewide, but believed to be extirpated. Grows 1 to 2 feet tall with yellowish-green flowers in late summer; prefers full to part sun in mesic, rich soils containing sand, silt or clay.

Gentiana andrewsii var. andrewsii (Bottle gentian) — [perennial forb] wet fields and moist, open woods, FACW; mostly west and southeast. Grows up to 3 feet, blue flowers in late summer. Prefers sun to part shade in moist to wet, medium textured, fertile, sandy, humusy loam with a pH of 5.8 to 7.2 at least 6 inches deep. Low tolerance for anaerobic conditions and limestone-based soils, but moderate adaptability to drought and light shade.

Gentiana catesbaei (Coastal plain gentian) — [perennial forb] Moist, open woodlands and clearings, reported only in Chester County, OBL; listed as extirpated. Grows 12 inches in full sun to part shade with purple flowers in summer; prefers mesic to moist sandy to silt loams.

Gentiana clausa (Meadow closed gentian) — [perennial forb] moist meadows, stream banks, and open woods in moist acidic soil, FACW; statewide. Grows up to 3 feet, blue flowers in late summer; sun to part shade in moist to wet, medium-textured, rich loam with a pH range of 5.8 to 7.2 at least 6 inches deep. Low tolerance for anaerobic conditions and limestone-based soils, but moderate adaptability to drought and some shade.

Gentiana linearis (Narrow-leaved gentian) — [perennial forb] Wet meadows, bogs, moist barrens, OBL; mostly northeastern Pennsylvania, but also in southwestern mountains. Grows to 12 inches with purple flowers in summer; prefers rich, mesic to moist humusy loams.

Gentiana saponaria (Soapwort gentian, harvestbells) — [perennial forb] swamps, open woodlands, FACW; listed as endangered in Pennsylvania. Grows 6 to 24 inches in full to part sun; purple flowers in summer. Prefers mesic to moist sandy loams.

Gentianella quinquefolia (Stiff gentian, agueweed) [annual forb] — thin woodland slopes, rocky meadows, stream banks, calcareous seeps, shaded limestone cliffs, FAC, mostly northeast, but also southern Allegheny Mountains south. Grows to about 2 feet in full sun to light shade on somewhat barren dry to mesic soils with clay or rocky materials, especially on high-quality sites where limestone is close to the surface.

Gentianopsis crinita (Eastern fringed gentian) [annual/biennial forb] — high quality wetlands including open wooded swamps, fens, wet meadows, stream banks, seepy slopes and swales in creek valleys, mostly eastern third of Pennsylvania, scattered west, OBL. Grows 1-3 feet with blue flowers in autumn on moist to wet, sandy, slightly calcareous soils in part sun to part shade.

Gentianopsis virgata (Narrow-leaved fringed gentian) [annual forb] — found in fens, wet meadows, marly shores, limestone crevices, calcareous flats, FACW+, but listed as extirpated. Grows 12-32 inches with attractive purple flowers in autumn. Grow in sun on mesic to wet, calcareous, sandy, gravelly or rocky soil.

Geranium bicknellii (Cranesbill) — [perennial forb] Dry, open woodlands and clearings, occasionally on rocky ledges; scattered throughout Pennsylvania and listed as endangered. Grows 18 to 36 inches with purple flowers in spring; prefers mesic to dry to mesic sandy to rocky soils in part sun, with cool to warm summer temperatures.

Geranium bicknellii (Cranesbill) [annual forb] — widely scattered in the Appalachians in dry woodlands, clearings and rocky ledges and listed as endangered. Grows to 20 inches with pink flowers in summer in dry to mesic sandy loams in full to part sun.

Geranium carolinianum (Wild geranium) [annual forb] — sandy savannas and woodland openings, rocky outcrops, dry barrens and hard fields, especially sandy Black Oak woodlands, generally southern Pennsylvania. Grows to 24 inches with white to pink flowers in late spring to summer on dry to mesic sandy, gravelly or clay soils in part sun to part shade. Some observations suggest the plant becomes abundant following wildfires because its seeds germinate in response to heat and/or light.

Geranium maculatum (Wood geranium) — [perennial forb] rich open upland woods, shaded roadsides and areas of fields, FACU; statewide. Grows 18 to 24 inches, with pink-purple flowers in spring; part sun to part shade in moist humusy loam, pH 5 to 7.

Geranium robertianum (Herb-robert) [annual forb] — rocky slopes, ravines, moist woods and river banks, generally eastern Pennsylvania — especially the glaciated plateau. Grows to about 15 inches with pink to purple flowers from late spring into fall on mesic to moist, well drained soils; technically native to Canada.

Geum canadense (White avens) — [perennial forb] upland dry to mesic open woodlands, woodland edges and openings and thickets, FACU; statewide. Grows 16 to 40 inches, white flowers in early summer; sun to part shade in dry to moist sandy loam of any texture and medium fertility at least 4 inches deep with a pH range of 4.5 to 7.5. Adaptable to anaerobic conditions and limesone soils, shade tolerant but not suitable for droughty sites.

Geum laciniatum (Herb-bennet) — [perennial forb] mesic savannas, thickets and woodland borders and moist meadows, FAC+; statewide. Grows 16 to 40 inches, with white flowers in summer; sun to part shade in moist, rich loam of any texture, pH 5.0 to 7.0, at least 12 inches deep. Low anaerobic and drought tolerance..

Wood geranium (Geranium maculatum)

Geum rivale (Water avens) — [perennial forb] bogs, peaty meadows and calcareous marshes, OBL; mostly northwest (Western Glaciated Allegheny Plateau), and scattered north. Grows 6 to 24 inches, flowers are yellowish with purple veins in early summer; full sun in moist to wet, silty, rich circumneutral loam with a pH between 4.8 and 7.0 and at least 12 inches deep. Moderate adaptability to anaerobic conditions, but intolerant of drought..

Geum virginianum (Cream-colored avens) — [perennial forb] scattered, mostly in southern Pennsylvania, in swamps, ravines and rich woodlands, FAC-. Grows to 24 inches in full to part sun with white flowers in summer; prefers rich, moist to wet silty loams with organic matter.

Gillenia trifoliata (Bowman's-root) — [perennial forb] dry to moist, upland woods and rocky banks; statewide, less common along northern tier. Grows 24 to 36 inches, white flowers in late spring and early summer; part shade to shade in moist, slightly acidic rich, rocky soil. AKA Porteranthus trifoliatus.

Gleditsia triacanthos (Honey-locust) — [tree/shrub] well-drained upland woodlands and borders, rocky hillsides, old fields, fencerows and rich moist stream banks, bottomlands and floodplains, FAC-; statewide, especially southeast. Grows to 65 feet; organically rich, moist, well-drained soils in full sun. Tolerant of a wide range of soils, wind, high summer heat, drought and saline conditions.

Glyceria acutiflora (Mannagrass) — [perennial graminoid] widely scattered in shallow water, muddy shores and wet swamps, generally Ridge and Valley, OBL.

Glyceria borealis (Northern mannagrass) — [perennial graminoid] in shallow water of streams and lakes and on muddy shorelines of ponds, lakes and streams, OBL. Mostly northeast; scattered elsewhere. Can reach 40 inches; sun to part sun in moist to wet, moderately fertile, silty loam of any texture and at least 14 inches deep with a pH range of 5.0 to 8.5. High anaerobic and low drought and shade tolerances and listed as endangered in Pennsylvania.

Glyceria canadensis (Rattlesnake mannagrass) — [perennial graminoid] bogs, swamps, wet woods and marshes near lakes, OBL; statewide. Can reach 36 inches; sun to part sun in moist to wet silty loam with a pH of 5.0 to 8.5 of any texture and at least 16 inches deep. Intolerant of shade and drought, but adaptable to anaerobic conditions and limestone-based soils.

Glyceria canadensis x grandis (Rattlesnake grass) — [perennial graminoid] scattered statewide in wet woodlands, swamps and marshes; OBL, a naturally-occuring hybrid.

Glyceria grandis (American mannagrass) — [perennial graminoid] wet woods and meadows, stream banks, swamps, and in the water of streams, ditches and ponds. Mostly north (northern Allegheny plateaus); scattered south. Can reach 48 inches; sun to part sun in moist to wet silty loam.

Glyceria melicaria (Slender mannagrass) — [perennial graminoid] swamps, bogs and wet soils, OBL; statewide. Grows 20 to 40 inches; sun to part sun in moist to wet, medium to fine textured, moderately fertile, silty loam at least 16 inches deep with a pH of 4.5 to 8.0. Intolerant of shade and drought, but adaptable to anaerobic conditions and limestone soils.

Glyceria obtusa (Coastal mannagrass) — [perennial graminoid] reported only in northwestern Monroe and in the Atlantic Coastal plain; prefers moist, sandy, peaty soils in wet woodlands, swamps and shallow waters of lakes and ponds; OBL and listed as endangered in Pennsylvania. Prefers medium to fine textured moderately fertile soils at least 4 inches deep with a pH range of 4.0 to 7.0; sun to part shade. Excellent for anaerobic conditions and intolerant of drought.

Glyceria septentrionalis (Floating mannagrass) — [perennial graminoid] very wet meadows, floodplain forests, swamps, pond and lake margins and in the shallow water of stream margins, OBL. Mostly west and south, especially southeast (Piedmont). Grows 3 to 6 feet in full to part sun and wet conditions; preferred soils combine some organic material with loam, clay or sand and shallow water is tolerated; may spread aggressively.

Glyceria striata (Fowl mannagrass) — [perennial graminoid] bogs, along lakes and streams, and in other wet places, OBL; statewide. Grows 20 to 40 inches; sun to part shade in moist to wet, medium to fine textured, silty loam at least 4 inches deep with a pH range of 4.0 to 8.0. Excellent for anaerobic conditions but intolerant of drought.

Gnaphalium purpureum var. purpureum (Purple cudweed) [annual forb] — scattered statewide except the northern tier in woodland clearings and edges and disturbed ground. Grows to 15 inches with greenish-red flowers in spring on dry to mesic sandy loams. AKA *Gnaphalium purpureum var. purpurea*.

Gnaphalium uliginosum (Low cudweed) [annual forb] — statewide in wet meadows, stream bsnks lake and pond shores or other frequently/sporadically moist disturbed sites. Grows to 10 inches with tiny brownish flowers in late summer on dry to mesic loams in full sun to part shade.

White avens (Geum canadense)

Goodyera pubescens (Downy rattlesnake plantain) — [perennial forb] dry to moist warm, deciduous or coniferous forests, FACU-; mostly southeast (Piedmont), scattered elsewhere. Grows 8 to 16 inches, with white flowers in summer; part shade to shade in dry to moist silty-sandy loam, pH 5 to 6.

Goodyera repens (Lesser rattlesnake-plantain) — [perennial forb] typically in shady, moist coniferous to mixed forests, often on ground covered with moss or humus and sometimes in bogs or cedar swamps; rare and mostly northeast to central Pennsylvania; FACU+. Grows 3 to 7 inches with white flowers in summer in part shade to shade on mesic to moist sites, especially in coniferous swamps.

Goodyera tesselata (Checkered rattlesnake-plantain) — [perennial forb] dry to moist upland coniferous or mixed woods, less commonly in swamps and near bogs, mostly northeastern

Pennsylvania and listed as threatened (FACU-).

Gratiola aurea (Goldenpert) — [perennial forb] very rare on sandy shores of ponds and moist stream banks in eastern Pennsylvania, OBL; listed as endangered.

Gratiola neglecta (Hedge hyssop) [annual forb] — statewide in floodplain forests, bogs, gravelly seeps, soggy meadows, muddy shorelines and poorly drained areas, OBL. Grows 4 to 12 inches with white flowers from spring to fall in sun to part shade on exposed, moist to wet muddy soil, including temporary standing water, and dies down after seeds mature.

Gymnocarpium appalachianum (Appalachian oak-fern) — [fern/ally] very rare on moist sandstone or talus slopes with cold air seepage on mountain slopes and summits dominated by maple-birch-hemlock forest; of conservation concern.

Gymnocarpium dryopteris (Common oak fern) — [fern/ally] cool, coniferous and mixed woods and at base of shale talus slopes often in pockets of humus. Ideal for the northeast. Fronds 9 to 12 inches; rhizome: wide or long creeping. Grow in part shade to shade in dry to mesic rocky humus.

Gymnocladus dioicus (Kentucky coffee-tree) — [tree/shrub] moist woods, especially lower slopes, and floodplains, 60 to 80 feet. Suckers to form colonies in native habitats; mostly southeast; scattered southwest. Grow in organically rich, mesic to moist soils in full sun; accepts soil of any texture, but avoid heavy clay. Requires a minimum soil depth of 36 inches and a pH range of 6.0 to 8.0. Tolerates drought, poorer soils and urban environments but not anaerobic conditions. AKA *Gymnocladus dioica.*

Hackelia virginiana (Beggar's-lice, stickseed) [biennial forb] — statewide in dry to moist wooded slopes and upland woodlands, FACU. Grows 1 to 3 feet with white to bluish flowers in late summer in part sun to part shade on a wide range of mesic, fertile loams.

Hamamelis virginiana (Witch-hazel) — [shrub] dry to moist woodlands, slopes, bluffs, and high hammocks, FAC-; statewide. Deciduous shrub or small tree that grows to 20 feet with yellow flowers in late fall to early winter in part sun to part shade. Prefers mesic to moist, moderately fertile, sandy organic loam, with medium to fine texture, at least 20 inches deep and a pH range of 4.5 to 6.2. Low tolerance for drought, limestone soils or anaerobic conditions. Not suitable for hedging and requires a 120 day growing season. The familiar astringent is distilled from the bark of young shoots. Among the most widespread shrubs in the region.

Hasteola suaveolens (Sweet-scented Indian-plantain) — [perennial forb] Shaded stream banks, rich woods, wet meadows; OBL. Scattered, mostly west (Central Appalachians, Western Glaciated and Southern Allegheny Plateaus). Grows 2 to 5 feet, white to cream flowers in late summer to early fall; prefers wet to wet-mesic well-drained somewhat organic soils. AKA *Cacalia suaveolens.*

Hedeoma pulegioides (American false pennyroyal) [annual forb] — statewide in dry upland rocky woodlands and glades, fields, pastures and along roadsides and trails. Grows 6 to 18 inches with blue flowers in summer on dry to mesic rocky or loamy soils in full sun to light shade; prefers barren or disturbed sites and more moisture in sunny sites.

Hedeoma pulegioides (American pennyroyal) [annual forb] — statewide in upland rocky woodlands, trails and glades, dry prairies, fallow fields and pastures. Grows 4 to 16 inches with blue-pink flowers in late summer in sun to part shade in dry to mesic (more mesic for sunny areas) rocky, loamy and especially disturbed ground.

Helenium autumnale (Common sneezeweed) — [perennial forb] meadows, moist riverbanks, wet fields, alluvial thickets and swamps, FACW+; statewide. Grows 3 to 5 feet, yellow flowers in late summer to fall; sun to part sun in moist to wet rich loam of any texture at least 6 inches deep with a pH range of 4.0 to 7.5. Intolerant of shade, drought and anaerobic conditions, but has low fertility requirements and a high tolerance for limestone-based soils.

Helianthemum bicknellii (Bicknell's hoary rose) — [perennial forb] sandy, dry rocky slopes, open woods and prairies. Mostly southeast; scattered elsewhere and endangered. Grows 8 to 24 inches, with yellow flowers in summer; sun to part shade in dry, sandy soil loam.

Helianthemum canadense (Frostweed) — [perennial forb] dry sandy or rocky ground, open woods and barrens. Mostly southeast; scattered elsewhere. Grows 6 to 12 inches, yellow flowers in early summer; sun to part shade in dry, gravelly loam.

Helianthemum propinquum (Frostweed) — [perennial forb] uncommon on barrens or other dry, sandy ground, especially eastern Pennsylvania. Yellow flowers in late summer; sun to part sun on dry sandy loam.

Helianthus angustifolius (Swamp sunflower) — [perennial forb] Very rare in sandy, open ground, including swamps, lower Bucks County, but believed extirpated; FACW. Grows 1 to 3 feet, yellow flowers in late fall; prefers wet somewhat circumneutral soils in part shade and a good choice for bog or pond planting.

Helianthus decapetalus (Thin leaved sunflower) — [perennial forb] open woodlands, woodland edges, savannas, meadows, thickets and lightly shaded areas along rivers, FACU; statewide. Grows 2 to 5 feet, yellow flowers in late summer; part sun to part, especially dappled, shade in moist sandy loam. Can be aggressive.

Helianthus divaricatus (Woodland sunflower) — [perennial forb] dry open woods and wooded slopes, thickets, shale barrens and roadsides; statewide. Grows up to 5 feet, yellow flowers in late summer; part sun to part shade in dry to mesic sandy loam, pH 5 to 7. Aggressive spreader.

Helianthus giganteus (Swamp sunflower) — [perennial forb] wet fields, swamps and ditches, FACW; mostly southeast (Piedmont) and west (Southern Allegheny Plateau), scattered elsewhere. Grows 6 to 10 feet, yellow flowers in late summer and fall; sun to part sun in moist, rich silty loam.

Helianthus hirsutus (Hairy sunflower) — [perennial forb] Dry, open sites including roadsides and woodland, especially oak, edges; mostly southwest. Grows 2 to 5 feet in full to part sun in loamy to sandy soils that are mesic to dry. Yellow flowers in late autumn; easy to grow, but can be an aggressive spreader.

Helianthus microcephalus (Small wood sunflower) — [perennial forb] Open, upland woods, rocky slopes and along roadsides, mostly west (Western Glaciated and Southern Allegheny Plateaus). Grows to 5 feet in full sun and prefers average to circumneutral, well drained soil. Yellow flowers from summer into fall.

Helianthus occidentalis (Sunflower) — [perennial forb] very rare in prairies, dry meadows, fields, glades and occasionally rocky open woods. UPL; reported only in Warren County. Yellow flowers in summer, 2 to 4 feet; dry to medium, well drained soils in full sun. Tolerates a wide range of dry to moist soils, but intolerant of heavy clays. Spreads by rhizomes to form large colonies.

Helianthus strumosus (Rough-leaved sunflower) — [perennial forb] fields, dry, open, upland woods and woodland edges; statewide. Grows up to 7 feet, yellow flowers in summer. Possibly hybridizing with *Helianthus divaricatus*; sun to part shade in dry, sandy loam, pH 5.5 to 7.

Heliopsis helianthoides (Ox-eye) — [perennial forb] open and sometimes rocky woods, thickets, prairies, stream banks; statewide. Grows up to 5 feet, with yellow flowers in late summer; full sun to part shade (where it may require support) in dry to moist sandy loam, pH 5.6 to 6.8.

Hepatica nobilis (Liverleaf) — [perennial forb] rich woods and dry rocky upland slopes; statewide. Two varieties — *obtusa* and *acuta* (sharp and round lobed leaves, respectively). Grows 6 to 8 inches, lavender to purple flowers in early spring; part shade to shade in dry sandy loam. pH 4 to 7, but prefers pH 4.5 to 6. Also known as *Hepatica americana*.

Hesperostipa spartea (Needlegrass, porcupine grass) — [perennial graminoid] very rare in dry prairies and open woodlands, as well as roadsides. Reported only in Lackawanna County. Grows 3 to 6 feet on dry rocky or sandy soils in sun to part sun, in medium textured soils at leats 10 inches deep, with a pH range of 5.0 to 7.5. Intolerant of shade and anaerobic conditions.

Heteranthera dubia (Water star-grass) — [perennial forb] in lakes, ponds, rivers and streams, statewide except southwest, OBL.

Heteranthera reniformis (Mud-plantain) —

[perennial forb] stream and pond edges, freshwater tidal flats, ditches, mostly eastern Pennsylvania, OBL..

Heuchera americana (Alum-root) — [perennial forb] rich woods, rocky slopes, shaly cliffs on rich, well-drained humus, FACU-; mostly southeast and west, scattered elsewhere. Grows 12 to 30 inches, greenish-white to pink flowers in spring; part sun to part shade in dry, sandy well-drained humusy loam, pH 5 to 7.

Hibiscus laevis (Halberd-leaved rose-mallow) — [perennial forb] rare along muddy alluvial shorelines and in swamps and marshes, sometimes in standing water, mostly southeast. Grows 5 to 7 feet in full to part sun with white to pink flowers in summer (flowers require sunlight to open properly). Prefers continually moist to wet, medium to fine textured, organically rich soil at least 12 inches deep with a pH between 5.5 and 7.2. Adapts well to anaerobic conditions, but not drought.

Hibiscus moscheutos (Rose-mallow) — [perennial forb] marshes, wet meadows, swampy open forests, OBL. Mostly southeast, scattered elsewhere. Large white flowers with crimson center in summer, 3 to 8 feet. Very late to appear in spring, then grows rapidly. Best in moist soils rich in organic matter; soil should not dry out and regular watering with fertilization helps. Prefers medium to fine textured soils at least 10 inches deep with a pH range of 4.0 to 7.2. Intolerant of shade and drought but an excellent choice for anaerobic conditions with full sun and good air circulation.

Hieracium gronovii (Hawkweed) — [perennial forb] openings in pine and pine-oak woods, bogs, sands; often hybridizes with H. venosum; mostly Piedmont and western Allegheny Plateau; UPL. Grows 1 to 3 feet with yellow flowers in late summer to early fall; prefers full sun to part shade and mesic to slightly dry sandy or rocky soil. Height varies with habitat.

Rose-mallow (*Hibiscus moscheutos*)

Hieracium paniculatum (Hawkweed) — [perennial forb] statewide in woodlands and forest openings, especially on slopes, with dry, rocky or sandy soils. Grows 1 to 3 feet with yellow flowers in late summer; prefers part sun to part shade on mesic to slightly dry sandy to rocky soil.

Hieracium scabrum (Hawkweed) — [perennial forb] statewide in woodland clearings and edges and dry fields, usually with sandy soils and often on disturbed sites. Grows 18 to 30 inches with yellow flowers in summer; prefers full sun to part sun in mesic to dry to mesic rocky loams and sandy loams.

Hieracium traillii (Green's hawkweed) — [perennial forb] generally south-central Pennsylvania and rare on dry woodland slopes, shale barrens and bluffs; listed as endangered. No cultivation data; may be very difficult to obtain from commercial sources. Grows to 24 inches with yellow-orange flowers in summer in sun to part sun on dry, rocky soils.

Hieracium venosum (Rattlesnake weed) — [perennial forb] dry, upland woods including slopes and edges, sandy hillsides and forest openings, statewide except northern tier counties. Grows to 18 inches in part shade to shade with yellow flowers in summer; prefers dry, sandy loams in open woodlands; part shade to shade in dry to moist organic sandy loam.

Hierochloe odorata (Vanilla sweetgrass) —

[perennial graminoid] very rare in moist meadows or river shores. Grows 18 to 36 inches, FACW; endangered reported only in Wayne, Butler, Erie and Allegheny counties. Grows 12 to 20 inches sun to part sun in moist, organic sandy loam.

Hordeum jubatum (Foxtail-barley) — [perennial graminoid] dry fields, roadsides, waste ground, FAC. Prefers medium textured soils at least 10 inches deep with a pH range of 5.0 to 8.5. Moderate drought tolerance but none for anaerobic conditions or shade

Hordeum pusillum (Little-barley) [annual graminoid] — found in dry, gravelly dolomite prairies and fields and sterile waste ground, reported in Bucks and Montgomery counties but listed as extirpated. Grows to 2 feet in full sun with a preference for dry to mesic, medium to fine textured soils at least 8 inches deep with a pH range of 6.2 to 8.0. Some tolerance for anaerobic conditions and limestone soils, but not shade. AKA *Criterion pusillum*.

Hottonia inflata (American featherfoil) — [perennial forb] floating aquatic in pools, swamps, streams, quiet backwaters; eastern Pennsylvania and believed to be extirpated.

Houstonia caerulea (Bluets or Quaker ladies) — [perennial forb] dry to mesic meadows, fields, upland open woods, and woods edges, FACU; statewide. Grows up to 16 inches, blue flowers with yellow centers in spring; sun to part shade in moist rich sandy loam, pH 5.5 to 7.

Houstonia canadensis (Fringed bluets) — [perennial forb] rare on rocky, dry slopes, mostly southwestern Pennsylvania. Grows to 16 inches with bluish-white flowers in spring; prefers sun to part shade in dry, sandy loam.

Houstonia longifolia (Long-leaved bluets) — [perennial forb] Dry wooded slopes, shale barrens and sandy fields, mostly south, especially Central Appalachians. Grows 1 to 3 feet, white, pink or purple flowers in early summer. Prefers dry to moist, acidic, sandy to gravelly loams in full sun to part shade. A good choice for rock gardens and relatively easy to cultivate.

Houstonia purpurea var. purpurea (Purple bluets) — [perennial forb] Very rare in open, moist rocky woodlands, stream banks and rocky slopes; scattered sites southwest. Grows 6 to 8 inches, pale blue white flowers in early summer; prefers part shade to shade in acidic, well drained, moist, loamy soils.

Houstonia serpyllifolia (Creeping bluets, Thymeleaf bluets) — [perennial forb] Rare along streams and in meadows; southwest (Southern Allegheny Plateau); believed to be extirpated. Grows 2 to 3 inches, light blue to lilac flowers in mid to late summer. Spreads by stolons to form a colony in moist sandy and slightly acidic soil in part sun to part shade (requires sunlight to bloom). Good for rock walls or flagstone paths.

Humulus lupulus var. lupuloides (Brewer's hops) — [perennial vine] moist alluvial soil, woods edges, thickets and waste ground; FACU; statewide. Twining vine to 30 feet. Greenish flowers in summer. Grow in sun to part sun in moist sandy loam. Used to flavor beer.

Huperzia lucidula (Shining firmoss) — [fern/ally] statewide in humus-rich soils of cool, moist conifer and mixed hardwood forests, infrequently on shaded, mossy acidic sandstone rock; FACW-. No cultivation data; may be difficult to find commercially.

Huperzia porophila (Sandstone-loving firmoss) — [fern/ally] very rare in Pike and Carbon counties, on damp, acidic, shaded sandstone, rarely on shale or exposed sandstone, of cliffs adjacent to waterfalls; FACU and listed as endangered in Pennsylvania.

Hybanthus concolor (Green-violet) — [perennial forb] generally southern Pennsylvania in rich mesic, especially alluvial, woodlands; FACU-. Grows 18 to 36 inches with green flowers in late spring to early summer; prefers part sun to part shade in mesic to moist, rich, loamy and slightly acidic soils with abundant organic matter such as fallen leaves.

Hydrangea arborescens (Wild hydrangea or sevenbark) — [tree/shrub] rich woods; rocky wooded slopes; stream banks and ravines, FACU; statewide, especially southwest (Southern Allegheny Plateau). Shrub to 6 feet with white flowers in summer; average, medium moisture, well-drained soil in part shade. Intolerant of drought.

Hydrastis canadensis (Goldenseal) — [perennial forb] mesic deciduous forests, often on clay soils. Mostly southeast (Piedmont) and southwest (Southern Allegheny Plateau). Tiny white flowers in spring, followed by dramatic red fruit. Grow in well drained, medium soil in part shade; prefers soils well composted with much leaf mold.

Hydrocotyle americana (Marsh pennywort) — [perennial forb] swampy thickets, boggy fields, wet woods and lake margins, OBL; statewide. Low creeping habit with white flowers in summer; sun to part shade in moist to wet marshy soils.

Hydrocotyle ranunculoides (Floating pennywort) — [perennial forb] typically shallow water, but also moist shores and wet meadows, south central and southeast Pennsylvania, OBL.

Hydrocotyle umbellata (Water pennywort) — [perennial forb] Very rare in muddy shorelines and shallow water, principally southeast; believed to be extirpated, OBL. Grows less than 12 inches in sun to shade in continually moist to wet muddy to sandy soil, including standing water up to 4 inches. Spreads to form a ground cover and bears white flowers in summer. Good for ponds and wetlands.

Hydrophyllum canadense (Canadian waterleaf) — [perennial forb] rocky upland wooded slopes, ravines and moist woods, FACU. Mostly southwest, scattered elsewhere. Grows 12 to 20 inches, white-pink to purple flowers in summer; part shade to shade in moist humusy soil.

Hydrophyllum macrophyllum (Large-leaved waterleaf) — [perennial forb] rare in southwest, south central calcareous rocky, mesic woodlands; endangered in Pennsylvania. Grows to 24 inches with green flowers in late spring on mesic to moist, circumneutral soils derived from limestone or dolomite.

Hydrophyllum virginianum (Virginia waterleaf) — [perennial forb] mesic wooded slopes and stream banks and in thickets, FAC; statewide. Grows 12 to 30 inches, white flowers in spring; part shade to shade in moist humusy loam, pH 6 to 7.

Hypericum adpressum (Creeping St. John's-wort) — [perennial forb] reported only in southern Bucks County in wet areas such as swamps, OBL; believed to be extirpated in Pennsylvania.

Hypericum boreale (Dwarf St. John's-wort) — [perennial forb] mostly northeastern Pennsylvania in wet meadows, swampy hummocks and open peat bog edges; OBL. Grows 4 to 16 inches with yellow flowers in late summer; prefers full sun to part sun on moist to wet, coarse to medium textured, moderately fertile soils, such as those on pond edges, stream banks and marshes. Requires a minimum of 8 inches of soil depth and a pH range of 4.4 to 6.0; intolerant of drought and limestone soils, but an excellent choice for anaerobic conditions.

Shrubby St. John's wort (*Hypericum prolificum*)

Hypericum canadense (Canadian St. John's-wort) [annual forb] — wet pond and stream shores and meadows, low thickets and swales, mostly east but scattered southwest, FACW. Grows 4 to 24 inches in moist to wet, sandy, muddy soils, with orange-yellow flowers in late summer.

Hypericum densiflorum (Bushy St. John's-wort) — [shrub] rare in sphagnum bogs, swampy meadows, rocky river banks, seepage slopes, pond and lake margins, moist pinelands; FAC+; southwest (Southern Allegheny Plateau). Grows 18 inches to six feet with yellow flowers in summer. Prefers moist to wet organic clay loams of any texture at leasst 18 inches deep with a pH between 4.0 and 7.5. Pefers full sun, but tolerates shade as well as anaerobic conditions but not drought or limestone-based soils.

Hypericum denticulatum (Coppery St. Johnswort) — [perennial forb] wet woodlands and bogs in Bucks and Adams counties, OBL; reported as extirpated in Pennsylvania. Grows 8 to 20 inches with yellow flowers in summer; prefers mesic to moist sandy loams of any texture in full to part sun, at least 10 inches deep with a pH range of 4.8 to 6.4; some tolerance for drought and anaerobic conditions.

Hypericum dissimulatum (Disguised St. John's-wort) [perennial forb] — widely scattered in eastern Pennsylvania in moist sandy to peaty soils, FACW. Grows 8 to 20 inches with yellow flowers in summer; prefers mesic to moist sandy loams in full to part sun.

Hypericum drummondii (Nits-and-lice) [annual forb] — prairies, fields, open woodlands and glades, riparian gravel bars, UPL, widely scattered west. Grows 1 to 3 feet with yellow flowers in late summer in dry to mesic, usually acidic, well-drained sandy loams, sun to part sun.

Hypericum ellipticum (Pale St. John's-wort) — [perennial forb] common in boggy areas, marshes, along streams and in swales, especially in sandy soils, statewide; OBL. Grows 9 to 24 inches with yellow flowers in summer; grow in full sun to part shade in moist, sandy loams.

Hypericum gentianoides (Orange-grass) [annual forb] — rocky prairies, bluffs, barrens, hillsides, open woodlands and glades, UPL, southern Pennsylvania, especially SE. Grows 4 to 12 inches in dry to mesic, acidic to circumneutral, rocky to sandy soil in sun to part shade with yellow flowers in summer.

Hypericum gymnanthum (Clasping-leaved St. John's-wort) [annual forb] — found in sandy, moist savannas and low areas along rivers, marshes and pond edges, OBL, reported only in Centre and Lehigh Counties and considered extirpated. Grows 1 to 3 feet in moist to wet peaty, muddy or sandy soils with yellow flowers in summer in full to part sun.

Hypericum majus (Canadian St. John's-wort) [annual forb] — along the Lake Erie coast in wet meadows, fens, shorelines, FACW. Grows 6 to 30 inches in mesic to wet sandy loams in full sun to part shade; yellow flowers in late summer.

Hypericum mutilum (Dwarf St. John's-wort) — [perennial forb] statewide in swamps, along streams, in moist fields and ditches, FACW. Grows 4 to 18 inches with yellow flowers in summer; prefers full sun to light shade in an acidic, sandy or rocky moist to wet, medium to fine textured, soil at least 8 inches deep with a pH range between 4.6 and 7.2. Some adaptability for anaerobic conditions but not drought or limestone-based soils.

Hypericum prolificum (Shrubby St John's-wort) — [shrub] rocky ground, dry wooded slopes, uncultivated fields, gravel bars along streams and in low, moist valleys, FACU; mostly southwest (Southern Allegheny Plateau); scattered elsewhere except northeast (Northern Glaciated and Unglaciated Allegheny Plateaus). Deciduous shrub to 6 feet with yellow flowers in early summer; average, medium moisture, well-drained soil of any texture at least 10 inches deep with a pH of 4.6 to 7.2. Prefers full sun to part shade. Tolerates wide range of soils, including dry rocky or sandy soils. Adaptable to anaerobic conditions, but not drought or limestone soils, and not a good candidate for hedging.

Hypericum punctatum (Spotted St. John's-wort) — [perennial forb] floodplains, thickets, moist fields and along roadsides, FAC-; statewide. Grows 20 to 40 inches, yellow flowers in summer; sun to part sun in dry to moist sandy loam of any texture at least 10 inches deep with a pH of 4.6 to 7.0. Tolerant of shade and anaerobic conditions, but not drought or limestone soils.

Hypericum pyramidatum (Great St. John's-wort) — [perennial forb] alluvial shores and in moist to mesic fields, rocky banks, and swamps, FAC. Scattered mostly east and northwest. Grows 30 to 60 inches, yellow flowers in summer; sun to part sun in dry to moist rich sandy loam, pH 5 to 6.

AKA *Hypericum ascyron*.

Hypericum sphaerocarpum (St. John's-wort) — [perennial forb] reported in Allegheny County on rocky shorelines, but native to western and southwestern Pennsylvania, FAC. Grows to 30 inches with yellow flowers in summer; prefers full to part sun in dry to mesic well-drained soils, with a tendency toward poor soils that limit competition.

Hypoxis hirsuta (Yellow star grass) — [perennial forb] dry to mesic meadows, fields, clearings, barrens and dry woods, FAC; statewide, except north-central. Grows up to 15 inches, yellow flowers in spring to summer; sun to part shade in dry to wet sandy, medium to fine textured, loam at least 7 inches deep with a pH of 5.2 to 7.3. Tolerant of light shade, anaerobic conditions, limestone soils and drought.

Ilex beadlei (Mountain holly) — [shrub] scattered in the Ridge and Valley and Glaciated Northeast and widely scattered northwest on woodland slopes. Shrub or small tree, with white flowers in spring and fruit in early fall; part sun to part shade; well drained soil.

Ilex laevigata (Smooth winterberry) — [shrub] eastern Pennsylvania in wet thickets, wooded swamps and on shorelines, OBL. Shrub or small tree with white flowers in spring and fruit in the fall; grow in full to part sun on low-elevation mesic to moist sites rich in organic matter.

Ilex montana (Mountain holly) — [shrub] cool moist rocky woods; mostly northeast, scattered north and at higher elevations along the Allegheny front. Shrub or small tree, grows to 30 feet with white flowers in spring and fruit in early fall; sun to partial shade; well drained soil.

Ilex mucronata (Catberry or mountain holly) — [shrub] swamps, bogs, moist woods, fens, OBL; mostly north (Western and Northern Glaciated and Northern Unglaciated Allegheny Plateaus); scattered elsewhere. Shrub to 10 feet with white-yellow flowers in spring and fruit in late summer; sun to part shade in moist to wet silty organic loam.

Ilex verticillata (Winterberry) — [shrub] wet woods, swamps, bogs and moist shores, FACW+; statewide. Shrub to 15 feet; sun to part shade in mesic to moist, medium to fine textured, organic loam at least 16 inches deep with a pH range of 4.5 to 7.5. Tolerates poorly drained soils, including swamps and bogs, but not anaerobic conditions, drought, limestone soils or hedging. Dioecious; only fertilized female flowers will produce the attractive red berries that are the signature of the species.

Winterberry (*Ilex verticillaata*)

Impatiens capensis (Jewelweed) [annual forb] — statewide in open, moist woodlands, partly or lightly shaded floodplains and streambanks, swamps, seeps and fens, and moist meadows, FACW. Grows 2 to 5 feet with orange-yellow flowers in late summer, in part sun to part shade; can spread aggressively by seed to form large colonies. Tolerates full shade and clay soils, but prefers mesic to moist humusy soils of any texture at least 14 inches deep with pH range of 6.4 to 7.4. Prefers in part shade to part sun; intolerant of anaerobic conditions, drought and limestone soils.

Impatiens pallida (Pale jewelweed) [annual forb] — statewide in swamps, muddy pond and stream edges, moist deciduous woodlands and soggy thickets, FACW. Grows 3 to 6 feet with yellow flowers in late summer and prefers part sun to part shade, moist to wet, moderately fertile, loamy to mucky soil of any texture at least 14 inches deep with a pH of 6.8 to 7.4. Intolerant of drought and anaerobic conditions, but a good choice for limestone soils.

Iodanthus pinnatifidus (Purple-rocket) — [perennial forb] Shaded thickets, ravines, banks, swamps, floodplains, creeks and stream edges, typically over limestone or sandstone in southwestern Pennsylvania; FACW and listed as endangered. Grows 1 to 3 feet with purple flowers in early summer; prefers part sun to part shade in moist to wet, rich loamy soil with much organic matter; plant tolerates temporary flooding.

Ionactis linariifolius (Stiff-leaved aster) — [perennial forb] dry rocky woods and edges; typically in acidic soils in pine-oak or pine-hickory woods, ridgetops, upland slopes and glades. Mostly east (especially Piedmont). Grows 12 to 24 inches, violet flowers in late summer to fall; average, dry to medium, well-drained soil in full sun to part shade. Prefers acidic, sandy soils, pH 4 to 7.

Ipomoea lacunosa (White morning-glory) [annual vine] — thickets, prairies, moist meadows, riparian banks and bars, shorelines, woodland edges, far southeast, FACW. Twining vine from 3 to 7 feet with white flowers in summer, growing in full sun and mesic to moist loams, clay loams or gravelly loams, ideal for fences and trellises.

Ipomoea pandurata (Man-of-the-earth) — [perennial vine] Upland thickets and along roads, commonly on calcareous soils, FACU, mostly across southern Pennsylvania. Twining herbaceous vine to 30 feet with white, trumpet-like flowers (a member of the morning glory family). Pefers full to part sun and mesic to dry conditions. The type of soil is unimportant; it often grows where there are rocky or gravelly slopes but can be rampant where the soil is moist and fertile; this plant can smother surrounding vegetation and it prefers some kind of structural support. Drought resistance is very good.

Iris versicolor (Northern blue flag iris) — [perennial forb] marshes, bogs and wet meadows, OBL; statewide except north and south central high elevations. Grows 24 to 60 inches, blue-violet flowers in late spring or early summer; sun to part sun in moist to wet rich silty loam, especially in pond margins.

Iris virginica (Southern blue flag) — [perennial forb] Rare in wetlands such as the margins of lakes, ponds and streams, mostly extreme northwest (Erie and Ontario Lake Plain) and endangered; OBL. Grows 1 to 3 feet, blue-violet flowers in early summer; prefers wet, acidic, boggy, sandy soils in full sun, but tolerates shade. Grow in soil at least 6 inches deep with pH between 4.8 and 7.3. No drought tolerance but an excellent choice for anaerobic conditions. Ideally roots should be under water for extended periods of time, otherwise they will grow slightly smaller in average garden soils that are uniformly moist. Spreads by rhizomes to form colonies.

Canada rush (*Juncus canadensis*)

Isoetes appalachiana (Appalachian quillwort) — [perennial graminoid] aquatic in shallow water of ponds, lakes and rivers, mostly central and western Pennsylvania.

Isoetes echinospora (Spiny-spored quillwort) — [perennial graminoid] mostly northeast in shallow water of cold lakes, ponds and slow-moving streams, OBL; aka Isoetes tenella.

Isoetes engelmannii (Engelmann's quillwort) — [perennial graminoid] statewide except for northern tier and far western counties as an emergent on clay, silty-sand or cobble river shores and in back-eddies of tributary streams; OBL.

Isoetes riparia (Shore quillwort) — [perennial graminoid] eastern Pennsylvania especially along the Delaware River; prefers shallow water of slow-moving streams and rivers as well as intertidal mudflats, OBL.

Isoetes valida (Carolina quillwort) — [perennial graminoid] Aquatic in ponds, slow-moving streams and sometimes woodland seeps, mostly southern Pennsylvania.

Isoetes x dodgei (Dodge's quillwort) — [perennial graminoid] very rare in eastern Pennsylvania in shallow waters of lakes and ponds, OBL, a naturally-occuring hybrid.

Isotria medeoloides (Small whorled-pogonia) — [perennial forb] Acidic soils, in dry to mesic second-growth, deciduous or deciduous-coniferous open forests with light to moderate leaf litter; often on slope bases or flats near canopy breaks; widely scattered and endangered in Pennsylvania; FACU. Rare native orchid that grows up to 10 inches in humusy leaf litter with small white flowers in spring.

Isotria verticillata (Whorled-pogonia) — [perennial forb] dry to mesic forests, sphagnum bogs and seeps with acidic soils, statewide except for northern tier counties, FACU. Orchid that grows up to 15 inches in part shade to shade, generally in humusy leaf litter with small flowers in spring.

Itea virginica (Tassel-white) — [shrub] very rare in swamps, wet woods, stream banks and moist coastal plain sites; OBL; mostly southeast. Grows 3 to 5 feet with white flowers in summer. Prefers sun, but adapts to part shade. Grow in average medium to wet soil, especially humusy soils that are medium to fine textured, at least 14 inches deep, with a pH between 4.0 and 7.5. Low drought and hedge adaptability, but because of high anaerobic tolerance, a good rain garden shrub and popular for erosion control.

Jeffersonia diphylla (Twinleaf) — [perennial forb] open rocky slopes and outcrops as well as rich moist woods, typically over limestone or other calcareous rock. Mostly southwest; scattered south-central and southeast. Very brief bloom with a single white flower in early spring; generally grown for its unique foliage. Grow in well-drained, mulched, circumneutral, continually moist humusy soils in part shade; tolerates full shade.

Juglans cinerea (Butternut) — [tree] rich woods of river terraces and valleys, especially in coves, on stream benches and terraces and on slopes, in the talus of rock ledges, and on other sites with good drainage, FACU+; statewide. Deciduous tree to 100 feet; moist, organically rich, well-drained soils in full sun. Prefers coarse to medium textured, moderately fertile soils at least 40 inches deep with a pH range of 6.0 to 7.0. Intolerant of shade, anaerobic conditions, drought and limestone-based soils.

Juglans nigra (Black walnut) — [tree] rich woods on wet bottomlands, dry ridges and slopes. Common on limestone soils, FACU; statewide except for north. Grows to 130 feet; deep, well-drained, medium textured soils that are moist and fertile, at least 40 inches deep and with a pH ranging from 4.6 to 8.2. Intolerant of shade, anaerobic conditions and drought, but excellent for limestone-based soils; require a 170-day growing season.

Juncus acuminatus (Sharp-fruited rush) — [perennial graminoid] wet meadows, swamps, marshes, stream banks, shores, ditches, and near springs on rock outcrops, OBL; statewide. Grows 8 to 30 inches; full sun in rich loam of all textures and at least 8 inches deep, pH 4.8 to 7.0, wet to shallow water; intolerant of drought.

Juncus arcticus var. littoralis (Baltic rush) — [perennial graminoid] rare along streams, and in wet meadows, fens and marshes, often slightly alkaline soils, FACW+; scattered statewide. Grows 12 to 36 inches in often calcareous silty loams at least 20 inches deep with a pH range of 6.0 to 9.0, including standing water. Low drought tolerance, but adaptable to all soil textures.

Juncus articulatus (Jointed rush) — [perennial graminoid] swamps and mud flats; wet ground in ditches, lake and stream margins, generally in calcareous soils of any texture and at least 8 inches deep with a pH range of 4.8 to 7.5; mostly northwest; scattered elsewhere. Grows 4 to 20 inches; full sun in rich loam, wet to shallow water.

Juncus biflorus (Grass rush) — [perennial

graminoid] rare in moist, open woods, gravel pits and ditches and boggy fields, FACW. Mostly southeast; scattered south. Grows 12 to 36 inches in silty loams of any texture at least 14 inches deep with a pH range of 4.5 to 7.0, including standing water. Shade tolerant, but not drought.

Juncus brachycephalus (Small-headed rush) — [perennial graminoid] widely scattered statewide, but mostly Erie County in muddy or sandy calcareous soils along shorelines, clayey seeps, marshes and springy or boggy fields; OBL and listed as threatened in Pennsylvania. Prefers moderately fertile soils of any texture at least 8 inches deep with a pH of 4.5 to 6.7. Low tolerance for limestone soils and drought.

Juncus brevicaudatus (Narrow-panicled rush) — [perennial graminoid] scattered statewide except far southeast, but concentrated in the northeast in moist, acidic, peaty sites such as emergent shorelines, bogs, swamps, swales and near springs; OBL.

Juncus bufonius (Toad rush) — [annual graminoid] moist soils in meadows, along lakeshores or stream banks, ditches, or roadsides, frequent in drawdown areas; usually in open sites and often becoming weedy, FACW. Scattered statewide but concentrated in the east, FACW. Grows in clumps 2-4 feet in sun to part sun in moist to wet circumneutral soils, including water up to four inches deep; good for average garden soils with constant irrigation. Grows 6 to 20 inches, sun to part sun in moist to wet rich loam of any texture at least 6 inches deep, with a pH of 4.6 to 7.5. Intolerant of shade and drought.

Juncus canadensis (Canada rush) — [perennial graminoid] swamps, marshes, bogs, swales, fens, lake and pond shores; prefers calcareous soils, OBL. Scattered statewide. Grows 12 to 48 inches; full sun in moist to wet rich loams of any texture, at least 12 inches deep, with a pH between 4.5 and 5.9; high anaerobic tolerance, but none for limestone soils or drought.

Juncus debilis (Weak rush) — [perennial graminoid] scattered in southern Pennsylvania in soft, mucky soils of small streams, swamps, river banks, mud flats, wet clearings and spring runs; OBL. Grows 12 to 36 inches; full sun in moist to wet rich loams.

Juncus dichotomus (Forked rush) — [perennial graminoid] sandy, well drained, moist to often wet soils in open woodlands, old fields, shores and clearings, scattered across southern Pennsylvania but concentrated in the southeast, FACW- and listed as endangered in Pennsylvania. Grows to 4 feet in sun to part sun, with a preference for coarse to medium textured soils at least 8 inches deep with a pH of 4.5 and 6.5. Good choice for anaerobic sites, but low tolerance for drought and limestone-based soils..

Juncus dudleyi (Dudley's rush) — [perennial graminoid] exposed or shaded sites, usually moist areas such as along stream banks, ditches, around springs. Scattered statewide. Grows 12 to 32 inches; sun to part shade in sandy to clayey loam.

Juncus effusus var. pylaei (Soft rush) — [perennial graminoid] swamps and marshes, and moist to saturated meadows, FACW+; statewide. Can reach 36 inches; sun to part sun in mesic to moist sandy, rich loam of any texture at least 24 inches deep with a pH range of 5.5 to 8.8. Tolerant of anaerobic conditions and drought, it does not adapt to limestone-based soils.

Juncus filiformis (Thread rush) — [perennial graminoid] rare on moist to wet soil along stream banks, pools, lakes or in meadow depressions; rarely in bogs. Mostly glaciated plateau area of Monroe County; scattered elsewhere. Grows 6 to 12 inches; sun to part sun in moist to wet sandy rich loam.

Juncus gerardii (Blackfoot rush) — [perennial graminoid] rare, can form extensive colonies in exposed estuary and coastal meadows and salt marshes just above line of high-tide line; also inland on waste ground, ballast and moist roadsides where de-icing salts are used. Mostly southeast (Atlantic Coastal Plain), scattered south. Grows 12 to 28 inches in full sun on wet, often salty, silt loams.

Juncus greenei (Greene's rush) — [perennial graminoid] very rare on dry sandy well-drained sites near lake shores, in sand dunes or pinelands; Monroe and Pike counties. Grows 10 to 30 inches; sun to part sun in dry sandy loam.

Juncus gymnocarpus (Coville's rush) — [perennial graminoid] concentrated in Schuylkill, Lebanon, Dauphin, Columbia and Northumberland Counties in sphagnum swamps, lake shores, low woods, springheads and seeps; OBL and listed as rare in Pennsylvania.

Juncus marginatus var. marginatus (Grass-leaved rush) — [perennial graminoid] bogs, shores, marshes and ditches in moist to wet clayey, peaty or sandy soils, FACW; statewide. Grows 10 to 20 inches; sun to part sun in rich, moist to wet, coarse to medium textured sandy, peaty or clay loam at least 8 inches deep with a pH range of 5.5 to 6.8. Tolerates anaerobic conditions, but not drought.

Juncus militaris (Bayonet rush) — [perennial graminoid] reported in Pike and Wayne Counties in mucky soils in the bottoms of shallow lakes, ponds and rivers, as well as shorelines, OBL and listed as endangered in Pennsylvania. Grows up to 5 feet in sun to part sun.

Juncus nodosus (Knotted rush) — [perennial graminoid] moist to wet fields, swamps, fens, marshes, swales, bogs in sandy often calcareous soils, OBL. Widely scattered, mostly northwest and east. Grows 6 to 18 inches; sun to part sun in moist to wet sandy circumneutral soils of any texture at least 18 inches deep, with a pH of 4.0 to 7.5. Adaptable to drought.

Juncus pelocarpus (Brown-fruited rush) — [perennial graminoid] scattered in northeastern Pennsylvania in sandy to peaty sometimes submersed soils of lakes, ponds, and bogs; OBL.

Juncus scirpoides (Sedge rush) — [perennial graminoid] moist to wet sandy or peaty soil in wet woodlands, meadows and along lake shores, including salt marshes; FACW and listed as endangered in Pennsylvania. Sun to part shade. Prefers coarse to medium textured, moderately fertile soils at least 10 inches deep with a pH between 5.6 and 6.8; no drought tolerance.

Juncus subcaudatus (Woodland rush) — [perennial graminoid] statewide in swamps, wet fields, bogs, stream banks and lake and pond shorelines, OBL. Grows to 4 feet in sun to part sun. Prefers medium to fine textured soils at least 8 inches deep with a pH between 4.5 and 6.0; high anaerobic but low drought tolerance.

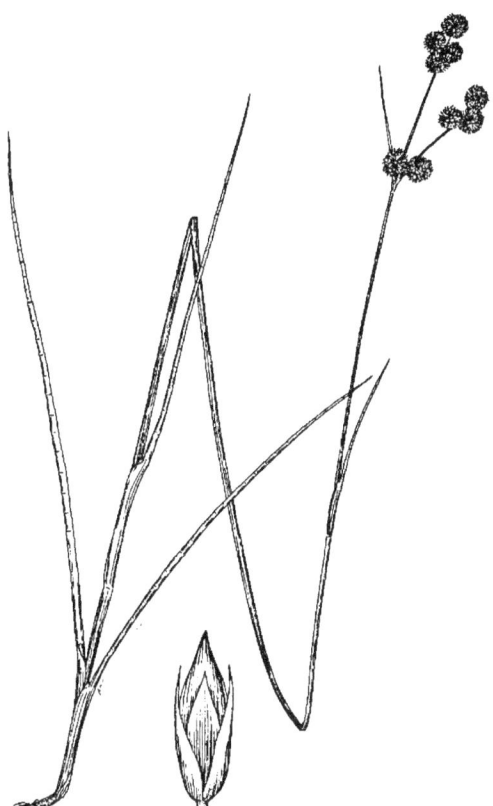

Sedge rush (*Juncus scirpoides*)

Juncus tenuis (Path rush) — [perennial graminoid] moist to dry and sometimes heavily compacted soil of woods, fields, waste ground and paths, FAC-; statewide. Grows 4 to 32 inches; sun to part shade in dry to moist loam of any texture, with a minimum depth of 6 inches and a pH range of 4.5 to 7.0. Intolerant of anaerobic conditions or drought.

Juncus torreyi (Torrey's rush) — [perennial graminoid] rare in calcareous wet meadows and swamps, sometimes on clay soils, and on wet sandy shores and the edges of sloughs and slightly alkaline watercourses, FACW; widely scattered statewide; endangered. Grows 18 to 30 inches in full sun in calcareous, moist to wet, coarse to medium textured, silty to clay loams at least 10 inches deep with a pH between 4.5 and 6.5. Intolerant of shade, drought and limestone-based soils, but adaptable to anaerobic conditions.

Juniperus communis (Common juniper) — [shrub] dry open woods, slopes, pastures; mostly southeast, scattered elsewhere. Slow growing to about 10 feet, spreading shrub, with yellow flowers in early spring; part sun to part shade in dry to mesic sandy loam of any texture, at least 14 inches deep, and with a pH range of 5.5 to 8.0. Highly tolerant of drought and limestone soils, but not anaerobic conditions or shade. Possible use as hedge. Declining due to deer browsing. Fruits used to flavor gin.

Juniperus virginiana (Eastern red-cedar) — [tree] upland to low (especially early successional) woodlands, old fields and fence rows, glades and river swamps, FACU; mostly southeast. Coniferous tree to 65 feet; average, dry to moist, well-drained soils in full sun. Tolerates a wide range of soils and growing conditions; minimum depth is 20 inches and pH range is 4.7 to 8.0. Prefers moist soils, but intolerant of anaerobic conditions; has the best drought resistance of any conifer native to the eastern U.S.

Justicia americana (Water-willow) — [perennial forb] Along the banks of or in the shallow waters of rivers, ponds, and lakes, statewide; OBL. Grows 1 to 3 feet, flowers that are white or light violet, with purple spots or other markings in the throat, throughout the summer. Aquatic; grow in moist soil or in a few feet of water in full sun to part shade. Suitable for any soil with a depth of 10 inches and a pH range of 5.4 to 7.6. Forms colonies on or near shorelines, including rocky riffles and shoals. Rhizomes and roots provide important spawning sites for many fish species and habitat for invertebrates.

Kalmia angustifolia (Sheep laurel) — [shrub] sandy or infertile soil, bogs, old fields, dry woods, barrens. FAC; mostly northeast and southeast . Grows to 3 feet with rose-pink to crimson flowers in early summer; part sun to part shade in mesic to moist sandy organic loam. pH 4.5 to 6.

Kalmia latifolia (Mountain laurel) — [shrub] dry upland sandy, acidic, rocky woods. FACU, statewide. Evergreen shrub to 15 feet with white to pink flowers in early summer; part sun to part shade in dry to mesic, coarse to medium textured, humusy, sandy loam at least 24 inches deep with a pH range of 4.5 to 5.5. Very slow growing, with feeder roots in an extensive mat near the surface; a broad blanket of decomposing oak leaves is important. Tolerant of shade and drought, but not anaerobic conditions or limestone-based soils. The state flower of Pennsylvania.

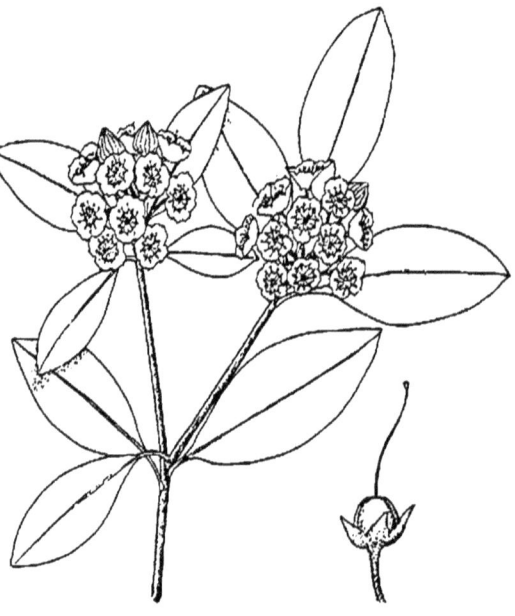

Mountain laurel (Kalmia latifolia)

Kalmia polifolia (Bog laurel) — [shrub] rare in peaty wetlands and bogs, OBL; northeast. Grows 6 to 36 inches with lavender flowers in summer; part sun to part shade in wet organic soils and peat. Grows in soils of any texture at least 12 inches deep with a pH range of 6.0 to 7.3. Tolerant of anaerobic condition and shade, but not drought.

Koeleria macrantha (Junegrass) — [perennial graminoid] very rare in generally sandy upland or high prairie sites, woods openings and open rocky slopes that are cool, semi-arid and somewhat infertile; a cool-season grass that goes dormant in late summer. Reported only as Bradford County; listed as extirpated. Grows to 18 inches in rocky or sandy, coarse to medium textured at least 20 inches deep with a pH range of 6.0 to 8.0. Tolerant of shade, limestone soils and drought, but not anaerobic conditions soils. AKA *Celeriac macrantha*.

Krigia biflora (Dwarf dandelion) — [perennial forb] moist fields and meadows, FACU. Mostly west, scattered elsewhere. Grows 4 to 24 inches, yellow flowers from late spring into fall; sun to part sun in dry to moist sandy loam.

Krigia virginica (Virginia dwarf dandelion) [annual forb] — dry, sandy prairies, shale barrens, slopes, savannas, dunes, fields, waste ground as well as rocky glade without limestone, UPL, generally east of the Allegheny Front. Grows 2 to 16 inches with yellow flowers in late spring to early summer in full sun, dry to mesic acidic, sandy loams; occasional wildfires are beneficial. Strong peference for open mixed mesophytic, northern hardwood, beech-maple, oak-pine, oak hickory woodlands.

Kyllinga pumila (Thin-leaved flatsedge) [annual graminoid] — along sandy to muddy shorelines in Philadelphia, Delaware and Allegheny counties, FACW. Grows to 12 inches in moist to wet sandy to mucky soils in full sun to part sun. AKA *Cyperus tenuifolius*.

Lactuca biennis (Blue lettuce) [annual forb] — statewide in moist woodlands, thickets, swamps, stream banks, FACU. Grows 2 to 6 feet with pale blue flowers in late summer in part shade to shade in mesic to moist loams.

Lactuca canadensis (Wild lettuce) [annual forb] — statewide in meadows, fields, prairies, savannas, woodland openings and limestone glades, thickets, lake borders, riverbanks, waste ground, more common in disturbed than high quality habitats, FACU-. Grows less than 12 inches with orange to yellow flowers in summer; prefers dry to mesic, fertile, loamy soil although poor gravelly and clay-loam soils are tolerated. Grow in full to part sun.

Lactuca canadensis (Wild lettuce) [annual forb] — statewide in prairies, woodland openings and limestone glades, thickets, savannas, riverbanks and lake shores, meadows, FACU-. Grows 3 to 8 feet with purple flowers in summer on mesic to moist rich soils in sun to part shade; poor gravelly soils and clay loams are tolerated.

Lactuca floridana (Woodland lettuce) [annual forb] — moist meadows, thickets and woodlands, FACU-, scattered in southern Pennsylvania; two varieties, *floridana* and *villosa* (the latter being more widely scattered). Grows 1 to 3 feet with purple flower in summer in mesic to moist, rich, loams that must be constantly moist; tolerates occasional wet conditions. Grows in part sun to shade. Although edible, it has a bitter flavor; young basal leaves are best.

Lactuca hirsuta (Downy lettuce) [biennial forb] — upland rocky woodlands, openings, clearings, borders and glades, savannas, prairies and fields as well as alluvial bottoms, widely scattered but generally along lower elevations of the western edge of the Allegheny front. Grows 2 to 7 feet, with red-yellow flowers in late summer on dry to mesic slightly acidic sandy to rocky soil.

Laportea canadensis (Wood-nettle) — [perennial forb] rich moist deciduous forests, often along seepages and streams, FACW; statewide. Grows 20 to 40 inches, tiny white flowers in spring; part shade to shade in moist, humusy loam. Stinging hairs on all parts causes brief burning or itching.

Larix laricina (American larch or tamarack) — [tree] cold, wet to moist, poorly drained swamps, bogs, and muskegs; also along streams, lakes, swamp borders, and occasionally on upland sites, FACW; scattered north, especially northeast. Slowly grows to 100 feet; sun to part sun in moist to wet, coarse to medium textured soils at least 40 inches deep with a pH of 6.0 to 7.0; intolerant of shade, anaerobic conditions, drought, heat, polluted areas and of dry, shallow chalky soils, but adapts to sites slightly drier than natural habitat.

Lathyrus ochroleucus (Wild pea) — [perennial forb] mostly northern Pennsylvania on typically dry, upland woodlands and slopes; listed as threatened in Pennsylvania. Grows 1 to 3 feet with greenish-white flowers in dry to mesic sandy or rocky soil with some organic matter; prefers part sun and cool summer temperatures.

Lathyrus palustris (Marsh pea) — [perennial forb] moist meadows, sand plains, swamps and thickets, FACW+. Scattered statewide, mostly southeast (Piedmont), and endangered. Grows up to 3 feet, red-purple flowers in early summer; moist to wet rich loam in full to part sun.

Lathyrus venosus (Veiny pea) — [perennial forb] Woodland slopes, sandy to rocky shorelines, railroad banks; scattered throughout mostly south, especially the Lehigh Valley. Grows 1 to 3 feet in a trailing habit in part shade with pink to purple flowers in summer. Prefers dry to mesic average soils.

Lechea intermedia (Pinweed) — [perennial forb] dry ridges and dry, sandy fields, mostly eastern and central Pennsylvania. Grows 6 to 24 inches with reddish-brown flowers in summer on dry sandy or rocky soils in sun to part shade.

Lechea minor (Thyme-leaved pinweed) — [perennial forb] dry woodlands and serpentine barrens, primarily in the Piedmont and Coastal Plain. Grows 18 to 24 inches in full to part sun in dry to mesic sandy or very rock soil; reddish-brown flowers in summer. Seeds can take several years to germinate.

Lechea pulchella (Pinweed) — [perennial forb] Open dry woodlands, sandy fields and barrens, primarily Ridge and Valley, Piedmont and Coastal Plain areas. Grows to 24 inches in full to part sun with reddish-brown flowers in summer; prefers dry to mois sandy soils in open fields and woodlands.

Lechea racemulosa (Illinois pinweed) — [perennial forb] Typically on shaly slopes and dry fields, throughout Pennsylvania. Grows to 24 inches with red flowers in summer in full to part sun on dry, sandy loams.

Lechea villosa (Pinweed) — [perennial forb] Sand plains, old fields and open woodlands. mostly eastern and northwestern Pennsylvania. Grows to about 18 inches with reddish-brown flowers in sun to part shade in dry to mesic rocky, sandy loams.

Ledum groenlandicum (Labrador-tea) — [shrub] wetter sites with low subsurface water flow and low nutrients; poorly drained habitats such as boreal forests, open conifer bogs, treeless bogs, wooded swamps, wet barrens, and peatlands, OBL; northeast. Shrub to 3 feet with white flowers in early summer; sun to part shade in moist to wet acidic organic soils, peat and muck. Flood tolerant. AKA *Rhododendron groenlandicum*.

Leersia oryzoides (Rice cutgrass) — [perennial graminoid] clayey to sandy heavy wet soils in meadows and bogs, frequently in standing water, OBL; statewide. Grows 30 to 80 inches; full sun in moist to wet mucky to sandy loams.

Leersia virginica (Cutgrass) — [perennial graminoid] damp to wet woods, often along streams, FACW; statewide. Grows 20 to 50 inches; part sun to part shade in moist, rich, coarse to medium textured, sandy loam at least four inches deep with a pH range of 4.5 to 8.5. Tolerant of shade, anaerobic conditions, limestone soils but not drought.

Leiophyllum buxifolium (Sand-myrtle) — [tree/shrub] very rare on dry sandy barrens and thin moist mountain woods, FACU. Shrub to 3 feet with whitish-pink flowers in late spring to early summer; part shade in moist, acid sandy peaty soil. Does not tolerate drought. Possibly extirpated. AKA *Kalmia buxifolia*.

Lemna minor (Duckweed) — [perennial forb] aquatic; still water of nutrient-average to nutrient-rich, lakes and ponds, and in streams, swamps and ditches, OBL; statewide except for high Alleghenies. Grow in shallow ponds and water features with slow-moving to still water with a pH between 4.1 and 8.8; intolerant of shade.

Lemna obscura (Little water duckweed) — [perennial forb] nutrient-average to nutrient-rich, quiet, shallow water in the Atlantic Coastal Plain; believed to be extirpated in Pennsylvania.

Lemna perpusilla (Duckweed) — [perennial forb] nutrient-average to nutrient-rich, quiet waters of marshes, bogs and ponds, widely scattered in eastern Pennsylvania, OBL.

Lemna trisulca (Star duckweed) — [perennial forb] cool-temperate aquatic; nutrient-average, quiet waters rich in calcium, forms tangled colonies in lakes, ponds, bogs, marshes, streams, OBL. Scattered, mostly east and northwest. Grow in shallow ponds and water features with slow-moving to still water with a pH of 5.7 to 7.0 low in calcium carbonate.

Lemna turionifera (Winter duckweed) — [perennial forb] nutrient-average to nutrient-rich, quiet waters of marshes, swamps, ponds and lakes, widely scattered in western Pennsylvania (OBL).

Lemna valdiviana (Pale duckweed) [annual forb] — aquatic found in mesotrphic, quiet shallow water, floating or on submerged debris, along the Delaware River but reported as extirpated, OBL. Prefers full sun and a pH of 5.7 to 7.0, low in calcium carbonate.

Lepidium virginicum (Poor-man's-pepper) [annual forb] — statewide in disturbed prairies but common in fields, lawns, gardens, waste places, FACU. Grows to 12 inches with white flowers in summer to fall in a wide range of dry to mesic soils, full to part sun; aggressive spreader.

Lespedeza angustifolia (Narrow-leaved bush-clover) — [perennial forb] reported only in Delaware County in moist, open, sandy ground, FAC; endangered. Grows 20 to 30 inches with reddish flowers in late summer; sun to part sun in dry to moist sandy loam.

Lespedeza capitata (Round-headed bush-clover) — [perennial forb] upland woods, thickets, prairies, glades and along streams, FACU-. Mostly southeast (Piedmont), scattered elsewhere. Grows 20 to 60 inches, yellow-white flowers, late summer; sun to part sun in dry to moist sandy loam.

Lespedeza hirta (Bush-clover) — [perennial forb] dry prairies, savannas, fields, meadows; statewide, except north-central (Northern Unglaciated Allegheny Plateau). Grows 24 to 48 inches, yellow flowers in summer; sun to part shade in dry sandy loams of any texture at least 9 inches deep with a pH of 5.8 to 6.9. Tolerates drought and limestone soils, but not shade or anaerobic conditions.

Lespedeza intermedia (Bush-clover) — [perennial forb] statewide in rocky, open dry woods and thickets. Grows 1 to 3 feet with pin flowers in late summer to early fall; prefers dry to mesic, well-drained somewhat sterile soils in part sun to part shade.

Lespedeza procumbens (Trailing bush-clover) — [perennial forb] In sandy to rocky soils of dry woods, fields and along roadsides, mostly Ridge and Valley and Piedmont, but also southwestern Allegheny Plateau. Grows to 3 feet with white-pink flowers in late summer; prefers dry to mesic, well-drained somewhat sterile soils in part sun to part shade.

Lespedeza repens (Creeping bush-clover) — [perennial forb] mostly southern Pennsylvania in dry, acidic and sterile soils of woodlands, banks and edges. Low-growing with white-pink flowers in summer; prefers dry to mesic, well drained soils in part sun to part shade.

Lespedeza stuevei (Tall bush-clover) — [perennial forb] reported only on sites in Bucks and Lancaster Counties in sterile dry soils of open woodlands and edges; listed as extirpated in Pennsylvania. Grows 20 to 60 inches in full to part sun in open fields, prairies, woodland edges and thin woodlands with white-pink flowers in summer; prefers dry to mesic sandy loams.

Lespedeza violacea (Slender bush-clover) — [perennial forb] dry upland woods, thickets and openings. Mostly southeast, scattered elsewhere. Grows 12 to 30 inches, violet-purple flowers in late summer; part sun to part shade in dry sandy loam.

Lespedeza virginica (Slender bush-clover) — [perennial forb] dry fields, stony banks, rocky woods. Mostly southeast, scattered elsewhere and absent in north (Western and Northern Glaciated and Northern Unglaciated Allegheny Plateaus). Grows 12 to 40 inches, violet-purple flowers in summer; sun to part shade in dry sandy loam.

Labrador-tea (*Ledum groelandicum*)

Leucothoe racemosa (Fetterbush) — [shrub] rare in swamps and moist thickets, shrub-free bogs, along marshy stream banks and forest edges; southeast, especially Atlantic Coastal Plain. An important shrub species in palustrine wetlands with deep, acidic, sandy, peat soils, FACW. Grows to 10 feet with white to pink flowers in late spring to early summer; part shade on moist, sandy acidic loam. Also known as Eubotrys racemosa.

Liatris scariosa (Northern blazing-star) — [perennial forb] Three varieties found in Pennsylvania: *var. scariosa* on limestone and sandstone outcrops, rock ledges, shale banks, flood plains and dry woods; *var. nieuwlandii* in prairies, glades, bluffs, open woods, red clays and rocky limestone soils; and *var. novaeangliae* in sandy fields and woodlands. All three mostly in Ridge and Valley province of the Central Appalachians, and all UPL. Grows 2 to 4 feet in full sun with lavender flowers in late summer. Prefers dry sandy to rocky, well-drained soils and while it will grow taller in fertile loams it may also need staking to support it. Intolerant of winter wet soils.

Liatris spicata var. spicata (Blazing-star) — [perennial forb] moist fields, meadows and swamps, usually over limestone, FAC+; southeast and west. Grows up to 6 feet, blue-purple flowers in late summer; sun to part sun in moist rich sandy loam at least 14 inches deep with a pH of 5.6 to 7.5. Adaptable to anaerobic conditions, but not drought or limestone soils.

Ligusticum canadense (Lovage) — [perennial forb] scattered in the southern Ridge and Valley in mountain woodlands, on stream banks and in wooded roadsides; FAC and listed as endangered in Pennsylvania. Grows in full sun to part shade, in a wide range of mesic to moist soils, to 6 feet with white flowers in summer.

Lilium canadense (Canada lily) — [perennial forb] wet meadows, moist rich woods especially edges, stream sides and river alluvia, bogs, marshes and swamps, FAC+; statewide. Grows up to 6 feet, yellow or red flowers in early summer; sun to part sun in moist to wet organic loam. pH 4 to 7.

Lilium philadelphicum (Wood lily) — [perennial forb] open dry woods, borders and clearings on well-drained soil, FACU+; mostly Central Appalachians and east; scattered elsewhere. Grows up to 3 feet, orange-red flowers in early summer; part sun to part shade in dry to moist sandy loam. pH 5 to 7.

Lilium superbum (Turk's-cap lily) — [perennial forb] moist meadows and thickets, pine barrens, swamp edges and bottoms, gaps and openings in rich forests; FACW+, statewide, but sparse in northeast and northern Piedmont. Yellow-orange with maroon spotted flowers in spring; prefers well-drained, average soils, mesic to wet in full sun to part shade. Spreads to form colonies.

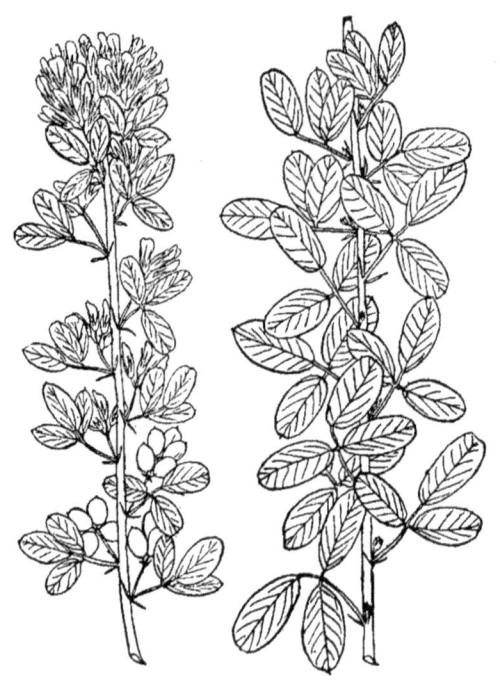

Bush clover (*Lespedeza intermedia*)

Limosella australis (Awl-shaped mudwort) [annual forb] — Tidal mudflats on the Atlantic Coastal Plain, OBL, but listed as extirpated. Grows to two inches with white flowers in late summer on muddy or sand coastal shorelines.

Linaria canadensis (Old-field toadflax) [annual forb] — serpentine barrens and sandy prairies, dunes, savannas fields, as well as rocky glades and river banks, widely scattered but most common in the Atlantic Coastal Plain. Grows to 18 inches with purple flowers in midsummer in sun to part sun on mesic, sandy and serpentine loams; benefits from occasional wildfires.

Lindera benzoin (Northern spicebush) — [shrub] moist sites in wooded bottomlands, ravines, valleys and along streams; found in many regional ecosystems, FACW-; statewide. Grows to 10 feet with yellow flowers in early spring; average, medium, well-drained, medium to fine textured, fertile soils at least 18 inches deep with a pH range of 4.5 to 6.0; full sun to part shade. Fall color is best in sunny areas. Tolerates full shade and anaerobic conditions, but not drought. Leaves used to make a mildly spicy herbal tea, hence the name.

Lindernia dubia (false pimpernel) [annual forb] — gravelly seeps, riparian and pond sandbars and margins, open woodlands and swampy thickets, OBL, scattered southeast. Grows 2 to 8 inches with white to violet flowers in late summer, full to part sun in moist to wet, muddy, sandy or gravelly soils, especially on sites with spring flooding. Several varieties: *dubia* (false pimpernel), the most common and statewide; *anagallidea* (Yellowseed false pimpernel), scattered southeast; *inundata* (flooded false pimpernel), limited to the Atlantic Coastal Plain.

Linnaea borealis var. americana (Twinflower) — [tree/shrub] rare in cool, dry to moist forests and woodlands, especially coniferous, in sandy acidic loam, and humus-rich swamps and barrens, FAC; widely scattered, mostly north. Trailing subshrub with pinkish-white flowers in spring; part shade to shade in moist to wet cool acidic humus. Low drought tolerance. pH 4 to 6.

Linum intercursum (Sandplain wild flax) — [perennial forb] southeastern Piedmont in clayey, moist thickets and serpentine barrens; endangered in Pennsylvania. Grows 12 to 36 inches, yellow flowers in summer; sun to part shade in sandy loam.

Linum medium var. medium (Yellow flax) — [perennial forb] moist sand flats in northwestern Erie County; FACU. Grows 12 to 36 inches, yellow flowers in summer; sun to part shade in sandy loam.

Linum medium var. texanum (Yellow flax) — [perennial forb] mostly Piedmont, but also Erie County in moist to dry woodland openings, open thickets and sandy fields, prairies and savannas. Grows to 30 inches with yellow flowers in summer; prefers sun to part shade in acidic clay.

Linum striatum (Ridged yellow flax) — [perennial forb] moist meadows, wet open ground and wet open woods, FACW. Mostly south, especially Piedmont, scattered north. Grows 12 to 36 inches, yellow flowers in summer; sun to part shade in moist, medium to fine textured, rich loam at least 2 inches deep with a pH ranging from 5.0 to 8.0. Intolerant of drought and anaerobic conditions.

Linum sulcatum (Grooved yellow flax) [annual forb] — rare in fields, woodlands and sandy barrens, generally in the east and listed as endangered. Grows 1 to 3 feet with yellow flowers in summer, blooming best in morning, on dry, open sites.

Linum virginianum (Slender yellow flax) — [perennial forb] common throughout except northern tier counties in old fields and dry open woods, stream banks, thickets and clearing and on shaly slopes. Grows 1 to 3 feet with yellow flowers in summer; prefers dry to mesic well-drained circumneutral soils in sun to part shade.

Liparis loeselii (Yellow twayblade) — [perennial forb] cool, moist ravines, bogs, fens, wet peaty to sandy meadows and exposed sands along lake edges, especially on open and disturbed habitats in relatively early stages of reforestation, primarily southeastern and northwestern Pennsylvania (FACW).

Lipocarpha micrantha (Common hemicarpa) [annual graminoid] — emergent and wet shorelines, FACW, in the Appalachians and listed as endangered. Grows to five inches in moist to wet soils in full to part sun.

Liquidambar styraciflua (Sweetgum) — [tree] rich, moist, alluvial clay and loamy soils of river bottoms, especially on the Piedmont Plateau, 75 to 130 feet; FAC+; mostly southeast; scattered elsewhere. Grow in deep, moist, moderately fertile alluvial loams of any texture with a minimum depth of 36 inches and pH range of 4.5 to 7.0. Intolerant of shade, anaerobic conditions, limestone soils and drought; can be aggressive in sandy, moist soils. Rapid growth.

Liriodendron tulipifera (Tuliptree) — [tree] rich woodlands on hills, bluffs and low mountains, FACU; statewide, except north-central. Grows to 150 feet with creamy-white flowers in spring; moist, organically rich, well-drained, coarse to medium loams with a minimum depth of 32 inches and pH range of 4.5 to 6.5. Grow in full to part sun; intolerant of shade, anaerobic conditions, drought and limestone-based soils.

Listera australis (Southern twayblade) — [perennial forb] edges of sphagnum bogs and the rich humus of low moist woodlands and marshes, most often in association with cinnamon fern (*Osmunda cinnamomea*) and royal fern (*O. regalis*); FACW and reported only in northwestern Warren County, endangered. Grows to about 12 inches with brown flowers in spring; prefers mesic to moist, rich, well drained loams in leaf litter.

Listera cordata (Heartleaf twayblade) — [perennial forb] widely scattered in northeastern and southwestern Pennsylvania in subacid humus of moist, mossy mixed hardwood-coniferous forests and cool, wooded sphagnum bogs, evergreen swamps; FACW+ and listed as endangered in Pennsylvania. Grows to about 12 inches with brown flowers in spring; prefers mesic to moist, rich, well drained loams in leaf litter.

Listera smallii (Kidney-leaved twayblade) — [perennial forb] scattered and listed as endangered in damp acidic humus of shady forests, bogs and sphagnum thickets of Appalachian Mountains, commonly under rhododendron. Grows to about 12 inches with yellow flowers in spring; prefers mesic to moist, rich, well drained loams in leaf litter.

Lithospermum canescens (Hoary puccoon) — [perennial forb] river bluffs, barrens and dry, rocky slopes, mostly Appalachian Mountains and Ridge and Valley. Grows 6 to 18 inches in full sun on dry to mesic loam, sandy loam or rocky material with yellow-orange flowers in late spring to early summer..

Lithospermum caroliniense (Golden puccoon) — [perennial forb] Very rare in open woods, sandy barrens and grasslands; endangered. Grows 1 to 3 feet, yellow flowers in late spring; prefers full to part sun with dry to dry-mesic sandy soils. Difficult to germinate and transplant, hence it is rarely cultivated.

Lithospermum latifolium (American gromwell) — [perennial forb] rich soils over limestone in woodlands and hilltops, southwestern Pennsylvania; listed as endangered. Grows 18 to 30 inches with yellow flowers from mid-spring to early summer; prefers slightly dry to moist, fertile and loamy soils with much organic matter and thrives in dappled sunlight in spring and light to medium shade in summer; seeds are reputed to be difficult to germinate.

Lobelia cardinalis (Cardinal flower) — [perennial forb] wet meadows, swamps, riverbanks and lake shores, FACW+; statewide. Grows 20 to 36 inches, with red flowers in late summer; sun to part sun in moist to wet, medium texture, humus rich, sandy loam at least 12 inches deep with a pH of 5.8 to 7.8. Tolerant of shade, drought, and limestone soils, but not anaerobic conditions.

Lobelia dortmanna (Water lobelia) — [perennial forb] aquatic; shallow waters of ponds and lakes, northeastern Pennsylvania in Wayne and Pike Counties, OBL and listed as threatened. Grows to 3 feet with pale purple flowers in summer; grow on the bed of shallow lakes and ponds, up to 40 inches deep.

Lobelia inflata (Indian-tobacco) [annual forb] — statewide in meadows, woodlands and old fields, FACU. Grows to 2 feet with blue to purple flowers in summer, in dry to mesic soils in full sun to part shade. All parts toxic in large quantities.

Lobelia kalmii (Brook lobelia) — [perennial forb] moist calcareous pastures, fens and swamps, mostly eastern Pennsylvania (OBL); listed as endangered. Grows 6 to 18 inches with lavendar flowers in summer; prefers full sun and consistently moist to wet calcarous sandy-peaty loams.

Lobelia nuttallii (Nuttall's lobelia) — [perennial forb] very rare in wet meadows, sandy to peaty moist thickets and low woods in the Atlantic Coastal Plain; listed as extirpated in Pennsylvania. Grows 1 to 5 feet with pale pink to lavender flowers in late summer; grow in wet, low, sandy loams.

Lobelia puberula (Downy lobelia) — [perennial forb] Rare in serpentine barrens and moist, sandy open ground such as prairies or fields and gravel pits, mostly southeast (Piedmont) and endangered; FACW-. Grows up to 30 inches in full to part sun with blue-violet flowers in late summer. Prefers moist to wet sandy loams.

Lobelia siphilitica (Great blue lobelia) — [perennial forb] swamps, moist meadows, stream banks and ditches, FACW+; statewide. Grows up to 5 feet, blue flowers in summer; sun to part sun in moist to wet silty loam.

Lobelia spicata var. spicata (Spiked lobelia) — [perennial forb] dry to mesic fields and open woodlands, FAC-; mostly south, sparse to absent in northern tier. Grows up to 36 inches, with pale blue to white flowers in summer; sun to part shade in dry to moist sandy loam.

Lonicera canadensis (Fly honeysuckle) —

[tree/shrub] cool, dry to moist woods upland woods, thickets, swamps, fens and sometimes along streams, FACU; statewide, except scattered southeast (Piedmont) Grows to 5 feet with pale yellow flowers in late spring to early summer. Part sun to part shade in moist sandy organic loam.

Lonicera dioica var. dioica (Mountain honeysuckle) — [perennial vine] rocky moist woods and thickets; FACU; mostly southeast (Piedmont), scattered elsewhere. Climbing woody vine or shrub, 3 to 6 feet; red to purple flowers in late spring. Grow in part sun to part shade in dry to moist circumneutral sandy loam.

Lonicera hirsuta (Hairy honeysuckle) — [perennial vine] rare in moist woods, swamps and rocky thickets; FAC; widely scattered northeast and northwest, and endangered. Climbing woody vine, to 10 feet; orange-yellow flowers in spring. Grow in part sun to part shade in dry to moist sandy loam.

Lonicera oblongifolia (Swamp fly honeysuckle) — [tree/shrub] bogs, marshes, swamps, fens; OBL; mostly northwest, endangered. Grows less than 3 feet with white/yellow flowers in summer; prefers moist to wet alkaline soils (pH >7.2) in part shade to shade.

Lonicera sempervirens (Trumpet honeysuckle) — [perennial vine] roadsides, woods, thickets; FACU; mostly southeast (Piedmont), widely scattered elsewhere. Woody vine, 10 to 20 feet; red-orange flowers in summer, red fruit in fall. Grow in sun to part sun in mesic to moist. medium to fine textured, loamy, well drained soil at least 10 inches deep with a pH range of 6.0 to 8.5. Tolerates shade, but will flower less; avoid anaerobic and droughty conditions; very popular with hummingbirds.

Lonicera villosa (Waterberry) — [tree/shrub] very rare bogs, swamps, wet thickets, swamps, treed fens and stream banks; widely scattered and endangered. Shrub to 3 feet with pale yellow flowers in late spring to early summer; sun to part sun in moist to wet organic loam.

Ludwigia alternifolia (Seedbox) — [perennial forb] swampy fields, wet woods, and the borders of streams and pond and lake shores, FACW+; statewide, except northern tier. Grows 16 to 48 inches, yellow flowers in early summer; sun to part shade in moist sandy loam. Common name comes from box-like seed pods.

Ludwigia decurrens (Upright primrose-willow) — [perennial forb] reported only on a sandy, alluvial beach in Lancaster County; OBL and endangered in Pennsylvania. Prefers medium to fine textured soils at least 10 inches deep with a pH range of 4.0 to 6.0. Tolerates shade and is a good choice for anaerobic sites but not limestone-based soils and droughty conditions.

Cardinal flower (Lobelia cardinalis)

Ludwigia palustris (Marsh-purslane) — [perennial forb] swamps, wet meadows, muddy shores, stream banks, ditches, OBL; statewide. Prostrate, creeping, floating stems; full sun in moist to wet mucky soils, including shallow water. Adaptable to soils of any texture, but requires a minimum depth of 10 inches and a pH range of 5.0 to 8.5. Intolerant of shade and drought, but an excellent choice for anaerobic sites with limestone-based soils.

Ludwigia peploides ssp. glabrescens (Primrose-willow) — [perennial forb] Rare in silty, muddy shorelines and shallow water, and regarded by many as troublesome aquatic noxious weed that invades water ecosystems and can clog waterways; OBL. Southeast . Grows creeping stems up to 12 feet long with yellow flowers in summer; full sun in mud or shallow standing water. Trim anytime to restrain spread.

Ludwigia polycarpa (False loosestrife) — [perennial forb] wet meadows and swales in the central Ridge and Valley; OBL and endangered in Pennsylvania.

Ludwigia sphaerocarpa (Spherical-fruited seedbox) — [perennial forb] reported only in southern Bucks County in Atlantic Coastal Plain swamps (OBL) and listed as extirpated in Pennsylvania.

Lupinus perennis (Blue lupine) — [perennial forb] dry fields, woods edges and along roadsides in sandy acidic soil. Mostly Central Appalachians and Piedmont, scattered elsewhere. Grows 8 to 24 inches, blue flowers in spring and early summer; sun to part sun in dry to moist acidic sandy loam, pH 5.5 to 7.

Luzula acuminata var. *acuminata* (Hairy woodrush) — [perennial graminoid] meadows, hillsides and open woods, FAC; statewide, except widely scattered southeast. Grows 5 to 15 inches; sun to part sun in rich, sandy loam.

Luzula echinata (Common woodrush) — [perennial graminoid] wet meadows and moist rocky deciduous woodlands, including slopes, alluvial woods, streamsides and occasionally in clearings; FACU, scattered statewide but concentrated in the Piedmont. Grows to 16 inches in part sun to part shade in dry to mesic woodland loams.

Luzula multiflora (Field woodrush) — [perennial graminoid] fields and meadows, clearings, open woods and roadside ditches, FACU; statewide. Can reach 30 inches; sun to part sun in dry to mesic sandy loam, pH 5.0 to 7.0.

Lycopodiella alopecuroides (Foxtail bog clubmoss) — [fern/ally] reported only in southern Bucks County in moist coastal plain woodlands, bogs and marshes; FACW+ and listed as endangered in Pennsylvania.

Lycopodiella appressa (Appressed bog clubmoss) — [fern/ally] Atlantic Coastal Plain on moist acidic soil of lakeshores, bogs and marshes; FACW+ and listed as threatened in Pennsylvania.

Lycopodiella inundata (Northern bog clubmoss) — [fern/ally] scattered except far western counties on moist acidic soils of sphagnum bogs, marshes and lakeshores; OBL.

Trumpet honeysuckle (*Lonicera sempervirens*)

Lycopodiella margueritae (Marguerite's clubmoss) — [fern/ally] reported only in Erie County in a bog; OBL.

Lycopodium annotinum (Bristly clubmoss) — [fern/ally] swampy or cool shaded often moist coniferous forests, mountain forests, and exposed grassy or rocky sites. Ideal for the north and south central regions. Stems 2 to 10 inches; rhizome: long creeping. Grow in part sun to shade in mesic to moist rich acidic humus of any texture and at least 10 inches deep with a pH reange of 4.0 to 5.3. Tolerant of shade and anaerobic conditions, but not drought or limestone-based soils.

Lycopodium clavatum (Common clubmoss) — [fern/ally] bogs, open woods and rocky barrens. Stems 2 to 10 inches; rhizome: long creeping. Grow in part sun to part shade in mesic to moist, rich acidic humusy soil.

Lycopodium dendroideum (Round-branch ground-pine) — [fern/ally] statewide in acidic soils, moist to dry in bogs, barrens, woodlands and second-growth shrub areas; FACU. Grows 4 to 12 inches in humus-rich, sandy, dry to mesic, well-drained soils.

Lycopodium obscurum (Flat branched groundpine) — [fern/ally] rich hardwood forests and successional shrubby areas. Stems 8 to 10 inches; rhizome: long-creeping. Grow in part shade to shade in mesic to slightly dry rich acidic humus.

Lycopus americanus (Water-horehound) — [perennial forb] mesic to moist hillsides and fields, moist thickets, wet ditches and swamps, OBL; statewide. Grows 6 to 24 inches, small white flowers in summer; sun to part shade in moist to wet rich, mucky soils that are medium to fine textured, at least 10 inches deep with a pH range of 5.2 and 7.8. Tolerant of shade and an excellent choice for anaerobic sites, but intolerant of drought.

Lycopus rubellus (Gypsy-wort) — [perennial forb] pond margins, river banks and bogs widely scattered in eastern Pennsylvania, especially the Atlantic Coastal Plain; OBL, listed as endangered in Pennsylvania. Grows in moderately fertile soils of any texture with a minimum depth of 10 inches and a pH between 5.2 and 7.2. Tolerant of shade and an excellent choice for anaerobic conditions, but not drought.

Lycopus uniflorus (Bugleweed) — [perennial forb] moist meadows, lake shorelines, floodplains and bogs throughout; OBL; sometimes hybridizes with L. virginicus.

Lycopus virginicus (Bugleweed) — [perennial forb] swamps, moist woods and stream banks, OBL, throughout; sometimes hybridizes with L. uniflorus. Prefers medium to fine textured, moderately fertile soils with a pH range of 5.0 to 8.3 and a minimum depth of 6 inches. Tolerant of shade and anaerobic conditions, but not limestone soils or drought.

Lygodium palmatum (Climbing fern or Hartford fern) — [fern/ally] rare in moist thickets, barrens, swamp edges, open woods, acidic, poorly drained and peaty soil. Good everywhere, but ideal northeast. Twining, climbing to 15 feet; rhizome: short creeping. Grow in full shade in acidic, peaty mesic to moist sandy loam rich with organic matter, pH 4 to 7. Can be challenging to cultivate.

Lyonia ligustrina (Maleberry) — [shrub] low, alluvial woods and thickets, wet meadows, bogs, and lakeshores, FACW; statewide except glaciated areas in the north. Shrub to 10 feet with white flowers in late spring; part sun to part shade in mesic to moist sandy clay organic loam.

Lysimachia ciliata (Fringed loosestrife) — [perennial forb] low moist ground and old fields, in floodplains and on stream banks, FACW; statewide. Grows 16 to 48 inches, yellow flowers in early summer; sun to part sun in moist sandy rich loam.

Lysimachia hybrida (Lance-leaved loosestrife) — [perennial forb] swamps, wet meadows, fens and pond margins, OBL. Mostly east and widely scattered elsewhere. Grows up to 5 feet, yellow flowers in early summer; full to part sun in mesic to moist organic, clay to sandy or rocky loam.

Lysimachia lanceolata (Loosestrife) — [perennial forb] mixed and deciduous forests, edges of wet meadows and fields, stream banks, sandy to rocky lake shores, swales in open prairies; FAC, mostly southwestern Pennsylvania. Grows 1 to 2 feet with yellow flowers in summer; prefers moist to mesic loams to clay loams of any texture at least 10 inches deep with a pH of 5.0 to 7.0. Grow in full sun to part sun. Shade, drought and limestone soil tolerant, but not suitable for anaerobic sites.

Lysimachia quadrifolia (Whorled loosestrife) — [perennial forb] dry to mesic hardwood forests, lowlands, fens, moist clearings, roadsides, and fields, rocky thickets and slopes, FACU-; statewide. Grows up to 3 feet, yellow flowers in early summer; full sun to part shade in a wide range of moist soils.

Lysimachia terrestris (Swamp-candles) — [perennial forb] swamps, flood plains, fens, bogs, stream banks, pond and lake margins and wet ditches, OBL; statewide. Grows 16 to 30 inches, yellow flowers in early summer; sun to part sun in moist rich loam.

Lysimachia thyrsiflora (Tufted loosestrife) — [perennial forb] bogs, swamps, marshes and wet woods, OBL. Northeast and north (glaciated plateaus). Grows 12 to 30 inches, yellow flowers in early summer; sun to part shade in moist to wet, medium to fine textured, rich loam at least 12 inches deep with a pH range of 4.8 to 7.2. A good choice for anaerobic sites, but not for limestone-based soils or droughty conditions.

Lythrum alatum (Winged loosestrife) — [perennial forb] swamps, marshes, fens, borders of lakes, areas along rivers and drainage ditches; FACW+, scattered and endangered, but most in southeast. Grows 3 to 6 feet, pink to purple flowers in late spring through summer. Prefers full sun in moist to wet sites, and is aquatic. Soil should be poorly drained and high in organic matter. Not to be confused with *Lythrum salicaria* (Purple Loosestrife), an invasive species, but *L. alatum* can be aggressive and is listed as a noxious weed in some states and banned for sale in Michigan.

Magnolia acuminata (Cucumber-tree) — [tree] scattered in cool moist oak-hickory forests, with a preference for bottomlands and north to east-facing, typically gentle slopes that are well-drained and deep; on steeper slopes it prefers coarser loams. Deciduous tree 40 to 70 feet; statewide, especially west. Best adapted to coarse to medium textured fertile soils at least 30 inches deep with a pH range of 5.2 to 7.0. The hardiest of the tree-sized magnolias, but intolerant of urban pollutants, anaerobic conditions, limestone-based soils and drought. Requires a 160-day growing season. Greenish-yellow flowers after 12 years. Grow in full sun to part shade in organically rich, well-drained moist loams.

Magnolia tripetala (Umbrella-tree) — [tree] rich woods and ravines, mainly in uplands, rarely on the coastal plain, FACU; mostly southeast; scattered southwest. Grows to 30 feet, with large white flowers in late spring, in part shade. Prefers medium to fine textured, mesic to moist, rich acidic, well drained sandy loam at least 12 inches deep and with a pH range of 5.0 to 7.5. Avoid anaerobic sites, limestone-bsed soils and droughty conditions.

Magnolia virginiana (Sweet-bay magnolia) — [tree] wet woods, swamps, swamp margins, savannas, hammocks, bogs, and floodplains, especially in acidic soils with poor to very poor drainage that are frequently flooded during winter or wet seasons, rarely in major river bottoms FACW+; mostly southeast; scattered southwest. Grows 60 feet; fragrant white flowers in spring. Grow in acidic, medium to wet, rich organic soil of any texture at least 30 inches deep with a pH of 5.0 to 6.9 in full sun to part shade; avoid anaerobic conditions, limestone-based soils, and droughty conditions.

Maianthemum canadense (Canada mayflower) — [perennial forb] dry to moist woods, rich and often sandy clearings, FAC-; statewide. Grows 6 to 8 inches, white flowers in late spring; part shade to shade in dry to moist sandy acidic loam, pH 4 to 5.

Maianthemum racemosum (False Solomon's-seal, feathery false lily-of the-valley) — [perennial forb] dry to moist deciduous woodlands, FACU-; statewide. Grows up to 3 feet, with white flowers in late spring; part shade to shade in dry to moist humusy loam, pH 4 to 6.

Maianthemum stellatum (Starry false lily-of-the-valley) — [perennial forb] moist to wet woods, marginal woodlands, oak openings and on stream banks, FACW. Mostly southeast and northwest; scattered elsewhere. Grows up to 24 inches, white flowers in spring; part shade to shade in moist to wet rich loam. pH 4 to 5.

Maianthemum trifolium (Threeleaf false lily-of-the-valley) — [perennial forb] often dense clonal patches in sphagnum bogs, and wet forests, OBL. Northeast and northwest (Northern Glaciated and Western Glaciated Allegheny Plateaus); scattered elsewhere. Grows up to 8 inches, white flowers in spring; part shade to shade in moist to wet rich loam.

Malaxis monophyllos var. brachypoda (White adder's-mouth) — [perennial forb] bogs, wet woodlands and wooded swamps, mostly northwestern glaciated areas, but also scattered northeast; FACW. Grows to 10 inches with flowers in spring; prefers part sun to part shade in rich, humusy loams.

Malaxis unifolia (Green adder's-mouth) — [perennial forb] moist to dry forests, swamps, heathlands and sand barrens, statewide except western counties; FAC. Grows to 16 inches with green flower in late spring to summer; prefers rich, humusy loams with much organic matter.

Malus coronaria var. coronaria (Sweet crabapple) — [tree/shrub] open woods, woodland edges and stream banks; statewide except north central. Grows to 35 feet with pinkish-white flowers in spring; part shade in moist, well drained humusy soil. Fruit very tart and acidic.

Matelea obliqua (Climbing milk-vine, Anglepod) — [perennial vine] scattered across southern

Pennsylvania in moist to mesic woodlands and edges, as well as red cedar thickets on limestone; listed as endangered.

Matteuccia struthiopteris (Ostrich fern) — [fern/ally] rich humus on rocky stream banks, moist alluvial flats, floodplains, mucky swamps and rich woods. Fronds 24 to 72 inches; rhizome: erect, but with wide-reaching stolons. Grow in part sun to shade in mesic to moist organic loams; pH 5 to 7.5. Dramatic vase-like habit; forms extensive colonies via multiple stolons; especially good for the southeast.

Medeola virginiana (Indian cucumber root) — [perennial forb] mesic woods and moist slopes; statewide. Grows 12 to 24 inches, greenish-yellow flowers in late spring; moist to wet soils in part shade to full shade, pH 4 to 6.

Meehania cordata (Heart-leafed meehania, Meehan's mint) — [perennial forb] Woodland slopes and banks, mostly southwest. Grows 3 to 6 inches in part shade to shade with lavender blue flowers in late spring. Tolerates dense shade and sun (as long as soil is moist). Good ground cover for shade and woodland gardens.

Melampyrum lineare (Cow-wheat) [annual forb] — dry to moist woodlands, bogs and barrens and parasitic on the roots of other plants. Two varieties: *americanum*, statewide, FACW, and *pectinatum* (narrowleaf cow-wheat) scattered east and FACU. Grows 3 to 16 inches in dry to moist peaty, rocky, sandy soils.

Melica nitens (Tall melicgrass) — [perennial forb] river banks and steep, rocky slopes, scattered in south central Pennsylvania and listed as threatened. Cool season grass from 1 to 3 feet with white flowers in spring. Dry to mesic open woods and grasslands in full sun to part shade.

Menispermum canadense (Moonseed) — [perennial vine] deciduous woods and thickets, along streams, bluffs and rocky hillsides, fencerows, mostly south, scattered north; FACU. Shade tolerant woody twining vine, 5 to 30 feet; whitish flowers in early fall. Grow in part sun to part shade in moist sandy loam.

Mentha arvensis (Field mint) — [perennial forb] swamps, wet meadows and moist banks, FACW; statewide. Grows 12 to 24 inches, blue-lavender flowers in fall; part shade in mesic to moist rich loam.

Menyanthes trifoliata (Bogbean or Buckbean) — [perennial forb] aquatic; bogs, sphagnum swamps and shallow water of ponds and lakes, OBL. Mostly northeast, scattered elsewhere. White flowers in late spring; grow in water gardens in mud or containers submerged in shallow water (3 inches over rhizome) in full sun to part shade. Best in peaty soils that are medium to fine textured, 10 inches deep, with a pH range of 4.8 to 6.5; ideal for anaerobic conditions, it is intolerant of limestone-bsed soils and drought.

Mertensia virginica (Virginia bluebells) — [perennial forb] river bottoms and floodplains, moist woodlands and forest clearings. FACW; statewide except Allegheny Mountains and Northern Unglaciated Allegheny Plateau. Grows 12 inches, blue flowers in very early spring before leaves are out; foliage dies back to the ground when the plant goes dormant in early summer. Grow part shade to shade in well-drained, rich, mesic to moist soils at least 4 inches deep with a pH range of 4.5 to 8.0. Low tolerance for anaerobic or droughty conditions. Slowly spreads by rhizomes, but freely from

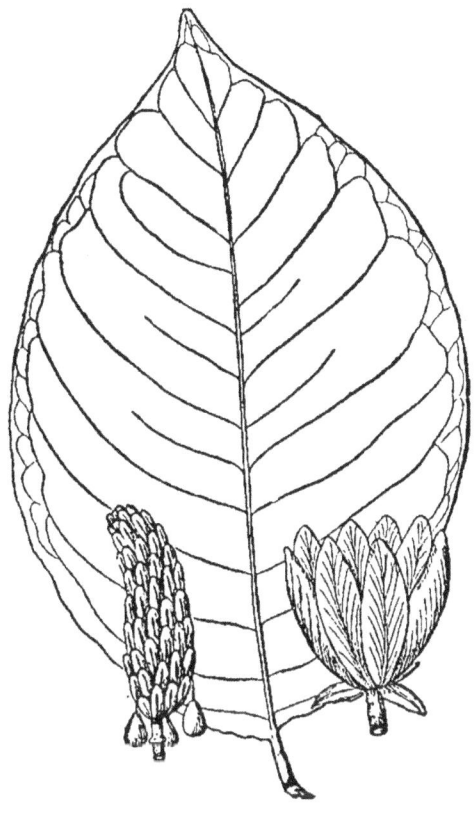

Cucumber-tree (Magnolia acuminata)

seed, ideal for naturalizing deciduous woodlands.

Micranthemum micranthemoides (Nuttall's mud-flower) [annual forb] — aquatic in tidal mud-flats of the Atlantic Coastal Plain, OBL, reported as extirpated.

Mikania scandens (Climbing hempweed) — [perennial vine] southeastern Pennsylvania, especially the lower Piedmont and Atlantic Coastal Plain in swamps and thickets; FACW+. Prefers moderately fertile, medium to fine textured soils at least 16 inches deep with a pH range of 5.7 to 8.7 in sun to part shade. Adaptable to anaerobic conditions, but not drought.

Milium effusum var. cisatlanticum (Milletgrass) — [perennial graminoid] cool rich woods, mostly north and south-central. Grows 4 to 8 inches; part shade to shade in mesic to moist humusy loam.

Mimulus alatus (Winged monkey-flower) — [perennial forb] seeps, swamps, stream edges, openings in floodplain forests, throughout except northeast and most concentrated in southeast; OBL. Grows up to 3 feet tall with blue flowers in summer. Prefers part sun with consistently moist to wet, medium to fine textured, rich soil with substantial organic matter at least 2 inches deep with a pH range of 6.2 to 7.8; tolerates full sun and light shade. Excellent choice for anaerobic conditions, but intolerant of drought.

Mimulus moschatus (Muskflower) — [perennial forb] wet shores, seeps and spring-fed swales, OBL. Mostly in the Delaware River Valley; scattered elsewhere. Creeping habit, with yellow flowers in summer; muddy moist to wet margins of garden water features in full sun to part shade.

Mimulus ringens (Allegheny monkey flower) — [perennial forb] sunny pond edges, swamps and wet meadows, OBL; statewide. Grows up to 6 inches, blue flowers in summer; sun to part sun in moist to wet rich loam.

Minuartia glabra (Appalachian sandwort) [annual forb] — on siliceous and sandstone rock outcrops in woodlands, UPL, reported as threatened; very widely scattered but most concentrated in the northeast. Grows to 8 inches in part sun to part shade in very rocky, sandstone sites with white flowers in spring to summer.

Minuartia michauxii (Rock sandwort) [annual forb] — prairies, savannas, meadows, fields and rocky ledges in the Appalachians and Piedmont. Grows 4 to 8 inches with white flowers from spring into fall, sun to part sun, in dry to mesic, calcareous gravelly soils.

Minuartia patula (Sandwort) [annual forb] — prairies, meadows, limestone barrens, rocky outcrops, alluvial shores in Carbon and Northampton Counties. Grows 2 to 12 inches with white flowers in spring to summer on shallow, calcareous limestone and sandstone-based soils in full to part sun.

Sweet crabapple (Malus coronaria)

Mitchella repens (Partridgeberry) — [perennial forb] dry to moist upland woods and sandy bogs, FACU; statewide. Trailing stems to 12 inches. White flowers in late spring, with long-lasting red fruits following; part shade to shade in moist rich humus. pH 4 to 5. Technically a subshrub.

Mitella diphylla (Bishops cap) — [perennial forb] rich, cool shaded sites in moist open woods and along stream banks, FACU; statewide. Grows 4 to 16 inches, white flowers in early spring; part shade to shade in moist rich sandy loam. pH 5 to 7, but prefers 6.0.

Mitella nuda (Naked mitrewort) — [perennial forb] very rare cool, mossy, mixed woods and cedar swamps, FACW-. Northeast and northwest (glaciated plateaus); endangered. Grows 2 to 4 inches, greenish-yellow flowers in late spring; part shade to shade in moist rich organic loam.

Moehringia lateriflora (Blunt-leaved sandwort) — [perennial forb] moist to dry woodlands and moist to mesic meadows, gravelly shores, swales, and low woods, FAC. Mostly east and west of the Central Appalachians. Grows up to 24 inches, white flowers in late spring; mesic to moist sandy loams in full sun to part shade.

Monarda clinopodia (White bergamot) — [perennial forb] moist woods, fields and floodplains; statewide. Grows up to 36 inches, white-yellow flowers in summer; sun to part shade in dry, rocky, sandy loam.

Monarda didyma (Bee balm) — [perennial forb] rich moist fields, meadows; bottomlands, thickets, woods and especially stream banks, FAC+; mostly west and east of the Central Appalachians. Grows 2 to 4 feet, red flowers in late summer; sun to part sun in mesic to wet, moisture-retentive soils. Prefers rich, humusy soils in full sun, pH 5.5 to 7.0.

Monarda fistulosa var. mollis (Horsemint) — [perennial forb] moist to wet prairies and upland open woods, UPL; statewide. Grows 20 to 48 inches, lavender flowers in late summer; sun to part sun in dry to moist. medium to fine textured sandy loam, pH 5.5 to 8.0, at least 4 inches deep. Excellent choice for anaerobic conditions, but intolerant of drought.

Monarda media (Bee balm) — [perennial forb] rich moist acidic soil on stream banks, thickets, low woods and ditches. Mostly west; scattered east. Grows up to 36 inches, purple flowers in summer; part shade in moist rich loam.

Monarda punctata (Spotted bee-balm) — [perennial forb] rare in savannas, prairies, meadows and pastures; UPL; endangered. Widely scattered statewide. To 24 inches, greenish pink flowers in spring to summer. Grow in full sun in dry, sandy circumneutral soils. Drought tolerant.

Monotropa hypopithys (Pinesap) — [perennial forb] humus of dry to moist forests, statewide. Grows 4 to 15 inches with pale yellow to reddish flowers in late summer to early fall — the earlier the bloom, the more pale it will be. Prefers humusy soil under leaf litter in deciduous forests and relies on appropriate fungi in the soil.

Monotropa uniflora (Indian-pipe) — [perennial forb] humus of dry to moist forests, statewide, FACU-. Grows 3 to 9 inches in forest soil humus with white flowers. Extremely difficult to cultivate and plants transplanted from the wild very unlikely to survive; relies on presence of appropriate fungi in woodland humus and forms either a symbiotic or parasitic association with mycorrhizal fungi through its roots.

Montia chamissoi (Chamisso's miner's-lettuce) — [perennial forb] along riverbanks, stream margins and wetlands in coastal valleys and mountains and moist, rocky ledges; reported only in northeastern Wayne County; listed as endangered in Pennsylvania. Grows to 12 inches with white flowers; prefers full sun to part sun.

Morus rubra (Red mulberry) — [tree] low elevation moist thickets and forests, stream banks and depressions; FACU; mostly south, especially southeast and southwest. Grows to 15 to 35 feet; prefers well-drained, moist soils of any texture, at least 24 inches deep with a pH range of 5.0 to 7.0, along streams or in sheltered coves.

Muhlenbergia capillaris (Hairgrass, Hair awn muhly) — [perennial graminoid] very rare in dry, exposed ledges, sandy prairies, FACU-. Only in Lancaster County; listed as extirpated. Grows to 3 feet in sandy moist soils of any texture, at least 9 inches deep, with a pH range of 5.8 to 6.8, in full sun. Tolerates anaerobic conditions, but not drought or limestone-based soils; prized for its stunning pink to lavender floral display in autumn.

Muhlenbergia frondosa (Wirestem muhly) — [perennial graminoid] thickets, clearings and forest edges and alluvial plains, FAC; statewide. Grows 20 to 40 inches; sun to part shade in moist, medium to fine textured, sandy loam at least 8 inches deep with a pH range of 5.9 to 7.9. Tolerant of shade and a good choice for limestone-based soils, but intolerant of anaerobic conditions and drought.

Muhlenbergia glomerata (Spike muhly) — [perennial graminoid] marshes, bogs, fens, meadows, lake shores and stream banks, prefers calcareous soils, FACW; statewide, mostly east. Grows 12 to 36 inches; sun to part sun in moist, rich, medium to fine textured, sandy loam at least 8 inches with a pH range of 5.3 to 7.5. Good choice for anaerobic sites, but not droughty conditions.

Muhlenbergia mexicana (Mexican muhly) — [perennial graminoid] bogs, swamps, lake margins, moist prairies and woodlands, FACW. Scattered statewide, mostly east. Grows 20 to 40 inches; sun to part sun in mesic to moist, medium textured sandy loams at least 8 inches deep with a pH between 5.5 and 7.5. Tolerates anaerobic conditions and limestone soils but not drought;.

Muhlenbergia schreberi (Dropseed or Nimblewill) — [perennial graminoid] dry to mesic woodlands and prairies, river banks and ravines, often in sandy to rocky soil, FAC; statewide. Can reach 36 inches; sun to part shade in dry to moist, medium to fine textured sandy loam at least 2 inches deep with a pH range of 4.5 to 7.5; tolerant of shade, limestone soils and drought, but not anaerobic conditions; can be invasive.

Muhlenbergia sobolifera (Creeping muhly) — [perennial graminoid] dry, rocky upland forests and oak woodlands, especially rock outcrops of limestone, chert or sandstone formations, generally eastern Pennsylvania.

Muhlenbergia sylvatica (Woodland muhly) — [perennial graminoid] statewide in moist, upland forests, along stream margins and in hollows, as well as rocky ledges of shale, sandstone or limestone, moist prairies and swamps; FAC+. Grows about 20 inches in part sun to part shade; prefers medium textured soils at least 8 inches deep with a pH range of 5.9 to 7.5. Intolerant of drought, limestone soils and anaerobic conditions.

Muhlenbergia tenuiflora (Muhly) — [perennial graminoid] Sandy soils over sandstone, chert or limestone on slopes composed of mixed hardwoods and oak-hickory combinations, statewide except northern tier. Grows 18 to 36 inches in part shade to shade, mesic to slightly dry loams, including till.

Muhlenbergia uniflora (Fall dropseed muhly) — [perennial graminoid] primarily northeastern Pennsylvania margins of glaciation on generally acidic, sandy or peaty soils in marshes and bogs, OBL and listed as endangered. Prefers medium to fine textured, moderately fertile soils at least 8 inches deep with a pH between 4.8 and 6.8. Good choice for anaerobic sites, but not for limestone-soils or droughty conditions and intolerant of shade.

Myosotis laxa (Wild forget-me-not) [perennial

Prairie dropseed (*Muhlenbergia schreberi*)

forb] — statewide except north central counties in or along rivers and streams, lakeshores, wetland margins and swamps, typically low elevations; OBL. Grows to several inches with blue flowers in summer in moist to wet soils, including shallow water, in sun to part shade.

Myosotis macrosperma (Big-seed scorpiongrass) [annual forb] — mesic woodlands, including slopes and bottomlands, and fields, FAC, reported only in Lancaster County and listed as reare. Grows several inches in mesic to moist soils in sun to shade with white flowers in spring.

Myosotis verna (Spring forget-me-not) [annual forb] — dry open woodlands, barren wooded slopes, and sandy savannas, prairies and fields; FAC-; statewide except the northern tier, but most concentrated in Bucks and Montgomery counties. Grows 6 to 18 inches in sun to part sun on dry to mesic, barren soils containing sand, gravel or clay; sometimes found in damp areas.

Myrica gale (Sweet-gale) — [shrub] rare in bogs, shallow water of lake and stream edges, OBL; northeast. Shrub to 5 feet with yellowish-green flowers in late spring; sun to part sun in wet to moist, medium to fine textured, sandy loam at least 14 inches deep with a pH between 5.0 and 7.8. Adapts to both anaerobic conditions and drought, but not limestone-based soils.

Myrica pensylvanica (Bayberry) — [tree/shrub] old fields, sand dunes, open woods, FAC. Mostly southeast and northwest; widely scattered elsewhere. Grows to 6 feet with yellowish-green flowers in late spring; sun to part sun in dry to moist sandy clay loam. Prefers moist, peaty or sandy, acidic soils, but tolerates a wide range of soils and growing conditions. Groups of plants need at least one male plant to pollinate female plants for fruit. Fruits have waxy coating used to make traditional bayberry candles. AKA *Morella pensylvanica*.

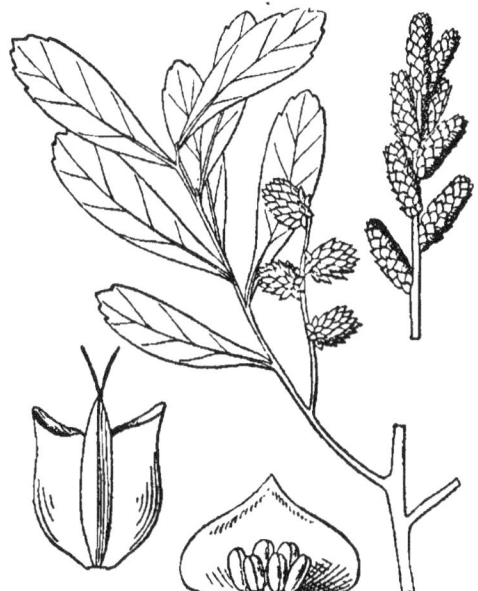

Sweet-gale (Myrica gale)

Myriophyllum farwellii (Farwell's water-milfoil) — [perennial forb] aquatic found in lakes and ponds in northeastern Pennsylvania, especially Pike County (OBL) and listed as endangered in Pennsylvania.

Myriophyllum heterophyllum (Broad-leaved water-milfoil) — [perennial forb] northeastern Pennsylvania ponds, especially in still water, OBL; listed as endangered.

Myriophyllum humile (Water-milfoil) — [perennial forb] found in lakes and ponds, especially eastern Pennsylvania; OBL.

Myriophyllum sibiricum (Northern water-milfoil) — [perennial forb] scattered in western and southeastern Pennsylvania in marshes, ponds and still waters of lakes and rivers; listed as endangered in Pennsylvania.

Myriophyllum tenellum (Slender water-milfoil) — [perennial forb] found in shallow waters of lakes in northeastern Pennsylvania, sometimes forming a thick turf on the bottom; OBL and threatened in Pennsylvania.

Myriophyllum verticillatum (Whorled water-milfoil) — [perennial forb] found in marshes and shallow ponds in Erie and Crawford Counties, OBL and listed as endangered.

Najas flexilis (Northern waternymph) [annual forb] — aquatic in lakes, ponds and reservoirs, especially in sheltered inlets, as well as spring-fed pools and upland sinkholes, OBL, scattered statewide. Grows 1 to 2 inches with white flowers in sun to shade in circumneutral silty to sandy muddy soils.

Najas gracillima (Slender waternymph) [annual forb] — aquatic, scattered statewide on shallow water of lakes, ponds and reservoirs, OBL. Grows 3 to 12 inches with white flowers in sun part sun in high quality wetlands. Good indicator of pollutants; water should be unpolluted, shallow to about 20 feet deep, mildly acidic to mildly alkaline, but relatively low in nutrients to reduce competition from algae and other plants and protected from strong wave action or currents.

Najas guadalupensis (Southern waternymph) [annual forb] — aquatic, scattered statewide in lakes, ponds, reservoirs and tidal flats, OBL, typically in about 3 feet of water in sandy, gravelly soil. Grows to about 25 inches with tiny white flowers, summer to fall, in full sun to part shade. Grows in soils of any texture at least 2 inches deep with a pH of 5.2 to 9.6; intolerant of shade and drought.

Najas marina (Holly-leaved naiad) [annual forb] — aquatic, in brackish or alkaline ponds and lakes, about 3 feet deep, OBL and very rare in the Allegheny Mountains.

Nelumbo lutea (American lotus) — [perennial forb] rare in ponds, lakes, marsh pools and swamps, as well as backwaters of reservoirs and lingering ponds in floodplains of major rivers; OBL. Creamy-white flowers in late spring to early summer. Widely scattered, mostly southeast (Atlantic Coastal Plain). Grow in any still-water pond or submerged pot; saucer-shaped leaves are up to 12 inches in diameter and plant requires room to spread/reproduce. Prefers moderately fertile soils of any texture at least 12 inches deep with a pH of 4.6 to 8.7. Intolerant of shade and drought.

Nuphar advena (Spatterdock, or yellow pond lily) — [perennial forb] aquatic; lake margins, ponds, slow moving streams, swamps and tidal marshes, OBL; statewide, mostly Central Appalachians and Piedmont. Grows in 1 to 3 feet of water in full sun to part shade. Can be grown in containers for water gardens; for natural ponds, plant rhizomes directly in the muddy bottom of poor sandy soil. AKA Nuphar lutea.

Nuphar microphylla (Yellow pond-lily) — [perennial forb] mostly eastern Pennsylvania lakes and ponds, but also in sluggish streams, sloughs, ditches and sometimes title waters; also in northwestern Erie County; OBL.

Nymphaea odorata (Fragrant water-lily) — [perennial forb] aquatic; quiet waters of acidic or alkaline ponds, lakes, sluggish streams and rivers, pools in marshes, ditches, canals, or sloughs, OBL. Mostly northeast (Northern Glaciated Allegheny Plateau), scattered elsewhere. White flowers from late spring to early fall; shallow ponds in silty to sandy soil.

Nymphoides cordata (Floating-heart) — [perennial forb] aquatic in ponds and lakes in northeastern Pennsylvania, especially in Pike County, OBL and listed as threatened.

Nyssa sylvatica (Sourgum or Black gum) — [tree] dry to middle and upper slopes and ridgetops, FAC; statewide except north-central. Grows to 100 feet; average, medium to wet soils in full sun to part shade. Prefers moist, coarse to medium textured soils at least 30 inches deep with a pH range of 4.5 to 6.0. Intolerant of anaerobic conditions, limestone soils and drought. Can spread by sucker growth.

Obolaria virginica (Pennywort) — [perennial forb] rich soils in southern Pennsylvania woodlands, especially the Piedmont. Grows up to 12 inches in leaf litter with whitish-brown flowers in spring.

Oclemena acuminata (Wood aster) — [perennial forb] typically on well-drained and acidic soils in a variety of forests but usually cool, and mesic to humid sites, occasionally in clearings or edges, mostly northern Pennsylvania — especially northeast — as well as the Allegheny Mountains in the southwest. Grows 8 to 30 inches with white flowers in late summer to early fall; prefers cool, mesic, well drained and acidic soils in humid part shade to shade, especially in red spruce forests.

Oclemena nemoralis (Leafy bog aster) — [perennial forb] prefers cold bogs and very poor fens, shorelines that are damp and sandy to acidic and peaty, cracks in acidic barren rocks; very rare in north-central Pennsylvania bogs and listed as endangered. Grows 8 to 30 inches with pale blue flowers in late summer to early fall; prefers sphagnum bogs and bog margins in moist to wet sandy, acidic soils.

Oenothera biennis (Evening primrose) — [perennial forb] dry fields, waste ground, and along roadsides, FACU-; statewide. Grows 20 to 60 inches, yellow flowers in late summer to fall; sun to part sun in dry to moist sandy loam of any texture with a minimum depth of 10 inches and a pH range of 5.0 to 7.0. Intolerant of shade, anerobic conditions but adaptable to drought.

Oenothera fruticosa (Sundrops) — [perennial forb] mesic meadows, fields and along roadsides, FAC; statewide. Grows 8 to 30 inches, yellow flowers, early summer. Two local subspecies, *fruticosa* and *glauca*; sun to part shade in dry to moist sandy loam of any texture at least 6 inches deep with a pH range of 4.5 to 7.0. Excellent choice for anaerobic and limestone soil sites and some shade, but not for droughty conditions.

Oenothera gaura (Gaura, biennial beeblossom) [biennial forb] — statewide except the northern tier on stream banks, floodplains, prairies, open woodlands and in moist meadows, FACU. Grows 3 to 6 feet with white to pink flowers in late summer to fall, often spreading into dense thickets crowding out other plants in part shade to shade in dry-mesic soils. AKA *Gaura biennis*

Oenothera laciniata (Cut-leaved evening-primrose) [Annual/Perennial Forb] — rocky woodlands, sandy fields and meadows, disturbed areas, scattered southeast, FACU. Grows 4 to 18 inches with white-pink-yellow flowers from spring to fall in sun to part shade on mulched, well-drained, sandy, somewhat calcareous soils including barren gravelly areas.

Oenothera nutans (Evening-primrose) — [perennial forb] a biennial found along roadsides, fallow land and old fields, scattered statewide. Grows to 12 inches with yellow flower in spring; prefers dry to mesic, well-drained soils in full to part sun.

Oenothera parviflora var. parviflora (Evening-primrose) — [perennial forb] biennial, mostly Piedmont in old fields and disturbed sites such as roadsides and railroad embankments. FACU-. Grows 1 to 4 feet with yellow flowers in dry sandy or gravelly soils in full to part sun, especially in fields and prairies.

Oenothera perennis (Sundrops) — [perennial forb] mesic pastures, shale slopes and along roadsides, FAC; statewide. Grows 4 to 24 inches, yellow flowers in early summer; sun to part sun in dry to moist sandy loam.

Oenothera pilosella (Sundrops) — [perennial forb] scattered, mostly Piedmont, along roadsides, in meadows and open woodlands, FAC. Grows up to 2 feet with yellow flowers in late spring. Prefers full to part sun with mesic, loamy soils high in organic content, at least 8 inches deep with a pH range of 5.8 to 7.2. Tolerates anaerobic conditions; easy to grow if not too dry, but can spread aggressively.

Omalotheca sylvaticum (Woodland cudweed) — [perennial forb] Open woods, boggy woods, rocky slopes, clearings, fields, borders of woods, roadsides, muddy banks, disturbed sites; extremely rare in Pennsylvania and known from a single example on a dry woodland hillside in Tioga County; aka Gnaphalium sylvaticum.

Onoclea sensibilis (Sensitive fern) — [fern/ally] open swamps, thickets, marshes, or low woods, in muddy soil in sunny wet meadows or shaded stream bank locations, often forming thick stands. Fronds 12 to 36 inches; rhizome: short creeping. Grow in part sun to shade in mesic to moist silty humusy loams, pH 4.5 to 7.5 but prefers acidic soil; available at many garden centers.

Ophioglossum pusillum (Northern adder's-tongue) — [fern/ally] scattered statewide in moist soils of open woodlands, meadows, fens, marsh edges and shorelines within glaciated areas. Grows to 10 inches in rich, moist, humusy soils in sun to part shade.

Opuntia humifusa (Eastern prickly-pear cactus) — [perennial forb] sandy habitats, especially openings on dry sometimes wooded hillsides; mostly southeast. Spreading, prostrate habit with yellow flowers in summer; sun to part sun in dry sandy loam, pH 5.5 to 7.

Orobanche uniflora (Broom-rape) — [perennial forb] in forests statewide and parasitic on the roots of many plants, FACU; listed by some as an annual and described in many states as a noxious, often quarantined, weed. Grows 3 to 8 inches with lavender flowers in late spring to early summer; perfers moist, rocky, sheldtered areas but more importantly requires a host plant such as sedums, saxifrage, sunflowers and goldenrods and the presence of a specific soil fungus related to those species. Transplants rarely survive a year.

Orontium aquaticum (Goldenclub) — [perennial forb] aquatic; shallow water of bogs, marshes, swamps, and streams, OBL; Central Appalachians and east, especially in northern Piedmont. Grow in water gardens in containers submerged in 6 to 18 inches of water in full sun. Leaves tend to emerge in water 6 to 9 inches deep, but mostly float in water 12 to 18 inches deep.

Orthilia secunda (One-sided shinleaf) — [perennial forb] dry to moist, coniferous, mixed, and deciduous forests and bogs, mostly eastern Pennsylvania, FAC.

Orthilia secunda (One-sided shinleaf) — [perennial forb] dry to moist, coniferous, mixed, and deciduous forests and bogs, mostly eastern Pennsylvania, FAC. Grows 4 inches with greenish flowers in summer; grows in sandy soils with a wide pH range in part shade to shade; prefers moist soils.

Oryzopsis asperifolia (Spreading ricegrass) — [perennial graminoid] on open, rocky ground dry, sandy to rocky soils in deciduous and coniferous woodlands with well developed duff across northern Pennsylvania and along the Allegheny front.

Oryzopsis racemosa (Ricegrass) — [perennial graminoid] generally eastern Pennsylvania in the Ridge and Valley, Glaciated Northeast and Piedmont regions in open rocky deciduous woodlands.

Osmorhiza claytonii (Sweet-cicely) — [perennial forb] rich upland woods and wooded slopes, FACU; statewide except for Central Appalachians. Grows 15 to 30 inches, white flowers in early summer; part shade to shade in moist rich loam.

Osmorhiza longistylis (Anise-root) — [perennial forb] upland dry to mesic wooded areas, shaded slopes and ravines, FACU; statewide. Grows 15 to 30 inches, white flowers in early summer; part sun to part shade in moist rich loam.

Osmunda cinnamomea (Cinnamon fern) — [fern/ally] swamps, stream banks, roadsides, Moist areas, acidic soils, frequently in vernal seeps, ponds and swamps. Fronds 30 to 60 inches; rhizome: erect with occasional offshoots. Grow in part sun to part shade in mesic to moist, medium to fine textured, acidic organic humusy to silty soils at least 12 inches deep with a pH range of 4.5 to 7.0. Moderate tolerance to anaerobic and droughty conditions, but not limestone-based soils.

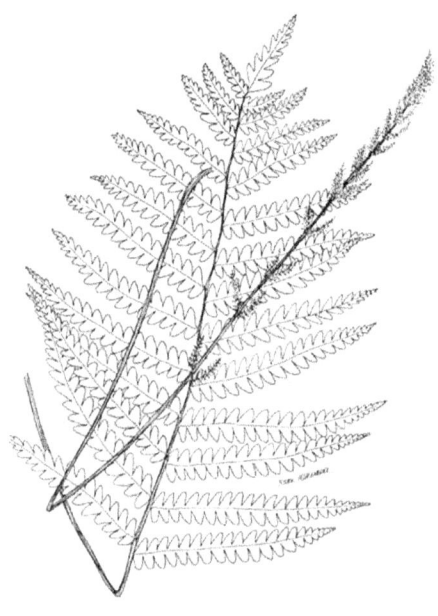

Cinnamon fern (Osmunda cinnamomea)

Osmunda claytoniana (Interrupted fern) — [fern/ally] oozy mud swamps, bogs, and stream banks; also, rich, mesic woods and open woods and shaded roadsides. Fronds 24 to 48 inches; rhizome: erect with occasional offshoots. Grow in part sun to part shade in rich, mesic to moist, medium to fine textured silty loam at least 12 inches deep with a pH range of 4.0 to 6.0. Tolerates anaerobic conditions, but not drought or limestone-based soils

Osmunda regalis (Royal fern) — [fern/ally] swamps, bogs, bluffs, stream banks in moist acidic soils; statewide. Fronds 24 to 60 inches; rhizome: erect with occasional offshoots. Grow in part sun to part shade in moist to wet silty organic loam of any texture and a minimum depth of 16 inches and pH between 4.0 and 6.0. Somewhat tolerant of anaerobic conditions, but not limestone based soils or drought.

Ostrya virginiana (Hop-hornbeam) — [tree] moist, open to forested hillsides to dry upland slopes and ridges, occasionally on moist, well-drained flood plains, FACU; statewide. Grows to 45 feet; average, medium, well-drained soil of any texture with a minimum depth of 16 inches and a pH range of 42 to 7.6, in full sun to part shade. Intolerant of anaerobic conditions.

Oxalis acetosella (Northern wood-sorrel) — [perennial forb] rich swamps, bogs and most woodlands, mostly northern Pennsylvania, but also south along the Allegheny front, FAC-. Grows 4 to 12 inches with lavender flowers in spring; prefers well-drained, mesic, sandy loams and silt loams in part shade to shade; excellent edge or groundcover plant.

Oxalis dillenii ssp. filipes (Southern yellow wood-sorrel) — [perennial forb] common statewide in woodlands, forest edges, along roadsides, disturbed ground and on diabase cliffs, especially southeastern Pennsylvania. Grows to 15 inches with yellow flowers throughout the season; prefers mesic to moist, well-drained humusy soils in full sun to part shade, especially on disturbed sites.

Oxalis stricta (Common yellow wood-sorrel) — [perennial forb] dry to mesic fields, lawns, gardens in shallow sandy loams to loamy tills, UPL; statewide. Prostrate to 20 inches, yellow flowers in summer; sun to part sun in dry to moist sandy loamy till, pH 4 to 6.

Common yellow wood-sorrel (*Oxalis stricta*)

Oxalis violacea (Violet wood-sorrel) — [perennial forb] dryish, acidic soils in glades, rocky open woods, fields and prairies, stream banks. Mostly south, especially southeast (Piedmont). Grows 6 to 9 inches, violet flowers in spring; part sun to part shade in dry to moist sandy loam; pH 4 to 7 but prefers 6 to 6.5.

Oxydendrum arboreum (Sourwood) — [tree] subxeric open slopes and ridges occupied by oaks and Virginia pine; less common in mesic sites like coves and sheltered slopes. Also along well-drained lowland areas along Piedmont streams not subject to flooding, in gently rolling areas, FACU; mostly southwest; scattered southeast. Grows 20 to 50 feet in full sun to part shade in well-drained, organically rich, mesic to moist, coarse to medium textured soils at least 30 inches deep with a pH range of 4.0 to 6.5. Part shade is tolerated, but flowering is diminished. Intolerant of urban pollution, anaerobic conditions and limestone-based soils.

Oxypolis rigidior (Cowbane) — [perennial forb] swamps, bogs, meadows, and moist sandy shores, OBL. Mostly southeast and southwest. Grows 4 to 5 feet, white flowers in late summer; sun to part shade in wet, sandy or clay loam.

Packera anonyma (Appalachian groundsel) — [perennial forb] in sandy or drying soils in open fields and woodlands, meadows, serpentine barrens and disturbed areas; UPL and rare in the Piedmont area of Pennsylvania. Grows 12 to 24 inches in dry to mesic sandy serpentine soil with yellow flowers in summer.

Packera antennariifolia (Shale-barren ragwort) — [perennial forb] slopes on shale barrens in Fulton and Franklin Counties; listed as endangered in Pennsylvania. Grows in clumps up to 10 to 20 inches on dry, sandy to rocky soil formed from shale; blooms late spring with yellow flowers.

Packera aurea (Golden ragwort) — [perennial forb] floodplains and in moist fields and woods, FACW; statewide. Grows 12 to 32 inches, yellow flowers in early summer; sun to part shade in moist to wet, medium to fine textured, rich loam at least 6 inches deep with a pH of 4.5 to 8.5. Low tolerance for anaerobic conditions or drought, ideal for limestone soils. AKA *Senecio aureus*.

Packera obovata (Ragwort, squaw weed) — [perennial forb] moist fields, meadows, upland woods and calcareous slopes. Western, south central and southeastern counties (including Carbon and Monroe) in Pennsylvania; scattered elsewhere Grows up to 30 inches, yellow flowers in early summer; sun to part shade in circumneutral humusy loam. AKA *Senecio obovatus*.

Packera paupercula (Balsam ragwort) — [perennial forb] moist meadows, peaty thickets, stream banks, prairies, meadows; in rocky, loamy soil; FAC. Mostly southwest, scattered elsewhere. Grows up to 30 inches, with yellow flowers in early summer; sun to part sun in moist sandy rich loam. FAC. AKA *Senecio pauperculus*.

Panax quinquefolius (Ginseng) — [perennial forb] rare in cool, moist, rich mesic woods, often on north-facing slopes; statewide. Grows up to 24 inches, greenish flowers in spring, red fruit in fall; moist, fertile, organically rich, medium moisture soils in part shade to full shade; pH 4 to 7 but prefers 4.5 to 6.

Panax trifolius (Dwarf ginseng) — [perennial forb] statewide in moist, rich woodlands. Grows 3 to 8 inches with clusters of small white flowers in mid- to late spring; prefers open to dappled shade in mesic to moist rich loams containing much organic material. An ephemeral the plant develops rapidly in spring but dies down in early summer.

Panicum anceps (Panic grass) — [perennial graminoid] low, sandy, moist soils in forests or in shaded, grassy pasturelands, pine savannas, borders of flood-plain swamps, mesic woodlands, roadsides, and upland pine-hardwood forests, FAC. Mostly southeast. Grows 2 to 4 feet in full to part sun on moist to wet sandy loams, but can adapt to waterlogged and very well-drained sites.

Panicum capillare (Witchgrass) — [perennial graminoid] fields, pastures, roadsides, waste places and ditches, FAC-; statewide. Grows 20 to 40 inches; sun to part sun in dry to moist sandy to clayey loam.

Panicum capillare (Witchgrass) [annual graminoid] — statewide in sandy to gravelly prairies, limestone and sandstone glades, riparian gravel bars, barren disturbed areas, FAC-. Grows 1 to 3 feet in full sun on dry to mesic, typically barren, circumneutral to alkaline soils containing sand, gravel or hard-pan clay.

Panicum clandestinum (Deer-tongue grass) — [perennial graminoid] clearings and edges in damp, sandy woodlands and thickets, FAC+; statewide. Grows 30 to 50 inches; part sun to part shade in moist sandy loam.

Panicum dichotomiflorum (Smooth panic grass) [annual graminoid] — statewide in savannas and praires, glades, riparian gravel bars, moist open woodland and meadows, FACW-. Grows 18 to 48 inches in full to part sun in mesic to moist, preferably fertile, soils of all textures with a minimum depth of 6 inches and a pH range of 4.8 to 7.0. Intolerant of shade and drought, but ideal for anerobic conditions and limestone-based soils.

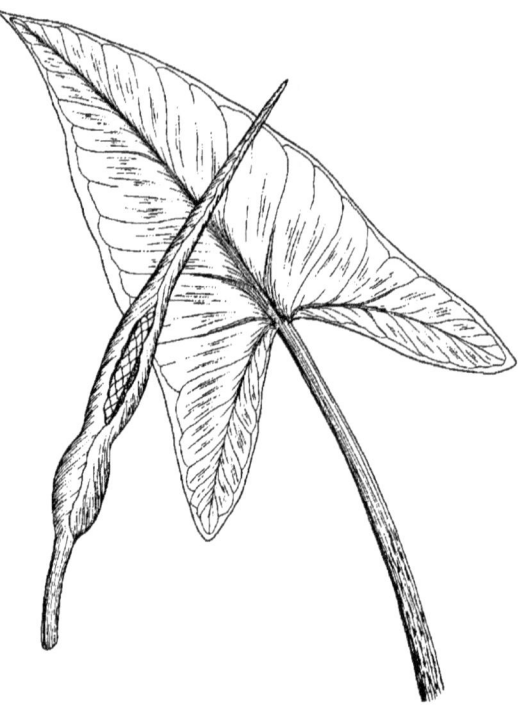

Green arrow-arum (Peltandra virginica)

Panicum dichotomum (Panic grass) — [perennial graminoid] statewide, especially southeast, on dry to moist sandy, clayey or rocky ground in woodlands or more typically in moist to wet marshes, bogs, swamps, low woods and pond and lake shores; FAC.

Panicum flexile (Old witchgrass) [annual graminoid] – meadows, fields, stream banks and swales, FACU, scattered southeast. Grows to about 3 feet in dry to mesic, circumneutral to alkaline sandy loams.

Panicum gattingeri (Gattinger's panicgrass) [annual graminoid] — statewide, especially Piedmont, on prairies, fields and cultivated ground, FAC. Grows 3 feet in full to part sun on dry to mesic, sandy loams.

Panicum philadelphicum (Panic grass) [annual graminoid] — scattered statewide except northern tier in fields, open woodlands, shorelines and rock crevices. Grows 1 to 3 feet in full to part sun in sandy, gravelly dry to mesic loams.

Panicum rigidulum (Long-leaved panic grass) — [perennial graminoid] rare in swamps, wet woodlands and flood-plain forests, wet pine savannas, marshy shores of rivers, ponds, and lakes; rarely in dry sites, OBL. Scattered southeast. Grows to 4 feet in sun to part shade in moist to wet, medium to fine textured, rich soils at least 6 inches deep with a pH range of 5.0 to 7.5. Ideal for anaerobic conditions, but intolerant of shade or drought. AKA *Panicum longifolium*.

Panicum tuckermanii (Tuckerman's panic grass) [annual graminoid] — Along the Lake Erie shoreline in sandy flats, FAC- and listed as threatened. Grows to 3 feet in full to part sun, dry to mesic sandy soils.

Panicum verrucosum (Warty panicgrass) [annual graminoid] — scattered southeast in meadows, swamp edges, marshes and near lakes, prefers coastal regions, FACW. Grows to 3 feet in mesic to moist sandy or silt loams; rare in dry woodlands.

Panicum virgatum (Switchgrass) — [perennial graminoid] dry slopes of open oak or pine woodlands, river banks, marshes, but especially mesic to wet tall grass prairies, FAC. Scattered statewide, especially in Delaware River Valley. Can reach 6 feet; full sun to part shade in average, medium to wet soils. Prefers moist, sandy or clay soils in full sun. Tends to lose columnar form and flop in rich soils and too much shade.

Parietaria pensylvanica (Pellitory) [annual forb] — deciduous woodlands, limestone glades, savannas (below trees), and thickets, statewide below the northern tier. Grows 4 to 16 inches with reddish-greenish flowers from spring to fall, dry to mesic loams, in part shade, but tolerates rocky soil in part sun.

Parnassia glauca (Grass-of-parnassus) — [perennial forb] boggy meadows or seeps on calcareous soils, OBL. Mostly east and west; endangered. Grows 10 to 20 inches, white flowers in late summer; moist to wet organic loams in full sun to part shade.

Paronychia canadensis (smooth forked nailwort) [annual forb] — statewide in woodlands, fields, clearings and waste ground. Grows 4 to 12 inches with greenish flowers in summer on dry to mesic sandy to rocky soil in sun to part sun.

Paronychia fastigiata (Hairy forked nailwort) [annual forb] — – three varieties in rocky woodlands, thickets and openings, generally in southern Pennsylvania. Grows to ab out 12 inches with greenish flowers in dry to mesic sandy to rocky soils. Distribution is the only major difference in varieties: *var. fastigiata* (Hairy forked nailwort) is found across the southern half of the state, while *nuttalli* (Whitlow-wort) is scattered in the southeast and *pumila* (Forked chickweed) is in the southern Appalachians.

Parthenium integrifolium (American fever-few, wild quinine) — [perennial forb] rare in dry to mesic woodlands and prairies. Widely scattered and considered extirpated. White flowers in early summer. Grow in well-drained, dry to medium average soils in full sun.

Parthenocissus inserta (Grape woodbine) — [perennial vine] alluvial thickets, ravines, woodlands, fields, scattered throughout. Woody twining vine, 30 to 50 feet. Green-white flowers in summer followed by blue-black berries attractive to birds. Grow in average, mesic, well-drained soil in full sun to part shade; tolerates full shade and a wide range of soil and climate conditions and is good for erosion control.

Parthenocissus quinquefolia (Virginia-creeper) — [perennial vine] open woods, fields, clearings, stream banks; FACU. Woody tendril vine, 30 to 50 feet. White flowers in spring, with fruit in late fall. Grow in average, medium, well-drained, medium to fine textured soil with a minimum of 16 inches in depth and a pH range of 5.0 to 7.5, in full sun to part shade. Intolerant of anaerobic conditions but well-adapted to drought and sometimes confused with poison ivy; vivid red foliage in fall.

Paspalum floridanum var. glabratum (Florida beadgrass) — [perennial forb] reported in sandy, moist soils in extreme southern Chester and Lancaster counties; FACW. Cultivated as an ornamental naturalizing grass, grows 3 to 5 feet with a 3 to 4 foot spread in full sun, mesic to moist, well-drained sandy soils, especially in low areas near streams.

Paspalum laeve (Field beadgrass) — [perennial graminoid] moist, sandy soils at lake and pond shorelines and fields in the southeast, FAC+, sun to part sun. Prefers coarse to medium textured soils at least 4 inches deep with a pH of 4.5 to 7.5. Some shade, drought and limestone soil tolerance but none for anaerobic conditions.

Paspalum setaceum (Slender beadgrass) — [perennial graminoid] Three varieties: *var. muhlenbergii*, widely scattered except northwest but concentrated southeast; *var. psammophilum*, widely scattered, mostly along the southern Delaware River; and *var. setaceum*, scattered in southeastern Pennsylvania, all FACU+. *Muhlenbergii* is found on dry to moist open ground, serpentine barrens, forest margins and disturbed areas, while *psammophilum* prefers sandy, maritime habitats and in dry fields and *staceum* occurs on dry, sandy soils on open ground typically at forest edges.

Passiflora lutea (Passion-flower) — [perennial vine] rare in rocky, moist woods and thickets; southwest, and endangered. Grows 12 to 15 feet with white flowers in summer; prefers moist, well-drained limestone sandy loam of any texture with a minimum depth of 12 inches and a pH range of 4.5 to 8.0; part sun to part shade. No tolerance for anaerobic or droughty conditions.

Paxistima canbyi (Canby's mountain-lover) — [shrub] very rare on calcareous slopes and cliffs where soils are associated with dolomite. Mostly south central counties. Endangered in Pennsylvania. Grows 1 to 3 feet in part shade on fertile, well-drained soils. Greenish flowers in spring.

Pedicularis canadensis (Forest lousewort) — [perennial forb] open dry upland woods, old fields, woods edges and mesic grasslands, FACU; statewide. Grows 6 to 16 inches, yellow to purple flowers in spring; sun to part shade in dry to mesic, medium to fine textured soils at least 6 inches deep with a pH range of 4.0 to 7.0. Intolerant of anaerobic or droughty conditions.

Pedicularis lanceolata (Swamp lousewort) — [perennial forb] swamps, fens, boggy sedge meadows and swales; parasitic on the roots of other plants. Throughout, but most concentrated in southeast; FACW. Grows 1 to 2 feet, yellow flowers in late summer; prefers full to part sun with wet to moist circumneutral loamy soils.

Pellaea atropurpurea (Purple cliffbrake) — [fern/ally] dry soils adjacent to dolomite glades and crevices of limestone and dolomite outcrops, bluffs, boulders and sink holes. Ideal for the southeast. Fronds 8 to 20 inches; rhizome: short creeping. Grow in part sun to part shade in dry to mesic sandy loam, pH 5.5 to 7.5 but prefers 6.5 to 7.5.

Pellaea glabella var. glabella (Smooth cliffbrake) — [fern/ally] generally southeastern Pennsylvania, often on limestone substrates, in moist to dry exposed calcareous cliffs and ledges, as well as masonry cracks.

Peltandra virginica (Green arrow-arum) — [perennial forb] emergent aquatic; bogs, swamps and ditches, and edges of ponds, lakes, and rivers, OBL; mostly east and west, scattered elsewhere. Grows 2 to 3 feet, green flowers in spring; water garden, bog, or pond areas in part shade, muddy soil in shallow water. Adapts to soil of any texture with a minimum depth of 16 inches and pH range of 5.0 to 8.8. No drought tolerance.

Penstemon canescens (Grey beard-tongue) — [perennial forb] Dry, rocky, shale outcrops and wooded slopes; in south, mostly Allegheny Mountains. Grows 12 to 18 inches in full sun with pale to dark violet flowers in late spring. Average, dry to mesic, well drained loams. Ideal for borders and rock gardens.

Penstemon digitalis (Beards tongue, Talus slope penstemon) — [perennial forb] old fields, meadows, prairies and mesic open woods and margins, FAC; statewide. Grows up to 60 inches, white flowers in summer; average, dry to medium moisture, well-drained soil of any texture with a depth of 8 inches and a pH range of 5.5 to 7.0, in full sun to part shade. Excellent choice for droughty conditions, but none for anaerobic or limestone-soil sites.

Penstemon hirsutus (Northern beard-tongue)

— [perennial forb] dry to mesic, open rocky slopes, fields, and roadside banks. Scattered statewide, mostly east and west. Grows 15 to 32 inches, violet to purple flowers in early summer; sun to part sun in dry rocky sandy loam; pH 5.5 to 6.5.

Penstemon laevigatus (Eastern beard-tongue) — [perennial forb] Moist meadows, rich wooded hillsides, roadsides; FACU. Mostly southwest. Grows 1 to 3 feet, full sun to shade, with purple flowers in early summer. Prefers moist, organic soils.

Penthorum sedoides (Ditch stonecrop) — [perennial forb] statewide in wet soils on stream banks, fresh-water marshes, beaver pond edges, floodplain forest pools, shorelines and ditches, OBL. Prefers fine textured soils at least 14 inches deep with a pH range of 5.0 to 7.0. Low anaerobic tolerance.

Persicaria amphibia (Water smartweed or Water knotweed) — [perennial forb] aquatic, found in very wet prairies and along shorelines, in swamps, ponds, and quiet streams, in mud or floating on still fresh water, OBL; statewide, especially in the Delaware River Valley. Two varieties; *emersum* (leaves don't float) and *stipulaceum* (leaves float); full sun to part sun in wet mucky soil or in water gardens. AKA *Polygonum amphibium;* not to be confused with the invasive *Polygonum cuspidatum* (Japanese knotweed).

Persicaria arifolia (Halberd-leaf tearthumb) — [perennial vine] shaded swamps, ponds, tidal marshes along rivers, wet ravines in forests; OBL; statewide, especially southeast. Annual vine; white to pink flowers in summer. Grow in moist to wet rich loams in sun to part shade. AKA *Polygonum arifolium.*

Persicaria careyi (Pinkweed) [annual forb] — low thickets, wet meadows, swamps and bogs,

Eastern beard-tongue (Penstemon laevigatus)

moist shorelines and woodland edges, FACW and listed as endangered, mostly along the eastern edge of the Appalachians. Grows to 4 feet with pink to rose flowers in late summer on moist to wet sandy and silt loams in sun to part shade. AKA *Polygonum careyi.*

Persicaria glabra (Denseflower smartweed) — [perennial forb] shallow waters and swamps in the Atlantic Coastal Plain, OBL, rare.

Persicaria hydropiperoides (Mild water-pepper) — [perennial forb] wet banks and clearings, shallow water, marshes, moist prairies, ditches, OBL. Mostly southeast, scattered elsewhere. Grow in full sun in mucky soil, standing water. AKA *Polygonum hydropiperoides var. hydropiperoides.*

Persicaria punctata (Dotted smartweed) — [perennial forb] Shallow water and lake, pond and stream edges, swamps, marshes, and floodplain forests, OBL; statewide. Grows 18 to 24 inches, white flowers in summer; prefers full to part sun in moist to wet mucky soil high in organic matter and tolerates standing water. AKA *Polygonum punctatum var. punctatum.*

Persicaria punctata (Dotted smartweed) [annual forb] — statewide in floodplain forests, swamps, swales, vernal ponds, muddy lake shorelines, and small streams, often along stagnant or slow-moving water especially in degraded wetlands, OBL. Grows 12 to 30 inches in sun to part sun, moist to wet mucky soil high in organic matter. Tolerates shallow standing water. AKA *Polygonum punctatum var. confertiflorum.*

Persicaria robustior (Large water-smartweed) — [perennial forb] peaty, wet ground and often in shallow water on stream and pond edges and in bogs, swamps or coastal plains; scattered in eastern counties and more concentrated in Erie and Crawford counties, OBL.

Persicaria setacea (Swamp smartweed) — [perennial forb] Shallow water and moist soils in alluvial woods and swamp forests, Erie and Crawford counties, OBL and listed as endangered in Pennsylvania.

Persicaria virginiana (Jumpseed) — [perennial forb] rich deciduous forests, floodplain forests, dry to moist woodlands and thickets, FAC; statewide. Grows 15 to 40 inches, white flowers in spring; sun to part shade in rich sandy loam. AKA *Polygonum virginianum*.

Phacelia dubia (Scorpion-weed) [annual forb] — woodlands, fields, thickets, floodplains, and shale barrens, scattered in south central Pennsylvania. Grows to about 12 inches with cream to light blue flowers in early spring in sun to part sun on dry to mesic sandy and silt loams.

Phacelia purshii (Miami-mist) [annual forb] — floodplain forests and alluvial clearing such as low, rich, open woodlands, especially along creeks, riparian bars, moist thickets and slopes mostly southwest but scattered southeast, UPL. Grows 6 to 20 inches in part sun to part shade in mesic to moist sandy to silt loams.

Phalaris arundinacea (Reed canary-grass) — [perennial graminoid] dry to wet, well to drained soil, especially in marshes, swamps, FACW; statewide. Grows 10 to 30 inches; full sun to part shade in dry to wet sandy rich loam.

Phaseolus polystachios (Wild bean) — [perennial vine] scattered across southern Pennsylvania, mostly east, in rocky woodlands, on bluffs, talus slopes and in thickets, as well as roadside banks and waste ground. Grows to 6 feet with pink flowers in late summer in dry, rocky soil in full to part sun.

Phegopteris connectilis (Long beech fern or narrow beech fern) — [fern/ally] cool shade, woods in moist loose humus, strongly to moderately acid soil, or on rocks in shaded rock crevices. Ideal for the northeast. Fronds 8 to 18 inches; rhizome: medium creeping. Grow in part shade to shade in mesic to moist rocky sandy humusy loam, pH 4 to 6.

Phegopteris hexagonoptera (Broad beech fern) — [fern/ally] moist woods, usually in full shade, often in moderately acid soils. Fronds 12 to 24 inches, rhizome: long creeping. Grow in part shade to shade in mesic to moist acidic well drained sandy to silt loams.

Phemeranthus teretifolius (Appalachian rock-pink) — [perennial forb] rocky to sandy thin soils, often near or on edges of sandstone, granite or serpentine outcrops; primarily found in Chester County and listed as threatened in Pennsylvania. Grows 3 to 8 inches with pink to lavender flowers in late summer to early fall; prefers full sun to light shade on dry to mesic sandy, gravelly loam.

Phlox divaricata ssp. divaricata (Wild blue phlox, Sweet William) — [perennial forb] rich, moist deciduous forests and bluffs, FACU. Mostly southwest; scattered elsewhere; absent in northern tier. Grows up to 12 inches, pale blue to white flowers in spring; humusy, medium moisture, well-drained soil of any texture, with a minimum depth of 14 inches and pH of 5.5 to 7.2, in part sun to part shade. Low tolerance for drought or anaerobic conditions. Another subspecies, *laphamii* is introduced, not native, and escaped from cultivation.

Phlox maculata (Meadow phlox, Wild sweet-William) — [perennial forb] Wet meadows, swamps, abandoned fields and thickets, low moist woods and riverbanks, FACW; statewide. Grows 12 to 32 inches, pink-rose to purple flowers in early summer; moderately fertile, medium moisture, well-drained soil in full sun to light shade. Prefers moist, organically rich, medium to fine textured soils at least 11 inches deep with a pH of 5.9 to 6.8, in full sun.

Phlox ovata (Mountain phlox) — [perennial forb] primarily in the central Ridge and Valley in edges and openings of sandy, dry woodlands; listed as endangered in Pennsylvania. Grows 4 to 6 inches with pink to lavender flowers in late spring; prefers slightly acidic, humus rich soil in part shade to shade and serves as an excellent groundcover in leaf-mulched, shady areas.

Phlox paniculata (Summer phlox, Fall phlox) — [perennial forb] meadows, thickets and along stream banks, often on calcareous substrate, FACU; statewide. Grows up to 6 feet, pink flowers in early summer; sun to part sun in moist to wet sandy rich loam, pH 5 to 7.

Phlox pilosa (Downy phlox) — [perennial forb] rare in dry open woodlands, prairies, roadsides and thickets. FACU. Southeast (Piedmont) and endangered. Lavender flowers in spring. Grow in sun to part shade in sandy to rocky slightly acidic, well-drained soils.

Phlox stolonifera (Creeping phlox) — [perennial forb] rich open woods and stream banks. Mostly southwest. Grows 4 to 6 inches, violet to rose purple flowers in spring; part shade to shade in dry to moist rich loam, pH 6 to 7.

Phlox subulata ssp. subulata (Moss pink) — [perennial forb] dry rocky ledges, slopes, clearings and fields. Mostly southeast, scattered elsewhere. Grows to about 6 inches, pink, purple or white flowers in spring; sun to part sun in dry sandy loam of any texture, at least 8 inches deep and with a pH between 5.7 and 7.5. Intolerant of drought, limestone soils or anaerobic conditions and listed as endangered. Another subspecies, *brittonii*, is very rare on shale barrens in the southwest.

Photinia melanocarpa (Black chokeberry) — [tree/shrub] swamps, bogs, wet and dry woods, barrens. FAC, statewide. Shrub to 10 feet; sun to part shade in average, medium, coarse to medium textured, well-drained soil at least 24 inches deep with a pH range of 4.4 to 6.5. Tolerant of wide range of soils, including both dry and boggy soils. Best fruit production occurs in full sun. White flowers in late spring. AKA *Aronia melanocarpa*.

Photinia pyrifolia (Red chokeberry) — [tree/shrub] pine bottomlands; swamps and moist woods; open bogs, FACW, statewide. Shrub from 18 inches to 10 feet, depending on habitat.; sun to part sun in mesic to moist, medium to fine textured sandy loam at least 20 inches deep with a pH of 5.5 to 7.5. Intolerant of shade. White flowers in late spring. AKA *Aronia arbutifolia*.

Phragmites australis var. americana (Common reed) — [perennial graminoid] marshes, lake shores, swales and ditches in wet, muddy ground, FACW. Mostly southeast and northwest, scattered elsewhere. Grows 3 to 12 feet; full sun in moist to wet, muddy soils of any texture with a minimum depth of 20 inches and a pH range of 4.5 to 8.7. Ideal for anaerobic conditions but intolerant of drought. A very aggressive spreader and considered invasive.

Ninebark (*Physocarpus opulifolius*)

Phryma leptostachya (Lopseed) — [perennial forb] rich woods, rocky limestone slopes and swamps, UPL; statewide except north. Grows 1 to 3 feet, purple flowers in summer; part sun to part shade in moist, rich circumneutral loam.

Phyla lanceolata (Fogfruit) — [perennial forb] Rare in wet to moist forests and along lakes, ponds and streams, OBL; scattered throughout, but most common southeast. Grows 6 to 20 inches in sun to part sun with pink to white flowers in spring; spreads to form a dense mat in average soil. Good groundcover for wet areas or pond edges.

Phyllanthus caroliniensis ssp. caroliniensis (Carolina leaf-flower) [annual forb] — moist alluvial areas, including gravel bars, along creek beds, and low thickets, moist valley depressions and ravines, far southeastern Pennsylvania and listed as endangered. Grows to about five inches with red-green flowers in late summer and fall on mesic to moist, gravelly to sandy loams in sun to part sun.

Physalis heterophylla (Ground cherry) — [perennial forb] fields, sandy or cindery open ground and cultivated areas; mostly southeast and west, scattered elsewhere. Grows 8 to 36 inches, yellow flowers in late summer; sun to part sun in dry, sandy loam.

Physalis pubescens var. integrifolia (Husk tomato) [annual forb] — sand and gravel bars and stream edges as well as fallow fields, cultivated and waste ground, FACU-, scattered southeast. Grows less than 12 inches with yellow-blue flowers from spring to fall in dry to mesic alluvial soils high in sand, silt and gravels.

Physalis subglabrata (Ground-cherry) — [perennial forb] mostly southern Pennsylvania on limestone uplands, fields, hedge rows and disturbed ground. Grows up to 40 inches with yellow-red flowers from mid-summer to early autumn; prefers full to part sun in mesic to moist fertile loams; lower leaves may yellow if too dry. Easy to grow, can be aggressive.

Physalis virginiana (Virginia ground-cherry) — [perennial forb] widely scattered in southern Pennsylvania rocky, dry disturbed ground. Grows 1 to 2 feet with yellow flowers in summer; prefers sun to part sun in dry, sandy prairie soils.

Physocarpus opulifolius (Ninebark) — [shrub] wet woods, moist cliffs, sandy or rocky stream banks, gravel bars and moist thickets, FACW- ; statewide. Shrub to 10 feet with white to pink flowers in late spring; sun to part shade in mesic to moist, well-drained soil of any texture with a minimum depth of 14 inches and a pH range of 4.5 to 6.5. Intolerant of shade, anaerobic conditions, limestone soils, but well suited for droughty sites.

Physostegia virginiana (False dragonhead) — [perennial forb] stream banks and along moist shorelines. Scattered statewide except northern tier. Grows up to 36 inches, pinkish-purple flowers in late summer; part sun to part shade in moist rich loam of any texture, at least 16 inches deep and with a pH between 4.7 and 8.0, although 5.0 to 6.5 is preferred. Moderate drought tolerance, but none for anaerobic conditions. Ideal for limestone-based soils.

Phytolacca americana (Pokeweed) — [perennial forb] moist to mesic thickets, clearings and forest openings, open ground and along roadsides. FACU+; statewide. Grows up to 10 feet, with greenish-white flowers in summer to fall; part sun to part shade in dry to moist sandy loam, pH 5 to 6.

Picea mariana (Black spruce) — [tree] bottomlands, peat bogs and dry peatlands, swamps, muskegs and transitional sites between peatlands and uplands, FACU-; mostly northeast; scattered elsewhere. To 65 feet; sun to shade in mesic to wet acidic humusy soils of any texture at least 16 inches deep with a pH of 4.7 to 6.5. Low tolerance for anaerobic conditions, limestone soils or drought. Shallow root system makes this tree susceptible to wind throw.

Picea rubens (Red spruce) — [tree] cool upland to sub alpine forests in climates with cool, moist summers and cold winters; on steep, rocky slopes with thin soils, and wet bottomlands; often on sites unfavorable for other species such as organic soils overlying rocks in mountainous locales, FACU; mostly northeast; widely scattered elsewhere. Grows to 100 feet on soils developed from unsorted glacial drift and till deposited on the midslopes of hills and mountains with thick mor humus. Adaptable to soils of any texture and moderate fertility at least 13 inches deep with a pH of 4.0 to 5.8. Intolerant of anaerobic conditions or limestone soils.

Pilea fontana (Lesser clearweed, bog clearweed) [annual forb] — widely scattered statewide in wetlands including spring heads, seepages, lake and stream shores, swamps and marshes, FACW+. Grows 4 to 20 inches with green flowers in late summer in boggy, springy soil, generally part shade to shade.

Pilea pumila (Clearweed) [annual forb] — statewide in shady wetlands including floodplains, seeps, small stream borders and low areas around vernal pools and poorly drained upland forests on sites typically dominated by *Acer saccharum* (sugar maple), *Acer saccharinum* (silver maple), *Plantanus occidentalis* (American sycamore), *Betula nigra* (river birch) and *Fraxinus pennsylvanica* (green ash). Grows 4 to 20 inches with green flowers in late summer to fall, in moist to wet humusy loamy soils, including temporary standing water, part shade to shade.

Pinus echinata (Short-leaf pine) — [tree] dry upland slopes, ridges, plains, bluffs and ravines between 700 and 2,000 feet in elevation; UPL;

mostly Central Appalachians. Grows 75 to 100 feet in dry, sandy to rocky acidic soils of any texture, at least 24 inches deep with a pH range of 4.0 to 6.0; prefers deep, well-drained soils having fine sandy loam or silty loam textures, often with clay components, in sun to part sun. Intolerant of shade, anaerobic conditions and limestone soils.

Pinus pungens (Tablemountain pine) — [tree/shrub] dry, shaly to sandy, often rocky uplands between 1,500 and 4,000 feet elevation; UPL; mostly Central Appalachians. Rarely grows over 65 feet. Prefers shallow, strongly acidic stony, infertile and excessively drained soils of any texture, at least 24 inches deep, with a pH or 4.5 to 7.0, in sun to part sun. Intolerant of shade, anaerobic conditions and limestone soils, but well adapted to drought.

Pinus resinosa (Red pine or Norway pine) — [tree/shrub] dry slopes and mountaintops and sandy soils in boreal forests, FACU; widely scattered, statewide. Grows to 120 feet; well-drained, dry to moist, coarse to medium textured, acidic to neutral soils at least 40 inches deep with a pH range of 4.5 to 6.0, in full to part sun. Tolerates poor soils but not anaerobic conditions, drought or limestone soils.

Pinus rigida (Pitch pine) — [tree] upland or lowland, sterile, dry to boggy acidic forests and barrens, FACU; statewide. Grows to 100 feet; dry, thin, infertile, and sandy or gravelly soils, ranging from rapidly draining to swampy limestone and sandstone. Prefers coarse to medium textured soils at least 20 inches deep with a pH of 3.5 to 5.1. Intolerant of shade, anaerobic conditions and limestone based soils.

Pinus strobus (Eastern white pine) — [tree] mesic to dry sites ranging from wet bogs and moist stream bottoms to xeric sand plains and rocky ridges, especially on northerly aspects and in coves, FACU; statewide. Grows to 130 feet; average, medium moisture, well-drained, medium textured soil, at least 40 inches deep with a pH range of 4.0 to 6.5, in full sun to part sun. Prefers full sun, fairly infertile sandy soils, such as well-drained outwash soils, in cool, humid climates with little hardwood competition. Tolerant of a wide range of soil conditions. Intolerant of anaerobic conditions, limestone soils, drought and many air pollutants such as sulfur dioxide and ozone.

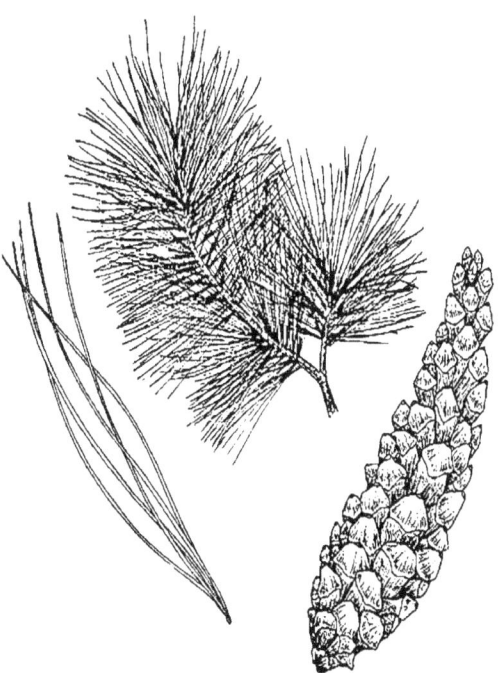

Eastern white pine (Pinus strobus)

Pinus virginiana (Virginia pine) — [tree] dry uplands, sterile sandy or shaly barrens, old fields, and lower mountains; barrens slopes and ridgetops. Mostly south, especially Central Appalachians, Southern Allegheny Plateau, Piedmont. Grows to 48 feet; full sun in sandy loam of any texture with a minimum depth of 20 inches and pH range of 4.5 to 7.5; will grow in poor, dry soils including clay. Intolerant of shade, anaerobic conditions and limestone soils but well adapted for drought.

Piptochaetium avenaceum (Black oatgrass) — [perennial graminoid] generally Atlantic Coastal Plain but widely scattered in the Piedmont on thin, sandy soils in rocky, open oak and pine woodlands; UPL.

Plantago pusilla (Dwarf plantain) [annual forb] — rocky ridges and open ground in the Atlantic Coastal Plain, UPL. Grows less than 12 inches with yellow-green flowers in spring on dry, sandy to rocky loams.

Plantago rugelii (Rugel's plantain) — [perennial forb] statewide in wet pastures and meadows, along roadsides, and disturbed ground; FACU. Low-growing rosette which produces stems bearing green, sometimes purple-tinted, flowers in summer.

Grow in full to part sun in mesic to moist, fertile loamy soil but avoid soils with high clay or gravel content; leaves wilt in drought.

Plantago virginica (Dwarf plantain) [annual forb] — dry, sandy prairies, barren slopes, rocky glades, fields, low meadows statewide except the northern tier, UPL. Grows 8 to 12 inches with greenish-white flowers in late spring and summer in full to part sun on dry to mesic sandy, rocky soils.

Platanthera blephariglottis var. blephariglottis (White fringed-orchid) — [perennial forb] widely scattered, mostly northeastern Pennsylvania in open sphagnum bog mats, moist sandy to peaty meadows as well as pine savannas, OBL. Grows up to 40 inches with white flowers in late spring to early summer; among the more showy native orchids. Grow in sphagnum moss on the edges of bogs in open, wet areas of spruce bogs.

Platanthera ciliaris (Yellow fringed orchid) — [perennial forb] bogs, moist meadows, and moist to wet woods, FACW; mostly southeast. Grows 15 to 40 inches, orange-yellow flowers in summer; sun to part shade in moist, rich loam.

Platanthera clavellata (Clubspur orchid) — [perennial forb] bogs, shores, moist woods, thickets, sunny openings, in damp deep humus; FACW+; statewide, except for southwest. Grows 5 to 15 inches, white flowers in late summer; sun to part sun in moist to wet sandy rich loam, pH 5 to 6.

Platanthera cristata (Crested fringed-orchid) — [perennial forb] prefers moist, sandy to peaty meadows, wet woodland flats, sphagnum bogs, swamps and seeping slopes; reported only in southern Montgomery County and listed as extirpated in Pennsylvania. Grows to 30 inches with deep yellow flowers in summer; prefers moist sandy to peaty soils in full sun to part shade.

Spreading Jacob's ladder (*Polemonium reptans*)

Platanthera flava var. herbiola (Tubercled rein-orchid) — [perennial forb] statewide, but especially Piedmont and Atlantic Coastal Plain in alluvial wet and open forests, riparian thickets, wet meadows, wet prairies, seeps, salt marshes; FACW. Grows to 30 inches in moist to mesic, rich alluvial loams, sometimes near seeps, with greenish flowers in late spring.

Platanthera grandiflora (Large purple fringed-orchid) — [perennial forb] statewide in rich mesic and especially sphagnum bog and swamp forests, meadows and old fields, seeps and thickets; FACW. Grow in rich alluvial mesic to moist soils; produces showy, fringed flowers — ranging from pale pink to deep lavender — in summer.

Platanthera huronensis (Tall green bog-orchid) — [perennial forb] Shorelines, bogs, wet meadows and moist woodlands in glaciated areas of northwestern and northeastern Pennsylvania, FACW. Grows to 30 inches with yellowish flowers in summer; prefers moist to wet silty loams in full sun to part shade.

Platanthera lacera (Ragged fringed-orchid) — [perennial forb] open alluvial and swamp forests, moist seepy slopes, moist riparian meadows, sand flats, prairies, old fields and roadside banks, statewide, FACW. Grows 12 to 30 inches with greenish flowers in mid-summer; prefers full to part sun in moist, acidic sandy and silt loams with peaty material and some gravel. Can be difficult to transplant.

Platanthera leucophaea (Eastern prairie fringed-orchid) — [perennial forb] in damp, calcareous soils of mesic to wet prairies, marshes, fens, meadows and lake shorelines; of conservation concern and reported only in Crawford County,

FACW+; listed as extirpated in Pennsylvania and threatened in the United States. Grows 12 to 24 inches with white flowers in early to mid-summer. Prefers moist, somewhat circumneutral soils with much organic matter in full sun to part sun.

Platanthera orbiculata (Large round-leaved orchid) — [perennial forb] statewide in rich, damp humus in deep shade of mesic to wet coniferous and deciduous forests and fen forests, statewide, especially northwest of the Piedmont; FAC. Grows to 30 inches with greenish flowers in part shade to shade in moist, acidic soils high in coniferous or deciduous organic matter.

Platanthera peramoena (Purple fringeless orchid) — [perennial forb] found in alluvial forests and stream banks and seepage slopes, wet wooded flats, thickets, marshes, moist meadows, ditches, thickets, southern Pennsylvania especially southwest, FACW. Grows 1 to 3 feet with purple flowers in mid-to late summer; prefers full sun to part shade in slightly acidic, moist loam to silt loam soils; difficult to transplant because of root relationships with soil fungi, and in some years it may not bloom.

Platanthera psycodes (Purple fringed-orchid) — [perennial forb] statewide except far southwest in open alluvial and swamp forests, stream banks, damp riparian meadows, moist and seeping slopes, marshes, roadside banks, ditches, old fields. Grows 1 to 5 feet with purple flowers in summer; grow in sun to part shade in humusy, well-drained slightly acidic soils high in organic content.

Platanus occidentalis (American sycamore) — [tree] alluvial soils near streams and lakes and in moist ravines, sometimes on uplands and on limestone soils; cultvated in parks and gardens and as a street tree, FACW-; statewide. Grows to 160 feet; average, mesic to wet, well-drained soils in full sun. Tolerates light shade. Prefers rich, humusy, consistently moist, coarse to medium textured soils at least 30 inches deep with a pH between 4.9 and 6.5. Generally tolerant of most urban pollutants, but not drought or limestone-based soils.

Pluchea odorata var. succulenta (Marsh fleabane) [annual forb] — tidal mudflats and sites in which salt hay mulch was used on the Atlantic Coastal Plain. Grows 1 to 3 feet with pink to purple flowers in late summer to fall in sun to part shade on moist to wet soils, especially in salt marshes.

Poa alsodes (Woodland bluegrass) — [perennial graminoid] statewide, but concentrated west and north in cool, mesic to moist woodlands and thickets; FACW-.

Poa autumnalis (Autumn bluegrass) — [perennial graminoid] moist Atlantic Coastal Plain woodlands; FAC and listed as endangered. Prefers coarse to medium textured soils at least 10 inches deep, with a pH range of 5.8 to 6.9. Low tolerance for anaerobic and droughty conditions and requires a 180-day growing season

Poa cuspidata (Bluegrass) — [perennial graminoid] southern Pennsylvania on dry woodland hillsides and banks, as well as forest openings.

Poa languida (Woodland bluegrass) — [perennial graminoid] widely scattered in moist woodlands and fens.

Poa paludigena (Bog bluegrass) — [perennial graminoid] widely scattered in shady bogs, fens and wet woodlands, typically under other plants; FACW and listed as threatened in Pennsylvania.

Poa palustris (Fowl bluegrass) — [perennial graminoid] wet meadows, shores, thickets, riparian and upland areas, FACW. Mostly north and east, scattered elsewhere. Grows 20 to 50 inches; sun to part sun in moist to wet, medium to fine textured, moderately fertile, silty loam with a minimum depth of 12 inches and a pH range of 4.9 to 7.5. Low tolerance to drought.

Poa saltuensis (Old-pasture bluegrass) — [perennial graminoid] dry to mesic rich open woodlands and thickets in thin soils over limestone. Mostly north, scattered south-central. Grows 20 to 50 inches; part sun to part shade in circumneutral dry to mesic loam.

Podophyllum peltatum (Mayapple) — [perennial forb] medium wet, well-drained soil in mesic woods, especially maple woods and clearings, FACU; statewide. Grows 12 to 18 inches, white flowers in spring followed by green fruits that yellow when ripe. Spreads by rhizomes to form huge colonies and appears to be ignored by deer; part shade to shade in dry to moist humusy loam, pH 4 to 7.

Podostemum ceratophyllum (Riverweed) — [perennial forb] aquatic found on rocks in rapidly flowing rivers and streams, statewide, but especially in the Delaware and Susquehanna rivers; OBL.

Pogonia ophioglossoides (Rose pogonia) — [perennial forb] sphagnum bogs, fens, moist acidic sandy meadows and prairies, open wet woods, pine savannas, sandy-peaty stream banks, and seepage slopes, OBL. Mostly eastern third of the state; scattered central and west. Grows 4 to 16 inches, pink flowers in summer; full to part sun in moist to wet acidic humusy loam.

Polanisia dodecandra ssp. dodecandra (Red-whisker clammyweed) — [annual forb] scattered statewide in mostly dry, sandy or gravelly alluvial soils on riverbanks, gravel bars and flood-scoured shorelines and grasslands, but also in glades and near bluffs. Grows to about 2 feet in full sun in dry to mesic rocky to sandy soil; stems may sprawl in moist, fertile soils. Because of ornamental flowers, popular for gardens, especially rain gardens.

Polemonium reptans (Spreading Jacob's ladder, Greek valerian) — [perennial forb] low moist woods, wooded floodplains, thickets at the base of cliffs and moist ground near streams, FACU; statewide. Grows 6 to 20 inches, light blue flowers in spring; part shade to shade in moist, rich sandy loam, pH 5 to 7. Cut back to avoid shaggy appearance after bloom, will green up again. Spreads by free-seeding, not rhizomes.

Polemonium vanbruntiae (Jacob's ladder) — [perennial forb] very rare sphagnum glades, swamps, and marshes, FACW; reported only in Wayne, Sullivan, Berks and Somerset counties. Grows up to 36 inches, blue flowers in summer; moist rich humusy soils in sun to part shade. Listed as endangered. AKA *Polemonium caeruleum ssp. van-bruntiae*.

Polygala cruciata (Cross-leaved milkwort) [annual forb] — sandy, shrubby prairies, pine barrens and Black Oak (Quercus velutina) savannas, as well as mountain bogs and boggy pastures, FACW+ and listed as endangered. Scattered in southern Pennsylvania, especially the Piedmont. Grows 4-12 inches with pink to white flowers in late summer, in mesic to moist, slightly acidic sandy loams; can withstand occasional temporary flooding.

Polygala curtissii (Curtis's milkwort) [annual forb] — Only in Chester county on dry, open serpentine barrens and listed as endangered. Grows to 16 inches with pink to violet flowers from late spring into fall in dry, sandy, serpentine loams in full to part sun.

Polygala incarnata (Pink milkwort) [annual forb] — Only in Lancaster County on dry, open serpentine barrens, prairies and glades, UPL and listed as endangered. Grows 8 to 24 inches with pink to pale rose flowers in summer on dry, sandy serpentine loams in full sun.

Polygala nuttallii (Nuttall's milkwort) [annual forb] — southeastern Pennsylvania in sphagnum bogs, peaty thickets and open woodlands, FAC. Grows 4-12 inches with reddish flowers in late summer in mesic to moist, sandy loams, sun to part shade.

Polygala paucifolia (Bird-on-the-wing) — [perennial forb] rich dry to mesic rocky, rich upland woods and wooded slopes, FACU; statewide except for far western edge. Grows 3 to 6 inches, rose-purple flowers in spring; part shade to shade in moist rich loam, pH 4 to 6.

Polygala polygama (Bitter milkwort) [annual forb] — upland prairies and savannas and wooded bogs, UPL; widely scattered but especially in the southern Appalachians. Grows 4 to 12 inches with rose-purple to white flowers in summer in full to part sun on dry to mesic sandy soils.

Polygala sanguinea (Field milkwort) [annual forb] — statewide in dry to moist prairies, savannas, glades and woodland edges, FACU. Grows 4 to 16 inches in dry to mesic, sandy, sterile and slightly acidic soils, especially poor soils.

Polygala verticillata (Whorled milkwort) [annual forb] — fields prairies, open woodlands, moist meadows, marshes and ravines, UPL, generally southern Pennsylvania. Grows 6 to 12 inches with greenish-pink flowers in summer in sun to part shade, moist, sandy soils, but does best in full sun. Three varieties: *verticillata*, statewide; *amigua*, south; and *isocycla*, scattered south.

Polygonatum biflorum (Smooth Solomon's seal) — [perennial forb] dry to moist woods in fertile, loamy soil; tall, robust plants are known as var. commutatum, FACU; statewide. Grows up to 6 feet, but more typically around 3 feet, with white-greenish flowers in spring and dark purple fruits following; part shade to shade in dry to moist rich loam. pH 4 to 6 but prefers 5 to 6.5.

Polygonatum pubescens (Hairy Solomon's seal) — [perennial forb] fertile, humus-rich moisture retentive well-drained soil in cool, shaded, dry to moist woods, wooded slopes and coves; statewide. Grows up to 36 inches, white-greenish flowers in spring; part shade to shade in dry to moist humusy sandy loam; pH 4 to 6 but prefers 5 to 6.5.

Polygonella articulata (Jointweed) [annual forb] — sandy banks, pine barrens lakeshores, beaches, riverbanks, plains and dunes, rare in southeastern Pennsylvania. Grows 4-20 inches with white to pink flowers in late summer in dry to mesic, acidic sandy soil.

Polygonum achoreum (Homeless knotweed) [annual forb] — disturbed aareas and waste ground, FACU; possibly extirpated, possibly introduced. Sprawling to 20 inches along the grouind with yellow-green flowers in summer on rocky, sandy soils in full to part sun.

Polygonum arifolium (Halberd-leaf tearthumb) [annual vine] — statewide except north central counties on sandy, wet ground near springs, in woodland bogs, thickets, swamps and wet meadows, often partially submerged, OBL. Grows 2 to 4 feet with pink to white flowers in late summer/fall in moist to wet, humusy silt loams. AKA *Persicaria arifolia*.

Polygonum erectum (Erect knotweed) [annual forb] — Riverbanks, old fields and waste groiund, FACU, generally across southern Pennsylvania. Grows to 20 inches with yellow to green flowers in late summer to fall on dry sandy and gravelly loams in full to part sun.

Polygonum pensylvanicum (Smartweed) [annual forb] — statewide in swamps, low riparian areas, marsh edges, degraded seasonal wetlands, prairie swales and pond shores, FACW. Grows 1 to 4 feet with pink flowers in spring in mesic to moist rich loamy circumneutral soils, of any texture at least 14 inches deep and with a pH between 4.0 and 8.5, in full to part sun; thrives on disturbed sites; temporary standing water is tolerated, making it a candidate for rain gardens. AKA *Persicaria pensylvanica*.

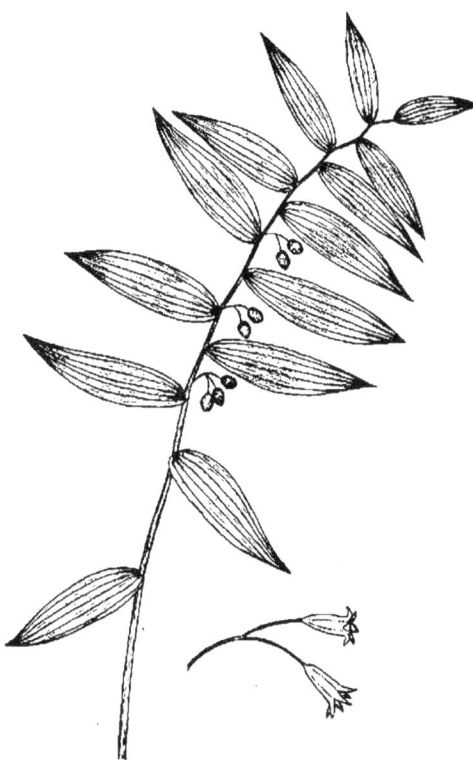

Smooth Solomon's seal (*Polygonatum biflorum*)

Polygonum ramosissimum (Bushy Knotweed) [annual forb] — Sandy shores and distrubed sites in Bucks and Monroe Counties, FAC. Grows to 3 feet and flowers in summer on sandy loams in sun to part sun. Two subspecies: *ramosissimum* and *prolficum*, the latter preferring saline sites.

Polygonum sagittatum (Tearthumb) [annual vine] — statewide in swamps, marshes, bogs, gravelly seeps, vernal ponds, soggy thicketrs and other low, moist ground, OBL. Grows 2 to 4 feet with white to pink flowers late summer to early fall, in part sun to part shade in moist to wet silt and sandy loams of any texture, with a minimum depth of 6 inches and pH range of 4.0 to 8.5, as well as gravels or peat moss; tolerates temporary flooding, but intolerant of shade and drought. AKA *Persicaria sagittata*.

Polygonum tenue (Slender knotweed) [annual forb] — dry fields, and serpentine and shale barren, mostly from the Appalachians eastward. Grows to 18 inches with greenish-white flowers in summer to fall on exposed sites with dry, acidic soils.

Polymnia canadensis (Leaf-cup) — [perennial forb] statewide, but mostly southwest, in moist, rocky, wooded hillsides, floodplains and roadsides, especially on calcareous soils. Grows 18 to 60 inches with white flowers from mid-summer into fall; prefers part sun to part shade in slightly dry to moist loamy to somewhat rocky soil with much organic matter; plant sizes vary depending on moisture and soil fertility and in cultivation may be short-lived.

Polypodium appalachianum (Appalachian polypody) — [fern/ally] eastern Pennsylvania, especially north, on a variety of substrates on rocky woodland slopes, cliffs, ledges, rocks and boulders.

Polypodium virginianum (Common polypody) — [fern/ally] rocks, boulders, cliffs, ledges, rocky woods; on a variety of substrates; statewide. Fronds 4 to 14 inches; rhizome: sort to medium creeping. Grow in part shade to shade in moist rich loam, pH 4 to 6.

Polystichum acrostichoides (Christmas fern) — [fern/ally] forest floors and shady, rocky slopes in organically rich loams. Fronds 12 to 24 inches; rhizome: multiple crowns. Grow in part shade to shade in slightly dry to moist organically rich, sandy or silt loam, pH 4 to 7. Found at most garden centers.

Polystichum braunii (Braun's holly fern) — [fern/ally] moist forest places such as cool rocky shaded ravines. Ideal for the northeast. Fronds 8 to 36 inches; rhizome: clump-forming. Grow in part shade to shade on cool sites in peaty, humusy moist loam.

Polystichum x potteri (Shield-fern) — [fern/ally] southern Wayne County in humus rich, circumneutral soils on shaded ravines and cool, rocky slopes.

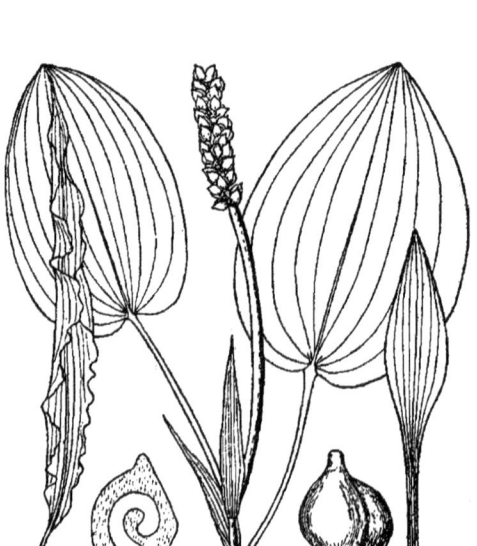

Heartleaf pondweed (*Potamogeton pulcher*)

Pontederia cordata (Pickerel-weed) — [perennial forb] emergent aquatic; pond and lake margins and swampy edges of lakes and streams, OBL. Mostly east and west. Grows 2 to 4 feet above water with light blue flowers in late summer to fall; full sun in mud at the margins of a pond or in containers of rich organic loams in a water garden under 3 to 5 inches of water. Adaptable to soils of any texture with medium fertility; minimum depth is 10 inches and pH range is 4.9 to 8.7. Intolerant of drought.

Populus balsamifera (Balsam poplar) — [tree] rare on river floodplains, stream and lake shores, moist depressions, and swamps, but will also grow on drier sites, FACW. Widely scattered statewide, endangered. Grows to 100 feet; alluvial gravel, deep sand, clay loam, silt, and silty loam with abundant soil moisture is needed. Adapts to soils with moderate fertility of any texture at least 30 inches deep with pH between 4.5 and 7.0. A good choice for limestone-based soils, but low drought tolerance.

Populus deltoides (Eastern cottonwood) — [tree] low elevation floodplains, wet areas and river banks on rich, alluvial soils, especially bare mud left after flooding; FACU-; mostly east, especially southeast. Grows 65 to 130 feet in full sun, preferably in fertile, deep, and moist but well drained soil of any texture, at least 24 inches deep with a pH range of 4.6 to 6.5. Intolerant of shade, but well suited for anaerobic conditions.

Populus grandidentata (Bigtooth aspen) — [tree] floodplains, gently rolling terrain, and lower slopes of uplands, FACU; statewide. Grows to 80 feet; prefers light sandy loams, sands, and loamy sands but adapts to coarse to medium textured soils at least 20 inches deep with a pH range of 4.8 to 7.2. Intolerant of shade, anaerobic conditions and drought.

Populus tremuloides (Quaking aspen) — [tree] moist upland woods, dry mountainsides, high plateaus, talus slopes, gentle slopes near valley bottoms, alluvial terraces, and along watercourses; statewide. Grows to 65 feet; soils ranging from shallow and rocky to deep loamy sands and heavy clays at least 32 inches deep with a pH range of 4.3 to 9.0. Prefers sites that are well drained, loamy, and high in organic matter and nutrients. Intolerant of anaerobic conditions and drought.

Portulaca oleracea (Purslane) [annual forb] — scattered statewide in fields and waste places, possibly introduced, FAC. Grows 4 to 9 inches with white flowers from late spring to early fall; full sun to part sun on dry to mesic, well-drained loams. Ideal as an annual groundcover for poor soils where other plants struggle, in rock gardens, hanging baskets; drought tolerant.

Potamogeton alpinus (Northern pondweed) — [perennial forb] aquatic in glacial lakes, ponds and slow-moving streams in eastern Pennsylvania; OBL.

Potamogeton amplifolius (Bigleaf pondweed) — [perennial forb] aquatic; waters of lakes, ponds, streams, and rivers, OBL. Mostly east and northwest. Green flowers in summer; full sun in shallow ponds with a pH range of 5.5 to 7.0; intolerant of shade.

Potamogeton bicupulatus (Snailseed pondweed) — [perennial forb] aquatic in acidic shallow waters of ponds, lakes, and streams, mostly northeastern Pennsylvania, OBL.

Potamogeton confervoides (Tuckerman's pondweed) — [perennial forb] aquatic in acidic waters of glacial lakes, ponds and bogs, especially higher elevations, northeastern Pennsylvania, OBL; listed as threatened.

Potamogeton diversifolius (Snailseed pondweed) — [perennial forb] shallow quiet water of ponds, lakes and streams, throughout Pennsylvania except northern-most counties, OBL. Requires pH range of 5.0 to 7.7.

Potamogeton epihydrus (Ribbonleaf pondweed) — [perennial forb] aquatic in statewide in ponds, lakes and streams, OBL.

Potamogeton filiformis var. borealis (Threadleaf pondweed) — [perennial forb] aquatic in calcareous, shallow waters of streams and ponds with a pH range of 5.4 to 7.0, statewide but widely scattered; OBL.

Potamogeton foliosus subsp. foliosus (Leafy pondweed) — [perennial forb] aquatic in slow to fast-flowing streams and lakes throughout Pennsylvania; OBL.

Potamogeton friesii (Fries' pondweed) — [perennial forb] aquatic in widely scattered in calcareous waters of lakes and slow-flowing streams; OBL.

Potamogeton gramineus (Grassy pondweed) — [perennial forb] aquatic in widely scattered lakes, ponds, streams and rivers, mostly northern Pennsylvania; OBL and listed as endangered.

Potamogeton hillii (Hill's pondweed) — [perennial forb] aquatic in alkaline marshes, ponds, lakes, and slow-moving streams, widely scattered but mostly Erie County, OBL and listed as endangered in Pennsylvania.

Potamogeton illinoensis (Illinois pondweed) — [perennial forb] aquatic in alkaline streams, rivers, lakes, ponds, and sloughs, statewide but mostly in Ridge and Valley and northeastern glaciated areas of Pennsylvania; OBL.

Potamogeton natans (Floating pondweed) — [perennial forb] aquatic; quiet or slow-flowing waters of ponds, lakes, and streams, OBL. Northeast and northwest; scattered elsewhere. Stems to 6 feet and green flowers in summer; full sun in ponds with a pH range of 5.8 to 7.0.

Potamogeton nodosus (Longleaf pondweed) — [perennial forb] aquatic; clear to turbid waters of lakes, streams, rivers, and sloughs, OBL; statewide, especially southeast. Greenish-white flowers in summer. Serves as an oxygenator in water gardens; grow in aquatic containers of sandy loam or rooted in muddy pool bottoms at depth of 6 to 24 inches with a pH range of 5.8 to 7.0, full sun to part shade.

Potamogeton oakesianus (Oakes' pondweed) — [perennial forb] aquatic in quiet acidic bogs, ponds, and lakes, OBL and mostly eastern Pennsylvania.

Potamogeton obtusifolius (Blunt-leaved pondweed) — [perennial forb] aquatic in medium to low-alkaline bogs, ponds and lakes and slow streams, reported only in Wayne County, OBL and listed as endangered.

Potamogeton pectinatus (Sago pondweed) — [perennial forb] Shallow brackish to alkaline waters of lakes, streams, rivers, and estuaries, OBL; scattered throughout, especially along the Susquehanna and lower Delaware Rivers. Grows up to 6 feet on nearly all bottom substrates in fresh to saline and alkaline water less than 10 feet deep, but poorly in waters with high turbidity. Considered a problem in recreational and irrigation waters.

Potamogeton perfoliatus (Perfoliate pondweed) — [perennial forb] aquatic; lakes, streams, rivers, and bays; statewide. Green flowers in summer; full sun in water features and ponds in silty loam.

Potamogeton praelongus (White-stem pondweed) — [perennial forb] Very rare in waters ranging from neutral to alkaline of lakes, rivers, and streams; OBL. Mostly northwest (Erie and Ontario Lake Plain) and endangered. Grow in full sun in water 3 to 10 feet deep in a soft sediment soil with a pH range of 5.8 to 7.0; prefers alkaline water. Tiny flowers in summer.

Potamogeton pulcher (Heartleaf pondweed) — [perennial forb] aquatic, widely scattered in shallow, acidic still to slow-flowing streams, lakes, ponds, and small rivers, including swamps and peaty to muddy shores, OBL and listed as endangered in Pennsylvania.

Potamogeton pusillus subsp. pusillus (Pondweed) — [perennial forb] aquatic, statewide in streams and marshes, lakes and ponds, especially northeastern Pennsylvania; OBL.

Potamogeton spirillus (Snailseed pondweed) — [perennial forb] aquatic in neutral to acidic shallows of ponds, lakes, and streams, statewide but mostly northeastern glaciated areas; OBL.

Potamogeton strictifolius (Narrow-leaved pondweed) — [perennial forb] aquatic in calcareous ponds, lakes and streams, very widely scattered, OBL and listed as endangered in Pennsylvania.

Potamogeton tennesseensis (Tennessee pondweed) — [perennial forb] aquatic in ponds and slow to fast moving streams and rivers, scattered in southwestern Pennsylvania; OBL and listed as endangered in Pennsylvania and of conservation concern nationally.

Potamogeton vaseyi (Vasey's pondweed) — [perennial forb] aquatic widely scattered in lakes, ponds, lagoons or slow-moving rivers, OBL and listed as endangered.

Potamogeton zosteriformis (Flat-stemmed pondweed) — [perennial forb] aquatic in lakes, ponds and slow-moving streams with a pH range of 5.8 to 7.0, mostly northwestern glaciated areas, but also east central Pennsylvania, OBL and listed as rare.

Potentilla anserina (Silverweed) — [perennial forb] Very rare on gravelly to sandy moist shores, OBL; northwest and southeast. Grows 6 to 9 inches in full sun in mesic to moist, medium textured, sandy loams to sand at least 10 inches deep with a pH range of 6.0 to 8.0. Yellow flowers in summer; most often used for erosion control and bank stabilization. AKA *Argentina anserina*.

Potentilla arguta (Tall cinquefoil) — [perennial forb] dry upland rocky ledges, fields and woods, UPL. Mostly along the Delaware River, widely scattered elsewhere. Grows 15 to 40 inches, white flowers in early summer; sun to part shade in dry to mesic, medium textured, sandy loam with a minimum depth of 10 inches and a pH range of 6.0 to 8.0. Intolerant of limestone-based soils, adaptable to anaerobic conditions.

Potentilla canadensis (Cinquefoil) — [perennial forb] statewide except scattered in northern tier counties in open, dry woodlands and fields. Grows 2 to 4 inches with white to yellow flowers in spring in full to part sun on dry, well-drained soils.

Potentilla fruticosa (Shrubby cinquefoil) — [tree/shrub] very rare on damp rocky ground, usually on limestone, FACW; reported only in Monroe and Northampton counties, endangered. Grows to 3 feet with bright yellow flowers, early summer through frost; well-drained, reasonably rich soil, but will tolerate clay, rocky, or slightly alkaline soils.

Potentilla norvegica ssp. monspeliensis (Strawberry-weed) — [perennial forb] statewide on disturbed ground and along roadsides; FACU. Grows 1 to 2 feet from a basal rosette with yellow flowers in summer; grows in full to part sun in dry to mesic well drained soils of any fertility.

Potentilla norvegica ssp. monspeliensis (Strawberry-weed) [annual forb] — statewide in woodlands, meadows, stream banks, lakeshores, FACU. Grows 1 to 3 feet with yellow summertime flowers in full to part sun on fertile to sterile soils including loams, clay loams, sandy loams and stony soil.

Potentilla paradoxa (Bushy cinquefoil) [annual forb] — sandy lake shores, river banks and bars, and low fields, along Lake Erie and in Lehigh County and listed as endangered. Grows 8 to 12 inches with yellow flowers in summer on moist to wet sandy loams erie lehigh county endangered; yellow flowers in summer sun moist to wet sandy soil in sun to part sun.

Potentilla simplex (Oldfield cinquefoil) — [perennial forb] dry upland woods, fields, meadows and along roadsides, FACU-; statewide. Prostrate stems to 20 inches, yellow flowers in late spring; sun to shade in dry, sandy loam. pH 5.5 to 7.

Potentilla tridentata (Three-toothed cinquefoil, shrubby fivefingers) — [perennial forb] rare on dry ridge tops and in open woods, northeast, and endangered. Grows 1 to 10 inches, white flowers in summer; sun to part shade in dry to moist sandy loam, pH 5.5 to 7. AKA *Sibbaldiopsis tridentata*.

Prenanthes alba (White rattlesnake root) — [perennial forb] moist open woods, along shady roadsides and in thickets, FACU. Statewide, especially southeast. Grows up to 8 inches, white and pinkish-lavender flowers in late summer into fall; part shade to shade in moist, well-drained soils. AKA *Nabalus albus*.

Shrubby cinquefoil (Potentilla fruiticosa)

Prenanthes altissima (Rattlesnake-root) — [perennial forb] statewide in open deciduous or mixed woods, shaded slopes, bluffs, and such disturbed areas as roadsides; FACU-. Grows 2 to 6 feet with greenish white flowers in late summer; grow in light to dappled shade in rich, loamy soil that is slightly dry to moist; rocky and sandy soils are tolerated. Plant size will vary widely depending on fertility, moisture conditions and light levels.

Prenanthes crepidinea (Rattlesnake-root) — [perennial forb] widely scattered in western Pennsylvania and listed as endangered; prefers moist, rich, deciduous woods, lowland or upland woods, thickets, low prairies, wet areas in rich soil; FACU. Grows up to 10 feet but more commonly about 3 feet in rich, humusy soils in part sun to part shade, with greenish-white flowers in late summer.

Prenanthes racemosa (Glaucous rattlesnake root) — [perennial forb] Very rare in bogs, marshy flats, tallgrass prairies, wet meadows and sandy alluvial soils of stream banks; FACW- and believed to be extirpated. Grows 3 feet, pinkish flowers in summer in full sun in wet to mesic, well drained sandy loams.

Prenanthes serpentaria (Lion's-foot) — [perennial forb] dry oak-hickory woodlands, clearings and edges, oak flats and pine woodlands, in Piedmont areas, especially Bucks, Montgomery, Chester and Delaware Counties. Grows up to 48 inches in sun to part shade with white to pale pink flowers in summer on dry to mesic, circumneutral soils.

Prenanthes trifoliolata (Gall-of-the-earth) —

[perennial forb] statewide in moist sandy or rocky oak-hickory woodlands, swampy thickets, cliffs and bluffs, as well as shale barrens. Grows to about 2 feet in part sun to part shade in rich, usually hickory, woodland soils that are well drained and slightly dry to mesic.

Proserpinaca palustris var. crebra (Common mermaid-weed) — [perennial forb] aquatic, scattered statewide in bogs, marshes, swamps and vernal ponds, OBL.

Proserpinaca pectinata (Comb-leaved mermaid-weed) — [perennial forb] aquatic in swamps or bogs, reported only in southern Bucks County and listed as extirpated; OBL.

Prunella vulgaris ssp. lanceolata (Heal-all) — [perennial forb] mesic fields, upland woods, floodplains, and along roadsides, FACU+; statewide. Grows up to 24 inches, violet-blue to pink or white flowers in summer and fall; sun to part sun in moist rich loam of an texture, with a minimum depth of 10 inches and a pH range of 5.4 to 8.0. Intolerant of anaerobic conditions but adaptable to drought.

Prunus americana (Wild plum) — [tree/shrub] riparian areas, but also moist to dry open to wooded prairie ravines, pastures, roadsides, fencerows, ditch banks, and natural drainage areas, FACU; statewide. Shrub or small tree to 20 feet with white flowers in spring; full sun to part shade in average, dry to medium, well-drained, coarse to medium textured soils with a minimum depth of 24 inches and a pH range of 5.0 to 7.0. Tolerant of anaerobic conditions but not drought or shade and an excellent choice for limestone-based soils. Control spreading with sucker removal. Fruit used to make jams and jellies.

Prunus angustifolia (Chickasaw plum) — [tree/shrub] very rare in roadside thickets, pastures, fields, fencerows, stream banks and other disturbed areas, usually uplands and bottomlands in open and wooded-open edge sites; scattered in southeast (Piedmont). Grows up to 20 feet in full sun to part shade on a wide range of coarse to medium textured soils with a minimum depth of 24 inches and a pH range of 5.0 to 7.5. Intolerant of shade, drought and anaerobic conditions, but a good choice for limestone-based soils.

Prunus maritima (Beach plum) — [shrub] rare on sand dunes or sandy soils near the Atlantic coast; southeast (Atlantic Coastal Plain), endangered. Grows 6 to 12 feet with white flowers in spring, followed by fruit that attracts birds and other wildlife. Fruits are considered poisonous and should not be eaten. Grow in full sun, sandy to gravelly soils at least 20 inches deep, with a pH range of 5.8 to 7.7.

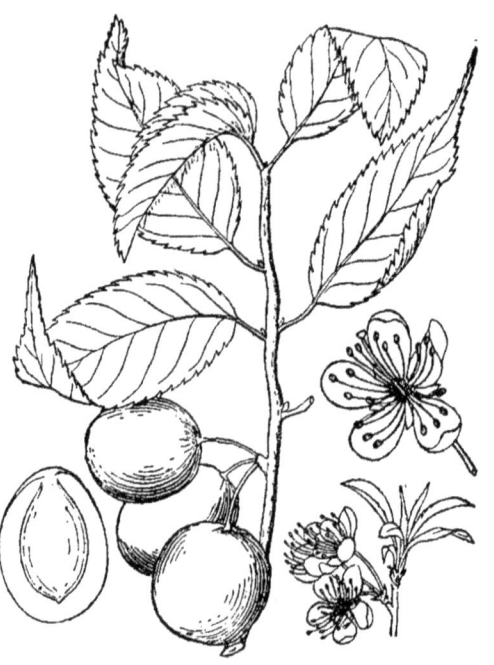

Wild plum (Prunus americana)

Prunus pensylvanica (Pin cherry) — [tree] areas characterized as water-shedding (rocky ridges, cliffs, dry woods, clearings) or water-receiving (sandy and gravelly banks, shores of rivers and lakes), FACU-; statewide. Shrub or tree to 40 feet with white flowers in spring; somewhat dry sites and shallow organic layers relatively low in nutrients. Soils very low in moisture may result in a shrub form of pin cherry. Adaptable to soils of all textures, requiring a minimum depth of 20 inches with a pH range of 4.3 to 7.3. Intolerant of shade, anaerobic conditions, limestone-based soils and drought.

Prunus pumila var. susquehanae (Sand cherry) — [shrub] open habitats with little shade from trees or other shrubs, typically along edges of openings or in stands where canopy closure has not occurred; scattered southeast. Sites are typically dry and excessively drained. Shrub to 5 feet with white flowers in spring; sandy, gravelly, and rocky soils, dunes, beaches, and outwash plains. Prefers coarse to medium textured soils at least 24 inches deep with a pH range of 5.9 to 7.0. Shade and limestone soils tolerant, but not anaerobic conditions.

Prunus serotina (Wild black cherry) — [tree] mesic woods and second-growth hardwood forests and old fields, especially on the Allegheny Plateau, on nearly all soil types. Prefers middle and lower slopes of eastern and northern exposures than the dry soils associated with south- or west-facing slopes, FACU; statewide. Grows to 100 feet with white flowers in spring; average, medium-moisture, well-drained, coarse to medium textured soils at least 36 inches deep with a pH range of 4.0 to 7.5. Intolerant of shade; grow in full sun to part part sun. A good choice for limestone-based soils but not suitable for anaerobic sites. Fruits used to make wines, jelly.

Prunus virginiana (Choke cherry) — [shrub] very acid to moderately alkaline, well-drained limestone residuum soil, at least 20 inches deep, of any texture, with pH ranging from 5.2 to 8.4, often in oak-pine forests, FACU; statewide. Grows 3 to 20 feet with white flowers in spring; sun to shade in dry to moist, circumneutral limestone-based sandy loam; intolerant of shade, poor drainage and prolonged flooding.

Pseudognaphalium macounii (Fragrant cudweed) [annual forb] — statewide in dry fields and barren ground, oak and pine savannas, rocky ridges and outcrops and woodland clearings or edges, generally biennial on the Allegheny Plataeu, UPL. Grows about 30 inches with white to yhellow flowers in summer to fall on dry to mesic well-drained gravelly to sandy loam; AKA *Gnaphalium macounii*.

Pseudognaphalium obtusifolium (Fragrant cudweed rabbit-tobacco, sweet everlasting) [annual forb] — statewide in dry clearings, woodland edges, fields, shale barrens and disturbed soils. Grows 9 to 30 inches with white flowers in late summer to autumn in full sun. Tolerant of a variety of dry to mesic soils, prefers a sandy loam with some silt and light shade is tolerated. AKA G*naphalium obtusifolium*

Ptelea trifoliata (Hoptree, Wafer ash) — [tree/shrub] gravelly areas, alluvial thickets and rocky slopes, FAC. Mostly northwest and southeast (Delaware River Valley); scattered elsewhere and endangered. Shrub or small tree to 10 to 35 feet in sun to part sun in well-drained, average, mesic to moist, coarse to medium textured soils at least 30 inches deep with a pH between 4.8 and 7.0. Intolerant of drought or anaerobic conditions.

Pteridium aquilinum (Northern bracken fern) — [fern/ally] sunny to partly shaded dry areas with infertile soil in barrens, pastures, and open woodlands in moderately to strong acid soil, abundant, forming large colonies. Fronds 18 to 50 inches; rhizome: very long creeping. Grow in sun to part shade in dry to mesic, sterile sandy to well drained, coarse to medium textured, silt loam, pH 4.5 to 7.0 at least 10 inches deep. Intolerant of anaerobic conditions. Unpalatable to deer and spreads to form large naturalized colonies.

Ptilimnium capillaceum (Mock bishop's weed) — [perennial forb] reported only in southern Bucks and Philadelphia Counties in wet soil along a stream; OBL and listed as endangered.

Pycnanthemum clinopodioides (Basil mountain-mint) — [perennial forb] dry slopes in the Piedmont. Grows 12 to 30 inches with white to pale lavender flowers in late summer, with a preference for dry to mesic well drained soils in sun to part sun.

Pycnanthemum incanum (Mountain mint) — [perennial forb] moist old fields, thickets, and barrens. Mostly southeast (Central Appalachians, Piedmont), scattered elsewhere. Grows up to 36 inches, with purple to white flowers in late summer; sun to part sun in dry moist sandy loam.

Pycnanthemum muticum (Mountain mint) — [perennial forb] moist woods, thickets, meadows and swales, FACW. Mostly southeast (Piedmont), scattered elsewhere. Grows 15 to 30 inches, purple to white flowers in late summer; sun to part shade in moist rich loam, pH 5.5 to 7.5.

Pycnanthemum tenuifolium (Mountain mint) — [perennial forb] moist fields, stream banks and floodplains, FACW. Mostly southeast (Piedmont), scattered elsewhere. Grows 20 to 30 inches, purple to white flowers in late summer; sun to part sun in moist rich loam.

Pycnanthemum torrei (Torrey's mountain-mint) — [perennial forb] upland thickets and woods, mostly southeastern Pennsylvania, listed as endangered. Grows 18 to 24 inches in sun to part shade with purple to white flowers in late summer; prefers well drained, mesic sandy to silt loams.

Pycnanthemum verticillatum (Mountain-mint) — [perennial forb] statewide in rocky meadows, woodlands, swamps, marshes and abandoned fields, FAC. Grows 2 to 4 feet with white flowers in mid to late summer. Easily cultivated in full to part sun in moist to slightly dry fertile loamy soil.

Pycnanthemum virginianum (Mountain mint) — [perennial forb] boggy fields, moist woods and floodplains, FAC; Mostly southeast, scattered elsewhere. Grows up to 36 inches, purple to white flowers in late summer; sun to part shade in moist, sandy loam, pH 5.5 to 7.

Pyrola americana (Wild lily-of-the-valley) — [perennial forb] moist to dry, deciduous or coniferous forests, and bogs, statewide except north central counties; FAC. Grows 6 to 15 inches with white-pink flowers in summer; prefers humusy soils in part shade to shade in leaf litter.

Pyrola chlorantha (Wintergreen) — [perennial forb] moist to dry coniferous and deciduous forests, generally eastern Pennsylvania; UPL. Grows 6 to 10 inches in part shade to dappled shade on mesic to moist well drained, humusy soils, with a preference for moist soil; whitish-green flowers in summer.

Pyrola elliptica (Shinleaf) — [perennial forb] bogs, fens, swamps and moist to wet coniferous woods; statewide. Grows 6 to 12 inches, white flowers in early summer; part shade to shade in dry to moist acidic loam, pH 4 to 6.

Quercus alba (White oak) — [tree] moist to fairly dry deciduous forests, usually on deeper, well-drained loams but sometimes on thin soils of dry upland slopes and sometimes on barrens, FACU. Grows to 100 feet; rich, moist, acidic, well-drained, coarse to medium textured soils at least 30 inches deep with a pH range of 4.5 to 6.8. Tolerates shade, but prefers full sun. Adapts to a wide variety of soil conditions with good drought tolerance, but not anaerobic conditions. Natural hybrid with *Q. prinus* is Saul oak.

Quercus bicolor (Swamp white oak) — [tree] low swamp forests, moist slopes, poorly drained uplands, FACW+; statewide. Grows to 70 feet; average, medium to wet, acidic soil of any texture in full sun. Requires minimum depth of 40 inches and a pH range of 4.3 to 6.5. Low drought and limestone soil tolerance, but adaptable to anaerobic conditions.

Quercus coccinea (Scarlet oak) — [tree] poor soils of well-drained uplands, dry slopes and ridges, but sometimes on poorly drained sites; statewide except north central. Grows to 70 feet; average, dry to medium, well-drained soil in full sun. Prefers dry, acidic, coarse to medium textured, sandy soils at least 48 inches deep, with a pH of 4.5 to 6.9. Intolerant of shade, limestone soils and anaerobic conditions.

Quercus falcata (Southern red oak, Spanish oak) — [tree] moist, but more often dry, sandy upland woodlands, typically south- and west-facing, sometimes on dry ridgetops, on or near the Atlantic Coastal Plain; FACU-; southeast. Grows to 80 feet; sandy, loamy, or clay soils of any texture, most commonly on red clay and glacial soils; does well on calcareous soils. Requires a minimum of 36 inches of soil depth, a pH between 4.8 and 7.0 and a 175 day growing season. Intolerant of anaerobic conditions, but an excellent choice for droughty sites.

Quercus ilicifolia (Scrub oak) — [tree] dry thickets and barrens in sandy, rocky, well-drained, nutrient-poor soils; statewide, but scattered north. Shrub to 15 feet; sun to part sun in dry to mesic, acidic sandy or gravelly soils.

Quercus imbricaria (Shingle oak) — [tree] mesic to somewhat dry uplands and slopes, sometimes in bottoms and ravines, FAC; mostly southwest; scattered east. Grows 40 to 60 feet in full sun in well-drained, humusy, rich, mesic to moist, coarse to medium textured soils at least 24 inches deep and with a pH range of 4.5 to 6.0. Intolerant of shade and anaerobic conditions. Formerly a source of shingles, hence the common name.

Quercus macrocarpa (Bur oak) — [tree] prairies, poorly drained areas, riparian slopes and bottomlands, typically on limestone and sometimes calcareous clays. Prominent in oak-basswood, upland oak-hickory and mix-oak communities, more often in coarsely-textured soil and less often on clays FAC-; mostly south, especially southwest. Grows 60 to 80 feet in medium to dry, average, well-drained soils of any texture, at least 28 inches deep and with a pH range of 4.5 to 7.5. Prefers full sun to part sun and well-drained mesic to moist loams, but is intolerant of anaerobic conditions. An excellent choice for droughty sites.

Quercus marilandica (Blackjack oak) — [tree] dry, sterile soils on ridges, rocky outcrops, disturbed fields, glades and especially serpentine barrens; southwest. Grows 30 to 50 feet in part shade on a variety of dry, acidic, coarse to medium textured soils at least 24 inches deep with a pH range of 4.6 to 5.6. Intolerant of shade, limestone soils and anaerobic conditions, but a good choice for droughty sites with a minimum of a 185-day growing season.

Quercus muehlenbergii (Chinquapin oak, Yellow oak) – Generally southwest, southeast and in the central Appalachians. Grows 40 to 60 feet in alkaline soils on limestone outcrops and well-drained upland slopes often in mixed hardwood forests, and sometimes on similar soils along streams, more often on southerly aspects. In cultivation, it appears to prefer moist, fertile, medium-textured and well drained soils in full sun, and may take up to 30 years before producing acorns. Grow on medium textured moderately-fertile soils with a minimum depth of 28 inches and a pH range of 5.0 to 8.0. Intolerant of shade and anaerobic conditions, but a good choice for droughty conditions and limestone-based sites. AKA *Quercus muhlenbergii*.

Quercus palustris (Pin oak) — [tree] poorly drained clay soils in bottomlands intermittently flooded during dormancy but not during the growing season, such as clay flats, depressions where water accumulates in winter, and clay ridges of first bottoms. Prefers level or near level moist uplands such as glacial till plains, FACW; statewide, except northern tier. Grows to 80 feet on average, mesic to wet, medium to fine textured soils at least 30 inches deep, with a pH range of 4.5 to 6.5. Intolerant of shade, drought and limestone-based soils, but adaptable to anaerobic conditions. Prefers moist loams, but tolerates poorly drained soils and occasional flooding.

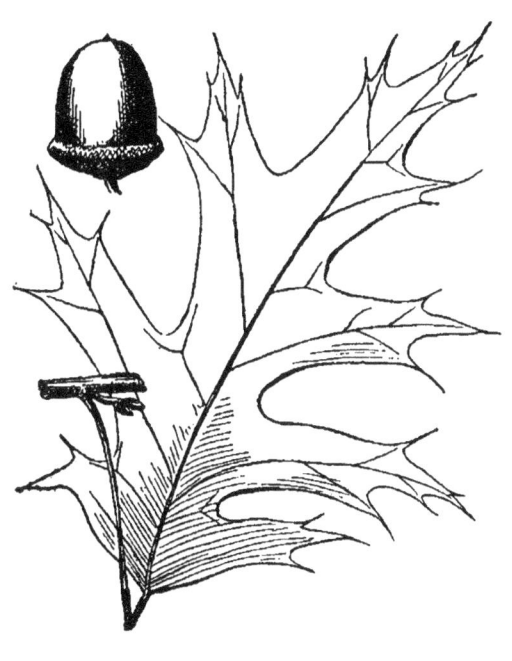

Red oak (*Quercus rubra*)

Quercus phellos (Willow oak) — [tree] rare in bottomland flood plains, but also on stream banks, terraces and sometimes poorly drained uplands. Does best on clay loam ridges of new alluvium and diminishes from bottomland to higher terraces; FAC+; mostly southeast. Grows 40 to 75 feet in full sun in well-drained, mesic to moist, medium to fine textured, moderately fertile soils at least 12 inches deep with a pH rang of 4.5 to 6.5. Intolerant of shade, anaerobic conditions, drought and limestone-based soils and but adapts to some urban pollution.

Quercus prinoides (Dwarf chestnut oak) — [tree] dry rocky soils, such as sandstone or shale outcrops associated with oak pine types; statewide except north. Shrub to 12 feet; part shade to shade in dry sandy loam.

Quercus prinus (Chestnut oak) — [tree] rocky, xeric, upland forest, dry ridges, mixed deciduous forests on shallow soils usually on south and west-facing upper slopes, FACW; statewide. Grows to 80 feet; dry, rocky, infertile soil with a low moisture-holding capacity, although can grow best in rich, well-drained soils along streams; ridge dominance is suggested by its ability to withstand drought.

Prefers coarse to medium textured moderately fertile soils at least 36 inches deep with a pH range of 4.5 to 6.5. Somewhat tolerant of shade and limestone-based soils, but not anaerobic conditions. *AKA Quercus montana.*

Quercus rubra (Northern red oak) — [tree] among the most common trees in Pennsylvania and found on rich mesic slopes and well-drained uplands, occasionally on dry slopes or poorly drained uplands, sandy plains, rock outcrops, and the edges of floodplains, usually on north- and east-facing slopes. Often found in lower and middle slopes, in coves, ravines and on valley floors, FACU-; statewide. Grows to 100 feet; average, dry to medium moisture, acidic soil in full sun. Prefers deep fertile, sandy, finely-textured soils with good drainage and a relatively high water table. Soils are derived from a variety of parent materials including glacial outwash, sandstone, shale, limestone, gneiss, schist, or granite. Adaptable to all soil textures with low fertility requirements, but needs a minimum of 36 inches of soil depth and a pH range of 4.3 to 7.3. Intolerant of anaerobic conditions and drought, somewhat tolerant of shade. Presence indicates a 100-day growing season.

Quercus shumardii (Shumard oak) — [tree] very rare on mesic slopes and bottoms, stream banks and poorly drained uplands. Prefers rich sites with moist, well-drained loamy soils found on terraces, colluvial sites and bluffs adjacent to large and small streams; FAC+; south-central along the Allegheny front. Grows 40 to 60 feet in full sun in well-drained, coarse to medium textured, dry to mesic, moderately fertile soils at least 40 inches deep with a pH range of 5.0 to 7.6. Intolerant of shade, anaerobic conditions, and limestone-based soils, but a good choice for droughty sites.

Quercus stellata (Post oak) — [tree] xeric to mesic uplands with southerly or westerly exposure, terraces of smaller streams in well-drained soil, dry gravelly and sandy ridges, dry clays, prairies and limestone hills, woodlands and deciduous forests, UPL; southeast; scattered in Central Appalachians. Grows to 100 feet; rich, moist, acidic, well-drained coarse to medium soils with a minimum depth of 36 inches and a pH range of 4.8 to 6.5. Intolerant of shade and anaerobic conditions, but a good choice for droughty sites. Adapts to a wide variety of soil conditions from poor dry sandy soils to moist heavy loams, especially where a heavy clay subsurface layer is within a foot of the surface or bedrock is within two or three feet. Also grows in deep sands and dry clay hills.

Quercus velutina (Black oak) — [tree] xeric slopes and upland areas, especially with southerly or westerly facing slopes, occasionally on sandy lowlands and poorly drained uplands and terraces; statewide. Grows to 100 feet; moist, rich, well-drained sites, but sensitive to competition on these sites and is more often found on dry, nutrient-poor, coarse-textured soils, especially sandy or gravelly sites or heavy glacial clay hillsides. Adapts to any soil texture with a minimum depth of 40 inches and a pH range of 4.5 to 6.5. Intolerant of anaerobic conditions, limestone-based soils and drought and needs a 140-day growing season.

Ranunculus abortivus (Small-flowered crowfoot) [Annual/Perennial Forb] — statewide in open low woodlands, clearings, borders and along paths, damp shores, especially riverbanks, old pastures and abandoned fields, FACW-. Grows 1 to 3 feet with yellow flowers from early spring to midsummer in part sun to part shade on mesic to moist, medium to fine textured, somewhat fertile soils with a ph range of 5.0 to 7.5 at least 4 inches deep. Mildly toxic, shade tolerant but not suitable for anaerobic or droughty conditions.

Ranunculus allegheniensis (Allegheny crowfoot) [annual forb] — generally southwestern Pennsylvania in fields, rich woodlands and rocky, calcareous slopes, FAC. Grows to 18 inches with yellow flowers in late spring in mesic to moist loams.

Ranunculus ambigens (Water-plantain spearwort) — [perennial forb] scattered statewide in swamps, marshes, ponds, muddy ditches and creeks, OBL. Grows to 10 inches with yellow flowers in spring; grow in moist to wet rich loams in sun to part sun.

Ranunculus aquatilis var. diffusus (White water-crowfoot) — [perennial forb] aquatic in mostly eastern Pennsylvania lakes and ponds, in and along streams and rivers, typically in slow moving water; OBL.

Ranunculus fascicularis (Early buttercup) — [perennial forb] rare in dry upland woods, grasslands and thickets, FACU. Scattered southeast; endangered. Grows 4 to 10 inches, yellow flowers in spring; sun to shade in dry sandy loam.

Ranunculus flabellaris (Yellow water-crowfoot) — [perennial forb] widely scattered in northwestern, south central and eastern Pennsylvania in quiet, shallow water and muddy shorelines; OBL.

Ranunculus flammula var. ovalis (Creeping spearwort) — [perennial forb] muddy, wet ground, including shores to shallow water; observed only in Pike, Northampton, Montour, Dauphin, Lancaster and Philadelphia counties; believed to be extirpated. Prostrate stems to 20 inches, yellow flowers in summer; sun to part sun in moist to wet, medium to fine textured, moderately fertile soil at least 10 inches deep with a pH range of 6.0 to 7.5. Tolerant of shade, and anaerobic conditions, but not limestone-based soils or drought.

Ranunculus hederaceus (Long-stalked crowfoot) — [perennial forb] shallow coastal plain water, moist depressions and the edges of lakes and ponds, southern Chester County, OBL and reported as extirpated in Pennsylvania.

Ranunculus hispidus (Marsh, Hairy buttercup) — [perennial forb] Three varieties: *var. caricetorum,* statewide in swampy woods, marshes, meadows, stream banks and alluvial thickets, ditches (FAC); *var. hispidus,* rich dry to mesic woods, usually oak-hickory, and meadows (FAC); *var. nitidus,*

Creeping spearwort (Ranunculus flammula)

wet, low woodlands, swamps, marshes and thickets, statewide (FACW). Generally grow to about 12 inches with yellow flowers in spring in sun to part shade. Prefers medium to fine textured, fertile, mesic to moist soils at least four inches deep with a pH range of 4.5 to 8.0. Tolerant of dappled shade, but not anaerobic conditions or drought and appreciates loams with decaying leaves.

Ranunculus micranthus (Small-flowered crowfoot) — [perennial forb] moist to dry woodlands, shale slopes, meadows, clearings, commonly on alluvium in southern Pennsylvania, FACU. Grows to 10 inches with yellow flowers in spring; grow in part sun to part shade on well drained mesic to slightly dry sandy to silty loams.

Ranunculus pensylvanicus (Bristly crowfoot) [Annual/Perennial Forb] — widely scattered, especially northwest and northeast, in wet meadows, stream banks, bogs, moist clearings, woodland depressions and marshy bottomlands, OBL. Grows 1 to 3 feet with yellow flowers in summer in moist to wet, fertile soils at least 4 inches deep with a pH or 5.0 to 7.5 in part sun to part shade. Intolerant of drought and anaerobic conditions.

Ranunculus pusillus (Low spearwort) [annual forb] — shallow ponds, swamps and swales, OBL; scattered south. Grows to 18 inches with yellow flowers in spring in moist to wet loams in full to part sun.

Ranunculus recurvatus (Hooked crowfoot) — [perennial forb] rich, low moist woods, FAC+; statewide. Grows 6 to 20 inches, yellow flowers in early summer; part shade to shade in moist rich loam.

Ratibida pinnata (Prairie coneflower) — [perennial forb] rare in prairies and thickets, as well as woodland edges. Mostly west; believed to be extirpated. Yellow flowers in summer; grow in well-drained medium moisture average soils in full sun. Prefers sandy and clay soils, but tolerates poor, dry soils. Grow in average, medium moisture, well-drained soil in full sun.

Rhamnus alnifolia (Alder-leaved buckthorn) — [shrub] rare in fens, calcareous marshes and wet thickets, OBL; mostly northwest; widely scattered elsewhere. Shrub to 3 feet with greenish flowers in late spring; moist to wet rich organic loam, full to part sun. Prefers medium to fine textured, moderately fertile soils at least 12 inches deep with a pH range of 4.0 to 8.0. Tolerant of shade and an excellent choice for anaerobic and limestone-based soils, but intolerant of drought and requires a 100-day growing season.

Rhexia mariana (Maryland meadow-beauty) — [perennial forb] rare in savannas and meadows; marshes and bogs, especially the Atlantic Coastal Plain; OBL and endangered. Grows 1 to 3 feet in full to part sun in slightly acidic, mesic to wet, fertile sandy loams. White to pink flowers in summer; good for water gardens and pond areas.

Rhexia virginica (Meadow beauty or Handsome Harry) — [perennial forb] rich, acidic sandy soil in moist open areas, OBL. Mostly southeast, scattered elsewhere. Grows 10 to 40 inches, dark pink flowers in late summer; sun to part shade in wet rich sandy loam.

Rhododendron arborescens (Smooth azalea) — [shrub] mountain bogs, forested swamps and stream banks, FAC; mostly southwest, scattered elsewhere. Grows 10 to 35 feet in part shade in mesic to moist, coarse to medium textured well-drained soils at least 12 inches deep with a pH range of 4.2 to 5.7. Tolerates low-fertility soils, shade, some anaerobic conditions but not limestone-based soils or drought. Requires a 185-day growing season. White flowers in late spring, among the last to bloom. Intolerant of drought.

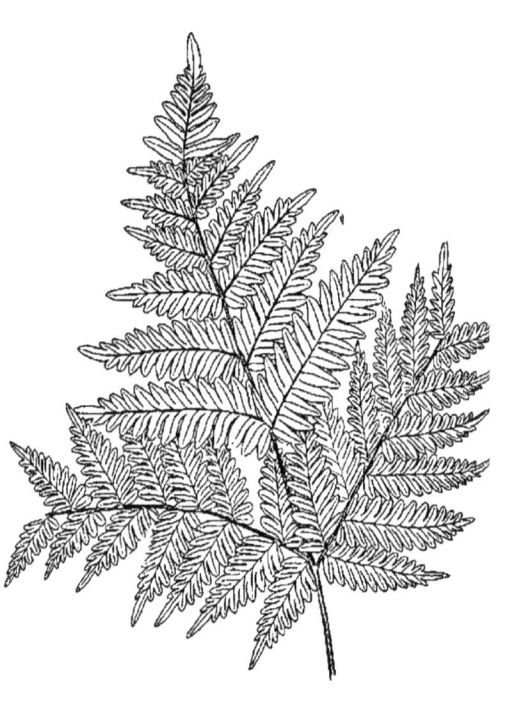

Northern bracken fern (Pteridium aquilinum)

Rhododendron atlanticum (Dwarf azalea) — [shrub] very rare in flat, moist, pine woodlands and savannas; reported only in southern York County and endangered. Grows 1 to 3 feet to form low colonies, sending up 1 to 3 foot, brief duration flowering stems with white to pinkish flowers. Grow in sandy, well-drained soil at least 12 inches deep with a pH between 4.2 and 5.7; prefers a dry to mesic habitat. Tolerant of shade, but not anaerobic conditions or limestone-based soils, and requires a 220-day growing season

Rhododendron calendulaceum (Flame azalea) — [shrub] very rare on south- and west-facing slopes in submesic to subxeric rocky open mountain woodlands; reported only in Somerset County and believed to be extirpated. Grows 6 to 12 feet with red, orange or yellow flowers in late spring to early summer. Grow in well-drained, mesic to moist, medium to fine textured soil soil in part shade; prefers pH range of 4.3 to 5.8 and a minimum soil depth of 14 inches. Needs a 200-day growing season. Some tolerance for anaerobic conditions, but not drought or limestone soils.

Rhododendron canadense (Rhodora) — [shrub] bogs, wet places with infertile, acidic soil, FACW; northeast. To 3 feet, with rose to purple flowers in spring; sun to part shade in mesic to wet, cold, coarse to medium textured, peaty soil at least 16

inches deep and a pH range of 4.0 to 5.3. Tolerant of shade, but not anaerobic conditions, drought or limestone-based soils.

Rhododendron canescens (Mountain azalea, Piedmont or southern pinxterbloom azalea) — [shrub] Generally southeast in dry to moist woods, pocosins, swamps and savannas, frequently along streams. Shrub to about 8 feet with pink flowers in spring, especially in acidic bogs in part shade. Grow in coarse to medium-textured soils at least 16 inches deep with a pH between 4.0 and 5.3. Prefers sun to part shade and a 120-day growing season. and is intolerant of anaerobic conditions, limestone soils and drought. Similar to *R. prinophyllum* and *R. periclymenoides*.

Rhododendron maximum (Rosebay) — [shrub] dry to moist woods, swamps, stream banks. FAC; statewide. Grows to 16 feet with creamy white flowers in early summer; part sun to part shade in mesic to moist, coarse to medium textured soils at least 18 inches deep with a pH range of 4.0 to 5.5. Forms vast woodland and woods edge colonies; manage as with any hybrid rhododendron. Well suited for droughty conditions, with low fertility needs, low anerobic tolerance and no limestone-soil adaptability. Needs a 150-day growing season.

Rhododendron periclymenoides (Pinxterflower) — [shrub] mixed deciduous forests along stream bottoms, bogs, shaded mountainsides and ravines, FAC; statewide. Grows to 10 feet with white to pink flowers in spring; part sun to part shade in mesic to moist, coarse to medium textured, well-drained soils at least 8 inches deep with a pH range of 4.3 to 5.5. Prefers cool, moist locations in part shade in acidic, humusy, organically rich, medium moisture, moisture-retentive but well-drained soils. Adaptable to anaerobic conditions and drought, but not limestone-based soils, and needs a 190-day growing season.

Rhododendron periclymenoides x prinophyllum (Azalea) — [shrub] very rare in woods, thickets, swamp margins. Grows to 10 feet with white or pink flowers in spring; part sun to part shade in mesic to moist acid sandy loam, pH 4.5 to 5.5. White or pink flowers in spring. A natural hybrid.

Rhododendron prinophyllum (Mountain azalea) — [tree/shrub] dry to moist woods thickets, rocky slopes, FAC; statewide. Grows to 10 feet with white to pink flowers in spring; part shade in rich humusy, acidic, medium moisture, well-drained soil in part shade.

Rhododendron viscosum (Swamp azalea) — [tree/shrub] swamps, bogs, stream margins and thickets, FACW+; mostly east. Grows to 10 feet; part shade in moist to wet acidic silty loam of any texture, at least 14 inches deep with a pH range of 4.0 to 7.0 and a 160-day growing season. Shade, flood and drought tolerant, but not suitable for limestone-based soils. White flowers in spring.

Rhus copallinum (Shining sumac) — [tree] hillsides, open woods, glades, fields and along the margins of roadsides; statewide. Grows to 20 feet; full sun to part shade in dry to medium, well-drained soils of any texture at least 14 inches deep and with a pH range of 5.3 and 7.5. Intolerant of poorly drained soils, shade and limestone-based soils, but adaptable to anaerobic conditions and drought. AKA *Rhus copallina*.

Rhus glabra (Smooth sumac) — [tree/shrub] open woodlands, prairies, dry rocky hillsides, canyons, and protected ravines; statewide. Grows to 15 feet; full sun to part shade in dry to medium, coarse to medium textured, well-drained soils at least 24 inches deep with a pH between 5.3 and 7.5. Intolerant of poorly drained soils, shade, anaerobic conditions and limestone-based soils.

Rhus typhina (Staghorn sumac) — [tree/shrub] old fields, roadsides, woods edges, statewide. Shrub or small tree to 30 feet; full sun to part shade in dry to mesic, coarse to medium textured, well-drained soils at least 24 inches deep with a pH range of 4.5 to 7.2. Intolerant of poorly drained soils and anaerobic conditions, but good choices for limestone-based soils and droughty sites. AKA *Rhus hirta*.

Rhynchospora alba (White beak-rush) — [perennial forb] statewide, but especially eastern Pennsylvania, in swamps and bogs; prefers acidic, boggy open sites, often on floating mats of peat, sometimes on rocky shorelines, and poor fens; OBL.

Rhynchospora capitellata (Beak-rush) — [perennial forb] statewide, but especially Piedmont, in moist to wet meadows, fens and bogs, on stream banks and in low, open flatwoods, including vernal ponds; OBL.

Rhynchospora fusca (Brown beak-rush) — [perennial graminoid] reported only in Luzerne and Sullivan counties in sands and peats of bogs, seeps and glacial lake and pond shores; OBL and listed as extirpated in Pennsylvania.

Rhynchospora gracilenta (Beak-rush) — [perennial graminoid] reported only in Lancaster County in a sphagnum bog; prefers moist to wet sandy, peaty soils of bogs, seeps, savannas and flatwoods; OBL and listed as extirpated in Pennsylvania.

Ribes americanum (Wild black currant) — [shrub] moist woods, marshes and thickets, FACW; statewide. Grows to 6 feet with yellow flowers in spring; sun to shade in mesic to moist soil of any texture at least 12 inches deep and a pH range of 5.0 to 7.8. A good choice for droughty sites, but poor for anaerobic conditions carries a disease that kills white pine.

Ribes cynosbati (Prickly gooseberry) — [shrub] moist, thin, usually rocky woods; statewide except southeast. Grows to 6 feet; part sun to part shade in moist rich loam. Yellow flowers; fruit: dull red to purple.

Ribes glandulosum (Skunk currant) — [shrub] mostly northern Pennsylvania as well as along the Allegheny front in wet woodlands including spruce-fir forests, conifer and conifer-hardwood woodland swamps, bogs, thickets and on moist, rocky slopes; FACW. Grows to about 16 inches high by 3 feet wide in part sun to part shade with a preference for dappled light, in well drained acidic to circumneutral sandy to silt loams; fruit is edible.

Ribes hirtellum (Northern wild gooseberry) — [shrub] moist, rocky woods; cliffs; bogs and fens, calcareous marshes, swamps, FAC; scattered statewide. Shrub grows 2 to 4 feet with yellow flowers and dull red fruit; sun to shade in mesic to moist rocky circumneutral soils. Carries a disease that kills nearby white pine (*Pinus strobus*).

Ribes lacustre (Bristly black currant) — [shrub] rare in mountain along streams, wet meadows, forests and cool wet woodlands, swamps, FACW; widely scattered north. Grows 3 to 4 feet with green flowers and black fruit; sun to shade in mesic to moist rocky soils at least 12 inches deep with a pH between 5.0 and 7.8. Tolerant of shade, but not drought or anaerobic conditions and carries a disease that kills white pine *(Pinus strobus)*.

Ribes missouriense (Missouri gooseberry) — [shrub] thickets, pastures, prairie ravines and rich upland woodlands on sites less than 2,000 feet elevation; endangered in Pennsylvania. Scattered in south-central counties. Grows 6 to 12 feet in part sun to part shade with white-greenish flowers in spring. Grow in loamy to rocky soil with organic matter to retain moisture, mesic to slightly dry conditions. Lack of flowers and fruit suggest too much shade.

Ribes rotundifolium (Wild gooseberry) — [shrub] throughout the Ridge and Valley as well as northwestern Pennsylvania in rich, rocky upland woods, slopes, boulderfields, grassy balds and heaths.

Robinia pseudoacacia (Black locust) — [tree] open woods on moist slopes and floodplains with a high probability of flooding in any given year, with pH minimum of 4.0, FACU-; statewide. Grows to 80 feet; rich, moist, often limestone-derived soils of any texture at least 36 inches deep with a pH range of 4.6 to 8.2; intolerant of shade, anaerobic conditions, and heavy or poorly drained soils, although tolerant of periodic flooding. Good choice for droughty sites.

Rorippa palustris (Marsh watercress) [annual forb] — poorly drained prairies, depressions, flats and swales, meadow sloughs, floodplain woodlands, thickets and estuaries, margins of ponds and small rivers and marshes, OBL, widely scattered, mostly Allegheny Plateau. Grows 18 to 40 inches with yellow flowers in summer in full to part sun on muddy soils containing clay or silt; flourishes in areas prone to occasional flooding.

Rosa blanda (Meadow rose) — [shrub] dry, open woods, hillsides, prairies, roadsides, widely scattered statewide. Shrub to 6 feet with pink flowers in early summer; full sun in dry rocky soils.

Rosa carolina (Pasture rose) — [shrub] dry, rocky or sandy fields and meadows, UPL; statewide. Shrub to 53 feet with pink flowers in early summer;

sun to part sun in moist to wet, coarse to medium textured, well-drained sandy soil at least 12 inches deep with a pH range of 4.0 to 7.0; best flowering and disease resistance in full sun with good air circulation and mulch. Use as a native alternative to the invasive multiflora rose. A good choice for droughty sites, but not for anaerobic conditions or limestone-based soils.

Rosa palustris (Swamp rose) — [shrub] swamps; wet thickets; marshy shores of streams, ponds and lakes, OBL; statewide. Shrub to 8 feet with pink flowers in summer; sun to part shade in mesic to moist, medium to fine textured rich soil at least 18 inches deep with a pH range of 4.0 to 7.0. Shade tolerant and adaptable to anaerobic conditions, but not limestone-based soils or drought.

Rosa virginiana (Wild rose) — [shrub] thickets, meadows, pastures, open woods, usually in a moist soil, FAC; widely scattered statewide except north-central. Shrub to 6 feet with pink flowers in summer; sun to part sun in dry to mesic, coarse to medium textured soils with moderate fertility and a minimum depth of 16 inches and pH range of 5.0 to 7.0. Somewhat adaptable to shade, but not anaerobic conditions, limestone soils or drought. Use as a native alternative to the invasive multiflora rose.

Rubus allegheniensis (Allegheny blackberry) — [shrub] old fields, open woods, clearings, FACU; statewide. Stems to 6 feet with white flowers followed by black fruit; sun to part shade in mesic, medium to fine textured soil at least 12 inches deep with a pH range of 4.6 to 7.5. Tolerant of shade and an excellent choice for droughty sites and limestone soils, but not for anaerobic conditions.

Rubus canadensis (Smooth blackberry) — [shrub] cool moist woods, rocky slopes, thickets; scattered north and Allegheny Mountains. Stems 3 to 10 feet with white flowers followed by black fruit;

Pasture rose (*Rosa carolina*)

part sun to part shade in moist sandy loam.

Rubus enslenii (Southern dewberry) — [shrub] widely scattered, but concentrated in the Piedmont on sandy banks; FACU.

Rubus flagellaris (Prickly dewberry) — [shrub] rocky to shaly slopes and cliffs and in fields, FACU; statewide. Stems prostrate and rooting at tips, with white flowers becoming black fruits; part sun to part shade in dry to moist sandy loam of any texture at least 6 inches deep with a pH between 5.0 and 7.0. Strong hedge potential, but low tolerance for anaerobic conditions, limestone soils or drought.

Rubus hispidus (Swamp dewberry) — [shrub] bogs, swamps, moist woods, thickets and barrens, FACW; statewide. Trailing stems that root at tips with white flowers becoming black fruits; part sun to part shade in dry to moist sandy loam of any texture at least 2 inches deep with a pH between 4.5 and 7.0. Intolerant of shade, anaerobic conditions or limestone soils.

Rubus idaeus var. strigosus (Red raspberry) — [shrub] rocky woods, clearings and thickets, FAC-; statewide except Central Appalachians. Stems to 6 feet with white flowers becoming red fruit; part sun to part shade in dry to moist sandy loam at least 12 inches deep with a pH range of 5.0 to 7.5; a good choice for droughty sites.

Rubus occidentalis (Black-cap raspberry) — [shrub] open woods; bluffs; thickets; stream banks; wet meadows, roadsides and pastures; statewide. Stems 3 to 6 feet with white flowers becoming black fruits; part sun to part shade in dry to moist, medium to fine textured, moderately fertile, sandy loam at least 12 inches deep with a pH range of 5.2 to 7.5. Good choice for limestone-based soils but not for anaerobic conditions.

Rubus odoratus (Purple-flowering raspberry) — [shrub] moist, shaded cliffs, ledges and rocky wooded slopes; statewide. Stems 3 to 6 feet with purple to maroon flowers becoming black fruit; full sun to part shade in mesic sandy loam of any texture at least 16 inches deep with a pH between 4.5 and 6.5. Intolerant of anaerobic conditions.

Rubus pensilvanicus (Pennsylvania blackberry) — [shrub] statewide in woodlands, fields, rocky banks and thickets. An upright, arching shrub to six feet with white flowers in spring leading to edible druplets up to three-quarters of an inch in diameter. Grow in rich, well-drained loams and sandy loams that are slightly acidic to circumneutral and dry to mesic. Prefers full sun to part shade; increase in light and moisture improves crop. Forms a dense thicket and good cover for birds.

Rubus pubescens (Dwarf blackberry) — [shrub] northern Pennsylvania, but scattered south, on moist slopes, and swampy to boggy woodlands, FACW. Grows to about 12 inches with white flowers in spring and fruit in summer; prefers mesic to moist, slightly acidic soils in part sun to part shade.

Rubus recurvicaulis (Arching dewberry) — [shrub] scattered statewide on dry, sandy to rocky soils; FACU.

Rubus setosus (Bristly blackberry) — [shrub] widely scattered in damp thickets and swamps; FACW. Grows to 3 feet with white flowers in spring and edible fruit in summer; grow in full sun to part shade in mesic to moist, well drained soils.

Rudbeckia fulgida (Eastern coneflower, Orange coneflower) — [perennial forb] two varieties: var. *fulgida* in prairies, pastures, open woods, scattered elsewhere; var. *speciosa* in mesic open woodlands and fields, mostly southeast. Both FAC and grow 2 to 4 feet with yellow to orange flowers in summer. Tolerant of hot, humid summers and some light shade; grow in well-drained, dry to medium average soil in full sun.

Rudbeckia hirta (Black-eyed Susan) — [perennial forb] mesic prairies, plains, meadows, pastures, savannas, woodland edges and openings, FACU-; statewide. Grows up to 36 inches, orange-yellow flowers in late summer. Two local varieties — *hirta* and *pulcherrima*; full sun in average, dry to mesic, medium to fine textured, well-drained soils at least 10 inches deep with a pH range of 6.0 to 7.0. Prefers moist, organically rich soils; intolerant of anerobic conditions, shade and limestone-based soils.

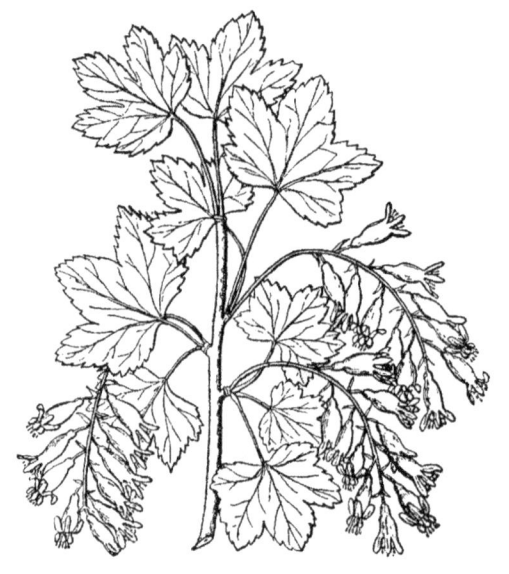

Wild black currant (Ribes americanum

Rudbeckia laciniata (Cut-leaf coneflower) — [perennial forb] moist, rich soils in fields, floodplains, open woods and thickets, FACW; statewide. Grows 2 to 9 feet, yellow flowers in late summer; sun to part shade in mesic to moist sandy loam of any texture at least 12 inches deep with a pH range of 4.5 to 7.0. Shade tolerant, and an excellent choice for droughty sites, but intolerant of anaerobic conditions.

Rudbeckia triloba (Three-lobed coneflower) — [perennial forb] mesic to wet woodlands, thickets, pastures, roadsides and meadows, frequently on limestone, FACU; statewide. Grows 18 to 60 inches, yellow to orange flowers in late summer; sun to part sun in dry to moist sandy loam.

Ruellia caroliniensis (Carolina petunia) — [perennial forb] very rare in sandy, open upland woodlands and stream banks; believed to be extirpated. Grows 1 to 3 feet, purple flowers in summer in part shade on moist to dry sandy soil; prefers soils without humus that are nutrient poor.

Ruellia humilis (Fringed-leaved petunia) — [perennial forb] very rare in woodland openings and edges, thickets; UPL. Reported only in Franklin County; endangered. Grows 18 to 24 inches with pale lavender flowers throughout summer, especially if kept moist. Grow in well-drained, dry to medium moisture average soils of any texture at least 4 inches deep with a pH between 4.5 to 7.5 in full sun to part shade. Tolerant of shade, but not anaerobic conditions or limestone-based soils

Ruellia strepens (Limestone petunia) — [perennial forb] rare in open woodlands and rich wooded slopes and bluffs, typically over limestone; mostly south; FAC. Grows 1 to 3 feet, lilac to lavender flowers, summer, in part shade on well drained, organically rich, medium to fine textured soils at least 6 inches deep with a pH range of 6.0 to 8.5. Tolerates nearly full shade, adaptable to anaerobic conditions and an excellent choice for limestone-based soils.

Rumex altissimus (Tall dock) — [perennial forb] river bottomlands and wet woods margins in rich alluvial soils, FACW-. Mostly southeast; scattered elsewhere. Grows up to 50 inches, reddish-green flowers in early summer; sun to part sun in moist, rich sandy loam.

Rumex hastatulus (Heart sorrel) — [perennial forb] found in moist to dry ruderal or alluvial habitats including river valleys sandy plains and meadows; in Pennsylvania, reported only in Delaware County in an alluvial meadow; FACU-. Grows to about three feet with reddish flowers in summer in full to part sun, mesic to slightly dry well drained silt loams.

Rumex verticillatus (Swamp dock) — [perennial forb] bogs, marshes, wet swampy meadows, swamps, wet alluvial woods and swales, including shallow water; OBL. Mostly northwest. Grows 3 to 5 feet, white-green flowers in late spring to early summer. Prefers light shade to full sun in wet, mucky soil, including standing water.

Sabatia angularis (Common marsh-pink, rose pink) [annual forb] — thickets, marshes, rocky glades, openings in rocky woodlands and edges, fields, meadows, serpentine barrens, southern Pennsylvania especially southeast. Grows 18 to 24 inches with pink flowers in summer in full to part sun on sandy, peaty loams to mesic loams including sand, silt and rocky or gravelly material.

Sabatia campanulata (Slender marsh-pink) — [perennial forb] coastal plain swamps, reported only in southern Bucks county and listed as extirpated in Pennsylvania.

Saccharum giganteum (Giant beardgrass) — [perennial graminoid] wet soils in Atlantic Coastal Plain swamps, bogs, swales and riverbanks; FACW+, listed as extirpated in Pennsylvania, aka *Erianthus giganteus*. Prefers coarse to medium, mesic to wet, moderately fertile, soils with a minimum depth of 24 inches and a pH range of 3.5 to 7.0. Intolerant of shade, limestone soils and drought.

Sagina decumbens (Pearlwort) [annual forb] — open pine woods, fields, pastures and open waste ground in Carbon, Bucks, Montgomery and Philadelphia counties. Grows to six inches with flowers in spring to early summer in dry to mesic, sandy loam.

Sagina procumbens (Bird's-eye) — [perennial forb] statewide in weedy, wet to damp, gravelly or sandy soils along roadsides, sidewalk cracks, margins of paths or lawns, pond and lake margins, coastal rocks and sands, and sea cliffs; FACW-. Grows 2 to 8 inches with greenish-white flowers in mid to late spring; grow in full sun to light shade in rocky to sandy soils that remain moist during spring; a good groundcover.

Sagittaria australis (Appalachian arrowhead) — [perennial forb] aquatic found in slightly basic to slightly acidic ponds, lakes and swamps as well as backwater pools, wet woods and alluvial meadows; southern Pennsylvania, especially lower Piedmont and Atlantic Coastal Plain.

Sagittaria calycina (Long-lobed arrowhead) [annual forb] — tidal mud flats and mucky backwaters of lakes and rivers, OBL in the Atlantic Coastal Plain and listed as endangered. Grows to four inches with white-yellow-red flowers in sun to part shade in mucky, moist to wet soils.

Sagittaria filiformis (Arrowhead) — [perennial forb] Aquatic found in ponds, lakes and drainage canals, OBL; reported only in lower Bucks County and listed as extirpated in Pennsylvania.

Sagittaria graminea var. graminea (Grass-leaved sagittaria) — [perennial forb] aquatic; streams, lakes and mudflats, erect or immersed or submerged in shallow water. OBL. Mostly eastern third of the state, scattered west. Blooms in summer; full sun in shallow water in silty soil.

Sagittaria latifolia var. latifolia (Wapato, or duck potato) — [perennial forb] aquatic; wet ditches, pools, and margins of streams, lakes and ponds, OBL; statewide. Grows 12 to 48 inches, white flowers in summer; plant in mud at the margins of a pond or in containers in a water garden, either along the shore or in up to 6 to 12 inches of water. Prefers medium to fine textured soils at least 18 inches deep with a pH range of 4.7 to 8.9. Intolerant of shade and drought, but excellent for anaerobic and limestone sites.

Sagittaria rigida (Arrowhead) — [perennial forb] aquatic; calcareous shallow water and shores of ponds, swamps, and rivers, occasionally in deep water, OBL. Scattered statewide, especially in eastern streams. Grows up to 3 feet, white flowers in late summer; plant in mud at pond edges or in containers in a water garden, either along the shore or in up to 6 to 12 inches of water.

Sagittaria subulata (Subulate arrowhead) — [perennial forb] rare along streams and brackish bays and mud flats in tidal shore areas, especially southeast; OBL. Grows 8 to 16 inches in silty to sandy soils. Often sold as an aquarium plant.

Salix amygdaloides (Peach-leaved willow) — [tree/shrub] moist to mesic, sandy, silty or gravelly lake shores, marshes, swamps, floodplains and the valley or trough between sand dunes; FACW; mostly northwest. Grows 35 to 65 feet on wet to damp limestone-based loams in sun to part shade.

Salix bebbiana (Long-beaked willow) — [tree/shrub] upland deciduous woods, moist to dry thickets and edges; ideally in recent deposits of alluvial silts and gravels along waterways or in silted-in, abandoned beaver ponds, FACW-; statewide. Shrub or tree to 32 feet; sun to shade in mesic to moist silty loam of any texture at least 16 inches deep with a pH range of 5.5 to 7.5, Intolerant of shade, drought and limestone soils. Short-lived and fast-growing. Susceptible to insect, disease, and wind damage.

Salix candida (Hoary willow) — [tree] reported only in southern Monroe and northern Northampton counties on calcareous soils of wet meadows and fens; OBL and listed as threatened in Pennsylvania. Adapts to soils of any texture at least 18 inches deep with a pH range of 5.7 to 7.6. Excellent choice for anaerobic sites and limestone based soils, but intolerant of drought.

Salix caroliniana (Carolina willow) — [tree] wet soils along stream banks and in swamps. To 20 feet; OBL, southwest. Grow in continually moist to wet, organically rich silty-clay loams of any texture with a depth of 20 inches and a pH of 4.5 to 8.8. Grow in full sun to part sun.

Salix discolor (Pussy willow) — [shrub] swamps and moist or wet woods, FACW. Shrub to 15 feet; sun to part sun in mesic to moist silty circumneutral loams of any texture with a depth of 20 inches and pH range of 4.0 to 7.0; statewide. Ideal for anaerobic sites, but not droughty conditions. Short-lived and fast-growing; cut back heavily every few years to encourage vigorous new growth.

Salix eriocephala (Diamond willow) — [shrub] banks of large streams, flood plains, wet meadows, shores and bottomlands, FACW+; statewide. Shrub to 20 feet; sun to part sun in moist to wet, medium to fine textured soils with a depth of 20 inches and a pH range of 4.0 to 7.0. Shade and anaerobic site tolernce, but not drought. Short-lived and fast-growing.

Salix exigua (Sandbar willow) — [tree/shrub] open to dense riparian communities along streams, gravel bars, lakeshores, and ditches, OBL; mostly west. Shrub or small tree to 30 feet; sun to part shade in moist to wet, sandy to gravelly loam. Favorable for stream stabilization because of profuse suckering.

Salix humilis (Upland willow) — [shrub] moist barrens and dry thickets, FACU; statewide. Shrub to 10 feet; two local varieties: *humilis* and *tristis*; sun to part sun in mesic to moist, coarse to medium textured soil with at least 10 inches of depth and a pH range of 5.9 to 7.0. Insert stems in the ground where they take root to form new stands. More drought tolerant than other willows.

Salix lucida ssp. lucida (Shining willow) — [tree/shrub] wet soils, especially in and near swamps, marshes, peat bogs and on sand banks along creeks, FACW; statewide. Shrub or small tree to 20 feet; sun to part sun in moist to wet, moderately fertile, medium to fine textured soils at least 10 inches deep with a pH of 5.8 to 7.2. Prefers poor drainage; low tolerance for drought.

Salix myricoides (Broad-leaved willow). — [tree/shrub] two varieties: *var. albovestita* (Shoreline willow) and *var. myricoides* (Broad-leaved willow); scattered statewide, except northern tier counties. Sandy lakeshores, swamps and calcareous slopes; FAC. Grows 3.5 to 13 feet in full to part sun in moist sandy loam.

Salix nigra (Black willow) — [tree] less sandy and wetter river margins, swamps, sloughs, swales, gullies, and drainage ditches, FACW+; statewide. Grows to 65 feet; fine moist to wet silt or clay, especially in saturated or poorly drained soil from which other hardwoods are excluded, with pH above 4.8. Adapts to any soil texture with medium fertility and a depth of at least 32 inches. Intolerant of shade, drought, limestone soils.

Salix petiolaris (Slender willow) — [tree/shrub] moist sedge meadows and swales, stream banks and openings in rich, moist, low deciduous woodlands; FACW+; scattered statewide. Forms clumps from 5 to 35 feet tall; prefers sunny sites in moist to wet rich loams.

Salix sericea (Silky willow) — [shrub] swamps, bogs, stream banks and low woods, OBL; statewide. Shrub to 15 feet; sun to part shade in moist to wet acidic sandy or clayey loam of any texture with a depth of 18 inches and a pH between 5.2 and 7.0. Excellent choice for anaerobic sites, but intolerant of drought and limestone-based soils.

Salix serissima (Autumn willow) — [shrub] fens, treed bogs, wet thickets, gravelly stream banks and lake shores, typically on calcareous soils; OBL. Mostly northwestern counties. Grows 5 to 15 feet in wet to wet-mesic circumneutral to alkaline silt and sand loams.

Salvia lyrata (Lyre-leaved sage) — [perennial forb] rock, rich open woods, wet to dry meadows and alluvial areas, in well-drained sand or loam, UPL; mostly southeast, scattered elsewhere. Grows 1 to 2 feet with purple flowers in late spring; medium to wet, average soils in full sun; prefers moist sandy soils, and tolerates very light shade. Tolerates heat and humidity.

Salvia reflexa (Lance-leaved sage) [annual forb] — rare on dry fields and prairies as well as riverbanks in southern Pennsylvania. Grows 1 to 3 feet with white to purplish flowers in summer on dry sandy to rocky loams.

Sambucus canadensis (American elder) — [shrub] woods, fields, stream banks, moist fields and swamps, FACW; statewide. Shrub to 10 feet with white flowers in

Black willow (*Salix nigra*)

early summer and purple fruit in late summer; average, medium to wet well-drained soil in full sun to part shade. Prefers moist, humusy soils. Spreads by root suckers to form colonies.

Sambucus racemosa var. pubens (Red-berried elder) — [shrub] stream banks, ravines, swamps, moist forest clearings and higher ground near wetlands, FACU; statewide. Shrub to 10 feet with white flowers in late spring becoming red fruit; sun to part sun in moist, well drained, medium to fine textured humusy soils at least 24 inches deep with a pH between 5.2 and 7.2. Low tolerance for drought and anaerobic conditions.

Sanguinaria canadensis (Bloodroot) — [perennial forb] moist to dry upland woods and thickets, especially on flood plains and shores or near streams on slopes, FACU; statewide. Grows 2 to 6 inches, white flowers early spring; part shade to shade in dry to moist rich sandy loam, pH 5 to 7, and spreads to form small colonies.

Sanguisorba canadensis (American burnet) — [perennial forb] swamps, bogs, meadows and floodplains, FACW+; mostly southeast; scattered elsewhere. Grows up to 50 inches, white flowers in summer; sun to part sun in moist to wet rich loam, pH 5.5 to 7.

Sanicula canadensis (Canadian sanicle, black snakeroot) [biennial forb] — statewide in mesic rich deciduous woodlands, rocky wooded slopes, north-facing bluffs, margins of shaded seeps, UPL. Grows 1 to 2 feet with white flowers in summer in part shade on slightly dry loamy soils with an abundance of organic matter. Popular in flower gardens.

Sanicula marilandica (Black snake root) — [perennial forb] statewide in woodlands, especially on limestone slopes, as well as bogs and barrens; UPL. Grows 1 to 4 feet in part shade to shade with greenish-white flowers in summer.

Sanicula odorata (Yellow-flowered sanicle) — [perennial forb] statewide, especially the Piedmont, in rich, moist woodlands, FACU. Grows 12 to 30 inches with greenish-white flowers in late spring to early summer; grow in part sun to part shade in mesic to slightly dry fertile, loamy soil; serves as good groundcover in shady areas.

Sanicula trifoliata (Large-fruited sanicle) — [perennial forb] biennial, scattered statewide on stream banks and moist woodlands, especially slopes. Grows to 30 inches with greenish-white flowers in late spring in mesic to moist, well drained humusy silt loams.

Sarracenia purpurea (Pitcher plant) — [perennial forb] sphagnum bogs and peatlands, fens, swamps, wet conifer woodlands, lake and pond margins, OBL. Mostly northeast (Northern Glaciated Allegheny Plateau) and northwest (Western Glaciated Allegheny Plateau), scattered elsewhere. Grows 4 to 8 inches, maroon to red flowers in early summer; full sun in acidic, humusy muck that is constantly damp but not watery, pH 4.5 to 5.5; a carnivore requiring insects for nutrition.

Sassafras albidum (Sassafras) — [tree] open woods on moist, well-drained, sandy loam soils, dry ridges and upper slopes, fencerows and old fields, FACU-; statewide. Grows to 65 feet; average, medium, well-drained soil in full sun to part shade. Prefers moist, acidic, sandy-loamy soils, at least 18 inches deep with a pH between 4.5 and 7.3, although it prefers pH 6.0 to 7.0. Tolerates dry, sandy soils, but not shade or anaerobic conditions. Good choice for limestone-based soils and requires a 160-day growing season. Can be aggressive, especially following disturbance such as fire.

Arrowhead (Sagittaria rigida)

Saururus cernuus (Lizard's-tail) — [perennial forb] wet soils and mud in lowlands and stream and lake edges, including still standing fresh or slightly brackish water to a depth of 6 inches; OBL; scattered throughout except northern tier. White flowers in late summer. In water gardens, plant in containers in shallow water, about 6 inches deep. In natural ponds, plant in sandy to muddy pond margins under shallow water or in boggy, moist soil. Prefers full sun to part shade, but will flower in full shade. Rhizomes spread to create colonies.

Saxifraga micranthidifolia (Lettuce saxifrage) — [perennial forb] rare in seepage areas and shaded streambeds, often among mossy rocks; OBL. Mostly southwest and the Lehigh Valley. Grows 1 to 3 feet, white flowers in late spring; prefers part shade to shade in continually moist, humusy soils.

Saxifraga pensylvanica (Swamp saxifrage) — [perennial forb] wet woods, bogs and swamps, OBL; statewide. Grows 8 to 30 inches, greenish-white flowers in late spring; part shade in moist to wet circumneutral soils.

Saxifraga virginiensis (Early saxifrage) — [perennial forb] rock crevices on dry to mesic rocky slopes, FAC-; statewide except north-central. Grows 4 to 12 inches, white flowers in spring; sun to part sun in dry to moist sandy loam, pH 5.5 to 7.

Scheuchzeria palustris (Pod-grass) — [perennial graminoid] scattered across northern Pennsylvania, especially glaciated northeast, in sphagnum bogs, marshes and lake margins; OBL and listed as endangered. No cultivation data; may be difficult to find commercially.

Schizachne purpurascens (False melic) — [perennial graminoid] scattered across northern Pennsylvania and along the Allegheny Front in rich dry to moist woodlands; FACU-.

Schizachyrium scoparium var. scoparium (Little bluestem) — [perennial graminoid] old fields, roadsides and open woods, FACU. Mostly southeast ; scattered elsewhere except north. Grows 20 to 45 inches; sun to part sun in dry to moist sandy loam of any texture at least 14 inches deep with a pH range of 5.0 to 8.4. Intolerant of shade or anaerobic conditions, but an excellent choice for limestone-based soils and droughty sites. Another variety, *var. littorale* (Seaside bluestem) is rare on sandy dunes and shores in Erie County, FACU.

Schoenoplectus acutus (Great bulrush) — [perennial graminoid] rare in freshwater marshes, fens, lakes and ponds, slow streams, commonly emergent in water up to 5 feet, OBL. Mostly west; endangered. Grows 3 to 6 feet in sun in moist to wet soil to standing water; alkaline tolerant and valuable for shoreline protection. Prefers medium to fine textured, moderaately fertile soils at least 14 inches deep with a pH range of 5.2 to 8.5.

Schoenoplectus fluviatilis (River bulrush) — [perennial graminoid] Mostly Atlantic Coastal Plain and Erie and Ontario Lake Plain on moist sandy shorelines and both tidal and non-tidal marshes; OBL and listed as rare in Pennsylvania, aka *Bolboschoenus fluviatilis*.

Schoenoplectus heterochaetus (Slender bulrush) — [perennial graminoid] reported only once in Carbon County in 1897 and believed to be extirpated in Pennsylvania; widely scattered elsewhere and appears to prefer fresh calcareous marshes and lakes, often emergent in water to five feet deep; OBL. Adapts to any soil texture, but prefers moderately fertile soils at least 18 inches deep with a pH range of 4.0 to 7.5. Intolerant of shade and drought.

Schoenoplectus pungens (Chairmaker's rush) — [perennial graminoid] scattered statewide, but especially the Atlantic Coastal Plain in fresh or brackish moist shorelines, marshes, lakes and fens, commonly emergent in water to about 30 inches deep; FACW+. Adapts to moderately fertile soils of any texture with a minimum depth of 14 inches and a pH range of 3.7 to 7.5. Intolerant of shade and drought.

Schoenoplectus purshianus (Bulrush) — [perennial graminoid] lake shores, ponds and ditches, often emergent with relatively little water to level fluctuations, OBL. Mostly southeast (Piedmont); scattered elsewhere. Can reach 36 inches; sun to part sun in sandy soils, shallow standing water.

Schoenoplectus purshianus (Weakstalk bulrush) [annual graminoid] — stream banks and margins, and pond shores, OBL; scattered statewide, but mostly in the southeast. Grows to 12 inches in moist to wet sandy soils, often emergent where there is relatively minor water-level fluctuation.

Schoenoplectus smithii (Smith's bulrush) — [perennial graminoid] Atlantic Coastal Plain, but also reported along Lake Erie in moist shores or coastal freshwater title flats with large fluctuations in water levels; sometimes on inland sandy to muddy shores, OBL and listed as endangered in Pennsylvania.

Schoenoplectus subterminalis (Water bulrush) — [perennial graminoid] widely scattered north and south central, especially in the glaciated northeast in quiet fresh water lakes, streams and bogs, submerged to emergent in depths up to 40 inches; OBL.

Schoenoplectus tabernaemontani (Great bulrush) — [perennial graminoid] fens, marshes, bogs, lakes, stream banks and sandbars, often emergent in water to 3 feet deep, OBL; statewide. Grows 18 to 30 inches; sun to part sun in sandy to silty soils, shallow standing water.

Schoenoplectus torreyi (Torrey's bulrush) — [perennial graminoid] shallow water of lakes, ponds and marshes, especially with fluctuating water levels, mostly central to northeast; OBL and listed as endangered.

Scirpus ancistrochaetus (Northeastern bulrush) — [perennial graminoid] widely scattered in central and eastern Pennsylvania in vernal ponds and mud holes where water levels fluctuate or in wet depressions, bogs, sinkhole ponds or pool edges; OBL and endangered both federally and in Pennsylvania.

Scirpus atrocinctus (Blackish wool-grass) — [perennial graminoid] moist to wet meadows, marshes, ditches and swales, FACW+; mostly northeast; scattered elsewhere. Grows 10 to 25 inches; sun to part sun in moist to wet rich silty loam.

Scirpus atrovirens (Black bulrush) — [perennial graminoid] marshes, moist meadows, swales, shores and ditches, FACW+; statewide. Grows 20 to 30 inches; sun to part sun in moist to wet rich silty loam.

Scirpus cyperinus (Wool-grass) — [perennial graminoid] marshes, wet meadows and swales, FACW+; statewide. Grows 30 to 60 inches; sun to part sun in moist to wet rich loam, including shallow water.

Scirpus expansus (Wood bulrush) — [perennial graminoid] marshes, wet meadows and swales, OBL. Scattered statewide, mostly east. Grows 12 to 30 inches; full sun in wet silty loam, including standing water.

Scirpus hattorianus (Bulrush) — [perennial graminoid] statewide in moist meadows, swamps, marshes, bogs and river banks; OBL. Grows 10 to 18 inches in sun to part sun.

Scirpus microcarpus (Panicled bulrush — [perennial graminoid] marshes, moist meadows, swales and ditches, OBL. Scattered statewide, mostly north and east. Grows 12 to 30 inches; full sun in wet silty loam, including standing water.

Scirpus pedicellatus (Wool-grass) — [perennial graminoid] scattered in glaciated northwestern Pennsylvania in wet shorelines, stream valley marshes, bog edges and boggy meadows; OBL and listed as threatened in Pennsylvania.

Scirpus pendulus (Rufous bulrush) — [perennial graminoid] marshes, moist meadows and ditches, often associated with calcareous substrates; mostly south, scattered elsewhere. Grows 12 to 30 inches; full sun in wet silty circumneutral loam, including standing water, of any texture at least 10 inches deep with a pH range of 4.9 to 7.0.

Scirpus polyphyllus (Leafy bulrush) — [perennial graminoid] swampy places and along streams, usually shaded by trees, OBL; statewide. Grows 12 to 30 inches; part shade in wet rich sandy loam, including standing water.

Scleria muehlenbergii (Reticulated nut-rush) [annual graminoid] — pinelands, savannas, bogs, meadows and prairies, OBL and listed as endangered, Atlantic Coastal Plain. Grows to about 25 inches in sun to part sun; rare outside of the coastal plain.

Scleria pauciflora (Few-flowered nut-rush) — [perennial graminoid] lower Piedmont in dry to wet pinelands, savannas, meadows, serpentine barrens, dry to mesic open woodlands, bogs and prairies; FACU+ and listed as threatened in Pennsylvania.

Scleria triglomerata (Whip-grass) — [perennial graminoid] scattered generally southern Pennsylvania, especially lower Piedmont, in moist to wet meadows, sphagnum bogs, moist serpentine barrens and open pinelands, prairies and savannas; FAC.

Scleria verticillata (Whorled nut-rush) [annual graminoid] — very widely scattered in marshes, bogs, savannas, calcareous meadows, pinelands and lakeshores, OBL and listed as endangered. Grows to 20 inches in moist to wet, marly, sandy or peaty soils in full to part sun.

Scrophularia lanceolata (Lanceleaf figwort) — [perennial forb] low woods, thickets, stream banks, and along moist roadsides, FACU+; statewide, especially southeast. Grows up to 6 feet, with yellowish-green flowers in summer; part shade to shade in moist, rich sandy loam.

Scrophularia marilandica (Eastern figwort) — [perennial forb] alluvial woods, river banks, moist shores and along roadsides, FACU-; statewide. Grows up to 10 feet, purple-brownish flowers in summer; part shade to shade in moist, rocky, rich loam.

Scutellaria elliptica var. *elliptica* (Hairy skullcap) — [perennial forb] shale barrens and open woodlands, especially on banks, in the Piedmont and Atlantic Coastal Plain.

Scutellaria galericulata (Common skullcap) — [perennial forb] scattered statewide in swamps, bogs and marshy meadows, especially northeastern glaciated areas; OBL.

Scutellaria incana (Downy skullcap) — [perennial forb] open rocky woods, clearings, on slopes and along streams, statewide except for northernmost counties and most common on the Southern Allegheny Plateau. Grows 2 to 3 feet in sun to part shade with blue flowers in early autumn; prefers average, well-drained soil, especially drier sandy to clay soils.

Scutellaria integrifolia (Hyssop skullcap) — [perennial forb] swamps, bogs and moist fields, FACW. Southeast, especially Central Appalachians and Piedmont. Grows 12 to 30 inches, blue flowers in late summer; sun to part sun in moist, silty loam.

Scutellaria lateriflora (Mad-dog skullcap) — [perennial forb] wet woods, stream banks and moist pastures, FACW+; statewide. Grows 12 to 30 inches, with blue flowers in late summer; sun to part sun in moist silty loam.

Scutellaria leonardii (Small skullcap) — [perennial forb] open woodlands and bluffs, shores, limestone glades, gravel and sand prairies; scattered statewide, mostly southeast. Grows to 4 inches in dry to mesic soils with purple flowers in late spring. Prefers shallow soils with sand or gravel, generally dry conditions; good for sunny rock gardens, but intolerant of taller plant competition.

Scutellaria nervosa (Skullcap) — [perennial forb] floodplains, stream banks and moist wooded slopes, mostly southern Pennsylvania especially east and west; FAC. Grows 1 to 2 feet, blue to violet flowers in late spring; prefers rich, well-drained soil in part shade.

Scutellaria saxatilis (Rock skullcap) — [perennial forb] scattered in southwestern Pennsylvania on rocky river banks and low woods. Grows 1 to 2 feet, blue to violet flowers in late spring; prefers rich, well-drained soil in part shade.

Scutellaria serrata (Showy skullcap) — [perennial forb] very rare in floodplains and rocky, humusy woodlands; mostly southeast (Piedmont, Atlantic Coastal Plain). Endangered. Grows 1 to 2 feet, blue to violet flowers in late spring; prefers rich, well-drained soil in part shade; ideal in groups for moist to dry woodland or shade gardens.

Sedum telephioides (Allegheny stonecrop) — [perennial forb] rare in extreme south central Pennsylvania on dry cliffs, ledges, shale barrens and in rocky woodlands. Grows 12 to 18 inches with white flowers in summer; prefers full sun to part shade in dry to mesic well drained soils. Drought tolerant.

Sedum ternatum (Woodland stonecrop) —

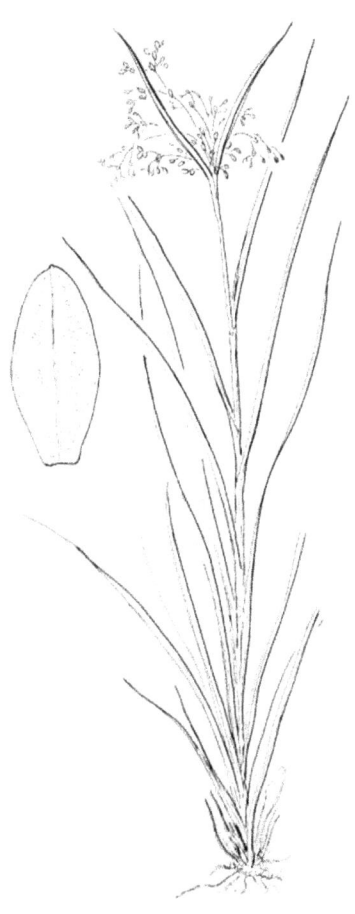

Blackish wool-grass (Scirpus atrocinctus)

[perennial forb] rocky banks, cliffs and woodlands, as well as damp sites along stream banks, bluff bases and stony ledges. Mostly southwest; scattered elsewhere. Grows 3 to 6 inches, white flowers in early spring; average, medium, well-drained soils in full sun to part shade, pH 5 to 7.

Selaginella apoda (Meadow spikemoss) — [fern/ally] swamps, meadows, marshes, pastures, damp lawns, open woods, and stream banks, in basic to acidic soil. Ideal for the southeast. Mat forming, low creeping multi-branched rhizome. Grow in part sun to part shade in moist to wet rich loam.

Senna hebecarpa (Northern wild senna) — [perennial forb] moist open woods, wetland edges, floodplains, and along roadsides, FAC; mostly southeast, also statewide except northern and western Allegheny plateaus. Grows 3 to 6 feet, yellow flowers in summer; part sun to part shade in moist, rich sandy loam, pH 5.5 to 7.

Senna marilandica (Southern wild senna) — [perennial forb] rare in dry open woods, openings and thickets; FAC+, mostly south. Grows 3 to 6 feet, yellow flowers in summer; well-drained, coarse to medium textured, sandy to clay medium moisture loams at least 12 inches deep with a pH range of 4.0 to 7.0 in full sun. Intolerant of anaerobic conditions.

Sericocarpus asteroides (White-topped aster) — [perennial forb] on dry, sandy, clay or shaley open soils in open pine to mixed woodlands and deciduous forest, fields and barrens, statewide. Grows to 24 inches in part sun to part shade with white flowers in late summer to early fall in well drained, acidic loams.

Sericocarpus linifolius (Narrow-leaved white-topped aster) — [perennial forb] on dry to moist sandy, clay or gravelly soils of open pine and deciduous forests, oak and pine barrens, serpentine barrens, fields, swamps, bogs and sandy disturbed ground; scattered in southeastern Pennsylvania and listed as endangered. Grows 18 to 30 inches with white flowers in summer in full to part sun, with a preference to dry to mesic, especially sandy, soils.

Setaria parviflora (Perennial foxtail) — [perennial graminoid] dry to moist open soil in the southeast, FAC. Prefers medium to fine textured soils at least 8 inches deep with a pH range of 5.0 to 7.0; intolerant of shade, anaerobic conditions or limestone-based soils; full sun to part sun.

Shepherdia canadensis (Buffalo-berry) — [shrub] rare on shaly, wet banks and lightly shaded depressions along Lake Erie; UPL; Mostly Erie County. Grows 6 to 8 feet with inconspicuous yellow flowers in spring; grow in circumneutral to slightly alkaline moist, rocky to medium textured soils at least 24 inches deep with a pH range of 5.3 to 8.0, in sun to part shade. Excellent choice for droughty sites, but not for anaerobic conditions.

Downy skullcap (*Scutellaria incana*)

Sicyos angulatus (Bur cucumber) [annual vine] — statewide, especially Piedmont, in moist floodplain forests and meadows, thickets, riverbanks. Grows to 24 feet with greenish white flowers in full to part sun on moist, fertile loamy to silty soils.

Sida hermaphrodita (Virginia mallow) — [perennial forb] in moist alluvial soils on south central Pennsylvania river banks; listed as endangered in Pennsylvania.

Silene antirrhina (Sleepy catchfly) [annual forb] — gravel, hill and dry sand prairies, dry open woods, rocky glades and thinly wooded bluffs. Grows to 32 inches with white to pink flowers in summer on dry to mesic rocky, sandy loams, especially poor soils.

Silene caroliniana ssp. pensylvanica (Fire pink) — [perennial forb] open, typically gravelly to rocky, usually deciduous woodlands; statewide, except northern and western Allegheny plateaus. Grows 9 to 12 inches, pink flowers in spring; average, dry to medium moisture, well-drained soils in full sun to part shade. Prefers sunny sites in dryish sandy or gravelly soils with some part afternoon shade.

Silene nivea (Snowy campion) — [perennial forb] mesic to moist alluvial woodlands and thickets, FAC; widely scattered statewide. Grows up to 8 to 12 inches, with white flowers in summer; sun to part sun in sandy, well-drained loam.

Silene stellata (Starry campion) — [perennial forb] wooded slopes, barrens and roadside banks; statewide except northern tier. Grows 12 to 36 inches, white flowers in summer; part sun to part shade in dry to moist sandy loam, pH 5 to 7.

Silene virginica (Fire pink) — [perennial forb] moist deciduous woodland slopes and bluffs; mostly west. Grows 12 to 18 inches with red flowers in late spring; well drained, dry to medium moisture, average soil in full sun to part shade; prefers moist, sandy to clay soils with excellent drainage in part shade.

Silphium asteriscus var. trifoliatum (Whorled rosinweed) — [perennial forb] prairies, dry thickets and meadows, roadsides and along railways, mostly southwest. Grows 4 to 6 feet, yellow flowers in late summer. Prefers dry, prairie habitats in full sun. AKA *Silphium trifoliatum var. trifoliatum*.

Sisyrinchium albidum (White blue-eyed-grass) — [perennial forb] very rare in prairies, rich open woods and open slopes, often on thin sandy to rocky soil. Listed as extirpated, but some doubt as to whether continental range should include Pennsylvania. Grows 1 to 3 feet, white flowers in late spring; prefers full to part sun on dry, sandy to gravelly well drained soil.

Sisyrinchium angustifolium (Blue-eyed grass) — [perennial forb] meadows, flood plains, moist fields, and mesic open woods; statewide. Grows up to 15 inches, with pale blue flowers in early summer; sun to part shade in moist sandy, medium to fine textured soil at least 4 inches deep with a pH range of 5.0 to 7.0. Intolerant of anaerobic conditions, limestone sois and drought.

Sisyrinchium atlanticum (Eastern blue-eyed-grass) — [perennial forb] Very rare in thin woods, open fields and coastal dunes that are sandy and dry to moist. Mostly southeast (Atlantic Coastal Plain); endangered. Grows 1 to 3 feet in sun on moist, slightly acidic sandy, peaty, rich loamy soil.

Sisyrinchium fuscatum (Sand blue-eyed-grass) — [perennial forb] marshy areas of moist pine barrens, reported only in Philadelphia County and listed as extirpated in Pennsylvania; aka *Sisyrinchium arenicola*.

Sisyrinchium montanum var. crebrum (Blue-eyed grass) — [perennial forb] dry to mesic open woods, roadsides and fields, FACW-; mostly northeast (Northern Glaciated Allegheny Plateau), scattered elsewhere. Grows up to 20 inches, with violet flowers in early summer; sun to part shade in dry to moist sandy loam.

Sisyrinchium mucronatum (Blue-eyed-grass) — [perennial forb] dry fields and prairies, moist open woodlands, rocky to sandy open shorelines, statewide except northwestern glaciated areas; FAC+. Grows 6 to 16 inches with blue flowers in summer; full to part sun in dry but preferably mesic well drained soils.

Sium suave (Water-parsnip) — [perennial forb] swamps, bogs, wet meadows, pond margins, OBL; scattered statewide. Grows up to 6 feet, white flowers in late summer; full to part sun in moist to wet rich loams.

Smallanthus uvedalia (Bear's-foot) — [perennial forb] statewide, especially south, on river banks and in ravines and thickets, prefers wet sites. Grows to 5 feet with yellow flower in late summer to early fall on moist to wet sandy and silt loams in full to part sun.

Smilax glauca (Catbrier) — [perennial vine] southern Pennsylvania in sandy, moist to dry soils of woodlands, thickets, swamps, fields and roadsides; FACU. Grows to 16 feet with yellow dioecious flowers in summer in a range of dry to moist, moderately fertile, soils of any texture at least 12 inches deep, with a pH of 4.5 to 7.5. Intolerant of anerobic conditions. Grow in sun to part shade, making it a good trellis plan for sunny edges or dappled shade.

Smilax herbacea (Carrion-flower) — [perennial vine] higher elevations in rich woods and floodplains, alluvial thickets, and meadows, often in calcareous soils, statewide; FAC. Climbing vine, 3 to 10 feet greenish-yellow flowers in early summer. Grow in part shade to shade in moist average soil.

Smilax hispida (Bristly greenbrier) — [perennial vine] swamps, moist woods thickets and roadsides, statewide. Climbing vine, 20 to 40 feet. Greenish yellow flowers late spring. Grow in moist loams in full sun to part shade. Tolerates wet soils.

Smilax pseudochina (False chinaroot) — [perennial vine] reported only in Delaware County, but prefers palustrine wetlands with deep, sandy, acidic peat soils as well as bogs, marshes and wet woodlands; FAC+ and listed as extirpated in Pennsylvania.

Smilax pulverulenta (Carrion-flower) — [perennial vine] southern Pennsylvania, especially the Atlantic Coastal Plain and adjacent Piedmont, in calcareous soils in rich woodlands and thickets.

Smilax rotundifolia (Roundleaf greenbrier) — [perennial vine] statewide except far northeast and southwest in dry to moist, occasionally riparian woodlands, borders, and hedgerows. Often a pioneer species. Grow in sun to part sun in medium textured, moderately fertile soils at least 12 inches deep with a pH range of 5.0 to 7.5; intolerant of shade, limestone soils and anaerobic conditions.

Solanum americanum (Black nightshade) [annual forb] — woodlands, fields, woods and moist disturbed ground, FACU-; very widely scattered in eastern Pennsylvania with white flowers in late summer, sun to part sun on well-drained loams.

Solanum carolinense (Horse-nettle) — [perennial forb] dry to mesic fields, roadsides, sandy stream banks, UPL; statewide. Grows up to 3 feet, pale violet to white flowers in summer; full to part sun in average sandy loam. Considered a noxious weed in many western states.

Solidago altissima (Canada goldenrod) — [perennial forb] dry to moist soils in fields and river banks as well as disturbed areas such as roadsides, FACU-; statewide. Grows up to 6 feet, yellow flowers in late summer and fall; sun to part sun in dry, sandy loam of any texture with a depth of at least 8 inches and pH range of 5.2 to 7.3. Intolerant of anaerobic conditions and drought.

Solidago arguta var. arguta (Forest goldenrod) — [perennial forb] statewide, especially east, in rocky conifer and deciduous forests, dry thickets and shaded roadsides. Grows 20 to 40 inches with yellow flowers in late summer to early fall; grow in mesic well-drained sandy to silt loams.

Solidago bicolor (Silver rod) — [perennial forb] dry open woods; statewide. Grows up to 40 inches; white flowers in late summer to fall; part shade in dry sandy loam, pH 5 to 6.

Solidago caesia (Wreath goldenrod) — [perennial forb] dry upland open woods, thickets and clearings, FACU; statewide. Grows 18 to 36 inches, yellow flowers late summer to fall; part sun to shade in dry to moist, medium to fine textured, rich loam at least 8 inches deep with a pH range of 5.5 to 7.0. Intolerant of anaerobic conditions or drought.

Solidago canadensis var. hargeri (Canada goldenrod) — [perennial forb] dry to mesic fields and along roadsides, FACU; statewide. Grows up to 6 feet, yellow flowers in late summer into fall; sun to part sun in dry to moist soil of any texture with a depth of 12 inches and pH range of 4.8 to 7.5.

Solidago curtisii (Curtis's goldenrod) — [perennial forb] rare in mostly Appalachian shaded, mesic thickets and woods; southwest and endangered. Grows 2 to 3 feet in rich well-drained soils, part sun to part shade; yellow flowers in late summer.

Solidago erecta (Slender goldenrod) — [perennial forb] rare in dry woods, disturbed open soils, road embankments; mostly south, endangered. Grows 12 to 24 inches, yellow flowers in early autumn. Grow in well-drained sandy to rocky soils in full sun. AKA *Solidago speciosa var. erecta*.

Solidago flexicaulis (Zigzag goldenrod) — [perennial forb] moist upland woods and rocky wooded slopes, FACU; statewide. Grows 18 to 36 inches, yellow flowers in late summer through fall; part shade to shade in mesic to moist, medium textured, rich loam at least 8 inches deep with a pH range of 5.3 to 7.0. Low tolerance for anaerobic conditions.

Solidago gigantea var. gigantea (Smooth

goldenrod) — [perennial forb] moist fields, woods, and floodplains, FACW; statewide. Grows up to 8 feet, yellow flowers in late summer through fall; sun to part sun in dry to moist, medium to fine textured soil at least 16 inches deep with a pH range of 4.0 to 8.0. Intolerant of anaerobic conditions.

Solidago hispida (Hairy goldenrod) — [perennial forb] dry sandy to gravelly soils in fields, meadows, dunes, open woodlands, rocky outcrops and sandy alluvium near streams and lakes, scattered southeastern Pennsylvania. Grows 1 to 3 feet with yellow flowers in late summer; average, dry to medium, well-drained soils in full sun. Tolerates poor, dry soils and light shade, but performs best in full sun in calcareous soils.

Solidago juncea (Early goldenrod) — [perennial forb] fields, meadows, rocky banks and along roadsides; statewide. Grows up to 4 feet, yellow flowers in late summer to fall; sun to part sun in dry to moist sandy loam, pH 5 to 6.

Solidago nemoralis (Gray goldenrod) — [perennial forb] fields, woods and roadsides in dry sterile soils; statewide. Grows up to 3 feet, yellow flowers late summer to fall; sun to part shade in dry to mesic, coarse to medium textured sandy loam at least 12 inches deep with a pH range of 6.5 to 7.5. Intolerant of shade and anaerobic conditions.

Solidago odora ssp. odora (Sweet goldenrod, anise-scented goldenrod) — [perennial forb] dry open woods and barrens. Mostly east of Central Appalachians. Grows up to 4 feet, yellow flowers in late summer to fall; sun to part shade in dry to moist sandy loam, pH 4 to 6.

Solidago patula ssp. patula (Spreading goldenrod) — [perennial forb] moist soils in swamp margins, boggy ground, wet meadows, roadside ditches, seeps, and the edges of wet woods, OBL. Statewide, mostly south. Grows up to 6 feet, with yellow flowers in late summer to fall; moist sandy loam in sun to part shade. Adapts to any soil texture with a depth of 6 inches and a pH range of 4.5 to 7.0. Tolerant of anaerobic conditions, but not drought.

Solidago puberula subsp. puberula (Downy goldenrod) — [perennial forb] eastern Pennsylvania except far north on sandy to rocky soils at the edges of deciduous and conifer woodlands, clearings, pond and stream margins, balds and along roadsides; FACU-.

Solidago rigida (Stiff goldenrod) — [perennial forb] rare in dry fields and prairies; UPL, widely scattered, mostly southeast (Piedmont), endangered. Yellow flowers in late summer to fall. Grow in full sun in well-drained, medium to dry moisture average soil. AKA Oligoneuronrigidum.

Solidago roanensis (Mountain goldenrod) — [perennial forb] rare in woods and clearings, rock crevices, edges of balds and rocky banks; southwest. Grows 12 to 36 inches in sun to part sun in well-drained, rocky soils.

Solidago rugosa (Wrinkle-leaf goldenrod) — [perennial forb] woods, fields, floodplains and waste ground, FAC; two local varieties, rugosa and villosa; statewide. Grows up to 4 feet, with yellow flowers in late summer into fall; sun to part shade in moist sandy loam at least 12 inches deep with a pH 5.0 to 7.0. Intolerant of anaerobic conditions.

Solidago simplex ssp. randii var. racemosa (Sticky goldenrod) — [perennial forb] calcareous rock crevices, ledges and cliffs and shorelines; reported only in Lancaster and Adams counties and listed as endangered in Pennsylvania. Grows to 30 inches with yellow flowers in late summer to early autumn on circumneutral, well drained sandy loams in full sun to part shade.

Solidago speciosa (Showy goldenrod) — [per-

Catbriar (Smilax glauca)

ennial forb] moist meadows and rocky woods and thickets; scattered statewide, especially southeast. Grows up to 6 feet, with yellow flowers from late summer into fall; sun to part shade in dry to moist sandy loam, pH 6 to 7.

Solidago squarrosa (Ragged goldenrod) — [perennial forb] statewide in dry, rocky mountain woodlands, thickets and fields, as well as rocky roadside banks. Grows to 4 feet with yellow flowers in late summer to early fall; prefers well drained, dry to mesic soils in full to part sun.

Solidago uliginosa (Bog goldenrod) — [perennial forb] bogs and wet areas, fens, marshes, and sometimes in wet woods, OBL; scattered statewide, mostly east and west edges. Grows up to 5 feet, yellow flowers from late summer into fall; sun to part sun in mesic to moist, well drained, medium to fine textured soil at least 6 inches deep with a pH range of 4.5 to 5.7. Excellent for anaerobic sites, but not limestone-based soils or drought.

Solidago ulmifolia var. ulmifolia (Elm-leaved goldenrod) — [perennial forb] wooded slopes, roadside banks and shale barrens; statewide, especially south. Grows up to 4 feet, with yellow flowers in late summer to fall; sun to part shade in dry rocky sandy loam.

Sorbus americana (American mountain-ash) — [tree] swamp margins, rocky hillsides, woodland edges, and roadsides, FACU; scattered statewide except southeast. Grows to 32 feet in newly-formed mineral-rich soils to shallow and infertile soils of any texture, at least 28 inches deep with a pH range of 5.3 to 6.8, in cool, windy, and humid conditions. Low tolerance for drought, anaerobic conditions and limestone soils

Sorbus decora (Showy mountain-ash) — [tree] rare in wet to mesic woods, cool moist rocky slopes, lake shores, FAC; northeast and northwest; endangered. Grows to 35 feet; part shade to shade in moist, circumneutral, poor to well-drained mesic to moist, fine-textured soil at least 36 inches deep with a pH range of 4.0 to 7.0. Low tolerance for anaerobic or drought conditions.

Sorghastrum nutans (Indian-grass) — [perennial graminoid] prairies, woodlands and savannas, including scrublands, FACU. Mostly southeast; scattered elsewhere except northern tier. Grows 3 to 6 feet; sun to part sun in dry to mesic sandy loam of any texture at least 24 inches deep with a pH range of 4.8 to 8.0. Intolerant of shade and anaerobic conditions, but a good choice for limestone-based soils.

Sparganium americanum (Bur-reed) — [perennial graminoid] lake and pond shores and shallow, neutral to alkaline waters, sometimes forming large stands, OBL; statewide. Grows 20 to 50 inches; sun to part sun in sandy to silty moist to wet loams, including standing water. Adapts to any soil texture at least 8 inches deep with a pH range of 4.9 to 7.3 with no drought tolerance. An excellent choice for anaerobic sites.

Sparganium androcladum (Branching bur-reed) — [perennial graminoid] rare on shores and quiet, circumneutral, shallow waters and wet meadows, OBL. Scattered statewide; endangered. Grows to 4 feet in a variety of wet to constantly moist soils and part shade to shade; can grow in water.

Sparganium angustifolium (Bur-reed) — [perennial graminoid] northeastern Pennsylvania in acidic, low-nutrient waters of lakes, ponds and streams, preferring shallow water but can go 15 feet deep; OBL. Grows in sun to part sun.

Sparganium emersum (Bur-reed) — [perennial graminoid] statewide except southeast in still to

Silver rod (Solidago bicolor)

slow-moving streams, lakes and bogs, especially those with some to high nutrient levels that are circumneutral to slightly alkaline; OBL. Grows in sun to part sun.

Sparganium eurycarpum (Broadfruit bur-reed) — [perennial graminoid] shores, ditches, low marshes, neutral to alkaline water on gravel, sand or mud, occasionally among boulders on wave to washed shorelines, OBL. Scattered statewide, especially southeast and northwest. Grows 20 to 50 inches; full sun in silty to sandy loam on pond edges or in standing water. Adapts to any soil texture, but requires 12 inches of depth and a pH range of 5.0 to 8.5. No drought tolerance, but an excellent choice for anaerobic conditions.

Sparganium fluctuans (Bur-reed) — [perennial graminoid] cold, still, acidic to neutral low-nutrient waters up to 6 feet deep; sometimes covers the surface with strap to shaped leaves, OBL; northeast (Northern Glaciated Allegheny Plateau). Can reach 6 feet; full sun in standing water on silty to sandy loam.

Sparganium natans (Small bur-reed) — [perennial graminoid] reported only in Tioga and Erie counties and prefers slightly acidic to circumneutral cool, still waters less than two feet deep in bays, lakes and ponds, pools and peat bogs; OBL and listed as extirpated in Pennsylvania.

Spartina patens (Salt-meadow grass) — [perennial graminoid] saline to brackish marshes, low dunes and sandy beaches, marsh ridges and tidal flats ranging from normal high tide to about 15 feet above sea level, FACW+. Mostly southeast (Atlantic Coastal Plain). Grows 1 to 4 feet in full sun in a wide range of soils from coarse sands to silty clay sediments. Grows in any soil texture with medium fertility and a depth of 10 inches with a pH range of 5.5 to 7.5. Intolerant of shade and drought, but high salinity tolerance.

Spartina pectinata (Freshwater cordgrass) — [perennial graminoid] marshes, sloughs and floodplains, especially those that are ice-scoured, OBL. Scattered statewide, especially Delaware and Susquehanna River Valleys. Grows 3 to 6 feet; sun to part sun in moist to wet silty and alluvial loam.

Sphenopholis obtusata (Slender wedgegrass) — [perennial graminoid] forests, marsh edges and prairies on mesic open sites, FAC-. Two varieties: *var. major* is statewide, mostly southeast; *var. obtusata*, mostly southeast; a hybrid, *x pensylvanica* is very rare on moist slopes and wet woods, scattered south. Grows 10 to 25 inches; sun to part sun in dry to mesic, coarse to medium, sandy loam with a depth of 18 inches and a pH of 6.0 to 8.5. Intolerant of shade and drought, but an excellent choice for anaerobic sites..

Sphenopholis pensylvanica (Swamp-oats) — [perennial graminoid] generally Appalachians and east in moist to wet sites in springy meadows, swamps, woodlands and stream margins; OBL. Grows to about 24 inches in sun to part shade.

Spiraea alba (Meadow-sweet) — [shrub] wet prairies, especially open ground along streams, lakes and bogs, and moist meadows, FACW+; statewide. Grows to 6 feet with white to pink flowers in late summer; sun to part shade in mesic to wet, well-drained soil. Prefers full sun; soil should not be allowed to dry out; grow in moist to wet organically rich loams of any texture with a depth of 12 inches and a pH range of 4.3 to 6.8. Can tolerate standing water but not limestone-based soils or drought.

Spiraea betulifolia var. corymbosa (Dwarf spiraea) — [tree/shrub] very rare on dry wooded slopes and steep shale hillsides, scattered in south-central counties. Grows 2 to 3 feet tall in average, well-drained soils in full sun; tolerates a wide variety of soils. White flowers in late spring on new wood.

Spiraea tomentosa (Hardhack or Steeplebush) — [tree/shrub] meadows, old fields, pastures, bogs and swamps, FACU-; statewide. Grows to 3 feet with white to pink flowers in summer; sun to part sun in mesic to moist moderately acid soil. Adapts to soil of any texture with a depth of 14 inches and a pH range of 4.5 to 7.0. Intolerant of shade and anaerobic conditions.

Spiranthes casei (Case's ladies'-tresses) — [perennial forb] very rare in mesic to dry meadows, barrens open woodlands, outcrops and old fields; mostly north central area; endangered. Grows 8 to 16 inches, yellowish to greenish-white flowers in late summer; prefers dry to moist; in sandy, acidic, sterile soil in sun to part shade.

Spiranthes cernua (Nodding ladies tresses) — [perennial forb] wet to dry open sites in fens, marshes, meadows, swales, prairies, open woodlands, riverbanks, shores, ditches, roadsides, and moist old fields, FACW; statewide. Grows 5 to 15 inches, white flowers in late summer and early fall; sun to part sun in moist medium to fine textured soils 8 inches or more deep with a pH of 4.5 to 6.5. Intolerant of shade and drought, but an excellent choice for anaerobic sites.

Spiranthes lacera var. gracilis (Southern slender ladies'-tresses) — [perennial forb] dry to moist woodlands, generally grassy meadows, prairies and old fields, including lawns, roadside banks, mostly southern Pennsylvania, especially Piedmont; FACU-. Grows to 30 inches with white flowers in summer to fall; prefers disturbed habitats such as grasslands, prairies and open woodlands, including lawns.

Spiranthes lucida (Shining ladies'-tresses) — [perennial forb] prefers calcareous soils on rocky to sandy river and stream banks, wet meadows, lake shores, seeps and fens, scattered statewide but mostly east and northwest; FACW.

Spiranthes magnicamporum (Great Plains ladies'-tresses) — [perennial forb] moist to wet prairies, meadows and fens on calcareous soils, reported only in Lancaster County and listed as extirpated in Pennsylvania; FACU-. Grows 6 to 16 inches in sun to part shade with white flowers in late summer in mesic to moist rich sandy and silt loams.

Spiranthes ochroleuca (Yellow nodding ladies'-tresses) — [perennial forb] statewide in dry to mesic open woodlands, thickets, meadows, old fields and barrens, including ledges and outcrops; FACW. Grows to 24 inches with pale yellow flowers in summer to fall; prefers disturbed habitats such as grasslands, shrublands and open woodlands.

Spiranthes ovalis var. erostellata (October ladies'-tresses) — [perennial forb] prefers humus in moist or damp woodlands, thickets and old fields, FAC; reported only in Franklin County and listed as endangered in Pennsylvania. Grows 3 to 12 inches with white flowers in early fall; prefers dappled to light shade on mesic to moist loams or clay loams with some decaying organic matter; requires specific strains of fungi in the soil with which to form symbiotic association with the root system and hence difficult to grow.

Spiranthes romanzoffiana (Hooded ladies'-tresses) — [perennial forb] very widely scattered, especially glaciated northwest, in rich open woodlands, moist to wet meadows, marshes, fens, seeps, bogs and coastal bluffs and dunes; OBL and listed as endangered in Pennsylvania. Grows to 20 inches with greenish-white flowers in late summer; grow in part sun to part shade in rich, humusy, well drained, mesic to moist, medium to fine textured loams at least 8 inches deep with a pH range of 4.5 to 8.5. Good choice for anaerobic sites, but not for limestone-based soils or droughty conditions.

Spiranthes tuberosa (Slender ladies'-tresses) — [perennial forb] Dry, open woodlands, grassy meadows, old fields, road edges, mostly lower Piedmont; FACU. Grows to 18 inches with white flowers in summer to fall; prefers dry to moist prairies, meadows, open woodlands in full sun to part shade.

Spiranthes vernalis (Spring ladies tresses) — [perennial forb] rare in old fields, dry to moist meadows and dune hollows, along roadsides; FAC. Southeast (Piedmont); endangered. White flowers in fall. Grow in full sun to part shade in medium moist, rich well-drained soil.

Spirodela polyrhiza (Greater duckweed) — [perennial forb] aquatic in lakes, ponds, swamps and on the margins of slow-moving streams, OBL; statewide. Adapted to medium to fine textured, moderately fertile soils with a pH of 5.0 to 8.6,

Sporobolus clandestinus (Rough dropseed) — [perennial graminoid] Dauphin and Lancaster counties sandy to rocky, dry soils, usually along coastlines but also on roadsides; listed as endangered in Pennsylvania.

Sporobolus heterolepis (Prairie dropseed) — [perennial graminoid] rare in mesic prairies, well-drained moraines, rock outcrops, glades, pine savannas and barrens, lightly grazed pastures, UPL; reported in Lancaster and Chester counties, and endangered. Grows 2 to 3 feet in well-drained, dry to medium average soils in full sun; prefers rocky, dry to mesic, medium textured soils at least 12 inches deep with a pH range of 6.0 to 7.2. Tolerant of drought, but not anaerobic conditions or limestone-based soils; slow to establish.

Sporobolus neglectus (Small rushgrass) [annual graminoid] — upland woodland openings, limestone glades, rocky openings and prairies, FACU, widely scattered south. Grows 5-10 inches in full sun on dry, sterile soils high in gravel or sand; intolerant of competition from taller plants.

Sporobolus vaginiflorus (Poverty grass) [annual graminoid] — statewide in upland woodlands, dry sand prairies, hill prairies, limestone and sandstone glades and fields, including serpentine barrens, UPL. Grows 6 to 12 inches in full sun on dry, barren soils high in sand or gravel.

Stachys hyssopifolia (Hedge-nettle) — [perennial forb] very widely scattered in eastern Pennsylvania on fields and river banks, bogs and shorelines, FACW+. Grows to 2 feet with white to purple flowers in late summer, in a wide range of preferably moist soils in full sun to part shade.

Stachys hyssopifolia var. ambigua (Hedge-nettle) — [perennial forb] very widely scattered in eastern Pennsylvania on fields and river banks, FACW+. Grows to 2 feet with lavender flowers in late summer in well-drained mesic to moist sandy and silt loams in full sun to part sun.

Stachys hyssopifolia var. hyssopifolia (Hedge-nettle) — [perennial forb] widely scattered in southeastern Pennsylvania on such disturbed ground as old fields, railroad tracks and ore pits; FACW+. Grows to 2 feet with lavender flowers in late summer in well-drained mesic to moist sandy and silt loams in full sun to part sun.

Stachys nuttallii (Nuttall's hedge-nettle) — [perennial forb] widely scattered wooded southern Pennsylvania mountain slopes; FAC and listed as endangered. Grows 20 to 40 inches, pink to white flowers in summer; wide range of soils, but prefers moist to wet rich soils in sun to part shade.

Stachys palustris var. pilosa (Hedge-nettle) — [perennial forb] very rare in wet meadows and marshes; scattered in south (Piedmont, Southern Allegheny Plateau). Grows 20 to 40 inches, pink to white flowers in summer; prefers moist to wet rich soils in full sun to part shade. Adapts to soils of any texture with a minimum depth of 10 inches and a pH range of 5.7 to 8.0. Good choice for anaerobic sites, but not for drought.

Stachys tenuifolia (Creeping hedge-nettle) [annual forb] — scattered statewide in floodplain forests, riverbanks, moist to wet meadows, fields,

Prairie dropseed (*Sporobolus heterolepis*)

swamps, seeps and thickets, FACW+. Grows 6 to 30 inches with pink-rosy flowers in summer in part shade on mesic to moist acidic clay and sandy loams of any texture, at least 10 inches deep and with a pH range of 5.7 to 7.4. Good choice for anaerobic sites, but not for limestone-based soils or droughty conditions.

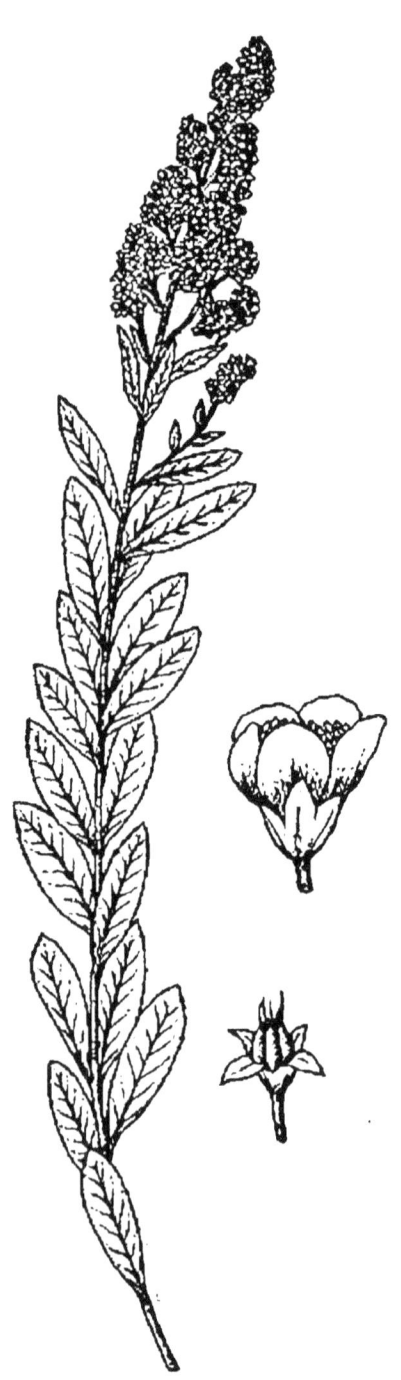

Meadow-sweet (Spiraea alba)

Staphylea trifolia (Bladdernut) — [tree/shrub] bottomlands, woodland thickets and moist soils along streams, FAC; statewide except north-central. Grows to 15 feet with white flowers in late spring; part shade to shade in dry to mesic sandy loam, but prefers a moist soil. pH 6.1 to 8.

Stellaria borealis (Northern stitchwort) — [perennial forb] scattered, mostly northern Pennsylvania on sphagnum swamps and stream banks, open marshy woodlands and grasslands, edges of low and floodplain forests and occasionally among boulders on talus slopes, FACW. Prostrate-growing with white flowers in spring; grow on moist to wet rich organic loams in full sun to part shade.

Stellaria corei (Chickweed) — [perennial forb] generally southwestern Pennsylvania in rocky woodlands, hillsides and bluffs. Grows 5 to 20 inches with white flowers in spring; grow on mesic, well drained soils in part sun to part shade.

Stellaria longifolia (Long-leaved stitchwort) — [perennial forb] statewide, usually on circumneutral to calcareous sites in wet meadows, marshy open ground, swamps, muskegs, and rich moist woodlands. Grows 5 to 20 inches in full to part shade on medium to fine textured, moist to wet loams at least 8 inches deep with a pH of 4.0 to 6.5. Excellent choice for anaerobic sites, but not for drought or limestone-based soils; white flowers in late spring.

Stellaria pubera (Great chickweed) — [perennial forb] mostly southeastern and southwestern Pennsylvania on moist, rocky ground in rich mesic forests and alluvial bottomland woods. Grows 6 to 12 inches with white flowers in late spring; prefers part sun in spring followed by dappled shade in mesic, well drained soil that includes a lot of decaying organic matter.

Stenanthium gramineum (Featherbells) — [perennial forb] mostly west central floodplains, fields, meadows and moist woodlands; FACW. Grows to 6 feet with white flowers in mid to late summer; prefers mesic to moist, rich, silt loams.

Streptopus amplexifolius (Twisted stalk) — [perennial forb] rare in rich, moist, coniferous and deciduous woods, seepy outcrops, often near waterfalls, FAC+; scattered northeast and endangered. Grows up to 36 inches, greenish-white flowers in summer; part shade to shade in rich loam, pH 5 to 6.

Streptopus roseus var. perspectus (Rose mandaria) — [perennial forb] cool to cold, moist woods and stream banks; Allegheny Mountains and northern plateaus. Grows up to 24 inches, with pink-rose flowers in early summer; part shade to shade in moist rich loam, pH 5 to 6. AKA *Streptopus lanceolatus var lanceolatus*.

Strophostyles helvola (Wild bean, Amberique-bean) [annual vine] — open, sandy and rocky woodlands, thickets, riparian sand and gravel bars and banks, sandy fields, southeast and widely scattered elsewhere, FACU. Grows 3 to 9 feet in full to part sun with pink flowers in summer on mesic to moist soils containing sand, loam, silt, or gravelly soil. Prefers disturbed soils.

Strophostyles umbellata (Wild bean, pink fuzzybean) — [perennial vine] Atlantic Coastal Plain and southern edges of Lancaster and Chester counties on sandy soils in woodlands, clearings and fields, as well as serpentine barrens; FACU. Pink to purple flowers in summer.

Stylosanthes biflora (Pencil-flower) — [perennial forb] primarily southeastern Pennsylvania in sandy fields and on rocky, shaly slopes and riverbanks. Grows 4 to 12 inches with yellow flowers in late spring to early summer; prefers full to part sun and dry to mesic, slightly acidic infertile soil.

Symphoricarpos albus var. albus (Snowberry) — [shrub] warm, dry woodland hillsides and rocky, open forest slopes, warm moist slopes, riparian benches and terraces. FACU-; scattered west, especially Allegheny Mountains. Grows 3 to 6 feet with white flowers in early summer; sun to part sun in dry to moist circumneutral soil composed of infertile sands and gravels. Adapts to soils of any texture at least 12 inches deep, with a pH range of 6.0 to 7.8. Will grow in part sun, but prefers more open sites tending toward limestone substrate. No tolerance for anaerobic conditions, but a good choice for droughty sites.

Symphoricarpos orbiculatus (Coralberry) — [shrub] open woodlands, shaded woods, thickets, stream banks and river banks; characteristic of *Quercus stellata* (post oak) woodlands, UPL. Mostly southeast; scattered west. Grows 2 to 5 feet with pink flowers in spring; sun to part shade on well-drained, mesic to moist, moderately fertile, medium to fine textured soils at least 18 inches deep with a pH range of 5.5 to 7.5. No anaerobic or limestone-based soil tolerance. Forms extensive colonies by rooting at nodes that touch the ground; control spread by removing suckers and runners.

Symphyotrichum boreale (Northern bog aster) — [perennial forb] prefers calcareous soils in cold bogs, fens, marshes, open cedar-tamarack-spruce swamps, wet meadows and swales, stream and pond edges, widely scattered in glaciated areas, OBL and listed as endangered in Pennsylvania. Grows 6 to 32 inches with white flowers in late summer to early autumn; prefers mesic to wet, circumneutral, organically rich silt loams in full to part sun.

Symphyotrichum cordifolium (Blue wood aster) — [perennial forb] rich, dry or moist woodlands, bluff bases, stream banks and moist ledges; statewide. Grows up to 5 feet, pale blue flowers in late fall; part shade to shade in dry to moist sandy loam at least 10 inches deep, with a pH of 5.7 to 7.5. Intolerant of shade and anaerobic conditions.

Symphyotrichum depauperatum (Serpentine aster) — [perennial forb] prefers serpentine or diabasic soils in open areas; reported in Chester and southern Lancaster counties and listed as threatened in Pennsylvania. Grows 10 to 20 inches with white flowers in late summer on serpentine or diabase soils in full to part sun.

Symphyotrichum drummondii var. drummondii (Hairy heart-leaved aster) — [perennial forb] very rare in open deciduous woods, clearings, thickets, stream banks, swamp edges; southwest; UPL. Grows up to 4 feet, bluish-white flowers in autumn. Prefers wet to dry mesic loamy to rocky soils in part shade.

Symphyotrichum dumosum (Bushy aster) — [perennial forb] Prefers moist to wet soils in open or wooded bogs, fens, sedge meadows, marshes, swamps, floodplains, flatwoods, pine-hickory forests, oak-pine thickets, secondary woodlands; also found on sandy to mucky or marly lake and pond shorelines and in interdunal hollows; mostly

Piedmont, FAC. Grows 1 to 3 feet with white to pink flowers in late summer to early fall; prefers mesic to moist calcareous sandy loams in full sun to part shade.

Symphyotrichum ericoides ssp. ericoides (White heath aster) — [perennial forb] dry to mesic meadows and fields, FACU. Mostly along the southern Delaware River, scattered elsewhere. Grows 10 to 50 inches, white flowers in fall; sun to part sun in dry sandy loam.

Symphyotrichum laeve (Smooth blue aster) — [perennial forb] dry woods, rocky ledges. Two varieties: *var. laeve*, common in mostly the Central Appalachians and Piedmont, while *var. concinnum* is very rare in the southeast. Mostly south central and eastern counties in Pennsylvania; scattered elsewhere. Grows 10 to 40 inches, pale to dark blue flowers in fall; sun to part shade in dry sandy loam at least 10 inches deep with a pH between 5.8 and 7.8. Intolerant of shade and anaerobic conditions.

Symphyotrichum lateriflorum (Calico aster) — [perennial forb] mesic to moist old fields, edges of woods, rocky woods, and waste ground, FACW-; statewide. Grows 10 to 45 inches, white flowers in autumn; sun to part shade in mesic to moist, medium to fine textured loam at least 10 inches deep with a pH of 5.2 to 7.5 but, prefers 6.6 to 7.0. Intolerant of shade and anaerobic conditions.

Symphyotrichum novae-angliae (New England aster) — [perennial forb] moist prairies, meadows, thickets, low valleys and stream banks, FACW-; statewide. Grows 3 to 6 feet, purple flowers in fall; average, medium, well-drained soil in full sun. Prefers moist, rich soils, pH 5.5 to 7.

Symphyotrichum novi-belgii var. novi-belgii (New York aster) — [perennial forb] rare in meadows, damp thickets, shorelines; FACW+. Southeast. Grows to 30 inches, white to blue flowers in late summer. Grow in well-drained, mesic to moist, medium to fine textured soils at least 10 inches deep with a pH range of 5.5 to 7.0. Intolerant of shade, drought and limestone-based soils.

Symphyotrichum oblongifolium (Aromatic aster) — [perennial forb] fields, prairies and openings, typically over limestone substrates. Mostly along the Allegheny front and in southwest. Grows 1 to 3 feet with lavender flowers in late summer; well drained, dry to medium average soils in full sun; prefers sandy soils and tolerates poor soils and drought.

Symphyotrichum patens (Late purple aster) — [perennial forb] dry, sandy, moist, open woods and old fields. Statewide except northern plateaus; most common in southeast. Grows 15 to 45 inches, blue flowers in fall; part shade to shade in dry to moist, medium to fine textured soil at least 10 inches deep with a pH of 4.9 to 6.9. Tolerant of shade, but not anaerobic conditions..

Symphyotrichum praealtum (Veiny-lined aster) — [perennial forb] open woods or thickets, wet prairies and meadows, lake and stream margins and moist banks, and oak savannas; FACW. Scattered statewide. Grows 20 to 60 inches in full to part sun, with blue flowers in autumn. Prefers wet, loamy soils.

Symphyotrichum prenanthoides (Zig-zag aster) — [perennial forb] swamps, stream banks and low woods, FAC; statewide. Grows 10 to 40 inches, blue to pale purple flowers in early fall; sun to part sun in moist, well-drained, medium textured soil at least 10 inches deep with a pH of 5.5 to 7.2. Intolerant of shade and limestone-based soils.

Symphyotrichum puniceum var. puniceum (Purple-stemmed aster) — [perennial forb] swampy ground of spring-fed meadows, stream banks and moist ditches, FACW; statewide. Grows up to 6 feet, blue flowers in early autumn; average, wet, well-drained, medium to fine textured soil at least 10 inches deep with a pH range of 4.5 to 7.5 in full sun. An excellent choice for anaerobic sites, but not drought or limestone-based soils. Listed as threatened in Pennsylvania.

Symphyotrichum racemosum (Small white aster) — [perennial forb] prefers moist to wet alluvial soils, often brackish, in bogs, swamps and swamp margins, low wet meadows, marshes, prairie swales, open bottomlands and flood plains, scattered statewide but primarily in the Atlantic Coastal Plain areas of extreme southeastern Pennsylvania; FAC. Grows 1 to 3 feet with pale blue flowers in late summer to early autumn in full sun to part sun.

Symphyotrichum shortii (Short's aster) —

[perennial forb] mesic, open, typically thin oak-hickory woodlands, woods edges, thickets and stream banks, calcareous hummocks, mostly southwest. Grows 2 to 4 feet, white flowers in autumn, with a preference to partial sun and mesic to slightly dry, circumneutral to slightly alkaline, loamy to rocky woodland soil. Richer soils produce taller plants, which may need support when in bloom.

Symphyotrichum subulatum (Salt-marsh aster) [annual forb] — salt, brackish and tidal marshes, OBL, on the Atlantic Coastal Plain. Grows 1 to 3 feet with white-lavender flowers in fall on moist to wet calcareous sandy and clay loams that are medium to fine textured, at least 6 inches deep and in a pH range of 5.6 to 7.0. Intolerant of shade, drought and limestone-based soils; no saline tolerance.

Symphyotrichum undulatum (Heart-leaved aster) — [perennial forb] dry woods, sandy slopes and old fields; statewide. Grows 15 to 45 inches, with blue-violet flowers in autumn; sun to part shade in dry sandy loam.

Symphyotrichum urophyllum (Aster) — [perennial forb] prefers open, dry to mesic, sandy to loamy and sometimes rocky soils over limestone in ravines, glades, fields, and open woodlands dominated by oak, sassafras, aspen or pine, sometimes on rocky, dry bluffs, stabilized dunes and savannas, as well as disturbed ground; statewide, but concentrated in west central and southeastern Pennsylvania. Grows 10 to 25 inches in full to part sun, on dry to mesic, well drained usually sandy to silty loams.

Symplocarpus foetidus (Skunk cabbage) — [perennial forb] swamps, wet woods, along streams, and other wet low areas, OBL; statewide. Grows 1 to 3 feet, yellow-brown flowers in early spring; part sun to part shade in moist to wet humusy loam of any texture with a minimum depth of 12 inches and a pH range of 4.0 to 7.0. Shade tolerant, but not drought or limestone-based soils.

Taenidia integerrima (Yellow pimpernel) — [perennial forb] rocky upland woods, bluffs, thickets and slopes, as well as prairies and savannas; statewide, mostly south and scattered elsewhere. Grows 16 to 32 inches, yellow flowers in early summer; part sun in poor, clay, rocky or sandy soils.

Taenidia montana (Mountain pimpernel) — [perennial forb] roadside banks and shale barrens in southern Bedford County; listed as endangered in Pennsylvania. Grows 1 to 3 feet with tiny yellow flowers; grow in full sun to part shade on dry, well drained sandy to rocky soils.

Taxus canadensis (Canadian yew) — [tree/shrub] cool moist rocky slopes or ravines under mixed coniferous (rarely deciduous) forest canopy; statewide. Declining because of deer browsing, FAC. Shrub to 5 feet; sun to part shade in mesic to moist sandy soil at least 24 inches deep with a pH range of 5.3 to 7.5. Shade tolerant but not suitable for anaerobic sites; an excellent choice for limestone-based soils that needs protection from winter sun and wind.

Tephrosia virginiana (Goat's rue) — [perennial forb] dry, sandy acidic woods. Mostly southeast (Central Appalachians and Piedmont) and southwest (Southern Allegheny Plateau). Grows 10 to 30 inches, yellow-white/pinkish purple flowers in summer; part sun to part shade in dry acidic sandy loam.

New York aster (*Symphyotrichum novi-belgi*)

Teucrium canadense var. *virginicum* (Wild germander) — [perennial forb] flood plains, lake margins, moist fields and meadows, FACW-; statewide. Grows 18 to 36 inches, purple to pink or cream color flowers in summer; sun to part sun in moist silty loam.

Thalictrum coriaceum (Thick-leaved meadow-rue) — [perennial forb] upland rocky, mesic woodlands and thickets as well as moist alluvium, scattered southwest, mostly in Bedford and Blair counties; listed as endangered in Pennsylvania. Grows to 60 inches in mesic, somewhat rich soils in part shade.

Thalictrum dasycarpum (Purple meadow-rue) — [perennial forb] very rare in deciduous woodlands along streams, damp thickets, swamps, and wet meadows and prairies; FACW. Reported only in Warren and Forest counties. Grows 3 to 5 feet with purple-white flowers in late spring; well-drained, medium moisture average soils in full sun to part shade; prefers rich humusy and moist soil in dappled light. Intolerant of hot and humid conditions.

Thalictrum dioicum (Early meadow-rue) — [perennial forb] rich, mesic to moist rocky woods, ravines, alluvial terraces, especially on north-facing slopes, FAC; statewide. Grows 10 to 30 inches; greenish to purple flowers in spring; part sun to part shade in moist rich loam, pH 5 to 7.

Thalictrum pubescens (Tall meadow-rue) — [perennial forb] rich mesic upland woods and wet meadows, thickets and stream banks, FACW+; statewide. Grows 2 to 10 feet, white to purplish flowers in summer; part sun to part shade in moist rich loam, pH 5.5 to 7.

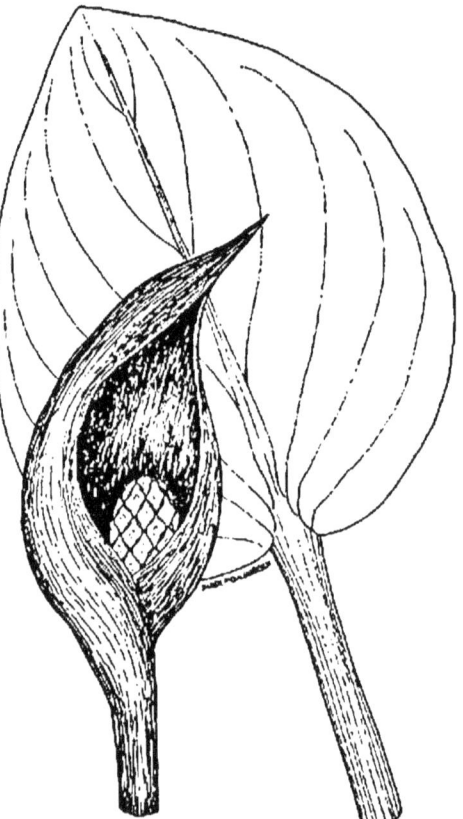

Skunk cabbage (*Symplocarpus foetidus*)

Thalictrum revolutum (Purple meadow-rue) — [perennial forb] dry open woods, brushy banks, thickets and barrens, UPL. Statewide except northern tier; most common southeast (Central Appalachians, Piedmont). Grows 2 to 6 feet, white flowers in early summer; sun to part shade in dry sandy loam.

Thalictrum thalictroides (Rue anemone) — [perennial forb] rich, moist deciduous upland woods, wooded banks and thickets; statewide except for Allegheny Mountains and Northern Unglaciated Allegheny Plateau. Grows 4 to 12 inches, white flowers, early spring; part shade to shade in rich humus, pH 4 to 7; goes dormant if the soil becomes too dry.

Thaspium trifoliatum (Meadow-parsnip) — [perennial forb] rich woodland slopes, ravines and woods edges. Two varieties: var. trifoliatum, mostly southeast (Piedmont) and var. flavum, mostly southwest (Southern Allegheny Plateau). Grows 12 to 30 inches, yellow flowers in spring; prefers full sun to part shade in mesic, well-drained soils.

Thelypteris noveboracensis (New York fern) — [fern/ally] terrestrial in moist woods, especially near swamps, streams, and in vernal seeps of ravines, often in slightly disturbed secondary forests, frequently forming large colonies; prefers dry oak, beech, maple and birch woods. Fronds 12 to 24 inches; rhizome: long creeping. Grow in high shade in mesic to moist humus rich sandy loam of any texture at least 6 inches deep with a pH range of 4.0 to 7.0. Excellent for anaerobic sites and shade tolerant. Can be used to form naturalized woodland colonies. Reported to be ignored by deer, hence the colonizing. AKA *Parathelypteris noveboracensis*.

Thelypteris palustris var. pubescens (Marsh fern) — [fern/ally] swamps, bogs, and marshes in soft rich muddy soil, also along riverbanks and roadside ditches, and in wet woods. Fronds 18 to 30 inches; rhizome: long creeping. Grow in part sun to part shade in moist to wet rich silty loam, pH 4 to 7 but prefers 4.5 to 6.5.

Thelypteris simulata (Massachusetts fern) — [fern/ally] mostly northeastern Pennsylvania, especially at the northern end of the Ridge and Valley in acid soils of shaded bogs, swamps and hummocks, often with sphagnum; FACW.

Thinopyrum pycnanthum (Saltmarsh wheatgrass) — [perennial graminoid] moist to wet disturbed ground in Philadelphia County (Atlantic Coastal Plain); FACW and aka *Elytrigia pungens*.

Tiarella cordifolia (Foamflower) — [perennial forb] moist, rocky deciduous woods and wooded slopes, FAC-; mostly Allegheny plateaus, north and west, sparse in Central Appalachians and Piedmont. Grows 4 to 14 inches, white flowers in spring; part sun to part shade in moist rich loam. pH 5.0 to 7.0.

Tilia americana var. americana (Basswood) — [tree/shrub] rich uplands on mid-slopes in mixed deciduous forests and occasionally swamps, FACU; statewide. Grows to 130 feet in sandy loams to silt loams; prefers moist to mesic, finer textured, well-drained loams at least 30 inches deep with a pH range of 4.5 to 7.5. Intolerant of anaerobic conditions, drought and limestone-based soils. Generally intolerant of air pollution and urban conditions.

Tipularia discolor (Cranefly orchid) — [perennial forb] rare in deciduous woodlands and stream banks, especially in acidic oak-pine woodlands and depressions under sweet gum canopies; FACU. Mostly southeast (Piedmont). Grows 4 to 10 inches, yellow-green-purple flowers in summer; prefers part sun to part shade in humus rich, well drained soils.

Torreyochloa pallida (Pale meadowgrass) — [perennial graminoid] widely scattered on lake and pond margins, swamps, marshes and bogs, OBL; two varieties: fernaldii and pallida.

Toxicodendron radicans (Poison-ivy) — [perennial vine] statewide in open woodlands, thickets, forest edges and roadsides and fencerows; FAC. Not a suitable landscape plant; may be difficult to find commercially.

Toxicodendron vernix (Poison sumac) — [shrub] wet soil of swamps, bogs, seepage slopes, and frequently flooded areas; in shady hardwood forests, OBL; statewide except north-central. Grows to 16 feet. Not a suitable landscape plant. All parts, in all seasons, will cause severe skin irritation if plant sap contacted.

Tradescantia ohiensis (Spiderwort, Bluejacket) — [perennial forb] rare in fields, thickets, rarely in woodlands, sometimes along streams; FAC. Scattered southeast and west; endangered. Blue flowers in early summer. Grow in well-drained dry to medium average soil in full sun to part shade; prefers acidic moist sandy soil in full sun.

Tradescantia virginiana (Spider lily or widows tears) — [perennial forb] dry to mesic upland wooded slopes, shale outcrops and moist fields, FACU; scattered south, especially Piedmont; absent in northern Allegheny plateaus. Grows 12 to 36 inches, blue to purple flowers in spring; sun to part shade in mesic to moist, mediu to fine textured, well-drained sandy loam at least 4 inches deep with a pH range of 4.0 to 8.0. No anaerobic tolerance. Prefers moist acidic soils, but tolerates poor soils.

Trautvetteria caroliniensis (Carolina tasselrue) — [perennial forb] rare in bogs, stream banks, wooded seepage slopes, mostly southwest; FACW-. Grows 18 to 40 inches, white flowers in summer on rich, humusy, mesic to moist loam in part shade.

Trautvetteria caroliniensis (Carolina tasselrue) — [perennial forb] rare in bogs, stream banks, wooded seepage slopes, mostly southwest; FACW-. Grows 18 to 40 inches, white flowers in summer on rich, humusy, mesic to moist loam in part shade.

Triadenum fraseri (Marsh St. Johns-wort) — [perennial forb] swamps, bogs, wet meadows and seeps, statewide but especially northern Pennsylvania, OBL. Grows 1 to 2 feet with red flowers in summer; prefers sun to part sun in moist to wet bogs, marshes, fens, shorelines.

Triadenum virginicum (Marsh St. Johns Wort) — [perennial forb] marshes, bogs, swampy woods, stream banks; OBL; statewide, especially Western

Glaciated and Northern Glaciated Allegheny Plateaus and Allegheny Mountains, scattered elsewhere. Grows 12 to 24 inches, pink to purple flowers in summer; mesic to moist rich loams in sun to part sun.

Trichomanes intricatum (Filmy fern) — [fern/ally] scattered statewide on heavily shaded, sheltered moist crevices and overhangs, typically on noncalcareous rock.

Trichophorum planifolium (Blue-curls, Bashful bulrush) [annual graminoid] — scattered in rocky hardwood forests and edges, usually with oak, often on hillsides, mostly southeast and listed as endangered. Grows to about 15 inches, flowering in summer in dry to mesic rocky well-drained soils in part sun to part shade.

Trichophorum planifolium (Club-rush) — [perennial graminoid] dry, rocky soils, typically on hillsides and slopes, in hardwood forests that often include oak; statewide, but especially southeast.

Trichostema brachiatum (False pennyroyal) — [perennial forb] shale barrens, dry slopes, rocky shorelines and open woodlands across southern Pennsylvania. Grow on calcareous sandy soils in full sun to part shade; purple flowers in spring.

Trichostema dichotomum (Blue-curls) [annual forb] — statewide, especially southeast, on fields, barrens, rock outcrops and open woodlands and clearings. Grows from 4 to 30 inches with blue flowers in late summer to fall in part shade to shade on dry, sandy, well-drained soils.

Trichostema setaceum (Narrow-leaved blue-curls) [annual forb] — shaly slopes and sandy banks, widely scattered in central Pennshylvania and listed as endangered. Grows 4 to 30 inches with purple flowers in fall in dry to mesic well-drained loams in part sun to part shade.

Tridens flavus (Purpletop) — [perennial graminoid] meadows, fields, roadsides and open woods, FACU. Mostly southeast (Central Appalachians, Piedmont), scattered elsewhere. Grows 40 to 50 inches; sun to part sun in dry sandy to clay soils of any textgure at least 10 inches deep with a pH range of 4.5 to 6.5. Intolerant of shade, anaerobic sites and limestone-based soils but an excellent choice for droughty conditions.

Trientalis borealis (Star-flower) — [perennial forb] moist to wet coniferous and mature northern hardwood forests, as well as bogs and open heath areas, mostly northern Pennsylvania; FAC. Grows 2 to 8 inches tall with a single white flower at the apex; prefers light or dappled shade and moist, acidic soil with peat or sand and relatively cool summer temperatures.

Trifolium reflexum (Buffalo clover) [annual forb] — found in rocky open woodlands including glades and edges, prairies and old fields and reported in both the southwest and southeast, but listed as extirpated. A non-stoloniferous clover, it grows 1 to 3 feet with red-pink flowers in summer on dry to mesic sandy, acidic loams in full sun to part shade.

Trifolium virginicum (Kate's-mountain clover) — [perennial forb] scattered in shale barrens in south central Pennsylvania, especially Bedford County; listed as endangered in Pennsylvania. Grows 4 to 6 inches in full to part sun, generally in coarse to gravelly soils over shale substrates.

Triglochin palustre (Marsh arrow-grass) — [perennial graminoid] moist and often calcareous, sandy shores, marshes and meadows; OBL, reported only in Erie County and listed as extirpated in Pennsylvania.

Trillium cernuum var cernuum (Nodding trillium) — [perennial forb] rich, moist, mixed deciduous-coniferous forests and swamps, FACW. Mostly southeast (Piedmont), scattered elsewhere. Grows up to 15 inches, white flowers in spring; part shade to shade in moist rich humus, pH 5 to 6.

Trillium cuneatum (Huger's trillium) — [perennial forb] rich, often upland woods, especially with limestone soils, along with less calcareous sites, sometimes old fields, ditches, or coal-mine tailings; scattered west and southeast (Piedmont). Yellow, purple, green and brown flowers in early spring. Grows 10 to 12 inches and more in rich, humusy, moist soils in part shade to shade. Similar to Trillium sessile, which lacks the height.

Trillium erectum var. erectum (Purple trillium) — [perennial forb] cool, rich, moist neutral to acidic soils of upland deciduous forests, mixed deciduous-coniferous forests, and coniferous swamp borders, FACU-; statewide, but widely scattered southeast

(Central Appalachians, Piedmont). Grows up to 15 inches, maroon flowers, spring; part shade to shade in moist rich loam; pH 4 to 7 but prefers 4.5 to 6.

Trillium flexipes (Declined trillium) — [perennial forb] rich forest floodplains, swampy woods and wooded slopes, typically over limestone; FAC. Scattered throughout south and west. Grows 1 to 2 feet, white flowers in spring; prefers part shade to shade in rich, humusy, constantly moist, well-drained soil.

Trillium grandiflorum (Large flowered trillium) — [perennial forb] rich deciduous or mixed coniferous-deciduous upland woods, floodplains, and along roadsides. Mostly west, scattered east. Grows up to 15 inches, white flowers becoming pink in spring; part shade to shade in moist rich loam. pH 6 to 7 but prefers 6.0.

Trillium sessile (Toad-shade trillium) — [perennial forb] rich woodlands, calcareous, clayey alluvium on floodplains and riverbanks and less fertile soils in high, dry limestone woods, FACU-. Mostly southwest, scattered elsewhere. Grows up to 12 inches, maroon flowers in spring; part shade to shade in moist rich loam.

Trillium undulatum (Painted trillium) — [perennial forb] deep acidic humus in mixed deciduous-coniferous woods; prefers deep shade except at higher elevations, FACU. Allegheny Mountains and northern Allegheny Plateaus; sparse in Southern Allegheny Plateau, Central Appalachians and Piedmont areas. Grows up to 15 inches, white flowers with rose-purple triangle in late spring; part shade to shade in moist rich loam, pH 4 to 6.

Triodanis perfoliata var. perfoliata (Venus's looking-glass) [annual forb] — statewide on dry to mesic sand or gravel prairies and savannas, lake borders, woodland edges and mesic to moist meadows, FAC. Grows 1 to 3 feet with blue to purple flowers in spring on dry, sandy calcareous loams in part shade to shade; reportedly deer resistant and considered an attractive ornamental.

Triosteum angustifolium (Horse-gentian) — [perennial forb] scattered in mesic to moist woodlands and thickets, southeastern Pennsylvania; FAC+. Grows 2 to 3 feet with white flowers in late spring to early summer; prefer light shade to dappled sunlight in mesic to slightly dry loamy or rocky soils enriched with organic matter.

Triosteum aurantiacum (Wild-coffee) — [perennial forb] statewide on rocky, moist limestone slopes and wooded ravines, especially Piedmont areas. Grows 2 to 4 feet with reddish-brown flowers in late spring to early summer; grow in light shade to dappled sunlight in sandy to rocky loams rich with organic matter.

Star-flower (*Trientalis borealis*)

Triosteum perfoliatum (Horse-gentian, wild coffee) — [perennial forb] open rocky woods and thickets, calcareous hillsides, scattered statewide. Grows 2 to 3 feet, purplish-greenish flowers in late spring; prefers light shade to dappled shade in slightly dry to mesic loamy or rocky soil with much organic matter. Fruits can be dried, roasted ground and used as a coffee substitute.

Triphora trianthophora (Nodding pogonia, three-bird orchid) — [perennial forb] widely scattered, but primarily in Piedmont in moist, humusy woodlands; UPL and listed as endangered in Pennsylvania. Grows to 12 inches with white flowers in summer; part sun to part shade in mesic to moist, humus rich loams.

Triplasis purpurea (Purple sandgrass) [annual graminoid] — sandy sites in prairies, savannas and along major rivers, including dunes, in the Atlantic

Coastal Plain and listed as endangered. Grows 1 to 3 feet in loams, clay loams and clay but prefers loose sand to sandy loam in areas of sparse vegetation, a pioneering stabalization species. Grow in full sun, dry to mesic soils.

Tripsacum dactyloides (Gammagrass) — [perennial graminoid] Rare in swamps and wet shorelines, FACW; mostly southeast (Piedmont). Grows 4 to 8 feet in full sun to part shade, in average, mesic and well-drained soil of any texture at least 20 inches deep with a pH range of 5.1 to 7.5; does well in shady locations near water but intolerant of limestone-based soils and drought.

Trisetum spicatum (Oatgrass) — [perennial graminoid] very rare in forests, moist meadows, rock ledges and scree fields, FACU. Endangered; reported only in Mercer and Lehigh Counties. Grows 4 to 20 inches; sun to part sun in dry sandy and rocky soils. AKA *Aira spicata*.

Trollius laxus (Spreading globe-flower) — [perennial forb] very rare in rich, moist calcareous meadows, swamps and moist, open woods, OBL. Mostly east-central (Hudson Valley and Lower New England Sections), widely scattered elsewhere; endangered. Grows 4 to 20 inches, yellow flowers in spring; part sun to part shade in moist, rich calcareous loam.

Tsuga canadensis (Canada hemlock, Eastern hemlock) — [tree/shrub] moist rocky ridges and hillsides, cool moist valleys, flats and ravines, especially on northern and eastern facing slopes, and swamp borders if peat and muck soils are shallow, usually above 1,200 feet, FACU; statewide. Grows to 100 feet; average, medium, well-drained soil in part shade to full shade. Prefers acidic cool, moist, humid conditions with good drainage; textures include sandy loams, loamy sands, and silty loams with gravel of glacial origin in the upper profile. Adaptable to coarse to medium textured, moderately fertile soils at least 28 inches deep with a pH range of 4.2 to 5.7. Low drought and no anaerobic or limestone tolerance. Has good hedging potential. Best sited in a location protected from strong winds.

Currently under attack by Adelges tsugae (wooly adelgid), a pest from Japan; once infected, a tree is usually dead within a few years.

Typha angustifolia (Narrow-leaved cat-tail) — [perennial forb] wet meadows, fens, estuaries, marshes, bogs, ditches, and along lake shores; OBL. Mostly southeast; scattered elsewhere. Grow in moist to wet rich organic soils, of any texture, at least 10 inches deep, with a pH of 3.7 to 8.5. Grows in shallow standing water, in full sun. No limestone or drought tolerance.

Typha latifolia (Common cat-tail) — [perennial forb] swamps, marshes, wet shores, ditches, or wet soil, OBL; statewide. Grows 3 to 9 feet and blooms in early summer; rich loams in full sun to part shade in water to 12 inches deep. Because it is an aggressive colonizer, many plant them in underwater containers. Grow in any texture soil with medium fertility and at least 14 inches deep with a pH range of 5.5 to 8.7. No drought tolerance.

Ulmus americana (American elm) — [tree/shrub] alluvial woods, swamp forests, deciduous woodlands, fencerows, pastures, old fields, waste areas, FACW-; statewide. Grows to 130 feet; average, medium moisture, well-drained soils in full sun. Tolerant of light shade. Prefers rich, moist loams with moderate fertility and any texture, at least 42 inches deep with a pH range of 5.0 to 8.0. Adapts to both wet and dry sites. Generally tolerant

Toadshade trillium (Trillium sessile)

of urban conditions and often planted as a street tree. Once a very common species, it fell victim to a fungus imported from Europe.

Ulmus rubra (Red elm or slippery elm) — [tree/shrub] moist rich soils on lower slopes, alluvial flood plains, stream banks, riverbanks and river terraces, and wooded bottom lands, sometimes on drier, limestone-origin sites, FAC-; statewide. Grows to 65 feet; average, medium moisture, well-drained soils of any texture, at least 40 inches deep, with a pH range of 5.0 to 7.5, in full sun. Tolerant of light shade. Prefers rich, moist loams. Adapts to wet and dry sites. Generally tolerant of urban conditions.

Urtica dioica ssp. gracilis (Great nettle) — [perennial forb] dry to mesic alluvial upland woods, margins of deciduous woodlands, along fencerows and in waste places, FACU. Statewide except sparse in the Allegheny Mountains, Central Appalachians and Blue Ridge Mountains. Grows 3 to 6 feet, greenish flowers in late spring; part sun to part shade in moist, rich sandy loam.

Utricularia cornuta (Horned bladderwort) — [perennial forb] aquatic in shallow pond and marsh water, as well as ditches; widely scattered statewide, but mostly northeast; OBL. No cultivation data; may be very difficult to obtain from commercial sources.

Utricularia geminiscapa (Bladderwort) — [perennial forb] generally Ridge and Valley region, especially north, in vernal ponds, bogs, along riverbanks, OBL.

Utricularia gibba (Humped bladderwort) — [perennial forb] rare aquatic; shallow water or exposed peat sand or mud flats, OBL. Scattered statewide, mostly northeast (Northern Glaciated Allegheny Plateau); believed to be extirpated. Yellow flowers in summer. An insectivore; water must be rich in microorganisms for it to survive; grow in full sun.

Utricularia gibba (Humped bladderwort) [annual forb] — sand or mud flats, exposed peat, in shallow water, widely scattered but concentrated in northeast, OBL; grows 1 to 6 inches with yellow flowers in spring and summer in full sun on wet sites (aquatic); because it is an insectivore, water must be rich in microorganisms.

Utricularia inflata (Inflated bladderwort) — [perennial forb] northeastern Pennsylvania ponds and lakes, OBL.

Utricularia inflata (Inflated bladderwort) [annual forb] — carnivorous aquatic in lakes and ponds, OBL, mostly northeast. Grows less than 12 inches with yellow flowers from spring to fall. The only bladderwort with floats.

Utricularia intermedia (Flat-leaved bladderwort) — [perennial forb] generally eastern Pennsylvania in lakes and on floating bog mats; OBL and listed as threatened.

Utricularia macrorhiza (Common bladderwort) — [perennial forb] statewide in ponds, lakes, swamps and marshes, especially concentrated northeast; OBL.

Utricularia minor (Lesser bladderwort) — [perennial forb] aquatic found in shallows of ponds, lakes and swamps in the northeast and northwest glaciated areas of Pennsylvania; OBL. Adapts to any moderately fertile soil texture at least 4 inches deep with a pH range of 6.5 to 7.5; intolerant of shade and drought.

Utricularia purpurea (Purple bladderwort) — [perennial forb] aquatic; suspended in lakes and ponds, OBL. Northeastern counties in Pennsylvania. Pink to purple flowers in late summer; full sun in soft, quiet water from shallow to more than 10 feet deep.

Utricularia radiata (Floating bladderwort) [annual forb] — shallow ponds and ditches in Bucks Counthy, OBL and listed as endangered. Grows less than 12 inches with yellow flowers in spring in still water and acidic soils. Considered toxic because it absorbs pollutants, pesticides and herbicides.

Utricularia resupinata (Northeastern bladderwort) — [perennial forb] Very rare carnivore in shores, shallows, quiet water, muddy-soil swamps; observed adjacent to Lake Erie but believed to be extirpated. A floating perennial up to 4 inches, white to pink flowers in summer. A challenging plant for water gardens.

Utricularia subulata (Slender bladderwort) [annual forb] — a carnivorous aquatic in wet soil and very shallow water, often among mosses, OBL, reported only in Chester County; yellow flowers in spring.

Uvularia grandiflora (Bellwort) — [perennial forb] rich, moist, deciduous forests and thickets, and forested floodplains. Mostly southwest (Southern Allegheny Plateau); scattered elsewhere. Yellow flowers in spring. Grow in well-drained medium moisture average soils in part shade to full shade; prefers humusy, moist soil in part shade.

Uvularia perfoliata (Bellwort) — [perennial forb] dry to mesic upland deciduous woods and thickets in acid to neutral soils, FACU; statewide. Grows 6 to 18 inches, yellow flowers in spring; part sun to part shade in moist rich loam, pH 5 to 6.

Uvularia sessilifolia (Bellwort) — [perennial forb] dry woods, moist hardwood coves, thickets and alluvial bottomlands, FACU-; statewide. Grows 6 to 18 inches, yellow flowers in spring; part sun to part shade in dry to moist sandy loam, pH 5 to 6.

Vaccinium angustifolium (Low sweet blueberry) — [shrub] dry woods and barrens, acidic soils, FACU; statewide. Grows to 30 inches with white flowers in spring and dark blue fruit in late summer; part sun to part shade in dry to mesic sandy loam of any texture at least 16 inches deep with a pH range of 4.7 to 7.5. Intolerant of shade, anaerobic conditions and limestone soils.

Vaccinium corymbosum (Highbush blueberry) — [shrub] statewide in moist, upland woodlands, open swamps, bogs, on the sandy shores of streams, ponds and lakes, in flatwoods, ravines and mountain summits, as well as upland ericaceous meadows, pine barrens and gray birch scrublands; FACW- and commonly available. Grows to 12 feet in full sun to part shade, in medium to wet but well drained acidic soils of any texture at least 16 inches deep, with a pH range of 4.7 to 7.5, under a good organic mulch; white to pink flowers in spring, fruit in summer. Shade tolerant. Parent of all popular hybrid blueberries.

Vaccinium macrocarpon (American cranberry) — [shrub] peaty woodlands, seepy areas and sphagnum bogs, OBL; statewide, especially northeast. Trailing shrub with white flowers in spring and the familiar red cranberry in late summer; sun to part shade in damp, acidic (pH 4.0 to 5.2), organically rich, well-drained soil in full sun.

Vaccinium myrtilloides (Sour-top blueberry) — [shrub] wet thickets and barrens, FAC; mostly northwest and northeast; scattered elsewhere. Shrub to 30 inches with greenish-white flowers in spring and dark blue fruit in late summer; sun to part shade in moist acidic sandy loam.

Vaccinium oxycoccos (Small cranberry) — [shrub] bogs, especially in cool areas, OBL; mostly northeast. Trailing shrub with white flowers in spring followed by red fruit; sun to part shade in moist to wet acidic sandy loam.

Vaccinium pallidum (Lowbush blueberry) — [shrub] dry, rocky hillsides, upland ridges, rocky outcrops and ledges, sandy knolls, shale barrens and upland swamps; statewide. Shrub to 3 feet with white flowers in spring and dark blue-purple fruit in late summer; part sun to part shade in dry to mesic sandy loam.

Vaccinium stamineum (Deerberry) — [shrub] dry woods, openings, barrens and clearings. FACU; statewide. Shrub to 6 feet with white flowers and spring and green fruit when ripe in late summer; part sun to part shade in mesic soils coarse to medium texture and at least 12 inches deep with a pH range of 4.0 to 7.0. Excellent choice for droughty sites, but not for anaerobic or limestone based. Shade tolerant.

Valerianella umbilicata (Navel corn-salad) [annual forb] — sandy wooded slopes, rocky banks along woodland streams, swampy woodlands, bottomland meadows and near springs at cliff bases, FAC, mostly in the southeast and southwest. Grows 1 to 3 feet with white flowers in late spring to early summer in part sun to dappled shade but consistently moist soils containing organic matter as well as sandy to rocky material.

Vallisneria americana var. americana (Tapegrass) — [perennial forb] aquatic; streams, lakes, rivers, OBL. Mostly Central Appalachians and northeast, scattered elsewhere. Grows up to 12 inches, produces green flowers; full sun, rich soil of any texture covered with sand in water 12 inches deep and a pH range of 5.0 to 8.8; no drought or shade tolerance. An important food source for turtles.

Veratrum hybridum (Slender bunchflower) — [perennial forb] mesic to dry, rocky, wooded slopes, mostly Piedmont; FACU and aka *Veratrum latifolium, Melanthium latifolium*. Grows up to 4 feet with white flowers in summer on dry to mesic well-drained loams in part sun to part shade.

Veratrum virginicum (Bunchflower) — [perennial forb] bogs, marshes, wet woods, savannas, meadows and damp clearings, FACW+. Mostly southeast (Piedmont); scattered elsewhere. Grows up to 7 feet, white flowers in early summer; full sun to part shade in moist to wet sandy to clayey loam. AKA *Melanthium virginicum*.

Veratrum viride (False hellebore) — [perennial forb] moist to wet woods, stream banks and seeps, FACW+; statewide. Grows up to 4 feet, with green flowers in spring; part sun to part shade in moist, rich loam.

Verbena hastata (Blue vervain) — [perennial forb] moist to wet meadows, flood plains and wet river bottomlands, stream banks and the edges of sloughs, FACW+; statewide. Grows up to 4 feet, with blue flowers in summer; sun to part sun in moist rich loam.

Verbena simplex (Narrow-leaved vervain) — [perennial forb] throughout southeastern Pennsylvania on shale barrens and such disturbed ground as fields, railroad banks and along roadsides. Grows 9 to 30 inches with lavendar flowers in summer; prefers full sun in mesic to slightly dry gravelly alkaline soils; will tolerate circumneutral sandy loams.

Verbena urticifolia (White vervain) — [perennial forb] moist meadows, fields, woodland borders, gravelly seeps, abandoned fields and waste ground, especially after site disturbance, FACU; statewide. Grows up to 4 feet, white flowers in summer; part sun in moist to mesic fertile loam.

Verbena urticifolia (White vervain) [Perennial Forb] — statewide in disturbed woodlands and borders, thickets, damp meadows, gravelly seeps and old fields, FACU. Grows 3 to 6 feet with white flowers in late summer to fall, part sun to part shade in mesic to moist fertile loam, clay loam or silt loam.

Verbesina alternifolia (Wingstem) — [perennial forb] moist slopes and lowlands in woodlands, including alluvial flats along streams; FAC. Mostly south. Grows 4 to 8 feet in full sun to part shade with yellow flowers in late summer. Prefers consistently moist and organically rich soils, but does well in average mesic well-drained soils.

Vernonia gigantea var. gigantea (Ironweed) — [perennial forb] floodplains, meadows and moist fields, mostly west (Western Glaciated and Southern Allegheny Plateaus); FAC. Grows 3 to 7 feet, purple flowers in late summer; prefers full sun to light shade in mesic to moist fertile, loamy soil. Sunny sites require more moisture than those in shade.

Highbush blueberry (*Vaccinium corymbosum*)

Vernonia glauca (Appalachian ironweed) — [perennial forb] rare in dry fields, open slopes and marshes; southeast (Piedmont, Atlantic Coastal Plain). Grows to 5 feet in full sun, with deep purple flowers in late summer; requires moist, loamy calcareous soil.

Vernonia noveboracensis (New York ironweed) — [perennial forb] stream banks and in wet fields and pastures, FACW+; statewide except north (northern Allegheny plateaus). Grows up to 6 feet, with brownish-purple flowers in summer; sun to part sun in mesic to moist, medium to fine textured, rich loam at least 6 inches deep and with a pH of

4.5 to 8.0. Prefers rich, moist, slightly acidic soils. Not suitable for anaerobic sites.

Veronica americana (American speedwell) — [perennial forb] moist riverbanks and stream edges and in ditches, OBL; statewide. Grows 4 to 10 inches, light blue to violet flowers in summer and fall; part shade in moist, humusy, medium to fine textured soils at least 6 inches deep with a pH range of 5.7 to 7.5. Low drought tolerance.

Veronica peregrina ssp. *peregrina* (Neckweed) [annual forb] — statewide in alluvial banks and open woodlands, FACU-. Grows to 12 inches with creamy flowers from May through October in sun to part shade on mesic to moist well-drained loams.

Veronica peregrina ssp. *xalapensis* (Hairy purlane speedwell) [annual forb] — found on moist fields, cultivated and waste ground in Lehigh, Bucks and Philadelphia counties, FACU-. Grows 3 to 12 inches with white flowers from May to October in sun to part sun on mesic to moist loamy soils.

Veronica scutellata (Marsh speedwell) — [perennial forb] wet woods, swamps, ditches and swales, statewide; OBL.

Veronicastrum virginicum (Culver's-root) — [perennial forb] moist meadows, thickets and swamps, FACU; statewide except north-central. Grows up to 6 feet, white or pink flowers in summer; sun to part sun in moist rich loam, pH 5.5 to 7.

Viburnum acerifolium (Maple-leaved viburnum) — [shrub] upland forests, woodlands, ravine slopes and hillsides in well-drained, moist soils; particularly tolerant of acid soils, UPL; statewide. Shrub to 6 feet with white flowers in spring; part sun to part shade in mesic to moist, coarse to medium textured, rich sandy loam at least 14 inches deep with a pH range of 4.8 to 7.5. An excellent choice for shady, droughty sites, but not anaerobic conditions.

Viburnum cassinoides (Witherod) — [shrub] swamps, moist upland woods and clearings and exposed rock crevices, FACW; statewide. Shrub to 15 feet with white flowers in spring; full sun to part shade in well-drained moist loams, but tolerates a wide range of soils including boggy ones.

Viburnum dentatum (Southern arrow-wood) — [shrub] moist woods and along stream banks. FAC; mostly southeast. Grows 6 to 10 feet with white flowers in spring; sun to shade in wet to dry acidic soils and sandy loams of any texture, with a pH range of 4.5 to 7.3; among the most adaptable of all the viburnums, but not for anaerobic sites. Suckers freely from the base and is easily transplanted.

Viburnum lantanoides (Hobblebush) — [shrub] rich, moist acidic woods, stream banks, ravines and swamps, FAC; mostly north and Allegheny Mountains. Shrub to 6 feet with white to pink flowers in late spring; part sun to part shade in mesic to moist, medium to fine textured sandy loam with a minimum depth of 14 inches and a pH range of 4.9 to 7.0. Shade tolerant and a good choice for anaerobic sites and limestone-based soils. Trailing stems take root where they touch the ground, creating hazards for walkers, hence the name.

Viburnum lentago (Nannyberry) — [shrub] woods, swamps and thickets with rich, moist soil, FAC; statewide, especially southeast. Shrub to 15 feet with white flowers in spring; part sun to part shade in average, medium, well-drained soil with medium to fine texture with a minimum depth of 14 inches and a pH range of 5.0 to 8.0. Low drought tolerance.

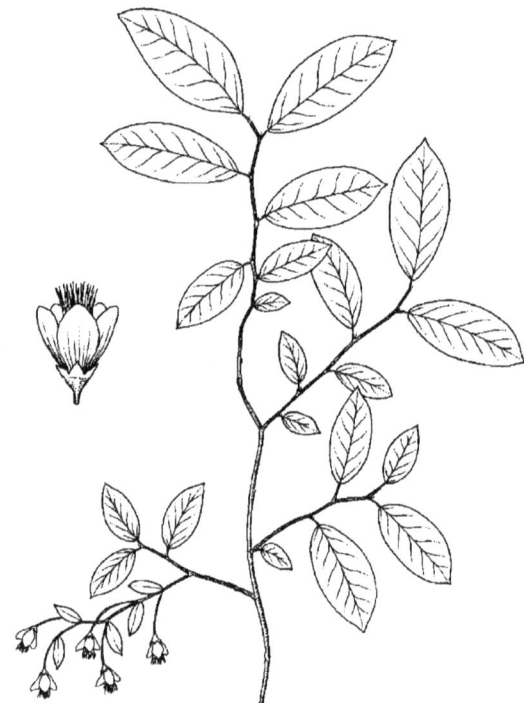

Deerberry (Vaccinium stamineum)

Viburnum nudum (Possum-haw) — [shrub] rare in low woods, swamps, bogs, OBL; southeast and endangered. Grows 5 to 12 feet with white flowers in spring; prefers moist loams in full sun to part shade, but tolerates wide range of medium textured soils at least 14 inches deep with a pH between 4.9 and 7.0. No anaerobic tolerance but a good choice for limestone based soils.

Viburnum opulus var. americanum (Highbush cranberry) — [shrub] swampy woods, bogs, lake margins, pastures, thickets, slopes and moist low places, FACW; widely scattered south, especially southeast. Shrub to 15 feet with white flowers in spring; full sun to part shade in moist to wet circumneutral (but not limestone) well-drained soil that is medium to fine textured, at least 14 inches deep and has a pH range of 5.5 to 7.5. Intolerant of shade and anaerobic conditions. Prefers loams with consistent moisture. *AKA Viburnum trilobum.*

Viburnum prunifolium (Black-haw) — [shrub] successional woods, thickets, old fields, roadsides, FACU; statewide except north. Shrub or small tree to 25 feet with white flowers in spring; sun to part shade in dry to mesic sandy loam that is medium to fine tetured and at least 18 inches deep with a pH between 4.8 and 7.5. Tolerates shade, but not anaerobic conditions and is an excellent choice for limestone based soils.

Viburnum rafinesquianum (Downy arrow-wood) — [shrub] rocky woods, old fields, dry slopes and banks; widely scattered statewide. Shrub to 5 feet with white flowers in spring; part sun to part shade in dry to mesic rocky sandy loam with a minimum of 14 inches of depth and a pH range of 4.5 to 7.1. Intolerant of anaerobic conditions, but a good choice for limestone-based soils. White flowers in spring.

Viburnum recognitum (Northern arrow-wood) — [shrub] swamps, boggy woods, wet pastures, stream banks, FACW-; statewide. Shrub to 15 feet with white flowers in spring; part sun to part shade in moist, humusy well-drained acidic loam that is medium to fine textured, at least 14 inches deep, and has a pH between 5.0 and 7.0. Low tolerance for drought, anaerobic conditions and limestone based soils

Vicia americana (Purple vetch) — [perennial forb] dry to moist, gravelly shores, thickets, meadows, and roadside banks, FAC. Widely scattered, mostly east. Grows up to 3 feet, blue to violet flowers in early summer; sun to part sun in moist rich loam that is coarse to medium textured, at least 10 inches deep and has a pH between 5.9 and 7.2. Intolerant of shade and anaerobic conditions, but an excellent choice for droughty conditions.

Viola affinis (LeConte's violet) — [perennial forb] rich moist, especially alluvial, woods, FACW; statewide. except north-central counties. Grows up to 16 inches, blue-violet flowers in spring; sun to part shade in moist, sandy loam.

Viola bicolor (Field pansy) — [perennial forb] fields, dry open woods and floodplain terraces, FACU; mostly south. Grows up to 10 inches, pale blue flowers with yellow centers in spring; sun to part shade in dry to moist rich loam.

Viola blanda (Sweet white violet) — [perennial forb] moist woods and swamps, FACW; statewide. Grows up to 16 inches, white flowers in spring; sun to part shade in moist rich sandy loam. Prefers humusy, moisture-retentive soils and forms large carpets in the wild by spreading through runners.

Viola canadensis (Canada violet) — [perennial forb] moist woods and swamps; statewide, but sparse in southeast (Central Appalachians and Piedmont). Grows up to 16 inches, white flowers with yellow centers in spring; part shade to shade in sandy humusy loam, pH 5 to 6.5. Naturalizes by vigorous seeding, not runners.

Viola cucullata (Blue marsh violet) — [perennial forb] bogs, meadows and swamps, FACW+; statewide. Grows up to 16 inches, pale purple flowers in spring; sun to part shade in moist to wet loam.

Viola cucullata x saggitata (Blue marsh violet) — [perennial forb] bogs, meadows and swamps; statewide. Grows up to 16 inches, blue to violet flowers in spring; part shade to shade in moist rich loam. AKA *Viola obiqua.*

Viola hirsutula (Southern woodland violet) — [perennial forb] open forests and forest clearings. Mostly southeast; scattered elsewhere and absent in northern Allegheny plateaus. Grows up to 16 inches, blue to violet flowers in spring; part shade in moist rich humusy loam.

Viola labradorica (American dog violet) — [perennial forb] moist woods and swamps, FAC; statewide. Grows up to 16 inches, pale blue flowers in spring; part sun to part shade in moist sandy humusy loam, pH 5 to 6.5. Aggressive spreader by runners and seeds.

Viola lanceolata var. lanceolata (Lance-leaved violet) — [perennial forb] moist, sandy shores, flats and bogs, OBL. Statewide, except absent in northern tier. Grows up to 10 inches, white flowers in spring; sun to part shade in moist sandy loam.

Viola macloskeyi ssp. pallens (Sweet white violet) — [perennial forb] bogs, swamps and wet woods, OBL; statewide. Grows up to 10 inches, white flowers in spring; sun to part shade in moist, humusy loam that is 4 inches deep with a pH between 6.0 and 7.3. Good choice for anaerobic sites.

Viola palmata (Early blue violet) — [perennial forb] statewide in dry, rich open woodlands and edges. Grows 4 to 6 inches with deep purple flowers; prefers sites in dappled sunlight during the spring, followed by partial sun or light shade during the summer. Grows best on loamy, well drained soils.

Viola pedata (Birdfoot violet) — [perennial forb] sandy or rocky barrens and dry forested slopes, UPL; Southeast, including Central Appalachians and Piedmont. Grows up to 16 inches, blue to violet flowers in spring; sun to part shade in dry to moist sandy loam, pH 4 to 7.

Viola primulifolia (Primrose violet) — [perennial forb] swamps, meadows and moist woodlands statewide, but especially Piedmont and Atlantic Coastal Plain; FAC+.

Viola pubescens var. pubescens (Downy yellow violet) — [perennial forb] dry to moist open woods and swamps, FACU; statewide. Grows up to 12 inches, yellow flowers in spring; part shade to shade in moist rich loam, pH 5 to 6.

Viola renifolia (Kidney-leaved violet) — [perennial forb] northeastern Pennsylvania on cool, wooded slopes and in wooded swamps, FACW.

Viola rostrata (Long-spurred violet) — [perennial forb] widely scattered statewide in moist woodlands; FACU.

Viola rotundifolia (Round-leaved violet) — [perennial forb] cool moist woods and banks, FAC+; statewide except southwest and south central. Grows up to 10 inches, yellow flowers in spring; part shade to shade in moist humusy loam; soil should not dry out and prefers cooler climates. Freely self-seeds and can become weedy.

Viola sagittata (Ovate-leaved violet, Arrow-leaved violet) — [perennial forb] dry woods, fields and edges, FACW; statewide. Two varieties: *ovata* (Ovate-leaved violet) and *sagittata* (Arrow-leaved violet). Grows up to 12 inches, blue-violet flowers in spring; sun to part shade in dry to moist sandy loam.

Viola selkirkii (Great-spurred violet) — [perennial forb] shaded ravines and similar cool woodlands in northeastern Pennsylvania. Grows 2 to 4 inches with pale purple flowers in late spring; prefers part shade to shade in mesic to moist, humusy well-drained soils.

Viola sororia (Common blue violet) — [perennial forb] moist woods, swamps, thickets, FAC; statewide. Grows up to 12 inches, blue flowers in spring; part sun to part shade in moist rich loam, pH 7 to 8. No runners, but aggressively spreads by seed.

Viola striata (Striped violet) — [perennial forb] common statewide in floodplains and moist, cool woodlands; FACW. Grows 6 to 12 inches with white flowers in late spring; prefers part shade to shade on mesic to moist, well drained loams rich with woodland humus.

Vitis aestivalis (Summer grape) — [perennial vine] open forests, woodlands, woodland borders and thickets; climbs nearly all hardwood and conifer tree species that grow in its range, statewide; FACU. Climbing vine, 15 to 30 feet; yellowish green flowers in spring, fruit in fall. Grow in deep, loamy, medium moisture, well-drained soils in full sun to part shade. Requires 16 inches of soil depth and a pH range of 5.3 to 7.0; low tolerance for anaerobic conditions.

Vitis cinerea var. baileyana (Possum grape) — [perennial vine] scattered in southwestern Pennsylvania in low woods; FACW. Prefers coarse to medium, moderately fertile soils at least 16 inches deep with a pH range of 5.4 to 7.0 and has a high drought tolerance.

Vitis labrusca (Fox grape) — [perennial vine] statewide, but especially southeast, along stream banks, in moist thickets and in rocky woodlands; FACU.

Vitis novae-angliae (New England grape) — [perennial vine] widely scattered central to northeast in moist to mesic mountain woodlands, ravines and roadside thickets; listed as endangered in Pennsylvania.

Vitis riparia (Frost grape) — [perennial vine] riverbanks and in alluvial thickets, statewide; FACW. Climbing vine, 30 to 70 feet; yellow-green flowers in May, fruit in late fall. Grow in sun to shade in moist, rich soil at least 16 inches deep with a pH range of 6.1 to 8.5.

Vitis vulpina (Frost grape) — [perennial vine] mostly southern Pennsylvania and widely scattered north, in woodlands, thickets, rocky slopes and sand dunes; FAC. Grows to 80 feet in coarse to medium textured soils with a pH of 6.0 to 7.5 and at least 16 inches of depth. Low drought tolerance.

Vulpia octoflora var. glauca (Six-weeks fescue) — [perennial graminoid] open woodlands and clearings, savannas, meadows, roadsides in dry and sterile soil; UPL. Mostly southeast (Piedmont), widely scattered elsewhere. Grows 4 to 16 inches; sun to part sun in dry to mesic infertile sandy loams.

Vulpia octoflora var. glauca (Six-weeks fescue) [annual graminoid] — fields, prairies, meadows, UPL, generally southeast and widely scattered elsewhere. To about 10 inches in dry, sterile soil, sun to part sun.

Waldsteinia fragarioides (Barren strawberry) — [perennial forb] moist rich woods and pastures;

Frost grape (Vitis vulpina)

statewide, but sparse southeast and southwest. Forms a mat to 6 inches in height with yellow flowers in spring; average, medium, well-drained soil in full sun to part shade. Tolerates a wide range of soils, but prefers slightly acidic humusy soil.

Wisteria frutescens (American wisteria) — [perennial vine] rare in alluvial woodland and river bank thickets, widely scattered statewide, FACW-. Grows 25 to 30 feet with white to purple flowers in early summer; sun to shade in moderately fertile, loam soil of any texture, at least 12 inches deep with a pH range of 4.0 to 7.0. Prefers a south to southwest position and sheltered from cold winds and early morning sun and a rich soil, but gardeners believe that results in excessive leaf growth.

Wolffia brasiliensis (Pointed water-meal) — [perennial forb] mesotrophic to eutrophic, quiet waters of lakes and ponds as well as slow-moving streams, widely scattered statewide; OBL. No cultivation data; may be very difficult to obtain from commercial sources.

Wolffia columbiana (Water-meal) — [perennial forb] aquatic; quiet waters of lakes, ponds, marshes, ditches and bogs. OBL; widely scattered, statewide. Grow in full sun in moderate to fertile shallow water; plant in silty loam.

Woodsia ilvensis (Rusty woodsia) — [fern/ally] sunny cliffs and rocky slopes, usually in contact with a variety of rocky substrates. Ideal for eastern part of the state. Fronds 3 to 8 inches; rhizome: erect to ascending. Grow in part sun to part shade in moist to wet acidic garden soil, pH 5 to 6.

Woodsia obtusa (Blunt lobed woodsia) — [fern/ally] cliffs and rocky slopes (rarely terrestrial); found on a variety of bedrock including both granite and limestone. Ideal for the southeast. Fronds 5 to 15 inches; rhizome: short creeping or ascending. Grow in part sun to part shade in dry to mesic sandy humusy loam, pH 5 to 7.5.

Woodwardia areolata (Netted chain fern) — [fern/ally] acidic bogs, seeps, and wet woods. Ideal for the southeast. Fronds 12 to 24 inches, rhizome: long-creeping. Grow in part sun to part shade in moist to wet rich loam.

Woodwardia virginica (Virginia chain fern) — [fern/ally] acidic swamps, marshes, bogs, and roadside ditches over acidic bedrock. Ideal for the northeast. Fronds 18 to 24 inches; rhizome: long creeping. Grow in high shade to dappled shade in acidic moist to wet garden soil.

Xanthium strumarium (Common cocklebur) [annual forb] — statewide, especially southeast in abandoned fields, cultivated ground and woodland edges, FAC. Grows to about 30 inches with yellow flowers in late summer on damp to seasonally wet, calcareous well drained soils in sun to part sun; toxic to animals.

Xyris difformis (Yellow-eyed-grass) — [perennial forb] in damp, sandy to peaty acidic soils of bogs, swamps, pond edges, poor fens, seeps and open sphagnous areas, glaciated northeast; OBL. Grows to 20 inches with yellow flowers in late summer to early fall; grow in sun to part sun in gravels, sands and peats found on the the edges of bogs and swamps.

Xyris montana (Yellow-eyed-grass) — [perennial forb] on exposed peat in floating sphagnous bog mats, poor fens, glacial lake shorelines, acidic seeps, streams and muskegs; northeastern glaciated areas, OBL and listed as rare in Pennsylvania.

Xyris torta (Yellow-eyed-grass) — [perennial forb] stream banks, pond shorelines, sandy swales and bogs, including moist disturbed sites, scattered statewide but mostly eastern Pennsylvania, OBL.

Zannichellia palustris (Horned pondweed) — [perennial forb] aquatic in lakes, ponds, streams, near springs and in tidal flats, widely scattered statewide but mostly southeast; OBL.

Zanthoxylum americanum (Prickly-ash) — [tree/shrub] calcareous soils or diabase along streams, on river bluffs, rocky hillsides and ravines and along roadsides; FACU; Mostly southeast (Central Appalachians, Piedmont). Grows 12 to 35 feet with inconspicuous flowers in rocky, calcareous soils (circumneutral to pH 7.2) in sun.

Zigadenus glaucus (Camass) — [perennial forb] reported only on a rocky slope in Huntingdon County. Grows to 24 inches with white flowers in spring; prefers moist calcareous well drained soils in full sun to part shade.

Zizania aquatica (Wild-rice) [annual graminoid] — Tidal and non-tidal marshes, primarily the Atlantic Coastal Plain but also along Lake Erie, but also ponds, lakes and borders of sluggish rivers, OBL. Grows to 11 feet with green flowers in summer in circumneutral moist to wet clay, loam or sandy soils in full sun.

Zizia aptera (Golden-alexander) — [perennial forb] woodlands, wooded slopes, thickets, glades, prairies, clearings and roadsides, FAC; mostly southeast (Central Appalachians, Piedmont), scattered elsewhere and absent in north (northern Allegheny plateaus). Grows 12 to 30 inches, yellow flowers in late spring; part sun to part shade in dry to moist rich loam, pH 5.5 to 7.

Zizia aurea (Golden-alexander) — [perennial forb] moist woods and meadows, thickets, glades and prairies; wooded bottomland, stream banks, floodplains; FAC-; statewide. Grows 12 to 32 inches, yellow flowers in late spring; average, medium moisture, well-drained soils in full sun to part shade; pH 5.5 to 7.